THE HISTORY OF DUNBLANE

DUNBLANE ABOUT 1890
G. W. E. Lockhart, R.S.A.

THE
HISTORY OF DUNBLANE

By

ALEXANDER B. BARTY, B.Sc., LL.B.

Solicitor, Dunblane

Foreword by

Very Rev. J. HUTCHISON COCKBURN, D.D., F.S.A. Scot.

Stirling District Libraries
1994

First published by
Eneas MacKay, Stirling.
1944

This edition published by
Stirling District Libraries
Stirling

ISBN 1 870542 29 0

Printed by
Cordfall Ltd.
0141 332 4640

Published with the assistance of

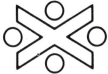 **BANK OF SCOTLAND**

A FRIEND FOR LIFE

TO MARK 300 YEARS OF BANKING SERVICE

CONTENTS

ILLUSTRATIONS

FOREWORD

To love one's countryside is inherent in patriotism, and to write its history is a high service both to the district and to the country. The life of even a quiet town and parish is a vivid reflection of the multitudinous and larger interests of the national life. In such a book as this we see how the historical events of our country affected the lives of ordinary men and women, the men of the professions, the farming community, the landed gentry. In it we trace the growth of social customs, the rise of traditions, the development of agriculture, architecture, education and social well-being; we see the minutiæ of life, often quaint and arresting, and as vital as things that happen in our own experience. Especially is this so when the town and district have so long a history as Dunblane, which saw the Roman legions tramp through its borders, welcomed the early Celtic missionaries of the Cross, was for long a centre of the Celtic Church, was chosen as a See of the Roman Catholic Church, and which was and is the junction of the road north and south with the road to the west; then the local history takes on an added importance and is linked notably with the wider affairs of the nation.

This history of Dunblane is the crown of long enquiry and patient study which its author did not live to see published. A sudden illness removed Mr. Alex. B. Barty from our midst, to the irreparable loss of Dunblane; but not before the manuscript was completed and much of it in print. For many years he had given most of his leisure to this labour of love, and he was quite remarkably fitted for the task. Born in Dunblane of a family whose connection with the district can be traced back for nearly 300 years, and which for well over a hundred years has carried on a legal business with large town and country connections, Mr. Barty had access to many private records which his scholarly mind enabled him to use with judgment and to weave into local and national history. Here in this book we have the background of the life of the people of Dunblane through the centuries, in the midst of which the Church has laboured since the days of St. Blane and his followers.

This is a most valuable contribution to local history, and I bespeak for it the warm support which it so richly deserves.

J. HUTCHISON COCKBURN,
Minister of Dunblane Cathedral.

THE CATHEDRAL MANSE,
    DUNBLANE.

ALEXANDER BOYD BARTY 1873-1940

PREFACE

Alexander Boyd Barty was born at Dunblane on 9th May, 1873. He received his early education at Clifton Bank School, St. Andrews. From there he went to St. Andrews University, where he graduated M.A. with Second Class Honours in Mathematics, and also received the Degree of B.Sc. He then served his legal apprenticeship with Messrs. Dundas & Wilson, C.S., Edinburgh, and studied law at Edinburgh University. He graduated LL.B. with distinction, and thereafter joined his father and his brother in the firm of Tho. & J. W. Barty, Solicitors, Dunblane. For the whole of his business life he was associated with that firm. His many appointments included that of Secretary of the Scottish Law Agents Society, Joint Agent of the Bank of Scotland, Dunblane, and Clerk to the School Board at Dunblane before the reorganisation of the control of education.

He had many interests outside his work. These included a deep interest in music, literature and country life. He was a keen sportsman, and proficient in various kinds of sport. But probably his greatest interest of all was in Dunblane—its people and its history, and in the Cathedral, which is the glory of Dunblane. He had been an elder of the Cathedral congregation since 1903, and Session Clerk since 1925, and was a Vice-Chairman of the Society of Friends of Dunblane Cathedral.

He died on 2nd March, 1940, when the manuscript of this book was already in the publisher's hands. It was doubtful at first if the publication of the book could go on in view of the author's death, and the difficulties of the times, but, happily, it has now been possible to arrange to proceed with the publication.

This book is the result of work and research extending over many years, the spare-time hobby of a busy man. The author collected his data and wrote the book gradually. There were often long intervals between the writing of one part and another. There is a danger of repetition when circumstances force an author to work in this way, and one found, when reading the proofs, that here and there events had been chronicled more than once.

Every effort has been made to ensure, by revision, that the book should be presented to readers as the author would have wished it, and that repetitions and redundancies have been eliminated. Some may, however, remain, as the author was not spared to make the final revision himself. It is hoped that such faults are few, and that the reader will overlook any undetected errors and appreciate the cause of them. A certain number of repetitions are, however, deliberate, since some information, relevant to two different topics, is necessary for the completeness of both.

I would like to record our grateful thanks to the Carnegie Trust for the Universities of Scotland, who have made a monetary grant to assist with the

PREFACE.

publication of this book; to the Society of Friends of Dunblane Cathedral, who have also given financial assistance; to the late Sir George Macdonald, who gave much valuable advice and assistance in connection with Chapter I.; to Mr. J. G. Fyfe, who has most carefully revised the whole work, and prepared the Index; and to the Very Rev. J. Hutchison Cockburn, D.D., who wrote the Foreword, and who has given us indispensable support and guidance in the various problems which have arisen. I would also like to thank all those friends who have helped us by their interest, advice and encouragement. Without the aid which they all freely gave it would have been impossible to carry out the publication.

With these explanations and acknowledgments, the author's family offer to the reader *The History of Dunblane*. They hope that it will be found interesting and of value.

J. W. BARTY.

PREFACE TO SECOND EDITION

The History of Dunblane by Alexander Boyd Barty was published in 1944 and has been out of print for many years. Now, fifty years after its original publication, a second edition has been prepared. This takes the form of a facsimile copy of the original text and its illustrations, to which has been added a new chapter covering the period from 1900 to 1994. Three new photographs have been added: one of A. B. Barty (facing Preface), one of the Leighton Library (front cover) and one of Scottish Churches House (page 275).

Alexander Boyd Barty died in 1940 when the original text was written but not published. His son, James Webster Barty, completed the arrangements for its publication and included a short biographical account of his father in the Preface. The additional chapter has been written by J. W. Barty and his daughter, Elisabeth Okasha. James Webster Barty OBE, MA, LLB was born in 1912 and was educated at the universities of St Andrews and Edinburgh. He succeeded his father in legal practice in Dunblane and also as Secretary of the Scottish Law Agents Society, of which he subsequently became President. He retired in 1984 but remains an Honorary Life President of the Scottish Law Agents Society. Elisabeth Okasha MA, PhD was educated at the universities of St Andrews and Cambridge. She is a lecturer in medieval English at University College Cork.

The authors acknowledge with gratitude the help given by:
Mrs J. D. Barnes, General Register Office for Scotland
Dr Ronald G. Cant, University of St Andrews
Mr Erskine Duncan, Dunblane
Mr J. S. Foster, Dunblane Hydro Hotel
Mr J. L. Gardner, Dunblane
Mrs E. M. Inglis, Stirling Area Office, Central Regional Council
Ms Isabel Kincaid, Local History Officer, Stirling District Council
Mr Charles King, Dunblane
Mrs E. Lindsay, Stirling District Library
Mr John G. Lindsay, Dunblane
Rev. Colin G. McIntosh, Dunblane
Mr Basil J. McKay, Dunblane
Mrs W. McLaren, Dunblane
Rev. Bryan Owen, Dunblane
Very Rev. Basil Canon O'Sullivan, Dunblane
Rev. Canon Dr G. Tellini, Dunblane
BT Archives, London, and BT Corporate Relations, Aberdeen
Central Regional Archive, Stirling
Queen Victoria School, Dunblane

Special thanks are due to the Bank of Scotland and the Society of Friends of Dunblane Cathedral for financial assistance in publishing this reprint.

The authors would also like to thank members of their family for their help and all those in Dunblane and elsewhere who took the time to answer questions and to check facts and figures. Especial thanks are due to Mr Herbert W. Gallagher who provided the photographs of the Leighton Library and the Scottish Churches House.

CHAPTER I.

DUNBLANE IN ITS EARLIEST DAYS.

A LOCAL historian wrote a few years ago, that nothing was known about Dunblane in prehistoric times or in the early centuries of the Christian era, but this is not altogether accurate. The district must have had a considerable population prior to the Roman occupation of Scotland, and this may be partly accounted for by the fertile soil on the hilly slopes in its neighbourhood and by the abundant supply of water in its river, burns and wells. While there was much flattened or hollow land which was marshy and unfit for cultivation prior to times when land was artificially drained, most of the countryside around Dunblane consists of gently sloping land with fertile soil where water would not lie and where vegetation would readily grow.

One of the proofs that the district was populated in early times is the existence of groups of standing stones at various parts of the parish or on land closely adjoining the parish. These are to be found on hillsides, hill summits, or high moorland or other high ground.

It has been pointed out by the late Mr. A. F. Hutchison, at one time Rector of Stirling High School, to whose writings the author is indebted, that the stones in this district, as a rule, point to a particular quarter of the compass, namely, to the North of the East ; that is, in the direction of the point where the sun rises at mid-summer, the inference being that they were erected there in pagan times by men who worshipped the sun or other pagan god. That, however, is pure speculation. All that can be said with certainty is that they were sepulchral in character.

One collection of standing stones is to be found on the moor a short distance to the east of Sheriffmuir Inn. There are altogether six stones still extant, in addition to which there is a small stone close to the public road below the hotel which differs in appearance from the others and does not seem to have had any connection with them.

Of the six stones only one is now standing. The first prostrate stone is 7 feet in length, 8 feet in circumference at the thicker end, and 6 feet at the top. On the exposed side, which, when the stone was erect, would be facing the south-east, appear over 20 cup-marks from one and a half inches to two inches in diameter. The purpose of cup-marks is still unknown.

The second stone in the same line, and about 75 yards distant, is not quite so high, but is rather larger in circumference. The third stone is somewhat out of position, but the fourth, which is only 4 feet in length, is in more exact line. Perhaps a portion may have been broken off at some time. There is an interval of 150 yards between this and the large stone which still stands erect, indicating the possibility that a stone is missing.

The erect stone, commonly called the Wallace Stone, is 6 feet in height and 14 feet in circumference, and it is four-sided. The last stone lies about 75 yards beyond, resembling a flattened pyramid. Its dimensions are larger than those of the Wallace Stone, being 10 feet in length and from 16 to 18 feet in circumference.

These stones are more or less in a line running south-west to north-east. There is a tradition that Sir William Wallace gained a great victory over the English at Sheriffmuir, and that the stones commemorated the success of the great Scottish patriot. The incident is narrated by Blind Harry, but, whether the victory is or is not historical, there seems no doubt that the stones date from a much earlier period.

To the east of Sheriffmuir and south of Greenloaning were found the remains of an ancient stone circle a short distance north-east of the farm house of Harperstone. The only stone now standing is 9 feet long, and 6 feet across the top. In the opinion of Mr. Hutchison it was the centre stone of a stone circle. The circle had a radius of about 15 yards with a similar distance between each of the larger stones.

The *Stirling Journal* of 6th May, 1830, makes reference to this circle, and records that about the middle of the previous century three vessels of clay were dug up which contained coins of very ancient date, as also specimens of ancient armour and some stones with inscriptions engraved thereon. The coins were for some time preserved by Mr. Monteath of Park, but have been lost trace of. Neither they nor the "stones with inscriptions" can have had anything to do with the circle. They must be much later.

Some of the most interesting of the standing stones in the district are on the farm of Glenhead, about midway between Dunblane and Doune, in a glorious situation from which an extensive view is obtainable in all directions. Three of these stones stand in a line and a fourth lies beside the most northerly of the three. The latter may have been one of the original group whose position had been moved in connection with agricultural operations. The most southerly stone is, as such frequently are, of an irregular pyramidal shape about 6 feet 8 inches in height and with a circumference of about 9 feet. Part of it may have been cut off or may have split at one time. The second stone, more squat or table-shaped, is four sided, two sides being 3½ feet broad and the other two 2½ feet. The height is 4 feet 6 inches and the circumference 12 feet. The top is flat and is covered with cupmarks 24 in number, one near the centre being larger than the others. The third stone is 6 feet in height and 2 feet 6 inches in breadth, while the fourth, lying beside it, is both higher and wider. The first three stones stand in a line N.E. and S.W. To the north of this line of stones, about a quarter of a mile away, stands a piece of rough sandstone 7 feet in height and 5 feet 6 inches in width. It is a most interesting stone consisting of a large flat slab standing on end, its shape being like a book. The north side is flat and even, but there are irregular markings on the south face. On the top where it is quite narrow there is at least one cup marking, but a fissure extends along this facing. The stone is unusually shaped as contrasted with ordinary standing stones.

There are other ancient stones of interest in the district such as the one on Whiteston Farm a short distance south of the public road to Perth, of large dimensions and having on its east side one large and seven smaller cups. It does not, however, form part of a stone circle.

The Battle or Gathering Stone at Sheriffmuir may have been at one time a standing stone which had been overthrown. Situated on the highest point of Sheriffmuir it seems undoubtedly to have a history extending many centuries before 1715. It has been known by various names, these including "The Beltane Stane," "The Carline's Stane," and the "Gatherums' Stane."

Without going into further details, it may be said that these stones bear witness to a population in the neighbourhood of Dunblane in prehistoric times.

It may be noted here that in 1928 an old stone coffin or tomb thought to date from the Bronze Age was found within a few feet of the N.W. corner of Dunblane Cathedral. It was about 4 feet in length and consisted of stone slabs without a top or lid. No relics were found inside.

Other stone cists have been found in Dunblane and neighbourhood of which the most interesting are the four which were laid bare when the second pair of Glenallan Cottages were erected. Behind the site of these cottages stood a mound of coarse gravel, part of which was removed when the foundations of these houses were built, the cists being under the highest part of this mound. Unfortunately 2 of the 4 were destroyed by the workmen before it was realised that the objects were of interest. Of the other 2 cists one was formed of 4 slabs of stone which met closely together at the corners, but had no cover. Its dimensions were 3 feet 3 inches in length, 2 feet 2 inches in breadth and 2 feet in depth. The contents consisted of a number of human bones, including part of a skull and 2 teeth. The fourth cist was formed of 4 stones rounded and worn with the flow of water; these were smaller than the stones of the first-mentioned cist. Two urns were found at the bottom of this cist but both were broken. They were small, about 5 or 6 inches in height, and made of very coarse material, but were to some extent ornamented. The cists were found about 15 to 16 inches below the surface, and evidently dated centuries before the time of Christ. In the first cist a bronze dagger or spearhead was found, measuring 4¾ inches in length and 1½ inches in width at the base. The base was neatly rounded with 3 rivets. When the dagger had been put into the cist, a handle had been attached to it. The dagger was of elongated triangular shape, and the metal was equally thick all over as if it had been cut out of a sheet of bronze.

Another stone cist was found at Cromlix in 1901 about 500 yards west of the Mansion House and about 10 inches below the ground. There remained the 2 stone ends, 1 side stone and part of a stone cover. It was about 3 feet 6 inches in length and about 2 feet in depth. At the bottom of the cist were stones with a thin layer of clay, but no bones or articles were found therein.

A further cist was found on 30th September, 1903, when a track was being cut for laying a drain at the Cathedral Hall, Dunblane. The top of it was 4½ feet below the surface of the ground, the length of the cist being 2 feet 8 inches, the width 1 foot 8 inches and the depth 16 inches. It consisted of 4 rough portions of local red-stone. Its only contents were 2 human teeth.

There exists a peat moss between the foot of Braeport and the choir of Dunblane Cathedral extending from the east gable of the Cathedral to the roadway of Kirk Street. The moss is about 5 feet 6 inches in depth and is about 2 or 3 inches below the surface. In this moss have been found bits of old ash and hazelwood, a right under-jaw Bone 13 inches long with 6 teeth of exceptional size, apparently that of a red deer, as also other bones of this animal. Some of the bones were neatly cut and may have been intended for use as tools, but had been left unfinished.

A number of arched passages and cellars of much later date are known to have existed in Dunblane. When the Cathedral Hall was being erected about 1903 an archway 15 feet in width and about 90 feet long was discovered over which the present building stands. This ran parallel to the wall of the churchyard and inside was found building stone. The facing stones were of a grey colour, but the principal portion was of local red sandstone. William Rae, who was then Beadle and Sexton, came on another archway about 18 inches to the north of the churchyard wall, but the side of this archway nearest the Cathedral had been previously removed.

The late John Robertson, antiquarian, Caretaker of the Dunblane Institute, came to the conclusion that the front of the Bishop's Palace faced the Cathedral with a gable towards the river, at an angle of about 30 degrees to the existing ruins with a circular tower containing a staircase where the two buildings met. This tower-way covered one-half of the present footpath from the Cross to the Haining, but, so far as can be ascertained from old titles, Robertson's theory is incorrect, the Bishop's Palace occupying the ground between this pathway and Dunblane Manse, and having the grass-yard as a garden and orchard.

The next interesting period in the history of Dunblane is that of the Roman occupation of Scotland. Dunblane was on the direct route between the camp at Camelon and that of Ardoch, and for many years the district was never without some Roman soldiers in these camps and in outposts, forts or signalling stations in the neighbourhood or passing along the main North Road. The road northwards from Camelon by Stirling is said to have been generally to the left or west of the present main North road. The tradition is that, from Bridge of Allan the road took the following route : Where the ground rises from the Carse of Lecropt near Bridge of Allan Station the road passed by Lecropt School through Park of Keir farm and crossed the river somewhere near the south end of Kippenross Tunnel. It then passed across the lawn of Kippenross House, through the parks, behind the gardens of the High Street houses and across the present Perth Road to the east of St. Blane's gate at Woodend House. The road skirted Holmehill and proceeded past the old buildings of Backcroft and onwards by the footpath past the Cemetery to Duthieston. Some writers have thought that it then followed the line of the present main road to Greenloaning, but this road was only constructed in the second half of the 18th century and a much earlier road to Ardoch and Crieff followed the line of the present Kinbuck road until north of the Glassingall North Lodge from which it continued eastwards in almost a parallel direction to the present Perth road until it came to a ford across the Allan a short distance below Greenloaning railway station. It seems more probable that the Roman road lay in that direction between Duthieston and Greenloaning rather than in the more obvious direction of the present main roadway. It is, however, only right to say that the local traditions with regard to the Roman road, as recorded by the late John Robertson, indicate that it passed, after Duthieston, along the direction of the existing main road to Greenloaning and that until recent days a Roman ditch on the north side was discernible. He also indicated that a spiral path was formerly seen on The Lady Mount, a knoll standing N.E. of Duthieston House, with traces of earthworks near the top.

The Romans doubtless had military posts and signalling stations in proximity to the road, at convenient heights. Various sites have been suggested, but in no single case has anything approaching proof been forthcoming.

One may, however, suppose that Dunblane was in the heart of a busy district during the days of the Romans in Scotland with Roman battalions passing northwards and southwards, as also waggons conveying provisions and military stores, while soldiers may have been resident at several stations within the parish.

Very little is known of the campaigns of the Roman generals in Scotland recorded by ancient historians, and no references have been traced in their writings to local places or events, while any local traditions that have survived are of so vague a nature as to be unworthy of record. Nor is there any evidence that the Romans left any impressions of culture or founded any seats of religion in the district.

The next period of interest in the history of Dunblane is that associated with the Celtic Saint Blane who gave his name to the township where he founded a church and a Christian community. One wonders why St. Blane selected this place in which to found a church and a seat of learning unless it be that a considerable population was resident there, that the land was suitable for agricultural operations and that there was a hillside which could be readily defended from an enemy's attack. But it must be kept in view that St. Blane was not the earliest Christian missionary to central Scotland. He was preceded by Ninian, Kessog, Fillan and others, and Blane may have passed through Dunblane when he accompanied his master Kenneth on his journeys to Abernethy and Fife.

In a very old manuscript Dunblane is described as being the principal city or chief seat of St. Blane. With regard to the Saint there is considerable information extant. In the Martyrology of Oengus under August 10th is recorded the death of " Fair Blaan of Kingarth." He is there described as " sound, of noble birth, well coloured." In the Martyrology of Tallaght St. Blane is referred to as Bishop of Kingarth in Bute.

Much has been done by the Reverend A. B. Scott, D.D., of Kildonan, to clear up the story of the life of St. Blane and to dis-entangle what had been super-imposed on the historical. The information which follows has been taken from his writings. A life of this early Brito-Celtic saint was written in 1505 by George Newton, Arch-deacon of Dunblane, but unfortunately it has perished, as also have the records of Kingarth.

Blane—the name meaning chief or leader—was born in the Island of Bute. The date is unknown, but is believed to be about A.D. 565. Blane's mother was named Ertha, but the name of his father is unknown and perhaps some mystery attaches to his birth. He is described as "a man of the country." Ertha was a sister of St. Catan, whose name is preserved in the word Kilchattan—that is the cell of Catan, erected a short distance from the church and community of Kingarth. Blane grew up under the protection of his uncle, who was of Iro-British descent. He received his early education at Kingarth under St. Catan at the school over which he presided. It is believed that the relics of early Christian days have established that, in the days of St. Blane, an advanced knowledge of art and the crafts existed.

Blane's education was completed at the Great School at Bangor in Ulster under St. Kenneth and St. Comgall, the Great. He is stated to have gone to Bangor about A.D. 581 and to have been ordained by St. Catan prior to his leaving Bute. Blane became the vowed Monk of St. Catan and to the end of St. Catan's life was subject to his discipline. It is recorded that Blane was baptised by St. Kenneth when he was about 12 years of age. The reputation of Bangor at this time was high throughout Western Europe and many of the most famous missionaries of the day were trained there. St. Catan had been one of St. Comgall's pupils and had made his vows to him, and Kingarth was a daughter monastery of Bangor.

Blane remained about seven years at Bangor under St. Comgall and it is believed that he went next to Aghaboe, of which community St. Kenneth was the head. After a few years under St. Kenneth, Blane was ordained Presbyter and sent forth on his first mission. Dr. Scott writes that he set sail due east from Bangor and landed on the coast of Cumberland, first making his way inland to the uplands. Blane resided for a time at " Appilby," now known as Appleby, a small town in Westmorland. Here Blane's aid was sought by a British chief, whose son was very sick. While one cannot accept the story that Blane brought back the lad to life, the lad's recovery was attributed to the assistance of Blane. The young man was named Colum and he became a pupil and fellow worker. He seems to have had his early training at the school at Kingarth, and later in life to have been placed at the head of the community founded at Dunblane where he was buried. It is said that Colum's father bestowed on Dunblane the revenues of " Appilby " and other lands in the north of England, and it is believed that the Culdees of Dunblane some centuries later did possess revenue from Cumberland. St. Blane worked northwards founding a number of churches including one at Greenock about A.D. 596.

On his return to Bute, he founded a community at Kilblane not far from Kingarth. Blane's Well and the monastic burial ground are known to this day.

Blane was probably about thirty years of age when he returned to Kingarth. He was ordained by St. Catan, a bishop of the Celtic type. He proceeded to organise his own community and training school while continuing under the direction of St. Catan and assisting him in his work. He then proceeded on a second tour visiting Kintyre, Inveraray and elsewhere and founding churches in various parts of Argyll.

It was during Blane's third missionary tour that he founded his community at Dunblane, sometime in the early years of the seventh century. Dr. Scott writes that he commenced this tour not earlier than A.D. 602, but not much later. He journeyed from the shores of the Firth of Clyde through the district of Lennox and along the valley of the Forth to the Devon Valley, turning again westwards and coming to Dunblane, where he founded a monastic community, and this came to be his chief seat. Other churches founded in this district at this time were the church at Muthill, St. Blane's on Lochearn, near the chief seat of the men of the Earn, and in the north part of Fortingall Parish.

The missionaries of the Brito-Celtic Church organised their work carefully, sought not to compete with each other and founded churches where there was need of such. The church at Dunblane occupied an important position on the north road after the crossing of the Forth on its way through the valleys of Strathallan and Strathearn inhabited by the Caledonians and the men of Fortren. Dunblane was no doubt visited by early missionaries when they passed north-eastwards to Abernethy, Dunkeld and elsewhere. Blane was associated in some of his missionary work with St. Kentigern, whose death occurred in A.D. 612. At that date, Blane was one of the best-known churchmen in central Scotland.

The sovereign of that portion of Scotland in which Dunblane was situated in the days of Blane was Nectan, who was a Christian. The name of Dunblane indicates the occupation of what had been a stronghold or fortified place or what became one. The permission of the overlord had to be obtained before a religious community could be founded. Such would be procured by Blane from Nectan. What had been a fort became the site of a monastery and the place was thereafter identified with the name of Blane.

It is thought that an intimate connection was maintained between the community at Kingarth and that at Dunblane, and probably St. Blane lived his later life in these two centres. While Dunblane was Blane's chief seat, probably he spent his last days at Kingarth of which he was head, while Colum presided at Dunblane where he was ultimately buried. Blane, known as " the mild of Kingarth," also " Blaan the Triumphant," died about 635 A.D. and was buried at the monastery founded by him in Bute. Dr. W. Douglas Simpson, however, ascribes his death to 10th August, 590.

Colum's death took place about 640 A.D. While it is not recorded that he succeeded St. Blane as Abbot of Kingarth and Dunblane, Dr. Scott is of opinion that this is implied from the references to Colum.

The connection between Kingarth and Dunblane was maintained for about two centuries, that is until after the destruction of many of the monasteries by invaders from Scandinavia about the end of the eighth century.

According to Dr. Scott's investigations, the first church at Kilbryde was founded by St. Briock (or Brite), a Briton who had been trained at Candida Casa during the time of St. Catan, and who had founded churches at Rothesay, near the Pass of Leny and at Annat Burn at Doune, as well as in North Perthshire.

Dr. Douglas Simpson suggests that the Abbey of Inchaffray was originally a foundation of St. Catan, for the Abbots held two of his churches, namely, the Church of Aberuthven and one at Stornoway.

David Camerarius, writing in 1627, quotes from a book of Archdeacon Newton, written about the year 1500, on the Acts of the Cathedral of Dunblane in which Newton claimed to have seen among the records of the Cathedral the autographum of the letter from Millitus and Justus, of date about 604, addressed to the Bishops and Abbots of Scotland. If Newton is correct in affirming this and if Camerarius is correct in his quotation, it is remarkable that the original of this important letter should have been in the archives of Dunblane Cathedral. By 1627 the letter could not be traced and the writings of Newton are no longer extant. Had they survived they would have been now of priceless interest and value.

In the Calendar of Saints, St. Blane was celebrated on the 10th day of August. In later centuries fairs were held in Dunblane three or four times annually, the principal fair, locally called the Grosset Fair, being celebrated on St. Blane's Day.

Dunblane has also been associated with a Roman Catholic Saint of Spanish origin known as St. Lawrence the Deacon, the date of whose martyrdom is said to have been the night between 9th and 10th August, A.D. 258. St. Lawrence was held in the highest reverence and many churches in Scotland, and elsewhere, were dedicated to him. No historical connection between Dunblane and St. Lawrence is known but there may have been some connection between St. Lawrence and St. Blane as these Saints were celebrated on the same date. Perhaps when the Celtic Church was replaced by the Roman Catholic, the latter saw that the name of St. Blane was held in such reverence that it was not advisable to endeavour to eradicate it, and they may therefore have chosen as Patron Saint of Dunblane the Saint who was celebrated on the same day as St. Blane in the hope that St. Lawrence would ultimately supplant the Saint of the Celtic Church.

The Coat of Arms of Dunblane contains a representation of both Bishops, St. Lawrence dressed as a Deacon holding in his right hand the book of the Gospel and also carrying a grid iron, he having suffered martyrdom by being grilled alive over a slow fire. His dalmatic ought to be red on account of his being a martyr, and in representations of him it is very often powdered with flames of gold. St. Blane is shown in bishop's vestments, his right hand raised in benediction and a pastoral staff held in his left hand. It has been said that the burgh seal of Dunblane (see page 30) dates from the 13th century, but other authorities ascribe it to a later date.

In the *Aberdeen Breviary*, it is provided that, in the Cathedral of Dunblane and in other churches dedicated to St. Blane, August 10th is to be observed as his festival, but elsewhere that date is to be the Feast of St. Lawrence. It has been said that the directions for the celebration of this festival given in the *Aberdeen Breviary* were the beginning of some biography now lost.

For some centuries the followers of St. Blane lived their quiet lives of industry and self-denial, but ultimately they fell away from their state of grace. Sons succeeded fathers and later generations appropriated for themselves what had been the property of the early Church until ultimately the Celtic Clergy ceased to be a source of uplift to the people and their order died out. Druidism, which long flourished in the district, was replaced in time by the Christian community of St. Blane and later by a community of Culdees. The latter was superseded by the Roman Catholic Church, to be followed in later days by the Presbyterian. If the latter is not true to the precepts of the founder of the Christian religion, it too will die.

The site of the fortified place of St. Blane was, in all probability, Holmehill. Here he and his followers would live in comparative security from attack. The ground is steep in all directions save to the north, while on the summit there is a considerable area of flat ground suitable for dwellings and cultivation. To the east and south there was a large morass known as Monthamyr or Mintockmyre, extending from what is now the Hydropathic gardens to the Minnow or Minnie Burn—perhaps a corruption of Mintock Burn. An old name for this is Alt Menych which has been translated as the Stream of the Hermit. (It now passes below the municipal tennis courts and underground through Dunblane under Balhaldie House garden behind the property of Mr. Gibson, Shoemaker, and the County Buildings and down the Millrow till it joins the River Allan). Below Holmehill to the south and south-west were thickets and bogs. We can well imagine St. Blane on the summit of Holmehill greeting the rising sun as it rose in its majesty on an early summer morn, or bidding it farewell as it sank in the west behind the high Grampian Hills. In early Christian days it was customary for a religious community to dwell a short distance from the church and it is probable that the church was situated on the flat ground near the left bank of the River Allan, where, in later years, the Cathedral was erected. In the earliest times the inhabitants of the district dwelt not in a community, but on the land which they cultivated and where their stock was grazed. Apart from the dwellings of the followers of St. Blane, it is not clear what was the site of the first village or city. There was an old Pictish hamlet of Pitzeavoch situated below Holmehill and an early village in the neighbourhood of Ramoyle. This word, locally pronounced " Ramule," is said to have been derived from the two words " Rath Maol " meaning either the ruined fortification or the fortification on the bare clear space. One has to keep in view that in early days there were no trees in the neighbourhood of Ramoyle, that some of the surrounding land was a moor and that part of it was known as the Blackcroft, this name surviving as Backcroft. It is interesting to notice that the word Holmehill is a modern form of Howmill and the second portion of that word has been thought to be Maol, which appears in the word Ramoyle. No mill has been traced to have existed about Ramoyle.

This was the place that became the chief city of St. Blane. It has been said, but erroneously, that St. Blane was buried in Dunblane—he was interred in Bute.

Of his successors in the early Celtic Church little is known. Dempster in his *Ecclesiastical History* refers to a St. Rumoldus as having been Bishop of Dunblane in Scotland, not of Dublin in Ireland, who ultimately suffered martyrdom in the year 772. St. Rumolde was worshipped on 1st July. Bishop Leslie refers to him as being Bishop of Dunblane in the 8th century. Particulars of other Abbots will be found in the writings of Dr. A. B. Scott. In Adamnan's *Life of St. Columba* there is given an account of the Battle of the Miathi—probably the same name as " Maeatae," a people who lived about the Hillfoots. The date is between 574 and 597 A.D. It is thought that Demyatt was the stronghold of this tribe.

In the 9th and 10th centuries the town of Dunblane suffered severely on two occasions. About the year 857, according to the Pictish Chronicle, the Britons of Strathclyde attacked the little city, destroyed it by fire and dispersed its inhabitants. Dr. Scott, however, while accepting the story that Dunblane may have been destroyed, wholly or partially, does not accept the truth of the reference so far as it attaches the blame to the Britons. Again in 912 Danish forces, commanded by Rognwald, landed on the banks of the Tay, marched through Strathearn and Strathallan, and reduced Dunblane to ruins.

From Lecropt to Menteith on the higher ground overlooking the Carse, there was a succession of forts erected for the protection of the Picts from British attacks, and the name of Keir is said to be derived from one of such forts (Caer).

Probably the lower portions of the Cathedral tower, built with the local redstone, were erected in Culdee days before the Roman Church was established in Dunblane. The tower may have served as a place of defence as well as a place of worship, and entrance was gained by a doorway several feet above the ground. There seems to have been, at one time, a church attached to the north side of the tower extending northwards.

The days of the Roman occupation were days of stir and excitement, those of St. Blane of quiet and spiritual uplift, those of the 9th and 10th centuries days of ravage and destruction followed by times when a strong community of Culdees existed in the neighbourhood, but, with the erection of Dunblane into a Bishopric of the Roman Church in the 12th century, a new era of development and prosperity commenced.

Any information about Dunblane in the 11th and 12th centuries is of a very meagre character, and such particulars have reference to the Bishopric, the Cathedral and its offices, with which this book is not primarily concerned. The exact date of the founding of the Bishopric is unknown, but it was during the reign of David I and has generally been ascribed to the year 1141, but the correct date may have been a few years later. There is no evidence that David I provided emoluments for the Bishop and Chapter. The diocese of Dunblane when the Bishopric was first created was probably co-terminous with the Stewartry of Strathearn. It is of interest to contemplate the probable reasons for the selection of Dunblane as the seat of a Bishop. Apart from its being probably the chief centre of population in the Stewartry, it had been for centuries identified with the early Celtic church and was, at this time, one of the chief centres of the Culdees. David I was desirous of replacing the Culdees by the Roman Church and, perhaps wisely, he appointed representatives of the Roman Church in districts where the Culdees had flourished and were still powerful. In Dunblane the Culdees for some time apparently formed the Chapter of the Cathedral, and no attempt was made to uproot them. Representatives of the Roman Church and Culdees continued to work together until in course of time the latter were entirely superseded. It was not a necessary rule, at these times, that the seat of bishops should be in the larger cities. While Dunblane was created into a Bishopric, an abbey—Cambuskenneth Abbey—was founded in Stirling. Dunblane Cathedral owed much, in early days, to the benefaction of Gilbert, Earl of Strathearn, who, prior to 1210, gave one-third of his possessions to the Bishop and Chapter of Dunblane. The significance of this gift has not, however, been determined. Some historians have thought that this gift merely represented the patronage of one-third of the churches in his Stewartry. It is improbable that the Bishopric owned at any time one-third of the lands of Strathearn.

While Dunblane was made the seat of a Bishop about the middle of the 12th century, it does not appear, as might be expected, in a list of Bishoprics existing in Scotland in the reign of Malcolm III, in the year 1057.

The lower sections of the Cathedral tower were probably erected in the 11th century. The names of successive Bishops from the middle of the 12th century are known. The limits of the diocese were defined, but there seems at first to have been no break from Culdee traditions and no development of Church organisation. That there was a Chapter, however, is clear from charters and other legal documents which have survived, dating from the 12th century.

As has already been mentioned, the family of the earls of Strathearn had a close connection with the early history of Dunblane. The first Malise, Earl of Strathearn, fought at the Battle of the Standard in 1138. He went into the fight in the fashion of his country wearing no armour, and it is narrated that he claimed that none of the Frenchmen in whom the King placed reliance would, with all their arms, be more forward in battle than he was.

Earl Gilbert succeeded his father, Earl Ferteth, in 1171. It is recorded that he adopted the Norman fashions, practised the usages of knight heraldry and united himself with Norman families in marriage. It has been claimed that Earl Gilbert was the founder of the See of Dunblane, but it is more accurate to say that the Bishopric owed him much for the magnificence of his endowment. The patronage of the Bishopric remained in this family until the abolition of the Earldom.

Malise, the last Earl of Strathearn of the Celtic race, lost his Earldom in 1334 for giving it to his son-in-law, John de Warren, an enemy of the King of Scotland. Earl Malise was one of the commanders of the Scots army at the Battle of Halidon Hill in 1333. He thrice married, but had no male issue. The fief reverted to the Crown who became patrons of the Cathedral.

During one of the restorations in the 19th century a gravestone was brought to view in the choir in which a knight and a lady were depicted in full size. This is believed to represent Earl Malise and his wife Joanna, daughter of Sir John Menteith. It may be noticed that the Earl is not represented cross-legged as Crusaders were, and his shield bears no device. It has been suggested that this was due to his having been attainted. The stone figures were above a coffin of lead which bore the date 1271.

It may be mentioned that Earl Gilbert was Justiciary of Scotland in 1178. His death occurred in 1223.

The claim that the benefaction to the Bishopric of Dunblane is due to Earl Gilbert rests on an old chronicle, which records his death and which, it is thought, was written in the Diocese or to have in some other way a connection with the records of Dunblane.

CHAPTER II.

DUNBLANE, 1200-1300.

THIS period is noted for the erection of the Cathedral of Dunblane which is perhaps the only local historical event of importance recorded in this century. While Dunblane had been a centre of religion from about the 6th century and while the land for a long period had supported a considerable population, there was no church of note until the Cathedral which now exists was built by Bishop Clement. The tower is certainly one hundred years older than the main portion of the Cathedral and a building had been attached to it at one time running northwards. Probably after the establishment of the Bishopric in the reign of David the First, a new church had been begun consisting of the Lady Chapel or Chapter House and perhaps the Choir, but the greater part of the present Cathedral was certainly built after the appointment of Bishop Clement—between 1240 and 1250.

There were, however, quite a number of men of note connected with Dunblane, but principally with the Cathedral. It is not proposed to give an account either of the history of the Cathedral or of the clergy—this is left to the historian of Dunblane Cathedral—but some notes may be given with regard to some of the Bishops of this See and other eminent men in the 13th century.

At the beginning of this century Jonathan, formerly Archdeacon of Dunblane, became Bishop. His death is recorded as occurring in the year 1209 or 1210 and his burial took place at Inchaffray. He was succeeded by William De Bosco who, according to Archbishop Spottiswoode, was Bishop before becoming Chancellor. He became Chancellor in 1211. He was succeeded by Bishop Abraham, bishop about the year 1220 whose name occurs in many old documents, and he again was followed by Radulfus who some years later is described as Bishop-elect of Dunblane while Robert was Earl of Strathearn.

There are various references to Bishop Osbert about the year 1230 and, according to Fordun, Osbert died in 1231. Osbert was succeeded by Clement in 1233, followed by Robert De Prebenda, regarding both of whom a good deal is known. The latter was still alive in 1282. Archbishop Spottiswoode includes one named Alpin as following on Robert. The last Bishop in this century was William, of whom we have some records. It is known that he was Bishop in 1290 and in 1292, but there is no record of the date of his appointment or of his death. According to Fordun, William sent in 1290 a letter addressed to Edward I concerning the succession to the Scottish throne and in 1292 he took an oath of fidelity to Edward I of England. Both he and Walter, then Archdeacon of Dunblane, were adherents of John Baliol, and the Bishop was chosen by the latter to act for him in a controversy between him and Robert the Bruce, 5th June, 1292.

It may be here noted that the Bishopric of Dunblane was closely associated in these years with the Earls of Strathearn. According to Fordun, as already mentioned, Gilbert, Earl of Strathearn, divided his lands into three portions, giving one-third to the Bishopric and one-third to the Abbey of Inchaffray and retaining the third portion to himself. It has been thought, however, that this merely refers to the patronage of the churches within the Earldom and that he had endowed the Cathedral of Dunblane with the patronage of one-third of the churches of his lands. The See may have been coterminous with the Earldom, and the Bishop is frequently styled as Bishop of Strathearn rather than of Dunblane. The Earls of Strathearn held almost regal powers over their possessions and the inhabitants therein and at this time they were patrons of the Bishopric. They claimed the right to elect Bishops and, if an appointment was made or confirmed by the Pope, he intimated this to the Earl as well as to the Chapter. We also find that John, one of the Deans of the Cathedral, is designated Dean of Strathearn in 1271. The Dean of Dunblane was usually the incumbent at Muthill as we find in the case of Donald about the year 1272. About this century Muthill was probably the second chief ecclesiastical centre in the district and in both places the Culdees were found at a comparatively late date after they had ceased to exist in other centres. The names of various Archdeacons in this century are recorded although the Archdeaconry appears only to have been endowed about 1239-40. It may be noted that Gilbert is referred to both as Archdeacon of Strathearn and Archdeacon of Dunblane. Another member of the Chapter to be found in this century is the Official who dealt with legal matters which were brought before the Chapter.

Of the other earls of Strathearn may be mentioned Malise, the fifth Earl, whose death occurred in 1271. He and his Countess appear to have been buried in Dunblane and their effigies in stone now lie in the north aisle of the nave, but were formerly in the chapter house, and previously in the north side of the choir west of the Bishop's Tomb. When the tomb was opened there was found on the lead coffin the above date.*

When Bishop Clement came to Dunblane he found the affairs of the Cathedral in a most unsatisfactory state. A great part of the possessions and endowments had been lost or dispersed by the Bishops. The Cathedral was without a Chapter and only one rural chaplain officiated in a church which was to a large extent roofless. There was no residence for the Bishop and the emoluments were insufficient to maintain him. So serious was the position that Bishop Clement went to Rome to lay the state of matters before Pope Gregory IX. The latter in 1237 addressed a letter to the Bishops of Glasgow and Dunkeld instructing them to visit Dunblane and to arrange if possible that a fourth of the tithes of all parish churches in the diocese should be assigned to the Bishop out of which the Bishop would be enabled to provide for a Dean and Chapter. If this provision was found not to be practicable the fourth part of the tithes was to be assigned to the Bishop and the seat of the Bishopric was to be transferred to Inchaffray. Fortunately that was not found to be necessary. In this letter of the Pope, reference is made to a representation by Bishop Clement that the possessions of the church had been seized and that the See had been vacant for more than 100 years, although elsewhere it is indicated that this should read as if it had been void for 10 years. It is not, however, by any means clear what is meant by this as there were certainly Bishops during the greater portion of the 100 years before Clement's appointment although it is possible that during the 10 years immediately preceding his appointment there was no resident Bishop in Dunblane.

An interesting writ was first published by the Reverend M. MacGregor Stirling in his *Notes on Inchmahome* (1817). This writ informs us that the Bishop of Dunblane had appealed to the Pope regarding the dilapidation of his church (which seems to have been in a lamentable condition) and the appropriation of its revenue by secular persons ; and it may be inferred from the terms of the agreement come to that the Earls of Menteith and their vassals were responsible for a good deal of the spoliation of the bishopric. In response to this appeal, the Pope (Gregory IX) issued a Mandate at Vitervi, 10th of June, 1237, to William, Bishop of Glasgow and Galdred (Geoffrey), Bishop of Dunkeld, directing them to enquire into the case and adopt suitable remedial measures. In pursuance of this mandate, the two Bishops held an investigation. The Bishop of Dunblane and Walter Comyn, Earl of Menteith, appeared before them ; and having stated their respective cases, they submitted themselves to the jurisdiction of the Bishops and their Court. The result was an agreement, accepted by both parties, of which the following were the principal provisions. The Bishop was to renounce all right claimed, or that might be claimed, by the Church of Dunblane, to revenues derived from the churches of the earldom of Menteith, in which the Earl had the right of patronage, and to desist from all complaints against him. The Earl was authorised " to build a House for Religious Men of the Order of St. Augustine in the Island of Inchmaquhomok, without impediment or opposition from the said Bishop or his successors." To these religious men were assigned, " in pure and perpetual alms, the churches of Lany and of the said Island, with all the liberties and easements" belonging "to the said churches" reserving his episcopal rights to the Bishop. The Bishop was not to be allowed to make perpetual vicars in these two churches, but to accept proper chaplains presented to him, who should be responsible to him " in spiritual and episcopal matters." The Earl, again, was to assign the Church of Kippen for a perpetual canonry in the Church of Dunblane, reserving to himself and his successors the right of presentation to the canonry, and to give over to the Bishop whatever right he held in the Church of Callander. References to the above are to be found in the Register of Inchaffray.

*The Countess was, according to MacGregor Stirling, the widow of Leod, the last of the Kings of Mann, ancestor of the MacLeods, and possibly aunt of Alexander, Lord of Lorne, who defeated Robert the Bruce at Dalry in 1306.

The instrument recording this agreement is dated at Perth on " the octave of John the Baptist," *i.e.*, the 16th of June, 1238 ; and it may be assumed that the building of the Priory was begun as soon as possible thereafter. It is understood that the original document cannot now be found in the Register House. The document (or a copy) forms the first item in an Inventory of Writs drawn up by William, 7th Earl of Menteith, in 1622.

It is interesting to note that in the case of the early Bishops they had no right to bequeath any of their estate by will. The Earls of Strathearn as patrons of the Bishopric claimed the whole goods of a Bishop on his decease. Theiner relates that an appeal was made by Bishop William to the Pope claiming the right for himself and his successors to bequeath the immovable estate however acquired. The Pope granted this right in the year 1291. Probably the Earls had originally regarded the Bishops as to a certain extent their representatives or stewards and it must be kept in view that the Bishops were not permitted to marry by the laws of the Church. This custom, however, so long as it lasted, probably led to the impoverishment of the Cathedral and its clergy.

In Dempster's *Ecclesiastical History* is mentioned a number of persons connected with Dunblane in this century. He records that Bishop Osbert was of good descent and of noble mind, a rhetorician, poet, philosopher and theologian, as well as a man distinguished for his piety. He is said to have been the author of a number of notable books. Dempster also records that a James Karden, a canon of Dunblane Cathedral and also of ancient lineage and of great talent, lived about 1294 and wrote some noteworthy theological volumes, and that Bishop Jonathan was a companion of the Carmelite Order, Rome being the place of his profession. He was sent to Scotland with the Pope's legate and employed to collect subsidies for the Holy War. He was said to have conducted himself most prudently and with singular learning.

Another author of this century was Hugo, Prior of Moy, a man of great sanctity and abstinence, born in Dunblane.

One of the most interesting men connected with Dunblane in this century was Simon Taylor who had studied in Rome and Paris, one of the first Dominican Monks in Scotland and closely connected with Bishop Clement. He was noted for his distinction in music, introducing sundry reforms in church music and writing works on this subject. He is said to have installed the first church organ in Scotland and to have brought church music to such perfection that Scotland might have competed with Rome in this art. Bishop Clement who, when he first came to Scotland, founded a monastery at Berwick, is described as a man full of virtue, distinguished in literature and piety. He wrote the life of St. Dominic, an account of the entry of the Dominican Order into Scotland and other works.

The Bishops were often engaged in work of national importance. Thus in 1277 Bishop Robert was, along with the Bishop of St. Andrews and two noblemen, appointed a commissioner on the question of the marches between England and Scotland, and in that capacity received letters of recommendation from Alexander III, King of Scotland, to Edward I of England.

In 1223 Bishop Abraham acted as mediator in a dispute between Robert, Earl of Strathearn, and the Abbot of Inchaffray. The matter was settled by the Earl swearing that he would never in all his life vex the Abbot or his Convent unjustly.

The Extracts from the Chronicles of Scotland, which Cosmo Innes thinks had been written in the diocese of Dunblane or had been in some other way peculiarly connected with Dunblane, record the death of Gilbert, the Earl of Strathearn, in 1223, and it is there stated that he was the founder of the Abbey of Inchaffray and of the Bishopric of Dunblane.

Bishop Clement, in addition to building Dunblane Cathedral, reorganised the ecclesiastical machinery. The clergy do not appear to have been connected with any order and accordingly the chapter was secular, not regular.

While the members of the Cathedral Chapter varied from time to time in the earlier years, it usually consisted of a Dean who was incumbent of the church at Muthill, a Precentor who was Abbot of Inchaffray, a Chancellor, an Official, a Treasurer and an Archdeacon, along with certain canons, one being the Abbot of Arbroath, coming in place of the church of Abernethy, dating from 1240, and another being the Abbot of Cambuskenneth dating from 1298. The other canons were incumbents of Crieff Primo and Crieff Secundo, Logie, Fordishall, Kinkell, Kippen, Monzie and Comrie.

Robert De Prebenda was Conservator of the Council at Perth in 1265.

Mr. Walter, Archdeacon of Dunblane, and Galfrys, Treasurer of Dunblane, were collectors of tithes in 1292 and received protection from Edward I dated at Berwick on 6th June of that year.

Theiner records the particulars of the tithe of ecclesiastical lands collected in Scotland by Bagimont. The total in the diocese of Dunblane for the first year, namely, 1225, was £108 9s. 2d. and was made up as follows :—

	lib.	sol.	den.
Abbas de Insula Missarum	24	13	3 (q)
Eccl. of Abernychi for Abbot of Abroth	6 marc.	4 sol.	
De Vicaria eusdem	2 marc.		
Abbas de Lindors	5	0	8
Prior de Insula S. Calmoth ...	6	13	5 (ob.)
De Prioratu of Abernythi	0	33	4
Ecclesia de Struan	3 marc.		
Ecclesia de Buthfuder	0	18	0
Vicarius de Kylmadoc	2 marc.		
Vicarius de Aberotheryn	0	7	0
Fioles	0	17	4
Ecel. de Glendelane	0	14	6
Eccl. de Muthuthe	0	28	8
Clemens Capellanus de Keldera Sua ...	0	2	0
Vicarius de Strughet	2 marc.	16 den.	
de Dunyn	0	12	0
de Druny	0	0	40
Ecclesia	0	16	0
de S. Maghot	0	20	0
De Duppeli ... ... nichil			
De Fossenwy	0	34	3
de Tullibothnyn nichil quia pauper			
Vicarius of Hughterardur	0	18	0
Eccl. de Tullalwy	0	0	3
De Garba de Logyn	0	42	8
Vicarius de Logyn	2 marc.		
De Eccl. of Kippen	3 marc.		
Eccl. of Cumery	0	24	0
de Aberful	0	12	3
de Killebrid	0	18	8 (ob.)
Vicarius de Gascrist	0	5	0
De Archidiaconatu	0	55	9
De Thesaurario	0	20	0
De prebenda Mag. R. de Strivelyn ...	0	0	32
domini J de Clacmana	0	0	32
Dominus Episcopus for his tenth ...	40 marc.		
Summa	108 lb.	9s.	2d.

This list is said to be imperfect as the names of certain churches are omitted.

In 1239 there was a dispute between the Abbot of Cambuskenneth and the Bishop of Dunblane with regard to the quarter teinds of Kincardine, Tullibody, and Tillicoultry Churches. The Bishops of Glasgow and Dunkeld, who were the auditors, considered that the churches had small revenue and were barely served and they ordered the Abbot and Convent to pay 4 marks yearly for the vicar who should officiate for them in the Cathedral of Dunblane, the Abbot and his successors in office to be canons. Cambuskenneth also was ordered to assign 4 marks to the church of Dunblane to be disposed of by the bishops at pleasure from after the death of Hugh De Bosco. Bishop Jonathan had, at an earlier time, confirmed the churches of Tullibody, Tillicoultry and Kincardine (on Forth) to the Abbot and Convent of Cambuskenneth.

The following are some additional notes regarding Gilbert, Earl of Strathearn. He succeeded his father, Earl Ferteth, in 1171. He, as has already been stated, assumed Norman customs, took charters for his lands, practised the usages of knight heraldry, connected himself by marriage with Norman families, and imitated David I in his munificence towards the Church. According to Fordun, it was he who founded the See of Dunblane, and his family had the patronage of the Bishopric until it was transferred to the Crown. In the earlier centuries the Earls protected the Culdees. His lands at one time seem to have extended from the Forth to the Moray Firth and from Loch Lomond to the east coast of Fife. In the time of Slezer (about 1693) it is said that there was a picture extant in the Cathedral representing the Countess of Strathearn and her children receiving a blessing from St. Blane while kneeling before him—this may have been a mural painting.

Principal Cunningham in his lectures refers to a Bull of Pope Innocent in 1200 which recognises the independence of the Scottish Church. The Bishop of Dunblane is referred to therein.

Bishop Clement consecrated the High Altar of Durham in honour of St. Mary on 5th June, 1240, which indicates that he was a man of note, whose fame extended beyond Scotland.

According to Theiner, William, Abbot of Arbroath, was consecrated Bishop in 1284 by the Bishop of Frascati.

The churches embraced in the Diocese as given by Bishop Walcott in *Scoti Monasticon* were as follows :—

PAROCHIALE DUNBLANENSE.

Aberfoil.	Prebend.
Abernethy.	Arbroath Abbey.
Auchterarder.	St. Mungo.
Abruthven.	St. Cathan. Arbroath Abbey.
Bondington.	Arbroath Abbey.
Blackford.	St. Patrick.
Comrie.	Paisley Abbey. Prebend.
Dron.	
Dunning.	
Dupplin.	
Foulis.	St. Methven.
Fordishall.	Prebend.
Gask.	Holy Trinity.
Innerpeffray.	
Kilmadoc.	Inchmahome Priory.
Kincardine.	St. Latan. Cambuskenneth Abbey.
Kinkell.	St. Bean. Prebend.
Logie.	St. Woloc. Prebend.
Kippen.	Prebend.
Lecropt.	Cambuskenneth Abbey.
Monzie.	Prebend.
Monedie.	
Monyvin'd.	
Madertie.	St. Ethernan.
Capeth Moothill.	The Dean.
Port.	
St. Madvins.	
Tullicultrie.	Cambuskenneth Abbey.
Crieff.	Prebend.
Logie Aithray	Nuns of North Berwick.
Strogeyt or Stroward.	St. Patrick.
Callendar.	St. Kessaig.

Fyndogask.
Tuelliallan.
Glendowan.
Fossowy.   Coupar Angus.
Baffudder.   Balquhidder.   Prebend.
Tulbothen.
Alva.
Dunbarnie.
St. Thomas Milnab.   (Prebend)   (which is probably the church sometimes
                                        referred to as Crieff secundo).
Tullibole.
Culross.

In 1219 Earl Gilbert of Strathearn granted a charter giving the church of Kilbryde and
eight churches in the neighbourhood of Auchterarder and Crieff to support the Abbey of
Inchaffray. Abraham, Bishop of Dunblane, Gilbert, Archdeacon of Strathearn, and Bricius,
parson of Crieff, were witnesses. The Bishop of Dunblane had in 1250 an income of £507 and
in 1282 an income of £607 13s. 4d. Apparently the income of the Bishopric fell off in the
14th century but this may have been due to the disturbed condition of the country. About 1258
slaves and their families were the subject of property in the same manner as cattle are at the
present day and that without being attached to any particular lands. Thus, it is recorded in
Dalrymple's *Annals* that Malise, Earl of Strathearn, granted to the monks of Inchaffray in pure
and perpetual loving kindness, Gilmoy Gillendes his slave with all his offspring for ever, and in
the same manner, John called Staraes, the son of Thomas, the son of Thore, with all his offspring.

Taking the Bishop's income as £507, on the assumption that £1 at that time is worth £5 at
the present, this emolument represented a very considerable annual sum.

In Stevenson's *Historical Documents*, volume 2, page 115, reference is made to the election
of Alpin, Bishop of Dunblane, on 15th October, 1296.

At that time Thomas of Inchaffray was called preceptor, Henry of Arbroath and Patrick of
Cambuskenneth, canons; John, dean; Walter, archdeacon; Peter, chancellor; Galfridus,
treasurer; Michael of Dundee and William of Gosford, canons.

In Dalrymple's *Annals* is recorded an account of the dispute at St. Andrews between
Gamelin, who had been elected Bishop, and the Regents during the minority of King Alexander
the Third, he having refused to purchase his bishopric. He had been consecrated by the Bishop
of Glasgow. Gamelin went to Rome to lay his grievances before Pope Alexander IV. Meanwhile the Regents seized the revenues. In 1257 the Pope pronounced judgment in favour of
Gamelin who was declared innocent of the charge against him and most worthy of a bishopric.
The Pope excommunicated Gamelin's accusers and the invaders of the See of St. Andrews, and
ordered the sentence to be solemnly published in Scotland by Clement, Bishop of Dunblane,
and the Abbots of Melrose and Jedburgh.

According to Fordun, during the winter of 1210 there was "great biting sharpness" and
flocks and herds perished. The severe weather began about the feast of All Saints and
lasted till Paschall.

It was during this century that Scotland was divided into sheriffdoms. The sheriffdom
of Perth was divided into quarters, but the district of Menteith and Strathearn had separate
jurisdictions and taxation. According to Cosmo Innes, the Culdees continued to act as the
Chapter of Dunblane Cathedral for over a century after they had been ousted at St. Andrews
and Dunkeld, and this was also the case at Brechin. They were protected by the Earls of
Strathearn.

It is said that David I endeavoured to reform the Culdees, but latterly superseded
them by monks brought from France and England, principally of the order of St. Augustine.
The Culdees usually married and the property which they held officially began to be appropriated
by individual members while there was a tendency to the priesthood becoming hereditary.

Both David I and his grandson William frequently resided at Stirling, and Dunblane
must have been well known to them.

There are various references in the register of the Abbey of Cambuskenneth to the Bishops of Dunblane and other church officials. In 1272, Robert, Bishop of Dunblane, consecrated the church of St. Servan of Alveth (Alva) on the Sunday after 14th February. He was a witness to a grant by Alexander, Lord of Stirling, to the church of an acre of land in Alveth near the spring of St. Servan. Bishop Robert's name appears in several charters about this time as a witness. In 1220 Abraham, Bishop of Dunblane, granted a charter in favour of the church of St. Mary of Stirling, of the churches of Tullibody, Tillicoultry and Kincardine (on Forth). In 1230 Bishop Osbert confirmed the above churches with lands, etc., to the Abbot and Canons of Stirling, that is of Cambuskenneth. In 1239 the Dean and Chapter of Dunblane Cathedral granted a charter of confirmation in which reference is made to previous bishops.

The church of Lecropt was formerly in the diocese of Dunkeld, but in 1260 an agreement was come to that it should pertain to the Abbey of Cambuskenneth in place of one half of the church of Kinclavin which had previously belonged to Cambuskenneth. In 1248 Bishop Clement was the principal witness to a charter by Alexander II confirming a grant of land at Cambuskenneth to the Abbey, as also a grant of fishing on the Forth between Cambuskenneth and Polmaise.

There was a school at Dunblane from an early date, the head of which was called the King of the scholars. The school had the right to receive " conveth " which is understood to have been an allowance of food. This right was renounced by an annual payment of 2s. to be paid yearly at Whitsunday. It is thought that the school was a survival of one under the ancient Celtic church. The resignation of this claim is recorded in the Chartulary of Lindores, the resignation being in favour of the Abbey of Lindores, Bishop Abraham undertaking to make the money payment.

In the time of Bishop Abraham there had been difficulty between Dunblane and Lindores regarding the church of Muthill. Bishop Clement had the matter re-opened on the ground that the church of Dunblane had suffered great injury. The Pope appointed the Bishop, Dean and Treasurer of Glasgow to enquire into the matter and their decision was that the previous settlement was just, but that the church at Dunblane was injured to some extent, and the Abbot of Lindores was ordered to pay annually 5 marks to the Bishop of Dunblane. In 1235, Bishop Clement accepted this decision and confirmed it. The confirmation was signed at Auchterarder by various officials including the Prior of the Culdees of Muthill and of Abernethy. About 1239 an arrangement was come to about the tithes of Feddal, Bennie and Concraig. These lands were in the parish of Muthill and diocese of Dunblane, but they belonged to Lindores. It was decided that Lindores would be free from payment of tithes provided they paid 6 marks yearly to the church of Muthill.

In 1261 there was a dispute between " Joachim of Kenbuc Knight' and the Abbey of Lindores as to the right of the Abbot to take wood from Curelundyn in Strathearn for repairing buildings on the lands of Feddal. Joachim agreed to allow wood to be taken and not to disturb the men of the Abbot provided he got previous notice.

When William was appointed Bishop in 1284 Pope Martin IV sent letters to the chapter, to the clergy and people and to the Earl of Strathearn, patron of the church. A similar course was taken at the election of Alpin in 1296, of Nicholas of Balmyle and of other Bishops.

The Abbey of Lindores had a mill at Feddal which brought them a rent of £8 a year.

The marches of the lands of Wester Feddal were determined by a jury in 1246. These had originally been crown lands within the thanage of Auchterarder.

Other Lairds of Kenbuc (Kinbuck) were, in addition to Richard referred to hereafter, Malcolm who swore fealty to Edward I in 1296, John who forfeited his lands in the reign of David II, Joachim who in 1341 helped to recover Edinburgh Castle by a successful stratagem, Sir Nicolas of Kinbuck, Archdeacon of Dunblane in 1360, Peter, who was groom to Robert, Duke of Albany, in 1402, Archibald, who sold " Lytel and Mikle Kynbuck " to Stirling of Keir in 1468, and Malcolm.

William the Lion died in Stirling Castle in December, 1214. His successors, Alexander II and Alexander III, frequently lived in Stirling and held Councils of Parliament there. Alexander III laid out extensive pleasure grounds called the "new park."

Bishop Ralph was Bishop-elect of Dunblane, but never seems to have been consecrated and he resigned before 1226 and probably earlier. Bishop Robert de Prebenda was bishop-elect at the end of 1258. He was a Canon of Glasgow and had not been consecrated by August, 1259. He seems to have been disappointed in not being made Bishop of Glasgow. He appears to have had property in the County of Nottingham and to have been favoured by Henry III. William of Arbroath, who succeeded him, was consecrated in December, 1284.

In a confirmation by Gilbert, Earl of Strathearn, about the year 1208, Richard, Knight of Kenbuc, was one of the witnesses. Richard's name appears in other charters. He was a son of Lugan and brother of Earl Gilbert's second wife Ysenda. In another charter Joachim of Kenbuc and Allan of Kenbuc are witnesses. Richard and Joachim gave part of the lands of Cambushinnie to Cambuskenneth Abbey. Sir Richard had a brother called Galfrid of Gask.

Malise, parson of Kilbryde, is a witness to a charter of Bishop Abraham about the year 1211.

After his appointment, Bishop Clement set about to gather in the emoluments of the bishopric which had been to some extent dispersed. The Bishop claimed certain tithes of the churches of Aberuthven and Thulliden. The matter was settled by the Bishop giving up his claims in return for an annual payment of £16 sterling, but in the same month Clement, out of compassion for the poverty of Inchaffray, remitted £6 of the amount awarded.

In 1239 the Chapter of Dunblane Cathedral confirmed to Inchaffray certain churches in the diocese, namely, Strugaith (Blackford), Auchterarder, Kinkell, Aberuthven, Dunning, Brandigask, Fowlis, Moneyvard, Thulliden and Kilbryde, under reservation of the sum of £16 payable to the Bishop and 20 marks to the Archdeacon of Dunblane. Some tithes were assigned for a prebend in Dunblane.

Bishop Clement was in charge of the Bishopric of Argyll about 1247. Earl Malise gave a portion of land in Dunblane called Tolauch to the church of Dunblane. This name was also spelt Culach.

There seems to have been a community of Culdees at Inchaffray before the Abbey was founded. The brotherhood there was converted into a priory of Austin canons by Gilbert, Earl of Strathearn. All the churches gifted to Inchaffray were dedicated to saints of the Celtic Church save the Church of the Trinity at Gask, but there may have been a Celtic church there. It is not clear whether the division into parishes took place before the diocese was created or if the diocese was first created and thereafter divided into parishes.

Although the estate of Keir did not belong to the family of Stirling in this century the ancestors of the Stirlings of Keir were resident in the neighbourhood. Alexander of Stirling lived between 1180 and 1245 and was the son of Peter who owned the lands of Cambusbarron. Alexander was Sheriff of Stirling and for some time Constable of Roxburgh, one of the chief Border strongholds.

Thomas of Stirling is also supposed to have been a son of Peter. He became Chancellor of Scotland and died in 1227. His name frequently appears in charters of King Alexander II.

Alexander, Sheriff of Stirling, was succeeded by John of Stirling, who lived from 1241 to 1270. John is presumed to have had three sons—Alexander of Cawdor, Sir John of Carse and Alva, and Sir William, the ancestor of the Keir line.

The original brass matrix of the old burgh seal of Dunblane is now in the British Museum. It was purchased at a sale of a Mr. Jamieson in 1839. It has been ascribed by Dr. Birch to the 13th century, but, in the opinion of Mr. A. P. Ready of the British Museum, it is probably the work of an artist of the 14th century, who had used, as a model, a seal of the earlier period. The wording on the seal is " S (igillum) commune Burgi Dunblanensis." The following description of the seal is taken from the book by the Marquis of Bute on *The Arms of the Baronial and Police Burghs of Scotland.*

" (Gules), within a Gothic temple (or) ; to the dexter the martyr St. Lawrence vested as a Deacon, holding in his dexter hand the Book of the Gospel, and leaning with his sinister hand upon a bed of iron bars ; and to the sinister St. Blane pontifically vested and mitred, his dexter hand raised in benediction, and his sinister hand holding a pastoral staff (all proper)."

The City of Dunblane was erected into a free barony in favour of the Bishops in the year 1442, but the burgh is of greater antiquity. The seal probably dates from the time of the original Earls of Strathearn, the last of whose line fell without issue at the Battle of Durham in 1346, the temporalities of the Cathedral of Dunblane being for long held from the earldom.

In the seal the left hand of St. Lawrence (see page 20) holds the frightful instrument of his martyrdom, which is represented by a sort of model or toy, but which ought, in Lord Bute's opinion, to be figured, as is the case on the town seal of the royal burgh of Forres, somewhat like an iron bedstead with crossbars.

In *Early Sources of Scottish History* by A. O. Anderson, we learn the following particulars with regard to Bishops of Dunblane.

On 23rd June, 1255, Pope Alexander IV permitted Master Robert De Prebenda, Dean of Dunblane, and others, proctors of the Prior and Chapter of St. Andrews, to borrow £500 of new sterling to pay their expenses homeward, binding the Bishop-elect (Gamelin) the Prior and Chapter and goods of the Church to repay the money. Robert, who was Dean of Dunblane, succeeded Bishop Clement, who died 1258. Before 1258 Gamelin was recalled by the King from exile and restored to the Bishopric of St. Andrews.

It appears from the Chronicle of Melrose that in 1259 Master Nicolas, Bishop-elect of Glasgow, returned from Rome without consecration. He had refused to pay money demanded by the Pope and Cardinals, and those who had gone to support him opposed him with all their might. Their leader was Robert, the Bishop-elect of Dunblane, who, blinded by his exultation, considered that, if the election of Nicolas were quashed, he could easily ascend to the Bishopric of Glasgow. Master John of Chean was, however, consecrated and Robert was sent off to his bishopric at Dunblane. Pope Alexander on 29th August, 1256, permitted Robert, Papal Chaplain, to hold two benefices in addition to the Deanery of Dunblane, and on 30th September, 1257, the Pope also allowed him to hold a further benefice.

On 13th August, 1259, the Pope permitted Robert, Bishop-elect, to increase his income by the revenues of the church of Kilmaling when vacant, the value of which was 10 marks, also to apply the first year's fruits of all benefices and dignities that became vacant in his diocese for the payment of the debts of the see.

On 22nd August, 1259, the Pope, at the request of Robert, permitted Master Ralph, rector of Loch Maben, and Master Richard Stirling, Canon at Dunblane, each to hold an additional benefice and permitted Robert to give benefices to three of his clerks. (The above notes are taken from Bliss).

Bishop Robert was in England in 1283 and on 11th September of that year when on his way to Scotland he received letters of protection while in England for two years. He died before 18th December, 1284, when, as already stated, Pope Martin IV wrote a letter to William, Bishop of Dunblane, approving of his election and appointing him Bishop. He had previously been Abbot of Arbroath. This letter states that Robert had died some time before. Similar letters were addressed to the Chapter of Dunblane, to the clergy and people of the see and diocese, and to Malise, Earl of Strathearn, patron of the church. William died about August, 1296, and the election of his successor Alpinius (Alpin) was confirmed on 16th October, 1296.

On 31st August, 1291, Pope Nicolas IV gave William Bishop of Dunblane permission to make his will, previous to which the Earls of Strathearn had taken the property of the Bishops at their deaths. It would appear that the effects of certain other bishops were claimed on their death by the King as patron. According to the Chronicle of Lanercost, Robert De Prebenda, along with Richard, Bishop of Dunkeld, more than all others that could be remembered, made so great a virtue of necessity by giving away their goods when death was imminent so that there was scarcely anything left for the patron to claim.

On 26th January, 1264, Pope Urban wrote to Bishop Robert on behalf of some Florentine merchants. According to Bower, Bishop Robert and Bishop Richard of Dunkeld were sent as delegates of the Scottish bishops to a council held in presence of Ottoban on 22nd April, 1268. At the instance of Ottoban and King Henry, Pope Clement ordered a 10th penny of the ecclesiastical revenues of Scotland to be paid to King Henry for the crusade. This was refused by the King and clergy of Scotland on the ground that they were all contributing to the crusade in a manner proportionate to the revenues of Scotland.

On 13th January, 1223, the Pope wrote to the Bishop of Dunblane and other bishops a letter praising the King of Scotland. The bishopric could not therefore have been vacant at that time.

Bishop Clement was consecrated by Bishop William of St. Andrews at Wedale, that is Stow, on 14th September, 1233. Bishop Jonathan was papal judge delegate from 1203 to 1210. He died in 1210 and was buried at Inchaffray. He was succeeded by Bishop Abraham. Ralph was Bishop-elect about 1224, but resigned before 12th January, 1226. Osbert died in 1231, a Canon of Holyrood. The See of Argyll was vacant from 1241 to 1248, during which time the diocese was administered by Bishop Clement. In a list of religious houses dated about the end of the 13th century the Chapter of Dunblane is said to consist of Culdees.

CHAPTER III.

DUNBLANE IN THE 14TH CENTURY.

WHILE the 14th century opened among stirring events for Scotland there are few records of historical occurrences connected with Dunblane. While not a large city it was of some importance as the seat of a bishopric and as a market town, but it was not the scene of any of the struggles of the wars for Scottish Independence although so closely situated to Stirling where Wallace gained his great victory at Stirling Bridge and Bruce his all-important success at Bannockburn. Stirling Castle, for some time one of the chief residences of the Scottish Kings, was a centre of hostilities in the days of Wallace and Bruce, this fortress changing hands seven times in 50 years. There is no record of the great hero William Wallace ever having been in Dunblane, although he may have passed through on his way to Stirling Bridge. Little is known of how Wallace fared after the Battle of Falkirk. He was betrayed by Sir John Menteith of Rusky, west of Thornhill, near to Port of Menteith.

Robert the Bruce must also have known the district well. Prior to the Battle of Bannockburn he had regained almost every stronghold in Scotland except Stirling Castle. An agreement was come to between Bruce and the English governor of the castle that if Edward II did not send an army to fight for the castle within a year he would deliver it over. Edward II came to Scotland in the following year, and on the 24th June, 1314, was defeated at Bannockburn, and Scotland was once more free from the yoke of the English Kings. On the morning before the battle the Scots soldiers were observed to kneel in prayer. Maurice, the Abbot of Inchaffray, passed along the front of the Scottish army barefooted and bearing a crucifix in his hands, exhorting the soldiers in few and forcible words to fight for their rights and their liberty. (Dalrymple's *Annals*, note page 170). Five years later Bruce, who was now established on the throne, appointed Maurice to be Bishop of Dunblane, in succession to Nicolas of Balmyle. Nicolas, who had at one time been Chancellor of Scotland, reigned as bishop from 1307 till his death in 1319 or 1320. He was previously parson of Calder (Caledor-Comitis), in the county of Edinburgh.

Bruce, in addition to promoting Maurice to the bishopric, conferred certain benefits on the Abbey of Inchaffray, granting to it the patronage of the church at Killin.

Unfortunately, Robert the Bruce died when his successor was but five years of age, and the heir in time proved himself an unworthy son of his great father. Hence we find that at the Parliament held at Edinburgh, on 10th February, 1333-4, the national liberties of Scotland were resigned, and among the parties to this disgraceful transaction was Bishop Maurice of Dunblane.

Maurice's successor in the bishopric was William, of whom little is known. He seems to have succeeded Maurice in 1347, and to have died in 1361. He had formerly been a Canon of Dunblane. The bishops who followed during the remainder of the century were Walter de Cambuslang or de Coventre, a former Dean of Aberdeen, appointed about 1361 or 1362, living in 1371, and dying about 1372, followed by Andrew, a former Archdeacon of Dunblane—Bishop from 1372 to 1380—and by Dugald Drummond, the brother of Annabella, queen of Robert the Third, who held office from 1380 to 1403.

It is recorded of Walter de Cambuslang, that he and the Earl of Douglas, the chief noble of his day, were the only persons who refused to do homage to Robert the Second at the Mount of Scone. They, however, took the oath on that occasion.

It is of interest to note that in 1289 a letter was addressed by the community of Scotland to Edward I of England, giving the names of the chief persons in the realm apparently in order of importance. The list begins with the Bishops of St. Andrews and Glasgow put together, followed by John Comyn and James Stewart, then follow the names of other Bishops, namely, Dunkeld, Moray, Aberdeen and William of Dunblane. Thus, the Bishop of Dunblane ranks here as the eighth person of importance in Scotland. Other Bishops follow in order, then Counts, the first being Malise, Earl of Strathearn, then Abbots, Priors, and Barons. Bishop William was formerly Abbot of Arbroath, and was Bishop of Dunblane from 1284 to

1296. In 1291 he swore allegiance to Edward I, and in that year he signed the Ragman's Roll at Stirling Castle. The Ragman's Roll was devised by Edward I of England, who ordered that the names of all landowners in Scotland should appear in a list under penalty of forfeiture of their land by any who did not sign the Roll, and this as a token of their subjection to Edward and in acknowledgment of his sovereignty. The name of Nicolas de Balmyle also appears on the Roll.

It appears from the Exchequer Rolls of Scotland that the contribution for the peace from the Bishopric of Dunblane in 1329 amounted to £112 19s., and in 1331 to £145 5s. 3d., which represents a considerable increase. In 1360, Sir Nicolas of Kinbuck, who was then Archdeacon of Dunblane, along with other persons, gave in an account of the third contribution for the King's ransom for the Stewartry of Strathearn. It may be noted that a similar account in respect of the Stewartry of Menteith was given in by Thomas de Carscapline. If the modern version of the name is Corscaplie, the popular derivation of the latter word, namely, " The Cross at the Chapel," must be incorrect.

From the Exchequer Rolls it is learned that Sir David Bell was Archdeacon of Dunblane in 1377, and that in 1384-6-8, and 1390, the Dean of Dunblane, whose name is not given, was paid at the date of the accounts £5 for his services as Chamberlain. In 1382 John of Kinbuck received a payment of £68, but for what is not stated.

It may be of interest to note that the first Nicolas, Abbot of Arbroath, was consecrated Bishop of Dunblane by Theodoric, Bishop of Rome, the second Nicolas by the Bishop of Ostia, and Bishop Maurice by the Bishop of Porto, a successor of whom consecrated William the Canon.

The church of Cambuskenneth sustained great losses through the war of Scottish Independence, and about that time the tower of the abbey was destroyed by lightning. On an appeal to Pope Clement V for assistance, the vicarage of the church of Clackmannan was bestowed on the Abbey, which church had become vacant on the appointment of Maurice of Strathearn to be Archdeacon of Dunblane. Edward I of England came to Cambuskenneth at the end of October, 1303, and remained there for about ten days. It is noted that he passed through Dunblane on 28th October, and again in the following year on 30th July, when proceeding northwards.

The activities of bishops were not confined to their dioceses or to church work, and while we know little of Bishop William who followed Bishop Maurice, it is recorded that he was one of the Scottish ambassadors who went to meet the English representatives to treat for peace at the village of Hextildesham in 1350, and again in the following year at Novum Castrum.

In 1304, according to the wardrobe accounts of Edward I, a brown palfrey was bought for the body of the King at Dunblane, in the month of August, from Basil Ballister. The price was £5 6s. 8d., and was paid at York on the 13th day of October by his own hands. It is also noted in the same year that the King gave 2/- to seven women who met him in the wood between Gask and Oggilwill (probably the modern " Ogilvie "), and sang before him as they were wont to do according to the custom in the time of Alexander, late King of Scotland. It was also in this year that the Cathedral roof was stripped of lead for use by the English army in their investment of Stirling Castle.

It may be of interest to reproduce the letter bearing date April 12th, 1304, from Edward I to the Prince of Wales, ordering him to provide lead for the siege of Stirling Castle, printed from the original draft preserved in the Public Records Office, in Stevenson's *Historical Documents of Scotland.*

" The King to the Prince greeting.

" Whereas we are afraid that we shall have want of lead for weights for our engines at the siege of Stirling Castle, we command you to procure and take as much lead as you can about the town of St. John of Perth and Dunblane and elsewhere, as well as from the Churches and from other places where you can find it provided always that the churches be not uncovered over the altars. And arrange and manage so that all the lead that you can thus procure shall come to us at the siege of the said castle. And upon these matters let us know your answer by your letters by the bearer of these presents. Kinghorn, 12th April."

We have a note of the valuation of the diocese of Dunblane in 1357 when the country was taxed for the ransom of David II. The old valuation of the see was £607 13s. 4d. Scots money and the true valuation £376 13s. 4d. Scots with £30 19s. 4d. additional as the value of the episcopal lands. The tithe of Dunblane would therefore be about £40 Scots.

In 1358 Nicholas of Kinbuck, Archdeacon of Dunblane, granted a deed which was attested by the seals of the Bishops of St. Andrews and Dunblane and the Constable of Scotland, which was not to be cancelled or in any way to be rendered null and void, whereby he bound himself and his successors Archdeacons of Dunblane to pay to the Abbot and Convent of Inchaffray 20s. sterling annually, representing the tithe and all other things which the Abbot and Convent were accustomed to receive from certain lands at Nessgask by reason of the Church of Gask-Christi.

According to Theiner, Nicholas, Abbot of Arbroath, who was elected Bishop of Dunblane on 13th November, 1301, was of the Benedictine Order and followed Bishop Alpin of blessed memory. In 1307 Maurice of Inchaffray, William of Lindores, Michael of Cambuskenneth, William of Eaglesham and Henry of Stirling, Canons of Dunblane, elected Nicholas II to fill the vacancy on the death of Nicholas I of goodly memory.

In 1309 William de Gospot, Canon of Dunblane, was allowed to participate in the fruits of the Canonry in absence. He held many benefices in Scotland and England.

The following is a description of the seal of Walter de Coventrie, Bishop of Dunblane from about 1358 to 1371. "It is oval, much damaged at the top. Virgin and child half-length and an angel on either side. In right central compartment a mitred abbot in the act of benediction with a crook in the left hand ; in the left compartment St. Catherine crown in right hand, sword in left, and words Johannis D. below all."

The reference made above to King Edward I meeting with seven women at the wood of Ogilvie near Blackford recalls a strange race of beings who occupied the hamlet of Buttergask which name appears in other forms such as Bithergirse. This hamlet stood on a moor about a mile south of Blackford. The inhabitants up to the beginning of the 19th century retained special racial features and their speech differed from all those of neighbouring lands, while their clothing was also of a strange fashion. James V of Scotland gave the chief a charter to the moor of Bithergirse to subsist while wood grew and water ran in return for a ram's horn spoon and a dish of kale-brose whenever he passed that way.

In this century the ancient, and at one time powerful, Celtic Earldom of Strathearn came to an end. Malise the last Earl forfeited his estates in 1345. He was one of the commanders of the Scots Army at the Battle of Halidon Hill in 1333—a disastrous fight for Scotland. Malise was thrice married, but left no male issue and the fief reverted to the Crown.

The chief proprietor in the district of Dunblane in the 14th century was probably the Chapter of Dunblane Cathedral. The lands of Kilbryde were at this time possessed by the Earls of Menteith. To the north of Dunblane the principal landowner was the family of Kinbuck who, in the following century, fell into penury and lost all their lands.

The estate of Keir was acquired by Lucas Stirling who lived between 1370 and 1449. Lucas was the grandson of John de Striwelye who was married to Mary, the aunt of John of Argyll, the last of the male line of the Lords of Lorne. John commanded the archers at the siege of Perth in 1339 where he was killed. Lucas acquired numerous lands during his lifetime, including Ratherne or Quoigs about the end of the 14th century. The lands of Keir were not obtained by him until 1448.

CHAPTER IV.

DUNBLANE IN THE 15th CENTURY.

THE principal landowner in the district at this time was Stirling of Keir. This old family had held land in the district for some generations before they acquired the property of Keir. The first Stirling of Keir was Lucas, who, as we have seen, acquired the lands of Ratherne or Quoigs about the end of the 14th century, and some time later certain lands in the Barony of Leysly in Fifeshire. In 1448 Lucas Stirling exchanged lands in the Barony of Leysly for part of Keir, then and later known as " The Keir." The word "caer" is an old British word meaning a fort or fortified place on rising ground, and a range of these ran along the northern face of the valley of the Forth and Teith towards Menteith. One of these forts was situated at Keir and hence the name. The mansion house of the Lesleys stood near the ford over the Teith, at or about Old Keir farm. This house, together with all papers not then at Ochiltree or elsewhere, was burnt in 1488 during the civil war. The present Keir House was commenced in 1489 by Sir William Stirling, son and heir of Lucas.

Lucas Stirling died between 1449 and 1452 and was succeeded by his son William, usually referred to as Sir William of Striveling of Ratherne. To the portion of Keir acquired by his father from Norman Leysly he added the other half of Keir known as Kerehawden (Haldane) from Walter Hawden of Kelore in 1455. Other important additions to the Stirling possessions were the lands of Lubnoch acquired from Janet of Kinross, Lady Kippenross, and the middle part of the lands of Schanraw and Garnortone bought from Archibald of Kinbuck of that ilk. He also acquired the lands of Little and Meikle Kinbuck in 1468. Born about 1420 he was thrice married and had 4 sons, William, his heir, John, William who was ordered in 1488 to restore to James Simson cattle, horses and goods taken by him from the place of Lekra (Lecropt) and Lucas who was involved in the encounter with Squire Meldrum regarding the widow Haldane of Gleneagles.

William, the eldest son, succeeded about 1471. On 26th April, 1472, he granted a Charter of Mortification whereby "for the health of the souls of King James (III), John Hepburne, Bishop of Dunblane, Luke Striuelyng, and Sir Willian Striuelyng, Knight, and Margaret, his spouse, the father and mother of the granter, and for the health of his own soul, and the souls of his wife, children, and ancestors, and of all faithful dead ; he granted to Almighty God, the Heavenly Choir, and the Blessed and Glorious Virgin Mary, and to her altar on the north side of the nave of the Cathedral Church of Dunblane, and to Sir John French, perpetual chaplain at the said altar, and his successors serving and to serve God there for ever, a toft and croft of the lands of Keyr lying in the town thereof the Lands of Schanrach, the Wodland, and Classingall, an annual rent of forty shillings from the lands of Kippanerayt, and the mill of Strowe, with three acres of arable land of the lands of Strowe, and the pasture of six beasts in the nether part of the same lands. To be held by the said chaplains in pure and perpetual alms, for performing divine service at the said altar, with license to Sir John French to possess any ecclesiastical benefice or chaplainry, with or without cure, for the whole time of his life ; but his successors were to reside in the city of Dunblane, and perform service at the said altar, and if they should be absent for two months without license from the granter and his heirs, the Chaplainry to become vacant eo facto. The presentation was to be with the granter and his heirs, who were to present a chaplain within two months after a vacancy, under a penalty of twenty merks, to be paid to the work of the Cathedral of Dunblane, and the presentation to devolve illa vice to the Bishop of Dunblane for the time. Dated at Keyr, 26th April, 1472, and Confirmed by John, Bishop of Dunblane, 10th May, 1472."

A similar charter was granted by his grandson, Sir John Stirling, on 2nd October, 1509. In 1473 the various lands of Sir William were united into a Barony.

In 1488 the Laird of Keir took the part of the young Prince James against his father James III, and it has been alleged that he was a party to the murder of James III at Sauchieburn, but this has not been established and there is ground for believing that he was in no way implicated in the tragic death of the King. The army of James III, after the battle, pursued the Prince and his supporters to Keir where James IV had taken refuge. He had to flee and the house was burned to the ground with all the owner's titles to his lands. After James IV was established on the throne on 9th January, 1489-90, he granted a new title for the Barony of Keir to be held from the Crown for payment of a pair of gold spurs at the Tower of Keir on the Feast of St. John the Baptist. The King conferred a knighthood on Sir William and, in 1488, gave him £100 Scots to the " byggin of his place." In 1489 £1000 was ordered by the Lords Auditors to Sir William Stirling " of the Kere, Knycht for dampnage and scathis sustenit in the distructioun and spuilyeing of his place of the Kere " (Acta dominorum audit page 130). Sir William's death occurred about 1503. He was twice married and had two sons, his heir being Sir John Stirling, and three daughters, one of whom, Catherine, married Archibald, Earl of Angus, known as " Bell the Cat."

Among the Keir charters is preserved the charter of Archibald of Kinbuck of that ilk to William of Stirling of Ratherne of the middle part of his lands of Glassingall sold in his great and urgent necessity for a certain sum of money to be paid by the said William, to be held of the King as Earl of Strathearn, reserving the lands of Schanroch and Garnortone. This charter is not signed, but the seal of the granter had been added when the deed was executed. The seal consisted of a cheveron between three bucks' heads cabossed. This was followed by a Procuratory of Resignation by Archibald of Kinbuck to King James II on 1st October, 1459, bearing the granter's seal. Shortly afterwards the Laird of Keir obtained a Royal Charter for the lands of Glassingall, Shanraw and Garnortone upon which an Instrument of Sasine was executed, the notary employed being John of Athrey, Treasurer of Dunblane, in the presence of certain venerable and discreet men including Master John Christinas, Chancellor and Official of Dunblane, and Sir Lucas Arnott, Chaplain. The title to the lands of Meikle and Little Kinbuck acquired in 1468 was completed by an Instrument of Sasine which proceeded on a precept of Sir William of Knollis, Presbyter of Torfychine, who had acquired the lands of Archibald of Kinbuck. William of Knollis was of the Order of Knights of John of Jerusalem.

The estate of Kilbryde, which had at one time belonged to the first race of the Earls of Strathearn, at this period was held in connection with the Earldom of Menteith. Sir John Graham, son of Malise, Earl of Menteith, traditionally known as " Sir John of the Bright Sword," obtained a title to the lands of Kilbryde on 7th April, 1469. He married Margaret Muschet, a member of an ancient family in the district. His death took place about 1490. On his death one third of Kilbryde passed to the husband of his only daughter, Drummond of Meggour, the remaining two thirds being acquired by Alexander, Earl of Menteith, his nephew. The erection of the Castle of Kilbryde has been attributed to Sir John Graham, but this has not been authenticated.

In 1487, James Muschet of Tolgarth acquired by decree of the Lords of the Council, certain lands at Kilbryde appertaining to Malise, Earl of Menteith, in respect of a debt of 400 merks, extending to an annual value of 20 merks, which lands the said Earl of Menteith and his heirs acquired right to redeem on payment of the said debt to James Muschet, with expenses, within a period of 7 years.

In 1495, King James IV confirmed a charter of Alexander, Earl of Menteith, in favour of his uncle Walter Graham and the heirs male of his body for payment " of one penny of 18 merks 6/8 of the lands of Kilbryde, namely from the Manis and those lands occupied by Thomas Henry Gibb, John Banks, John Muschet, John Wynds, And. Clark, Donald Clark, John Aneris, John Danskin, Christie Aneris, Makglas Vidua and John Brown." The witnesses of the charter included Bishop James Chisholm, Dean John Drummond and Will Forbes the Official.

King James afterwards reclaimed the lands of Kilbryde, as previously possessed by Alexander, Earl of Menteith, and gave these to Henry Shaw. Shaw again granted his lands of Kilbryde to Mariot Forestare, son of Walter Forestare of Torwood.

The tragic story of the murder of Lady Anne Chisholm of Cromlix by Sir Malise Graham, the Black Knight of Kilbryde, is related in Marshall's *Historic Scenes of Perthshire* and elsewhere, but apart from Malise Graham, Earl of Menteith, no man bearing this name has come down to history as being in any way connected with Kilbryde Estate. The property remained in the hands of the Earls of Menteith until 1643.

Doune Castle, one of the best examples of Scottish architecture of the 15th century, was one of the principal residences of the Earls of Menteith. It is said to have been built by Murdoch, Duke of Albany, superseding an earlier structure which had come into the possession of Robert, the great Duke of Albany, on his marriage to Margaret, Countess of Menteith. Like Falkland Palace, it was forfeited to the Crown on the return of James I from captivity in England in 1424, when, after trial, Murdoch, Duke of Albany, his two sons and his father-in-law, the aged Earl of Lennox, were all executed at Stirling. In 1431 Doune Castle was the dwelling place of James, the heir to the throne, then six months old, for whose use 48 lbs. of almonds were sent. James II frequently resided there and a record is preserved of the provisions supplied about 1451-4. On the staff kept at the castle were a chaplain, watchman, porter, park-keeper, gardener and keeper of the castle, and seeds of cabbage, scallion and onions were supplied for the garden. The King stayed there when hunting in the Royal Forests at Glenfinlas, but a hunting lodge consisting of a hall and two chambers was erected at Glenfinlas in 1459. The Castle of Doune was a dower house of the queen of James II and was also part of the jointure of the queens of James III and James IV.

At one time the Lairds of Kinbuck were men of some importance and were among the largest landowners in the district, but during this century they alienated most, if not all, of their possessions. A large part was acquired, as already mentioned, by Stirling of Keir. On 4th February, 1470-1, Malcolm of Kinbuck, a provident man, by his procurators, resigned and quit-claimed forever for him and his heirs, by staff and baton in the King's hands all and sundry his lands of Easter Glassingall and Wester Glassingall lying in the Earldom of Strathearn which resignation being made the King gave and bestowed the said lands to " Alexander Broys, son of Alexander Broys of Stanhuis, and husband of Marjorie de Kinbucks."

The city of Dunblane, the lands in the immediate neighbourhood and many lands at a little distance were the property of the Bishopric of Dunblane.

The Earldom of Strathearn having become merged in the Crown—the title continuing to this day to be held by a member of the Royal family—the patronage of the Bishopric became vested in the Crown who became the feudal superior of the lands. This was declared by the Parliament held by James II in Perth in 1442 during the bishopric of Michael Ochiltree. While the city of Dunblane was declared a free barony in favour of the bishops in this year, it is considered that the burgh is of greater antiquity as the matrix of a burgh seal now preserved in the British Museum has been ascribed to the 13th century or in any event not later than the 14th century. It may be of interest to record the names of the lands belonging to the Bishopric in 1442, most of which names are still in use. These include the following :—City of Dunblane, Brigend, Cascaplymore, Cascaplybeg, Cornileyis, Achwlay, Drumdowles, Ramule, Barbuskis, Achinvy, Classingalbeg, Buthirsgask, Brecache, Ardachis, Gadnachy, Kerè-decani, Tulmoquhousk, Tourechane, M uthill, Dromlechacy, Renybeg, Dergale, Fyndale, Clenes, Kerepon, Culuchibeg, Glentarky, Belach, Cragarnot, Lundyden, Thom-decani.

Towards the latter half of the 14th century Robert II, the Steward, grandson of Robert the Bruce, was King and he was succeeded in 1390 by his eldest son, Robert III. The Duke of Albany, the brother of the latter, was, however, virtual ruler of Scotland as was also his successor, his son Murdoch. One of the offices held by them was Keeper of Stirling Castle and Duke Robert died there in 1420. On 16th July, 1420, a National Council of the Church of Scotland was held at Perth. William Stephen, Bishop of Dunblane, was chosen Conservator of the Privileges of the Church of Scotland and in that capacity presided at the Council. In 1424 James I returned from captivity in England and he came to reside at Stirling Castle in May, 1425. The severity of James I led to his assassination at Perth in 1437. He was succeeded by James II, who, after being crowned at the Abbey of Holyrood House, came also to reside at Stirling Castle. After his unfortunate death in 1460 Stirling Castle became the favourite residence of his successor, James III, who erected there a Parliament Hall and a Chapel. His death occurred at Sauchieburn in 1488 and he was buried in the Abbey of Cambuskenneth where his queen had been previously interred. His son, James IV, also lived much at Stirling Castle.

One of the most notable events in the history of Dunblane in the first half of the 15th century was the erection of the first bridge over the River Allan, built by Bishop Finlay Dermoch, formerly Archdeacon of Dunblane, who became Bishop about 1406 and who died in 1419.

The bridge is said to date from 1409 and to have been of a width of 12 feet and a breadth of 42 feet. A tradition is recorded by Pocoke that the arch of the bridge was not found to be strong enough and was rebuilt, but, although it has been added to twice in modern times, the original bridge, now over 500 years old, remains. The tomb on the north side of the choir beside the site of the High Altar, is ascribed by tradition to be that of this Bishop, but some writers throw doubt on this. They consider that this was the customary position of interment of the Bishop who built the Cathedral and that the tomb should be that of Bishop Clement. Prior to the erection of this bridge the town of Dunblane appears to have been entered from the south by a road from the Bridgend to a ford in the River Allan, a short distance above the bridge, with a road leading from the east side of the river to Millrow. The bridge was, of course, originally saddlebacked and the street at both ends was much lower than at present. It is not known when the present High Street was first made, but it no doubt dates from a date subsequent to the building of the bridge. The Darn Road, which originally left the High Street at its junction with the New Road, dates from early times, and it led not only to the Meal Mill of Kippenross near Millad's Cottage, but also to the Crofts in the parks formerly known as the Cow Park and to the road round the rear of the gardens of the High Street houses.

Bishop Finlay Dermoch was not the only Bishop of Dunblane who was a bridge builder. Michael Ochiltree, previously Dean of Dunblane and as such incumbent of Muthill Church, was appointed Bishop in 1429 and crowned James II at Holyrood in 1437. He erected a bridge at Braco over the River Knaic and the Bishop's Bridge over the River Machany at Culdees. It is believed that some of the oak stalls still preserved in the Cathedral were his gift. There is a tradition that this Bishop was deformed by lameness and that difficulty arose over his appointment on this account. His tomb is preserved in the south-east corner of the nave at Dunblane Cathedral.

Important duties in the realm were frequently performed by the Bishops in early days. Bishop William Stephen, one of the first Professors at St. Andrews University and afterwards Bishop of Dunblane, between 1419 and 1429 was one of the auditors in the taxation of the goods and rents of burgesses for the ransom of James I, and in the following year he was sent on an embassy to Rome. At this time Dean Michael Ochiltree administered the Royal Alms on behalf of James I. In January, 1429-30, Bishop Michael was one of the ambassadors to England to obtain redress for certain grievances. In 1449 Bishop Robert Lauder was granted a safe conduct when sent as an ambassador to England, and in the same year it is recorded that he sat in Parliament. While the bishops were all summoned to meetings of Parliament it may be noted that a burgess of Dunblane sat in the Parliament of 1482 in the reign of James III. Various actions decided by the Lords Auditors have local references, some of which are noted in the chapter on the 16th century to follow. One may be mentioned here of date 13th October, 1479: "The Lords Auditors decreet and deliver that William of Stirling of the Keir, William his brother, and David Arnot shall freith a Reverend Father in God Johne, Bishop of Dunblane, and Robert Covin of the sum of £26 8s. for the quhilk they became dettour for them to Matthew forest burges of Stirling." John Hepburn was Bishop of Dunblane from about 1467 and was succeeded by the first of the three Chisholm Bishops about 1486. The other Bishops of Dunblane in the 15th century are Robert Lauder (already mentioned), bishop from 1447 to 1466, and Thomas whose name appears only once in the records in 1459 and who may therefore have only been a bishop quo-adjutor. The poverty of the diocese of Dunblane throughout the centuries is frequently referred to. It is somewhat surprising to observe in a Vatican record dated 6th September, 1419, that the church of Dunblane had been of old most sumptuous in its buildings, its glass windows, its ornaments and vestments, its many relics and jewels; sad to relate by this date, on account of mortality, the evils of the times and the thinness of the revenues so greatly reduced, the Bishop, Dean and Chapter were unable to maintain the fabric befittingly, and they supplicated the Vatican for aid. It is not recorded whether a favourable answer was returned by the Pope.

One case recorded in the Acts of the Lords Auditors of Causes having a local reference is of date 10th May, 1491, where "the lords auditors decreet and delives that Alexr. Bannerman sal content to pay to Maister Walt Small Chanoun (Canon) of Dunblane £6 of lent siller for the quhilk the said Alexr. was bunded be ane bill subscribit with his hand shewin and producit before the lords."

Reports of other local cases are to be found in the Acts of the Lords of Council of which the following are extracts :—

3rd February, 1484.—" Johne of Drummond dene of Dunblane on the ta part sued Arthur Oliphant, Patk. Ranaldson, Walt Ranaldson and James Ralesne on tother part annent the tack of the lands of est Kere and Cludy beg with the part pertaining to the dene and chapellanes of the Cathedrall Kirk of Dunblane."   On 10th March, 1490, William Stirling in Dunblane raised an action against Laurence Lodd Oliphant, Sheriff of Perth " For wrangus execution of his office in taking from him guids and corn, etc., as under written,

" Out of lanraky eight oxen, twenty-two ky.

" Out of coigge (Quoig) of Strathallan six oxen, fourteen ky.

" Out of brigland eight oxen, nine ky.

" Three young cattle, twelve sheep, a black horse."

Not only was the Sheriff of the County sued by a residenter of Dunblane, but even the bailies were not free from being taken to court.   On 29th October, 1495, John of Kinross accused Richard Sinclare and John of Row, bailies of Dunblane, of "Wrangus spoliacioun of twa potts, a pan and one wob of lynyng contenand seix eln out of the said Johne's land that tenement liandin the toun of Dunblane betwix the land of Thomas Ranaldson on the south parte and the land of Duncan Campbele on the north pte."

Alexander Brois did not retain his lands at Kinbuck for a long period.   In 1485 the sale by him of Glassingalls to John Drummond of Cargill was confirmed.   In 1493 John, Lord Drummond, was proprietor of the Cambushinnies as well as of Glassingalls.

At the end of the 15th century there was a considerable population resident on Kilbryde. In 1494 the Mains or Home Farm of Kilbryde was in the possession of Walter Graham, uncle of the Earl of Menteith who also possessed certain lands occupied by the following persons— Thomas Henrici, Gilbert Henrici, Johne Bankis, Joh Wyndis, And. Clerk, Donald Clerk, Joh Aneris, Joh Danskin.   The names of other persons resident on Kilbryde in 1491 include the following :—Gilbert Muschet, Gilbert Herisoun, John Patone, Melhope Dansell, wedow, Morris Clerk and William Glass.

Prior to the Reformation much legal business was transacted in Dunblane particularly in the courts presided over by Church dignitaries.   Where there was much legal work the Church commonly made the appointment of an Official who acted as judge.   The names of various Officials of Dunblane Cathedral appear in the Records.   The following sample may be given of a case tried by the Official of Dunblane of the time, taken from the Records of Stirling Burgh, 26th August, 1476.   " Before John Fresare, official of Dunblane within the cathedral church of the same, sitting in judgment in the usual consistorial place, compeared John Stewart lord Dernly on the one part, and John Haldane of Rusky, in name and behalf of Agnes Menteth, his spouse, on the other part, which John Lord Dernly presented certain citatorial letters against the said Agnes in a cause of bastardy, who being thrice called and not compearing, John Haldane, her spouse, craved to be admitted in the cause, the other party that it was a personal cause, and therefore she should compear personally, etc., the judge with counsel of his assessors, admitted the said John Haldane as pledge procurator for the said Agnes, his spouse, who bound himself to stand in law for her under caution of 1000 merks.   Present Vmfrid Cunyngham of Glengernock, Mr. Martin Wan, chancellor of the cathedral church of Glasgow, William Elphinstoun, official of the same, John Drummond, dean of Dunblane : Patrick Sandelandis, Rector of Calder and others."   One might also insert an account of the installation of a Canon of the Cathedral taken also from the Stirling Burgh Records 4th August, 1476.   " Sir William Ingleram, chaplain, presented letters of collation of John, Bishop of Dunblane, under his round seal, etc., directed to Mr. John Drummond, dean of the cathedral church of Dunblane, which, being received by the said dean with due reverence, he past to the choir and chapterhouse of the said cathedral church, with the said William and witnesses, and assigned the said William to a stall in the choir and place in the chapterhouse called the canonry and prebend of Cummery, and gave him real and corporal possession of the said canonry and prebend."

Justice ayres were also frequently held in Dunblane.   In 1444, in which year one was held in Dunblane, provision was made for an annuity to the chaplain doing duty in Dunblane

Cathedral from the fruits of justice ayres held in Strathearn, and in 1450 there was a similar provision in favour of Chaplains of the Choir.

Among some of the numerous officials of the Cathedral in this century whose names appear in the records as holding public office may be noted Sir Donald of Bute, Dean and an Auditor of Accounts in 1406-08 : David Lutherdale, a Canon, one of the Auditors in 1473, and Clerk of the Household in 1477 ; Henry Alane, at one time Clerk of the Accounts and of the Household and afterwards Archdeacon, and an Auditor of Accounts in 1495-6. He let crown lands at various times. Sir William Murray, a Canon of Dunblane Cathedral, was at one time Customer of the Burgh of Stirling.

Other noteworthy names are those of Master John Mosset (probably the same name as Muschet) who was Commissar of Dunblane in 1474, and John Cristisoun, Chancellor in 1448.

We find various records of the Bishops of Dunblane travelling, in the 15th century, on church or public business. Thus in 1425 a safe conduct was granted to certain ambassadors of Scotland, including Bishop William Stephen, who were going to Rome, the protection to last from January to Pentecost. Again in 1452 Robert, Bishop of Dunblane, journeyed to Canterbury along with the Bishops of Glasgow and Moray and certain noblemen to visit the King of England on national business. In 1473 the Lords of the Kirk offered £2000 to the King, the portion falling to be contributed by Dunblane being £100. In 1494 it appears that the Bishop of Dunblane contributed £20 to the building of Tarbert, that is of Tarbert Castle, which was then being rebuilt by James IV in connection with his expedition into Kintyre against the Lord of the Isles.

While the country north of Dunblane seems to have been almost destitute of trees until the end of the 18th or beginning of the 19th century we find that as early as 1461 timber grew well on the banks of the Allan south of Dunblane. In that year 14 great timbers were carried from the woods on the river banks at Kippenross to Stirling where they were cut and planed and afterwards used at Ravenscraig Castle, Fifeshire.

CHAPTER V.

DUNBLANE ABOUT 1500.

As Scotland advanced greatly in wealth, culture and importance under the rule of King James IV, 1488 to 1513, so the city of Dunblane may be said to have reached the height of its prosperity about this time, due partly to the importance of its cathedral, partly to the influence wielded by the chief inhabitants of the district and to some extent to its proximity to Stirling Castle, which was one of the chief residences of the King. It may be of interest in the first place to picture the appearance of the town about this time.

A stranger from the south, probably travelling on horseback, entered Dunblane by the bridge erected by Finlay Dermoch almost a hundred years previously. The original bridge was about twelve feet wide or about half the width of the bridge before its improvement in 1927, and the roadway at each end was lower, the bridge rising with an arch in the centre. There was a city gate at the east side of the Bridge known as the Netherport. The High Street had no doubt been made by that time—probably soon after the building of Finlay Dermoch's bridge— but it was not known as the High Street in early days, this name being usually applied to Kirk Street. Prior to the 15th century the Millrow was the main street at the south end of the town. A road branched off at the east end of the bridge where the Darn Road commenced, and this led through the Park, now part of Dunblane Golf Course, to Ochlochy and to an old road behind the High Street Gardens joining the Holmehill Road at Woodend. This park, formerly known as the Cow Park, from Kippenross North Lodge to the Darn Road was divided into Crofts, some of which formed endowments of the altars in the Cathedral. The houses in the High Street mostly consisted of one-storeyed thatched dwellings, and the width of the street did not exceed the width of the portion at the Bank of Scotland, while at some places it was even narrower. There was no road past the present County Buildings. There were old houses about where the shop of D. B. Macintosh, barber, stands, but these were entered from Arnott's Close off Kirk Street and they had gardens behind extending towards St. Blanes House. The Cross was also narrower in these days, the buildings on the west side extending into the present roadway, and a Market Cross stood some-where near the Cathedral gate. Sinclair's Wynd existed at that time, and the road between the high walls below Holmehill garden was known as the road to Mintock or Mento Myre, that is the myre where the mintock berries grew. There was a road up by the present English School, although there was none round by St. Mary's Church. The road, after passing Holmehill Lodge, turned to the left across by Backcroft and Ardennan. The ground about the Hydro-pathic gardens and the lower part of the Hydropathic grounds was known as Mintock Myre, called in later years " The Boggs," while the ground about Backcroft seems to have been moor land. The main street was, however, up Kirk Street and Braeport, and at Braeport stood the north gate of the town, known as the Overport. It is difficult to determine the exact position of this city gate, but it would seem to have been near the foot of the brae about the north-west corner of the Dunblane School playground. The houses in Kirk Street and Braeport were the larger houses of the city and were chiefly occupied by the dignitaries of the church. There was a considerable population in Ramoyle, which was outside the city proper, and was generally referred to as a separate community or suburb, as was also the Bridgend. The land between the street of Ramoyle and the Laighhills was cultivated as crofts. The road to Doune was, of course, by the Old Doune Road, but there was also a road to Kilbryde, which was then a separate parish with a church, church lands and minister. A considerable number of the inhabitants possessed Acres, or pieces of land extending up to about three acres, either within the city or immediately adjoining it. One has to keep in view that the roads were not paved or macadamised, but were little more than tracks, and in any mental picture which may be conjectured one must imagine the appearance of the district before it was so much altered by railway construction. Thus, across the Allan from the Cathedral, there were meadows and fertile land belonging to the bishop. The railway embankment now runs through these.

The houses of the inhabitants were in these days huddled closely together. Not only were the streets narrow, but there were many dwellings up closes immediately adjoining the houses in the front streets, particularly about Kirk Street, The Cross and Sinclair's Wynd, while there were also byres and stables situated there, for many of the citizens kept a cow and other live stock dwelling beside them.

The importance of Dunblane as a city at this time arose chiefly from the presence there of the Cathedral. The exterior of the building probably differed little from its present external appearance. The tower was about this time completed to its present height, and the bishop of the day—Bishop James Chisholm—added parapet walls to the choir and made other minor additions. The whole cathedral was at this time roofed and in regular use. The history of the Cathedral is, however, a matter for later consideration. The church-yard was, of course, not so extensive, as houses protruded into the present ground along the east boundary and partly on the north and south boundaries. It is probable that it was not greatly used at this period for burial purposes and there is no trace of early tombstones, while local fairs and markets were held there.

The Palace of the Bishop was a large and imposing building occupying a considerable portion of the ground from the Bishop's Close to the present Manse. There seem to have been stables connected with it, and a porter's lodge, which stood at The Cross. Quite a number of vaults or vaulted passages proceeded from or under the Palace, one going in the direction of the Manse from the existing ruins, another passing under the burial ground of the Rev. Dr. Blair towards the Cathedral, another under the site of the Cathedral Hall, and a fourth under the coach-house at the Cross belonging to the Manse. The grassyard or Bishop's Yard between the Palace and the River Allan formed the policies of the Palace, and the old well there was known as the Bishop's Well. The water which fed this well came from a spring in Kirk Street, which is now led into the burgh sewer there, and the Bishop's Well is now water-less.

Dunblane being an important ecclesiastical city, the various officials of the Cathedral had residences within its bounds, and many of the aristocracy and leading families in the district had also houses in Dunblane. The Earl of Menteith, who was one of the most powerful men of his time, had a residence where the present building of the Bank of Scotland stands, while the Earl of Perth's Dunblane home at a later date was opposite the Leighton Church at the north end of Kirk Street.

One has to keep in view that the clergy of the day were not only amongst the wealthiest in the land—the Archbishop of St. Andrews was said to be the richest man in Scotland—but their influence extended far beyond ecclesiastical matters, they frequently holding important official positions, and being frequently entrusted by the King and Government with important missions. Thus, the Dean of Dunblane, at this time, Walter Drummond, held the post of Lord Clerk Register, and the Bishop, after the death of James IV, was one of the guardians of his successor during his minority. He also acted on several occasions as ambassador to England, sat as a judge and attended as a member of Scottish Parliaments.

It may be of interest at this stage to have some particulars of the more important personages living in the neighbourhood at this time. The family of Keir is the one with the longest continuous history. The owner, about 1500, was a Sir William Stirling, who seems to have added largely to the family estate. He sided, as we noted in chapter iv, with the nobles who took the field against James III, and it has been alleged that he was one of the three persons who pursued the King from the battlefield of Sauchieburn, also known as the field of Stirling, the others being Patrick Gray of Kyneff and a man named Borthwick, said by James Grant, the author of *The Yellow Frigate*, to have been at one time a Prebend of Dunblane Cathedral. According to Grant, whose novel makes a good story, but is not in all details good history, it was Borthwick who assassinated the King (but whether this be so or not, there is no evidence that Sir William Stirling was directly concerned in it). It was this Sir William who founded a Chaplainry at the altar of the Virgin on the north side of the Cathedral of Dunblane, which he endowed with a croft of the land of Keir lying in the town of Dunblane, the lands of Shandroch (Shanraw) and Wodlan (Woodlands) and an annual rent of 40s. from the lands of Kippenrait. Sir William Stirling of Keir was succeeded by his eldest son Sir John about 1503. Sir John also added largely to the family estates, acquiring among others Kippendavie and Blackford. In 1509 he granted to the Altar of the Virgin an

annual rent of £20 Scots for performing of Mass and prayer at the Altar.   He was one of the
guardians of James V after the death of his father.   The lands of Cadder were acquired through
the marriage about 1534 of James, heir of Sir John Stirling, to Janet Stirling of Cadder.   Sir John
was killed about the year 1539 at the Bridge of Stirling, by David Shaw of Cambusmore and
George Dreghorn who were pardoned for the slaughter.   He was murdered for having assassinated Buchanan of Leny, whose daughters and co-heirs he stripped of a great part of their estate.
Shaw is said to have been instigated to this by the widow of Leny.   Sir John added about 30
properties to the Keir possessions betwen 1527 and 1535.

The estate of Argaty was, until after the succession of James I to the throne, the property
of the powerful Duke of Albany, who, on the King's orders, was arrested, tried and executed at
Stirling Castle along with his sons and aged father-in-law.   In 1498 the lands of Argaty consisting of Argaties and Lundies were gifted by James IV to Sir Patrick Home of Polwarth in return
for war services and these remained in the ownership of his descendants until recent years.
In 1501 Sir William Stirling of Keir entered into a contract with Sir Patrick Home that Sir
William's eldest son John, should marry Sir Patrick's eldest daughter, or failing her some other
daughter, the marriage to be celebrated when John Stirling became fourteen years of age and
Sir Patrick's daughter, twelve.   The contract does not seem to have been implemented, however, as Sir John Stirling's wife was the daughter of Sir Walter Forrester of Torwood.

The estate of Kippenross was then the property of a family of the name of Kinross of Kippenross.

In 1516 John Kinross of Kippenross was indebted to Sir John Stirling of Keir, and being
unable to pay cash he bound himself to infeft Sir John in the lands of Auchlochy and Spittal
Croft and " Merzonis Akir " at the Bridgend of Dunblane under reversion to John, upon a
payment of 610 merks on the high altar of the Cathedral Kirk of Dunblane.

About 1533 there were disputes between Keir and John Kinross about money matters in
which Master Henry Spittal acted as Procurator for Kinross.

One wonders if the croft mentioned above took its name from this man or some ancestor
of his.

The owner of Cromlix estate was Sir James Chisholm.   The Chisholms of Cromlix are
said to have been a branch of the family of Chisholm who settled in the Borders in the reign of
Alexander III.   (See Marshall's *Historical Scenes in Perthshire*).   The first Chisholm to possess
Cromlix was an Edmund Chisholm who came to Perthshire in the 15th century.   This family
supplied the last three Bishops of Dunblane.   The Chisholms were staunch adherents of the
Church of Rome and, for some time after the Reformation, were concerned in various schemes
for restoring the Roman Catholic religion.

Bishop James Chisholm was a son of Edmund Chisholm.   As a young man he was a chaplain to King James III.   He was sent to Rome to Pope Innocent VIII in the year 1486 who afterwards conferred the Bishopric of Dunblane upon him.   His death occurred in 1533.   Bishop
James had a brother named Thomas, and Sir James Chisholm of Cromlix and Bishop William,
who succeeded him, were his half-brothers.   His father's second wife was Janet Drummond,
daughter of James Drummond of Coldoch and niece of the first Lord Drummond.

Bishop William Chisholm was consecrated at Stirling by Gavin Dunbar, Archbishop of
Glasgow, in 1527.   He had several children, one daughter Jean Chisholm, whose mother was a
daughter of the Earl of Montrose, being married to Sir James Stirling of Keir.   He died in
1564 and was buried in the Cathedral of Dunblane.   Bishop James Chisholm executed a number
of improvements to the Cathedral including the erection of the parapet wall on the tower and
choir.   He also endowed chaplainries of the choir.   Bishop William, known as the Robber
Bishop, was in every way a contrast to the former and much of the property of the Bishopric
was dispersed at his hands, being bestowed chiefly upon his bastard children.

The second Bishop William Chisholm, who was a son of James Chisholm and Jean Drummond (a daughter of John Drummond of Innerpeffray and the Lady Margaret Stewart,
the daughter of James IV and the Lady Margaret Drummond), was made Bishop of Dunblane
about 1564, but his appointment being made after the Reformation in Scotland he was never
established as Bishop in Dunblane.   He was a man of great ability and a valued councillor of
Mary Queen of Scots who entrusted him with many important commissions.   Later he retired
to France where he became Bishop of Vaison.   Later in his life he became a Carthusian monk

and died in Rome. It is believed that had he lived a short time longer he would have been appointed a cardinal.

His brother John, also son of the third Chisholm Laird of Cromlix, lived much in France and is said to have been a secret agent of the King of Spain and correspondent of the Scottish lairds who favoured papacy. The fifth Chisholm Laird of Cromlix, also called Sir James, was Master of the Household of James VI. He was at one time in correspondence with the agents of the Church of Rome, but in 1595 he appeared before the General Assembly at Montrose and, declaring his adherence to the reformed faith, was admitted to the Reformed Church. His youngest son, Alexander Chisholm, was appointed Parson of Comrie, and another son Walter was Bailie of Dunblane. His second son Alexander succeeded him as Bailie and held the office for a long period. The fifth Chisholm Laird of Cromlix was succeeded in turn by his sons, James and John, but neither left issue and on the death of John the estate passed to the house of Drummond. The estate of Innerpeffray was connected with Cromlix for some centuries until recent years, through the marriage of Jean Drummond of Innerpeffray to Sir James, the third Chisholm Laird of Cromlix. Cromlix and Innerpeffray together passed from the Chisholm family to the Drummonds through Jean Chisholm who married James Drummond, first Lord Madderty.

There seem to have been four Drummonds Deans of Dunblane at the end of the 15th and beginning of the 16th centuries. The first was John Drummond, Dean in 1478 and Parson of Kinnoull, the second son of Walter Drummond of Cargill. He is described as having been a very bold churchman and to have thrust himself into the Deanship at his own hand giving rise to a proverb afterwards applied when anything is taken possession of without warrant: " You take it as Drummond took the Order." He was one of the Pope's knights and was known as Sir John. He had a son, Sir William Drummond, who succeeded his father as Dean, and several daughters. Sir William had at least two sons, Malcolm Drummond, a Notary, and David Drummond, from whom several families about Dunblane took origin. Sir William was Parson of Forteviot before he became Dean. He was Dean in 1494, but in 1495 one finds Walter Drummond in office.

Walter Drummond was the second son of Sir Malcolm Drummond of Cargill. In 1496 he was Chancellor of Dunkeld and in 1500 Dean of Dunblane and Parson of Kinnoull. He was a brother of the first Lord Drummond. There was a chamber in Drummond Castle called after him Walter's Chamber. Walter Drummond feued the lands of Deanston which took its name from him. He received permission to marry and one son was John Drummond who succeeded him as Dean and was Parson of Kinnoull and who solemnised the marriage of the queen of James IV to the Earl of Angus. From the Exchequer Rolls of Scotland it appears that Walter Drummond was Clerk of the Registers and of the Council for which he received a fee of £22 and a gown. He was allowed 32s. as a payment for eight " barilibus " of salmon. Dean Walter Drummond and John, his son, are said to have been buried within Drummond's Aisle in the Cathedral upon the south wall where descendants of the family were also afterwards buried. There was also a William Drummond Dean of Dunblane after 1527 and before 1534 during the time of Bishop William Chisholm.

The most powerful family in these days connected with Dunblane was that of the Earl of Menteith, the owner of the estate of Kilbryde, with a residence in the town of Dunblane. The Earls of Menteith were of ancient lineage, but the first line of earls terminated with the execution by James I of Murdoch, second Duke of Albany. The Duke's lands, which included Doune Castle and the lands from the neighbourhood of Doune westwards beyond Aberfoyle, were forfeited and passed into the possession of the Crown. It may be of interest to note here that there are various traditions as to the scene of the capture of the Duke of Albany, one story identifying the place with Murdoch's Ford on the old road between Doune and Dunblane where a small stream is crossed about a mile from Dunblane. Another tradition states that he was taken from his castle on an island in Loch Ard, but he seems to have been arrested when attending Parliament at Perth.

In 1427 James I granted the Earldom of Menteith to Malise Graham who had previously held the earldom of Strathearn, of which the King had deprived him, but the whole lands formerly held by the Duke of Albany were not made over to the new Earl. His principal residence was on Inchtalla, an island in the Lake of Menteith. The first Earl was sent to England as a hostage and security for payment of the King's ransom in 1427 and he remained there till 1453, when he was allowed to return on condition that his eldest son took his place. In a charter, dated 1466, James III refers to the singular favour which he bore to his beloved cousin Malise, Earl of Menteith. When the nobles rebelled against James III in 1487 he remained faithful to the King, and although he had attained a great age he commanded a division of the royal army at the battle of Sauchieburn. He died in 1490. The Earl appears to have had five sons and one daughter, one of his sons being John, who is referred to as " of Kilbride " of which property he received a charter under the Great Seal in 1469. He is known in tradition as " John of the Bright Sword," indicating that he had been a warrior of fame, but there is no record of any martial exploits which earned him this title. Part of the old Castle of Kilbryde said to have been erected about 1460 is still extant. As already stated, Sir John left an only daughter who succeeded to one-third of Kilbryde, the other two-thirds part going to the next Earl, his nephew.

The first Graham Earl of Menteith was succeeded by his grandson Alexander, who with other noblemen and gentlemen entered into a bond to James IV wherein they engaged to do their utmost to suppress crime within their bounds and bring criminals to justice. This Earl lived until 1536 or 1537. About 1508 he was deprived of the lands of Kilbryde which were given to Henry Schaw, a soldier who had gained distinction, but the lands came back to the Menteith family and remained in their possession for another century. The importance of Dunblane as an ecclesiastical centre, along with their ownership of Kilbryde, accounts for the Earls of Menteith having a residence in Dunblane.

There are recorded at this time many associations between the royal family and Dunblane and district. The first King of Scotland definitely known to have lived in Stirling Castle is Alexander I. His younger brother David I, the founder of the Bishopric of Dunblane, succeeded him in 1124. Stirling Castle was one of his chief residences. Alexander I and William the Lion who succeeded David I both died in Stirling Castle. The latter was followed in succession by Alexander II and Alexander III, who frequently lived in Stirling and who laid out an extensive pleasure ground which was called the New Park. Various Kings James resided much in Stirling, and this was the favourite residence of James III. He built a Parliament Hall and a new chapel at the Castle. Much of the business of the state was transacted by James IV at Stirling. He made great improvements within the Castle and its neighbourhood. Part of the low ground below the Castle Rock was converted into a garden and planted with vines and fruit trees, flowers and vegetables. One reads that in June, 1508, the King's gardener travelled twice to Holyrood with strawberries for the King. James III was a man with some amiable qualities, but with distinct points of weakness. He lost the sympathy and support of many of the nobles, suffered defeat at Sauchieburn and having sustained injuries from a fall from his horse was murdered shortly after at a mill to which he had been taken. He was buried in Cambuskenneth Abbey where his queen had previously been interred. His successor, James IV, is an interesting figure in Scottish history. He ascended the throne on the death of his father in 1488 while still quite a young man. If his father ruled in a weak and indolent way, his son showed an entirely different disposition. He resolved to restore order throughout the land and took vigorous means to enforce the law, but he was impulsive and passionate. During his reign Scotland developed to a wonderful extent in riches and importance. James IV did much to develop the Scottish navy which had been started by his father, and large boats were built with foreign timber at Airth and Newhaven. His reign, however, concluded in misfortune at the battle of Flodden in 1513. An historian had written that his virtues came to nothing while his faults brought him disaster. As a military leader he was inclined to rush into battle before making his plans, and it would appear that, had he had any military capacity or had entrusted his army to the guidance of some soldier who had ability, the battle of Flodden would not have been lost.

James IV appears to have been frequently in Dunblane and district and probably he sometimes resided with Bishop James Chisholm in the Bishop's Palace. He also lived from time to time at Doune Castle and elsewhere west of Dunblane, as he was attached to hunting and other sports, and frequently hunted at Glenfinlas or in the Menteith and Aberfoyle district.

The first Parliament of James IV was held in Edinburgh in October, 1488, at which Bishop James Chisholm was present with four other bishops. The country was divided up into various portions and power given to noblemen to put down crime therein. One district consisted of Strathearn and Dunblane, which were placed under the care of the Earl of Atholl, Lord Drummond and Robertson of Struan.

In the account of the Drummond family written by General William Drummond, first

Viscount Strathallan, he gives an interesting estimate of the character of the first Lord Drummond, who is described as being a wise, active and valiant nobleman. He left written in his own hand advice to his heirs who were to succeed to his estates, urging them to " know themselves, to crave assistance from God to direct them aright, to eschew intemperance and sloth, to better the estates left to them and not to disperse such by false pretexts of liberality, to maintain a good name and to act discreetly." Lord Drummond seemed specially anxious that what his heirs succeeded to without labour on their part should not be dispersed.

He died at Drummond Castle in 1519 at the age of 89 and was buried at Innerpeffray.

In the year following the accession of James IV (1489) the Earl of Lennox, who had been a strong supporter of James III, led a revolt. Dumbarton was held by his friends. Lennox with an army intended to cross the River Forth at Stirling and proceed to Dumbarton, but hearing that the King's supporters were in possession of Stirling he moved westwards up the River Forth and encamped on a level plain called Talla or Tilly Moss, about sixteen miles from Dunblane to the west of the Lake of Menteith and the River Forth. One of his men seems to have deserted and brought intelligence to the King and Lord Drummond, who were at the time in Dunblane. They resolved to attack Lennox without loss of time, and in the middle of a dark October night they marched forth from Dunblane at the head of a force hastily gathered together. They took Lennox by surprise and completely defeated his army, following on which the Castle of Dumbarton surrendered. After the battle the King returned to Stirling by Kippen, where he left an angel (24/-) as a thank offering for his victory. James, Bishop of Dunblane, appears to have been with the royal forces at the siege of Dumbarton Castle. There is an entry in the Treasurer's Accounts of a payment made " till ane odir man that pass to Dunblane for the mytir and the stafe."

He also appears to have been at Dumbarton on another occasion in 1489 as there is an entry in the Treasurer's accounts of a payment of £5 "to Mussche to pass for the Bishops of St. Andrews, Brechin, Dunblane, and the Abbots of Arbroath, Dunfermline, Lundories and Scwne to cum to Dumbartane."

Before passing on one might notice an entry in the Treasurer's accounts on 29th March, 1497, of a payment given to Sir John of Kilgour of Dunblane in part payment for the mending of the " Kings revin arras clothes 40s."

The Castle of Doune was also a royal residence from the time the lands of the Duke of Albany were forfeited after James I ascended the throne. Sums of money expended on the maintenance of the Castle and in payment of its officials appear in the Chamberlain's accounts in the time of James I. Doune Castle and the Stewartry of Menteith were part of the dowry of the queens of James II, James III and James IV. James I and his family were at the Castle of Doune in 1431, and James II and James III frequented the district for hunting. James IV was at Doune Castle in 1490 and in the district at later dates, while Queen Margaret, after his death, frequently resided there.

Margaret Drummond forms one of the closest ties between royalty at this period and Dunblane. The home of her early days was the Castle of Stobhall, on the Tay, about eight miles above Perth, where the Drummonds had resided since 1360. The family had previously been Thanes of Lennox and had held vast estates in the west. The first Drummond to live at Stobhall was the father of Annabella, queen of Robert III, and he was thus the grandfather of James I. Margaret's father was John, the first Earl of Drummond, born in 1439, a man, apparently, of great ability and much trusted by James IV. He was four times sent to England on missions of peace. It is said that when he died twenty-five of his descendants were wearing coronets. Lord Drummond was given a licence to build Drummond Castle in 1491. Margaret was his eldest daughter, born in 1472. In a *History of the Family of Drummond* written by the first Lord Strathallan in 1681 she is described as a "Lady of rare perfections and singular beauty." King James IV became deeply enamoured with her and Lord Strathallan wrote that the King was affianced to her in order to have made her his queen without acquainting his nobles or Council. Some writers, such as the historian Tytler, have been of opinion that the attachment of James for Margaret Drummond commenced during the lifetime of his father, they relying on certain payments in the Treasurer's Books for Lady Margaret, but it seems clear to the more recent historians that these payments were for behoof of an aunt of the King. It is, however, certain that Margaret Drummond resided with the King in Stirling and had a daughter,

Margaret, born in 1497. For some years negotiations had been proceeding for the marriage of Margaret Tudor, daughter of Henry VII of England, to James IV, and, as the time drew nearer for the completion of this union, the King's infatuation, says Tytler, for Margaret Drummond increased. He maintained a splendid establishment for her and gave her large sums of money and rich clothing, and lands to her relatives. At this stage she and her two sisters, Euphemia Lady Fleming and Sybilla, were suddenly and mysteriously poisoned at Drummond Castle, following upon a meal. In *Scenes from Perthshire in Bygone Days* it is said that Lord Drummond was from home when this occurred, but that the family physician, David Drummond of Milnab, was living at the Castle at the time, that he also suffered from poisoning and was reduced, it is said, to a state of helplessness from which he never quite recovered. The three sisters seem to have been somewhat hastily interred in separate graves in the choir of Dunblane Cathedral, the Dean of which was their uncle Walter Drummond, and their father brought from Italy three slabs of marble, each weighing over a ton, which were placed over their graves. This tragic event occurred at the end of 1501 or early in 1502. Various reasons have been ascribed for the assassination. Some writers have thought that the act was inspired by the family of Kennedy, a daughter of Lord Kennedy being a rival for the affections of the King. Some have thought that Lord Drummond was not a favourite with others of the nobles who dreaded having his daughter as queen, particularly as a former king, Robert III, had married a Drummond. It is unlikely that the cause of the tragedy will ever be cleared up, but the most probable explanation is that the party in the state who favoured a marriage between the King and the English princess as a means to procure peace between the countries considered it necessary to remove Margaret Drummond as an obstacle in the way of this marriage. No action appears to have been taken to bring the perpetrators of the crime to justice, which is remarkable when one considers the affection which James clearly bore to Margaret, and the power which Lord Drummond exercised in the country, and one wonders whether the King, either from a sense of duty or from some other reason, was not in some way privy to what had been done. The tragic death of Margaret Drummond does not appear to have affected the relationships between her father and her lover. The King seems afterwards to have visited Drummond Castle, where the young child Margaret Stuart remained for some time. One reads that " The Nurse that brocht the King's dochter frae Drummond to Strivelin " was paid £3 10s. on 18th June, 1503. The child was for some time at the Palace of Stirling, but was afterwards taken to Edinburgh Castle where she was brought up. In June, 1502, the King seems to have given to Margaret Stuart thirty French crowns and to her nurse three French crowns. In February, 1502-3, £5 was paid to the Priests in Edinburgh for "to do dirige and saule masses " for Margaret Drummond, and in the same month priests at Dunblane were paid a quarter's fee of £5 for performing the same offices. Similar entries appear in the Treasurer's books during the later days of James IV. Whether this was the outcome of remorse or of genuine affection cannot be determined, but one cannot but recall that James IV sided with the nobles against his father and did penance for the remainder of his life for sharing in the revolt which ended in his father's death. Margaret Drummond is believed to be the heroine of an old and beautiful song named "Tayis Bank."

In 1517 an incident occurred in the life of Sir John Stirling, the then Laird of Keir, which is worthy of reference, particularly as it forms the subject of an old romantic poem by Sir David Lindsay of The Mount, one of the greatest of the early Scottish poets. The poem goes by the name of " Squire Meldrum " and the circumstances are also recorded by the historian, Lindsay of Pitscottie. Squire Meldrum was Laird of Bines in Kinross-shire and he was enamoured with the widow of John Haldane of Gleneagles, who was killed at Flodden in 1513. Her married life had probably been a short one as she lived for forty years after her husband's death. Her father was provost of Edinburgh. Meldrum wished to marry her, but was unable to do so without a licence from the Pope. Luke Stirling, an uncle of the Laird, was also an admirer of the Lady, and sought the help of his nephew to assist him to carry her off by force. Sir John Stirling with a company of men followed Meldrum betwixt Leith and Edinburgh, and near Holyrood Chapel with fifty armed men he attacked Meldrum, who had only five men with him. According to Pitscottie, the Laird of Keir's principal servant was killed, the Laird seriously wounded and twenty-six of his men hurt and slain. Meldrum was badly wounded on the legs, arms and body, but escaped death along with all his men, and he is said to have lived for fifty years thereafter. The Duke of Albany, the Regent, was absent at the time in France, leaving a

Monsieur de la Batie in charge, with a guard of Frenchmen. It was reported to him that Laird Meldrum was slain, and he at once sounded an alarm and called on men to follow him that he might revenge the slaughter. With his men he followed the aggressors until he overtook them at Linlithgow, where he captured them and took them prisoner to the Castle of Edinburgh to await the return of the Regent. These incidents are also graphically told in Lindsay's poem, composed about the year 1550. The Poet refers to Sir John as " a cruel knight full of envy and a tyrant without mercy."

As Sir William Stirling of Keir (who died in 1503) had sided with the young prince, afterwards James IV, against his father James III, so his son and successor, Sir John Stirling, took the part of the Queen Mother, widow of James IV, against certain of the nobles who opposed her. In 1526 a summons of treason was directed against Sir John, the Earl of Eglinton and others. It seems that he had opposed the forces of Angus, Argyll and Lennox in whose hands the young King was. Sentence of forfeiture was pronounced on 19th November, 1526, for treasonable convocation of the lieges at Stirling and for leading a host and army and fighting at the Burgh of Linlithgow. King James thereafter for good service and for money paid to himself granted to George Douglas, brother of Archibald Earl of Angus, the lands and barony of Keir with the fortalice, manor, mills, cruives, fisheries, annexis, etc., including the power of appointment of two chaplains within the church of Dunblane, as also the lands of Auchlochy in the barony of Kippenross, the piece of land " Marionisaker " at the end of the town of Dunblane and the lands of the " Tua Classingawis " and other lands all of which pertained to the King in respect of the forfeiture of Sir John Stirling. In the following year, however, the latter was restored to his estates and honours and the sentence of forfeiture was rescinded and later in the year he accompanied Lennox in an attempt to rescue the young King from the hands of the Douglases. " Classingaw " is now known as Glassingall.

One obtains some interesting information about local affairs and people from the Lord Treasurer's Accounts. Quite a number of the officials of the Cathedral have held office as auditor of these accounts, such as Sir David Luthirdale, in 1473-4, a Canon of Dunblane, also Hendry Alane or Alansone, Archdeacon of Dunblane and Auditor in 1492 and 1496.

In 1494 it is noted that £20 was received " frae the Bishop of Dunblane to the biggin of Tarbert"—that is, to the re-building of Tarbert Castle in Kintyre in connection with the expedition of James IV against the Lord of the Isles.

James IV seems frequently to have worshipped in St. Mawarrokis Chapel, Lecropt. He was there on 19th April, 1497, and gave 14s. as an offering. A month later when leaving Stirling for Linlithgow he commanded payment of 15s. 6d. to the Priest of St. Mawarrokis.

A man of some note in Dunblane about the year 1500 was George Newton, who held the office of Archdeacon. Among a number of books written by him was one entitled *The Acts of the Cathedral of Dunblane,* and it is narrated that he affirmed that he had seen the original of the letter from Mellitos and Justice (who were appointed Bishops to the East Saxons and Kent respectively by Augustine, Archbishop of Britain) to the Abbots of Scotland, among the records of Dunblane. George Newton left money at his death for masses to be said daily at the High Altar in the Cathedral for all time coming.

Walter Drummond, Dean of Dunblane, the uncle of the sisters who were poisoned, was private secretary to James IV and Lord Clerk Register. There were frequent disputes about the valuable fishing rights in the River Forth at Stirling and in 1501 Dean Walter Drummond acted as arbiter in a controversy between Cambuskenneth Abbey and the Town of Stirling. In 1513 he attended the General Council of the Realm held at Perth, along with Bishop James Chisholm. His predecessor in the Deanship of Dunblane was John Drummond, his uncle. Another official of the Cathedral at this time was Sir Andrew Macbreck, who was Chancellor between 1520 and 1526. It is thought that he was Almoner to James IV. Further particulars regarding Walter Drummond are found in Malcolm's *House of Drummond* from which it appears he had been Rector of St. Andrews and afterwards Chancellor of Dunkeld in 1496, being appointed Dean of Dunblane shortly after.

On 11th July, 1521, an important ecclesiastical event took place at Cambuskenneth. Abbot Mylne of Cambuskenneth, who was afterwards appointed the first President of the Court of Session founded by James V, had rebuilt part of the Abbey building, particularly the great altar, the chapter house and part of the cloister house, and he had also laid out two

D

new cemeteries.   The Bishop of Dunblane on the Abbot's invitation dedicated the buildings. Bishop Chisholm was assisted by Archdeacon George Newton, John Chisholm, Prebender of Kippen, and James Wilson, Prebender of Glendowane.   John Tulydaf, Warder of the Minorities of Stirling, preached on the efficacy of dedication after Mass had been celebrated.   Amongst the large concourse of people who attended were Lord John Erskine and Sir James Haldane of Gleneagles.   An account of the proceedings was written by James Blackwood, Presbyter of the diocese of Dunblane and Notary Public, and is preserved in the Register of Cambuskenneth.

In the reign of James IV there was a dispute between Cambuskenneth and the Bishop of Dunblane with reference to the patronage and emoluments of Kippen Church.   The king had made a gift of these to the Abbey of Cambuskenneth, but the Bishop of Dunblane disputed the validity of the gift on two grounds, namely, that the church and revenue therefrom were already the property of Dunblane and that, in any event, the Abbot of Cambuskenneth was already a Canon of Dunblane in respect of Kincardine Church, which belonged to the Abbey, and could not hold a similar appointment in the same diocese.   The dispute was adjusted by the Bishop of Dunblane and Abbot Andrew of Cambuskenneth at Dunblane on 13th March, 1510, with consent of the King to the effect that the Rector of Kippen should be a Canon and Prebend of the Cathedral Church of Dunblane, that the vicarage, manse and £20 Scots yearly from the Rectory should pertain to him, and that the Abbot and Convent should have the fruits of the Rectory under deduction of the yearly sum of £20.   This agreement was embodied in letters, dated 1st April, 1511.

Many of the Clergy within the diocese held appointments in connection with the Cathedral and were members of the Chapter.   Such were, of course, not in constant residence, but they had manses in Dunblane where they resided when on duty.   Particulars of such will be found in a later chapter.

Light is thrown on old Dunblane through entries in the Exchequer Rolls of Scotland and the Treasurer's accounts.   A number of payments to Dean Walter Drummond who was Clerk of the Register and Council are noted.   Thus in 1501 he was allowed £37 for household expenses, the same sum being allowed to the Earl of Lennox and other peers, while on another occasion he received £22 for his fee and gown.   Another person to receive material for a garment was the Laird of Keir, who, in 1507, was given by the King 7 ells of black damask "for ane cote." The damask cost 25s. an ell.   In 1505 and also in 1506, he was given a coat, doublet and hose.

At this time there were three Fairs in Dunblane held at Whitsunday, St. Blane's or St. Lawrence's Day (10th August) and All Hallows Day.   Purchases were not infrequently made for the King at these fairs.   Thus the Treasurer of the King's household on 9th August, 1513, handed over £300 for the purchase of oxen at the Fair of Dunblane.   In that year 7 score 3 oxen, that is 143 head of cattle, were bought at Dunblane by the "Maister of Work and Maister Flescher of divers prices at a cost of £208."   On 15th May, 1531, Robert Gibb was given £20 to buy a horse for the King at Dunblane Fair.   £20 was given to Andrew Aytoun on 21st May, 1506, to buy 4 cart horses at Dunblane.   Dunblane Fairs were not only well known for the cattle and horses sold at them, but there seems to have been a considerable trade in Dunblane for saddlery and on 15th July, 1505, a furnished saddle was bought in Dunblane at the Royal expense.   There were traders then as now who sought to gain wealth at the expense of their fellows and in 1538 a proclamation was made in Dunblane against forestallers, that is persons who sought to buy up goods brought to fairs before they were exposed for sale with the view to creating a monopoly and allowing the purchasers to control prices.   One has to keep in view that in these days there was much less ready money throughout the country and that shops were comparatively few and that the principal buying and selling took place at fairs.   Thus the local people who made boots and shoes did not sell them from day to day in a shop, but brought them to a fair when the farmers and crofters would bring cattle and sell them at the fair and then purchase boots and shoes for their family.

Horses, beds, etc., were hired by James V for use when hunting.   In August, 1538, John Tennand received expenses for taking beds, tables, etc., from Dunblane for the hunting and remaining there during the hunting.   This would probably be to Glenfinlas which was a Royal forest and a place frequented by the King for hunting.   On 23rd September, 1539, 10 horses were hired from Stirling, and 7 from Dunblane, for the Royal hunting at Glenfinlas, the rate paid for each being 2/- a day.

At the beginning of the 16th century Stirling was probably the chief centre in Scotland for the manufacture of guns. In 1508 a man was sent to Dunblane on horseback to get a stone of flokks, that is cloth with the nap raised for smoothing the moulds of guns. He was paid 3/- for his trouble and the price of the flokks was 4/-.

There are numerous references in these accounts of payments to Margaret Drummond and to her daughter. Thus on 24th June, 1502, £21 was given to Margaret Drummond (apparently the child of the King), and 41/- to her nurse. Sometimes it is not quite clear to whom Margaret Drummond refers. At an earlier date the person bearing this name appears to have been an aunt of the King, while other payments refer to sums given to Margaret Drummond's child, although the latter is usually referred to as her daughter, or as Margaret Stuart. The priests who sang masses in Dunblane Cathedral for the repose of Lady Margaret's soul received a fee of £5 quarterly, and on 20th May, 1505, they were given an extra £1. Similar payments are recorded both in Edinburgh and Dunblane during the lifetime of James IV.

In 1504 we learn that the "neuris of Drymmyn was dischargit of the bairn," that is of Margaret Stuart, the King's daughter. She was then past 7 years and apparently did not require a nurse longer. £14 was paid to the nurse on 16th December, 1504. Margaret Drummond's daughter on 11th June had been brought to her father at Stirling Castle from Drummond when the nurse received 5 crowns, which would be worth £3 10/-.

Margaret Stuart's education was carried on in Edinburgh Castle where she was for some time under the charge of Sir Patrick Crichton of Cranston-Riddell and his wife. Along with her resided Marjory Lindsay, who was probably a companion, and two Moorish or negro girls as attendants. Ample provision was made for their clothing, and all seem to have been well provided with dress. £100 or so was allowed for the boarding of the four girls. Lady Margaret Stuart learned dancing from "Guilliame the Taubroner", whose fee was £4 7s. 6d. a quarter. The King's daughter and companions were supplied with shoes by John Davidson, cordoner, that is shoemaker, and particulars of her clothing, trimming, ribbons, etc., are found in the Treasurer's accounts. She was married in 1510 at the age of 13 to Lord Gordon, son of the third Lord Huntly, by whom she had two sons. Her husband died in 1517, but she afterwards married Sir John Drummond of Innerpeffray.

The King displayed an interest in the raising of the tower of Dunblane Cathedral, and the building of the parapet to the choir, and on one or two occasions he gave drinksilver to the Bishop of Dunblane for his wrights and masons. Payments were also made by the King to the poor folk inside Dunblane, as for example, 9/- on 26th May, 1505. On 8th February, 1507, 14/- was given as an offering from the King in Dunblane. On the other hand Bishop James Chisholm frequently sent presents to James IV. Thus, in March, 1504, he sent a man with pikes, in March, 1508, two live cranes, and in March, 1512, a fed ox. The Bishop's messenger was rewarded with a present of money varying from 5/- to 10/-. Bishop James sent an ox to King James V in 1526, for taking which his servant received 14/-. In August, 1505, the Laird of Keir sent a servant to the King with a gift of pears, and his messenger received 9/-. In these days letters were sent usually by messenger on horseback, and one reads of frequent communications being sent to the Bishop, or other personages of importance, such as the Sheriff of Dunblane, about whom, it may be added, one hears little. On 5th November, 1546, a messenger was dispatched to Dunblane for the cursing upon the "Slaarres of the Cardinal," his remuneration being 22/-. In the following August all kirk men at Dunblane were warned to come to the army, and be in Edinburgh by the 31st, while in June, 1548, messengers were sent to Dunblane after the first sight of the Spanish Navy, to cause them to thresh corn and bring victual to Edinburgh.

It was in this year that the property of Kippendavie was acquired by the Laird of Keir from Ruthven of Crichton. Keir exchanged this property for the Mains of Meigle.

Kinross, Laird of Kippenross, was in trouble in 1532 for the "slochter of Umquhile John Towert in Pettindreycht" (Pittindreich). On 29th October William Christesoun, messenger, was paid 27/- to pass to take surety of Kinross, and his accomplices to underly the law in the Tolbooth of Edinburgh on 15th November. On 16th November, Archibald Hogg, messenger, was paid for passing to summon an assize to William Kinross in Kippenrait, charged with the slaughter of John Towert.

On 11th June, 1506, a charter was confirmed of Janet Stewart, spouse of John Kinross of

Kippenross, who had sold to Arch. Makclauchlane the lands of Letter in the Stewartry of Menteith, and County of Perth, under an annual payment of 16/8 to the King, with the usual services. The witnesses were Henry White, Official, three of the Cathedral chaplains, and John Row and Richard Sinclair, two leading citizens of Dunblane.

CHAPTER VI.

DUNBLANE IN THE 16th CENTURY.

THIS period in the history of the City is one of strife, turmoil and declension. With the overthrow of Roman Catholicism and the establishment of Protestantism in Scotland, Dunblane ceased to be a centre of religious and political importance. In the latter part of the century the Cathedral fell into disrepair, and the Bishop's Palace and many of the homes of the clergy and aristocracy became ruinous. As it was a time of religious upheaval, it will be of interest in the first place to outline the course of events connected with the Cathedral and the clergy. It is, of course, a mistake to lay the destruction of all the cathedrals and abbeys of Scotland at the feet of the Reformers, and, while altars were overthrown and images destroyed within Dunblane Cathedral by a band of men under Argyle and the Prior of St. Andrews in June, 1559, the fabric itself does not seem to have been in any way injured as is explained later in this book.

Although Scotland had declared for Protestantism, for a long period after 1560 a struggle continued between the supporters of the old faith and of the Reformed. Mary Queen of Scots was a devoted Catholic, and many of the nobles sided with her, while at Rome and on the Continent the Roman Catholic faith had great power and influence, and its supporters were ever ready to take advantage of any possible opening which might arise for its reintroduction. Probably Dunblane as a cathedral city and a centre of the Catholic religion had many adherents of the old faith after 1560, and we read of lands possessed by the Catholic clergy and officials for a considerable time after the date of the Reformation. At that date William Chisholm I, known as the " Robber Bishop," a man who had done much to dissipate the property of the church, and whose character was held in little regard, was still Bishop of Dunblane.

In 1558 the Bishop is referred to in a French paper as the President of the Bishops. He was one of a few Bishops who did not favour the reformed religion in 1560. He did not sign the Confession of Faith, but agreed to stand with God's word and consent to abolish all abuses to the contrary.

In 1559 Randolph wrote that the Lords wished to take their open adversary, the rich Bishop of Dunblane, intending to make him pay well. He died in 1564 leaving his estate to his eight daughters. Randolph elsewhere suggests that his children numbered ten or twelve in addition to those begotten of his own daughter.

In 1561, notwithstanding the Reformation, his nephew William Chisholm II was appointed co-adjutor to his uncle. He again was a man of great ability and devoted to the church in which he had been reared, while, although hated by his opponents, no reproach can be passed on his personal character. Finding no scope for work in the church in Scotland he largely devoted himself to political action and he was one of the most trusted servants and friends of Mary Queen of Scots, who frequently sent him as her ambassador to France and to Rome. Thus, in 1565, he was sent by Queen Mary to the Pope and in her commission she mentions that she was under great obligations to him for the important services he had rendered. He seems to have made his influence early felt, as the Papal Legate in Scotland in 1562 wrote in such terms, also remarking that he was justly held in high esteem and regard by all good men. One of the missions entrusted to him was to obtain the necessary dispensation for the marriage of Queen Mary and Darnley in 1565, and in the following year he assisted at the baptism of Mary's son, James, and was in the same year sent to the Papal Court as Queen Mary's ambassador. So great faith had Queen Mary in the Bishop's ability and prudence that she selected him for the delicate mission of going to France in 1567 to excuse her action in marrying Bothwell. In Calderwood's *History of the Church of Scotland* the story of the Bishop's interview with the King of France and the Queen, his mother, is narrated. It is stated that when the Bishop began to extol Bothwell and to excuse the contracting of the marriage without their knowledge, the Queen interrupted him and confounded him by producing letters from Scotland which told that in the Bishop's short absence Bothwell had fled and the Queen was a captive. Some of those present smiled and some laughed, but no one thought that anything had befallen her which she had not deserved.

Bishop William Chisholm's abilities and devotion to the Roman Catholic religion made many enemies for him in Scotland, and in 1567 he was ordered to the Tolbooth of Edinburgh for saying mass, administering sacraments, and holding communion with the Pope, while his accusers went the length of charging him with being a participator in the murder of Darnley. In that year the Regent Moray passed sentence depriving him of his see and of his property and revoking his licence from Queen Mary for travelling abroad. This was followed in 1574 by a Declaration of Outlawry, and any dealings with William Chisholm or certain other ecclesiastical leaders were forbidden under pain of death. In 1585 an Act of Restitution was passed, but his name was expressly excluded. Nevertheless in that year he came to Scotland as the Nuncio of the Pope to James VI and he was again in Scotland in 1587 on an embassy from Philip of Spain and the Pope. Evidently King James regarded him with favour, as the records of the Privy Council show that in 1587 the King "restored William, some time Bishop of Dunblane, from the sentence of forfeiture and reponed him in his lands and heritages for certain good causes which had moved His Majesty." This decree was rendered largely inoperative by Parliament annexing a condition that the Bishop must not return until he reconciled himself to the Kirk and ministers thereof without which his home-coming would be subject to the penalty of death. William, of course, declined to acknowledge the Protestant faith although his brother Sir James Chisholm of Cromlix ultimately did so and was received into the Reformed Church. William Chisholm was thus compelled to leave Scotland although at the instigation of the King some further time was given to him to arrange his affairs. The leniency of King James may be accounted for by the intimacy which had existed for some generations between the Royal family and the Chisholms. We have already seen the close relationship between Bishop James Chisholm and James IV. Sir James Chisholm of Cromlix was Master of the Household of James VI and his wife Jean was a granddaughter of James IV and Margaret Drummond.

One need not follow further the career of Bishop William Chisholm who left Scotland for good at this time, further than to mention that, having resigned the Bishopric of Vaison, he became a Carthusian monk, finally becoming Procurator General of his Order about 1592. He died and was buried in Rome, the Pope delivering an eulogy upon him on the occasion of his funeral. His virtues and learning and the facility shown by him while preaching in French were held in high esteem. Knox referred to him as one of the chief pillars of the papistical church. He acted as one of the commission who pronounced Bothwell's marriage null and void. It may be of interest to note that when William was appointed Bishop of Vaison in 1570 it was on the condition that his appointment was to cease on his restoration to the Bishopric of Dunblane.

He was succeeded as Bishop of Vaison by his nephew, also named William Chisholm. James VI appears to have interested himself on his behalf to secure his promotion. He visited Scotland in 1603 as Nuncio of the Pope, but although anxious to visit his old home of Cromlix, he was not permitted to do so.

It has been generally thought that Bishop William Chisholm II, when compelled to leave Scotland about 1565, took with him the Chartulary and whole records of the Cathedral and diocese, but whether this be true or not, these have entirely disappeared and all efforts to trace them have proved unsuccessful.

The first Protestant minister in Dunblane following on the Reformation was Robert Pont or Kypont or Kynpont, who was appointed on 30th June, 1562, to minister at Dunblane till the next Assembly. He was born at Culross in 1524 and studied at St. Leonard's College, St. Andrews, afterwards studying law at a foreign university. After returning to Scotland he joined the Reformed Church and was present at the first General Assembly held on 20th December, 1560. He did not remain long in Dunblane, being soon after his appointment removed to Dunkeld. At an Assembly held at Perth on 2nd July, 1563, he complained that the Bishop of Dunblane had lately said mass in Dunblane Cathedral, contrary to the Act of Parliament under which all who said mass or attended mass were subjected to penalties. It is related that on one occasion Pont was violently assaulted on the head with a weapon by a certain Captain Lauder.

Perhaps one might mention here that in 1569 four priests of Dunblane were condemned to death at Stirling, for saying mass contrary to the Act of Parliament. Regent Moray remitted their lives and modified their sentence as follows :—"The priests to be bound to the Market Cross with their vestments and chalices in derision, the people casting eggs and other villainy at their faces by the space of ane hour, their vestments and chalices being afterwards burned to ashes." By Act of Parliament dated 24th August, 1560, the saying of Mass had been prohibited under pain of confiscation, banishment and death, the same punishment being meted out both to those who said mass and the hearers, but despite this the Roman clergy seem to have continued a more or less precarious career in Dunblane for some considerable time after the Reformation, of which more later.

After the removal of Robert Pont to Dunkeld, there seems to have been an interval of some years in which there was no Protestant clergyman in Dunblane. In 1567, Robert Montgomery was translated from Cupar to Dunblane. He had also Kilbryde parish under his charge, while his stipend appears to have amounted to £200 Scots money. In 1572 he was appointed to Stirling. When the Archbishopric of Glasgow became vacant he was offered the see by the Earl of Lennox on condition that Lennox should receive the whole revenue of £4,080 Scots save £1000 which was to go to Montgomery. The General Assembly taking up the matter, excommunicated Montgomery for having entered into this arrangement, but at a later date he submitted to their authority, obtained permission to be admitted a pastor over a flock, and was appointed minister of Stewarton in 1589. He died in 1609. When Montgomery was minister of Dunblane, Duncan Nevin, the local schoolmaster, occupied the post of reader in the Cathedral. Montgomery was succeeded at Dunblane in 1572 by Robert Menteith, who had previously been minister at Alva and who was translated in 1578 to Dollar.

Following on the Reformation the number of clergy of the Reformed Church was insufficient to fill all the charges in Scotland and many parishes had to be content with the appointment of a reader. Readers were not empowered to marry, baptise or celebrate the communion, but they conducted service in church from a printed prayer-book. While they lingered on for some time after 1581 in country parishes, readers were abolished in that year. The name of the reader at Dunblane in 1574 was Alexander Wratoun, with a salary of £20. At this time Michael Learmonth was minister of Kilbryde Parish, and he had the help of a reader, Alexander Anderson, whose stipend was 20 merks and the kirk lands. Learmonth had under his charge readers at Leny, Kilmahog and Callander, each with a stipend of £16 Scots money, while the minister of Kilmadock, Alexander Fergy by name, had readers at Kincardine, Lecropt and Logie under him with salaries of the same amount and occupation of the church lands.

In 1572, the Concordat of Leith made provision for the establishment of bishops in the Church of Scotland, these being elected to enable the nobility to draw the larger part of the revenues attachable to the sees. Such Bishops were named in derision "Tulchan," which is the Gaelic name for calf skins stuffed with straw, it being the custom to place such before cows to induce them to give their milk more readily. In 1574 Andrew Graham was presented to the Bishopric of Dunblane under the name of preacher, although it was notorious that he had not been one. The General Assembly accordingly ordered him to exercise in the Magdalene Chapel, Edinburgh, before the Bishops, Superintendents and Commissioners, but especially before the ministers of Edinburgh, on Romans, Chapter v., verse 1. Graham seems to have passed his test satisfactorily. He had the parish of Dunblane assigned to him by the General Assembly in 1576, but was deposed by the Presbytery in 1594 for being "non-resident and having at na tyme preichit God's Word, ministrat the sacraments nor execut discipline thereat the space of sevin zeiris bygane." Andrew Graham appears to have been the youngest son of the Earl of Montrose, but Calderwood says of the Laird of Morphie that his presentation to Dunblane was by the Regent. His performance of his duties seems to have been at all times unsatisfactory, as in 1576 a complaint was made against him of not teaching or residing in the diocese or having a flock. His reply at that time was that he had received none of the fruits, that he had been " deseased " for three weeks past and he promised amendment. While in 1578 he submitted himself to the authority of the General Assembly, complaints were again made in 1580 that there were many papists and ex-communicants in Dunblane and no order taken with them, that he had let the benefice to William Stirling without the consent of the Assembly, that there was only a reader at Muthill Church, that the sacrament was observed at Easter, and that the sacraments were bought and sold at Auchterarder. Graham, in reply, blamed Stirling for not having obtained the permission of the General Assembly, but admitted that he had not been so diligent as he might have been. Graham's stipend as Bishop was in 1585, £208 8s. 4d., ½ boll wheat, 8 chalders 13 bolls of barley and 32 chalders 6½ bolls of meal.

Andrew Young became minister of Dunblane in succession to Robert Menteith in 1578, having been translated from Foulis Wester.   It is recorded in Melville's diary that he was one of two ardent hearers of John Knox, and that he wrote down Knox's sermons, translated some into Latin, and read them in the hall of the College instead of his own orations.   He was appointed by the Privy Council in 1589 along with two other ministers for the maintenance of true religion in the Stewartries of Strathearn and Menteith with the diocese of Dunblane.

As was remarked above, the Reformation was not immediately followed in Dunblane by a clearance out of the clergy of the old faith.   The bishop remained in possession till 1567 and in that year provision was made for " sex scoir laidis of peatties and eighteen laidis of turves " for the palace, which then must have still been inhabited.   The manses of Abernethy, Comrie and Balquhidder were in 1572 in the possession of their Catholic owners, although Robert Leytoun, a Prebendary and Perpetual Vicar of Logie, disposed of his manse under reservation of a chamber for his occupation when in residence in Dunblane.   In 1572 John Leirmonth, Perpetual Chaplain of St. Blais, held as part of the endowments of this altar, the Dovecot Croft with the Dovecot, a rood of land, garden ground and a tenement, while in the same year, Henry Drummond, Chaplain, had possession of St. Michael's Croft.   Roger Gordon was Dean of Dunblane, 1558-1570, and James Chisholm Archdeacon from 1574 to 1582.   On the other hand, John Burdoune, Minister of Balquhidder, held the emoluments of the Lady Altar for part of his stipend.   We have seen that there were priests performing the rites of their religion in Dunblane in 1569 and that in 1580 there were many papists dwelling in the city and no order taken with them, while in 1587, despite the efforts of the ardent follower of Knox, Andrew Young, the Bishop who had lately come home was drawing all after him " in the same old dance."   Apart from the violence done to the four priests of Dunblane, little feeling seems to have been exhibited between the supporters of the old and new faith in Dunblane, and they existed together quite a long time before the Reformed Church attained the final mastery.

It is of interest to ascertain at what date the nave of the Cathedral fell into disrepair and became ruinous.   It does not appear to have been in the best state of preservation prior to the Reformation, as one reads that Bishop William Chisholm had recently rebuilt the west portion of the north aisle—that is, the aisle of St. Blais.   The Reformers cannot be blamed for the subsequent state of ruin which befell this noble building.   Their instructions were merely to take down the images, cast down the altars and purge the Kirk of monuments of idolatry.   Care was to be taken of the desks, windows, doors and glass and iron work.   When the body of armed men from Perth entered the Cathedral in June, 1559, it is recorded that they had little time to spend at Dunblane and that the invaders quickly marched off to Stirling.   Their visit was a short one, and it is clear that little, if any, damage was done to the building.   The Cathedral probably suffered neglect in the years following the Reformation through the absence of Protestant clergy in charge and through its poverty arising from the dissipation of the property of the Bishopric. Between 1560 and 1567 the only minister in charge was Robert Pont, who only remained for a short time, and, as the Catholic clergy were forbidden to conduct services, the Cathedral no doubt suffered from want of hands to care for it.   In 1588 the General Assembly appealed to King James to interpose to avert the ruin which threatened Glasgow and Dunblane Cathedrals and Dunfermline Abbey.   The Assembly approached the King with regret for the decay of these kirks, which were ruinous and would not be able to be remedied without hasty repair, and they asked the King to cause the Bishop of Dunblane to have the Cathedral repaired. Evidently although the condition of the Cathedral was then serious, it was still not beyond repair, and it may be inferred that the nave was still roofed.   One would gather that the Reformed Church held worship in the nave at this time although in the following century the nave was popularly known as " the old church."   It would seem, however, that the choir of the Cathedral had become the Parish Church before the year 1622, and in all probability the nave became roofless and a ruin between 1588 and 1622 through continuous neglect, combined with want of pecuniary means, extending over a period of years.   This is fully dealt with in Chapter VII.

Mention might be made of the appointment in 1592 of Mr. William Stirling at Dunblane " to make careful advertisement of all kind of practices against the religion of all priests, Jesuits and resetters of them and all other weighty enormities that shall fall out and come to their knowledge," Mr. Stirling to report directly to Mr. Walter Balcanquall in Edinburgh.

It was some little time after the Reformation before presbyteries were formed, the first being that of Edinburgh about 1581-3. Eight parishes, latterly in Dunblane Presbytery, were at first included in that of Stirling, but sundry of the brethren alleged that there might be a presbytery in Dunblane as well as in Stirling, and one seems to have been formed for Dunblane some years later. In 1593 the General Assembly ordained that the Presbytery of Dunblane be transported to Auchterarder with liberty to the brethren of Dunblane to resort either to Auchterarder or Stirling as they pleased, but, in the event of the Kirk of Auchterarder being not sufficiently repaired before next General Assembly, and a sufficient stipend provided for a minister, the Prebytery should be re-established in Dunblane. There seems accordingly to have been no Presbytery of Dunblane between 1593 and 1608, but the Presbytery of Dunblane was re-established in the latter year and has since continued to this day. It was united to the Presbytery of Stirling after the Union of the Churches in 1929.

Prior to the time of Bishop William Chisholm the First, a great portion of the lands in the neighbourhood of Dunblane was the property of the Church. These included what are now Cromlix and Glassingall estates, a considerable portion of Kippendavie and Corscaplie, and most of the lands in and about the city of Dunblane. The dispersion of these Church lands is dealt with in a later chapter.

In 1593, an Act of Parliament was passed in favour of " Maister Patrik Galloway and Johnne Duncansoune, Ministers, anent the temporalitie of Dunblane." The following is a copy of the act :—

" To his heines Dalie orators, Johnne Dunkesoun and Mr. Patrik Galloway, his graces ministers in yeirlie pensioun for all the dayes of yair lyftymes.

" All and haill the few ferms, fewmales, canis, custumes, annuellis, fuices, ariages, cariages and utheris dewties whatsumever of the lands of the temporalitie of the bishopric of Dumblane efter specified To witt of the lands of Glencorkie, Bello, annuell of pitbr., Clevage, findall, dergall, ledmachany, Mylne of his, drumlatochie, glassingall beg glenquhany, Corskaplies easter and wester, annuellis of the toun of D & custumes thereof & of the faires of the samy ; Ardochis over & nether ; brigend, ramynyle ; mylne of dumblane ; cromlixes, Auchinleyes ; blewbittergask ; eister bittergask ; barbus lythell ; Tanroquhan, craginquhills, Thomerclay ; eister Drumaquhence, midle Drumaquhence ; benebrig ward of Muthill ; ganzlochan ; brotoche, Keirprone ; cluthybeg ; damskeir ; Cragarnally ; Auchinbie ; Aneulis of eister Culingis ; & of eister egglismagirdell ; deenstoun ; als Thomercany or Sancutholme and of lundies."

Prior to the Reformation much civil power was wielded by the church authorities. When James V instituted the Court of Session in 1537, it consisted of a President and seven lay and seven clerical members. The first President was Abbot Mylne of Cambuskenneth and one of the first members Master Henry White of Dunblane. In 1560, Commissary Courts were established to execute certain powers previously wielded by ecclesiastical courts. Their chief duty was the receiving and recording wills and inventories of the estates of deceased persons who had died within the district of the commissariat, the executors receiving confirmation or authority to deal with such estates. The officials appointed were a Commissary and a Commissary Clerk and such a court was established at Dunblane for the district of the diocese. At first this court also dealt with minor actions arising out of debt claims and slander, disputes between husband and wife and certain minor offences, while protests of unpaid bills could be registered in such a court. The Commissary Court of Edinburgh, erected in 1563, had powers of reviewing the decision of the district Commissary Courts, and such courts continued until the year 1823, when the duties of Commissary were taken over by the Sheriff. There still continued a Commissary Clerk who might or might not be the Sheriff Clerk, but Commissary Courts were finally abolished as separate courts in 1876. This work has been carried on continuously at Dunblane save for a short period in the time of Cromwell when he removed the commissary work from Dunblane to Perth, but after the Restoration the old practice was resumed and the commissary business of Dunblane district transacted there.

One or two incidents which occurred during this period at or in Dunblane are worthy of note. In 1535, James V had granted to Sir James Stuart of Beith, a gentleman of his bedchamber, the custody of Doune Castle, then a royal residence. He was a brother of Lord Methven, the third husband of Margaret Tudor, widow of James IV, who resided much there. This appointment had long been held by the Edmonstons of Duntreath. In 1543—other writers give the year as 1547—a fight took place in the High Street of Dunblane (another writer says at Murdoch's ford) with the result that Sir James Stuart was killed by his predecessors, Sir William Edmonston of Duntreath and his brother Edmonston of Spittal, from whom the King had withdrawn the appointment in 1535. Doune Castle then came into the possession of the son of Sir James Stuart—Lord Doune. Lord Doune's eldest son married the daughter of the Regent Moray and was afterwards known as " the Bonnie Earl of Moray." The Captain of Doune Castle was the patron of the Chaplainries of St. Fillan within and without the Castle.

About 1578, the inhabitants of Dunblane were much disturbed by their prospective forced removal from the occupation of the lands held from the Bishop which they had long possessed. A supplication was presented to the King by the " native tennentis and Kyndlie possessours of the temporal lands pertaining to the Bishopric of Dunblane, who had held these lands as takis-men and tennentis for tyme past the memorie of man paying thankfull payment of their dewtie and dew service none having cause to complain of them." These were people whose ancestors had previously occupied the land which they at that time held. Their complaint was that Mr. Andrew Grahame "quha is provest to the said Bishopric be nenis of Johne Erll of Montrose in process of tyme will not faill to remove theme fra their saidis Native & Kyndlie rowmes quhairby ane thousand of your Sovereign Lord's comonis and pure people wilbe put to uter (extreme) heirschip and extreme beggartie." They prayed the King to ordain the Bishop to allow them to go on as before and that the letting of the " tennentis rowmes over their heads suld on na wayes be confirmit and it suld not be lesum (permitted) to Lord Bishop to let tak rentall or uther richt be resson quhairof they may be removit. They payand their maillis and dewties thankfully and uther dew service."

The Bishop had feued these lands of Dunblane to the Earl of Montrose. The Earl replied that he would not put out the " Kyndlie Tennentis," but the King granted their petition and Montrose's appeal was not heeded to. An Act of Parliament concerning the kindly tenants of the Bishopric was passed on 25th July, 1578, followed by a second Act in 1579.

There had been in 1575 litigation between the tenants of the Bishopric against Mr. Robert Montgomery, now minister at Stirling and the Earl of Montrose. The following is a copy of the Decree, dated 30th June, 1575.

" Decreet in complaint at the instance of James Kynross of Kippenross, John Reid in the Hall, Cryistie Cairnis, James Belchis, John Cairnis, Isobell Neilsoun, John Reid in the Hous, Andrew Adie, Jonet Hart, John Glas, Cryistie Crommie, Robert Roiss, Andrew Fogo, Wm. Coward, Robert Reid, Robert Coward, Wm. Henrysoun, John Finlaysoun and remanent tenants and occupiers of the Bishopric of Dunblane, against Mr. Robert Mungumry, Minister at Stirling on the one part and John Earl of Montrois Lord Graham on the other part, narrating that whereas said Mr. Robert M. alleges that there is due to him for his stipend as minister at Stirling 4 chalders 14 bolls 3 firlots meal out of the Thirds of said Bishopric and has obtained letters of horning charging said tenants to pay the same, and that said Earl Montrois alleging that he has the escheat of Wm. sometime bishop of Dunblane has also obtained letters of horning against said tenants charging them to pay to said Earl their teinds and ferms of said Bishopric, and so the said tenants are thus double charged and being first charged by said Mr. Robert they have made payment to him *bona fide*. Whereupon the said tenants compearing by Mr. Henry Kinross their procurator and said Mr. Robert being personally present and said Earl being summoned and not compearing the Lords of Council decern the said tenants to answer, obey and pay to said Mr. Robert M. so long as he remains minister of said Kirk, and suspend the letters of horn-ing of John Earl of Montrois."

Lindsay of Pitscottie, the old Scottish historian, records that Mary Queen of Scots held a Parliament in Dunblane in December, 1558, at which she secured consent to the Dauphin being crowned King of Scotland and to new seals being made and the old seals broken up. These decisions were, however, reversed soon after.

In 1579 the Earl of Atholl, Chancellor of Scotland, died at the seat of the Earl of Montrose, Kincardine Castle. He was said to have been poisoned by means of ground glass. His body was conveyed through Dunblane on 7th July, and was taken to Edinburgh on 8th July, and interred in St. Giles Kirk.

During this period another fight took place between local families, namely, between the Stirlings of Keir and the Sinclairs of Galwauldmoir. The cause of the dispute was the lands of

Auchinbie, now part of Kippendavie Mains Farm. These lands had been in the possession of the Keir family for some generations and Archibald Stirling of Keir had given them to his son, James Stirling of Kippendavie. William Sinclair, on the other hand, claimed them as having purchased them from the crown as Kirk lands formerly belonging to the Bishopric, but which had been annexed after the Reformation. The fight took place in Dunblane on 3rd June, 1593, with the result that James Stirling and William Sinclair and his sons, Edward and George, were all slain. Three years later the quarrel was made up by the Sinclairs giving up their claim to the lands and a contract was entered into between Sir Archibald Stirling of Keir, Dame Jean Chisholm, Lady Keir, his mother, and William Sinclair then of Galwauldmoir, dated 8th April, 1596. Sir Archibald and his mother forgave the slaughter of James Stirling by what was known as a " Letter of Slanes," while William Sinclair and his brother, James, gave a similar letter on their part. James Stirling, who lost his life in this fight, had been given in his youth, the rents of one of the chaplainries of the Cathedral for his support at the schools. In 1587, the Lairds of Keir and Kippenross are included in a list of Highland landlords where " broken men presently dwell." In 1589, Mar and Home rode to Dunblane and Doune with three hundred horse in search of Bothwell, but found him not.

The lands of Auchinbie had been acquired from the Dean and Chapter of Dunblane by James Stirling of Keir in 1549 for certain payments (see page 74) to Sir William Drummond, Sacristan of Dunblane, a free passage through the lands to the city of Dunblane being reserved for the inhabitants and their " weinis and drawand cairtis " for peats, turfs, stones, wood and other portable things. On 3rd February, 1549, Bishop William Chisholm confirmed the appointment of William Blackwood, clerk, to the Chaplainry of St. Mary within Dunblane Cathedral on the presentation of James Stirling of Keir, but subject to this condition that the chaplainry be served by an honest chaplain until Blackwood was promoted to priest's orders.

In 1579, King James VI confirmed an appointment by William, Bishop of Dunblane, of his " well-beloved brother, James Chisholm of Cromlix and his heirs and successors as their undoubted and irrevocable Bailie over all the tenants, possessors and others whatsumever dwelling within the Lordship of Dunblane, to be holden the said office with all fees and privileges to the said James and his successors in fee and heritage for ever." Along with the appointment the said James Chisholm received the sum of £40 yearly from the readiest of the rents of the Bishopric. He was to act as judge in all disputes arising within the Lordship and Regality of Dunblane, while all trespassers were to be pursued before him for their demerits. This letter of Bailerie was dated at Dunblane, 3rd June, 1565.

In the Leighton Library at Dunblane there is preserved the manuscript of a satirical poem entitled " Rob Stene's Dream." The poem appears to have been written about the year 1591, and the handwriting is understood to be of that period. The poem chiefly deals with the politics of the day and warns King James VI, who is referred to in the poem as "the Royal Lion," against sundry of his councillors. It refers to the King bringing home his bride, daughter of the King of Denmark, across stormy seas in May, 1590, and it expresses an ardent hope that he might be blest with a son and heir. The person most severely handled in the poem is referred to under the designation of Laurence or the Fox. It is not known who is depicted, but it has been suggested that it was the Chancellor, John Maitland, Lord Thirlestane. The author of the poem is unknown. No poet is known to have existed of the name of Rob Stene, but it is almost certain that the name is fictitious. The author of the poem must have been a man of education and culture and his composition has very considerable merits. Nothing is known of how the manuscript came to be in the Leighton Library.

Reference may here be made to one or two notable persons resident in or natives of Dunblane or district at this period. Some distinguished scholars are mentioned in Dempster's *History of Scotland*, one of whom was David Reid, Professor in the College of the King, who had many honours conferred upon him. He wrote a number of books, principally in defence of Mary Queen of Scots against the " English Jezebel " as he termed good Queen Bess. He ceased teaching in 1586, the date of his death being uncertain. Another scholar was David Scott, who became a professor at Paris. He wrote numerous works which were highly esteemed by Dempster. He was elected to the Academy of Paris in 1554 and died 1573. Thomas Smeton, another native of Dunblane, became a professor of Latin in Paris. He seems at first to have been a member of the Society of Jesus, but is said to have become " a vile apostate and heretic." He afterwards taught secular scholars. His death took place in 1578, probably in Edinburgh.

A notable man in the ranks of the Reformers was John Row, born at Row in Lecropt Parish in 1526. He was educated at the Grammar School, Stirling, graduated M.A. at St. Andrews and practised as an advocate in the Consistory Court at St. Andrews. In 1550 he was nominated Agent of the Clergy of Scotland at the Court of Rome, and he resided in Italy for seven or eight years, becoming a Doctor of Law of Padua University. He returned to Scotland in 1558 for health reasons, but with the appointment of Pope's Nuncio. Following on a discussion with Robert Colville, Laird of Cleish, Row embraced the Protestant faith and became a strong supporter of Knox. He was one of the six ministers who framed the Covenant of Faith. His ministry was chiefly in the city of Perth, then the second burgh in Scotland, where he was sole minister and where he died, much regretted, in 1580.

The most important men in the district at this time were undoubtedly the Bishops, who held considerable power not only in ecclesiastical, but also in civil matters. Bishop William Chisholm I, who was a half-brother of the good Bishop James Chisholm, was a man of very different character from his predecessor. Known as "the Robber Bishop," he gave away much of the possessions of the Church to his illegitimate children and other relatives. In 1543 he accompanied Cardinal Beaton when courts were held in Stirling, Perth and elsewhere for the purpose of trying heretics. These dignitaries were attended by the Earl of Argyll, who was Lord Justice General, and the Earl of Arran, and by soldiers with several pieces of cannon. At Perth five men were condemned and hung and one woman drowned, the latter because she refused to pray to the Virgin Mary. A number of citizens of Perth who sympathised with the sufferers were banished from the town, including one bearing the name of Laurence Pullar. The Provost of Perth at this time was Alexander Macbreck, M.A. Fettis, the local historian, conjectures that he may have been related to Sir Andrew Breck (or Macbreck), Royal Almoner and Chancellor of Dunblane Cathedral at the beginning of this century.

William Chisholm was a member of Parliament when the Confession of Faith was submitted, but neither he nor any supporter of the Roman Church protested. Tardy protests were made at a later date, but this did not prevent the passing of various Acts of Parliament in August, 1560, forbidding the celebration of Catholic rites under the severest penalties. On 2nd June, 1561, Chisholm's nephew was appointed Bishop of Dunblane. The elder William Chisholm died in 1564, and is said to have been buried within Dunblane Cathedral. He had a son, James Chisholm, for whom he bought twelve ox-gangs of land in Lothian in 1544. An ox-gang measured about thirteen acres. His daughter Jean, whose mother was a daughter of the Earl of Montrose, was married to Sir James Stirling of Keir in 1542. The Bishop undertook to pay the ordinary expenses of the couple for five years and the bride received a dowry of a thousand pounds from James Chisholm of Glassingall, along with a lease of teind sheaves for nineteen years.

Sir James Chisholm of Cromlix was also a prominent adherent of the Roman Church. He is said to have been involved with the Earl of Huntly in the capture of Donibristle Castle and murder of the Bonnie Earl of Moray. In 1595 he appeared before the General Assembly and craved mercy for his apostacy and renounced the Anti-Christ with all his errors. He was received into the bosom of the Reformed Church, and absolved from the sentence of excommunication previously pronounced. He is said to have been buried within Dunblane cathedral, his tombstone exhibiting the family arms with the inscription " Hic Jacet Honorabilis vir Jacobus Chisholm eques auratus de Dundorn ! "

As has been mentioned, the owner of Keir about this time was Sir James Stirling, who was married to Jean Chisholm, " cousingness " to William Chisholm, Bishop of Dunblane, in 1542. Sir James Stirling had been previously married to the heiress of Cadder, but the marriage was annulled. Sir James Stirling took part in the trial of the Earl of Morton for the murder of Darnley as one of two Commissioners, and he pronounced sentence of death on Morton. He was a member of the Parliament of 1st August, 1560, which brought forward the Confession of Faith. His death took place at Cadder in 1588. Sir James gave his son and heir, Archibald, the estate of Keir in 1579, and he afterwards succeeded to Cadder. Sir Archibald gave his *fourth* son, also named Archibald, the lands of Kippendavie in 1594. He was thus the first Stirling of Kippendavie. The estate of Kippenross never belonged to the Keir family, the owners in the sixteenth century being of the name of Kinross. The property of Kilbryde was still part of the possessions of the Earls of Menteith, while the estate of Argaty was owned by Homes of

Argaty, a branch of the Homes of Polwarth who had acquired this estate from James IV about 1497 or 1498. The owner of Argaty about 1550 was still George Home, the second laird of that name, who was succeeded by his eldest son, Alexander Home, some time after 1562. A brother of the latter, named David Home, was accused of treason and convicted and afterwards executed on 8th December, 1584. The charge against him was inter-communing with the Earl of Mar and other traitors, including David Erskine, some time Commendator of Dryburgh, and of receiving letters from these men, and from his nephew, Patrick Home, servant to the Earl of Mar, received through Robert MacWillie, whom he had received in his own house, committed in the summer of 1584. A thousand crowns were offered in vain for his life, and to the great wrath of the populace, his head was placed on the Nether Bow Port of Edinburgh. A graphic account of his execution is given by Calderwood, the historian. George Buchanan wrote that his brother Patrick was also executed, but this seems to have been a mistake. Some writers refer to David Home as "of Argaty," but probably he was never proprietor of the estate, although he was the third son of George Home, the second laird of this family. Alexander Home, who was married to a Campbell of Glenorchy, died about 1574, and was succeeded by Patrick Home, who lived until about 1629.

Alexander Home, son of Home of Polwarth, is known as "the Poet-Preacher of Logie." He was born in 1560 and was minister of the Parish of Logie at the end of the sixteenth century.

The romantic story of Sir James Chisholm of Cromlix and Helen Stirling is worthy of recall. Sir James, the fifth Chisholm of Cromlix and a great grandson of Margaret Drummond and James IV, was betrothed to Helen Stirling, daughter of William Stirling, who resided in Dunblane, and who was a younger brother of the Laird of Ardoch. The Stirlings' maternal grandfather, Harry Sinclair, had received the lands of Ardoch from Bishop William Chisholm. Helen appears to have had great personal attractions, and she and Sir James, who had been companions from youth, were betrothed. The wedding, however, was postponed until after Sir James would visit his uncle, William Chisholm, Bishop of Vaison, and another uncle, Sir John Chisholm, who had married a wealthy lady and also lived in France. Before leaving Scotland, Sir James arranged to correspond with his fiancee and transmit his letters through a friend who was to convey them to his sweetheart. His friend, however, in course of time, became fascinated with the lady and kept back letters which Chisholm sent for her. At first the letters became less frequent and ultimately ceased—at least so it appeared to Helen Stirling. She continued for some time writing to Sir James, but the intermediary saw that no replies reached her, and he himself pretended to write on her behalf without success. The latter persuaded Helen that he was dead or false to her. She learned, however, that his letters were reaching Cromlix and brought good news of his health and advancement in France. Ultimately the false friend informed Helen that he had learned that Sir James had fallen in love with a French lady of noble family and was about to marry her. He secured a promise of marriage from Helen, and arrangements were made for its celebration, after considerable delay, and it was only with reluctance that Helen gave her consent. The wedding day arrived. After the bride had appeared in bridal attire and the marriage ceremony had been completed, the bride within the banqueting hall turned and denounced her husband as the basest of villains. He had betrayed the confidence of his friend and kept back her lover's letters and had failed to forward her letters to him. She announced that Sir James Chisholm would yet appear to vindicate his honour and to avenge the wrong done. The guilty man was said to have been covered with confusion and to have slunk away from the gathering with his friends, while the bride remained in her father's house. Sir James was already on his way home to Scotland, and he hastened to join his betrothed. The marriage was annulled and the two lovers were shortly after united in wedlock. Their sons, James and John, were afterwards the last Chisholm lairds of Cromlix. A well-known poem entitled "Cromlet's Lilt" is said to have been composed by Sir James on the voyage home while believing that Helen Stirling had proved false to him, giving expression to his deep grief and sorrow. The poem is well worth preservation and is now given in the form quoted in *Historic Scenes in Perthshire*.

" Since all thy vows, false maid,
  Are flown to air,
And my poor heart betrayed
  To sad despair,
Into some wilderness
My grief I will express,
And thy hard heartedness,
  O cruel fair !

" Have I not graven our loves
  On every tree
In yonder spreading groves,
  Though false thou be ?
Was not a solemn oath
Plighted betwixt us both,
Thou thy faith, I my troth,
  Constant to be ?

" Some gloomy place I'll find,
  Some doleful shade,
Where neither sun nor wind
  E'er entrance had ;
Into that hollow cave,
There will I sigh and rave,
Because thou dost behave
  So faithlessly.

" Wild fruit shall be my meat,
  I'll drink the spring ;
Cold earth shall be my seat ;
  For covering
I'll have the starry sky
My head to canopy
Until my soul on high
  Shall spread its wing.

" I'll have no funeral fire
  Nor tears for me ;
No grave do I desire,
  Nor obsequies.
The courteous redbreast, he
With leaves shall cover me,
And sing my elegy,
  With doleful voice.

" And when a ghost I am,
  I'll visit thee,
O thou obdured dame,
  Whose cruelty
Hath killed the kindest heart
E'er pierced by Cupid's dart;
No grief my soul shall part
  From loving thee.

Sir James afterwards became Master of the Household to James VI with whom he was a great favourite.   It was intended at one time that he should proceed to Spain on a mission on behalf of the adherents of the Roman Catholic faith, of which he was long a stout supporter, but as already mentioned, he in 1595 was admitted a member of the Reformed Church by the General Assembly at Montrose.   According to another version of the romantic story of Sir James and Helen Stirling, Sir James appeared on the day of the intended wedding and threw the false bridegroom out of the house, and, according to a tradition, killed him, but this has not been authenticated.

Reference has already been made to the forced marriage of Janet of Cadder to James Stirling, the heir of Keir, in 1534.   In carrying through this marriage Sir James Stirling of Keir appears to have received considerable assistance from a Thomas Bischop.   Bischop is referred to as a " servitor " or " servand " of Keir, but this word was probably used in the sense of secretary. Bischop's life as traced by John Riddell is an interesting one.   The son of a burgess of Edinburgh, who owned considerable property in that city, he is found acting as a Notary Public in 1533, when he witnessed a deed affecting Sir John Stirling.   He acted as a Notary Public for Sir James Stirling in 1539 and about 1541, while still servitor for Sir James Stirling, he himself married Janet, the first wife of his master.   He averred that his marriage was " with love of Keir " who gave him 300 merks, some lands, 200 gold crowns, two daggers, Scottish Chronicles and two platts of Edinburgh and Stirling Castles.   Bischop afterwards became private secretary to the Earl of Lennox, who was descended from Mary, sister of James IV, and father of Darnley, who married Mary Queen of Scots.   He had just returned from Europe where he had taken a distinguished part in the wars in Italy.   Lennox sent Bischop to England in 1544 to obtain redress against the Earl of Arran, Governor of Scotland, and Cardinal Beaton, when he was described as " Our Secretary and lawful procurator to treat with the Commissioners of Henry VIII."   He was also entrusted to negotiate with Henry VIII for the wedding of Lennox to Lady Margaret Douglas, his niece.   The marriage was arranged, and the outcome of it was Darnley, who became nearest heir to the English throne after Mary Queen of Scots.   Bischop had the honour of Squire conferred on him by the English Crown and was evidently held there in high regard.   On the other hand Shrewsbury referred to him in a letter as " a lewd practising Scot and a naughtie person."   Janet of Cadder seems to have obtained a safe conduct to England and to have remained attached to her husband.   His Scottish property was forfeited in 1545 in respect of his conspiring with the English, but, although continuing to live in England, he still exercised great influence with Lennox, whom he strove to keep Protestant while his wife endeavoured to make him a Catholic. When Mary Queen of Scots contemplated marriage with Bothwell, Bischop wrote a remarkable letter to Sir James Melville which he asked Melville to show the Queen. This Melville had the courage to do. The terms of the letter show Bischop to have been a man endowed with ability and patriotism. In 1568 a poem was written in defence of Mary Queen of Scots against the Earl of Moray which led to Bischop being confined in the Tower of London as the supposed author. The authorship of the poem has never been established, but it would seem that Bischop had a share in the writing of it. He returned to Scotland in his old age under a remission from James VI in which honourable mention is made of his faithful services to Queen Mary.

On 13th July, 1592, Ardoch House was attacked by Sir Robert Crichton of Cluny who took away his half-sister Marion, by force. She was under the guardianship of Henry Stirling, then proprietor of Ardoch. With some bold companions and horsemen he obtained access to the house under pretext of searching for the Earl of Bothwell, then an outlaw in hiding. After they had brutally assaulted the lady of the house and plundered it, Marion was carried off. Legal proceedings were instituted for her restoration, and as the raiders failed to produce her they were outlawed, but it does not appear that they suffered any definite punishment. The lady was, however, ultimately recovered, and later on married with the consent of her guardian.

It may be of interest to note that in the last year of the century (1600), the Privy Council prohibited the killing of heron in Strathearn and surrounding districts east of the " stopis of Kilbuc " (Kinbuck) under severe penalties.

CHAPTER VII.

THE DECAY OF DUNBLANE CATHEDRAL FOLLOWING THE REFORMATION.

THE opinion formerly held by many that the fabric of Dunblane Cathedral suffered damage at the hands of the Reformers about the year 1560 is incorrect. Early in the 16th century it was repaired and certain embellishments were made during the bishopric of James Chisholm, but it seems to have deteriorated during the time of his brother, Bishop William Chisholm. It is true that the aisle of St. Blais was repaired by him and it is probable that he had a special interest in this aisle as the altar was under the patronage of the Chisholms of Cromlix, but, if this aisle required repair in the middle of the 16th century, it is very probable that other parts of the cathedral were not being maintained as they ought to have been, and it is known that by the year 1588 the work of decay had advanced considerably.

The aim of the Reformers was not to destroy the ancient places of worship, but to clear the churches of images therein and of all monuments of idolatry.

The terms of the warrant for clearing the Cathedral of Dunblane as recorded in Henderson's *Annals of Dunfermline* is as follows :—

" Trist friendis, after maist hearty commendacioun, we pray you faill not to pass incontinent to the Kyrk of (Dumblaim) and tak doun the haill images thereof, and bring furth to the Kirk Zayrd and burn theym oppinly. And siclyk cast doun alteris, and purge the Kyrk of all Kynd of Monuments of idolatrye. And this ze faill not to do, as ze will do us singulare emplesour ; and so committis you to the protection of God :—Fro Edinburgh—1559.

(Signed) Ar. Argyle,

James Stewart,
Ruthven.

" Faill not, bot ze tak guid heyd that neither the dasks, windocks, nor
  durris be ony ways hurt or broken, eyther glass in wark or iron wark."

The instructions, therefore, were to take down and burn the whole images, cast down the altars and clear the Cathedral of its idols, but explicit directions are given that the desks or stalls windows and doors, glass and iron work should be in no way damaged.

In the *Book of Perth* by Mr. J. P. Lawson, M.A., 1847, appears the following account of the clearing of Dunblane Cathedral by armed men headed by the Earl of Argyle and Lord James Stewart, Prior of St. Andrews.

" On a beautiful morning towards the end of June, 1559, as the people were attending mass in the Cathedral a noise as of armed men was heard within the surrounding Court (they had marched all night from Perth). Presently a band of warriors entered by the Western portal and advanced towards the choir in two lines, the one led by the Earl of Argyle and the other by the Prior of St. Andrews. The worshippers in the body of the Church, rising from their prostrations retreated into the aisles, while those within the choir forgetting their devotions, rose up and turned with inquiring eyes towards the intruders, who, halting in their double array, nearly filled the body of the Cathedral. Some of them were completely armed, while the greater part wore the garb of citizens but each had a rope or halter suspended round his neck. One of the officials at the altar descending the steps and advancing towards the balustrade which divided the choir from the main body of the Church said :—
' O My Lord of Argyll and you, my Lord Prior, what means this martial array in the House of God and what the symbols thy followers wear. Me thinks if they betoken penance it were fitter to enter this threshold as suppliants than as conquerors.'

" ' We come Dean,' replied the Earl, ' to set forward the reformation of Religion according to God's word and to purify this Kirk and in name of the Congregation warn and charge you that whatsoever person shall plainly resist these our enterprises we by the authority of the council will reduce them to their duty.'

" ' And moreover,' added the Prior, ' we with 300 burgesses of Perth whom ye see here have banded ourselves together in the Kirk of St. John now purified from its idolatry and bound ourselves by a great oath, that we are willing to part with life as these symbols round our necks testify, if we turn back or desist. So therefore, shall we with all the force and power which God shall grant unto us execute just vengeance and punishment upon you; yea we shall begin that same war which it was commanded the Israelites to execute against the Canaanites : i.e., contract of peace shall never be made till ye desist from your open idolatry and cruel persecution of God's children.'

" ' We are here in the peacable exercises of our holy religion,' replied the Dean, ' if there be persecutors within these walls, they who violate the sanctuary are the men.'

" ' Peace,' interrupted the prior, ' we are not here to wrangle but to see the commands of the Council executed. Say if ye and your brethren are willing to obey and of your own consent to remove the stumbling blocks, even these monuments of idolatry.'

" ' Most reverend Father and you most puissant Earl,' answered the Churchman. ' We who are here are but servants or menials, so to speak. Whatsoever our will may be our power reacheth not to the things whereof ye speak—Our beloved Bishop is even now with the Queen Regent, conferring doubtless of these mighty matters. To him your request shall be made known and by his orders we shall abide and act.'

" The Prior and Earl conferred a short time together when the latter again addressed the Dean.

" ' We are even now on an expedition of great weight and moment, which brooketh not delay, but turned aside to warn the lieges of Dunblane of the danger of upholding the errors and enticements of Papistry else we had not departed without leaving this house stript of these vain trappings. Ye are now in our power, time presseth and we cannot trust Wm. Chisholm. This therefore will we do:—'we will not advance beyond this barrier nor disturb those assembled in it, but with our own hands will we cast down the images and destroy the altars which on every side ye have reared to Gods of your own making.' The words were scarcely out of the speaker's mouth when the shrines were entered and the images and pictures displaced, and trampled underfoot."

" To the brook with them, 'cried the Prior ; and the armed multitude rushing out at the portal by which they had entered bore the relics to the banks of the Allan and cast them in. It was the work but of a few moments and the troops were again marshalled on their way to Stirling. The multitude within the Choir, saw what passed with an air of stupified wonder and leaving the services of the morning unfinished gradually withdrew to their respective houses, wondering at the things which they had witnessed."

All the information available points to the clearing of the Cathedral nave occupying a brief time during which altars were cast down and images destroyed, the debris being thrown into the river Allan. After the brief visit the invaders passed on to take similar action in Stirling.

In later years one reads of 32 stalls, along with the Bishop's seat and Dean's seat, still remaining in the Cathedral while the 3 steps of the High Altar remained until after 1799. In 1569, priests of Dunblane were still in possession of vestments and chalices. It may be concluded, therefore, that no interference took place with the fabric of the building during the short visit of the invaders from Perth and there is no evidence of the visit of the Reformers being repeated on any later date. In all likelihood, the majority of the inhabitants of Dunblane still favoured the Roman Catholic party. The Bishops Chisholm possessed great power in the district and were closely identified with many of the principal land-owners, while the Cathedral clergy all had residences in the city. The inhabitants probably regarded the proceedings of the Reformers with disfavour or at least took no active part in the work of demolition either on the occasion of this visit of the armed warriors from Perth or at any later date.

How then is the state of decay, into which the Cathedral fell between 1559 and 1588, to be accounted for ? During that period the Reformed Party in the Church of Scotland was in a struggling condition. The sympathies of Queen Mary were entirely with the Catholic Church and, while Cathedrals were in the hands of the Reformers, no help would be given by the Crown for the maintenance of such buildings. The properties of Dunblane Cathedral, consisting of the city of Dunblane and much land in the surrounding district to a large extent had passed to private persons. The Church of Scotland was not properly organised and there were few clergy to

E

administer the rites of religion according to Protestant usages. As we have already seen, there was a minister of the Reformed Church in Dunblane Cathedral only for a short period between the years 1559 and 1567 and perhaps the work of decay set in then. It may have been aggravated by acts of vandalism happening where there was no representative of the Reformed Church to maintain order, but there is no record of this occurring in Dunblane. Even when Protestant clergy were settled they may have been unable, through lack of funds, to carry out repairs necessary to restore and maintain the ancient building.

In the 5th session of the General Assembly in the year 1588, " it was ordained that an article sould be given in to the king bearing regrait for the decay of certane Kirks which are ruinous and without hastie repaire are not able to be remedied, namely, Glasgow Dumfermline and Dumblane, and that his Majestie sould be desired to caus the Earle of Huntlie now Abbot of Dumfermline to repair Dumfermline, the Bishop of Dumblane, Dumblane."

It is not known whether this appeal to the Crown was effectual, but, if any repairs were executed at this time, they were of a minor nature and insufficient to prevent the nave becoming the ruin that it was for 300 years. In all likelihood the roof remained in existence in 1588, although probably in insufficient repair, while the nave may still have been in use at that time as a place of worship, but by 1622, that is 34 years later, the nave was roofless, and the choir was being used as the parish church. In 1660 the nave was familiarly known as " the old Church."

At the beginning of the 16th century under Bishop James, the Cathedral had attained its height of embellishment and was more richly endowed than at any other time. By the end of the century it was a ruin, the larger portion roofless and its possessions in secular hands, but it had not suffered in these respects at the hands of the Reformers.

CHAPTER VIII.

THE ALTARS OF DUNBLANE CATHEDRAL, THE MANSES OF THE CLERGY AND RESIDENCES OF THE LAIRDS, AND THE CROFTS OF DUNBLANE.

THE ALTARS IN DUNBLANE CATHEDRAL.

THERE seem to have been at least 7 altars in Dunblane Cathedral prior to the Reformation. These include the High Altar situated at the east end of the choir, raised three steps above the floor of the Choir, the Altar of the Virgin Mary in the Keir Aisle, the Altar of St. Stephen in the North Aisle west of the last, the Altar of St. Blais at the west end of the North Aisle, the Trinity Altar opposite the latter in the South Aisle, the Altar of St. Nicolas in the Drummond Aisle east of the tower and entrance door, and the Altar of St. Michael, east of the last in the South-East Aisle, probably below the Holmehill window. These Altars had their patrons who had the right to appoint chaplains and they were endowed with tenements and crofts in Dunblane.

The Stirlings of Keir were patrons of St. Michael's Altar to which belonged a tenement and yard on the south of the property called Greenyeards, now known as the Union Bank House, that is between the Bank House and the Millrow. St. Michael's Croft was situated in what used to be known as the Kippenross Park or Cowpark which extended from behind the High Street towards Ochlochy and the Darn Road. St. Michael's Croft was bounded on the east by the Mony Burn and on the west by the Dovecot Croft which stood above the Stirling Arms garden. In 1692, Janet Wright succeeded to it. In 1753 the lands were worth £21 Scots yearly to the Kirk Session. One has to keep in view that at that time there was no New Road or cutting where the New Road now is and that the land immediately above the High Street was more or less flat and all in grass or under cultivation.

The Altar of St. Nicolas standing in the South-East Aisle (known as Drummond's Aisle) was repaired and endowed by Walter Drummond, Dean of Dunblane, shortly before 1509. In 1535-36 it was in the patronage of John, Lord Drummond. The endowments bestowed by Dean Walter Drummond in 1509 included 10 merks yearly from Easter and Middle Cambushinnie described as in the Stewartrie of Strathearn and an annual rent of £13 9s. from a tenement and croft in Dunblane of George Sinclair on the south side of the " Wynd yt leads to Mento Myre " (that is Sinclairs Wynd), next the stream called Ald Menych Burn, as also three tenements and one house in the city, with the lands of Whitehill in the Lordship of Glendevon. It is probable that it was this Sinclair who gave its name to Sinclair's Wynd. The Ald Menych is the Minnie or Money Burn. This endowment is referred to in an old Kilbryde paper as being for the " sustenance of ane Chaplain at *St. Ninians* Altar." For " St. Ninians " should be read " St. Nicolas." The croft of St. Nicolas stood to the north of Holmhill near to Ramoyle and included a tenement and garden bounded on the north by Glenhomie (Glenwhommie) and by the Archdeacon's croft and the Archdeacon's garden on the east. The Altar of St. Nicolas at one time belonged to the Earls of Perth, and Lord Drummond of Stobhall in 1662 succeeded to it from his father John, Earl of Perth. It was afterwards disponed to William, Viscount Strathallan, with consent of George Drummond of Blairdrummond, Chaplain of that Altar.

Walter Drummond, who was private secretary to James IV, provided that the Chaplain to the Altar of St. Nicolas should celebrate divine service there at the Altar for the salvation of the souls of the King, the Queen, Prince Arthur, John, Lord Drummond, his brother, and Elizabeth, spouse of the said John, and of the deceased John Drummond, Dean of Dunblane.

St. Nicholas was born in Patara, a seaport town, in the latter half of the third century. He became Bishop of Myra in Asia Minor. His festival was celebrated on 6th December. He was the guardian saint of sailors and of children. His name is preserved in the form of Santa Claus.

The Altar of St. Blais was built and repaired by William, Bishop of Dunblane, and was in the patronage of the Lairds of Cromlix who had the power of appointment of the " Chaplain at the Altar of the most precious cross of our Lord Jesus Christ, called the Chapel of St. Blais." The Croft of St. Blais was known as the Doucot or Dove Croft. The Doucot was built on the croft above the first portion of the Darn Road which formerly ran from the fruiterer's shop to the New Road. Attached were tenements, barn and garden, the croft running behind the gardens of the High Street. St. Blain's House was, 100 years ago, known as St. Blain's Rood, but the name St. Blain, which is more familiar, may have been confused with that of St. Blais. The Altar stood where a canopy is still seen recording the burial place of the Strathallan family who became proprietors of the possessions of the Altar. Sir James Chisholm of Cromlix, Knight of the Gilded Spur, is said to have been buried there. The endowments of the Altar of St. Blais also included three crofts, namely, Waterstoun's, Kiln Croft and Long Croft. In 1567 the Altarage was worth £4 13s. 4d. In 1572 the King confirmed a charter by the Chaplain of the Altar of St. Blais to James Blackwood of the Dovecot Croft—the tenement being then ruinous. At this date Bishop William Chisholm was Patron and John Leirmonth was Chaplain. The Drummonds of Cromlix succeeded the Chisholms in the patronage.

On 29th December, 1674, Lieutenant-General William Drummond of Cromlix, Patron of the Chaplainry and Altar of St. Blais, and immediate lawful superior of three crofts of land in Dunblane commonly called Waterstoun's Croft, Kiln Croft and the Long Croft, approved of letters of alienation and disposition of the said crofts granted by Mr. John Sinclair sometime of Glassingall Beg to Duncan Drummond of Balhaldies and his heirs, reserving always to himself and the person appointed to the said chaplainry feu-duties, rents and sums payable from the three crofts of land with the Kiln Barn and yards. General Drummond was then a prisoner in Dumbarton Castle. It may be mentioned that St. Blais was Bishop of Sebaste in Cappadocia in the time of Diocletian, and the instrument of his martyrdom was a comb such as was used by wool-combers. The celebration of his anniversary on 3rd February was observed in Bradford up to 1825. He was represented, on such occasions, sitting on a white horse with a Bible in his right hand and a comb in his left. At one time no labour was permitted on this day and bonfires were lit.

The Lady Altar or St. Mary's Altar was in the patronage of the Stirlings of Keir and reference is made to it in a Keir Charter, dated 1472. It was endowed by William Stirling of Keir for the health of the souls of King James III, John Hepburn, Bishop of Dunblane, Luke Stirling and others, with a toft and croft of his lands, the lands of Ichanrach, the woodland of Glassingall and an annual rent of 40s. from the lands of Kippenrait and 3 acres of arable land with the pasturage of six cows. In 1472 Sir John French was Chaplain of the Altar. In 1509, John Stirling of Keir further endowed it with an annual rent of £10. In 1573 Our Lady Altar in Dunblane was assigned to John Burdone, minister of Balquhidder, for part of his stipend. Its yearly revenue at this time was £20. On a vacancy occurring it fell to the patron to make an appointment within two months thereafter, failing which, the patronage fell to the Bishop. The chaplain was under obligation not to absent himself from duty for more than two months at any time. A longer absence involved the loss of the appointment. Our Lady Altar stood in the Keir Aisle on the north side of the nave. As the chapel to the north of the choir is commonly known as the Lady Chapel it has been sometimes thought that the north aisle of the nave at one time continued without interruption along the north of the choir, but this is improbable. In 1549, Sir John Forfar was inducted chaplain on the resignation of Sir James Blackwood, by delivery by the latter of the vestments and altar missal.

Sir James Stirling of Keir, who was also patron of St. Michael's Altar, in 1574, presented his son James Stirling with the emoluments of Our Lady Altar " for his support at the Schuils." There was then a vacancy in the chaplainry through the failure of the chaplain Sir William Blackwood to appear before the Superintendent of the Diocese to attest his faith to the King. It may be mentioned that James Stirling to whom was presented the chaplainry of Our Lady Altar in 1574 was afterwards presented by his father to the church of Baldernock in 1588. He became minister of Strathblane in 1597 and is said to have died father of the Church in July, 1650, in the 63rd year of his ministry.

The patron of the Altar of St. Stephen the Martyr was the Bishop of Dunblane. In 1511 a yearly payment of 6s. 8d. pertained to this Altar from a croft on the east side of Dunblane. The rents belonged to the Bishopric in episcopalian times, and Bishop Leighton presented these to John Graham, Commissary Clerk at Dunblane, who in turn gave them in 1691 for the benefit of the Leighton Library.

The Trinity Altar was founded by Master Henry White, Official of Dunblane, and also " Canon of the Cathedral Kirks of Murreff, Dunblane and Brechin, Rector of Sanct Modoce, Lord of Auchnagufe and Laird of the third part of the lands of Kintulach and of the mill of the same beside the Brig of Earn within the Parochin of Dunbary." This is referred to in an old Cambuskenneth Charter, dated 1533-34, by William, Bishop of Dunblane, James, his brother, formerly Bishop, then Administrator General of the Bishopric, the Dean and Chapter, the Official and Sir Steven Culrois, Chaplain of this Altar. Reference is made to the annual rent of 17 merks the gift of Henry White from the said lands of Kintulach and the mill for the support of the Trinity Altar. Henry White was one of the first members of the Court of Session founded by James V.

In the Kirk Session Records we read that Alexander Whithead, surgeon in Stirling, made an application in 1662 to have the aisle and burial place at the south and west end of the Cathedral called " the ferquhaires yle or Trinity Altar " with the dues and casualties thereto belonging, over and against the Laird of Cromlix's aisle. Sir Colin Campbell was given a right of burial in this aisle. In 1690 Harie Blackwood, Bailie of Dunblane, took proceedings against those who paid duties to the Trinity Altar of which he had the liferent.

The minister of Logie, a Prebend of the Cathedral, had a manse in Dunblane, but no emoluments were attached to this appointment. He was, however, liable in a payment of two merks to the titular of the Trinity Altar. In 1695 the sum of 17 merks was paid annually to the Altar from properties in the parish of Dumbarton.

The High or Great Altar was endowed by George Newton, Archdeacon of Dunblane, and on 18th January, 1532, a charter was granted by John Stirling of Keir to the 12 chaplains of the Choir of Dunblane and their successors providing an annual rent of £12 which had been purchased by Newton as a bequest for the saying of masses at the Great Altar daily. During Newton's lifetime the money was in the hands of the Fratres Minores of Stirling. Bishop James Chisholm had 10 years earlier erected 9 chaplainries of the Choir into perpetual chaplainries. In 1562 Bishop William Chisholm, with the consent of the Chapter and Chaplains of the Choir, sold the lands of Sauchinthome, that is Deanston, with wood or grove and fisheries. The Choir owned certain properties in Dunblane which in 1493 included the croft given by John Forfar, Chaplain, known as Monthamyr and Braedfute's tenement in Dunblane. The steps of the High Altar in the choir existed till 1799 or later.

In the *Red Book of Menteith* there is an account of the foundation of another altar in Dunblane Cathedral under the following circumstances. Lady Margaret, the only child of Sir John Graham, and his wife, the Countess of Menteith, born 1334, was married at the age of 14, to John, son of the Regent Moray. He died three years later and six months thereafter she married the Earl of Mar, who in 1354 divorced her, according to Fordun, " at the instigation of the devil." A third husband, married in 1359, was John Drummond of Concraig, but as these parties were related within the forbidden degrees of consanguinity, a dispensation had to be obtained from Pope Innocent Sixth in 1360, which dispensation is printed in Theiner's *Vetera Monumenta*. One of the conditions to the dispensation was that the parties should erect an altar within Dunblane Cathedral, endow it with a yearly sum of 10 merks, supply the necessary books and furnishings, and also provide an endowment of five silver merks for two poor maidens on their marriage. Lady Margaret, who was then Countess of Menteith, and her husband were to have the right of patronage. John Drummond died soon afterwards and in the following year, 1361, his widow married for the fourth time at the age of 26 or 27. Her fourth husband was Robert Stewart, third son of the Earl of Strathearn, afterwards King Robert II, and Margaret had again to apply to the Pope for a Dispensation in respect of her fourth marriage, which is also printed in *Vetera Monumenta*. This was granted on condition that husband and wife founded a chapel to the honour of God in the city or diocese of Dunblane and endowed it with an annuity of twelve silver merks payable to one perpetual chaplain. In respect of his marriage Stewart became Earl of Menteith and, after his wife's death, Duke of Albany and, later, Governor of Scotland. It has not been ascertained what Chapel was founded by them, or what altar, if any, was erected and endowed in Dunblane Cathedral.

THE MANSES OR RESIDENCES OF THE CATHEDRAL CLERGY.

Dunblane was entered from the north by the Overport or gate which stood on the Braeport. At this gate the dues on merchandise brought into the town were collected by the tacksman who had acquired the right of collecting such in return for a yearly rent or payment. The majority of the old manses were situated in the Braeport or elsewhere in the neighbourhood of the Cathedral.

A teind barn stood on the north-west side of Braeport, where the house now stands named Bishop's Barn and here were gathered the goods payable in kind to one of the clergy as part of his emoluments. The barn stood outside the gate. Across the street from the Bishop's Barn, but a little lower down the hill, was the Manse of Abernethy with garden ground behind, adjoining the lands of Holmhill to its north and east. The Manse of Abernethy was also known as the Abbot of Arbroath's Manse, as Abernethy latterly became attached to the Abbey of Arbroath and the Abbot was a member of the Chapter of the Cathedral as Prebendary of Abernethy. 100 years ago this house was possessed by Mrs. Malloch. A little lower down the Braeport on the same side as the Manse of Abernethy was the Manse of the Treasurer. The Manses of the " Abbot " and Treasurer, also of a prebender—it is not said of which—are shown on the Ordnance Map as having been situated on the west side of Braeport, but this seems to be erroneous. In *Perthshire Illustrated,* published 1843, the Prebend of Monzie's Manse is shown as situated in Braeport below the Manse of he Treasurer, but this is incorrect as the Manse of Monzie was on the west side of Braeport either near the site of the Leighton Church or north of it.

According to the Titles of Cromlix estates there were certain manses in the Braeport which were contiguous below the Treasurer's Manse—these were the Manses of Balquhidder, Aberfoyle, and Logie. The Manse of Balquhidder, south of the yard of theTreasurer and north of the Manse of Aberfoyle, was bounded on the east by Pitteocaleoch and on the west by the public street. It was conveyed in 1578 by the Prebend of Balquhidder to Thomas Drummond of Corscaplie and was then a waste piece of ground.

The property of the Parsonage of Aberfoyle was bounded by the yard of Balquhidder on the north, the Manse of Logie on the south, the common way to Ramoyle on the west, and the Howcroft belonging to John Kinross on the east. The Howcroft was a piece of land in the hollow below the hill of Holmhill behind Dunblane Public School. In 1619 the Parson of Aberfoyle granted a precept of Clare Constat to John Drummond of Corscaplie for infefting him in the waste piece of land belonging to his parsonage.

The Balquhidder and Aberfoyle Manses were afterwards conveyed by Drummond of Corscaplie to the Earl of Perth.

It has been said that the Manse of Logie was situated in Arnot's Close or at its north end, but this is erroneous. The Manse of Logie was sold in 1567 under reservation of a chamber in the south part for the use of the vicar.

In 1558 Roger Gordon, Dean of Dunblane, conveyed to Malcolm Drummond of Borland the Dean's Croft commonly called the Howcroft, the yard commonly called the Dean's Yard, and also the croft known as the Langcroft. The Howcroft, as has been mentioned, was east of the Manse of Aberfoyle. In 1589, Robert Drummond exchanged the Dean's Yard for an acre of land of Ramuile. Langcroft was also known as Laichale Croft, and was probably situated to the north-west of Ramuile.

In 1624 John Kinross, brother of the late Laird of Kippenross, conveyed to Harry Kinross, advocate, his nephew, and Margaret Drummond, his wife, his tenement in Dunblane along with Howcroft, Langcroft or Laichale Croft, an acre of Ramuile called Glenquhonnie containing three acres and the west land called the new yard. These lands were afterwards acquired in 1671 by General William Drummond and the lands included Whitecroft's acre. The lands of Ramoyle extended in various directions from the street now known by that name. It is probable that the modern name of Whitecross is a corruption of Whitecrofts. The property of Ledcameroch was formerly named Whitecross and the northern portion belonged to Cromlix estate.

General William Drummond acquired the Manses of Balquhidder, Aberfoyle and Logie in 1684 from the Earl of Perth as well as the patronage of St. Nicolas' Altar, the Earl reserving power to bury within Drummond's Aisle.

The proprietors of Cromlix also owned a piece of land between the lands of Glenquhonnie on the north and the Cathedral kirkyard on the south. The situation of this was apparently west and north of the Leighton Church. To the west of this property was the manse and croft of the " Dean " and to the east was the Manse of Monzie. By the Dean's Manse is probably meant the Manse of the Archdeacon and in a later title it is referred to as the Archdeacon's Manse. The Manse of Monzie (in ruins) and garden in the city of Dunblane were conveyed in 1513 by William Scott, Rector in Monzie, to John MacIlvoire under reservation of a decent chamber and stable as often as he and his successors should come to Dunblane for which an annual payment of 13s. 4d. was stipulated. The Manse of Monzie thus stood between the Archdeacon's Manse and garden and the lands of William Merser. Merser's lands were north of Ramoyle near the property known as Shaw's Buildings. The Manse of Monzie is said to have been sometimes referred to as the Manse of Comrie. The statement that the house of the Prebend of Monzie occupied the site of the house of the schoolmaster of Dunblane, that is where the infant department of Dunblane School now stands, is incorrect.

The Archdeacon's Manse in 1839 was said to be at the south-west corner of Mr. McInnis' Garden. The Rev. J. G. Christie described this site as " in front of ruins of an old barn and at a narrow road leading up past the old well," and states that the Archdeacon's Manse had a large garden and dark cellars. In the titles of the property in Braeport of the late Duncan McOwan, his property is said to be bounded on the East by the " High Street " and on the west by the manse and yard of old belonging to the Arch Dean of Dunblane.

In 1839 the Chancellor's Manse was said to have been " where Mr. John Sharp, Car and Drosky keeper has his house." Rev. J. G. Christie stated that this is now the Union Bank House, but there is no trace of a John Sharp occupying the Bank House in the middle of the last century. The Chancellor's Manse rather appears to have occupied the site of the property of Mr. James Lennox, grocer, as it is described as being south of My Lord's House, that is the town house of Lord Strathallan. It is well-known that Lord Strathallan's lodge was situated where Dunblane Prison now stands and one must keep in view that until modern times there was no street from the High Street to the East Church and onwards. This house is sometimes referred to as the Nether Lodging and the property he acquired north of the Cathedral as the Upper Lodging. The latter was apparently the Archdean's Manse acquired by Lord Strathallan from Chisholm of Cromlix. In the map of Dunblane in *Perthshire Illustrated* the Chancellor's Manse is shown as standing about opposite to the entrance of the County Buildings, but this is probably incorrect to some extent, as it would not then be south of my Lord's House.

Dr. Patrick Gordon Stewart in 1839 wrote that the Bishop's Palace was possessed by the Rev. Mr. Anderson (Minister of the United Presbyterian, now the Leighton Church). There is obviously some confusion here as the Palace of the Papal Bishops had been in ruins for some centuries before Mr. Anderson's day. During his stay in Dunblane Mr. Anderson occupied more than one house, one being the three-storeyed house at the south end of Kirk Street which has a small piece of ground and a low wall in front of it. This house may have been occupied by some of the Episcopalian bishops in the 17th century. An old building which stood between the Leighton Library and the Manse garage, in front of the present Cathedral Manse, was the Dean's Manse and was occupied latterly by the parish ministers of Dunblane until it was removed about 1828 or 1829. This was probably the Manse of the Dean in Episcopalian times although not in the days of the Roman Catholic clergy. The building on the opposite side of the Cross, entered by an outside stair, bears the arms of the family of Pearson of Kippenross and it has been frequently referred to as the Dean's Manse. The first Pearson was Dean of Dunblane Cathedral until the abolition of Episcopacy in the reign of Charles I. When Scotland ceased to be Episcopalian, Pearson lost his deanship and, although he made frequent efforts to regain office, he was unsuccessful. It was probably his private residence and it was not the manse of the Dean of the Cathedral.

The principal proprietors in the district had residences in Dunblane with the possible exception of the Stirlings of Keir. The latter owned a house in Stirling, but appear not to have had one in Dunblane. Next Dean Pearson's house and to the south of it was the residence of the Campbells of Kilbryde standing where the Burgh Chambers now stand. Further south was Lord Strathallan's house and the Drummonds of Balhaldie lived in Balhaldie House. The Earl of Perth had a residence opposite the Leighton Church and the Meeting House Loan leading down to the Haining.   This was a ruin in 1839.   It probably stood where the headmaster's house now is.   The Earl of Menteith's home stood on the site of the Bank of Scotland and the Earl of Montrose is said to have had a house on the opposite side of the High Street.   Dr. P. G. Stewart wrote in 1839 that the Bishops after the Reformation occupied the house then possessed by Patrick James Stirling, Writer, Dunblane, which was the Union Bank House, then known as Greenyeards, and this is probably correct, although Rev. J. G. Christie was of opinion that Bishop Leighton and his successors lived in a house between the Cross and the Kirk Street, that is in Cross Street.   There is ground for thinking that the Bishops in the reign of Charles II occupied a property described as south and west of the Dean's Manse, which points to the Union Bank House.

In 1579, the Bishop of Dunblane feued to William Stirling, Rector of Aberfoyle, the " great building" commonly called the Lodge, girnells and stables with the Bishop's meadow for payment of 3s. 4s. for the house and 10s. for the meadow.   In a Charter of Confirmation following thereon the property is described as "the Bishop's waste edifice or fore-dwelling house measuring 30 ells south and north with a part of the Bishop's close commonly called the Outer close adjacent to the houses along with that piece of the Bishop yard or orchard within the walls with the green valley, with the office of Bailie and the Bishop's whole other lands."   This seems to refer to the site of the Bishop's Palace and the ground in the valley between the Palace and the River Allan and perhaps the Bishop's Meadow across the River Allan extending westwards. It would thus appear that the Bishop's Palace was in ruins in 1579, but that the Bishop claimed the right of the disposal of the property.   Sir James Chisholm of Cromlix acquired these subjects along with Easter Corscaplie in 1592.

Crofts of Dunblane.

To the south-west of Dunblane in the neighbourhood of Springfield Terrace in the 16th century were acres occupied by some of the inhabitants who had held these from father to son for generations.   Other parts of the lands surrounding the city were divided into crofts particularly behind the gardens of the High Street and between these and the Darn Road, also in the neighbourhood of Balhaldie House and surrounding Holmhill to the south and west and in the neighbourhood of Ramoyle.   Quite a number of crofts lay between the road to Mintochmyre and the Monie or Minnie Burn.   The road to Mintochmyre led from Sinclair's Wynd between Holmhill and Balhaldie House to the myre which lay in the low ground below Dunblane Hydropathic.   The Monie or Minnie Burn came down from Ochlochy past Woodend through the garden of Balhaldie House below the Free (or East) Church and, turning there, below the Co-operative Store Buildings behind the County Buildings and down the Millrow to the River Allan.

In 1674 General Drummond of Cromlix, Lord Strathallan, as patron of the Altar of St. Blais was the immediate superior of three crofts known as Waterstoun's Acre, Kiln Croft, and the Lang Croft, with the Kiln barn and yards.   He approved of the disposition granted by John Sinclair sometime at Glassingall Beg to Duncan Drummond of Balhaldies made on the 29th December, 1671, reserving payment of the feu duties and other rights exigible from these crofts. These crofts were all in the neighbourhood of the property now known as Balhaldie House. Waterstoun's Croft lay between the road to Mintochmyre and the Monie Burn with Forfar's Croft to the east of it and Bank's Croft to the west.   Kiln Croft lay further to the west, being bounded by Bank's croft, otherwise known as Craigarnhall's Croft on the east, with the Monie Burn to the south and west and the road to Mintochmyre on the north.   Further to the west of Kiln Croft was the croft on the Wellbrae and further to the north-west was the tenement of John Dunkin's, previously the tenement of Lord William Drummond of Riccarton.

As has been mentioned, Forfar's Croft lay east of Waterstoun's Croft and beyond that lay Dion's Croft, probably in the neighbourhood of St. Mary's Church or Parsonage, to the north of which was land known as Lochinfauld which lay between Mintochmyre and the Holmhill road. These crofts apparently occupied the ground from the East Church hall by Woodend and St. Mary's Church.

It has been mentioned already that the Dean's Croft lay to the east of Dunblane Public School and was also known as Howrcroft.   At the top of Braeport to the north-east of

Glengyle house was the croft known as Howmilnhead which was bounded on the east by a path or road known as the north way to Mintochmyre. To the north of Howmiln Croft was the croft of Nicholas Stirling. The Howmilnhead Croft was bounded on the east, south and west by the Meikle Barn Croft and Lang Croft. To the east of the Meikle Barn Croft were lands of Ramoyle. The croft known as Saltie Croft should have been mentioned previously. It lay to the west of Mintochmyre and to the south of Lochinfauld. A further croft in the neighbourhood of Ramoyle was Kemp's Croft which lay to the north of Meikle Barn Croft.

Details have already been given of other crofts belonging to Altars of the Cathedral lying in parts immediately adjoining the city. Of the crofts in the land of Kippenross Park between the back of the High Street and the Darn Road was one known as Scott's Croft, the boundary of which was the Monie Burn on the east with St. Nicholas' Croft on its south, the croft of William Blackwood on the west, and the croft of Walter Brewster on the north.

The Doucot Croft lay to the east of the garden of the Stirling Arms Hotel above the first portion of the old Darn Road between the fruiterer's shop and the New Road now closed up.

Rowe's Croft or Rood lay north of the Doucot Croft, with the yard heads (of High Street) on the west, the Monie Burn on the north and Henry Drummond's Croft on the east. A William Ker in 1666 owned a tenement of land with barn and garden to the east of the public way leading to the Bridge of Dunblane, between the public road and the land of Robert Rowe. On the south of this property was George Henry's house and garden with the cubicle of the deceased James Blackwood, Rector of Sanquhar, on the south, and the house and garden of John Milne on the north. Among the owners of the Doucot Croft were William Blackwood and in 1723 Sir James Campbell of Kilbryde.

CHAPTER IX.

DISPERSION OF THE PROPERTY OF THE BISHOPRIC OF DUNBLANE.

ABOUT the 15th century and earlier, the Bishop and Chapter of Dunblane were the principal landowners in this district. In 1442 " the King, with the consent of the Council of Bishops, Abbots, Priors, Earls and Barons confirmed to Michael, Bishop of Dunblane, and his successors and to the Chapter all and whole the lands, annual rents and possessions after specified, viz. : Civitatem Dunblanen, Brigend, Cascaplymore, Cascaplybeg, Cornileyis, Achwlay, Drumdowlis, Ramule, Barbuskis, Achinvy, Classingalbeg, Buthersgask, Brecache, Ardachis, Gadnachy, Kere-decani, Tulmoquhousk, Tourechane, Muthill, Dromlecachy, Renybeg, Dergale, Fyndale, Clenes, Kerepon, Caluchibeg, Glenkarky, Belach, Cragarnot, Lundyden, Thom-decani, the annual rent of 4 merks from Pitlour, 6 merks from Aulich, 11 merks from Eglismagrill, annual rent of 19 merks 6 shillings and 8d. from Monyvard, Moyhe and Kelty, annual rent of 40s. from Eister Culyns, which were united in a barony of regality to be held by the said Bishops and their successors and the Chapter of Dunblane blench of the Kings of Scotland, the King ordaining that the said Bishop, his successors and Chapter should hold and possess the said barony in full liberty, from the Crown of Scotland." These properties received considerable additions prior to the time of Bishop William Chisholm I. Rev. J. G. Christie estimated that they included between 40 and 50 crofts in Dunblane, but that the emoluments were shared by 34 clergy.

While Bishop James Chisholm further endowed the Cathedral of Dunblane during his Bishopric, his successor, the first Bishop William Chisholm, dispersed a large portion of the patrimony of the Cathedral by conveying the estate of the Bishopric—in many cases to relatives, particularly to his daughters and their husbands.

The lands of Corscaplie with the teinds were sold sometime before 1571 to John Charters of Kinfauns and Janet Chisholm, his wife, for 1200 merks and for payment of $7\frac{1}{2}$ merks of augmentation, along with 11 bolls of grain or 6s. 8d. per boll with a duplicand of $7\frac{1}{2}$ merks on the entry of each heir. The minister of Dunblane still receives from the owner of Corscaplie the sum of £8 13s. 4d. Scots which is equivalent to $7\frac{1}{2}$ merks and 11 bolls at 6s. 8d. a boll. The sale was confirmed by the King in 1571.

The lands of Auchenby, situated at Kippendavie Farm between Kippendavie and Lanrick with Drummagoun on the west, were purchased by James Stirling of Keir in 1549 for a payment of 40s. plus 13s. 4d. of augmentation to be paid to Sir William Drummond, Sacristan of the Church of Dunblane, and his successors with right to the Dean, Bishops, Presbyters and citizens to pass with drawn carts for peats, stones, turf and other portable things of weight. (See also page 59.)

The following properties in or near Dunblane were transferred for the small annual payments mentioned on or before the dates specified: 1511, 7s. 11d from Rottearns and Quoigs acquired by Stirlings of Keir; 1532, £12 from Bowton being the church lands of Kilbryde; 1555, £2 from property belonging to the Altar of St. Blais; and 1595, £28 13s. 4d. from the lands of Claveg.

Over, Nether and Middle Cromlix (which include Waterside and Hutchison Farms) and Over and Nether Auchinlay with corn and waulk mills were conveyed in a charter by the Bishop of Dunblane to Sir James Chisholm of Dundurn and Agnes Beaton, his wife, dated 1509. Blew-buttergask or Wester Buttergask was added to the above lands in subsequent charters. The payment for Cromlix lands was 10 pounds Scots, for Auchinlays and the mill five merks, and for Buttergask three merks. Later on, the twelve merk lands of Bridgend, the three merk lands of Ramule, the mill in the city of Dunblane, Easter Buttergask, Barbuss and Lichhill were all added, along with Greenyards in Dunblane. James Chisholm of Cromlix also acquired half of the lands of Cambushinnie from William Muschet, the lands of Cullens, formerly part of Kippenross, and half of Wester Feddals in the Barony of Feddals and Regality of Lindores. He also acquired lands about Braco.

John Chisholm of Cromlix appeared to get into debt and in 1658 he disponed his lands to Sir James Drummond of Machany, David Drummond of Innermay and Harie Blackwood, indweller in Dunblane. They had power to sell these lands to pay off debt. In 1665, Harie Blackwood disponed his one-third share of the lands to Sir James and David Drummond. General Drummond in 1671 acquired from Sir John Sinclair of Glassingall a portion of the lands of Ramule called Drummagoun.

General Drummond also acquired the lands of Innerpeffray, but part of these were sold in 1700 to John Drummond of Colquholzie, and these lands were purchased in 1762 by the Archbishop of York, the Drummond owner of Cromlix at that date. A charter, dated 1825, was granted with the consent of William Stirling, Writer, probably an uncle of Patrick James Stirling, LL.D., Solicitor, Dunblane.

The lands of Easter Corscaplie were acquired as a feu from Bishop William Chisholm by David Ramsay, son of the Laird of Ochtertyre, in 1548. This did not include the Bishop's Meadow which it is understood extended from opposite the Cathedral for some distance westwards, where the railway line to Oban now is.

That " great building", commonly called the Lodge, girnells and stables were acquired by William Stirling, Rector of Aberfoyle, from the Bishop of Dunblane in 1579, as also the Bishop's Meadow formerly part of Easter Corscaplie. The Bishop's Yard or Orchard and the Green Valley were also conveyed to William Stirling. Stirling of Keir succeeded as heir to the parson of Aberfoyle who was his father.

In 1587, the Prebender of Balquhidder granted a charter to Thomas Drummond of Corscaplie and Elizabeth Stirling, his wife, of his waste piece of land, situated between the land belonging to the Manse of Aberfoyle, on the south, the street on the west, the yard of the Treasurer of Dunblane on the north and Pettescaleoch on the east.

John Drummond of Wester Corscaplie acquired the Manse of Logie about 1619, and also in the same year a waste piece of land belonging to the parsonage of Aberfoyle. It stood betwixt the How Croft on the east, the commonway to Ramule on the west, the Manse of Logie on the south, and the yard of Balquhidder on the north. John Drummond afterwards conveyed the Manses of Logie, Aberfoyle and Balquhidder to the Earl of Perth in 1662.

In 1558 a Feu Charter was granted by Roger Gordon, Dean of the Cathedral, with consent of the Chapter, to Malcolm Drummond of Borland of the Dean's Croft, commonly called the How Croft, the Long Croft and the Dean's Yard. Long Croft was also known as Laighhill Croft.

The Lands of Glassingall Mor were acquired by Stirling of Keir along with the lands of Ochlochy before 1526.

The Lands of Glassingallbeg and Drumdowlis were held by Edward Sinclair of Galwaldmoir of William, Bishop of Dunblane, from 1546 in return for six score loads of peats, one day's work of three horses for carting lime from the Forth and the services of a horseman and footsoldier in the time of war.

In 1547 the King confirmed a charter of William, Bishop of Dunblane, and the Dean and Chapter in favour of Edward Sinclair of Galdwaldmoir and his spouse for two hundred merks of the lands of Glassingallbeg, Drumdowlis with six merks annually and augmentation and the services including those of three men to carry wood from the meadows of Muthill.

Among other lands of the Bishopric that were sold, from which feu-duties were payable to the Dean of Dunblane, were Deanskeir (said to be Keirblane or Keirallan, near Braco), the town and chaplainry lands of Deanston, with woods and fisheries, acquired in 1562 by John Drummond, natural son of Malcolm Drummond. Deanslundie (that is West Lundie), Gogar and Craigarnhall. The Charter of Deanston by Bishop William Chisholm was granted with consent of the Chapter and Chaplains of the Choir, the names of the latter being " James Forsyth, Robert Hendersoun, Alexander Andersoun, Tho. Rob, Rob Sinclair and Wal Johnesoune."

At one time the customs of the city of Dunblane were payable to the Bishopric, but these also became the property of the Lairds of Cromlix, along with the office of Bailie of Dunblane.

The lands of Drumdruils and Haughheads were held of the Bishop of Dunblane till 1690. They were afterwards held of the Crown for a yearly payment of 16 merks at Whitsunday and Martinmas and the services of a third part of a man and horse.

The estate of Ardoch at Braco was conferred by Bishop William Chisholm I upon Henry

Sinclair who, in 1560, married a niece (or possibly a daughter) of the Bishop. Sinclair was Dean of Glasgow.

The lands of Keirblane were granted to William Sinclair of Galewaldmore by Roger Gordon, Dean of Dunblane, in 1558 for sundry payments in money and kind.

In 1576, the King confirmed a charter of William, Bishop of Dunblane, with consent of the Chapter by which was transferred " in eternal feu to William Sinclair of Bankis and Elizabeth Stirling, his spouse, the lands of Fyndale and Durgall extending to 6 merks lands in the parish of Muthill and county of Perth, which the said William and Elizabeth had held from the Feast of Pentecost, 1561, of his predecessor in the said Bishopric." Durgall is now known as Dargill.

James Blackwood, Clerk to the Chapter of Dunblane Cathedral, acquired in 1556 the teinds of the lands of Shanra (now known as Shanraw) and other lands from Bishop William Chisholm.

In 1572 the King confirmed a charter by John Learmonth, Chaplain of the Altar of St. Blais within the Cathedral, with consent of William, Bishop of Dunblane, the Patron of the Chaplainry, to John Blackwood, Jun., of the Dovecot (Doucot) Croft with the Dovecot built thereon, the tenement being ruinous and great expense required for the repair. The croft is described as bounded on the west and south by the road to Ochlochy (the first portion of which was the first part of the Darn Road now closed up, commencing at High Street), by the Croft of the deceased Henry Drummond, Chaplain of the Altar of St. Michael, and by that of Edward Sinclair on the east and the hood road of Robert Row (perhaps the lands of St. Blane's House) and tenement of William Wright and George Drummond on the north.

There is appended hereto an Extract from the Rental of the County of Perth as at 4th August, 1649.

EXTRACT from Rental of the County of Perth, by Act of the Estates of the Parliament of Scotland, 4th August, 1649, edited by William Gloag, Depute Collector of Cess. Perth, Morisons, Printers, 1835, page 82.

DUNBLAIN PARISH.

Earle of Perth, for Cambusbyne, Kinbuicke Litle and meikle, with the Mylne and Glassingall, one thousand threescore six pounds, thirteene shilling, four pennies	1066	13	04
Laird of Keir for Coiges, Glenyback, and Over Keir, six hundreth threescore six pounds, thirteene shilling, four pennies	666	13	04
Laird of Keir, for the Teynd dewties of Balhadies, threescore pounds	0060	00	00
Earle of Airth, for the Baronie of Kilbryde and Auchinloch, seven hundreth threttie three pounds, six shilling, eight pennies	0733	06	08
Laird of Cromlix for the Rent of the Bishopric, two hundreth twentie pounds	0220	00	00
Lady Cromlix, for her conjunct fie lands eight hundreth fourscore nyne pounds	0889	00	00
Laird of Urquhill, for Rottearns, Easter, Wester and Midle, and Mylne fyve hundreth and eight pounds	0508	00	00
Lady Kippendavie, for Auchinlay, Shaura, Woodlands, Lenrick, Kippendavie with the Mylne, four hundreth twentie fyve pounds	0425	00	00
Mr. James Persone for Kippenross, Kippenrait, and Mylne, fyve hundreth threescore fyteteene pounds, six shilling, eight pennies	0575	06	08
Laird of Cromlix for his lands in this parish one thousand seven hundreth pounds	1700	00	00
Henrie Sinclair, for Glassingall and Drumdulles, three hundreth threttie pounds	0330	00	00
John Drummond, for Corshaple, one hundreth fytie six pounds	0156	00	00
Walter Chisholme, for his wadsett and ackres in Dunblain, one hundreth fourtie eight pounds, six shilling, eight pennies	0148	06	08
John Keir, of Auchinlochie, for Auchinlochie, fyve hundreth pounds	0500	00	00
John Michell, for his fewed ackres in Auchinlochie, three score three pounds, six shilling, eight pennies	0063	06	08
William Corser's heirs for their ackres	0012	00	00

Thomas Gillespie, for his ackres six pounds ten shillings	0006	10	00
James McGrouther, for his ackres fyve pounds	0005	00	00
James Buchanan, for his ackres, six pounds ten shillings	0006	10	00
William Graham for Bowtone, one hundreth pounds, six shilling, eight pennies	0100	06	08
David Muschet, for his part of Glassingall, two hundreth fourtie-four pounds	0244	00	00
Duncan Drummond for his half of Balhaddies and Mylne, one hundreth fourtie pounds	0140	00	00
Patrick Drummond for his half of Balhaddie and Mylne, one hundreth fourtie pounds	0140	00	00
Mr. James Drummond for his part of Glassingall, one hundreth twelve pounds	0112	00	00
Margaret Drummond, for her ackres in Dunblain, thirteene pounds, six shilling, eight pennies	0013	06	08
William Drummond for Mersers Croft, six pounds thirteene shilling, four pennies	0006	13	04
James Browster for his ackres in Dunblain three pounds, six shilling, eight pennies	0003	06	08
David Blackwood, for his ackres in Dunblain, twentie pounds, thirteene shilling, four pennies	0020	13	04
John Stirling for little Quoiges, one hundreth fourtie fyve pounds	0145	00	00
Summor eight thousand nyne hundreth nyntie seven pounds	8997	00	00

CHAPTER X.

DUNBLANE, 1600-1660.

AMONG the more stirring incidents of this period in this city may be noted the murder of John Murray by Gavin Drummond of Kildees in the town of Dunblane which, says a contemporary annalist, was "like to make a grave stir betwixt the Murrays and Drummonds, but by the wise providence of His Majesty's Privy Council and the ready obedience of their chiefs to quiet matters for the public peace the businesses were remitted to an ordinary course of law." (See Balfour's *Annals of Scotland*, Volume 2, page 53).

In the Register of the Privy Council one reads of a scuffle which took place at the Bridgend in 1621. John Monteith at the Mill of Keir and John his son made complaint to the Privy Council on sixth December, 1621, that William McIlroy at Park of Keir had come to them on 7th October at the Bridgend of Dunblane and thereafter uttering threats and reproaches had given the elder complainer a stroke on the head with the "gairds" of a sword and felled him to the ground. He then trod on him and bruised him with his feet and when the young Monteith came to his father's relief McIlroy attacked him with the drawn sword wounding him on the head and various parts of the body. The elder Monteith lay bedfast for a time and by sixth December was not able to go about his affairs. The Lords of the Privy Council ordered the defender to be denounced a rebel.

In the 17th century superstition was very prevalent in the minds of the majority of the inhabitants of Scotland and belief in the existence of witches and warlocks was almost universal. It is worth recalling the circumstances connected with the trial of Wattie Bryce as narrated by John Monteath in his *Dunblane Traditions*. Whatever characteristics may have distinguished him and whatever powers he may have wielded "the maist part of ye inhabitants in ys town and nither pairts about it stuid ever in sic fear yt they never durst accuse" Bryce of witchcraft or of dealings with the Devil. After the appointment of Adam Bellenden to the Bishopric "ye haill town and sundrie gentillmen yrabout" approached the Bishop with their complaint against Bryce. It will be noted that the gentry did not seem to have been so unanimous as the town's people in their complaint. In consequence of this application the Bishop on 13th May, 1615, wrote a letter from Scone applying for a commission to the Laird of Keir, Sir George Muschett of Burnbank, James Kinross of Kippenross and William Blakwoode and John Morisone Bailyies of Dunblane for putting this man to inquest he being one "yt haid dune grett mischief" by his sorceries and witchcraft. The Bishop's letter was addressed to the Rev. John Rollok of Edinburgh who applied to the Privy Council to obtain the necessary permission which was duly procured and transmitted to Dunblane and Wattie was in a short time "fast in bandis." The "Evil-ane" was observed by those who apprehended him "girnin" in his very face while the onlooker with "holy fear" gave thanks that "the Devil durst gang nae farer than the tether wad lat in.'

The appointed commissioners met within the Tolbooth of Dunblane to hold their inquest, and to the credit of the lairds it may be said that they evinced none of the ignorance and superstition so prevalent amongst the general population. The Laird of Keir proposed that the prisoner should be allowed to be present along with his accusers and that he should be permitted to cross-question the witnesses, a proposal which seems to have been contrary to the usual practice. Kippenross and Burnbank supported the proposal while the bailies sturdily opposed it on the ground that none of the accusers would have the courage to tell the truth in the presence of their adversary. The Laird of Kippenross, however, took a firm attitude, his resolve being to see the matter fairly sifted and he indeed showed that he had little sympathy with the accusations. "Beilzie Morrisone" reminded the Commission that the great King James was a true believer in witches, nay that the Great and ever blessed John Knox was a believer in the existence of witches, and that every godly minister of the true Reformed Kirk of Scotland believed in the Bible and in witches. Keir and Kippenross were little moved by reference to such authorities and merely pitied the credulity of those who embraced such superstitions in their faith, while Kippenross remarked that ministers in the new Kirk were illiterate and ignorant. Burnbank himself bore testimony to the character of the accused whom he had known for 40 years as an honest, industrious and sagacious man. The Bailie when about to appeal to the authority of the Rev. Robert Rollok a " man of gritt, knowledge and learned in all ye wisdom of ye Egyptians " was interrupted by the lairds who ordered Bryce to appear. The prisoner, having asked leave to speak, complained that during the three days and nights since his apprehension he had not been permitted to sleep, that the two Bailies had tortured him most cruelly with a view to extorting a confession that he was a warlock and in compact with the Devil, and he complained that he had been " stabbet wi swords, dirks and daggers " by the Bailies' attendants and sometimes by themselves in many parts of the body while bound and unable to protect himself. Burnbank turned to the Bailies enquiring if Wattie had told the truth, which they could not deny, but pled that this was the usual custom and was necessary for the extortation of confession from such enemies of God and man as warlocks were. Burnbank, who had been roused to extreme anger, proposed that they should apply torture to the Bailies themselves in order to make them make a like confession and suggested that the Laird of Cromlix, the Lord of the Barony, should be sent for, whereupon the two Bailies withdrew from the Bench. Evidence was then called, but the lairds were not long in being satisfied that the complaints were unfounded and the Court in a short time discharged the prisoner. Monteath concludes by saying that the Laird of Cromlix a short time afterwards found means to have the Bailies hanged at the Gallow-lee of Dunblane, but this sounds somewhat like an addition made from a sense of poetic justice, for one has to keep in view that the Bailies owed their appointments to the Laird of Cromlix for whom they discharged certain duties and who were no doubt men trusted by him. It is, therefore, very improbable that he inflicted such condign punishment.

In the Kirk Session Records of 2nd August, 1660, one comes across a case connected with a Helen Bryce and one wonders if she were a descendant of Wattie Bryce. References are frequent in the Records of Kirk Sessions to the offence of seeking one's health from a woman, implying an invocation of hidden powers to effect a miraculous cure. The Session Records narrate that Helen Bryce gave in a supplication to the Session against Alexander Jack alleging that he had slandered her in as much as he had come to her and on his knees sought his health from her. The Session supported this charge of slander and ordained Jack to satisfy publicly upon the Stool of Repentance for his sin.

The trial of Wattie Bryce no doubt discouraged similar proceedings in Dunblane for many years to come, but did not altogether allay superstitious fears or stop superstitious practices in the way of effecting miraculous cures. In 1648 it is recorded that in this district witchcraft, turning the riddle, fortune telling and superstitious cures were common. Thus, in the Session Records of 1659, we find that a Catherine McGregor was accused of using and charming with water out of the superstitious well at Cullines. She was ordained to appear before the Kirk Session on 3rd March, 1659, when she appeared and confessed that she did take water out of the well above Cullines and did take it into Stirling and did give it to a woman, but denied that she had washed the woman in Stirling with the water or had sprinkled her with it. Details of the case are narrated in Chapter XI.

In a Cathedral City its early history centres round that of the Cathedral and its officials. The Episcopalian Bishop at the end of the 16th century was Andrew Graham. He demitted office prior to February, 1603, when he was succeeded by George Graham, M.A., promoted from Scone. Bishop George Graham was a member of the Court of High Commission 1st April, 1610, and suitor for the Archbishopric of Glasgow in 1615, but in August of that year he was translated to Orkney. His successor was Adam Bellenden, M.A., whose name also appears as Bannatyne or Ballantyne. Bishop Bellenden was for a time the minister of Falkirk and in his earlier years was strongly opposed to Episcopacy. He is described as being " an eager opposer of ' Hierarchie,' " in 1606. He was appointed Bishop of Dunblane on 23rd September, 1615, consecrated before 3rd April following, and admitted on 14th April, 1617. He became a Doctor of Divinity of St. Andrews University in that year, and in 1621 was a member of the Parliament which ratified the Articles of the Assembly at Perth. He owned the lands of Kilconquhar in Fifeshire and when minister of Falkirk in 1606 complaint was made against him that he was living in the Canongate (Edinburgh) and not in his diocese. He then craved the appointment of a helper as his estate was too far from Falkirk, but he was ordained to serve the Church in person and reside within his parish or demit the charge. Bellenden seems to have exhibited strong feeling towards Bishop George Graham whom he called " the excrement of Bishops who had licked up the excrement of Bishoprics." (Calderwood's *History of the Church of Scotland*.) However, when George Graham left Dunblane for Orkney Bellenden licked up his Bishopric. Calderwood explains that he accepted the Bishopric with the view to patching up his broken lairdship. It may be that Bellenden had been annoyed that Graham should get the Bishopric of Dunblane in preference to himself.

During his period of office he was successful in adding to the emoluments of the Bishopric. In 1617 King James by Act of Parliament considering the meanness of the Estate of the Bishopric and understanding that their rents were altogether unable to furnish the necessaries of the private family of a Bishop much less to bear his expenses in Parliament and at Ecclesiastical Conventions, with the consent of the Abbot of Crossraguel, incorporated the Abbacy in the Bishopric of Dunblane, as well as the Priory of Monymusk, with all lands and kirks, fishings and other profits as if the same had been mortified to the said Bishopric at its first foundation, reserving the liferent rights of the holders of these benefices. Bellenden was present at Holyrood when the communion was administered there in 1617 in the English form, according to the orders of King James, the recipients receiving the bread and wine on their knees. In the following year he received from Lord Madderty one thousand merks on condition of his intervention to save his Lordship from paying great stipends. The Deanery of the Chapel Royal, at first attached to Stirling and afterwards to Holyrood House, was attached to the Bishopric of Galloway until 1621 when the Bishop, being unable to discharge the duties, resigned office. King James dissolved the Deanery from the Bishop of Galloway and worked it into a benefice at the disposal of His Majesty, the recipients to be called Deans of the Chapel Royal. The deed of gift was made out under the Great Seal in favour of Bellenden who was appointed Dean for life and the charter was confirmed by Act of Parliament, 1621. The Deanery remained united to the Bishopric of Dunblane till the Bishopric was finally swept away at the Revolution. Bellenden's successors were Bishop Wedderburn, 1636, and the three Bishops following the Restoration, namely, Bishops Leighton, Ramsay and Douglas. At the Revolution in 1688 the endowments reverted to the Crown and they are now devoted to the endowment of Professorships in the Faculty of Divinity in the Scottish Universities. (*History of the Chapel Royal of Scotland* by Charles Rogers.) It is stated in Calderwood's *History* that Bellenden and the Bishop of St. Andrews in 1624 were " gaping for a fine from a man who would not conform." In 1621 Bellenden sued the widow of the Bishop of Galloway for documents connected with the Chapel Royal, one of the witnesses being his eldest son James. He was admitted a member of the Privy Council in that year. In 1635, on the death of the Bishop of Aberdeen, the King conferred the vacant Bishopric on Bellenden. It appears that Archbishop Laud had received authority from King Charles in 1633 to correspond with Bellenden on the Regulation of Worship in the Chapel Royal and he seems to have written several letters to Bellenden showing dissatisfaction with him both as regards doctrine and ritual. As Dean of the Chapel Royal he was considered a person who should take a leading part in connection with the new liturgy, but, as he proceeded negligently in this affair, says Calderwood in his *History*, "Laud thought it necessary to provide another better disposed." Baillie in his *Letters* also mentions that Bellenden was removed from the Chapel Royal to Aberdeen as one " who did not favour well enough Canterbury's new ways."

In October, 1633, Charles I wrote to Bellenden to preach "in his whites " and also that " copes " should be used at the Lord's Supper in the Chapel Royal. Bellenden was ultimately deposed by the Glasgow Assembly in 1638 when the Moderator remarked that Mr. Patrick Simson said to him " he never liked Mr. Adam Ballantyne, for he was too violent against Bishops without any light or good reason and therefore he feared that he should never be trusted." (Sprott's *Introduction to Scottish Liturgies*.)

James Wedderburn, D.D., a Professor of Divinity at St. Mary's College, St. Andrews, succeeded Bishop Bellenden at Dunblane. He was consecrated on 11th February, 1638, and was deposed and excommunicated by the General Assembly on 6th December, 1638, as " he had been the confidential correspondent and agent of Laud, Archbishop of Canterbury, in introducing the new Liturgy and Popish ceremonies." He died in England in the following year, aged 54. According to Baillie's *Letters* the appointment of Wedderburn had been suggested by Spottiswood. Wedderburn had left St. Andrews for England in 1636 and according to Baillie had been " fugitive from Church discipline for his Arminian lectures to his Scholars there, but was sent back by Laud to Scotland to weave out the web which he had began at St. Andrews." Laud speaks of him as " a man recommended to him as having very good parts of learning." He had lived long with Mr. Isaac Casaubon " who was not like to teach him any Popery." He, however, referred to him as " a mere scholar and a bookman." In a letter, dated 19th September, 1635, addressed to Bishop Maxwell of Ross, Laud refers to Bishop Wedderburn as follows:— " I thank you for your care of Dr. Wedderburn ; he is very able to do service, and will certainly do it if you can keep up his heart. I was in good hope he had been consecrated as well as my Lord of Brechin ; what the reason is I know not, but 'tis a thousand pities that these uncertainties abide with him. I pray commend my love to him, and tell him I would not have him stick at anything, for the King will not leave him long at Dunblane, after he hath once settled the Chapel aright, which I see will settle apace if he keep his footing."

Wedderburn, who was a native of Dundee, had studied at Oxford and during his stay in England between 1626 and 1635 had held various appointments as Rector and Prebend. After Wedderburn's return to Scotland he began to take a leading part in connection with the Liturgy which was followed by a change of plans, namely, the destruction of the edition which had been partially printed and a closer imitation of the English Liturgy. Copies of the new Liturgy were issued from the Press in April, 1637, and it was the reading of it in St. Giles on 23rd July, 1637, that was the signal for a popular outbreak which ended in the Great Rebellion. (Sprott's *Introduction*).

In 1593 the General Assembly had ordained that the Presbytery of Dunblane be transported to Auchterarder with liberty to the brethren of Dunblane to resort either to Auchterarder or Stirling as they pleased, but with the proviso that should the Kirk of Auchterarder be insufficiently prepared before the next General Assembly and a sufficient stipend not provided for a minister with manse and glebe, the Presbytery should be re-established in Dunblane. There seems to have been no Presbytery at Dunblane between 1593 and 1608. There is a register of the Presbytery commencing in 1616 with gaps between 9th April, 1628, and 11th April, 1648, and from 2nd October, 1688, to 26th April, 1698, when it was temporarily united to Stirling. The minister of Dunblane at the close of the 16th century was Andrew Young and he was succeeded in 1606 by Ninian Drummond, M.A., the fifth and youngest son of Henry Drummond, founder of the family of Riccarton. He obtained his degree at the University of Glasgow in 1582 and was one of those who sympathised with the brethren at Linlithgow prior to their trial for holding an Assembly at Aberdeen contrary to the pleasure of the King. He was translated to Kinnoull in 1611. William Fogo, a graduate of St. Andrews University in 1613, was presented to the Deanery of Dunblane by James VI in 1618. He demitted prior to March, 1624, having been translated to Callander. He was succeeded by James Pearson, son of Alexander Pearson, Merchant Burgess of Edinburgh, who graduated M.A. at Edinburgh University on 2nd May, 1615. He was presented to the Deanery of Dunblane by James VI on 3rd March, 1624. He read the Service Book to his congregation in 1637, but signed the Supplication against it some time after. He had twelve hundred merks mortified to him in 1641. He was deposed in the latter end of 1649. From 1650 to 1652 the minister of Dunblane was Alexander Gibson, M.A., who previously held the second charge of South Leith and was afterwards translated to Ayton. Pearson appears to have endeavoured to obtain re-entry in 1652, but was unsuccessful. He and his son were sued by the Kirk Session of Dunblane for stipend for the year 1651. The Session were unable to recover any part of it until the year 1672 when his son compromised the matter by payment of five hundred merks. The latter was an elder in Dunblane Kirk in 1659 and also during Bishop Leighton's time. His father was the first of the Pearson Lairds of Kippenross.

The last minister prior to the Restoration was Thomas Lindsay who graduated M.A. at Edinburgh University in 1639 and was admitted in 1653. His death occurred in 1673 at the age of 54. He appears to have left no estate beyond some utensils and books and it is recorded that his debts exceeded his goods. His wife's name was Helen Wood by whom he had two sons, Thomas, appointed Bursar of the Synod in 1668, and James, apprenticed to a skinner in Edinburgh.

There is a reference in the Kirk Session records of 1652 to a paper of Mr. James Pearson anent his re-entry to the Kirk of Dunblane. Two of the elders, Andrew Ker and John Ker, con-

F

fessed to having signed the paper, urged thereto by a Henry Sinclair. Being much grieved, they submitted themselves to the Session and disclaimed the subscription of the said paper. At the same time it was resolved " to interrogate Johne Robisone concerning the said paper."

Up to 1618 there was a separate parish of Kilbryde distinct from Dunblane, but at a meeting of the Commissioners for Plantation of Kirks held at Edinburgh on 18th February of that year, at which Adam Bellenden was present, the parishes were united. This had been found convenient as the Kirks of Dunblane and Kilbryde did not provide sufficient stipends for a minister as required by the Act of Parliament. The Kirk of Kilbryde was accordingly annexed to the Kirk and Parish of Dunblane " to remain as part of the Parish of Dunblane in all times coming and the whole tenants and inhabitants of the Parish of Kilbryde were ordained to repair to Dunblane as to their Parish Kirk and there was mortified to Andrew Young, then minister of Dunblane, and to his successors the sum of seven hundred merks yearly out of the teinds of Dunblane as sufficient stipend for the charge and for the furnishing of the elements of the Communion." £24 yearly from the Parsonage teinds of Kilbryde with the Vicarage teinds were assigned to the schoolmaster of Dunblane. The Decree of Annexation dated 18th February, 1618, was pronounced by the Commissioners of Parliament for Plantation of Kirks. The summons was at the instance of the Lord Advocate and the Procurator for the Kirk and was executed against Lord Madderty, the Earl of Perth and the Bishop and Dean of Dunblane. Those who attended the proceedings before the Commissioners were Mr. Andrew Young, then minister of the Kirk of Dunblane, with one Reverend Father in God, Adam, Bishop of Dunblane, Patron of the said Kirk and Titular of part of the teinds, Lord Madderty, and Mr. John Drummond, Procurator for the Earl of Perth. Lord Madderty was Titular of the teinds of Kilbryde and the Earl of Perth lessee of the teinds of Cambushinnie and Kinbucks. The seven hundred merks stipend was to be contributed, 90 merks by the Earl of Perth out of the teinds of Nether and Middle Cambushinnie and the lands of Little and Meikle Kinbucks, the Bishop of Dunblane to contribute 310 merks out of the Bishop's teinds and three hundred merks out of the teinds of Dunblane pertaining to the Deanery. The yearly sum of £24 for the schoolmaster was to be paid out of the Parsonage teinds of Kilbryde by Lord Madderty, the Titular, and the Master of Madderty, his lessee.

It may be of interest to learn how the fabric of the Cathedral fared at this time. It is unknown when the nave became unroofed or became so dangerous as to forbid the holding of services there, but probably worship ceased to be held in the nave about the end of the 16th century. (See page 66.) The holding of church services was thereafter restricted to the choir alone. It is said that an old seat belonging to the Keir family which stood in the choir of the Cathedral bore the date 1620, which seems to indicate that the choir was in use by that date as the Parish Church.

From the early part of the 17th century until the end of the 19th century the choir was disfigured by the erection of galleries or lofts, as they were called at that time. The Session Records of 1653 show that two lofts were built at a cost of £533 6s. 8d. at which time £333 6s. 8d. was expended on " ye glassen windows of ye Kirk." It may also be noted that the expenses of seeking out a minister and entertaining ministers to preach in time of vacancy cost the Session £165 13s. 4d. It was at this time that Mr. Thomas Lindsay was appointed minister and the Session Records bear that at his entry " there was not one penny Scots to pay the above sums withal " (See page 87).

A few years later, namely, in 1664, we find the Kirk Session giving liberty to build another loft with right to enter thereto through a window. In old engravings of the Cathedral at the end of the 17th, and up to the beginning of the 19th century, one sees depicted a short stair leading to an entrance through the south-eastmost window to the east end of the choir. This gallery seems to have been removed about 1820.

For some centuries there was no communication between the nave of the Cathedral and the Lady Chapel or Chapter House. This dates from January, 1654, when a certain William Brown, who had committed an offence, appeared before the Kirk Session with his cautioner. He was ordained on the next Lord's day to sit on the pillar as the last day and in commutation of his penalty to " big up the entry from Keir Yle to the Vestry." This door was re-opened at the restoration of the Cathedral in 1870 when the existing stone stair to the apartment above the Lady Chapel was discovered. This had been built up for over two hundred years. It would appear from the Kirk Session Records that the parish school was conducted in the apartment above the Lady Chapel or in the Chapel itself about 1653 and for long after.

Very little regard seems to have been taken to preserve the beauties of the ancient building or to preserve its sanctity, but it is fair to record that on 5th May, 1659, it was "enactit" by the Kirk Session that no "Mercat either at Whitsunday, Lawrence or Hallowday be any more keepit in ye Kirk yaird of Dunblane and ye Kirk yaird be built with all expedition." On the other hand we read of the Synod of Dunblane in 1649 passing a resolution concerning the "Monuments of idolatry which are in the province and in particular the Cross standing in the Churchyaird of Dunblane" which was ordered to be demolished. Presumably this was done, but, had such an object still existed, it could not have failed to be of the greatest interest. Whether it was due to their sins or their virtues the Synod of Perth and Stirling in April, 1655, received a visitation, while meeting in Dunblane Cathedral, from a party of soldiers under the command of an English Officer called Lieutenant Belvine who, having intruded on the meeting, commanded the Synod to dissolve, affirming he had received authority to that effect from his superior Officer. The Moderator called on him to show his order and to inform the Synod from whom he had it, but both requests were refused, and he ordered his party to use violence if the meeting was not dissolved. Some Members of the Synod were violently removed and against this the Moderator protested as contrary to the liberties of the Kirk of Scotland. He also protested that it should not be prejudicial to the Synod to meet again at their ordinary time and sooner when they should be called thereto. After prayer by the Moderator the Synod dissolved.

About 1654, bodies of Royalists were in the neighbourhood of Dunblane, and Castle Camp-bell, which was the property of the Marquis of Argyll, was burned down. A garrison had been left at Dunblane during the previous winter with orders from General Middleton to burn all strong houses near the hills. In June and July, 1654, General Monck, whose headquarters were at Dalkeith, marched by Dunblane to Perth and Aberfeldy in a campaign against Middleton's troops.

Among other visitors to Dunblane during this period was Archbishop Laud. As he rode past the Cathedral he was heard to remark "A goodly Church." "Ay," replied a bystander, "it was a brave Kirk afore the Reformation." "Deformation, fellow," retorted the Prelate as he continued his way. (*Scoti-monasticon*).

In 1647, Dunblane appears to have had the misfortune along with other districts of Scotland, of being visited by plague. At a meeting of the Synod at Dunning in November of that year James Pearson of Dunblane was the only representative of the Presbytery who was present, and he declared that "the infection was raging in the bounds of the Presbytery."

In 1659, serious illness befell the horses of the district, so much so that the Church ordered that a fast be held in respect of the prevalence of sin in the district and of the plague afflicting the horses. The conjunction of these matters which demanded a day of repentance makes one wonder whether the district would have troubled with a day of mourning for their sins had it not been for the serious loss that was being occasioned by the horse plague.

It may be noted that in the year 1650 a tolbooth or public gaol was erected east of the Kirk Style, that is the main entrance gate to the Cathedral Churchyard. This building was in existence until the 19th century and was erected from stones which had formed part of the old Palace of the Bishops. In front of the Kirk Style stood the "Mercate Cross."

From this time onwards much light is thrown on the life of Dunblane through the records of the Kirk Session which with certain blanks continue from 1650 to the present day. It may be interesting to note the names of the elders present at a meeting on 4th April, 1652, which are as follows :—"Harie Blackwood, Walter Cheisholme, James Sinclair, Johne Morisone, Robt. Gair, David Thomsone, Wm. Robisone, George Henrie, Andro Ker, Jon. Robisone, Jon Ker, and Thomas Cairnes." Most of these names are familiar in Dunblane at the present day. It is observed from the sederunt that certain elders were absentees and at the following meeting held a week later such were questioned for their reasons for absence which were sustained at the meeting, but the absentees were "gravlie exhortit be the Moderator to keep pre-ceislie in tyme coming." Other names found in the Session records at this time include such familiar names as Matthew Finlayson, Archibald Duthie, John Brown, Walter Clerke, James Buchanan, Janet Mershel, Malcolm Adie and David Chrystie.

Considering the population of Dunblane at the time one would have thought that there was more than a sufficiency of elders, but in 1654 a resolution is recorded to appoint, owing to the paucity of elders, deacons, "who may assist the Session with a view to their being publicly received as elders after they have learned for the space of a year or thereby if found qualified and if no objection is taken by the Congregation to their appointment."

In 1652, certain of the elders complained that they had no proper seat in church, but were forced to stand in time of divine service. The Session accordingly ratified a formal resolution anent the appointing for themselves the two foremost long "fermes" and the beadles were ordained to ask intruders on these seats to remove. In the event of their not removing, the offenders were to be censured and held to be dissolvers of the Session and handed over to the magistrate for a money penalty for the use of the poor. This forms one of many illustrations of the power acquired by the Kirk Session over the people of the town, the civil authorities being bound to execute their decrees.

It would appear that the Session held its meetings at first on Sundays, but in 1654 it was enacted that henceforth the Session should meet on Thursdays weekly, the hour of meeting being 10 a.m. precisely. It was also ordained that every absent elder should consign 12s. Scots for each day absent from the Session before he give in his excuses. If his reasons for absence were not satisfactory the money consigned was forfeited and placed in the Poors' Box.

In 1661 the day of the Session meetings was altered from each Thursday to the first Monday of each month.

From time to time the Kirk Session made enquiry into the conduct of their respective members. Thus in 1653, after the appointment of Mr. Thomas Lindsay as minister, Robert Caddel, the Session Clerk, being removed from the meeting, enquiry was made concerning his discharge of his duties which enquiry being satisfactory he was continued in office. It was then agreed to delay the trial of the elders for a time. On 25th January, 1655, and at other times, we find that the whole elders and deacons were removed and everyone interrogated regarding each other's carriage, duty and ability. On that occasion one of the elders, John Reid by name, was found wanting and was suspended for his incapacity.

The elders, in addition to sitting in judgment on their neighbours, had other duties to perform, particularly with regard to the care of the poor, while in 1657 we find that they are recommended to be "carefull in their respective divisiones for reconceilling all yat are at variance before the Communion." They were also bound to attend the taking of the collection and, if absent without relevant excuse, an elder forfeited the amount of the collection of the preceding week.

Among the matters which concerned the Session in 1653 was the negligence of Family Worship and they resolved accordingly to try all the families within the congregation with the view to ascertaining whether they were deficient in those religious duties with certification that every head of a family would be proceeded with before the Session if found deficient.

Various regulations were laid down by the Session with regard to baptisms and marriages. It was enacted in 1653 "that before Baptism the parent, if in life, in health and in country, or otherwise the vice-parent, should come to the Clerk and give in the child's name with three or two witnesses at least, who were to sit upon a seat provided for that purpose by the Treasurer." As in the case of the elders' "fermes" the parents' seat appears to have been invaded from time to time with the result that the Session had later to ordain that neither old nor young should presume to sit within the range about the pulpit except scholars and men who had children to be baptised. In 1672, Thursdays and Sundays were fixed for baptisms. Some time previously the Session had ordained that no one having a child baptised on the Lord's Day should make any banquet on that day. It is also recorded in 1672 that a man was sued before the Session for using "ane unlawful way of baptising his child."

It may be worth recording here, as illustrative of the formal procedure observed in Church matters, a petition by Anna Chisholm, daughter of James Chisholm of Cromlix, for the baptism of the child of herself and her husband, Lieutenant Harlow. The petition was duly granted conditionally on a cautioner being found for the child's Christian education. Henry Sinclair of Glassingall bound himself to see that the child was educated in the discipline and doctrine of the Church of Scotland. The following are extracts from the Kirk Session Records.— "This day thair wes ane supplicatione presentit be Anna Cheisholme the laull dauter of umqle

Jas. Cheisholme of Cromlix Kngt. for baptism of hir chyld laulie procreat betwixt hir and Lieut. Johnne Harlow qrof the tennor follows—" The ryt reverend the Minr. and Eldars of the Kirk Sessionne of Dunblane. These humblie entreat for the benefite of baptisme to my chyld procreat in laull marriage being borne of honall. parents wtin the paroche I have lived from the vombe and that not haveing givin offence: to any baptizme conform to the constitutiones of the Church (I hope) will not be denyed uponn the humble and earnest desyre of your humble supplicant.

(signed)   A. Cheisholme.

" The Sess. accepts of the supplicatione and unanimouslie concludes the chyld to be pntlie baptized with the provision thair be cautionne fund for its Christiane educatione."

" Compeirit Henrie Sinclaire of Glassingall wha heirby enactes himselfe that he shall faithfullie honestlie and christianlie see to the educatione of the daughter of Anna Cheisholme callit Helene Harlow in the professione discipline and doctrine well professed in the Church of Scotland as if she were his own not permitting hir to his power to be ensnaired by any false doctrine and is content thir presents be regrat in the Sess. book of Dunblane as ane standing law agt. him in testimonie qrof. thir presents are subt be him at Dunblane 22nd January, 1654.

(Signed)   H. Sinclaire."

Various regulations were adopted from 1650 to 1654 with regard to proclamations and celebrations of marriage. In 1654 the Session ordained that after the examination of the bridegroom and bride before the Session they be " bookit" by the Clerk in the book set apart for that purpose, but a provision was made that if " ye shamefastness and modestie " of any did not permit them to make so public an appearance either or both parties might be "bookit" in private before the minister and two elders on consigning at least £4 Scots for the use of the poor, but if the parties be of quality they were to pay according to the discretion of the Session.

The wasteful expenditure incurred at weddings was the subject of frequent legislation in early times in Scotland. It is dealt with by the Kirk Session of Dunblane in 1650, and in 1654 the Session found that notwithstanding the steps already taken anent the curbing of the exorbitant prices and extraordinary number of people at " pennie brydals " many had transgressed and the Session accordingly ratified the Act of 1650 to the effect that a bride and bridegroom should not have at their wedding more than three people accompanying each, and before the marriage was celebrated the parties had to consign a sum of money to be bestowed upon pious uses if they transgressed or permitted any " unbeseeming carriage " at their bridal. From further entries in the Session records it would appear that wasteful expenditure had not been abolished within the parish. In 1656 it was ordained that consignation money would be forfeited if piping and dancing were permitted at a bridal. Three persons only were permitted to attend bride and bridegroom and the cost of the marriage supper was not to exceed 6s. 4d. Weddings had to take place prior to 11 a.m. under forfeiture of a dollar.

It would appear that, as early as 1653, provision was made for the recording in a book the baptisms, marriages and deaths of young and old, thus anticipating what only became the law of the land in 1854.

While the members of Session had not only to attend diligently all meetings of Session, as well as all religious services, they had also to behave themselves with decorum at such meetings, and in 1654 we find rules laid down regarding their behaviour. Thus, any speaker at a Session meeting had to do so uncovered and was only permitted to speak if the Moderator asked him. Further, all had to behave themselves gravely and authoritatively and were ordained not to take away anything spoken in Session under a penalty of 6s. Scots, while if any member continued to offend after two or three admonitions the penalty was deposition.

The Kirk Session at this time ruled the people with a rod of iron and it is remarkable how they acquired such authority and how their interference was not more frequently resented and defied. In particular, the rules with regard to Sabbath observance were particularly stringent as may be illustrated by indicating some of the charges which were considered sufficiently grave to be worthy of a summons of the culprit. Thus, James Gray in 1657 was called to appear before a meeting of Session for weighing and bearing away lint on the Sabbath Day, and John Robison for flitting his fauld. In 1658 a poor woman was dealt with for setting out sheets and blankets on the Lord's Day and the offence of another was washing puddings. It was no doubt quite proper in these days that many of the offences recorded in the books should have been dealt with such as the case of Henry Finlayson who " was taken with drunkenness by the constables at night after the Communion, deriding piety." Many of the Sabbath offences involved drunkenness or the consumption of liquor during the time of sermon, and we also find offenders dealt with for fighting in church, for disorderly conduct in church and for cursing and swearing on the Lord's Day. For fighting on the Lord's Day Isabel Lennox was ordained to make public repentance and pay 10s., while for drunkenness James Wilson forfeited the considerable sum of £6 and he had also to make public satisfaction. Scolding women seem to have met with severe reprobation as the Session ordained that every one who repeated the offence to her husband was to pay £20 Scots. The doings of the poor farmers was a source of concern and such were frequently proceeded against for grinding corn, removing stock or doing some harvest work probably in times of late and bad harvests. So far as the efforts of the Session were concerned to put down Sunday drinking, and these were numerous, they are certainly to be commended, while they also made an endeavour with the Magistrates to stop dealing in merchandise and keeping shops open on Sundays. Other Sabbath offences appear very trifling, such as kindling a fire for washing, and even the mucking of a byre, a desirable operation, probably not too much indulged in in these days, brought a man into conflict with the Church. The offence of one poor man was that he had not curbed the swearing and cursing of his wife and family. In October, 1658, enquiry was made as to how the people had observed the Sabbath in time of harvest when the elders replied that they " did keep the Sabbath verie poore as in former tyme " which indicates that the bad habits which the Session sought to cure were not of recent acquisition.

It may be interesting to note that the ringing of the Church bell was under the control of the Kirk Session and that the hours of ringing were as follows:—"The first bell at 7 a.m., the second at 8.30, the third at 10 a.m. precisely and the fourth at 2 p.m. precisely, the hours being the same summer and winter." One observes that it was only in the case of the two latter bells that the ringing is prescribed at the precise hour. Perhaps some latitude was given with regard to the morning bells. On Sundays the congregation was summoned to attend at the second bell to hear the Catechism. In October, 1660, the Session enacted that a voluntary contribution should be collected throughout the parish for helping to cast the great bell. The minutes read that for the greater encouragement of all ranks of persons within the parish to contribute largely and willingly to the bell it was ordained that the bell should ring at the burying of such persons that gave a voluntary contribution for the founding of the bell. This would no doubt be a considerable inducement to the parishioners to give generous subscriptions.

In the early days there were many Acts of Parliament dealing with vagrants and beggars, who, as a rule, were only permitted to beg within certain areas and such at one time were required to carry a badge. In the 17th century the Session sought to regulate what strangers were to be permitted to settle in their midst, and in 1653 we find them concerned over the number of persons who had come to reside without " testificats," houses having been let to " loose and licentious livers " with the result that an evil report had been brought on the parish by their profanity and wickedness. Householders were accordingly ordained not to receive any person into their dwelling without testification produced to the Session or Minister within two days of their entry. No vault, house or cottage was to be let to any person not of approved conversation and quality unless the landlord undertook responsibility for the stranger's Christian carriage. A few years later these regulations were strengthened by the Kirk Session imposing a penalty of 40s. with liability to Kirk censure on all which received strangers without testimonials.

If the decrees of the Kirk Session were not obeyed, the Session obtained the assistance of the civil authorities as, for example, in the case of a Janet Stewart who was committed to the Bailie of Dunblane to be put out of the town for disobedience to the elders of the Session and for drunkenness.

While the doings of the Session may seem, in modern days, frequently to have been harsh, one has to observe that the elders were also moved by kindly considerations. Thus in 1656 a collection was ordained for the benefit of Peter Blair taken by the Turks with his two sons. In June, 1659, the Session ordained that a collection be taken for a poor blind lady.

It is understood that the churchyard at Dunblane Cathedral was not always in use for burial although it had been at a very early date, but in 1660 intimation was made from the pulpit that all within the parish of Dunblane, who claimed rights to burial places within the kirkyard, should attend eight days later to prove their rights under penalty, should they not appear, of losing the right of burial at any particular place.   In the following month there seems to have been a dispute between two local men as to the ownership of a grave-stone.   The Session intimated that anyone who gave 5s. to the Treasurer should have this stone.

In 1652 the churchyard dyke appears to have been out of order as four of the elders were ordained " to meet on the morrow betwixt 7 and 8 forenoon to cognosce upon and to mak close ye Kirkyeard dyke with yews or other things necessary."   The same men were entrusted with the sale of the grass of the churchyard to the best advantage in the Session's interest and were directed to think upon a commodious way for the scholars' entry to the school which was held in the Lady Chapel or more probably, at this time, in the apartment above the Chapel.

Further instances of the powers, duties, and actions of the early Kirk Sessions in Dunblane are given in Chapter XII.

During this period a Commissary Court flourished at Dunblane.   About 1638 the Commissar was Mr. John Rollo or Rollok and Mr. Henry Blackwood, son of William Blackwood, was appointed by Mr. Rollo, Commissary Clerk.   During the years from 1631 to 1638 the following acted as depute Clerk—Walter Chisholm, James Pearson, John Forrest, and Andrew Young.

While this was not an age of mechanical genius and the help of science was seldom invoked for the relief of labour, there was quite a number of mills in this neighbourhood.   Seven corn mills have been noted as being in existence about the middle of the 17th century, namely, at Dunblane, Auchinlay, Kilbryde, Keir, Kippenross, Balhaldie and Quoigs.   There were also waulk mills at Auchinlay, Kippenross and Keir, and a lime kiln at Kilbryde. The purpose of waulk mills was for fulling or strengthening of cloth woven by hand in the homes. Lint was extensively grown in the neighbourhood of the town and spun and woven in the homes.

When the Rev. Thomas Lindsay became Minister of Dunblane in the year 1653 the finances of the Church of Dunblane appeared to have been at a low ebb as will be seen from the following financial statement which shows that the Kirk Session were in debt to nearly £1500 and had " not one penny Scots to pay it withal "—

" For Mr. Allexr. Gibson.

To James Blaikwood furnishments to his house fourscore seventeen pounds fifteen shilling.

To Bailie Chesholm for house meal (that is, rent) threescore five pounds thretteen shilling four pennies.

To David Lambe by Bund for borrowet money ane hundreth pound.

To John Fisher vintner threescore fifetene pound ten shilling.

To John Armour baxter fourscore sextene pound fiftene shilling saxpence.

To David Thomsone Elder, Smyth fourtene pound seven shilling six pennies.

Whilk same in the haill comes to £446 : 1 : 4
                                    (really £450 : 1 : 4).

As also the building of two Loaftes   £533 : 6 : 8

For ye Glassen windowes of ye Kirk   333 : 6 : 8

And for expenses in seeking out a Minister and intertaining of Minrs. to preach in the tyme of the vacancy of the Church £165 : 13 : 4.

" Whilk is just in the haill £1133 : 6 : 3 (really £1032 : 6 : 8) so that the Compt. of the money dispersed for the Church of Dunblane by the Minister and Session since his entrie will extend in haill to £1509.   (Really £1482 : 8 : 0) of all at his entrie their was not one peny Scots to pay it withall."

It may be of some interest to note some particulars as to the principal families resident in the Parish at this time.   The lands of Kilbryde were until the 17th century the property of the Earls of Menteith although they were situated in the Stewartry of Strathearn.   About the end of the previous century, somewhere about 1590, John, sixth Earl of Menteith, had a litigation with the Dowager Countess, his mother, regarding the titles of Kilbryde.   The latter, whose name was Lady Margaret Douglas, counterclaimed against her son for assault in respect of his forcible entry into Kilbryde Castle and the Earl was put under caution.   It would seem that at this time

Kilbryde Castle was the dower house of the widowed Countess. Earl John, before completing fifteen years of age, entered into a marriage contract with Mary, sister of Duncan Campbell, of Glenorchy, and a few years later his residence was given as Kilbryde. Probably the Castle of Inchtalla had by this time fallen into ruin. He died in December, 1598, and was succeeded by his only son William, seventh Earl of Menteith, a man of great ability who latterly met with great misfortune. He became early in the 17th century the most powerful man in Scotland, but his laying claim to the Earldom of Strathearn led to his downfall. On his marriage he conveyed the Barony of Kilbryde to his bride. His son, Lord Kilpont, was born about 1613, and on his marriage about 1632 his wife was infeft in the Barony of Kilbryde. Earl William in 1630 renounced the Earldom of Strathearn, but retained the lands of Kilbryde. Lord Kilpont rendered valuable services to King Charles for which he received on two occasions his special thanks. He was very happily married to Lady Mary Keith, but on 5th September, 1644, he was murdered at Collace in the camp of the Marquis of Montrose by James Stewart of Ardvorlich. He was buried in the Chapter House of Inchmahome and his wife was so much affected by the death of her husband that she lost her reason. For a long time thereafter a bitter feud existed between the Grahams and the Stewarts. The details of the murder are to be found in Sir Walter Scott's *Legend of Montrose*. The story as narrated by the Stewarts of Ardvorlich is to the effect that James Stewart and Lord Kilpont commanded independent companies in the army of Montrose and while they served together lived and slept in the same tent. Some Irish having joined the army of Montrose under Alexander MacDonald committed some excesses at Ardvorlich which lay in the line of their march from the west, of which Ardvorlich complained to Montrose. He, not having received satisfaction, challenged MacDonald to single combat, whereupon Montrose, it is supposed, on the advice of Kilpont, laid both men under arrest. Montrose forced a reconciliation between them, but, a few days after the Battle of Tippermuir, following on an entertainment given to the officers in honour of the victory obtained, Stewart of Ardvorlich being heated with drink blamed Kilpont for the part he had taken and reflected upon Montrose for not giving him proper reparation. Kilpont took the part of Montrose, the argument developed into high words and finally Ardvorlich, a man of violent passions, struck Kilpont dead with his dirk. He immediately fled and threw himself into the hands of Montrose's enemies. It is very probable that this account of the tragedy is substantially correct, although the earlier story was to the effect that Stewart, having laid a plot for assassinating Montrose, had murdered Lord Kilpont owing to his refusal to take part in the assassination.

The fortunes of the Earl of Menteith rapidly became worse. In 1643 the ownership of Kilbryde passed to Sir William Ruthven of Dunglass under a decree of apprising. The latter disponed the estate in 1662 to John Stirling of Bankell, a branch of the family of Stirling of Keir, and it was from Stirling of Bankell that Kilbryde was acquired by Sir Colin Campbell of Aberuchill. The connection of the Earls of Menteith with this parish thus came to an end in 1643. The eighth Earl of Menteith who died in 1694 was the last Earl. He died in poverty although he had large claims against the Crown which were admitted to some extent, but never paid. The few lands remaining to him he conveyed to his relative the Marquis of Montrose.

The estate of Kippenross belonged to the Pearson family. It was purchased in 1630 from the old family of Kinross who had long been lairds and it remained in the Pearson family for 148 years. The Kinross family had been for some time, prior to this, in penurious circumstances, and in 1619 James Kinross of Kippenross was sued for remaining at the horn as a rebel and enjoying at the same time his estate. James Pearson, the first of Kippenross, was born in 1594 and was inducted minister of Dunblane by Bishop Bellenden in 1623. He received the appointment of Dean of Dunblane from James VI in the following year. He is said to have inhabited the house at The Cross in Cathedral Square which bears the Pearson coat of arms. On the overthrow of Episcopacy Dean Pearson was deprived of his appointment. One finds various references to him in later minutes of Kirk Session showing that he had striven hard to obtain re-appointment as minister of Dunblane. Dean Pearson's son appears to have taken an interest in Church affairs in Dunblane and to have been an elder.

The owner of the estate of Argaty in the first part of the 17th century was Patrick Home who died about 1629. He was succeeded by Henry Home who died in or before 1659 survived by his widow Mary Muschet and numerous sons. His heir was George Home, writer in Edinburgh, but the affairs of the latter being involved in debt, George Home conveyed the estate in

1659 to his immediate younger brother, Major John Home. The conveyance was written by Robert Cadell, writer in Doune, one of the witnesses being Alexander Stewart, Doctor of the Grammar School at Doune.

The Laird of Keir at the beginning of the 17th century was Sir Archibald Stirling, whose father had conveyed the estates of Keir to him in 1579. Sir Archibald was appointed Admiral Depute of the West seas and lochs " at the float and tak of the herring in the year 1601." He was first married to the youngest daughter of the second Lord Drummond and his second wife was a daughter of Lord Ross. Sir Archibald died in 1630 leaving a numerous family. A sister married John Napier of Merchiston, the inventor of logarithms. His eldest son was educated at the University of Glasgow and was married to the eldest daughter of Home of Wedderburn. He died before his father, being killed in Dunblane in 1593, and his only son, Sir George Stirling, became the next laird in 1630. Sir George first married a cousin, Margaret, daughter of Lord Ross, at the age of 17, his bride having barely completed 15 years. Their wedded life lasted little over two years. The young wife was buried in Holyrood Chapel in March, 1633. An account of the funeral is preserved in the Lyon Office Record of Funerals. Sir George Stirling was married in all four times. His last wife, Lady Margaret Livingstone, was married for the third time in 1668 to Sir John Stirling of Keir, a second cousin of her previous husband.

Sir George sided with Montrose concerting measures in favour of Charles I in 1641 in which he was associated with Lord Napier and Stewart of Blackhall. They were all committed prisoners to the Castle of Edinburgh, but in the following year they were fully exonerated by the King.

The Commissioners for sequestrating the estates in the time of Cromwell threatened to take Sir George's estates from him in respect of his having entered England with the King's army, but it was fortunate that men deponed that he had never entered England and his estates were respited. In 1652 he was appointed a Commissioner for treating for a union between Scotland and England with power to attend the English Parliament, and in the following year Cromwell granted him authority to pass from London to Scotland without trouble or molestation. He joined in a petition to Cromwell's Council to have the parishes in the neighbourhood of Dunblane disjoined from the County of Perth and added to the Sheriffdom of Stirling, but the petition was not acceded to. Sir George Stirling died in June, 1667. He had no family and was succeeded by his cousin, Sir Archibald Stirling, Lord Garden. His will dated 1664 provided that his body must not be dissected, but that it should be interred in his aisle in Dunblane Kirk without show, trumpets or convening any but friends at a near distance.

It was in 1594 that Kippendavie became a separate estate through the gift of it and other lands by Sir Archibald Stirling of Keir to his son Archibald. The latter was married about 1617 to Jean Mushet, daughter of the Laird of Burnbank. He died between April, 1645, and April, 1646, his successor being his eldest son, George Stirling. George Stirling, the second Laird of Kippendavie, died at an early age without family and was succeeded by his brother John. The residence of the lairds appears to have been at Auchinbee which is now part of Kippendavie Mains Farm.

Another branch of the Stirlings of Keir has existed since 1613 when, on the occasion of the marriage of Sir John Stirling, the second son of Sir Archibald Stirling of Keir, the latter made over the estate of Garden which he had acquired from Sir James Forrester whose family had possessed Garden for a number of generations. The eldest son of the first Stirling of Garden was educated at the University of Glasgow, studied Law, travelled in France for some time and sided with the Royalists in the time of Cromwell. He was appointed in 1661 one of the Senators of the College of Justice. His death took place in Edinburgh in 1668 and his interment took place at Dunblane. He was twice married and had four children by his first wife and ten children by his second.

The names of the principal proprietors appear among the elders of Dunblane Parish Church at this period. Thus, in 1659, we find the names of Sir George Stirling of Keir, James Pearson of Kippenross, John Stirling of Kippendavie, and James Stirling who for a time owned part of Kilbryde.

The lands of Keir prior to the separation of Kippendavie extended from the Teith in the direction of Dumyat and northwards to Greenloaning and southwards by the east bank of the River Allan but did not include the town of Dunblane or generally speaking any lands to the west and north-west of Dunblane.   The Keir lands included besides Keir and Kippendavie, the Quoigs, Lanrick, Kippenrait, Glassingalls, Glenbank and Lany.

In the middle of the 17th century James Chisholm was Laird of Cromlix.   His brother, John Chisholm, succeeded him in the ownership of this estate and completed his title thereto in 1657.   In addition to the lands of Over, Middle and Nether Cromlix and Over and Nether Auchinlay with its corn and waulk mills, he owned land at Feddal and Nether Ardoch, as also Easter and Wester or Blew Buttergask, Easter Corscaplie with the Bishop's Meadow, Barbush, Laichhill (spelt Leithall) and the lands of Bridgend and Ramoyle.

The heritable office of justiciary and bailie of the lordship and regality of Dunblane also pertained to the Lairds of Cromlix and they were patrons of the Altar of St. Blais.   In 1642 Cromlix also owned the lands of Cullins.

The Cromlix estates at this time thus included most of the land to the north and west of the River Allan from Dunblane, where they marched with Kilbryde and Keir to beyond Green-loaning, and also certain lands in the neighbourhood of Dunblane on the south-east side of the Allan.

The possessions of Cromlix included the cornmill in the city of Dunblane.

Among antiquities preserved in the Cathedral are two interesting articles dating from the 17th century which had been in the possession of Mr. Mackinlay, the Beadle of Dunblane Cathedral in the middle of the 19th century, and were afterwards preserved by his daughter, Mrs. Bruce, and ultimately gifted by her to the Kirk Session.   One is a funeral or dead bell with the initials "S.B." thereon, which are understood to stand for St. Blane, and the date, 1615.   The bell was rung to intimate either the passing away of one of the local inhabitants or for the purpose of summoning them to a funeral.   The other article is an ancient pulpit sand glass, such as was fixed on pulpits to indicate to the minister how time had flown since the commencement of his sermon. The sand in this glass runs through in an average time of 14 minutes, but this varies to the extent of a couple of minutes.   It was used in days of lengthy sermons, but the ministers did not restrict their sermons to one glass.   A sand-glass—probably this one—was purchased in Edinburgh in 1695 for use in Dunblane Cathedral for 12s.

Chapter XI.

DUNBLANE AS IT APPEARED TO SOME ANCIENT WRITERS.

It is of interest to recall the impressions which the little town of Dunblane made upon travellers in the 17th and 18th centuries. One of the earliest accounts is that contained in Franck's *Northern Memoirs*, written in 1658, but not published till 1694, and republished in 1821.

" *Theophilus.* What town is this ?

" *Arnoldus.* Dirty Dumblain; let us pass by it and not cumber our discourse with so inconsiderable a corporation ; our itch after (Machany) Mockeny puts a spur to quicken our expectation ; for who knows but the various alteration of weather may in some measure frustrate those expectations we may have of those admirable streams to answer our designs ?

" *Theop.* Do what you please.

" *Arn.* Truly I think it but time lost, to survey the reliques of a ruinous heap of stones that lean o'er the verge of a river, facing the mountains. The houses, it's true, are built with stone, but then to consider them low and little, it plainly demonstrates there's nothing eminent but narrow streets and dirty houses; a convincing argument there's no scavengers amongst them. And for their house-wifery, let that alone ; for if you touch it you sully your fingers. There is a market place such an one as it is ; but as for merchants there's no such thing in nature. But a palace there is and a Cathedral too, otherwise Dumblain had nothing to boast of.

" But there is one thing remarkable and that's the house of Domine Caudwel (a formal pedagogue) that absolved the thief, and concealed the theft, so lost his breeches, for you must know the good woman his wife was a notable comer, one of the first magnitude ; who with two more of her consorts (as I was told, at a four hours' drinking), guzled down as much ale and brandy, wine and strong waters, as amounted to the sum of forty pound Scots. But wanting money to pay her reckoning she liberally pawned her husband's breeches ; and he like a fop to redeem his wife's reputation, would never redeem his breeches, lest suspecting they should smell of the tears of the tankard. And here, as reported, was celebrated that famous union of Doh and Doris, stark love and kindness, a custom inviolable. Here also resided jovial Bille (Bailee) Sincleer.

" Now you are to consider that this pittiful pedling corporation of Dumblain, has little or no trade among them, except now and then a truck with a brandy-man, a tobacco merchant or a brewster-wife ; for ale, tobacco and strong waters are the staple of the town ; And so let us leave them to pursue our intended design for Minever and Dromon-Castle (Drummond Castle) that stands distant about some three miles from the Bridge of Ardoh ; where there runs a small rivulet of a rapid motion paved with a slaty bottom, but the access difficult."

The "Domine" referred to was Robert Caddell, Schoolmaster of Dunblane from 1652-1657, who also held the appointments of Session Clerk, Reader and Precentor. He was afterwards transferred to Doune.

The foregoing account does not give too flattering an impression of Dunblane with its low built houses, crushed together, narrow and dirty streets and ruined buildings, its inhabitants given to excessive indulgence in liquor and its trade restricted to dealing in tobacco and strong drink.

The author is specially interested in streams and angling and he refers to the Forth as the "most portable" river in Scotland—"a river meandering and torpid below the Bridge of Stirling but with streams above, especially towards the flourishing fields of Monteith" which he preferred to the Allan.

About the same time, namely, in 1693, there was published Slezer's *Theatrum Scot.*, a volume which contains most interesting drawings of Dunblane Cathedral and of many of the finest buildings and ruins in Scotland. Reference is made—at page 61—to Dunblane as a pleasant little town on the banks of the River Allan where ruins of the bishop's and regular canons' houses are to be seen. The writer refers to the very fine dwellings of Lord William Drummond, Viscount of Strathallan, who derived considerable revenues from the adjacent country. The Cathedral is described as of excellent workmanship, a part of which remained entire and in the ruins thereof, it is said, there was then an ancient picture representing the Countess of Strathearn with her children kneeling asking a blessing from St. Blane clothed in his pontifical habit.

The latter account gives a pleasanter impression of the little ancient city, but probably with the restoration of Episcopacy in 1660, and under the rule of Bishop Leighton and his successors, and with the help of distinguished laymen resident in the district, such as Lord Strathallan and Sir Colin Campbell, Dunblane had between 1658 and 1693 become more prosperous. Being a city of a Bishopric, clergy and nobility would be attracted to it, bringing to it also a retinue of servants and a certain degree of wealth.

The following notes from an account of Dunblane were written by Mr. McGoun, the parish schoolmaster, and included in Macfarlane's *Geographical Collections*—compiled about 1723.

Dunblane is there said to be 11 miles from Stirling and 20 miles from Perth. It contained at this time about 330 houses, had four yearly fairs and one weekly market on Thursdays. There was a large teind barn outside the north part of the city, and outside the south part was a stone bridge over the Allan. The barn belonged to Cromlix Estate. There was abundance of white marle south of Slamabach (Slymaback) which was much used for dunging the ground. The Kocksburn flowed from the Moor south-west of Pandrich and joined the Allan opposite Kier Crous (Cruives).

"Auldwharrie Burn rises out of the green forrat half a mile south-east of Glentay (Glentye) and out of the Revar Burn. It joins the Allan immediately below the corn mill and Crous of Kippenross, opposite the Corn Mill of Keir.

"The Ardoch (or Kilbryde) Burn had three heads—(one) Loch Bu haik (Mahaik), (two) Garn-ald and (three) Auld na sai (or Ilay Burn).

"Among the chief houses in the Parish are the houses of Bouton (that is near Kilbryde Chapel) and Kippendavie. The Kippendavie Burn rises in Glentay and after flowing half a mile forms the east end of line of battle of Sheriffmuir fought in 1715. The Burn crosses the Kings Highway at Sparkside where there is a handsome stone bridge."

"The Plewghie Burn joins the Allan a little above the Bridge of Kinbuck." Buttergask is spelt "Buttercasque."

In Bishop Pocock's *Tours in Scotland between 1747 and 1760*, published by the Scottish History Society in 1887, there are particulars with regard to Dunblane as it appeared to this writer. His information however is not entirely accurate. He writes from Stirling on 8th September, 1760, to a sister (Letter No. 59, page 291) as follows :—
" Dear Sister,
          " Dunblane though a poor town as to buildings, is very pleasantly situated on the river Alan consisting chiefly of one street built parallel with the river, and the Cathedral is at the end of it. There was anciently a Convent of Culdees here, which continued after it was made a Bishop's See by David the II. St. Blaan was head of the convent in the reign of Kenneth the III from whom it has its name, Dunblane (Blanes hill or fort). The first Bishop whose name is met with is about 1150 ; Bishop Finlay called Dermoch built the bridge before 1419, which is a fine arch 42 feet wide and twelve broad ; it appears to have been pulled down and new built, and the tradition is that the Bishop thinking it weak, built another arch over a new one to make it stronger. The tower is at the side of the present building of the Cathedral and appears to have been at the Westend of a fabric which joyned on to it, and might have been the first church, perhaps of the Culdees ; two Gothic stories of a light-coloured stone appear to have been built on five Saxon stories of red freestone, the same as the rest of the present buildings. The body of the Church consists of eight light Gothic arches, over each of them are two Gothic windows and in the isles a Gothic window to each division into four parts. The West window is very fine and lofty, and built double, so that there is room to go between the inner and outer window. The door is beautifull and consists of about a hundred members, computing every minute member. The Quire only is the present Church, and consists of six windows on the South side, that which is farthest to the East and to the West being narrower than the others, and consist of two parts, the others of four. There is only one on the North side answering to the most Eastern window on the South side. The East

window is extremely beautifull ending in four parts at top, adorned with circles between the Gothic arches, and there are as many Gothic arches in the middle ; on each side of it is a long Gothic window, and all of them rise to the top of the Church.   The isle continues the whole length on the north side, but is now divided to the north of the Quire into a School and vestry ; the four stalls on each side at the west end of the Choir remain with the fine ornaments over them of carved Gothic pilasters, and there are 13 stalls on each side, a division being made at the sixth as for the Chantor and Treasurer.   There is a Sepulchral nich on the south side of the Choir.   The church yard is over the river, which is to the west of it.   To the South was the Bishop's house, the ruins of which are seen, where were demolished by undermining, it extended all down to the end of the library, opposite to it were the Canons houses which are still standing.   In a street to the East of the Church are remains of the small house in which Bishop Leighton and the reformed Bishops lived.   The see of Dunblane at the Reformation was computed to be worth £313 one of the least whose rents were paid in wheat, beare, meal and oats.   At the West end of the spot on which the Bishop's house stood is a library founded by Bishop Leighton who sent his books to it ; but gave some to the library at Glasgow.   There is a good collection of books in Divinity, and they lend them to every one who enters his name and gives half a guinea for the use of the library.

" They have a small manufactory of linnen and thread and shoes which they send to Glasgow.

" There is a Seceding house set up here on their displeasure being taken that the patron of the living could not accept of their recommendation, but they do not differ in doctrine. The Tenants of the Patron and some others set up the person they would have put in as a Lecturer in the Kirk and raise a subscription of £50 a year.   There is a pleasant walk a measured mile long over the river to the south east, terminating at a Gentleman's house, called Kippenross, where there is a Sycamore which measures at the root and branches 34 feet round, and 18 at the smallest part, four great branches grow out of it.   There are plantations on each side of the walk, it is mostly hanging ground to the river, and on the whole very beautifull.

" I rid a mile and a half to Sheriffmuir to see the place of battle between the Duke of Argyle and the Rebels under Lord Mar in 1715.   The King's forces were encamped four days on an eminence defended by a vale and extended half a mile down to Dunblane, the Rebels on a moor to the north west of the Allan.   They met on the height of the hill, and the right wing of the enemy broke the left of the King's forces and pursued them to the lines, but finding that Argyle had broken their left wing, they returned and were cut to pieces, about 1,000 of the enemy falling.   We saw several little risings where 'tis supposed the dead were buried.   They pursued them even through the Alan and up the mountains, and several of the enemy were drowned in the Alan.

" We had here a pleasing view of the neighbouring country which includes Strathallan, the Strath on the Forth, and extends almost to Monteith and Lough Loumond, all very fine, though much intermixed with heath.   Most of the gentlemen of this country are of the Church of England, but some of their ladies go to the Kirk."

In Camden's *Britannia* published 1789, Dunblane is described as being situated in a rich and fertile bottom in an amphitheatre of hills and as being a pleasant little town of one long narrow street tolerably well built, at the head of which is the shell of a magnificent Cathedral built in a simple style of architecture by David I in the beginning of the 12th century. The writer refers to the choir as being crowded and deformed, like all Gothic buildings in this country, the nave, which is walled off from it, being full of modern gravestones.

It has of course to be kept in view that David I had no part in the building of Dunblane Cathedral (he merely founding the Bishopric) and that the greater portion of the Cathedral was erected in the 13th century.

In Robertson's *Account of Agriculture in Perthshire in* 1799, references are made to the Cathedral which is described as unroofed and going to decay, yet generally grand.   It is noted that in the choir there are 32 stalls for Prebends with grotesque figures carved upon them, such as a cat, a fox and an owl, and it is suggested that they are emblematic of the peculiar qualities of these animals, like the ancient hieroglyphics of Egypt.   It is noted that the three steps of the High Altar remain and that several graves of Bishops and Deans in the area are covered with coarse blue marble stones.   These no doubt refer to the graves of the sisters Drummond.

CHAPTER XII.

THE KIRK SESSION IN ITS EARLY DAYS—1652 to 1700.

ONE of the most surprising institutions connected with the Church in Scotland is that of the Kirk Session, a body which in a short time acquired a remarkable hold over the life of the community. It was unknown in connection with the Roman Catholic Church and may be regarded as peculiar to the Presbyterian form of church government. The Kirk Session Records in Dunblane date from 1652—that is from a short time after Episcopacy was overthrown in the reign of Charles I. It is uncertain whether there had ever been an earlier volume of Session Records than this and it is unknown when the Session of Dunblane was first instituted. The earliest extant volume, consisting of a small quarto book bound in vellum, commences without explanatory or prefatory statement with the record of a meeting held on 4th April, 1652. It is possible that the Kirk Session had been in existence for some little time prior to this date without any written record having been kept, or there may have been earlier volumes than those which survive, but of these matters nothing is known. At that time Dunblane was without a minister. Dean Pearson, a strong Episcopalian, had lost his office and no Presbyterian minister had as yet been found to take his place. The meeting was presided over by " Magister John Edmonstone," who was probably the minister of the parish of Lecropt, transferred later in that year to the parish of Kilmadock. As mentioned in a previous chapter the names of the elders who were present at this meeting were " Harie Blackwood, Walter Cheisholme, James Sinclaire, John Thomsoune, Rob Zair, David Thomsoune, William Robisoune, George Henrie, Andro Ker, Ion Robisoune, Ion Ker and Thomas Cairns." The name of Harie Blackwood is prominent in the history of Dunblane at this time while Chisholm was probably a descendant of the Cromlix family as he seems to have been Bailie of Dunblane. The other names are to be found in the records of the city from that time to the present day. These were not all the members of Session for one finds at a later date the names of a number who were absent from the first meeting, and one also learns that if an elder had not a valid excuse for absence he had at next meeting to pay a considerable penalty.

The minister of the parish was Moderator or chairman, and, while he had no vote on any matter under discussion, he exercised somewhat despotic power. At a meeting on 27th July, 1654, the following rules were adopted :—" It is enactit that in tyme of sessionn 1d. non shall speake except the Moderator aske 2d. That when any speak they shall and be uncovered 3d. That non speak to any delinquent except the Minister 4d. that elders and deacons behave themselves gravelie and authoritativelie as becomes thame in thair place and that they doe not take away anything spoken in Session." The Moderator thus kept effectual control of the proceedings, only allowing those members upon whom he called to speak while he himself was free to speak without restriction. The members of Session other than the minister were the elders and deacons, but the latter had no duties except with business connected with the funds of the Church and lesser powers.

While for about ten years the form of Church government in Scotland was Presbyterian, Episcopacy was restored soon after the Restoration of the Stuarts to the throne in the person of Charles II. It is remarkable that the advent of Episcopacy is unnoticed in the Session Records and seems to have had no influence on the actions of the Kirk Session. This may be, to some extent, accounted for by the policy of Bishop Leighton who endeavoured to rule in a mild and persuasive way so as to commend Episcopacy to the people. It will be found that about this time the lairds and chief persons in the district became members of the Kirk Session. These included the Lairds of Keir, Kippenross, Kippendavie, Sir Colin Campbell of Aberuchill and Kilbryde and Lieutenant-General Drummond, Lord Strathallan. Probably their sympathies were largely with Episcopacy, but they seem to have willingly taken part in the business of the Session, and Sir Colin Campbell and Lord Strathallan evidently carried much weight in the deliberations of this body. Thus it is frequently recorded that consideration was delayed until the Lieutenant-General was present, while in any matter of delicacy or requiring the help of a trained legal mind the Session never turned to Sir Colin Campbell in vain. After Episcopacy was again abolished at the Revolution the lairds took a less active part in the business of the Kirk Session although Sir Colin Campbell performed all work entrusted to him until his death early in the 18th century.

The powers of the Kirk Session were wide and the discipline exercised by them was strict. While they had a case under consideration the Civil Courts were forbidden by the Law of the land to deal with the matter. If the Civil power endeavoured to interfere with the jurisdiction of the Kirk Session or other Church Court, the Lord Advocate would intervene to stay the hand of the Civil authority. On the other hand if the Kirk Session had difficulty in enforcing culprits to implement the sentences pronounced upon them, the arm of the civil law would come to its aid. At first the sentences pronounced by the Session seem in most cases to have been harsh, but it must also be recognised that the Records disclose many acts of kindly consideration. While much time was occupied in dealing with breakers of the moral laws, complaints were not confined to breaches of the seventh Commandment. The sanctity of the Sabbath Day was a matter of the greatest concern to the Kirk Session and the views which it held were as extreme as those of the Pharisees in the time of Our Lord. One of the most common and most trivial of offences to be dealt with was that of pulling kale on the Sabbath, while any acts of agricultural labour were deemed worthy of punishment. Thus on 23rd October, 1653, a farmer at Kilbryde was proceeded against for binding his corn on Sunday. The farmer appeared and confessed that " he band ane stook of corn on the Lord's Day being unbound on the Satternsday night and rain likely to be on the morrow." His explanation was not deemed satisfactory and he was ordered to stand in his seat on the following Sabbath and be publicly rebuked. Other offences on the Lord's Day were winnowing corn and mucking a byre. A farmer charged with the latter offence stated that the byre was " mucket " by some children without his knowledge, he being in the Kirk at the time. This reasonable excuse was not accepted and the farmer was publicly admonished on the following Sunday " in respect he aucht to have tane ane better care of his family."

On 20th September, 1657, Catherine McGregor appeared and confessed bearing home some lint on the Sabbath, but as she was not compos mentis, she was privately admonished. Another breach of the Sabbath frequently mentioned in the Minutes is that of " vaging " through the fields, and, when the taking of a Sabbath walk was forbidden by the Session, it is not surprising that Sunday golfing was deemed an offence. It is more surprising to consider that any person was so bold as indulge in this wickedness. Even the worthy Bailie Chisholm, himself a member of Kirk Session, broke the Sabbath of a time by the leading of corn on the Lord's Day at night. He explained that it was between 9 and 10 at night that he yoked to the work. His penalty was a fine of £6 Scots for the use of the poor and he was suspended from his office of eldership for a time.

Another offence committed on the Sabbath Day was that of slaying of fish. A James Hutchison admitted this charge, his explanation being that he was forced thereto by the " Inglishes quho did strick his wife " with grievous results to her. The Session seems on this account to have regarded him more kindly as he was ordained only to make public repentance from his seat whensoever he was required to do. Perhaps the most trivial act regarded as Sabbath breaking was that of leaving out clothes on the Sabbath which was deemed to be an offence.

Another matter about which the Session concerned itself was that of scolding and quarrelling or of one libelling the character of another. This salutary rule was, however, observed, namely that, if a person who alleged that his character had been libelled, failed to establish the charge before the Session he was himself dealt with for having brought an unfounded charge.

Dunblane had not at the time an enviable reputation for sobriety and consequently we read of numerous cases of persons taken in drunkenness. On 18th May, 1660, Martha Abercrombie confessed that she had drunken " but two chopines of aill " with her son and that she had been a little mistaken with it. An admonition was deemed sufficient in her case. Two husbands and wives admitted a charge of drinking in their own houses during the sermon and were ordered to satisfy publicly from their seats the next Lord's Day. It was deemed a more serious charge when the drunkenness occurred on the Sabbath, and particularly during hours of public worship. One of the duties devolving on the Session was to search the town during the period of afternoon service with the view of ascertaining who were idling their time at home and who were indulging in liquor, a duty which frequently fell on the elders who had taken the collection at morning service. Sometimes we read that the Session endeavoured to enforce regular church attendance by inflicting penalties for absence. Thus James Gray in 1657 was warned that, if he did not attend church regularly, he would be fined 40s.

The Session also took cognizance of acts of violence. Isobel Crambe was cited before the Session " for bleeding of her neighbour's lass on the head to the effusion of blood " for which she was admonished. In 1665 John Buchanan, flesher in Dunblane, was dealt with for beating his wife and "raging with her so oft." John's defence was that his wife " was a provoker of him to it and that he had often times reasons to do the same." The Session had probably good ground for not being satisfied with the defence and he was put under caution for £40 Scots that he would give no just occasion for any outfall or squabbling with his wife in future. His wife had, however, to bind herself to give no occasion of provocation to her husband, as otherwise she would be found liable in the same penalty.

In addition to acts of Sabbath profanation and of immorality the Kirk Session were concerned, to a minor degree, with neglect of family worship. It is gladly noted that no cases are recorded of trials for witchcraft which in certain parts of Scotland were so numerous at one period of its history, leading to the deaths of many harmless, but ignorant or mentally afflicted persons, principally older women. Such prosecutions chiefly arose out of the superstitious fears and gross ignorance of the accusers and would not have been tolerated in a more enlightened age.

There are, however, in the Kirk Session Records of this period one or two references to witchcraft. In 1654 the Session agreed to summon Margaret Lawson for alleged cursing of Edward Maltman unlawfully, Maltman being also summoned to appear before the Session. On the 15th June, " Margaret Lausonne and Edward Maltman baith present. The sd. Edward being questioned why and how he sought his healthe from Mart Lasonne, confesses that at being in the rig (that is the ridge of the field) sowing in gude health at the 12 houre of the tent day of March, 1654, Mart Lasonne prossit his way twice who bade him at ill will for being causit be ane sojer to take her meal for the sojers use against her will to Dunblane, and she expressing to his father yt same morning that she had not forgott to be revenged on his sonne, but to do him a dishort (to do him harm) within a short time ; within halfe ane hour he fell downe on the rig and did sweit exceedinglie and continued so to the second day of May at qlk tyme the said Margaret being sent for be his mother Helen Bryce he askit he being lying in his bed his healthe in ther words Margaret Lausone give me my healthe for God's sake and she trembling and muttering many words in to herself he forthwith fand himselfe to gett healthe daylie and is now weill." This statement was corroborated by Edward Maltman's mother, father and others. Margaret Lawson said in her own defence that "she absolutely denied that she went that morning to James Maltman, Edward's father, and at any tyme ever said yt she had any quarrell against his sone or yt she promised him ane dishort in short space. But confessit she came to the sick man and yt he sought his healthe from hir and that she mutterit some words and tooke him be his hand and said God send you his health and that he gaide (went) ane ill gait to seik health from her yt morning." The Session had long deliberation as to what should be done but in the end Edward Maltman was put under discipline for being unlawfully healed, and Margaret Lawson was reported to the Presbytery. The charge against Margaret Lawson was that she had brought a serious illness on Maltman through some powers which she possessed as a witch she having conceived illwill against the lad's father, while Maltman had committed an offence in having sought the aid of the evil powers which the woman possessed to cure him of his illness.

A few years later a second case occurred where the person charged was a Catherine McGregor whose offence was that " she lives and charms with carrying water out of ye superstitious well of Cullens." Catherine appeared before the Session on 3rd March, 1659, and on being interrogated confessed that she did take water of the well above Cullens and did take it into Stirling and did give it to a woman. She denied having washed the woman with it or having sprinkled it over her, but confessed that she did " cast ye fairie wispe yat stopped ye stope in the fire." She also admitted having gone several times to Stirling after this manner and that she met the woman a third time at a house in Bridge of Allan and that she only received 12s Scots for her travell and lost 6s. of it. The poor woman seems to have had much labour and incurred some risk for little gain, one half of which she lost.

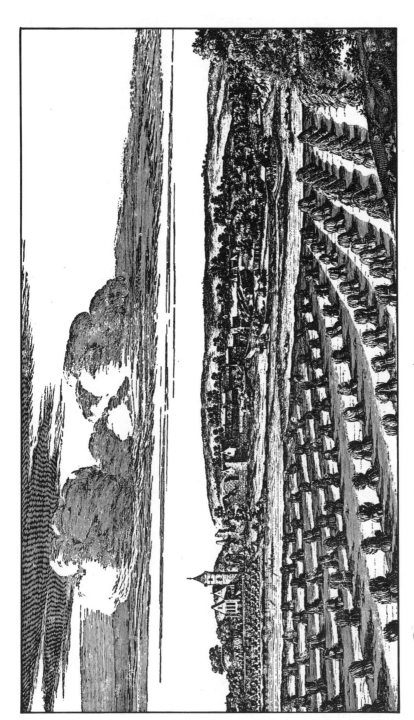

Prospectus Oppidi DUMBLANI . The Prospect of the Town of DUMBLANE .

From Slezer's "Theatrum Scotiae," London, 1693

By courtesy of the Society of Friends of Dunblane Cathedral

ARGATY

Reproduced by courtesy of D. C. Bowser, Esq., and Mrs. Bowser, of Argaty, and the proprietors of " Country Life "

Walter Reid, who was tenant at Cullens, gave evidence that one of his stirks did not return from watering after Catherine McGregor had accused him of reporting her to the Session—and he accordingly blamed her for doing away with one of his cattle. The Session records the words used by her for charming which had probably been handed down from generation to generation and had become somewhat mutilated in their descent through the ages. It may be of interest to some readers to have the charm repeated here.

> " Sainct Jon lay in ye mouth of a lyon
> And he forgot himself to faine
> And something came to him with atreinne
> Will yat it bund him be stake and stane
> Will it brunt him to ye baine
> For all the ills yat ever may be
> Let it never byde with thee
> But in ye deid and into ye slaine
> And let it never come again to thee
> Ryse up Mother Marie for deir John's sake
> And charme this man with yor ten fingeres
> With your great gold rings
> For blood and melt for shotes and grippe
> For all the ills yat ever may be
> Let it never come again to thee
> But into ye deid and into ye slaine
> And let it never come again to thee."

The well referred to in this case may be the spring at Cullens which supplies the mansion house of Cromlix. It could not have been the mineral well which is situated some distance from Cullens on Crofts of Cromlix. Evidently the wells of Cromlix had earned a reputation for healing as one reads in Beveridge's *History of Culross and Tulliallan* that Robert Cusing in Kincardine on Forth was charged with having gone to a man of Kilbuck-Drummond for John Aitken in Torryburn " for seeking health to his wife." The case proceeded from which it appeared that a man Young had been healed by the help of Robert Cusing who had sent him to a man Drummond in Kinbuck. Drummond had directed Young to go to a south-running water, put in his neck and wash himself three times all over and go three times about in a contrary direction to the sun and say " all the evil that is on me be on the gowen." The gowan plant referred to, called the lucken gowan (or globe flower), was held in great repute as a charm.

A case of alleged witchcraft in this district is referred to in the Records of the Privy Council of Scotland.

On 18th December, 1664, the Privy Council were informed that Barbara Drummond, spouse of William Robison in Tenantry of Kilbryde, was suspected of witchcraft, charming and sorcery. The Privy Council remitted to certain lairds in the district and the Provost and Bailie of Stirling to put her to trial, and on 22nd December, 1664, they ordered her to be taken to the Tolbooth of Stirling. On 15th June, 1665, there is a further reference to Barbara's case. She presented a petition stating that she had been for twelve months imprisoned in Stirling and still remained there in great misery. The Privy Council ordered the persons to whom her trial had been entrusted to meet within fifteen days under pain of being denounced and their property forfeited. Later on she presented a further supplication narrating that she had been kept for three years in prison at Dunblane, Edinburgh and Stirling, stating that her accusers were afraid to appear to try the commission and that she was still in a most miserable condition and starving. The Commissioners were ordered to appear before the Privy Council to answer for not carrying out their commission. The end of Barbara Drummond's case is not recorded.

While the Kirk Session wielded great power over the lives of the community and administered justice sternly or even at times with harshness, many instances are, however, recorded both of acts of benevolence and public spiritedness of which a few instances may be given. In October, 1677, a collection was taken for certain men who had been made captives by the Turks. In February, 1683, a poor widow was given a donation to help her son John to a trade and at the same meeting the Session ordained that a boll of meal be given to the Lady of Knockhill, a poor gentlewoman. On several occasions collections were taken to defray the expenses of surgical operations. Thus, in April, 1654, two elders from Keir supplicated the Session in favour of a poor girl in the Keir who was diseased of the " stoune." The Session considered the request very reasonable and that the poor girl was an object of pity, particularly as she had neither parents nor friends. It was accordingly resolved that the whole elders in their respective divisions with their deacons should set about taking a collection, and it was remitted to the minister and Harie Blackwood to send for the doctor and agree with him " for hair (her) cutting this week." In June, 1682, Henry Dewar in Rottearns applied to the Kirk Session for some help as his wife was unable to supply their child with milk whereupon it was agreed to give him £6 Scots quarterly for the nursing of his child.

A collection was taken in 1684 for the benefit of the town of Kelso when £65 12s. Scots money was contributed.

The Session Records disclose the result of the collection for the poor girl in the Keir, and the receipt of the surgeon, William Soutar by name, is given. It appears that he was paid £42 4s. 6d. for the surgical operation. In all, £66 17s. 2d. was collected in the parish. The doctor's man was given £6 for his assistance and drink money and the balance after payment of all charges was handed to John Robison (Robertson) for furnishing for the poor patient such things as the doctor prescribed.

In 1695, a similar operation had to be performed on the son of Robert Dawson. A general collection throughout the parish yielded £52 Scots. It is pleasing thus to find that the sternness directed against moral failings was blended with kindness towards those in trouble and suffering from serious sickness.

Among other matters which the Kirk Session dealt with was the admission of strangers to the parish and the licensing of beggars. In 1653, as already noted, it was ordained that no one should receive any person into his family or let a vault, house or cottage to such who is not of "approven converse and qualitie" until he be assured of the stranger's Christian carriage. In March, 1654, it was reported to the Session that a certain woman's life and conversation was not good. She was ordered to supply testimonials and the penalty of disobedience was banishment from the town by the hands of the Bailie. At the same time the Session ordered that no family should employ a certain servant from Stirling before she produced testimonials, while at a later meeting the Session ordered that any one receiving strangers, travelling vagabonds or idle persons without certificates of character should suffer a penalty of 40s. Scots.

In the Minute of 16th October, 1656, reference is made to the application of John Brown who seems occasionally to have acted as a teacher in Dunblane. " This day the Session having taken to ther consideration the desire of Mr. Jone Brown to have ane testimoniall, the Session considering that he had no residence amongst them, but yat now and then he taught in Dunblane at his coming to the toune, and that having no residence no testificatt could be askit of him by them and therefore they could not give one, or at least the requiring of one from this place was not needful. But the Minister asking all and every one of the Elders if yai had anything to say against his honest carriage and speciallie if yai had seen him drunk at any time they all being posit (asked) declairit they knew nothing against his carriage and could not positivelie say yai saw him drunk and ordaines him for ane testimonial to have extract hereof."

The usual punishments imposed by the Kirk Session on offenders were public censure in Church or private censure at a meeting of Session or the imposition of pecuniary penalties. Culprits were frequently ordained to sit in sack cloth at Divine Service, but it seems doubtful whether the degrading of a man or woman in this way achieved any good results either in the life of the defaulter or by impressing the other members of the congregation.

In December, 1653, the Session approved of John Duthie being paid £7, his price for making a stool of repentance. Another form of punishment is referred to in 1669 where Patrick Mulland, for misbehaviour before the Congregation when he should have satisfied for slandering John Cramb, was ordained to sit next Lord's Day in sackcloth or otherwise to be put into the brankes. The brankes made of iron were put over the culprit's head with an iron bit to go into his mouth.

In September, 1701, the herd lads and young boys seem to have caused trouble and disturbance within the Church particularly in the lofts during divine worship. The Session accordingly directed their Treasurer to have a whip made with a long handle having several rings for the use of the Church Officer in deterring and restraining the herds and boys. It is reported in a subsequent minute that the whip had been made, but there is no record of whether its use proved effectual.

Some interesting information about the Cathedral at this period is derived from incidents mentioned in the Kirk Session minutes. From some time before 1600 the nave had been unroofed, and the choir only used as the parish church. The large arch between the nave and choir had been built up. About the middle of the 17th century there were two galleries known as the east and west lofts at the east and west end of the choir. The entrance to the east loft was through the eastmost of the south windows by a stone stair erected outside. The westmost loft seems at this time to have been reached by a stair from the interior of the choir at the west end. The pulpit was near the south wall about the middle of the choir where the church was entered by a door under one of the south windows. The main entrance for the congregation seems to have been by a door in the west gable.

There were frequent applications to the Kirk Session for liberty to erect seats. The seats in the choir were usually private property, the owners obtaining permission from the Session to erect or place a seat and paying a small sum annually for the site. Some seats were, however, erected by the Session, who let sittings in such, the income derived being expended in the care of the poor. In 1656, the Session, in respect that he had never had a seat for his wife and family, gave permission to Mr. Lindsay (the Minister) to erect a seat where the pulpit formerly sat, and Mr. Lindsay offered to leave the seat for the use of his successors. In January, 1661, John Stirling of Kippendavie, Harie Blackwood, Bailie in Dunblane, and John Graham of Cromlix supplicated the Session for the use of four pews in the west end of the choir opposite to the entry of Kippenross seat upon the right hand as they entered in at the large choir door. Kippendavie and Harie Blackwood were allowed three seats between them and John Grahame, the fourth, and the yearly charge for these was 1s. sterling per pew. In the following year the Session found it desirable to erect three benches for scholars to provide them with a seat of their own. The Session employed John Fife to do the work for wages, he providing deals of those he had at one time borrowed from the Session. This points to the Session wishing to get something back from John Fife for having kept the deals which the Session had lent to him.

In 1668 there seems to have been further difficulties about seats. John Stirling of Kippendavie gave in a supplication regarding the room west of the pulpit formerly possessed by him but now by Bailie Chisholm. At the next meeting Bishop Leighton was present with the Dean and others when the request of Kippendavie was granted and apparently Bailie Chisholm was compelled to give way. At this meeting John Graham, Commissary Clerk, was given room next to Kippendavie for himself and his family of two children, while Harie Blackwood was given a site under the east loft in the middle of the church as one enters at the east little door. Alexander Chisholm, Bailie of Dunblane, was given room under the east loft between Harie Blackwood's seat and that of the Laird of Keir. The position of the east door referred to is not at present known.

Bishop Leighton, while present at one or two meetings of Kirk Session, did not frequently attend. His duties in his diocese, and in Edinburgh and London took him frequently from home and one can understand how he would gladly avoid attendance at such meetings where purely parochial matters were under discussion, principally cases of discipline. His attendance at the above meeting was probably due to a desire to bring about peace where a heated controversy had arisen over church sittings. In 1673 and 1674, we find Bishop Ramsay attending meetings of the Session and delivering sermons prior to proceeding with the business. The presence of the last Bishop of Dunblane, Bishop Douglas, at a Session meeting is recorded in 1687. Attendance of the Bishops was, however, exceptional.

One would gather that the east and west lofts had been erected about 1653 as a note of the cost appears in the Session minutes at that time when one also learns that the windows in the choir had been glazed.

In 1694, the Session, finding that the entry to the pulpit from the south door was very inconvenient both for the ministers and those parents who had children for baptism, appointed the minister and James Robertson (Robison) in the Park (of Keir) to remove their seats from the south wall three feet towards the middle of the church to give a convenient entry from the south door, the seats to come $6\frac{1}{2}$ feet from the door north-west and eastwards and James Robertson's seat to take in the pillar of Balhaldie's Loft.

The Kirk Session also took charge of the churchyard. In 1654 they enacted that no market was to be kept in the kirkyard at any future time and that the churchyard wall was to be built with all expedition, while on 18th May, 1660, as already noted on page 87, they ordained intimation from the pulpit that all within the town and parish who claimed rights of burial within the churchyard should attend on the Tuesday following the intimation to prove their rights, failing which they were to lose any right to interment in any particular place.

In 1661, an application was made by Alexander Whitehead, surgeon, in Stirling, to have a confirmation of right of burial at the south-west end of the Church of Dunblane over and against the Aisle of the Laird of Cromlix which Whitehead alleged had pertained to the Farquhars from the first foundation thereof, the Aisle being called Farquhar's Aisle or Trinity Altar. He claimed to be the heir of Thomas Whitehead and Marion Farquhar. The Session upheld his claim. A short time later this ground was gifted by the Bishop, with consent of the Chapter, to Sir Colin Campbell of Kilbryde. This minute indicates the site of the Trinity Altar which stood on the south wall nearly opposite the Strathallan Tomb on the north wall.

In 1687, two silver cups for use at the Communion were presented by John Graham, the Commissary Clerk, at a meeting of Session which the Bishop attended. The cups were said to be 18 ounces in weight and to hold upwards of a chopin and to bear the name and arms of the donor. It was provided at the time of the gift that the cups should be at John Graham's command when he pleased to call for them. In 1700, he supplemented his gift by presenting two similar cups which were handed over by his son, John Graham, Junior. The cups were of similar size and no proviso was attached to the gift. These cups are still in use at the celebration of the Lord's Supper. Some two years later the Session purchased on their own account another pair of cups of similar design which cost them the sum of £144 Scots.

Although Bishop Leighton was anxious to have John Graham appointed Commissary Clerk in Lanarkshire it would appear that he remained in Dunblane, his death occurring about 1702.

In some parishes doubt has existed as to whether the grass of the churchyard was the property of the Minister or of the Kirk Session. The Kirk Session Minutes of this period indicate that the Session claimed the right to the grass and that it was their custom to sell it. (See page 87).

On 25th September, 1693, the Session appointed two windows to be struck out on the south side of the church, that is of the choir, one on each side of the pulpit that the people might the better see to read, and on 23rd November, 1694, John Don, glazier, submitted his account to the Session for glazing the two new windows in the south side of the church. It would thus appear that prior to 1693, there must have been two fewer windows in the choir than at the present time. Captain Slezer's drawing of the Cathedral seems to show the six windows which now exist. Was his drawing made rather later or did he put in the windows before they had been supplied?

In 1694, the Session also ordered "glasses" to be put into the schoolhouse because the children could not sit therein for cold. The Lady Chapel was in use at that time as the school and without heating and without glass must have been a bitterly cold place in winter, the sun penetrating it at no season of the year.

It is not known when a clock was first supplied for the Cathedral Tower, but on 10th May, 1702, Robert Thomson, the Keeper of the Town Clock, applied for a gratuity. The Treasurer was instructed to allow him £2 5s. for that year only, the Session to be under no obligation to continue payment in future years beyond what they should see fit.

As mentioned on page 86, the people of Dunblane were not dependent on the clock alone for giving them the hour of day. The Church bell was rung by order of the Kirk Session at 7 a.m., at 8.30 a.m. and at 10 o'clock precisely. The bell was also rung at 2 o'clock afternoon. In 1695 the Session ordained that a new leather be put to the tongue of the bell, that 4s. be paid for a pound of tallow for the bell towes and that the bell be rung at 6 a.m. on Sabbath mornings to wake and raise the people.

Various entries in the Kirk Session Records refer to soldiers stationed in Dunblane. One occurs in 1683 and another in 1700. At the latter date three young women, apparently sisters, were reported to the Session " for their offensive carriage with soldiers," and on 31st March they were sharply spoken to and rebuked for such conduct, but, as the Session could find no clear ground for bringing them before the congregation, they were dismissed with an admonition.

The Records of this period record various gifts made to the Kirk Session for behoof of the poor. A sum of 600 merks, being stipend mortified by Mr. Alexander Gibson, some time minister at Dunblane, for the poor of the parish, was in the hands of James Pearson of Kippenross, and great difficulty was experienced in obtaining payment. This money had been borrowed by James Pearson, Senior, father to the Laird of Kippenross. Ultimately the Session had to restrict their claim to 500 merks Scots and to discharge their right to bygone interest in order to get a settlement with Mr. Pearson and a Bond was executed by Kippenross in favour of the Session and delivered to the Kirk Treasurer.

On 6th October, 1672, John Graham announced to the Session that their late Bishop— Bishop Leighton—had mortified £1024 Scots Money to the Session of Dunblane, the annual rent being for the use of the poor which money was then in the hands of Commissary Bordie for which gift John Graham delivered papers to John Thomson, the Treasurer. Lieutenant-General Drummond and John Graham and their heirs were named Trustees by Leighton. The Session also experienced great difficulty in obtaining the cash from Bordie.

Again on 12th October, 1684, John Graham conveyed another gift to the Session in his capacity of executor to Captain John Fleming, his brother-in-law, who, on his death bed, had willed to the Kirk Session the sum of 200 merks Scots for the poor of the parish. The money was paid over by Mr. Graham to George Robertson, then Kirk Treasurer. At a later meeting it was arranged to lend this sum to Pearson of Kippenross—a somewhat strange resolution considering the difficulty the Session had in recovering the money in his hands which was mortified by Mr. Gibson. On 28th January, 1703, John Graham, Junior, handed over the sum of 200 merks Scots bequeathed by his father, now deceased, for the poor of the parish along with a sum of interest since the mortification of the money. The Session expressed themselves very sensible of the pious deed of their late good friend and returned their hearty thanks to his son.

It may be noted that in 1696 the Session ordained that before any money was bestowed on indigent persons that such should come before a meeting and be exhorted to be religious and fearers of God. One wonders whether, if a poor person declined to do so, assistance would have been refused him.

It is disappointing that in these Kirk Session Records no reference is made to any constitutional upheavals in the country or to any historical events. The numerous alterations in Church government, the Restoration and Revolution, the changes in the Monarchy all passed unheeded. With the return of Episcopacy under Charles II there is no modification in the procedure or spirit of the Kirk Session and there is only a slight difference observable when Episcopacy was abolished after James II was driven from the Throne. It is to be noted that after the Revolution the lairds (with the exception of Lord Aberuchill) ceased to be members, their sympathies being probably with the Episcopalian form of government. The rule of the Kirk Session, however, became milder and in place of dealing with wrongdoers before the Session or in presence of the congregation, the elders were frequently deputed to remonstrate privately with offenders.

Further information about the early Kirk Sessions will be found on pages 81-87, 153-154, and in p. 209 ff.

CHAPTER XIII.

BISHOP LEIGHTON AND DUNBLANE.

THE most distinguished name in Scottish history connected with Dunblane is that of Bishop Leighton, one of the leading figures in the religious struggles of the time of Charles II, one who was a ripe scholar, an able linguist, a powerful preacher, a man of singularly fine character, and completely detached from worldly aspirations. It was during the most important part of his career that Leighton occupied the Bishopric of Dunblane.

While it would be impossible here, as it is unnecessary, to give a full account of the life of this saintly man, one must recall the principal events in his earlier days to enable the reader to appreciate what occurred during his residence in Dunblane between 1662 and 1671-2.

Leighton was of Scottish descent of a family of some distinction resident at Ulyshaven near Montrose. His birth was in 1611 or perhaps 1610. While his grandfather was a Papist his father, Alexander Leighton, was a strong opponent of Episcopacy and had acted as a Presbyterian minister in London and Utrecht. He also practised for some time as a medical man. Dr. Alexander Leighton published several works. One, printed in 1628, entitled *An Appeal to the Parliament* or *Zion's Plea against the Prelacie*, led to barbarous punishments being inflicted by the Star Chamber on the author, including mutilations and branding, fines and lifelong imprisonment. Although his writings may have contained invectives of a vigorous nature, Leighton's father has been described as kind and loving, eminent for learning and piety, and one who only spoke of his persecutors in terms of forgiveness. Little is known of Leighton's mother save what may be gathered from his letters to her, and even her name is unknown. Bishop Leighton seems to have been much attached to her and her early death made a deep impression upon him.

He entered the University of Edinburgh in the winter of 1627, where he had a distinguished career. Bishop Burnet wrote of him in later years that he had the greatest command of the purest Latin that ever he knew in any man and that he was a master both in Greek and Hebrew and in the whole compass of theological learning. He was noted for his quickness of parts and charming vivacity of thought and expression. Burnet writes that even in his early days he was counted as a saint and he came to be possessed with the highest and noblest sense of divine things that he had ever seen in any man.

During his term of college life at Edinburgh, it is interesting to recall that the saintly, serious-minded Leighton got into trouble through writing a poem " Lampooning the Lord Provost " who was *ex officio* Rector of the University, for which offence he was excluded from the University for some little time, he being reponed on the return to Edinburgh of Sir James Stewart, his guardian.

Leighton having completed his degree of Master of Arts in July, 1631, his thesis being Logic and Natural Philosophy, went abroad and spent some years, principally in Douai, France. It had been his father's desire that he would enter the ministry of the Church of Scotland, but shortly before Leighton left the University his father had become a victim of the Star Chamber, and the King and Archbishop Laud were fighting for the extermination of Presbyterianism. In 1641, Leighton's father was released by the Long Parliament and his son in the same year returned to Scotland receiving licence as a preacher from the Presbytery of Edinburgh in July of that year. He was ordained a few months later to the parish of Newbattle about six miles from Edinburgh. In Newbattle Leighton found a seat of labour which must have been congenial to his spirit. There stood the ruins of an ancient Abbey amid scenery of great natural beauty. Two members of his Kirk Session were the Earl of Lothian and Sir John Murray, a member of Privy Council, while the poet Drummond of Hawthornden lived within a short distance.

The Records show that he took his share of the duties falling to the country clergymen both in his parish and at meetings of Presbytery, Synod and Assembly. Bishop Burnet states that he disliked the Covenant, but, notwithstanding, he signed it along with his parishioners in 1643. Many of Leighton's writings which have been preserved until the present date and which still influence the minds of serious men and the religious thought of Scotland, were written by Leighton during his early career as minister at Newbattle. Burnet tells us that there was a majesty and beauty about his preaching that left a lifelong impression upon him. His preaching was distinguished by such majesty of thought and language that a wandering eye was never seen and whole assemblies often melted in tears before him.

In 1652 Leighton was in London endeavouring to obtain liberty for those ministers who were in confinement in England and on his return at the end of the year he sought to be released from his charge. The Presbytery were averse to losing him, but they ultimately released him in order that he might accept the Principalship of Edinburgh University. While continuing a Presbyterian throughout this period Leighton probably lost sympathy with the Covenanters, disliking the severities shown to many worthy men and the bitter controversies of these days.

Leighton was highly qualified for holding the important position of head of the Edinburgh College. He revived the custom of addressing students once a week in Latin and these addresses are still extant and are regarded by some as the most interesting of his writings. He seems to have taken a great interest in the students and to have been an influence for good amongst them. He also endeavoured to further the interests of the University in other ways, and in 1658 he waited upon Cromwell with the view to obtaining an increased endowment for the University with successful results. He continued as Principal of the University for nine years until changes were brought about by the Restoration of Charles II to the throne when Leighton's connection with Dunblane commenced accompanied by his adopting Episcopacy.

How is this remarkable change to be accounted for in one of such sublime character and one who was the loving son of a father who had suffered such cruelty at the hands of the Bishops? It would appear that during his years at Newbattle his calm and gentle spirit had wearied with the continual controversies and with the intolerance of his co-presbyters. He had naturally a broadminded and tolerant spirit and his desire was to unite all the faithful in one Church, wide enough to embrace all types of religious people of a Protestant nature. He regarded theological disputing on points of ecclesiastical difference as of less importance than righteousness and personal religion. One has to keep in view that he had resided for considerable periods in England, France and other European countries and that he personally preferred more beauty of religious form than was to be found in Presbyterian worship in Scotland, although he considered such of less importance than humility of spirit. He had probably lost all hope of modifying the harshness of Presbyterianism and in accepting Episcopacy it was his desire that the latter system should be developed in a modified form which in course of time would gather into one national Church all elements of religious thought in Scotland.

Leighton's connection with Dunblane commences from the latter half of 1661 when Episcopacy was restored by Act of the Scottish Parliament and by public proclamation at the Market Cross of Edinburgh. Probably he would not have accepted a Bishopric had it not been for his brother, Sir Elisha Leighton, who had become a Roman Catholic and who had some influence at Court. Charles II might well see that in a man of Leighton's high character and reputation he was obtaining a valuable assistant for carrying out his schemes. In any event it is recorded that the King appointed Leighton Bishop " of his own proper motion." His brother seems also to have had considerable influence over him as it is said that he concealed from him his vicious tendencies and made a great show of piety while the Bishop was genuinely attached to all his relatives. It is said that Leighton could have obtained from the King a much more important Bishopric than the one he selected, possibly even the Primacy. He chose Dunblane no doubt partly from want of confidence in his own abilities, but principally because of its small emoluments, worldly position and riches making no appeal to him. Associated with the Bishopric of Dunblane was the Deanery of the Chapel Royal. Leighton's whole income from these posts has been estimated at about £200.

Leighton, with three other Bishops appointed at this time, was consecrated in Westminster Abbey after Leighton and Archbishop Sharp had been re-ordained. Following on their consecration a sumptuous feast was held and it was not long before Leighton's eyes were opened to the worldly selfishness of his colleagues and the officiousness of the nobles forming the Scottish Government.

The four Scottish Bishops left London in April, 1662. Leighton, learning that it was intended that they should be received with much ceremony and show in Edinburgh, left his companions at Morpeth and entered Edinburgh privately.

Leighton soon took over his duties in Dunblane. He sought to rule his diocese by gentle methods enforcing no oaths on the clergy which they objected to give, avoiding controversy, displacing no ministers from office and endeavouring to heal divisions. There was, after all, little change in the order of service or in the government of the Church following on the Restoration of Episcopacy in this diocese and, had the King and the Scottish Government followed the methods of Leighton, there would have been no rebellion and none of the hardships and cruelties of the Covenanting times.

Bishop Leighton first met the Synod of Dunblane on 15th September, 1662. His diocese included the Presbyteries of Dunblane and Auchterarder with a few additional parishes. Few ministers were absent from this first meeting at which the Bishop propounded certain proposals all of which were unanimously approved. Although Leighton was frequently absent on business connected with the Church, he devoted himself, so far as other duties permitted, to those of his diocese, visiting each parish annually and setting a living example to all by the humility and unselfishness of his life. He appears to have spent on his personal wants merely sufficient to provide the necessaries of life and the remainder of his income was given to the poor. While in his own case he had agreed to be re-ordained, he did not force re-ordination on any minister in his diocese. While he from time to time took part in the proceedings of the Presbytery and Kirk Session, he did not coerce them and, apart from his acting as perpetual Moderator of the Synod, there was little change in the government of the Church in his diocese. As a rule, the Presbyteries at this time appointed their own Moderator. By 1665 Bishop Leighton was expressing a very great desire to be relieved of his Bishopric. He was weary of disputings and considered that what was contended for was of far less importance than Christian meekness and charity which were set at nought. He proceeded to London in that year to interview the King, begging him to release him from his charge. He described the proceedings of the Government of Scotland as so violent that he could not concur in planting Christianity in such a manner while, so long as he retained his Bishopric, he felt he was in some way accessory to the violence. The King appears to have been influenced by what Leighton told him as he assured him that violent measures would be put an end to and Leighton returned home inspired with a new hope that conciliation would take the place of coercion. Unfortunately Leighton was doomed to disappointment and the promises he had received from the King came to nought. The reader cannot but wonder why Leighton retained his association with men of the type of Archbishop Sharp and with the persecutors of the Covenanters, but this sprang from the hope cherished by him that he might be able to modify violence and to reconcile the opposing parties. At last, in 1669, some milder measures were adopted and worthier men acquired an influence in Scottish affairs. Archbishop Burnet of Glasgow was removed and Bishop Leighton was put in charge of his see. For some time Leighton discharged his duties at Dunblane as well as acting as administrator of the See of Glasgow. He last attended the Synod of Dunblane on 10th October, 1672, although he seems to have accepted the Archbishopric of Glasgow in 1671. For some time previous he had resided partly in Dunblane and partly in Glasgow. He seems to have accepted only one-fifth of the emoluments of the Archbishopric. One cannot follow here Leighton's vain endeavours to secure moderation and conciliation in the west of Scotland. Soon we find him again anxious to be relieved of office in 1673. He tendered his resignation to the King who would not accept it, but agreed to give him liberty to retire after a further year. He returned to London in the following year and obtained his release. His last days were spent with his sister, Mrs. Lightmaker, and her son in retirement at Broadhurst Manor, Sussex. His death took place on 25th June, 1684, in the Bell Inn, Warwick Lane, London, to which he had gone, at an urgent request, to meet the Earl of Perth, Lord High Chancellor of Scotland, who wished to consult him. He was buried in the church of Horsted Keynes.

Among Leighton's principal associates in Dunblane were General Drummond, the first Viscount Strathallan, and Sir Colin Campbell, of Kilbryde, Lord Aberuchill, of whom an account is given elsewhere. For John Graham, the Commissary Clerk, the Bishop had the highest regard and he conferred on him the endowments of one of the Cathedral Altars of which he was patron. Later on the latter bestowed the income coming to him in this way upon the Leighton Library. About 1671, Leighton selected John Graham for appointment as Commissary of Lanark. From a letter addressed by the Bishop to the Duke of Lauderdale it would appear that he had been much importuned by candidates for this post and he had been offered large sums by them to secure appointment. In this letter Bishop Leighton refers to Graham as a man of approved honesty and ability, worthy of a better place than had been bestowed on him. John Graham will always be remembered in Dunblane as the donor of two silver communion cups, still in use in Dunblane Cathedral, which bear his crest and initials and the hallmark of 1695.

While Leighton's actions in Presbytery, Synod and higher courts of the realm are recorded and tell of the wonderful personal characteristics which distinguished him, particularly his love of peace and hatred of controversy, his unworldliness and humility, few traditions have been handed down connected with his life in Dunblane. He was much concerned with the hardships which the poor suffered, but his charity was dispensed in secret. The affairs of State took him frequently from Dunblane to Edinburgh, London and elsewhere, but when in his diocese he regularly visited all its parishes. He had, therefore, little leisure to bestow on his fellow-citizens, and what time he had was spent in contemplation and reading his beloved books. The town of Dunblane in Leighton's time was a city of little importance. The dwelling houses were old and mean, and the inhabitants, numbering a few over one thousand, were for the most part ignorant, uneducated, gossip-loving and drunken, if one judges by the records of the Kirk Session. Notwithstanding, Leighton seems to have loved this spot, the ancient ruin, the walk by the riverside and the beautiful mountainous scenery which surrounds it. In 1673 he made a bequest to the poor of the parish of Dunblane of £1,024 of Scots money and later on he bequeathed his library for the clergy of the diocese with £100 to provide a room in which to keep it.

It is not by any means clear where Leighton resided in Dunblane. Various suggestions have been made, but it would appear that he occupied at one time a small house, bounded on the north by the Greenyards and on the west by the Minnie Burn. Greenyards is the old name of the present Union Bank House. The Minnie Burn flows below the Co-operative buildings and the Dunblane Prison down the south side of the Millrow and across the Millrow into the River Allan. These directions indicate that Leighton lived on the brae from High Street to the Millrow. According to other accounts he lived to the south of the site of the Cathedral Manse, but an eighteenth century writer says he lived in Cross Street.

Some distinguished authors have thought that the path above the Grass Yard, known as the Bishop's Walk, received its name from its being a favourite walk of Leighton, but when one considers that the Grass Yard should be called the Bishop's Yard, and was the garden of the Bishop's Palace, that the old well there is known as the Bishop's Well, and that the close between the Cross and the Haining was known as the Bishop's Close, these names evidently refer to Bishops of earlier days. In any event there is not sufficient ground for holding that this pathway acquired its name from Leighton.

The ordinances of religion in Leighton's time were celebrated in the choir of the Cathedral and it must have been a dull and disfigured place. As already noted, about 10 years before Leighton came to Dunblane two galleries or " loafts " had been erected, one across the large east window, the other on the west division wall between choir and ruined nave. It was about this time that the passage from the Keir Aisle into the Lady Chapel was built up by order of the Kirk Session which passage was only rediscovered towards the end of last century. In Leighton's time churchgoers used movable chairs or stools. The pulpit then stood between two of the choir windows facing northwards, with the reader's desk in front within the railed place set apart for the Stool of Repentance and for people desiring baptism for their children. At the one side of the pulpit was the minister's seat and on the other the seat of the scholars. After the introduction of pews about this time, seat rents were charged by the Kirk Session, the income derived being used for the benefit of the poor. No steps seem to have been taken to beautify the place of worship and the minds of men were too much engrossed with the affairs of the State and the Church to conceive a scheme of rebuilding the waste places. All that was done to the old Cathedral was to mend the steeple roof and keep up the old walls where these were tottering.

Leighton was a lover of beauty and order in matters of worship and, had he lived in happier times, would perhaps have been the restorer of the Cathedral. In 1658, that is 3 years before the restoration of Episcopacy, the Rev. Thomas Lindsay became minister of the parish of Dunblane. He is said to have been a man of some energy and force of character. He gave up Presbyterianism when Episcopacy was re-introduced and was Dean of Dunblane during Leighton's stay there. His stipend was augmented through the kindness of Leighton, but it is recorded

that, when he died, he left more debts than goods.   While the Bishop entrusted the Dean with
the performance of certain duties while he was absent, one does not gather that there was any
close intimacy between them.   The Kirk Session records indicate that minister and elders were
a more active body before than after the Restoration.   The parish schoolmaster at the time was
David Wilson and the scholars were taught within the vestry which was cold, poorly lit and not
well supplied with school furnishings.   The Bailie of Dunblane then was Alexander Chisholm
and the Beadle William Simpson.

The Presbytery records of 1663 refer to a contest between the Ministers of Dunblane and
Callander regarding a yearly payment of 80 merks by John Buchanan of Arnprior to the Bishop.
The Ministers ultimately had to confess that neither had a right to the payment.   Bishop Leighton thereupon asked the Presbytery to dispose of the 80 merks and settle to whom this sum should
be paid, as also payments of a similar amount received for the two previous years.   In the
following year the Presbytery, not having disposed of the matter, Bishop Leighton suggested
that, as no decision would probably give satisfaction, the money should be expended for the
relief of the poor unless the Presbytery should think that either of the ministers had established
a good claim to the money.   The Presbytery, however, at its next meeting resolved to recommend
that the minister of Callander should receive the money in view of the smallness of his stipend
at which decision the Dean of Dunblane protested.   Leighton does not appear to have taken
any prominent part in the proceedings of the Presbytery although on frequent occasions he was
present.   He did not act as Moderator nor preside at these meetings.

While Leighton showed his unselfishness in the matter of stipend payable to him from
Arnprior, it may also be mentioned that he allowed the minister of Dunblane to draw 350 merks
annually from the rents of the Bishop.   His successor, Bishop Ramsay, however, claimed this
money and the minister of Dunblane was so much the poorer.

Any stories preserved of the Bishop are somewhat trivial.   The Reverend Dr. Blair tells
of the Bishop's manservant who was on terms of familiarity with him.   John left the Bishop in
his house one day when he went fishing in the Allan, locking in the Bishop by mistake.   When
he returned Leighton remarked to him that when next he went to fish he must be sure to lock
the door " past," that is past the hole so as to leave the door open.   Two anecdotes are related
in a book entitled *Scotland and Scotsmen*.   One refers to the ruse of his men, who in order to get
liquor stated to the Bishop that his horses would only drink at a burn two miles away where
there was an alehouse.   One day through the men's conduct a suit of clothes was ruined with
rain, and a friend, wondering that the Bishop said no angry word, he remarked " would you have
me lose my coat and my temper too."   The other story connected with Leighton has reference
to a young woman, widow of a minister in the diocese who told the Bishop as he walked in the
Haining that she had had a revelation the previous night.   On his enquiring what it was she
informed him that it was that the Bishop and she were to be married.   His reply was to the
effect that such a revelation was not a good one unless it was revealed to both the parties concerned.

It is disappointing that a man of such eminence as Bishop Leighton left so little impression
upon his Cathedral City.   Any traditional stories are trifling and perhaps not authentic, and one
cannot point to any work begun or carried out by him for the good of Dunblane during his
period of residence.   This may have been due to his nature, which was above petty and parochial
matters—it was the larger, higher issues that appealed to him—but nevertheless, he acquired a
love for the city of his see and ultimately he left provision for the poor of Dunblane and his
library for the use of the clergy.   A man who was so spiritual and so detached from worldly
affairs could not have been appreciated in the somewhat sordid conditions of Dunblane
at this time.   One wonders why it was that Bishop Leighton took no steps for the improvement of Dunblane Cathedral which at that time was internally a very unattractive building.   He
would have had the support of eminent men such as Lord Strathallan, Lord Aberuchill, John
Graham, the Commissary Clerk, and the principal lairds in the district, all of whom were at one
time or another members of the Kirk Session, but he may not have had the energy and physical
vigour to take this work in hand, and, after all, his mission in life was not the building up of waste
places, but the reconciliation of opposing religious factions.

CHAPTER XIV.

THE SYNOD OF DUNBLANE IN THE 17th CENTURY.

It was fortunate for the clergy and inhabitants of Dunblane and district that during the stirring times which followed the Restoration in 1660 there should have been a man at the head of ecclesiastical affairs so broad-minded and so free of prejudice and narrowness as Bishop Leighton was. So light was his rule and so liberal was his policy that he at no time came into conflict with any in his diocese who differed from him about ecclesiastical matters or methods of Church government. The Episcopalian regime followed on the Presbyterian in this district naturally and without conflict between the Bishop on the one hand and Kirk Sessions, Presbyteries and Synods on the other hand. These bodies continued to perform their functions in the diocese of Dunblane without serious change. The proceedings of the Synod are recorded in the register preserved in the Leightonian Library at Dunblane and published in 1877 by John Wilson, D.D., then Clerk of the Synod of Perth and Stirling. The Synod comprehended the parishes within the Presbyteries of Dunblane and Auchterarder with the addition of a few adjacent parishes. The members of the Synod were the parish ministers and there were no lay members.

Soon after Leighton's consecration at Westminster he convened the first meeting of his Synod for 15th September, 1662, or earlier than the date on which it had been fixed to meet, namely, the second Tuesday of October. At the first meeting the Bishop read and afterwards "propounded some few particulars which by the unanimous voice of the Synod were approved." The minute states that, as there was nothing further to do at this meeting, no clerk was nominated, but the Bishop left a written note of the particulars aforesaid which are duly recorded. In the Bishop's directions he advocated that all diligence be used for the repression of profaneness, the dealing with offenders and the advancing of piety. In his directions for worship he emphasized the reading of larger proportions of Scripture and that the Lord's Prayer, Doxology and Creed be frequently in use. He recommended the use of daily prayer in the churches and of private prayer in families, and that the younger people and ignorant be catechised. The Bishop concluded with an appeal to all ministers, to be lovers of peace, endeavouring to quench useless debates and contentions.

At the next Synod on 28th April, 1663, Mr. John Edmonstone, minister of Kilmadock, then Moderator of the Presbytery of Dunblane, was the preacher. The Bishop proposed that a Clerk be elected and, after a vote had been taken, the choice fell on Master David Wilson, reader and schoolmaster at Dunblane. It was then agreed that the meetings of Synod be held on the accustomed dates, namely, the second Tuesdays of April and October, which have continued to be the dates of meeting until the present day. Bishop Leighton declared at this meeting that each member of the Synod had as full and free liberty of voting in all things as they had in former times.

Thereafter during Leighton's tenure the custom was for the meetings of Synod to extend over two days. On the first day a meeting was held in the forenoon and was usually adjourned to meet again at 4 p.m. At the forenoon meeting it was customary to appoint a committee to transact certain business, and this committee met, as a rule, at 3 o'clock prior to the second session. On the second day the meeting met at an early hour which was not always recorded, but seems sometimes to have been at 8 a.m.

Bishop Leighton was a regular attender and indeed was remarkably seldom absent for one whose duties must have frequently taken him from home. When present he acted as Moderator, but, in the event of his being absent, his place was taken by Mr. Thomas Lindsay, Minister and Dean of Dunblane. When this occurred, the Synod appears to have held a short sitting and dispersed as speedily as possible.

From a perusal of these minutes one learns this of Leighton that he alone of the brethren made any permanent or deep impression, and that although he never sought to impose himself on the brethren. The elevating thoughts suggested and measures proposed seem all to have been his but, while the proceedings of the Synod were guided by his hand, one cannot detect that he at any time tightened the reins. His influence was characterised by deep earnestness and elevation of thought, and, while he advocated changes of a minor nature when he deemed such necessary, contentions were hateful to him as a lover of peace. Entire harmony appears to have prevailed among the whole members and between them and the Bishop, and one finds him commending them for their unity, and concord and good conversation, and exhorting them to continue therein. At the close of the Synod on 25th April, 1668, Bishop Leighton having, as on other occasions, commended the brethren for their unity and concord, and having exhorted them to be more and more exemplary in holiness, modesty and gravity, even, as the minute narrates, " in the externals of their hair and habit," urged them to greater abstraction from the world and to the duties of their high calling. This seems to suggest that the brethren were not altogether distinguished for tidiness in their persons and attire and that this had proved disturbing to one so unworldly and so much engaged in the contemplation of higher things as the good Bishop was. Some of the brethren appear to have been dilatory in the payment of what was due by them, and, although the Bishop himself despised worldly possessions, he appears to have had no sympathy with those who did not pay such sums as they were under obligation to give. Frequent references are found to the Clerk of Synod having not received his dues and the Bishop approved of his pursuing for the same. The Bursar, maintained by this Diocese at the University, had also difficulty in always recovering his Bursary and at times was in distress through failure to obtain payment.

There were certain matters in which Bishop Leighton was specially interested. He was most desirous, and properly so, that the Sacrament of the Lord's Supper should be more frequently dispensed, and one learns from the minutes that some years elapsed without any dispensation in the parish, while it was seldom observed more than once a year. Leighton frequently referred to the neglect of family worship and urged on the brethren to impress the desirability of this on their flocks, while the prevalence of swearing and profaneness is on numerous occasions adverted to by him. He also strongly urged that a reverent attitude be adopted at prayer whether by kneeling or by standing, but, while his remonstrances were well received by the brethren of the Synod, they seem to have produced little effect, else the Bishop would not have required to repeat them so frequently.

The Synod met for the second last time during Leighton's Bishopric on 11th April, 1671. On that occasion he was not present as he had gone to Glasgow, but, having been uncertain as to his return, he had left instructions with the Clerk that the Dean should preside in his absence and a letter was read to the meeting which is perhaps as characteristic of the man as anything he ever penned. It contains the following passage :—" Let prayer the converse of the soul with God, the breath of God and man returning to its original—frequent and fervent prayer the better half of our whole work and that which makes the other half lovely and effectual." Later in this letter the Bishop continued, " But you will possibly see that it is he himself that speaks these things to us. Alas I am ashamed to tell you, all I dare say is this, I think I see the beauty of holiness and I am enamoured with it, though I attain it not . . . . . . And I trust, dear brethren, you have the same desire and design and follow it both with more diligence and with better success."

Bishop Leighton met the Synod of Dunblane for the last time on 10th October, 1672, when the business appears to have been of a routine nature. The meeting terminated with his exhorting the brethren to love amity amongst themselves and be very careful amongst their flocks.

Bishop James Ramsay, the successor of Bishop Leighton, first presided over the Synod of Dunblane on 30th September, 1673. The work of the Synod was carried on under him with little change. Bishop Ramsay appears to have endeavoured to follow in the footsteps of his distinguished predecessor, but, although this is obvious, one feels that he failed to exercise the same authority over the brethren or to fill them with the same high inspiration. It is noteworthy that the Presbytery books were very often not produced for inspection and that the reasons given were seldom satisfactory, as, for example, that the books were not ready. With these exceptions, however, the work proceeded much as in Leighton's time and there was little want of harmony although a considerable time was taken up with the case of Mr. William Spens, minister of Glendevon, who was ultimately excommunicated for the views expressed by him. In the Bishop's address to the Synod he refers to prayer, paraphrasing Leighton's famous reference, and suggests that at least three brethren should meet together once a month to hold a prayer meeting amongst themselves. The Synod continued to meet forenoon and afternoon on their day of meeting and sometimes on the following morning about 9 a.m. The afternoon meeting tended to be held later in the day. In April, 1674, it was at 4.30, and in October, 1677, at 6 p.m.

Collections were frequently ordained for benevolent and public objects. Thus, it was ordained that a collection be taken to buy off slaves in the hands of the Turks, and in April, 1682, a deputation appeared from the Burgh of Dumbarton for a voluntary contribution towards the building of a stone bridge over the river of Leven. The Bishop and Synod found that the said work was not only pious and charitable, but very much conducive to the good of the Kingdom. The ministers were enjoined to recommend this from their pulpits and to canvass their principal parishioners, and the Bishop seriously recommended the brethren to attend to this vigorously.

In October, 1676, the Synod was troubled by Donald MacVicar, minister at Aberfoyle, who had not met with the brethren for some years, the supposed reason being that he was owing money and that his creditors had taken out caption against him. Robert Kirk, minister of Balquhidder, was ordered to go to Aberfoyle and obtain a list of the debts and see about a reasonable offer for satisfying the creditors, and, if the said Mr. Donald MacVicar did not make a reasonable offer and comply with what the Presbytery thought just, they were ordered to censure him. In April, 1677, ministers were ordered to reside within their parishes and attend diligently to their work and not be absent for more than four weeks in a year or above two weeks at any time without permission, otherwise they should be suspended. In October, 1678, the Synod ordered that a register of rents and revenues be compiled in each Presbytery giving exact information of glebes, size and condition of manse and true information of emoluments belonging to churches, schoolmasters and the poor.

There was still difficulty in getting the ministers to administer the Communion and in 1679 the brethren of the Presbytery of Dunblane reported that they had not celebrated this owing to trouble throughout the land during the year. In October, 1680, the Presbytery book of Dunblane was not produced as the clerk was taken up about some serious concernment when he should have made this book ready. There had been a dispute for some time about the right of burial in the south aisle of the nave at the west end which was claimed by an Alexander Whitehead and also by Sir Colin Campbell. Alexander Whitehead's relict in April, 1681, suggested that it should be divided between them. Sir Colin not being present, the Synod remitted to the Presbytery of Dunblane to deal with the matter at their next meeting. In October, 1681, most of the heritors and elders of Kinkell and Trinity Gask complained of offences and misdemeanours of their minister, Richard Duncan. It was agreed to deal with the case on the 26th October, but there is no record of what took place then. Duncan had been admitted prior to November, 1674. He was tried as an accessory to the murder of a child whose remains were found under the hearthstone of the manse and condemned to death by the Steward of Strathearn and executed in 1682. A reprieve was obtained in his favour and, while the bearer of it approached on horse back, the execution was hurried on so that the messenger arrived too late. In October, 1682, the Bishop enquired at the brethren if the 29th of May was well observed. It was reported that it was observed by some, but was deemed out of date by others. This day had been appointed by Parliament as a day of thanksgiving for the Restoration of Charles II, on 29th May, 1660.

Bishop Ramsay's last Synod was on 16th April, 1684. The Synod had to deal with two men from the parish of Kippen. One named William Harvie, who was charged with having said that if the Communion had been in winter when bread was scarcer, there would have been more then to take grey bread than would have come now to take wheat bread. The charge was proven by two famous witnesses. He was ordered to receive instruction in the mystery of the Sacrament and to pay £10 "which if he did not pay thankfully without stress of law he was ordained to pay £30 as also to sit in sack-cloth." The other Kippen man named John Henrie was charged with having asked "Will there be any pipes and tobacco at the Communion?" He failed to appear and was ordered to pay £20 thankfully, or, if not paid thankfully, £60 as well as "to satisfy in sack-cloth." Having disposed of these cases Bishop Ramsay bade the Synod farewell.

The next Synod on 14th October, 1684, was presided over by Robert Douglas, the new Bishop. The Bishop recommended the brethren to contribute to the inhabitants of Kelso who had suffered through a recent fire. In April, 1686, a similar request was made for the distressed people of Newburgh who had suffered great loss by fire.

Bishop Ramsay was at one time minister at Kirkintilloch and afterwards at Linlithgow.

In 1670, he was appointed to Hamilton and made Dean of Glasgow, and in 1673 Bishop of Dunblane.   He boldly advocated ecclesiastical reform and political moderation.   A friend of Leighton's, he gave him important assistance in his efforts to effect a union between Episcopalians and
Presbyterians.   He was also a friend of Bishop Burnet.   He took an active part in drawing up the
Glasgow Remonstrance against the Act of Supremacy, advocating the calling of a national Synod
and proposing the compilation of a Liturgy.   He gave offence to the Court party and stirred up
the resentment of Archbishop Sharp through whom a Royal letter was sent down commanding
that he be transferred to the Bishopric of the Isles.   Ramsay proceeded to London to protest,
and a controversy took place between him and Sharp.   The letters are recorded in Wodrow.
In 1676 Bishop Ramsay was restored to the See of Dunblane.   The Synod did not meet between
April, 1674, and October, 1676.   He was transferred to the See of Ross and was deprived at the
Revolution.   He died in Edinburgh on 22nd October, 1696—it is said in great poverty—and he
was interred in the Canongate Churchyard.

A letter was received by the Provost at Dunblane addressed to " The Lord Mayor of
Dumblane, Ireland," from J. S. Visser, Santpoort, a town in Holland a short distance outside
Amsterdam, dated 17th July, 1935, in which Mr. Visser mentioned that he had received from a
friend a red copper stamp bearing the following inscription :—*Sig : Iacob. Epis : Dum-
blanen : ac Decan : Sacel Reg.*   The stamp was found in the soil in the neighbourhood of a
small village, Nieuwe Niedorp, situated between the towns of Den Helder and Alkmaar, near a
very old smithy.   Beside the smithy, there was of old a sluice, where passengers paid their fee
to the smith who was in charge of the sluice.   The inscription bears that the seal was that of
James, Bishop of Dunblane and Dean of the Chapel Royal.   On the seal is depicted a coat of
arms showing a shield bearing an eagle surrounded by two serpents, whose heads touch above
and whose tails touch below.   Above the shield is a bishop's mitre with five pearls on the band
below and on each side of the mitre a ribbon with fringes hung half-way down the shield.

The arms were those of Bishop James Ramsay who was the only Bishop of Dunblane of the
name of James, who was also Dean of the Chapel Royal.

On 22nd August, 1935, Colonel Archibald Stirling of Garden called on Mr. Visser, but he
was unfortunately from home.   The latter afterwards sent him a wax impression of the seal,
which is retained among the antiquities of Dunblane Cathedral.   It has not been discovered
how the seal came to be in the place where it was found.   Scottish clergymen no doubt frequently travelled or sojourned in Amsterdam and elsewhere in Holland, and it has been conjectured that the Bishop may have dropped the seal when taking money from his purse to pay the
smith.

Bishop Douglas was related to the House of Angus.   He studied at Aberdeen and was
licensed about 1650.   His cousin, the Duke of Hamilton, made him Parson of Hamilton and
Dean of Glasgow.   He was elected Bishop of Brechin, consecrated 1682, and transferred to
Dunblane, 1684. He sat in the Convention of Estates in March, 1689, and was deprived in April,
1689.   He retired to Dundee with a considerable pension, where he died in 1716 in his 92nd
year " full of piety as of years."

A strange figure in the Presbytery of Dunblane was Robert Kirk, minister of Balquhidder
from 1664 to 1685, when he was transferred to Aberfoyle.   His father was his predecessor in
Balquhidder and their whole goods, house, etc., had been destroyed by the rebels and they had
spent their whole patrimony in legal proceedings against the barbarous Highlanders and in
educating seven sons.   Kirk graduated in Dundee in 1661, and afterwards studied theology at
St. Andrews.   He was the author of the first Gaelic Psalter and superintended the edition of an
" Irish " Bible for the use of the Highlands.   He wrote a curious work entitled *The Secret
Commonwealth*—a book about elves, fauns, fairies and the like as described by those who have
the " second sight."   He died in 1692, dropping down in a fit at a mound known as
" Fairy Knowe."   Some believe that he had been carried off by the fairies and a report went
abroad that he had appeared to a near relative informing him that he was a captive in
Fairyland.

In the 17th century Scotland suffered much from pestilence and Civil War.   At the Synod
of Dunning in November, 1647, James Pearson was the only member of the Presbytery
of Dunblane present and no member was present from Stirling.   Superstitious practices were
very common, such as witchcraft and supernatural cures.   The Synod were also concerned

regarding monuments of idolatry and in particular with regard to the cross standing in the church-yard of Dunblane which was ordered to be demolished.

The Deans of Dunblane at this time were Thomas Lindsay and Gaspar Kellie. Lindsay was the son of a minister at Walston and was appointed helper and successor to James Pearson in 1653. He was appointed Dean of Dunblane after Episcopacy was restored. He seems to have been in poor health and in pecuniary difficulties before his death in 1673. His son, Thomas, was Synod Bursar in 1668.

Gaspar Kellie took his degree at Edinburgh in 1664 and was appointed Dean of Dunblane about 1674. He was deprived at the Revolution for not praying for William and Mary. He opened a meeting house in Edinburgh near the Fountain Well and preached there till 1717, when he was prohibited by the authorities.

CHAPTER XV.

THE BUILDING OF THE BIBLIOTHECA LEIGHTONIANA.

THE most interesting building in Dunblane, apart from its Cathedral, is the house in which the library of Bishop Leighton is preserved—a plain erection standing almost within the confines of the parish Manse. The building consists of one long apartment entered from an outside stone stair beneath which are two cellars or vaults for a long time used as a plasterer's store, and latterly as a painter's. The Library itself is lit by two windows to the west and south and is a wood-lined apartment with bookcases round its walls, 16 in number, and low presses for books in the centre of the room, and it is furnished with a plain square table and a dozen chairs. The Library building was erected within a few years of Leighton's death which occurred on 25th June, 1684.

Bishop Leighton's Will, written by his own hand at Broadhurst, Sussex, on 17th February, 1683, provided that, when the day came which he so much wished for, when he should be set free of his prison of clay, his money and goods were to be devoted to charitable uses. He provided for only one legacy, namely this :—" My books I leave and bequeath to the Cathedrall of Dunblane in Scotland to remain there for the use of the Clergie of the diocese." Leighton then appoints his sister, Sapphira Lightmaker of Broadhurst, and her son, Edward Lightmaker, to be the executors of his Will. Mr. Edward Lightmaker immediately after his uncle's death, by a letter, dated 8th July, 1684, communicated this bequest to Robert Douglas, Bishop of Dunblane, explaining that it was Leighton's desire that he or his mother, soon after his death, acquaint Bishop Douglas of his desire to send his books to the Church at Dunblane to remain there for the use of the ministers and students. Mr. Lightmaker also informed Bishop Douglas that it was Bishop Leighton's desire that £100 should be provided from his estate for providing a room somewhere near the Church. Leighton had apparently suggested to his nephew that a room might be built out of some of the ruinous walls that were without the Cathedral or out of the ruins of the Bishop's Palace. He had suggested that the room should be well lit and handsomely furnished with presses, shelves, desks for reading at and chairs or stools to sit on. Mr. Lightmaker, not wishing to burden Bishop Douglas too much with the provision of the building and its furnishings, also communicated with Sir Hugh Patterson of Bannockburn, who had formerly looked after Leighton's business affairs, asking him to give his assistance. A long correspondence followed with reference to the arrangements for conveying the books from Broadhurst to London, thereafter to be taken by sea to Scotland, and for transmitting the £100 for the erection of the Library. Mr. Lightmaker " pitched upon a verie worthie gentleman," Master Edward Haberfield of Middle Temple, London, to assist him in the work, while the Bishop of Dunblane obtained the help of Sir Hugh Patterson and John Graham, the Commissary Clerk of Dunblane, an intimate friend of Leighton, both of whom were then resident in Edinburgh. £100 may not appear to be a large sum wherewith to erect a library, but Bishop Leighton's object was, no doubt, to acquire as simple a building as possible for the use to which it was to be put and not to serve as a memorial of the donor or as a means of perpetuating his memory. The object of the gift was to benefit the local clergy, not to advertise the learning and scholarship of the donor.

The Bishop of Dunblane having offered his best endeavours for carrying out Leighton's bequest, Mr. Haberfield, on 25th October, 1684, wrote Bishop Douglas that he had paid in the £100 for provision of the building to James Foules, Merchant Factor at London, who would pay the money to Sir Hugh Patterson in Edinburgh in November. Mr. Haberfield conveyed a request from Mr. Lightmaker that the Executors provide a room for a library and one for the keeper and that it be made larger than would hold the Bishop's Books in the hope that other donors would follow the worthy example of Leighton. The local representatives were asked not to stint themselves to the £100 and what more they spent would be met by the Executors. The latter explained that the books could not be sent before spring owing to the condition of the roads in Sussex, and the Bishop, Dean and Chapter of Dunblane were asked to authorise some person in England to receive the books from the Executors, a receipt to be given for the same. The Executors had a suitable instrument prepared which they required should be sealed with the Common Seal of the Chapter of Dunblane, but, while taking such cautionary measures, they also acted generously and undertook to defray the expenses of conveying the books to Scotland.

The preparation of a suitable instrument was entrusted to John Graham, who, besides being Commissary Clerk of Dunblane, was Clerk to the Chancellary Chamber at Edinburgh, and this was duly signed and sealed by the Bishop and Dean. In due course the books were despatched by ship from London and safely received at the port of Leith and were afterwards conveyed to Dunblane. After the £100 had been sent down from London, Sir Hugh Patterson went to Dunblane and gave his advice for the building of the Library, and he and John Graham did everything that lay in their way to forward the work, although being resident in Edinburgh and having public duties there, they were unable to supervise its progress. On delivery of the money Bishop Douglas sent Mr. Lightmaker a receipt explaining that the sum would not be sufficient to accomplish the work as they desired it, but that the moneys given would be frugally expended and an account submitted of the disbursements when the work was accomplished. Bishop Douglas then sought the help of Lieutenant-General Drummond (Lord Strathallan), commanding His Majesty's Forces in Scotland. His Lordship readily gave his assistance, having "a profound reverence to the memory of that most excellent person B. Leightoune," one of his great intimates, as also having a generous propensity to promote public good works. Bishop Douglas refers to Lord Strathallan as a man of many and great parts, a statesman, a soldier and a good patriot, the accomplishments of a gentleman being very eminently found in him. Bishop Douglas was fortunate in enlisting his help, as Lord Strathallan "did contrive the fabric and everything as it stands," and he and his tenants provided horses for the carriage of lime, stone, slates and timber. The building was devised by James Robison in the Park of Keir, his Lordship's Chamberlain, and Mr. Robison settled the contracts for the work, received the money sent by the Executors and expended faithfully and frugally at Bishop Douglas' oversight. Unfortunately, during the progress of erection, Lord Strathallan died.

A parcel of ground having been bought for the foundation of the house, the work was proceeded with, but owing to troubles and broils in the country it was for a time much foreslowed. On the completion of the work Bishop Douglas summoned Mr. Robison, the Master of Works, with the tradesmen, and had an account of all expenditure drawn up when it was found that the total cost of the building amounted to £162 2s. 6d. sterling. The Bishop having communicated the detailed account to Mr. Lightmaker and his mother, they at once forwarded the balance of £62 2s. 6d., but to that they added a further sum of £10 for distribution among Lord Strathallan's servants and a further £10 to Mr. Robison to be bestowed as he thought fit. Mr. Lightmaker's letter, dated 12th September, 1687, mentions that he had paid these sums to Mr. Haberfield to be forwarded to Mr. Foules. This letter refers to the stone which Lord Strathallan had desired should be provided, namely, a very rich stone of white marble, oval in shape, having upon it the Coat of Arms of Archbishop Leighton with the inscription engraven thereon "Bibliotheca Leightoniana" set on a pedestal of white marble cut in the form of a mort head with a gilded mitre placed on the top to be set up in the middle of the front wall or frontispiece of the house towards the street. In a letter, dated 24th May, 1687, Mr. Lightmaker refers to his intended gift of £200 for providing a salary for the Keeper of the Library and mentions that he proposes to send a bundle of manuscripts in Leighton's own writing which were in his study at the time of his death. A catalogue of Bishop Leighton's books in his own handwriting, with the exception of the last two pages containing a list of the books purchased shortly before his death and added by his nephew, was also sent to Dunblane. This catalogue was duly received and put under the care of the Librarian. Mr. Lightmaker apologises in this last letter for delay in writing as he had been suffering from great indisposition of body, rendering him wholly unfit for business. He also mentions that Bishop Leighton had ordered that any writings found by him in an outward room next to his bedchamber should be burned, and he asks Bishop Douglas to purchase for him copies of any of Leighton's writings which might be in print.

The manuscript sent down by Mr. Lightmaker contained a number of miscellaneous "observes, sentences and selected aphorisms" which the Bishop had been pleased to note for his own use in his writings, promiscuously written, some sentences in Latin, others in Greek

H

and some in French, there being of these three manuals in octavo and others stitched or loose. After the books had arrived at Leith they were conveyed by the Bishop to Dunblane and stored in a room of Lord Strathallan's lodgings or town house which stood opposite the Library where Dunblane Prison now stands. The trunks and chests were all found safe without detriment, the books having been extraordinarily well packed up with "great circumspection." Bishop Douglas narrates that "the books form a signal memorial of the piety and bounty of that famous, devout and religious donor in order to the advancement of piety and learning for the glory of God and advocation of the Church and to the never dying memory of that most religious and devout saint who now rests from his labours and his good work follows him."

On 25th July, 1688, Mr. Haberfield wrote on behalf of Mr. Lightmaker enquiring if the £200 sent for the provision of a salary for the Librarian had been invested. Bishop Douglas and some friends whom he had consulted were of opinion that the money might best be lent to the Magistrates of Stirling, and the Bishop accordingly proceeded to Stirling and arranged with the Magistrates to lend this money on a bond and on the Bishop's instructions James Robison paid over £200 to the Treasurer of the town of Stirling.

It may be of interest to note that the £200 given by Lightmaker to provide a salary for the Librarian and for the upkeep of the Library as well as the £100 bequeathed by Leighton for the poor of the Church of Dunblane were, according to an article written by the Rev. Dr. Robertson of St. Ninians, lent under bond to the town of Stirling at Lammas, 1688. It is recorded in the accounts of the Burgh that the money borrowed from the "Bibliothec" of Dunblane and from the poor of Dunblane was employed for repaying debts to Christian Harwell and John Harlaw, her husband, and the laird of Boquhan. The interest or rent, as it is called, was paid from time to time, but not punctually as appears in the Burgh accounts. Thus in August, 1695, James Robertson (Robison) of Park of Keir was paid rent on 2000 merks due to the poor in Dunblane for the two years to Whitsunday, 1694, and Mr. Robert Douglas, Keeper of the Library at Dunblane, received at this time one year's rent to Lammas, 1694.

Dr. Robertson stated that the Burgh accounts of Stirling for the years 1703 to 1709 are lost, but these loans appear to have been repaid before 1709. The money in turn was lent to the town of Edinburgh. The endowment of £200 is still intact in the hands of the Library Trustees, but one regrets to say that Leighton's gift for the poor cannot now be traced.

Bishop Douglas then called on Dr. Fall, Principal of the College of Glasgow, to inspect the Library and to advise as to how the house might be best ordered. Dr. Fall came to Dunblane and a meeting was held in the Library House on 9th August, 1688, at which were present Mr. Gaspar Kellie, Dean of Dunblane, Dr. Fall, John Graham and George Robertson, Writer in Dunblane. The meeting first reviewed the fabric and its contents and found everything well done and in good order, "three desks being provided for reading, 12 chairs of turkie lether, an iron chimney, thongs and shoufles." The desks and chairs, as also a table, are still extant. The meeting then considered as to the arrangements for the preservation of the books and as to the duties of the Librarian. It was arranged that he receive salary from Whitsunday, 1688, and that he have the house and the vaults under the Library, the Librarian to be a student of Divinity, a man of piety and fidelity, of good parts, sober and trusted. An oath was to be administered to him for the faithful discharge of his duties and the wording of which was approved by this meeting. It was also approved that he give caution for the proper discharge by him of his duties, that nothing should be lost by his neglect. It was further provided that the Librarian should not hold office for more than three or four years in order that other young men have the advantages of holding this office. No formal opening took place on the completion of the Library, but at this meeting Rules were drawn up for the working of the Library, one of which was that the Bibliothecarius or Librarian was to deliver an anniversary discourse in the month of April yearly at the close of the Synod. The Librarian was ordained to attend on week days from 10 to 12 and from 2 to 4 and to keep the Library neat and clean and the shelves free from dust, moths and cobwebs. On the motion of Dr. Fall it was agreed to appoint as Librarian Mr. John Littlejohn, son of the Rev. David Littlejohn, formerly minister of Blackford, whose death had taken place in 1683. John Littlejohn had been a Presbytery bursar and was licensed in 1686.

On 29th July, 1690, the Privy Council considering that the books of the late Bishop Leighton lying in the town of Dunblane, might, during the existing troubles of the kingdom, be either embezzled or destroyed, ordained a Bailie of Dunblane, James Robertson in Park of Keir, to transport the books in their boxes to the Castle of Stirling " to be keeped during the present troubles and, after the peace is settled, ordained the said books to be sent back to Dunblane, and they gave order to Captain John Erskine, Governor of the Castle of Stirling, to send a guard to convey and secure the books in their transport, to receive the books at Stirling conform to ane inventar, to subscribe the same, and to put the books in a secure place."

On 8th August, 1690, that is ten days later, the Privy Council again took precautions for the safety of the Library, remitting to Sir Colin Campbell and Sir John Lauder of Fountainhall to make certain enquiries and take certain steps. There is no trace in the Privy Council Records of any report from these judges.

Dr. Fall himself lost his appointment in Glasgow in 1690, but in the following year he was appointed Precentor of York and he received additional appointments some years later. Five letters written by him from York are preserved with the Leighton papers. Three of these, written in 1704, are addressed to Mr. Michael Potter, minister of Dunblane. In a letter, dated 24th April, 1704, Dr. Fall intimated that Mr. Lightmaker and his mother wished to add a further sum of £100 to the sum of £200 previously given by them and then invested with the town of Stirling. One half of the interest on this additional sum was to be given to the Library Keeper in augmentation of his salary and the interest of the other half was to be expended on the repair and maintenance of the fabric. Dr. Fall expressed a hope that the whole sum of £300 would be placed in the best and surest way and that no time should be lost as Mr. Lightmaker was in a very precarious state of health. A deed of donation by Mr. Lightmaker of this additional sum of £100 is preserved, his instructions being as indicated in Dr. Fall's letter. The £100 was sent down by bill and delivered to a son of Mr. Potter. The Lord Advocate was consulted as to how it would best be invested and he agreed to use his influence to get the town of Edinburgh to accept the money as their security was the best in the Kingdom. Letters follow from Mr. Potter, Jun., to his father from which it appears that the former had to solicit the help of the Lord Advocate as Mr. Pringle, Dr. Fall's friend in Edinburgh, had been too ill and Sir James Campbell of Aberuchill had declined to speak to the Lord Advocate " on account of some affairs betwixt them."

On 28th April, 1706, a report was sent to Dr. Fall stating that the Library and books had been inspected and found in very good condition and that necessary repairs to the fabric had been ordered, but that they had found that several of Bishop Leighton's works were not in the Library and they observed that the catalogue of the books had apparently been taken by Dr. Fall while volumes of the Bishop's manuscripts had been sent to Mr. Lightmaker for printing. In Dr. Fall's reply he mentions that the catalogue which he had taken from Dunblane for printing had been handed over by him to Mr. Lightmaker and that he assumed that Bishop Leighton's manuscripts were in the hands of Mr. Lightmaker's Executors, part of which had been transcribed for the press and others had been printed. Unfortunately the manuscript catalogue consisting of 18 pages, 16 written in Bishop Leighton's hand and two by the hand of Mr. Lightmaker, has never been traced, nor have the manuscripts sent to Mr. Lightmaker for printing.

The constitution of the Library was established by a formal deed of gift, dated 11th December, 1701, signed by Mrs. Lightmaker and her son. It narrates the original bequest by Leighton, the steps taken to give effect to his wishes, appoints Trustees and nominates Mr. Robert Douglas, Library Keeper. Mr. Douglas was a son of the last Bishop of Dunblane (Bishop Douglas), and had previously been minister of Bothwell Parish. He seems to have retired at the Revolution and taken up residence in Dunblane. He died in 1746, leaving to the Library his own books and 300 merks in money.

The investment of the £300 given by the Lightmakers was a source of frequent trouble to the Trustees. The towns of Stirling and Edinburgh were not desirous of retaining these sums and the Trustees had to accept repayment. Mr. Stirling of Keir had the first sum of £200 on loan for some time, but in 1747 he repaid it and it was afterwards lent to merchants in Edinburgh. Sir James Campbell of Aberuchill and Kilbryde borrowed it from the Trustees who found difficulty in obtaining payment of the interest and ultimately repayment of the capital. The Trustees of the Library were to consist of the Dean or Minister of Dunblane, the Laird of Cromlix (Successor to Lord Strathallan), the Laird of Kilbryde, two members of the Presbytery selected by the Synod, Sir Hugh Patterson of Bannockburn and his heirs, and Mr. John Graham, Commissary Clerk, and his heirs. The heir of John Graham was in

1740, his grandson, then Secretary to the Royal Bank of Scotland, but the direct successors of Graham and Patterson, if there be any, are not now known. The Lairds of Kilbryde and Cromlix, the minister of Dunblane and the two members appointed by the Synod, form the Trustees at the present time. The £200 lent to Edinburgh merchants continued in their hands till 1754, when it was lent to Sir William Stirling of Ardoch. The £100 was then still in the hands of the Laird of Kilbryde. In 1786, the £200 was lent to Mr. David Russell, probably son of Mr. Russell, Bailie of Dunblane, who entertained the Duke of Cumberland at Allanbank, his house in Dunblane, prior to Culloden. The £100 had been repaid by this date and lent to Mr. Stirling of Keir. Ultimately in 1817, the £100 had to be recovered from Keir to meet the expense of repairs on the Library. In 1818 an attempt was made to obtain a grant from the Exchequer to help the Library, but this and other like endeavours in later years proved abortive and the Library continued to suffer from insufficient funds to enable the Trustees to maintain the building and preserve the books in the best possible way until recent years during which valuable help has been given by the Society of Friends of Dunblane Cathedral.

For a long time in the 19th century little interest was taken in the Library, and, except on the mornings of Presbytery Meeting days when some of the ministers arriving in Dunblane at an early hour assembled there prior to their meeting, the building was seldom opened, fired or aired. In 1924 new oak doors were presented by Mrs. Stewart, Ault Wharry, who also paid the expense of some minor alterations, and in 1926 the Trustees were able, with Mrs. Stewart's help, to have the interior thoroughly cleaned and repainted, the windows repaired, the bookcases washed and the books dusted and their bindings treated with a preservative mixture. While little had been done in the way of preserving the contents of the Library, it was then found that, apart from dust which had gathered during many years, the books were in a better condition of preservation than could have been expected and were probably in a better state than many books of like age in the large city Libraries maintained by public funds.

A few particulars with regard to the contents of the Library may be of interest. Bishop Leighton's gift consisted of nearly 1400 volumes of which it is stated that over 1200 are still on its shelves. 1363 original volumes were at first arranged in six presses along with which were sermons, treatises and other pamphlets stitched together and numbering 149. The latter were put up in six bundles, the last containing 11 catalogues and 13 pair of theses, but of the catalogues only 4 are now to be found and of the theses only 5. The surviving theses date from Leighton's student days. The collection is interesting as a whole as illustrative of what the Library of a scholar and theologian consisted of in earlier times. There are many examples of beautiful printing from continental presses, as from Paris and Amsterdam, while in the case of a number of the books there are beautiful bindings. Some bear inscriptions from the authors while others appear to have been purchased by Leighton second-hand. One of the chief points of interest consists of the notes in Bishop Leighton's hand-writing. These are written not only in Latin and Greek, but in several modern languages. It has been noted that no remarks are to be found on the writings of famous Puritan authors of which there is a considerable number of volumes. There is little doubt that the *Imitation of A' Kempis* was the favourite book of Leighton and he refers to it as one of the best books that ever was written next to the inspired writers. There are three copies to be found in the Library, one of which can be carried conveniently in the pocket and may have been the constant companion of the Bishop. Certainly it has been much used and many leaves have notes and jottings thereon. Various gifts have been made to the Library from time to time, one of which, that of Douglas, has already been referred to. The Library includes a large number of commentaries including twelve volumes by Calvin, twelve by Grotius and nine by Erasmus, many volumes of sermons and devotional works and volumes by writers contemporary with Leighton. Many books are written in Latin or Greek, but there are a few by Scottish authors dealing with Scottish subjects. The oldest book in the Library is said to be Herbert's *Expositio*, bearing date 1504. There are a few manuscripts still preserved in the Library, one being the account of its founding written by Bishop Douglas and Dean Kellie which was printed by the Bannatyne Club. Another most interesting manuscript is a satirical poem, entitled *Rob Steen's Dream*, dating apparently from about the time of the marriage of King James VI. The authorship of this poem, which exhibits considerable poetical merits, is unknown, and it is interesting to conjecture how it had found its way into the Leighton Library. Could it have been in Bishop Leighton's possession from his early days ? This poem was reprinted by the Maitland Club in 1836.

The successors of Robert Douglas as librarian included Mr. Coldstream, parish school-master, appointed 1746, and his son who succeeded him both as schoolmaster and librarian. Other holders of the office until recent years were also parish schoolmasters.

It has been recorded that Bishop Leighton, who was the patron of the rents and endowments of the Altar of St. Stephen, presented these to his friend, John Graham, Commissary Clerk, for life. The latter is said to have passed on the emoluments to the Library, but no further information has been obtained as to this gift.

While some of the books are valuable, much of the interest in the Library is personal to the founder. Leighton had the habit of writing notes and quotations on the margins of his volumes, and the Rev. William Blair, D.D., of the Leighton Church, Dunblane, counted 206 books on which some such markings are to be found. The Rev. W. West, who edited the chief edition of Leighton's works, and who spent a lifetime in the study of the Bishop, his writings and Library, designed to write his life, but died without accomplishing this. Mr. West had transcribed a list of these notes. Unfortunately his manuscripts seem now to be amissing.

While many of Leighton's books were the works of his favourite authors, there are many volumes by Puritan writers which seem to have been little handled, and it is thought that Bishop Leighton had not been in close sympathy with such writers. The presence of these and some other volumes in his Library may be accounted for by their having formed part of the Library of his father. Among some of the books which attracted the attention of Dr. Robertson of St. Ninians were the works of Justin Martyr, beautifully printed by R. Stephens, Paris, 1551, in the original binding, Walton's *Biblia Polyglotta* in six volumes, first edition, magnificently printed, and the works of St. Augustine printed by Plantin of Antwerp, 1577. The letterpress of Plantin's books is said to be remarkable for its accuracy as well as distinctness of type.

While the works in Latin, Greek, French, Italian and Spanish attest the scholarship of Leighton, the works of devotional writers such as De Sales and Thomas A'Kempis point to the spiritualmindedness of their owner and such indeed were his intimate friends.

It has been pointed out by Bishop Knox in his study of the life and times of Leighton that, while he lived in the Golden Age of English poetry, Shakespeare being still alive in his early youth and Milton, Ben Johnson and Dryden being contemporary with him, no volumes of these great poets are to be found. At one time the Library possessed the poems of George Herbert with notes in Leighton's writing, but this volume has disappeared and almost the only poetical works are those of the Greek dramatists and Latin poets. The works of Scottish theological writers of his day are also absent, and even the works of Bunyan are not to be found. The author most largely represented is said to be Jeremy Taylor, 14 volumes of whom are in the Library. Many volumes of the Cambridge platonists and of the mystics are on the book shelves.

A number of the books are interesting as having been owned by persons of some distinction. Thus, the Rev. W. J. Couper refers to a volume of Plutarch printed at Basle, 1542, which belonged in 1569 to the Duke of Norfolk, the suitor for the hand of Mary Queen of Scots. A Latin grammar published at Edinburgh in 1679 was the work of Patrick Dykes, sometime schoolmaster at Doune, and was recommended by the Synod of Dunblane. Several of the books were gifted to Leighton by their authors, one being from his dear friend, Scougal of Aberdeen, namely, *Life of God in the Soul of Man*. Dr. Couper is of opinion that the pocket edition of the *Imitation* was that published at Cologne in 1622.

The bindings in the Leighton Library were carefully examined in 1934 by Mr. J. B. Oldham, Librarian of Shrewsbury School. He found that one book (10 E 10) bore the arms of James VI of Scotland and may have come from his library, although not necessarily so ; that another book (9 G 2) came from the library of William Kerr, Earl of Lothian and friend of Leighton, when in his early days he was minister of Newbattle ; a third book (G F 5) bears the arms of Cambridge University, and another (10 C 17) the arms of the town of Goss in Zealand. 10 D 9 was a prize awarded at Leyden School.

The Library includes an Order of Prayer according to the use of Spanish synagogues.

(The best account of the contents of the Leighton Library is the paper entitled *Bibliotheca Leightoniana Dunblane,* by the Rev. W. J. Couper, M.A., D.D., printed in the proceedings of the Society of the Friends of Dunblane Cathedral, 1932).

CHAPTER XVI

THE LANDS OF CROMLIX IN THE 16th AND 17th CENTURIES.

FOR the greater part of the 16th and 17th centuries, the lands of Cromlix in the parish of Dunblane were the property of successive members of the family of Chisholm. The greater portion of these lands, including Cromlix itself and the Auchinlays, belonged to the Bishopric up to the 16th century. The last three Bishops prior to the Reformation were, of course, members of the Chisholm family.

In 1669 Cromlix was acquired from the last Chisholm Laird by Lieutenant-General William Drummond, afterwards the first Viscount Strathallan, and these lands passed in succession to the second Lord Strathallan, to Robert Drummond, Archbishop of York, to Robert Auriol Drummond, to the Earl of Kinnoull, and in the latter part of the 19th century to Captain Arthur Drummond, R.N. For some of these lands payments were due by the Laird of Cromlix to the Bishop and he had also to supply certain goods. Thus for Easter Buttergask it fell to the proprietor of Cromlix to supply 220 loads of peats and twenty-six poultry, from the lands of Barbush—formerly Barbuss—twelve poultry and two loads of peats, and from Bridgend and Ramuile (Ramoyle) twenty-four capons, twenty-four poultry and one swine, together with " arriages and carriages, used and wont."

The following lands were embraced in the estate of Cromlix :—

(1) The twelve merk lands of Bridgend with the pendicle thereof called Smith Land and the Corn Mill of Dunblane with mill-lands, multures, sequels and knaveship.

(2) The three merk lands of Ramoyle with the land known as Howmiln—the old form of the name Holmehill.

(3) The five merk land of Easter Corscaplie.

(4) The Bishop's Meadow of old pertaining to Easter Corscaplie and adjoining thereto.

(5) Over and Nether Auchinlays with the corn mill and waulk mill thereof.

(6) Over Cromlix, Middle Cromlix or Waterside and Nether Cromlix or Hutcheson Farm.

(7) Barbuss and Lichell, that is Barbush and Laighhills.

(8) The tenement or lodging with the yard commonly called the Nether Lodging lying to the East of the public way and to the north of the Chancellor's or Dunblane Manse, and south of the Monyburn with the tenement which belonged to John Lamb also to the north of the Nether Lodging.

(9) The tenement with yard, stable and pertinents called Greenyeards (Greenyards) in the city of Dunblane to the west of the public way to the south and east of the Bishop's Manse and yard and to the north of the tenement and yard which sometime belonged to the Altar of Saint Michael.

(10) The tenement with yard and pertinents which sometime belonged to Robert Morrison.

(11) The aisle built and repaired by William, Bishop of Dunblane, called the "Isle of St. Blasines," at the North West part of the Kirk of Dunblane along with the patronage of the Chaplainry in the Kirk of the Altar of the Most Precious Cross called "the Chapel of St. Blasines" with power to nominate chaplains to the Chaplainry.

(12) The acres of land called Glenwhonie and the piece of land between orchard dyke of the over place and the Lichell Burn, two acres of land called the Black Croft lying at the back of Corscaplie's Yard and sometime belonging to Henry Kinross, Sheriff Clerk of Perth, an acre of land called Bogside acre sometime belonging to Henry Sinclair and half of Mercer's Croft, all on the north side of the town of Dunblane.

(13) The lands of Drummyon, which formerly had belonged to the said Henry Sinclair.

(14) The heritable office of Justiciary and Bailliary of the Lordship and Regality of Dunblane and all other lands and heritages belonging to the said Bishopric.

(15) The tolls and customs of yearly fairs and weekly markets.

(16) The sum of £40 usual money of Scotland as formerly paid by the Bishop of Dunblane to the Bailies of the said Lordship.

(17) The lands of Wester Cambushinnie.

(18) The lands of Easter Cullyngs with the mill thereof.

(19) The Lands of Wester Cullyngs.

(20) The house and orchard on the east side of Dunblane called Corscaplie's Lodging which at one time belonged to John Drummond of Corscaplie, afterwards to the Earl of Perth, and thereafter to Lord Strathallan.

(21) The Altar of St. Nicholas and the Aisle commonly called Drummond's Aisle, disponed by the Earl of Perth with the consent of George Drummond of Blair Drummond, the Chaplain of the said Chapel, to the Viscount of Strathallan.

The Smith Land referred to in Bridgend was apparently land which belonged to a blacksmith as this is referred to in very early documents. The corn mill of Dunblane existed at least from the 15th century, but probably considerably earlier. The lands of Ramoyle extended much more widely than the present part of Dunblane now known as Ramoyle. It included part of Holmehill, the old property of Backcroft and other lands extending to Whitecross. It is interesting to note the old spelling of Barbush and Laighhill, which corresponds exactly to the local pronunciation of these words by natives of Dunblane. Greenyards is the property now owned by the Union Bank of Scotland. The Blackcroft was the land afterwards known as Backcroft—in some old Titles there is reference to the Muir of Ramoyle. Backcroft lay between the Ramoyle and the Perth Road, south of Anchorfield.

The Bishop's Meadow lay on the west side of the River Allan across the river from the Bishop's Orchard extending westwards where Springbank Mills now stand. The Nether Lodging was afterwards known as My Lord's House or Strathallan's Lodging and occupied the site of Dunblane Prison. Corscaplie's Lodging probably stood where the house of the schoolmaster of Dunblane now stands, east of the Leighton Church.

The property of Cambushinnie, forming part of Cromlix, was acquired from William Muschet, a family which owned much land in the neighbourhood of Kinbuck, but more in the neighbourhood of Doune and Thornhill. Cullyngs was formerly in the barony of Kippenross, and half of Wester Feddals, formerly in the Barony of Feddals and the regality of Lindores, was also owned by the Cromlix family.

Another property at one time owned by the Chisholms for which a title was obtained in 1623, included houses and yards in Dunblane bounded by the Cathedral Kirkyard on the south, the manse and crofts of the Dean on the west, the lands of Glenwhonie on the north and the lands of Robert Henderson and the Manse of Monnie on the east. There seems to be no doubt that by the Dean's Manse is meant that of the Archdeacon who is called in other titles the Archdean. The Archdean's Manse is believed to have stood in Meeting House Loan between the site of the Leighton Church and McLaren's buildings, the land attached extending northwards.

In 1650 John Chisholm of Cromlix appears to have been in financial difficulties. He conveyed his estates to Sir James Drummond of Machany, David Drummond of Invermay and Harie Blackwood, indweller in Dunblane, for payment of his debts and for relief of obligations undertaken by them.

In 1665 Bishop Leighton confirmed their title to Chisholm's lands excluding Feddals, Cambushinnie and Cullyngs as well as the tenement called the Upper Lodging or Archdean's Manse. In the same year, Harie Blackwood conveyed his one-third share of these lands to Sir James Drummond and David Drummond. Ultimately in 1669 Sir John Chisholm of Cromlix with their consent conveyed the lands to Lieutenant-General Drummond, the Notary Public employed being John Graham. Lieutenant-General Drummond also acquired other lands belonging to Sir John Chisholm. In 1670, Robert Freebairn, Archdean of Dunblane, confirmed his title to the Upper Lodging or Archdean's Manse. In 1671, General Drummond acquired from John Sinclair of Glassingall part of the lands of Ramuile (Ramoyle) called Drummagon, which was probably in the neighbourhood of Ledcamerach or about the site of Dunblane Hydropathic. In 1673, he completed a title to the Croft at Ramoyle called Glenquhonie—Lichell Croft, the Howcroft and a Croft called White Croft's Aiker (which was possibly the land at Whitecross), and a waste piece of ground called Newyard.

The first Lord Strathallan also acquired the lands of Innerpeffray situated a few miles from Crieff near Highlandman railway station and on the left bank of the River Earn. These lands were originally given by King James IV to the first Lord Drummond, the builder of Drummond Castle. Lord Strathallan was nominated to this estate by Lord Madderty, the owner, under the reservation of a liferent to himself and his wife.   Half of the lands of Wester Cambushinnie were obtained in 1571 by James Chisholm and Jean Drummond his wife from William Muschet in exchange for Wester Spittalton of Cessintully.   The other half of Wester Cambushinnie had belonged to the family of Kinross of Kippenrait from the early 16th century, but was acquired by the Earl of Perth in 1624.

The lands of Cullyngs were acquired in 1495 by an Archibald Buchanan from a Malcolm Nicholson, and at that early date there was a mill at Cullyngs.   For some time it was the property of Kinross of Kippenross and was part of that Barony.   It was acquired by Sir James Chisholm in 1619.   Previous to that date, the Barony of Kippenross consisted of Kippenross, Kippenrait, Auchlochie, and Cullyngs, with corn and waulk mills and cruives, the owner in 1616 being James Kinross.

Easter Corscaplie excluding the Bishop's Meadow was originally feued by Bishop William Chisholm to Ramsay of Ochtertyre, in 1548, and Sir James Chisholm acquired the former in 1592.

The Bishop of Dunblane in 1579 feued to William Stirling, Rector of Aberfoyle, the great building commonly called the Lodge, girnells and stables, with the Bishop's Meadow for payment of 3s. 4d. for the houses and 10s. for the meadow.   In a Charter of Confirmation which followed thereupon, the property was described as "the Bishop's waste edifice or fore dwelling house measuring thirty elns south and north with a part of the Bishop's own Closs commonly called the outward Closs, and that piece of the Bishop's Yard or Orchard within the walls along with the green valley and the office of Bailliary and Justiciary and the Bishop's whole other lands." This applies to the remains of the Bishop's Palace, which so soon after the Reformation had become a ruin.

These subjects were afterwards acquired by Sir James Chisholm of Cromlix.   Bridgend and Ramoyle were obtained by the latter through a charter of Bishop William Chisholm in 1565.

As early as 1502 the owner of Cromlix had acquired the Archdean's house or Manse with the yard adjacent from James Chisholm, Archdean of Dunblane.   The Manse of Balquhidder was obtained by Thomas Drummond of Corscaplie in 1578 from the minister and prebend of Balquhidder and was then a waste piece of ground.   It lay between the ground of the parsonage of Aberfoyle on the south and the yard of the Treasurer of Dunblane on the north with Pitteocaleoch on the east.   John Drummond of Wester Corscaplie acquired the Manse of Aberfoyle which was between that of Balquhidder and Logie.   The Manse, therefore, of Abernethy and Arbroath, the Treasurer's Manse and the Manses of Balquhidder, Aberfoyle and Logie were all contiguous on the east side of Braeport and bounded on the east by Pitteocaleoch and the How Croft or Dean's Croft.   These properties were all conveyed by Drummond of Corscaplie to the Earl of Perth in 1662.

Roger or Rodgers Gordon, Dean of Dunblane, conveyed to another member of the Drummond family, Malcolm Drummond of Borland, the Dean's Croft, the Long Croft and the Dean's Yard.

In 1624, John Kinross, brother of the late Laird of Kippenross, conveyed to his nephew, Harry Kinross, Advocate, and Margaret Drummond, his wife, who was a daughter of Drummond of Corscaplie, the waste piece of land called the New Yard, How Croft, Glenwhonie, containing three acres, and Longcroft or Lidiale Croft.   Harry Kinross, who became Sheriff Clerk of Perth, and John Drummond of Corscaplie came under obligation for 2,000 merks on the marriage of their sister, Janet Drummond, who conferred this obligation on her daughter and this was ultimately acquired by Lieutenant-General Drummond about 1670.   The latter obtained a Decree of Adjudication in 1671 and thus acquired the above lands.   Bishop Leighton afterwards granted a Charter of Confirmation.

The right of Bailliary and the whole customs of Dunblane were acquired by Sir James Chisholm from King James VI in 1590, and the whole feu, rents and other property in Dunblane holden by him to the value of £114 Scots in the following year.

Archbishop Robert Drummond received from the Government £400 as compensation in respect of the abolition of heritable jurisdiction in 1746.

MAJOR-GENERAL SIR JOHN BURNETT STEWART'S CHARTERS.

A number of interesting Charters were presented by Sir John Burnett Stewart for preservation in the Record Office of the General Register House, some of which relate to Dunblane.

Number 28 is a precept of Clare Constat by Adam, Bishop of Dunblane, to Sir James Chisholm of Cromlix, Bailie of Dunblane, to infeft William Drummond of Rickartoune, as heir to his great-grandfather in the following properties (1) The barn of the deceased Donald Malloch lying to the east of the high road from the Market Cross to Holmehill bounded on the south by the tenement which belonged to the Altar of St. Nicholas and on the north by the Manse of Kippen.

(2) A tenement bounded by the lands of St. Nicholas on the north, that is on the opposite side of the lands of St. Nicholas from the previous property.

(3) The yards lying to the east of the last property bounded on the north by the croft of the Dean of Dunblane which was below Holmehill and behind the playground of Dunblane School.

(4) The tenement between the highway leading to " Montokmyre " on the east, the house of William Sinclair of Drumdoules on the south, the Monnie Burn on the West and Polcak on the north. This property stood somewhere about the site of Dunblane Institute or Balhaldie House. There is no information known as to the site or meaning of Polcak.

(5) A croft with the Monnie Burn on the east, Auchlochie on the south, the Doucot Croft on the west and St. Michael's Croft on the north.

(6) A croft situated on the west side of the Monnie Burn, but its situation is not elsewhere described. A precept of Clare Constat was granted by Bishop Leighton in 1671 for infefting Ninian Drummond of Wester Glassingall in these subjects.

Title Number 30 is an Instrument of Sasine by Harie Blackwood giving infeftment to William Robertson, Junior, Merchant in Dunblane, and Beatrix Drummond, sister of Duncan Drummond, Laird of Balhaldies, in " a tenement Little Yaird and Valley three elns in breadth at the back of said tenement called Greenyairds (that is the Union Bank House) bounded by the common Street on the East, the tenement of William Robertson, Senior, on the South, the orchard of the late Bishop on the West, and the outmost wall of the Bishop's principal Manor and dwelling house with the Little Yaird and tenement of Andrew Lamb on the North."

Number 31 is an Instrument of Sasine in favour of James Robertson of Park of Keir, in that acre of land called Bridgend of Dunblane known as " Jeonet Lambus Aicker " (that is Janet Lamb's Acre) that tenement called " The Smythie Hous " in the town of Bridgend and that " hospis or house with yards and part of Bank (presumably River Bank) adjacent, south of the Bridge."

Some of the properties referred to above were situated on the east side of Kirk Street or to the rear thereof, and the gateway in Kirk Street opposite the east end of the Cathedral no doubt derived its name from one of the Drummonds of Rickarton.

Number 36 consists of a Charter by Bishop Leighton to John Cramb, Commissary Clerk, Dunblane, of " the teind Sheaves of Glassingall, Wester Wodland, Schanrell (now Shanraw) and Cokpla (Cockply), said to be in the Parishes of Dunblane and Strogeith." Strogeith is generally understood to be the old name of Blackford, but the lands now known as Strageath are situated near the railway line between Muthill and Crieff railway stations. This charter is signed by the Bishop, Dean, Chancellor and Treasurer, as also by the Rectors of Comrie and Glendevon and the Prebends of Monzie, Kippen and Logie, and the Parson of Aberfoyle. Some charters also bear the signatures of the Archdeacon and the Subdeacon, but in Episcopal times these offices may not have been filled.

CHAPTER XVII.

LIEUTENANT-GENERAL WILLIAM DRUMMOND—
FIRST LORD STRATHALLAN.

ONE of the most distinguished names associated with the history of Dunblane is that of Lieutenant-General William Drummond, who resided in " My Lord's House," Dunblane, in the latter half of the 17th century. His residence stood where the prison of Dunblane was afterwards erected. He was an intimate friend of Bishop Leighton, took a warm interest in local matters and was a member of Dunblane Cathedral Kirk Session.

General Drummond was the second son of John Drummond, second Lord Madderty, and his wife, Helen Lesley, who was the oldest daughter of Patrick Lesley, Commendator of Lindores. He was the great-grandson of Lady Margaret Stuart, daughter of James IV and Margaret Drummond. He became a student of St. Leonard's College, St. Andrews, at an early age, where he showed great capacity exceeding that of his fellow students, but he was attracted to an active and adventurous life rather than to that of a student. He joined the army and saw service in Ireland under Sir Robert Monro in an expedition sent to put down the Irish Rebellion. He then had the rank of Captain and he early attracted the attention of his superior officers by the manner in which he performed his duties.

Returning some years later from Ireland he took part in the engagement at Stirling, where the forces of Argyll were defeated by the royal army under Sir George Monro. The royal forces, being at this time disbanded, he went south to London and was present at the beheading of King Charles I, an incident which made a deep impression upon him. He left next day for Holland to meet the Prince, and was the first to salute him as King. He commanded a brigade at the Battle of Worcester, where it is said he broke through three regiments of the enemy, but had eventually to retreat. General Drummond, after fighting most gallantly, was taken prisoner and removed to Windsor, but, escaping, he reached Paris, where Prince Charles was then residing. Returning to England he landed near Yarmouth, and proceeded northwards by Newcastle and Kelso to Edinburgh, disguised as a carrier driving an old horse with a load of cheese.

Finding that there was no hope at this time of bringing about the restoration of the Stuarts to the throne of Great Britain, General Drummond obtained leave to go to Muscovia, the Emperor of Russia and the Imperial Army being then before Riga. The Emperor of Russia appointed him a Colonel and soon after Lieutenant-General. He performed his duties with great distinction and on one notable occasion he saved the Russian army from destruction by the Poles.

After the restoration of the Stuarts to the throne in 1660, he was recalled to Britain by Charles II. He acted as Major-General from 1666 and was present, with a troop of horsemen raised by him, at Rullion Green where the Covenanters were defeated. He was made a member of the Privy Council in the following year.

In 1669 an Act of Parliament was passed in favour of Lieutenant-General Drummond who was Heritable " Baylie " of Dunblane, authorising him to hold a fair and market at Dunblane. The Act states that " the Regall town of Dunblane has been for time passed memory in the habit of keeping yearly, three fairs, to wit, Whitsunday, Lawrence day and Hallowday." General Drummond was authorised to hold a fourth fair " to be kept on the 1st day of March yearly called St. Monance day, with a weekly market to be holden weekly upon Thursday within the said town of Dunblane in all time coming for buying and selling of horse, nolt, sheep, fish, flesh, meal, malt and all sort of grains."

In 1671 he let the custom of the three markets or fairs to James Crichton, Vintner, Dunblane.

He was appointed by the Council in 1673 to report on the condition of the highways in Perthshire. He was termed " Overseer of Highways " and later Sir George Kinnaird was appointed to act with him, but at a later date the Lord Privy Seal was nominated in his place.

He was active in organising militia forces in Perthshire and he represented the county in Parliament from 1669 to 1674 and from 1681 to 1682 and was also in the only Parliament of James II in 1685. General Drummond was a member of the Convention of Estates summoned by Lauderdale in June, 1678.

In August, 1674, he was deprived of his command of Major-General of the forces in Scotland, and in the following month was ordered to report himself a prisoner in Dumbarton Castle. No explanation has been given of this. He was a man of high principle who did not seek personal advantage and his devotion to the royal family was undoubted. He had served the Stuarts with extraordinary devotion and had constantly risked all on their behalf. The Royal Warrant gives no ground for his arrest, nor does the Minute of the Privy Council give any reason for this step being taken when they directed the Lord Lyon to put the order into execution. Wodrow states that he had held converse with intercommuned persons and Burnet that he had been in touch with fugitives in Holland. The following is Bishop Burnet's account of the incident :—

" A certain Carstairs in 1674 was seized on a paper of instructions from the Prince of Orange being found in his possession. He had been sent over from Holland to England. The Prince (of Orange) said when asked about it that it was only meant for a direction for carrying on the levees of some regiments that the King had allowed the Dutch to make in Scotland which the King did the better to excuse his letting so many continue in the French service. Howsoever mention being made of money to be paid and of men to be raised and a complement being ordered to be made to Duke Hamilton, this looked suspicious. Duke Lauderdale made use of it to heighten the King's ill opinion of the party against him. And, because Lieutenant-General Drummond was of all the military men he that had the best capacity and the greatest reputation, he moved that he might be secured. The method that he took in doing it showed that he neither suspected him, nor regarded the law. The ancient method was to require men to render themselves prisoners by such a day. This was a snare to many, who, tho' innocent, yet hating restraint went out of the way, and were proceeded in an outlawry ; but an Act of Parliament had been made condemning that method for the future. Yet Duke Lauderdale resolved to follow it. And Drummond knowing his innocence rendered himself as required and was kept a year in a very cold and inconvenient prison at Dumbarton on the top of a high rock. This, coming after a whole life of loyalty and zeal, was thought a very extraordinary reward to such high pretensions."

In the following year, 1675, General Drummond on account of ill-health applied for liberty to take exercise without the prison and the petition was communicated through the Duke of Lauderdale to the King, who allowed the Captain of the Castle to permit him to take exercise in the fields for one month on condition that the General give security that he return to the Castle nightly. In March, 1675, this was continued for another month. He was released from Dumbarton Castle by Royal Warrant in February, 1676. During the period of his confinement he retained the command of the Perthshire Troop. It was the custom at this time for the Militia to meet annually for training at Auchterarder about the end of June. Soon after his release he was restored to his command as Major-General.

In 1678 he accompanied the Duke of Hamilton and others to London to plead against the severities practised by the Privy Council on the Covenanters at a time when all heritors were forbidden to leave Scotland without royal permission. Probably it was his objection to such harsh treatment that had led to his confinement at Dumbarton. He was present at the Battle of Bothwell Brig in 1679 with Monmouth's army, when he was second in command, but his chief expedition against the Covenanters was during the years 1682 to 1685. He worked energetically for securing peace in the Highlands.

In 1682 he was appointed Major-General of the Ordnance and proceeded to replace old artillery with cannon of the latest pattern. The nobles, however, who were in charge of the national strongholds, objected to this, and he was prohibited from interfering with their charges. In 1685, General Dalziel, with whom he had been much associated throughout his life both at home and in Russia, died and General Drummond succeeded him as Lieutenant-General of the Forces in Scotland with an annual salary of £800 and an allowance of £100 for a secretary and a like sum for procuring intelligence.

In 1686 he was summoned to London by King James II to confer on religious toleration. He declined to agree to the proposal of the King to give full liberty of conscience to the Roman

Catholics while prosecutions of the Covenanters continued, which attitude he continued to maintain. He did not lose favour at Court in consequence.

General Drummond was knighted at a date between 1678 and 1681, and on 6th September, 1686, he was created Baron Drummond of Cromlix and Viscount Strathallan. In 1684 he succeeded his brother David as Baron Madderty.

In 1687 he was appointed Governor and Keeper of the Castle at Inveraray and thereafter he took a lease of the parks at Inveraray. In the following year he was repaid £600 which he had expended on fortifications there.

After a lingering illness he died on 23rd March, 1688, at the age of 70 and was buried at Innerpeffray on 4th April, 1688. His wife, Elspeth, who was the daughter of Sir Archibald Johnston of Warriston, and the widow of Thomas Hepburn of Humbie, predeceased him in 1679. He left a son, William, second Lord Strathallan, who also left an only son, William, third Lord Strathallan. The former died in 1702 and the latter in 1711. William Drummond, the fourth Lord Strathallan, was a cousin of the last-named.

The fourth Viscount took part in the '45, and was killed at the Battle of Culloden. The first Lord Strathallan also left a daughter, Elspeth, who married the sixth Earl of Kinnoull.

Before his death Lord Strathallan made all arrangements for the disposal of his affairs, gave presents to the servants and thereafter asked that he be no longer troubled with business affairs.

He was a man of distinguished appearance, and, although he had led an active life and had had a long military career, he was said to have acquired great learning and to have been able to discourse on all subjects, moral, political, historical and theological. His manner is said to have been meek, calm, affable and courteous and he was beloved by everybody. He is said to have been a prudent and courteous advisor and to have been of easy access to all men. If he broke into anger it was to reprove what was base, mean or vicious. A sense of religion pervaded his life and he was a devoted Christian. He was filled with charity to his neighbours. Cameron of Lochiel in his MSS. memoirs described him as " an honest man, a faithful and sincere friend and an incorruptible patriot."

Bishop Douglas of Dunblane wrote of Lord Strathallan on his death as a man eminently accomplished as a soldier, a statesman, a scholar and a good patriot who at his death witnessed his piety by giving 4,000 merks to the poor of the parish of Dunblane.

Lord Strathallan acquired the estate of Cromlix in 1669 and from time to time thereafter he added to the property by the purchase of additional lands and houses in Dunblane and neighbourhood.

Lord Strathallan's mother was a daughter of Sir James Chisholm of Cromlix and a sister of two of the Chisholm Bishops of Dunblane.

Much of the information contained in this chapter with regard to Lord Strathallan's career and his personal attributes and character was obtained from the sermon preached at his funeral at Innerpeffray by Dr. A. L. Monro, Principal of the College of Edinburgh. The sermon was printed for Joseph Hindmarsh at the Golden Ball over against the Royal Exchange, Cornhill, 1693.

As is narrated elsewhere, he took a keen interest in the erection of the Leightonian Library and gave great assistance in making arrangements for the housing of Bishop Leighton's books.

The smaller of the old Cathedral bells was founded by General Drummond, Lord Strathallan, in 1687 and refounded at the expense of the Kirk Session in 1723, the work being done by Robert Maxwell, Edinburgh.

CHAPTER XVIII.

HARIE BLACKWOOD.

A COMPLEX CHARACTER.

THE name of Harie Blackwood is to be found frequently in old papers connected with Dunblane about the middle of the seventeenth century. He was a Bailie of Dunblane and a Notary Public residing at The Cross where the Burgh Chambers now stand. He was related to the Chisholms of Cromlix.

He was one of the leading elders of Kirk Session in 1652 and was appointed along with George Henrie, a commissioner to the Presbytery of Perth anent the transportation of Mr. Robert Young. They obtained a precept for summoning the parishioners of Dunbarnie to hear the reasons of transportation. After sundry procedure Blackwood and fellow commissioners reported that on account of the delay and partiality of the Presbytery, they had been forced to appeal to next Assembly. It appears from the Kirk Session Minutes that Mr. Young, so much sought after by the Kirk Session, objected to the call formerly given that it was of old date. The Session ratified the call and of new invited him to the ministry of Dunblane. Harie Blackwood seems to have taken a prominent part in these proceedings.

He was frequently engaged in litigation, sometimes as pursuer and sometimes as defender. He took proceedings in 1690 on behalf of Bruce of Bordie, Commissary of Dunblane, against the feuars and others who paid duties to the Trinity Altar in Dunblane Cathedral, of which he had the liferent. No list of feuars or properties is given.

On 1st January, 1693, Harie Blackwood, as Notary Public, proceeded to the house of George Robertson, writer in Dunblane, accompanied by representatives of the Presbytery of Stirling and Dunblane and of the Kirk Session of Dunblane and required him to hand over to two members of the Session, the Session books, the writs of the various mortifications, the poor box and the bonds of money for the poor and the silver cups and other utensils of the Kirk of Dunblane. The said George confessed—" The having of the maist pairt these utencils except ye Session buik qlk he could not command." He excused himself from delivering the mortcloths and the two silver cups without acquainting Lord Strathallan and John Graham, the donors. The said George eventually transferred the Session Books, silver cups and other utensils to the Kirk Session.

In 1699 James Lucas, a servant of John Drummond of Cromlix, assigned to Sir Colin Campbell of Kilbryde, Lord Aberuchill, a decree in his favour against Harie Blackwood. A precept of poinding by John Drummond against Harie Blackwood followed on a decree obtained before Alexander Chisholm, Depute Bailie, at the instance of James Lucas, decerning Harie "to pay the soum of threttie two pund, sex shillings and eightpence Scots money" with interest.

Harie himself had difficulties in recovering money due to him. Thus he obtained a decree for a hundred merks against Jean Wright in Dunblane in 1677. As she failed to implement the decree she was put to the horn and denounced rebel and this was followed by the forfeiture of her moveables and those of her husband, Thomas Gillespie.

On another occasion, a decree of apprising was granted against Harie Blackwood, indweller in Dunblane, and Walter Graham, fiar of Boquhapple. Such proceedings were intimated in Dunblane at the Cathedral or within the kirk-yard, similar intimations regarding properties in Menteith being intimated within the Knowe of Doune near the Castle of Doune. This particular apprising affected the following properties in Dunblane of Harie Blackwood, namely, the Dovecot-croft and Dovecot and pertinents within the city of Dunblane, a lodging and tenement on the east side of the Cross a little beneath the Mercat Cross, as also certain properties on the west side of the street from the Cross to the Bridge between the High Street and Millrow, as also a property in the Millrow bounded by the water of Allan, some other properties of no interest and finally a piece of ground in the village of Bridgend opposite the Shieling Hill as also the lands of Greenyards, Shandraw, Duthieston, Bithergask, Lessengallie, Cockplae and others in the Parish of Dunblane. These proceedings show that Harie Blackwood owned a considerable amount of property in Dunblane and in its neighbourhood.

In 1667 poor man Duncan Ure, indweller in Dunblane, obtained a decree against Black-wood in the Court of Session by which he was ordained to restore and deliver to the complainer " ane brewing cauldron spullzied and violently away taken from the complainer upon the twelfth day of February, 1664, in as good condition as the same was at the time of the said spullziane or the soume of three score punds scots, as the price thereof, and also to refound to the complainer the soum of ten shillings Scots money as the proffitts of the said cauldron, qlk he must have made thereby from ilk weik since the wrongus spullziane of the said cauldron."

In 1657 Harie Blackwood had a litigation with a neighbour, John Lamb, whom he accused of having erected a building to his prejudice beyond the boundaries of his (John Lamb's) property.

Harie Blackwood was also in difficulties in the year 1667, when proceedings in the form of horning and poinding were directed against him as principal and John Chisholm of Cromlix as cautioner for a debt of one thousand merks. He seems on this occasion to have borrowed that sum from Patrick Ross, burgess of Perth, for payment of which David Murray, tutor of Aber-cairney, was cautioner.

There are further references to the doings of Harie Blackwood in the Commissary Court Records of Dunblane. Thus, in 1665 there is reference to a lease by John Chisholm of Cromlix to " Harie Blackwode in Dunblane and John Blackwode his son, of the lands of Over and Nether How Mylne (Holmehill) the grass and pasturage of the same lying within the dykes thereof as the same lies in length and breadth within the precinct of the lands of Ramoyle at the upper part of the city of Dunblane." The lease was to run for life and the rent fixed was nominal.

In the same year Harie Blackwood granted an Obligation to " Jeane Chisholm relict of umquhile Collene Campbell of Ardbeith (perhaps Ardbeich) my mother-in-law " for payment of 100 merks and a chalder of victual. His wife was the daughter of a daughter of the family of Chisholm of Cromlix.

In 1671 John Chisholm of Cromlix assigned to Harie Blackwood the sum of £3000 Scots being the balance of a sum of 12,000 merks contained in a bond " by William Earle of Airth as principal and umquhill John Lord Kinponnt (Kilpont) Sir James Grahame Knight umqulk John Graham of Rednoch, William Graham of Boquapple, John Graham of Duchray, and Patrick Menteith of Arnbeg as cautioners." The bond was originally granted in 1643.

A similar assignation by Chisholm to Blackwood follows in which Blackwood is referred to as " my weill beloved and trustie freind."

On 16th December, 1680, Harie Blackwood granted a discharge to the Earl of Menteith and Sir Colin Campbell of certain sums of Vicarage Teind due by them.

On 26th February, 1681, Sir Colin Campbell of " Aberurquhill," Knight, as having " the right of the Chaplainrie called trinitie altar situated within the Cathedral Kirk of Dunblane having expirience of his dewtifull respect and cair appointed Harie Blackwood pror actor and factor to uplift, collect, ingather and receive any rents and duties payable to the said altarage by any person or persons addebtet and in use of payment thereof."

At the same date a Factory by James, Bishop of Dunblane, to Harie Blackwood, dated 13th January, 1680, was recorded. It narrates that the Bishop as the lawful and undoubted patron of " the trinitie altar situate within the Cathedral Kirk of Dunblane and Chaplainrie thereof now vacant by the decease of James Cunningham, lawful son to the deceased William Cunningham in Edinburgh," who had received the life rent of the chaplainry and of the yearly rents of the same and having experience of the dutiful service and care of Harie Blackwood in Dunblane tending to the will of the Bishop and his successors in that see, nominated the said Harie Blackwood as attorney factor and commissioner with authority to collect the yearly rents and duties of the said Trinity altarage from the heritors, feuars, and occupiers of the lands or tenements belonging to the altarage during the life-time of the said Harie Blackwood.

There are one or two references in the Privy Council Records to Harie Blackwood, Bailie of Dunblane, such as on 15th June, 1665, where Jean Brown, wife of James Riach, Dunblane, complained that when she was on her way to Edinburgh to prosecute Harie Blackwood and others for wrongful imprisonment and other crimes, the Bailie pulled her from her horse and put her in prison and kept her there for a long time, with the result that the diet passed in Edinburgh before she got there and the defenders were assoilzied. She was not successful in her case as it was alleged that she was imprisoned for failing to find caution for a debt due by her.

On 1st May, 1672, Walter Smith, writer in Edinburgh, complained that Harie Blackwood was indebted to him and imprisoned in the Tolbooth of Dunblane, but that he was allowed so much latitude that he could escape when he pleased, so much so that it was no prison. Smith craved warrant to remove him to the Tolbooth of Stirling. The Privy Council granted warrant to the Bailies of Dunblane to deliver the prisoner and to the Magistrates of Stirling to receive and imprison him.

Harie Blackwood or Blaikwood, as his name was sometimes spelt, was the son of William Blaikwood, Bailie of Dunblane in 1612. The latter gifted the larger of the two bells which were hung in the Cathedral tower until a set of chiming bells was gifted by Lord Blanesburgh. From the inscription on this bell it appears that it was founded in Edinburgh in 1612, and was in regular use until 1657, when it was broken by unskilful handling. The bell was refounded by Harie Blackwood at Brimin, by M. Clavdigage in 1660, he being then Bailie in Dunblane. It was re-cast in 1809 by T. Mears & Son, of London, from funds of the Kirk Session, the Session Minutes recording that this Bell had been " rent by the carelessness of John Dougall," in May, 1795. The unnecessary immortalising of the name of the culprit indicates a feeling of great impatience at what was considered the stupidity of this man.

CHAPTER XIX.

THE CAMPBELLS OF ABERUCHILL AND KILBRYDE AND THE BARONY OF KILBRYDE.

IT may be of interest to learn somewhat of the history of the family of Campbell of Aberuchill and Kilbryde, the proprietors of the latter estate for the last 250 years. Their descent is from the Campbells of Argyll, who claim to trace their origin from Constantine, grandfather of Arthur of the Round Table, and son of Androen, who was invited to this island by the Britons and crowned king about 450 or 455A.D. There is extant a pedigree of the Argyll family, of which the writer has a copy, compiled before 1685, in which it is affirmed that the " last sixteen deschants cane be yet proven by Wryts that are yet extant." The author of this pedigree claimed that the family of the Earl of Perth, from which the Cromlix family is descended, were also derived from the Campbells of Argyll, but this seems to be open to question, although the families were long intimately connected. The original name of the family of Campbell was O'Dwyne or MacDwyne, and the name of Campbell is said to have been first assumed in 1057 on a marriage of the heiress of Campbell of Lochow with Gillespie Campobellus, a Norman. The first Campbell to assume the title of Argyll instead of Lochow was Sir Duncan Campbell, Lord Justice General of Scotland, created Lord Campbell in 1445. It is strange to find that he had a son named Archibald Roy Kilbrid, for Kilbryde Estate did not come into the hands of the Campbells until 200 years later. Lord Campbell, in 1432, conveyed to his son, Colline Downaroibh, the lands of Glenorchy, and he became the first of the Breadalbane family. He was known as " Black Colin of Rome." He was married four times, his fourth wife being Margaret, daughter of Luke Stirling of Keir. Sir Colin Campbell of Glenorchy rendered important services to the Crown, receiving from King James III a charter of the lands of Lawers for good and faithful services rendered in the capture of Thomas Chalmers, one of the murderers of James I. A son of Sir Colin Campbell of Glenorchy and of Margaret Stirling of Keir succeeded to Lawers. A descendant of Sir Colin Campbell married Alexander Home of Argaty. Sir John Campbell, first baronet of Lawers, married his cousin, Beatrix of Glenorchy, and his second son, Colin, was the first Campbell of Aberuchill and the ancestor of the Kilbryde family.

At the end of the sixteenth century ill-feeling existed between the Campbells of Glenorchy and those of Lawers, which resulted in the latter leaving their original home in the neighbourhood of Ben Lawers, on Loch Tay side, and settling on the lands of Fordie, near Comrie, which has since been known as Lawers. The estate of Aberuchill, which is also in the Comrie district, was acquired by Sir John Campbell of Lawers from William Mory of Abercairney in 1594, and in the following year Sir John made Aberuchill over to his second son, Colin, who obtained a Crown Charter in 1596. Colin Campbell, first laird of Aberuchill, had numerous brothers and sisters, his eldest brother being Sir James of Lawers, and his next younger brother, Archibald Campbell, prior of Strathfillan, whose portrait is preserved in Kilbryde Castle. He was a man of great ability, and entrusted with important duties by the king. The first Campbell of Aberuchill was married to Jean, the oldest daughter of Harie Drummond of Riccarton, a branch of the family of the Earl of Perth. The families of Argyll and Aberuchill continued to be intimately associated, and they rendered to each other services of great importance. In 1612, Archibald, Earl of Argyll, Lord Justice General, granted a commission to Colin Campbell of Aberuchill, to apprehend or pursue to the death all persons of " that most unhappy and barbarous raice of the name of MacGregor, His Majesty's Rebels." We do not know what success Colin Campbell attained in carrying out this warrant, but certain MacGregors were afterwards tried for burning and destroying " the haill houses and biggings upon the forty merk land of Aberuchill pertaining to Colene Campbell." A further document is preserved amongst the Kilbryde papers, dated 1615, referring to the trouble occasioned by the treasonable Sir James MacDonald and the need for a substantious order to frustrate his treasonable designs. The King gave an order to pursue him and his accomplices by land and sea, and not to leave off pursuit "till they be suppressed and brought to their tragical and miserable end." All the lieges between sixty and sixteen were summoned to prepare themselves in their most substantious and warlike manner with forty days' victual.   Colin Campbell seems to have given Argyll assistance in this matter, as also did the prior of Strathfillan, who was Bailie of Kintyre.   Argyll on this occasion drove the MacDonalds out of Kintyre and Islay.   MacDonald, after his long life of bloodshed and rebellion, escaped to Spain, and ultimately had a peaceable death "among his beloved books in England."   Colin Campbell, first laird of Aberuchill, died in 1618, soon after the suppression of the rebellion of the MacDonalds.   There are a number of letters still in existence from Argyll to him, in which he is addressed in familiar terms, such as " My truest freind Colene Campbell of Abruchill," and signed " Your loving Cousing, Argyll."   Colin Campbell, first laird of Aberuchill, was succeeded by his son, James, in 1618.   He was married to Ann, daughter of Patrick Hepburn, Apothecary Burgess in Edinburgh, a man of some wealth and importance.   James died in November, 1640, and was succeeded by his son, Colin, third Laird of Aberuchill, born in 1637 or early in 1638. It was he who afterwards acquired the property of Kilbryde.   Nothing is known of his early days, save that he was only two or three years of age when he succeeded to Aberuchill.   He was admitted an advocate in 1664, and very early obtained appointments through his relatives, the Earl of Loudon and the 9th Earl of Argyll, who conferred on him the Sheriffship of Argyllshire in 1668.   The Earl of Argyll in 1680 was due Sir Colin 18,000 marks, and commission was granted to him to uplift feu-duties of certain lands including the Barony of Menstrie.   He represented the burgh of Inveraray in the Scottish Parliament from 1669 to 1674, and was also Provost of the burgh.   Sir Colin Campbell had no seat in Parliament from 1674 to 1690, when he was returned for Perthshire as one of its four members, retaining his seat until 1702.   Sir Colin was married first to Margaret Foulis of Ratho, who died in 1666, and afterwards to Catherine, sister of the 1st Earl of Cromartie, a man of great talent, and estimable in his private life, but one who was said to have sworn all the most contradictory oaths and complied with all the opposite Governments for 60 years from 1648, and was humble servant to them all.   The owner of the estate of Cromlix during part of the lifetime of Sir Colin Campbell, first laird of Kilbryde, was Lieutenant-General William Drummond, first Lord Strathallan, whom we have already noted.

In 1667, Sir Colin Campbell bought from Robert Stirling of Coldoch the superiority of the five merk land of Dullatur, for which there was a yearly rent of " four score staine of cheese, qrof fortie staine be laid at the Castle of Campbell yearly, and for ilk staine of the ither fortie staine of cheese to paye three shillings and four pennies, as also the feu-duty of ten merks of the lands of Glennie."   These superiorities still belong to Kilbryde.   In the same year, 1667, Sir Colin Campbell of Kilbryde also acquired from Robert Stirling of Coldoch, Ashentree, Dunrobin, Spittalton, Calziemoir, and Calziemuch.   The lands of Coldoch in prehistoric times had extended to the north shore of a great arm of the sea which covered the Carse of Stirling.   The soil is very rich and fertile.   Sir Colin afterwards sold Coldoch lands to John Edmonstone of Cambus Wallace.   In 1676 he bought the fourth part of the lands of Wester Row, most of which now belongs to Inverardoch Estate.   He also acquired from David Moir of Leckie, in 1679, the farm of Greenyards, which now is part of Keir Estate.   The estate of Kilbryde was bought by him in 1669, but it was some years later before he obtained a proper title to the estate.   After his purchase of Kilbryde it became his chief residence when not engaged at his legal duties as an advocate, Lord of Session, or Privy Councillor.   When at Kilbryde he attended meetings of Kirk Session, and he received a grant of the Trinity Altar in the Cathedral for a burial place as also of the Chapellanry of this altar.   The altar stood at the south-west end of the Cathedral opposite St. Blais Altar.   The rights of patronage and its emoluments were reserved by the Bishop.   In 1670, Sir Colin received a fit and convenient place for hearing the Word of God upon the north wall west of the seats of John Drummond of Cromlix with $1\frac{1}{2}$ ells of ground for building "a foreseat and buncker" with power to put a cover on his seats.   He represented the Kirk Session in the Presbytery of Dunblane, and was also a member of General Assembly, but he appears to have taken no active part in this work, though in 1692 it is noted that he went to Linlithgow with the minister of Alloa and Mr. Douglas to present a call from the parish of Dunblane to Mr. Michael Potter, minister at Bo'ness.   Mr. Potter accepted the appointment, and was minister of Dunblane till 1718.   It would appear that Sir Colin was one of the victims of the Darien Scheme, but only to the extent of £500.   Sir Colin was probably not blameless in connection with the Glencoe massacre.   It seems to have been partly due to him that Glencoe's oath of allegiance was erased and never submitted to the Privy Council, of which he was a member.

I

When the facts became known, he resigned his seat in the Privy Council, and was afterwards fortunate in escaping with a simple censure. He died in Edinburgh in 1704, and was buried in Kilbryde Church or Churchyard, but the site of his grave is unknown. No stone or tablet records the fact.

In 1693 he received, by Act of Parliament, a grant of £17,000 Scots to meet the loss which he had sustained at the hands of the MacGregors and other Highlanders through the frequent harrying of Aberuchill, but it is not known whether this sum was paid and probably it was not. He was empowered by Act of Parliament in 1695 to hold a yearly fair at the Kirkton of Kilbryde. The succeeding proprietors of Kilbryde need only brief notice. The second laird of the Campbell family was James, Sir Colin's second son, his elder brother having died in his father's lifetime. Sir James was a member of the highest society in Edinburgh, but was of extravagant habits, and dispersed a considerable portion of the wealth accumulated by his father. He was an elder of the parish of Comrie, and lived much at Aberuchill. In 1729 the Kirk Session of Dunblane were much concerned as to the filling up of the vacancy, as the whole people were determined to call to the parish of Dunblane Mr. Simpson, minister of Fowlis. The Session Clerk, Mr. McGoun, solicited the help of Sir James Campbell to obtain a right settlement of this " poor, desolate, and numerous congregation." Mr. Simpson was ultimately elected, and was minister in Dunblane during the '45.

Sir James was first married to a wealthy Fife lady, Jean Dempster of Pitliver, and secondly to Jean, daughter of the Earl of Loudon. His only son, Colin, who died before his father, was married to Catherine Nisbet, of Direlton. Numerous letters of his, written from London, are still extant, and show that he had more interest in country affairs than in the life of a town. He returned to Edinburgh, and was admitted to the Scottish Bar in December, 1718. A letter written in 1739 by Mr. Steven, factor on the Auchmethie property of the Campbells, has been preserved. Mr. Steven had found his factory not so easy as he imagined, and complained of meetings with the tenants with their "sundry altercations and jouglings," the letter going on to state that the factor was sorry that the smallness of his fee was not adequate, and unless the laird considered his transactions worth 5 per cent. and charges attending the different meetings of tenants, he begged leave to demit his charge, of which he thought it mannerly to give timeous advertisement. Sir James appears to have married a third wife, named Sarah Cleghorn, probably of Strathvithie, Fife. In 1723 Sir James's son and brother jointly urged him to purchase the property of Drumdroulls (Drumdruils), on the ground that it had one of the best fruit orchards in the shire, both as to kinds and quantities, and also contained a lime quarry of as good lime as ever they had seen. The purchase was not made, probably because Sir James was in constant need of money, and had not the means to purchase additional lands. He had expended in 1738 a large sum on improving Lawers House under the directions of the famous William Adam. Sir James and his brother, Colin, who acted as his factor for some time, ultimately had a serious quarrel. Colin was residing in 1745 at Pinkie House, near Musselburgh, where Prince Charles Edward found shelter on the night following the Battle of Prestonpans.

The sisters of Sir James Campbell, the second baronet, seem not to have been well provided for by their father, and in 1712 one of them wrote mentioning that she had boarded herself " with Mrs. Gowdielocks for £12 Scots for ane year."

Sir James Campbell, the third baronet, led the Scots Greys at Fontenoy. He was first married in 1754 to Margaret Ball, heiress of Captain William C. Ball, Lord Commissioner for Scotland, and secondly to Mary Ann Burn. He died in 1812, aged 89. Sir James had five sons and one daughter by his first wife. The only daughter was married to William Pearson of Kippenross. Sir James's second wife is said to have been the governess of his children. Her portrait shows her to have been a handsome and clever woman. Sir James's second family consisted of four sons and four daughters. In 1772 he sold the old family property of Aberuchill for a small price. He had an expensive litigation with reference to the estate of Auchmethie, which he was unfortunate to lose. His estate became impoverished from various causes, one of which was the obligations he had to undertake for his family. The two eldest sons of this baronet were boarded when very young with William Coldstream, schoolmaster in Dunblane, whose merits are recorded on a monumental slab in Dunblane Cathedral. The cost of their board and tuition per annum was £9, with an additional allowance of £2 to provide tea. It is noted on a receipt which is preserved, that " while the bairns are away with Sir James or Lady

Campbell 15s. per month may be discounted." The eldest son died while young. Sir James's second son, Alexander, left Scotland in 1773, aged 16, for Jamaica. A number of interesting letters from him are still extant. He was first upon Content Estate, the property of Patrick Stirling, one of the Kippendavie family. In 1774 Alexander Campbell wrote home that Patrick Stirling had handed over the charge of other estates to a brother, and adds that he " does not think that Mr. Stirling is just now in a capacity to buy Kippenross," which points to the Pearsons at that time having the sale of Kippenross under consideration. The estate of Content in Jamaica was valued at the time at £250 an acre. Alexander Campbell seems to have been industrious and respected in the island, but he experienced considerable trouble with his younger brothers, particularly with James, who had become addicted to drinking and lying, so that no situation could be found for him. Alexander remarks in a letter to his father, that if James had been in the Navy these bad habits might have been boxed out of him by his fellow-blackguards. A letter written in 1782 records that Alexander is investing his savings in the purchase of new negroes, whom he will hire out on lease at 10 per cent. interest. He had afterwards difficulty with a younger brother, Thomas, for whom he obtained a post on a vessel trading between London and Jamaica. Thomas gave up his post to take command of a privateer of 6 guns. Thomas cost Alexander about £70, but he recouped himself by obtaining a pipe of Madeira wine earned by Thomas as prize money of the value of about £100. In 1812 Sir James Campbell died, and Alexander returned from Jamaica to assume the family estates. He was married in 1816, at the age of 59, to Margaret Coldstream, Crieff, whose usual residence appears to have been in Glasgow. He had a family of one daughter and six sons, but only four of the sons survived infancy. Sir Alexander died in 1824 at the age of 67. Some stories are still recalled regarding Sir Alexander Campbell. He walked about his estate carrying a heavy whip, which it was thought he had used while in charge of natives in Jamaica. He was fond of fishing, and was accustomed to fish in the Kilbryde water seated on a chair on the bank of the river. On one occasion he annoyed his attendant, who, in retaliation, lifted him in his chair and placed him in the middle of the stream, leaving him there. A manservant attended the arrival of the mail at Dunblane daily to get letters for the laird. He went on horseback, dressed in red breeches and white stockings. On one occasion, when he arrived with the letters at the Castle 10 minutes late, Sir Alexander struck him with his heavy whip for his dilatoriness. It was remarkable that the wife of this ex-slave owner lived until 1871. Sir Alexander Campbell was succeeded by his eldest son, Sir James, in 1824, when the latter was only six years of age. He was educated in Edinburgh, and in March, 1840, he was married to Caroline Bromley, daughter of Admiral Sir Robert Bromley of Stoke Hall, Newark, Notts. He had a long, happy married life of sixty years. Sir James was of handsome appearance and attractive manner, and one could not but recognise on first acquaintance that he was of high birth and ancient lineage. He held an important position for many years under the Department of Woods and Forests, but, although greatly attached to Kilbryde, he was never able to reside on his property. He was succeeded by his only son, Sir Alexander Campbell, who, after education at Harrow, obtained a commission in the Royal Horse Artillery, retiring with the rank of Colonel after 33 years' service. His eldest son, James Colin Campbell, was killed in the South African War while in charge of an armoured train. His second son, the present baronet, succeeded his father in 1914, a few months before the outbreak of war. He served with the Scottish Horse and Lovat Scouts (10th Cameron Highlanders), and for some time after the war resided near Nairobi, Kenya Colony. He was married in January, 1921, to Miss Janet Moffat, daughter of ex-Provost Moffat, coalmaster, Hamilton.

THE BARONY OF KILBRYDE.

The Barony of Kilbryde was at one time part of the possessions of the Earls of Menteith. Some authorities have held that in early days the district of Menteith was one of the seven great districts into which Scotland was divided, but the lands of Kilbryde were apparently in the neighbouring earldom of Strathearn. The first Earl of Menteith appears to have been Gilchrist, who witnessed the signature of Malcolm IV in 1164. In the 13th century Kilbryde belonged to the Comyns. John Comyn of Kilbryde was confined in the Castle of Nottingham by the King of England prior to going to fight for Edward I of England in France in 1297. The later Earls of Menteith were descended from David, Earl of Strathearn, son of Robert III.   It is known that the lands of Kilbryde were the property of John, son of Malise, Earl of Menteith, in 1469.   His wife was Margaret Muschet.   He was traditionally known as Sir John of the Bright Sword.   His father was the first Graham, Earl of Menteith, and the eldest son of Patrick Graham of Kilpont, West Lothian, whose mother was the only child and heir of the Earl of Stratherrn and Caithness.   In 1546, the 4th Earl of Menteith received sasine of the lands and mill of Kilbryde.   In 1571 the Lands of Kilbryde are referred to as " £20 lands of old extent within the Stewartry of Strathearn."   In 1587 there was litigation between John, the 6th Earl of Menteith, and the Dowager Countess with regard to the titles.   The latter, as already noted, counter-claimed for damages in respect of his forcible entry of Kilbryde Castle, the Earl being put under caution.   William, the 7th Earl of Menteith, born in 1589, rose, it was said, from comparative obscurity to be the most influential nobleman in his country.   He became a Privy Councillor and Justice-General of Scotland, receiving in 1628 a pension of £500 a year.   Unfortunately, this Earl's fall was even more rapid than his rise.   It originated from his claim to the Earldom of Strathearn, which had been taken from Malise, Earl of Menteith, by James I. The King gave him (the seventh Earl) the title of Earl of Strathearn in 1621, and he then became the first nobleman in Scotland.   The Earls of Breadalbane and Seaforth prepared memorials to King Charles I, setting forth reasons why the Earl of Menteith should not be allowed to retain the Earldom of Strathearn, and pointing out that this involved the acknowledgment that the Earl of Menteith was the lawful heir of King Robert, making himself equal, if not superior, to His Majesty.   It was also reported to the King that the Earl of Menteith had said he " had the reddest blood in Scotland."   He was in consequence deprived of all his dignities, including the titles of Menteith and Strathearn, and much of his possessions.

Kilbryde was one of eleven parish churches gifted by Abraham, Bishop of Dunblane, and Gilbert, Earl of Strathearn, for the support of the Abbey of Inchaffray, being known as the Church of St. Bridget of Kilbryde.   Kilbryde appears in Bagamond's Roll as paying 18/8½ of tithe. In 1444-5 James II created the lands of the Monastery of Inchaffray into the free Barony of Cardinay, these including the church lands of Kilbryde.

On 20th January, 1494, King James IV confirmed a charter by Alexander, Earl of Menteith, who had given to his uncle, Walter Graham, lands at Kilbryde of the value of 18½ merks, including the Mains and lands occupied by certain crofters, namely, " Thomas and Gilbert Hendry, John Banks, John Paton, William Glass, Andrew and Donald Clark, John Wyndis and John and Christie Aneris, John Danskin, Widow Makglas and John Broun, all lying in the Stewartry of Strathearn and County of Perth."   The witnesses include James, Bishop of Dunblane, John Drummond, the Dean, and Will Forbes, Official of Dunblane.

In 1510 Walter Graham was given other lands to the value of 18½ merks, belonging to the Earl of Menteith.

On 7th May, 1487, King James by virtue of decrees of the Lords of Council in 1485-86 confirmed some lands of Kilbryde to James Mushet of Tolgarth in respect that Malise, Earl of Menteith, was held to pay him 300 merks and had been unable to do so, but on condition that the Earl and his heirs might buy back the lands within seven years on payment of the money due.   The lands were estimated as being worth 20 merks annually.

On 29th April, 1508, King James IV gave to his familiar, Henry Shaw, a soldier and his heirs, for faithful service, the lands of Kilbryde and others which were in the hands of the King on account of the alienation of the major part of the Earl's lands, which Alexander, Earl of Menteith, alleged were part of the lands given by the King when the Earldom of Menteith was given in exchange for the Earldom of Strathearn.

On 7th June, 1509, the King confirmed a Charter of Henry Shaw by which he granted to " Mariota Forestare, daughter of Walter Forestare of Torwood, his lands of Kilbryde with the Mill, tenements and tenandries."

About a month later King James IV granted to "his Familiar, Malcolm Drummond of Megour, a third part of the lands of Kilbryde with a third part of the Mill, which the King had granted to Henry Schaw and which Henry Schaw had personally resigned."   Drummond had married the only daughter of Sir John Graham of the Bright Sword.   In 1532, Alexander, Earl of Menteith, was granted a third of Kilbryde and a third of the mill which had been alienated to Henry Shaw and others who had resigned them.

The tithes of the church of Kilbryde in 1275 and 1276 were given by Thiener at 18/8.

In 1630 the teinds of the Barony of Kilbryde amounted to £390 less tax duty of £24 payable to Lord Madderty, leaving a free rent of £366.   In that year the teinds of the Kirk of Kilbryde were estimated to be worth 21 bolls of Victual.

The Kirk Lands of the parish of Kilbryde were commonly known as Boutoun, and in 1630 were worth £80 and Chalder victual £120.

Little is known about the clergy of Kilbryde, but as early as 1178 there is a reference to John, Parson of Kilbryde, who witnessed a charter of Bishop Simon of that year.   In 1567, following upon the Reformation, Michael Learmonth was appointed Reader at Kilbryde, having also under his charge Lany, Kilnahug and Calendreth with a stipend of £80 along with the Kirk lands.   In 1572 he was permitted to be Exhorter and he was transferred to Kincardine in 1584.   In 1576 Lany only was included along with Kilbryde under its minister.

Alexander Anderson was Reader at Kilbryde in 1574 with a stipend of 20 merks, and Kirk lands to the value of £4.   In 1576 Master John Sinclair became Reader at Kilbryde with a stipend of £20.

In 1555 the Kirk lands of Kilbryde were feued to Robert Row of Callentois and his wife, Marion Edmonstoun for a yearly payment of 42/- by Alexander, perpetual Commendator of Inchaffray.   They had been feued in 1503 to Robert Row of Caldercois for a yearly payment of 20/- with 2/- augmentation and previously to John Row, his father.   The church of Kilbryde was previously let to Robert Row and his ancestors under several leases commencing 1491.

In 1698 they were the property of Lord Strathallan after being for a time in the possession of the family of Graham of Drumlane.

It is not known whether there was any minister at Kilbryde later than Michael Learmonth. In any event the parish was united to Dunblane in 1618.

In 1571 King James VI with consent of the Bishop and Chapter confirmed John Charters of Kinfauns and Janet Chisholm his wife, in the lands and town of Crosschapel with the teinds of the same held by Robert Row and his tenants for a yearly payment of 7 merks and 6/8 of augmentation with eleven bolls or 6/8 per boll with a duplicate of $7\frac{1}{2}$ merks at the entry of each heir.   The witnesses were " James Chisholme of Cromlix and Jo Lermonth, Vicar of Dunblane." It will be noted that this charter was granted sometime after the Reformation and when there was no Bishop or Chapter.

John, Lord Graham and Kinpont, obtained a charter of the Barony of Kilbryde and Kinpont in 1633.   He is referred to at a later date as Lord Kinpont and Kilbryde.

In 1643 Sir William Ruthven of Dunglas obtained a decree of apprising for payment of debts due by the Earl of Menteith, amounting to over twenty-three thousand pounds Scots money and £1180 sheriff's fee.   Under this process Sir William Ruthven secured the title to the lands of Kilbryde and he acquired the teinds from the Earl of Loudon in 1659.   In 1662 his heir conveyed the lands to John Stirling of Bankell and his wife, Elizabeth Dick.   The latter sold them in 1669 to Colin Campbell of Aberuchill, first baronet of Aberuchill and Kilbryde and his spouse, Katherine Mackenzie.   Sir Colin, not being satisfied with the title, obtained in 1677 a further disposition by William, Earl of Menteith, who had now regained this title.   It was this unfortunate Earl's son and heir, Lord Kilpont, who was slain by Stewart of Ardvoirlich in Montrose's camp in 1644 at the age of 31 and buried in the Chapter House at Inchmahome. His grandson, the eighth Earl of Menteith, was the last of his house.   The last Earl seems to have been the most unfortunate of all, and his life may be described in his own words as " wrapt in a labyrinth of never-ending trouble."

Sir Colin acquired the Chaplainry of the Trinity Altar in Dunblane Cathedral in 1680 and a right of burial there in 1683.   At another time Harie Blackwood was liferented in these duties.

The present estate of Kilbryde commences at Ormelie House, Doune Road, and includes the holdings of Stockbridge, Corscaplie, Auchinteck, Nether Grainston, and Torrance Farms, Belland Pendicle, and the policies and parks around Kilbryde Castle.   Until November, 1920, it also included the farms of Nether Glastry, Dalbrack, and Bows, comprising about 4000 additional acres.   The boundaries of the estate acquired by Sir Colin Campbell in many respects differed from the modern estate of Kilbryde and did not include Stockbridge, Bowton and Corscaplie Farms, or the land adjoining Dunblane, which was only purchased about 70 years ago. Part of the lands of Cromlix appear to have been originally in the Barony of Kilbryde, while lands known as Bowton or Kirklands, now part of Corscaplie Farm, situated on the right-hand side of the road leading from the Kilbryde Road to the Chapel, formed a separate estate with a Mansion House.   The Barony of Kilbryde, when purchased by John Stirling in 1662, included the following lands:—"Glassrie, Dalbrack, and Park Lands, Sappeltown, Town and lands of Carrenne, Mylne and miln lands of Newbole, Blairbanes, Tenendrie, Grayngtoun, and the Chapland."   The Glassrie is, no doubt, the modern Glastry; Blairbanes may be Braelane or Blairloaning (part of Dalbrack), and Grayngtoun is Grainston.   "Tenendrie" is now part of Nether Grainston, and the Chapland may represent Chapel lands.   About 100 years later we find that there were 20 or more farms at Kilbryde, exclusive of Stockbridge and Corscaplie (as compared with 4 at the present time), some of which were probably small pendicles, and in many cases the present farms were occupied by two tenants, as in the case of Auchinteck, where the lands are described as "head and foot and upper and lower town of Auchinteck."   It is said that about 150 years ago there was a population of 700 persons in the Barony of Kilbryde, but although a household frequently numbered 14 to 16 exclusive of servants, it is difficult to know how the housing problem was overcome if the population approached half that number.   Possibly the earliest reference to the Church of Kilbryde is in a charter by Abraham, Bishop of Dunblane, dated about 1211, giving to the Canons of Inchaffray the Church of Abruthven at the presentation of Gilbert, Earl of Strathearn.   The charter is signed by the Earl, two of his brothers and a son, and certain ecclesiastical dignitaries, including Malaise, designed Parson of Kilbryde.   Earl Gilbert had, at the foundation of the Priory of Inchaffray, granted to it five churches, but before his death he added other six, one of which was that of Kilbryde.   The grant of these churches was confirmed by the Chapter of Dunblane in 1239.   In 1491-92 the Abbot of Inchaffray leased the fruits of the Church of Kilbryde for nineteen years to his well-beloved friend, John of Row, for a payment of £10 a year, payable at Mid-summer and Candlemas, "Jone to pay all costs effeiring to the Abbey for said Church," including the stall in the Church of Dunblane.   Similar leases amongst the charters dated in the first half of the sixteenth century were granted by the Commendator of Inchaffray to other members of the Row family.   After the Reformation the possessions of the Priory became Crown possessions, and in 1609 the lands pertaining to Inchaffray, including the Kirk lands of the Kirk of Kilbryde, were erected by King James VI into a temporal Lordship in favour of John Drummond, eldest son and heir of Lord Madderty. The Kirk lands of Bowton were in the possession of Thomas Graham, a great-grandson of Malise, first Earl of Menteith, about the end of the sixteenth century.   His mother was a Stirling of Keir.   There was apparently a glebe at Kilbryde, as in 1697 William Graham of Bowton paid five years' rent of the glebe of Kilbryde, amounting to 100 merks Scots to Mr. Potter, minister of Dunblane.   At this time the schoolmaster of Dunblane received a payment of twenty-four pounds Scots money and 20 merks out of the teinds of Kilbryde.   The smithy and smithy lands at Kilbryde, occupied for some generations by the Dougalls, is known as Belland, which is said to be a corruption of Bedell's land.   It was probably possessed in ancient days by the beadle of the Kirk.   The Castle of Kilbryde was one of the residences of the Earls of Menteith, whose principal home was at Inchtalla, Lake of Menteith.

The old castle is believed to have been erected in the fourteenth century, and there is a possibility that Mary Queen of Scots may have resided there or visited it on one or more occasions. Till the Castle was restored in 1877-78, it had remained unaltered for centuries.   Up to that time the north-west portion had been protected by a high wall surrounding a courtyard.   As a child Queen Mary lived at Inchmahome for a short time, and when she went to France the Earl of Menteith is said to have accompanied her.   At a later date she lived for a period at Doune Castle, and after the death of the Earl of Menteith of that time his widow resided for some time at Kilbryde.   A bedroom in Kilbryde Castle is still known as Queen Mary's bedroom, and until lately there was in the possession of the Campbell family, at Kilbryde, a pair of hunting gloves which were said to have belonged to the Queen, and which had been handed down from generation to generation.   There were also until recently two pieces of tapestry which were associated with her, and an old Dutch cabinet in the Castle containing numerous drawers, with hand-painted scenes, which is said to have belonged to her.   Two other traditions connected with her name are that she planted the original daffodils which adorn the glen each spring, and that she used to go hawking on the farm of Glenwhilk, which seems at one time to have been in the Barony of Kilbryde.   While such traditions may or may not be true, there are grounds for believing that Queen Mary lived, at least on one occasion, in the old Castle of Kilbryde.

During the last 100 years many of the ancient buildings on the estate of Kilbryde have disappeared, leaving little trace of their sites. According to a Kilbryde Rental of 1798 there were 21 farms or small holdings on Kilbryde and in three cases farms were jointly held by two tenants. The tenants were bound to supply the laird with 295 hens, 2 stone of butter, 8 stone of cheese and 300 wads of peats, and to drive a large quantity of coal. About 1806 many of the smaller farms at Kilbryde were united. Quite a number of humble dwellings clustered round the neighbourhood of the old Kirk. On the south side after passing the cross roads on the brow of the hill above the Ardoch stood two cottages or more, known as Brighills. The last occupant of one was William Don, a tailor, who was born in 1777, and whose father, Daniel Don, was butler at Kilbryde Castle, and lived in Craigengelt. During his latter days the gable of his house had to be supported by wooden beams, and the walls could barely be held together until his own life flickered out. The last tenant of the neighbouring house was a man named Campbell and his married daughter. On the road up to Grainston Farm and the Chapel, known as the Road to Cullings or the Highlanders' Road, were a number of cottages of the low thatched type, one of which was occupied by the local shoemaker and another by the bellman. On the opposite side of this road were the lands of Bowton, and a small house used to stand there. Continuing up the Grainston Road one arrived at the farm of Nether Grainston—the name is a corruption of Grangeton or Home Farm—on the left, and on the right the farm of Tenandry, situated on the top of the hill, the site of which is distinguished by the trees that used to surround the farm town. It is said that there were at one time a number of cottages at Tenandry, as well as the farmhouse. There has been a smithy for a long period where the present smithy stands, but the innermost part of the present buildings there was formerly the school of Kilbryde, still numerously attended about 1832. On the opposite side of the Kilbryde Road, in front of the modern cottage now known as " The Green," stood a public house of the same name. A story is still related in connection with " The Green," how a certain farmer and his friends adjourned there on the completion of sowing their land, how they continued their festivities for some days, and on emerging from the public-house they found that the grain which they had completed sowing before adjourning for refreshment had already sprouted. The story is not, however, so alarming as it at first appears, as the old Scottish barley, known as " Bere " (which was not sown until the middle of May) has been known to sprout on the second day after sowing.

There were several pendicles or crofts on the estate, such as Shank Pendicle or Stepps on the right-hand side of the present Doune Road, at its junction with the farm road from Auchinteck on the west side of the Paffray Burn ; the Gardener's Croft, part of Blenboard ; Newhouse Pendicle, and Dalchanzie beside the burn behind Auchenlay Pond, and near Tenandry. Other farms which have become absorbed in Nether Glastry and the Brack Farms are :—Upper Grainston, the steading of which stood in the present rabbit warren, and Braelane or Blairloaning ; Allan's Hill, the site of which was near the west end of the Glastry Plantation, overlooking the Argaty Springs; and Towrie Farm, to the north-west of Lerrocks Farm, near the Argaty Quarry, which the late Mr. W. B. Bruce stated, but on what grounds the writer cannot say, was formerly the site of a hunting lodge of the Scottish kings, who were accustomed to hunt in that neighbourhood. It may be mentioned that West Lundie, a farm west of Towrie, was at one time called The King's Lundies, but in earlier times The Dean's Lundies. Allan's Hill and Towrie are now part of Nether Glastry Farm, and Upper Grainston, and Blairloaning part of The Brack Farm. The Bows Farm was at one time in the occupation of three tenants, with three separate farm towns known as Wester, Easter, and Middle Bows. The name is a corruption of the Bow House. Greenyards farm (also called Banks of Row) formerly in the parish of Lecropt, belonged to Kilbryde in 1798. The old farm of Blenboard, or Blainboard, is now part of Torrance, and the buildings are occupied by the estate forester. The meal mill of Kilbryde stood on the right bank of the water, beside the old smithy road which comes from the direction of Doune and Easterton Farm, and joins the Kilbryde Road at the end of the two bridges. On a rising piece of ground to the north-west of the mill stood the Sheiling Hill, where the grain was carried to be sifted when Providence provided a suitable day and a drying wind. The Shieling Hill was a necessary adjunct to every mill in the early days, and the name is preserved in connection with Dunblane and innumerable other mills. The last meal miller at Kilbryde was of the name of Congleton, one of whose daughters married Henderson, the gamekeeper, a cousin or other near relative of the notorious Heather Jock. There are many quaint customs recorded in connection with country mills. These were usually provided at the expense of the laird, and in order to recoup himself and to secure an adequate rent from the miller he bound all his tenants to have their grain milled at the estate mill, and they had to make payments to the mill, whether they carried the grain there or elsewhere.

It may be of interest to note that it was claimed for Alexander Fergusson, whose ancestors and successors long occupied West Lundie Farm, that he was the inventor of fanners for sifting grain, and that following on his invention he was summoned by the Kirk Session of Kilmadock to answer for the offence of seeking to improve on the works of Providence by inventing a mechanical arrangement which was to displace the forces of nature. His son, John, also claimed to be the inventor of the first threshing mill worked by horse power, about 1790, but in a newspaper cutting which recorded the death of Michael Stirling, some time farmer at Glassingall, who died at Craighead in 1796, he was said to have invented the first threshing mill in Scotland in 1758, and to have threshed his whole grain with it yearly thereafter.

As has been already mentioned, the lands of Kilbryde were constituted a Barony, of which the laird of Kilbryde was, of course, the Baron. No records have been preserved of the Barony Court at Kilbryde, but there can be little doubt that such courts were held from time to time. Such were presided over, as a rule, by a notary or writer, appointed Bailie by the Baron, and attached to the court were a Prosecutor, the Clerk of Court or Chancellor, an officer sometimes called Sergeant, and a Deemster, the official who announced the sentence of the Bailie. No doubt the Baron himself would preside in the earlier days, and perhaps in later times in small courts. Just as Parliament originally consisted of all Barons who held lands from the Crown, who were bound to attend under penalties, so all holding land from the Baron were under obligation to attend the Barony Court. Barony Courts are known to have been held as early as 1385. It is not known where they met at Kilbryde, but the probability is it would be in the neighbourhood of the Castle. The proceedings in such courts began by the officer " crying " the court, that was calling all to draw near. The roll was then read over, and persons absent were fined. The court dealt with criminal cases other than the more serious crimes known as the four pleas of the Crown, and some Barons had power to inflict capital punishment where they had a grant of Barony with pit and gallows. The word " pit " is used in connection with the drowning of female prisoners, who, when sentenced to death, were drowned rather than hung on the gallows. Where a jury was required to determine the case, 15 jurymen or other number were selected and sworn, the hearing of the evidence proceeded with and sentence pronounced. The holding of the court was the source in some cases of considerable revenue to the laird. At the end of the Barony Courts held at Stitchill and possibly elsewhere, the officer cried the assize of bread and ale. This was an intimation of the prices which might lawfully be charged for these commodities within the Barony until the next court was held. Notice was also given that no brewer was to sell his ale till the " ale conoure (taster) have assayed thereof." It is thus strange to find that hundreds of years ago rules existed controlling the prices of foodstuffs and the testing of liquor to secure that it was not unduly watered. The Barony Court also dealt with all questions of debts, claims for damages, and other civil claims, and we find that it imposed levies for public purposes, such as for education, to pay for the ringing of the bell at 4 in the morning and at 8 at night, and for supporting wounded soldiers. It laid down regulations restricting the nature of festivities on the occasion of weddings, as at Stitchill, where the Court ordered that only the bride and bridegroom, blood relatives, and four friends on each side were to be present. As it was important to encourage local industries, those arranging a wedding feast were bound to procure their bread and ale from those supplying these in the district. Thus the bride of James McDowel was mulcted, for having her wedding outside the Barony in the sum of £10 to the laird and 10s to the local miller. There was a rule that all bridal ale was to be bought within the Barony " if it were gud " and the price reasonable. Heavy fines appear to have been inflicted for damaging trees. Thus in one case a fine of £10 was inflicted, one half of which was given to the poor. The fines for commission of crimes were considerable. Two men were "emerciated" in £50 each for beating one another " in an unchristian manner," and had also to find caution for 100 merks for future good behaviour. A woman was fined £40 for scolding and a man £5 for slander. Swearing cost a culprit 10s. and another left this sum behind for " being sensibly drunk." The fine inflicted on tenants for absence from a Barony Court was 2s. 6d., along with a fee to the Officer of Court. Parents at Stitchill were penalised £10 if they did not keep their children at school.   Men attending at the mill with grain, who had their horses stabled overnight, were ordered by the court at Urie to hold them in the stables between 11 p.m. and sunrise.   The Urie Court extended its jurisdiction apparently beyond the tenantry to the fowls of the farmyard, for the court in 1624 ordered " everie ffoull that gans amangis their naichtbours' corn shall pey ane peck of aits or bear quhairin they pastur." While the administration of justice may at times have been harsh, and although abuses may have latterly crept in, one must admit that in the earlier days of Scottish history the Baron's Court exercised a judicious control over the district when probably no other means could have been devised for effectively dealing with crime and for settling petty disputes.   Although the powers of such Barons were greatly curtailed in 1747, it is still competent for a Baron to impose a fine not exceeding 20s., or to sit in judgment in a dispute of a value not exceeding 40s.

CHAPTER XX.

ARGATY: ITS OWNERS AND ITS BARONY BOOK.

Argaty and its Lairds.

From 1497 to Date, with Notes appended on the Barony Book of Argaty, 1672-1699.

The history of the estate of Argaty has not been traced beyond the year 1497 or 1498, when it was gifted by King James IV to Sir Patrick Home of Polwarth. In all likelihood the lands of Argaty and the Lundies were the property of the Earls of Menteith prior to the condemnation, for high treason, of Murdoch, Duke of Albany, in 1425, in the reign of James I Doune Castle, which seems to have been built by Robert, Duke of Albany, father of Murdoch, was one of the principal residences of the Earls of Menteith, and the lands of Argaty were in the Stewartry of Menteith. It is, therefore, very probable that they were amongst the lands forfeited to the Crown by James I, when he secured the condemnation of the Duke of Albany, his sons and father-in-law, at Stirling. In any event, these lands were in the hands of the Crown when gifted to the ancient family of Home in the year 1498.

The Crown Charter is dated 20th May, 1498, and was granted for " good, faithful and thankful service in war against the old enemy, the English, and otherwise in time of peace."

As this interesting and beautiful property was held for many generations by Homes it may be of interest to give a brief account of the family, which is said to have flourished in Scotland from the middle of the thirteenth century. According to the Douglas Peerage the family derived its descent from the Saxon Kings of England and the Princes, whose descendants were at a later date Earls of Northumberland. The first to adopt the name appears to have been Sir William Home, a descendant of Dunbar, Earl of March. Sir William having married his cousin Ada, daughter of Patrick, fifth Earl of March, succeeded to the barony and lands of Home, which had been gifted to his wife by her father. He then assumed the surname of Home and adhered to the armorial bearings of the Earls of March. His death occurred about 1266. Among his descendants were the Earls of Dunbar, Home, and Marchmont, and Lord Polwarth.

Sir Patrick Home, who was the first owner of Argaty of this name, was twice married. His second marriage, which took place in 1491, was to Ellen Shaw, daughter of Shaw of Sauchie, on whom the blame has been laid for the death of James III after the battle of Sauchieburn. James IV is said to have granted a charter in August, 1497, of the lands of Argaty and the Lundies in favour of Sir Patrick Home, who had espoused his cause, and Ellen Shaw, his wife, and the longest liver of them, and their heirs-male. Sir Patrick Home had one son by his first marriage, who succeeded to Polwarth, and the oldest son of the second marriage, George Home, by name, succeeded to Argaty and the Lundies. George Home married Margaret Erskine, second daughter of Lord Erskine of Mar. It is not known when they died, but George Home was still alive in 1562.

As the family of the Earl of Moray is descended from Sir James Stewart of Beith, who did not come to the Doune district till 1528, the Homes of Argaty could claim, until they sold their lands in 1917, that they were the oldest County family resident in that district.

George Home, besides owning Argaty, was proprietor of Rednock. His oldest son was Alexander Home, who was married to a Campbell of Glenorchy, and who succeeded his father sometime after 1562 and before 1574, when Alexander himself died. The second son of George Home was named Patrick, and he acquired from his parents the lands of Corriechrombie on the shores of Loch Lubnaig granted to them in 1531. Patrick Home's death was in 1572. The third son, David Home, was accused of treason, convicted and afterwards executed in Edinburgh on 8th December, 1584. It would seem that he had sided with the Earl of Angus and other disaffected nobles, and that he had held Stirling Castle on their behalf. The charges against him were of inter-communing with the Earl of Mar and other traitors, including David Erskine, sometime Commendator of Dryburgh, and of receiving letters from these men and from his nephew, Patrick Home, servant to the Earl of Mar, received through Robert Macwillie, whom he had received in his own house, committed in the summer of 1584. An effort was made to save his life and a sum of a thousand crowns was offered with that object, but this proved unsuccessful. His head was placed on the Nether Bow Port, to the great wrath of the populace. As already noted, a graphic account of the execution is given by Calderwood the historian. The historian Buchanan states that his brother, Patrick, was also executed, but this is understood to be erroneous, as Patrick Home was then resident in England. Some writers refer to David Home as of Argaty, but probably he was never owner of the estate.

It does not seem clear who owned Argaty, following on Alexander Home, who died in 1574, but apparently he was succeeded by Patrick Home, his son and lawful and nearest heir. This Patrick Home, whose wife was Margaret Haldane, died in January, 1629. The lands of Argaty in 1619 are described as " Over Argatie, Nether Argatie and Easter Argatie, and Mill of Argatie and the pendicles of Argatie, viz., the lands of Glenquhill, Boghall, Cranochallum, and a pendicle occupied by William Faill." He in turn was succeeded by Henry Home, who died in or before 1659, survived by his widow, Mary Muschett, a Muschett of Burnbank, and numerous sons. Henry Home also succeeded to the Lundies on the death of Captain Patrick Home, brother of his grandfather, prior to 1629. His heir, George Home, was a writer in Edinburgh, but he having fallen into debt conveyed the family possessions to his immediate younger brother, Major John Home, in 1659, in return for a considerable sum of money paid and in consideration of his disburdening his brother of certain very urgent creditors. The Conveyance was written by Robert Caddell, writer in Doune, one of the witnesses being Alexander Stewart, Doctor of the Grammar School at Doune. Major John Home was married in 1660 to Jean Drummond, Lady Kippenross, the widow of the Laird of Kippenross. Shortly before his death in 1670, he conveyed Argaty to his younger brother, Henry Home. Major John Home left no children, and his wife was appointed executrix by her husband.

Henry Home, who succeeded Major John Home and who was his immediate younger brother, was baptised in July, 1633. Henry's wife was Janet Moir of the family of Moir of Leckie, and their marriage took place prior to 1680. Her " tochergude " was 5000 merks. Henry died in 1689, and was succeeded by his son, George, who had been baptised at Kilmadock in March, 1686. The new laird could only have been about three years of age at the death of his father. He lived until 1751, but, although a strong supporter of the Stewart Kings, he was unable, owing to his age, to take any part in the Rebellion of 1745. He was the last Home of Argaty in the direct male line. It is mentioned in a letter by the Earl of Marchmont to the Earl of Seafield, dated 1701, that George Home's property was reduced to a small matter through his ancestors having sustained severe losses and contracted large debts by their close adherence to the cause of Charles I, but in that year the lands were erected by Crown Charter into a free Barony to be called the Barony of Argatie.

The three Home lairds of the latter half of the seventeenth century all saw some military service. George Home, who succeeded in 1659, served as a private in the Life Guards from 1667 to 1678. He was in the Captain's Squadron of Lieutenant-General Drummond's Troop in 1667. The Life Guards was the first corps levied in Scotland after the restoration of the Stewarts to the throne in 1660. It was raised in 1661, and the private soldiers were all sons of nobles and gentlemen. They received pay at the rate of 2s. 6d. a day.

His brother, John Home of Argaty, held a commission as Major, and was Captain of the 3rd Company of Perthshire Militia in 1668. He also held a commission as Chamberlain of the Lordship of Menteith and Strathearn.

Henry or Hairie Home, his successor, described " Brother to Argettie," served in the Life Guards for a number of years from the date of their being raised, and in 1688, the year before his death, he was in command of the 2nd Division of the Perthshire Militia, who were summoned to muster at Dunblane between 27th October and 9th November.

George Home left no children, but a number of sisters, the eldest of whom was Mary Home, married to George Stewart of Ballochalan. Mary Home and George Stewart were afterwards succeeded as lairds of Argaty by their two eldest sons, David and George. David seems to have died before 1776, as his brother George, who was his heir, completed a title to Argaty estate in that year. There were also two younger brothers, namely, James Stewart, Sheriff Clerk at Kinross, and William Stewart, a merchant in Annapolis, Maryland, U.S.A. The Stewarts in

Annapolis, who had fled thither after the battle of Culloden, suffered financially during the War of Independence, in which they sided with Britain, part of their family estate of Doden, ten miles south of Annapolis, having of necessity to be sold, but their fortunes were retrieved at a later date.   The Stewarts of Ballachallan were descended from Alexander Stewart who purchased the estate of Annat from Muschett of Burnbank in 1621.   His second son, Duncan, was the first owner of Ballachallan.   His son George Stewart succeeded him and he in turn was succeeded by his eldest son, David Home Stewart of Argaty, who granted a Deed of Entail in 1768.   David Home Stewart conveyed Ballachallan, Wester Brackland and other lands to his brother, Doctor George Stewart, in Annapolis about 1775.   He had previously conveyed the lands of Annat to him in 1767.   George Stewart was succeeded by his eldest son, George, who dropped the name of Stewart and was known as George Home.   His first wife was a daughter of Mr. Paterson of Bannockburn (married in 1777), and in 1785 he married his second wife, Jean Monro of Auchenbowie.   George Home died in October, 1787, leaving an infant daughter, Sophia, aged two months, who was his heir.   At that time there was doubt whether, under the Entail, Sophia Home was entitled to succeed her father or whether George Home's brother, namely, Charles Stewart, was now the heir.   The point was decided in 1791 in favour of the infant child, Sophia.   It may be of interest to note that in the Deed of Entail granted in 1768, David Home Stewart restricted his successors from selling or burdening the estate for a period of 30 years, except with the consent of the Laird of Keir and certain other local proprietors. The lands of Ballachallan were sold by the tutors of Miss Sophia Home to James Dundas, Clerk to the Signet, in 1796.   The lands of Annat had been previously sold by the tutors of Miss Sophia Home to the Earl of Moray.

Sophia Home, born in 1787, seems to have been married in 1803 at the age of 16 years.   Her marriage contract was signed on the 8th and 9th August of that year.   Her husband was David Monro, a son of Alexander Monro, the second Professor of Anatomy at Edinburgh University, son of Alexander Monro, the first Professor.

The family of Monro trace their descent from Sir Alexander Monro of Bearcrofts, whose eldest son, Colonel George Monro, married Margaret Bruce of Auchenbowie about 1721. Auchenbowie had been the property of the Bruces since 1506.   A brother of Colonel Monro, John Monro, was a surgeon in Edinburgh and father of the three famous Professors of Anatomy, father, son and grandson, all bearing the name of Alexander Monro.   The first of the name purchased the estate of Auchenbowie from his cousin George.   His eldest son, John Monro, succeeded him and in turn was succeeded by his elder daughter, Jean, who, as noted above, married George Home of Argaty in 1785.

John Monro, the father of the first Professor of Anatomy, is said to have been the originator of the scheme for the foundation of a Medical School in Edinburgh and also of an Infirmary. His son accomplished his ideals, became Professor of Anatomy at the age of 22 and, through the instigation of his father, other lecturers on medical subjects were appointed.   He acquired a European reputation and brought fame to the University of Edinburgh.   He never resided at Auchenbowie, but enlarged it for the benefit of his eldest son.   His wife was the daughter of the 11th Laird of Sleat, and through her George Home Binning Home claimed to be the heir-general and representative of the Earl of Ross and Lords of Skye.

Sophia Home's husband, David Monro, had assumed the name of Binning, as the estate of Softlaw had been purchased and settled on him under the will of a distant cousin, William Binning of Wallyford, in 1796.   The Binnings of Wallyford claim descent from a farmer, named William Binnock, who was the hero of the story of the capture of Linlithgow Castle from an English garrison in the year 1311, narrated by the poet, John Barbour, in *The Bruce*, written in 1375.   Binnock was employed to take in hay to the Castle, and concealing eight men in his waggon as it stood in the gateway, he cut the traces so that the portcullis could not be lowered. The guard was overpowered and the Castle taken.   According to tradition, Robert the Bruce awarded Binnock with the lands of Easter Binning about four miles to the south-east of Linlithgow.   The earliest reference to a Binning as owner of Easter Binning is William de Benyng in 1429.   The first Binning of Wallyford was William Binning, Lord Provost of Edinburgh, 1675-1677, who bought this estate, which is in the parish of Inveresk, in the former year.   A descendant named Katherine Binning married Professor Alexander Monro, the second.   Their younger son, David Monro, was named heir in the will of William Binning of Wallyford, who directed his trustees to buy a property and entail it on him and his heirs. His trustees accordingly bought the estate of Softlaw for him and he assumed the additional surname of Binning. His marriage was soon broken by the death of Sophia in 1806, before she had completed her nineteenth year. Sophia left two sons whose portrait was painted by Sir Henry Raeburn in the year 1811, the sale of which picture procured what was, at the date of sale, a record price for a Raeburn. The older of the two boys, born in 1804, took the name of George Home Monro Binning Home, and lived till 1884. He succeeded to the estate of Argaty, which belonged to his mother, on her death, and to the estate of Softlaw on the death of his father. He was an advocate by profession. He married, in 1839, Catherine Burnett, daughter of Lieutenant-Colonel Joseph Burnett of Gadgirth. They had six children, but all died young. His widow lived until 1894. Known popularly as " auld Binnie," he was described in the press as a public-spirited, intelligent, and patriotic man who had done much to improve the land and breeds of cattle, as well as the "moral relations of the people where that was thought desirable." He was much interested in Shorthorns, and kept a large number of saddle horses, while he made a practice of riding over all rights-of-way in the district once a year in order to keep such open. He claimed to be the heir-general of the Earls of Ross and Lords of Skye, and also of the Lords of the Isles as the heir of his great-great-grand-mother, Isabel Macdonald, daughter of Sir Donald Macdonald of Sleat.

The following pen portrait has been drawn from information supplied by one who knew Mr. Binning Home well in his later years. "An aristocrat of the severe type, handsome with high forehead, clear blue eyes under knitted eyebrows, sandy-grey hair, side whiskers and moustache, and severe chin and lip, a man not to be trifled with, and one who admitted that he had no superior. His usual dress, characteristic of the man, consisted of a short-frock-shaped coat, in summer always of grey alpaca, white beaver top-hat, white moleskin breeches, high riding boots, and a collar supported with layers of tie. Thus clad he looked the picture of a Victorian country gentleman. He was always an early riser, and before breakfast he was off to the stables, and, mounted on his favourite mare, he rode round his estate inspecting the work in progress. He breakfasted at nine, partook of a light mid-day meal of biscuits, milk, and fruit, and dined about 6 or 6.30, on Sundays at 4.30. He was in bed by 9.30 or 10 p.m., and he expected all the members of his household to do likewise. He did much draining of the land by the laying of drain pipes, and employed a large number of Irish workers for this, while he was the first person in the district to plant turnips and potatoes in drills.

"He was greatly interested in the breeding of Shorthorn cattle, and many of his animals obtained distinctions at the leading shows. One of the dreams of his life was realised when in the early 'sixties his Shorthorn bull, Van Tromp, won the gold medal for the best bull at the Royal Agricultural Show in England. In his latter years a severe misfortune befell him in the loss of the pick of the herd, Amelia, Princess, and Dot, which were slaughtered by the local authority on account of an outbreak of pleuro-pneumonia on an adjoining farm—a loss which he never forgot and an injury which he never forgave. In his early manhood a Yeomanry officer, he was always an excellent horseman and rode to within a year of his death. He bred and broke in horses to his last days, and hunted with the Stirlingshire hounds and local harriers until disabled by a serious accident to a shoulder. Being a road trustee he saw that on the side of each road was a suitable riding path on which no metal might be laid. For many years he drove a pair of grey horses in a long, heavy built phæton, with an old-fashioned rumble behind for footmen, and this he took with him when he visited France. He, however, brought home from Paris a heavy brougham, also with a rumble, called the Clarence, of which he was always proud. He had artistic tastes and attainments, and frequently between 1850 and 1870 had pictures hung in the Academy. Although a trained lawyer he never practised. He was also interested in architecture, and Argaty house was added to from plans of his own in 1861 and following years. Mr. Binning Home had some knowledge of geology, and was an intimate friend of Professor Geikie of Edinburgh, with whom he had a lengthy correspondence on the formation of red sandstone. In politics he was a staunch Conservative. No one, whether a friend, tenant, or servant, could venture to express views differing from his own without encountering retorts, often expressed in the strongest of language. In his early days he was a strong Episcopalian, and drove each Sunday to Stirling to attend service, but latterly he was a member of the Established Church and regularly attended the Parish Kirk of Kilmadock. He took the deepest interest in local affairs, and a part in county administration at Dunblane. He was a keen sportsman and a good shot of the deliberate type. He never missed a 12th of August on Argaty moor. The bag on that day was restricted to 20 brace of grouse, and on any subsequent day to 10 brace. He was most considerate to his farm tenants and interested in their welfare, but there was a reserve which was never broken. He was ready, however, at all times to consider any suggestion which might be made to him in the way of improvements. During his lifetime he rebuilt the buildings on all his farms, reclaimed and drained large areas of land, and planted considerable areas with trees. To sum up, he was a typical laird of the early nineteenth century, self-opinionated to a degree but notwithstanding progressive in his opinions on matters of agriculture and estate management and with an intuitive insight into the future."

His brother, Alexander Binning Monro, the other son of Sophia Home, was a Writer to the Signet. He succeeded to the estate of Auchenbowie, the property of his grandmother, Jean Monro, on her death, and on the death of the laird of Argaty in 1884, he succeeded to the entailed estate of Softlaw. He did not, however, succeed to the estate of Argaty, which was left by his brother, George, to his grand-nephew, George Home Monro, the eldest son of his nephew, Alexander Monro.

George Home Monro, the last laird, took the name of Home on his succession. He and his brother, Alexander E. Monro, came from New Zealand to Scotland as boys, and were educated at King William College, Isle of Man. George qualified as a Doctor at Edinburgh University, practised for some time in Nottingham and Liverpool, was for a time employed on medical work with a Life Insurance Company in China, and during part of the War period was Port Health Officer at Shanghai. After succeeding to Argaty, he let the mansion house and estate shootings to a number of successive tenants for some years, but, ultimately, on the death of Mr. Rogerson, the last tenant, he resolved to sell the estate, from which he received little income on account of the heavy burdens upon it, and as he had no hope of ever being able to live on his property. The estate was accordingly advertised for sale, and was ultimately purchased in 1917 by Mr. Thomas Henderson. Dr. George Home Monro Home succeeded to the estate of Softlaw on the death of his father. This is an agricultural property a few miles from Kelso, but without a mansion house, and this Dr. Monro Home also sold. The estate of Auchenbowie is still in the possession of the Monro family.

Argaty has now fallen into the loving hands of those, who, within a short time, have effected many important improvements and added greatly to its adornment. The development of its natural beauties has proved a joy to its owners, and to all who take a part in the work or are privileged to be onlookers.

THE BARONY BOOK OF ARGATY, 1672-1699.

(Preserved in the Historical Department, H.M. Register House, Edinburgh).

While barony courts existed throughout Scotland for some centuries, there seem to be comparatively few barony books still extant. Two, namely, those of the baronies of Urie and Stitchell, which have been published, convey important information as to rural customs and the administration of justice in Scotland in the Middle Ages, and, while the only volume of the Argaty barony records preserved to this day covers but a short period, it gives an interesting picture of the life of the district and of the relationships between the proprietor and his vassals.

When the record starts, the proprietor of Argaty was Harie Home, and at the court held on sixth January, 1672, Robert Drummond in Kilbryde was his bailie. Drummond does not appear to have held this office long, which may be accounted for by the fact that the laird had borrowed heavily from him and had mortgaged part of his lands to Drummond, who was put in possession of the rents of that portion. He could not in these circumstances have with propriety acted as bailie, considering that his duties as bailie would frequently clash with his interests as mortgagee.

For some time Robert Caddell of Banks acted as baron bailie, but, during the latter part of the period, the bailie was Andrew Clerk in Downe. So far as the barony of Argaty is concerned, although the laird was frequently present in court, the proceedings appear to have been conducted by the bailie, and it was he who pronounced judgment. It was only right that this should be so, considering that the laird was so often the claimant in the cases which came before the court. It is interesting to note that on the death of Harie Home, his widow, Janet Moir, the liferentrix, held the next court, namely, on 1st January, 1690, Andrew Clerk in Downe being associated with her as her ladyship's bailie. It is therefore by no means a new incident in the administration of justice in Scotland for a lady to be on the bench. Her ladyship, however, did not continue to grace the courts with her presence, as in the following years we find two or more of the tutors of the young laird representing him. The barony books have numerous references to other officials, one of whom bore the familiar title of Procurator-Fiscal and another was the Officer of Court. The latter office was held by residents on the estate. There was also usually present in court one who acted as Clerk of Court. The Barony Officer appears to have been remunerated by an allowance of grain payable by the tenants. At the court held on 16th December, 1693, the bailie ordained the whole tenants within the barony to pay yearly to the officer six firlots of wheat of which twelve pecks were to come from Lundies and Maynes of Argaty, and the other twelve pecks from the rest of the barony.

While the suits that appeared before the court were principally concerned with matter for rent and arrears of rent, we have records of prosecutions for various criminal offences. At the court held on 12th July, 1683, " a bill of complent was given in be the procuratour fiscall and Duncane Fergusone his informer againes Alexander Mitchell laufull soune to Alexander Mitchell in Argatie, and after examination of both parties, they are found to be both gultie of blooding and streiking each of them wtheris, theirfoir the balyie wnlaws ilk ane off them in tuentie pundis Scotis to be payed to the procuratour fiscall withine terme of Law; and in the maine tyme the said balyie ordaines ilk ane of them to find cautioune to wtheris to keip the pace in tyme cuming wnder the paine of ane hundreth pundis Scotis; and in obedience to the qhuich comand for keiping of the said pace Alexander Mitchell findis James Adame in Lundie cautiouner for him and lykuayes the said Duncane Fergusone finds Andro Thomsone in Argatie cautioune for him."

The penalties were very considerable, as although the present value of Scots money is only one-twelfth of money Sterling, the value of money at that time was probably twelve times what it is now, and the fine imposed for " blooding and streiking each other," was perhaps equivalent to a fine of £20 at the present day.

"On 28th August, 1688, a bill of complent was given in by George Thomsone in Argatie, procurator fiscall and Johne Caydan in Lundie and Janet Scobie his spouse, his informers, against James Millar thair to the effect that the informer's spouse while keeping hir oune kows wpone Sunday last wpone ane haind lye quhich the informer had purchased from Harie Chrystie leit tenant thair, the said James Millar came to the informer's spouse without anie ground or resone to turne off the saidies kowes of the foirsaid gras and did put a hand to the informer's wyfe and did throw hir doune and did draw her throug the said lye by and attour severall wthir abuses hawing shakine of all fear of God; James Millar failing to appear in Court, the balyie onlaws him in the soume of fyve pundis for his contamasie and disobedience and in the soume of tuelf pundis for the foirsaid ryot and wthir abuses to be payed to the procuratour fiscall within terme of Law; and he was ordained to keip good neibourhead to wtheris in all tyme cuming wnder the pain of tuentie pundis. As the offence was committed on the Sunday previous there had been no loss of time in putting the law in force, while the penalties imposed were, as in the previous cases, severe."

On 7th December, 1694, at a court presided over by George Moir of Leckie and David Muschet of Calyechatt two of the tutors of George Home, the young Laird, " the Baillyie vnlawes George Squyre in fyve punds Scotts for wrongous intromissioune with certaine peattes pertaining to James Adame, the said fyne to be paid to the procuratour fiscall under the paine of poynding."

At the court of 8th April, 1696, presided over by the same tutors, " George Squyre in Easter Argatie" was again in trouble and was fined " fyve pund for streacking Patrick Ogylbie on the Sabath last, as well as a further sum of fyve pund for his contumacie and disobedience for refusing to depone to the circumstances being personallie cited thairto."

The maintenance of a mill for grinding the corn was of great importance in rural districts, and tenants were under obligation not only to take their grain to the mill on the estate, but to maintain the water lade and the thatching of the roof of the mill premises. If a tenant took his grain elsewhere he became liable to the miller for certain quantities of grain or payments, the miller being entitled as his remuneration to receive a certain proportion of the tenants's corn.   On the other hand, it was the miller's duty to supply certain quantities of grain to the laird by way of rent.   There are numerous references in the Argaty Barony Book to complaints by the millers of that time against the tenants bound to Argaty Mill who had failed in the performance of their obligations as also complaints by the laird against the millers.   On 5th November, 1687, " Robert McCutcheon, tacksman of the mylne of Argatie, complained of Hary Chrystie in Lundie for abstracting sixteen bolles of corn yearlie for three yeires bygone which sould have been grunnd at the said mylne and have payed full multer thairfore.   The Bailie decernes Chrystie to pay ane peck for each boll suae abstracted, he failing to appear in Court and depone thairupon."   The miller's remuneration thus appears to have been one-sixteenth of the quantity presented for grinding.

On 25th November, 1692, Robert McCutcheon appears to have been in fault for sending " insufficient meall yearly to the girnell of Argatie, in which case the tutors ordained McCutcheoune in all tyme cuming to make gude and sufficyent meall frie of dust and seids wnder the paine of tuentie punds Scotts."   This decree does not appear to have been effectual as at the following court on 16th December, 1693, a further complaint was given in against McCutcheon for supplying " insufficient meall for crope 1692.   The meall was producit and inspected and found altogidder insufficient with the result that the baillyie fined the miller tuentie pundis and ordained the officer to charge and poynd thairfoir and the said Robert was ordained to sell his meall yeirlie at the mercattis of Sterling."   The poor miller at this court was in further difficulties, there being a bill of complaint against him for cutting timber within the said barony.   The matter being referred to his oath he refused to depone and the bailie fined him five pounds.   Notwithstanding the trouble he had got into McCutcheon was at the same court appointed one of four " birleymen of the said barony for sighting of houses and utheris."   The duty of birleymen or burlawmen was to act as valuators or arbiters in questions between two tenants or between a tenant and his landlord, and at this court the birleymen and officer were ordained to sight Walter Drummond's barn and " whatevir they ordained that Walter should have, the tutouris were to provide."   This seems to indicate good relationships between the tutors and their tenants when the former were willing to agree to do such repairs to a farmer's barn as other tenants considered were necessary.

At this period the tenants, of course, paid only a small sum of money rent, but had various duties to perform for the laird in accordance with their leases, such as tilling his land, keeping up the park dykes, supplying and driving peats to the mansion house, and supplying grain, fowls, butter, and other commodities of the table.   On 7th December, 1694, the court fixed money equivalents for services not performed or goods not delivered, and we find that tenants and cottars within the barony had to pay 1s. for each load of peats not delivered at Argaty House. Those that were liable in payment of yarn were required to pay 18s. for each spynle not delivered, 40s. Scots was the value of a wedder, 14s. the equivalent of a boll of hors corne, four merks the price of a stone of butter, and four shillings the value of a hen.   Apparently the laird of Argaty had the privilege of asking payment in cash for the foregoing in place of delivery of the goods.

In the report of the first court held on 6th January, 1672, there is a record of a complaint by the tenants that the Lady Kippenross was threatening to compel them to carry their yearly quota of peats where she pleased.   The bailie ordered the tenants to take them where they had been used to stack them in former times, namely, to the place of Argaty, and to none other place.

At the following court held on 13th July, 1672, Harie Home, the laird, produces an assignation by Jean Drummond Lady Kippenross in his favour of her Ladyship's life-rent rights in the lands and barony of Argaty and Lundies from the Whitsunday preceding.   Her Ladyship did not trouble the laird and tenants further.

There is only one instance of action being taken by a servant against his master.   In that case, Donald Deor (Dewar) complained against John Mackison for £4 Scots of bygone wage owing by him to the said Donald.   The baillie ordered Mackison to pay same to the pursuer in respect of Mackison's admission of the debt.

At the court held on 13th July, 1672, it was found necessary to appoint birleymen to decide all matters debatable betwixt neighbour and neighbour, when " thriehonnest men " were appointed, any two to be a quorum.   These men were duly sworn to *fideli administratione* without partiality to any, and were given power to determine any differences " anent eatten cornes, sighting of housses and utheris, and to call and hold courtis for that effect." A complaint having been given in at this barony court " by the tennents of the Maynes of Argaty against the cottaris ther abuseing the medow and sauch bushes within the medow the same was referred to the cognition of the said Birlawmen." Another instance in which the birleymen were called into action is recorded in the proceedings of the court held on 10th April, 1673, in a complaint by Donald Macnab against John Mackison for corn alleged to have been eaten by Mackison's stock. Macnab had appealed to the birleymen who had estimated the quantity eaten at six firlots. Mackison called upon the said Donald to purge his own gear and other goods of the said scathe—that is, to swear that the damage had not been done by Donald's own beasts. Donald refused to depone thereon, whereupon Mackison went free, as where a party to a cause refused to give his oath he was held to be admitting his opponent's case.

On a number of occasions one comes across instances of the laird imposing restrictions in the interests of good husbandry. Thus on 5th November, 1687, the baillie ordained " each tennent having a pleugh of land to sow yearlie ane firlot of pease, and each cottar to sow ane peck under the penalty of tuentie shilling for a tennent or fyve shilling for a cottar." At the same time, " each tennent was ordained to plant six barren trees within their enclosures yearlie and each cottar three such trees, the laird supplying the trees and the tennents being under penalty of a merk for failure." It has to be kept in view that the countryside was, generally speaking, very deficient in wood and shelter, and it was a most desirable thing to encourage the rearing of timber on an estate, particularly as agricultural implements were made of wood. The same injunction as to planting of " peis " is found in the record of the last court held at Argaty on 7th February, 1699, the penalty for failure being a fine of 40s.

It was important then, as it is now, that all farm manure should be applied to the land, and on 28th August, 1688, it was enacted that none of the tenants or cottars should sell or put away any manure off the ground in all time coming under the pain of £10.

While there was at this time little in the way of fencing, and few dykes on an estate unless round the policies or park of the laird, the owners of animals were under obligation to prevent their stock trespassing on the lands of their neighbours, destroying their crops or eating their corn. John Moir complained against "the haill tennentis of Argaty for pasturing sheip and uther bestiall within the park of Argatie let by the laird to him and the baillie ordained the officer to poynd for thrie schillingis four pennies for each sheep fund pasturing within the park and to forbid any of the tennantis goeing throw the park under the paine of fourtie schillingis. The penalty for a hors or kow found pasturing in the park was half ane merk, or 6s. 8d."

The laird on several occasions had to complain of mischievous persons breaking down his yard and dykes, and on 5th January, 1674, Johne Makison in Argaty and John Muile were fined on their own admission twenty shillings for this offence and Moir ordained to build his yard dyke before the first of March.

At a court held on 22nd May, 1686, the tenants, in accordance with an Act of Parliament of James VII, and the Laird, for his interest, bound and obliged themselves and their families, cottars and servants to live " peacablie and regularlie, frie of all fanaticall dissorderis." The undertaking was signed by the laird, and apparently by John Moir, Notary Public, on behalf of the tenants with the exception of one named Andrew Thomson, who may have had the distinction of being the only tenant on Argaty who knew how to write. At the same court a complaint was given in by the laird that the tenants had each received "ane lippie of meall" for each three loads of peats brought by them to Argaty, and that he was not pleased with this arrangement. The Bailie found that there was " no maister in the cuntrie who gave the lyke to his tennentis and ordained that the tennentis should onlie have their meatt for the conveying of the peatts, the refreshment to consist of thrie meallis for ilk fyve loads and that in place of the lippies of meal." The bailie at this court forbade any person to shoot any hares, partridges or grouse under the penalty of twenty pounds to be paid to the procurator-fiscal.

On 20th February, 1680, a complaint was given in to the barony court by James McIlduine in Corscaplie against "Johne Makisone in Argatie regarding ane ox given for hire by Makisone to McIlduine till the following Beltane and which ox was sold by Makisone to Sir Coline Campbell of Kilbryde." McIlduine had delivered the ox at the request of Sir Colin's servants out of his plough. The dispute was referred to the oath of McIlduine, who was present, but he refused "to depone thairupon and the court accordingly assolyied Makisone fra the matters complained of and fra the sum of half a merk a day" which McIlduine appears to have claimed from the time of the removal of the ox.

At the court held on 16th January, 1697, there is a reference to what in later years was known as a love darg, that is, a day's ploughing given by tenants of an estate to a newcomer to help him on with the ploughing of his farm. At this court the tutors of the Laird and the Bailie ordained all the tenants to bring their whole ploughs to Middle Argaty possessed by Robert Mitchell and there to till four yokings in due time of the year under the penalty of 20s. Scots for each person that should fail in each yoking. The penalty was payable not to Mitchell, who lost the yokings, but to the tutors.

At the court held on 29th January, 1698, the Procurator-Fiscal gave in a complaint against the whole tenants and cottars within the barony for selling and buying meal by measure and not by weight, contrary to the Act of Parliament. The matter was put to the various land-holders when numerous tenants seem to have confessed buying or selling by measure. The bailie fined each of the transgressors £20, the penalty to be paid to the Procurator-Fiscal. As ten tenants admitted guilt the fines amounted to £200, a very large sum to be made forthcoming from the estate.

It is satisfactory to be able to record that a perusal of this barony book leaves the impression on the reader, that, on the whole, justice was meted out between laird and tenant and between fellow-tenants, with wonderful impartiality.

CHAPTER XXI.

DUNBLANE 1700-1800.

DUNBLANE during the 18th century did not flourish. Much of its former importance was derived through its being the seat of a Bishopric which brought within its bounds the numerous officials of the Cathedral and induced many of the proprietors of estates within the diocese to maintain a town residence within the city, which they occupied for part of the year. Episcopacy ended in 1689, and thereafter the Cathedral was a parish church and not the central place of worship in a wider district.

During the 18th century there was little building done within Dunblane or its immediate neighbourhood. The Cathedral, with the exception of the choir, was ruinous and there was little trade. During the first half of the century Dunblane was a centre of considerable activity on behalf of the exiled Stuarts. During the second half it was distinguished for ecclesiastical dissensions. Some information about the impression made by Dunblane on eighteenth century writers will be found in chapter xi.

While there were some houses of considerable size in Dunblane, such as that of Lord Strathallan, most of the dwellings were of a poor description. They were all closely packed together, some on the main streets which were narrow, and some up pends off these streets or in vennels which led from one street to another. Beside the houses, in many cases, were cow byres or pigsties. Many of the inhabitants had holdings of land in proximity to the town for many made a living of agriculture. The houses were built with very thick walls tapering as they rose from the ground, but frequently only about 6 ft. high. The gables were thicker than the side walls. The roofs were made with the trunks of trees with divots laid thereon, covered with thatching.

The administration of justice was to a large extent in the hands of the Bailie of Dunblane, an office vested in the Lairds of Cromlix who were wont to appoint a depute to act on their behalf. The Bailie again or his depute nominated officials to assist him in the maintenance of order and administration of justice, who were termed Quartermasters. Thus, on 6th November, 1734, the Bailie nominated and appointed Patrick Dow in Bridgend of Dunblane, William Stirling, merchant, John Gillespie, merchant, and William Murray, weaver in Ramoyle of Dunblane, to be Quartermasters within the said city and in Ramoyle and Bridgend of Dunblane. Stirling and Gillespie were residenters within the city and Dow and Murray in the areas outside its gates.

On 1st January, 1724, the Bailie appointed John Bryce and Henry Kerr, merchants in Dunblane, William Moir in Ramoyle and James Lucas in Bridgend to be Quartermasters for the ensuing year with all powers and privileges to that office pertaining or committed by former Acts of Court.

On this occasion the Bailie having been informed that country people passing home in the night had been attacked and threatened and abused by people said to be living in the town or territory of Dunblane, ordered the quartermasters to make up lists of all the inhabitants and summon them before him that their circumstances might be inquired into. (*Records of Regality.*)

John Don or Dow, Bailie in 1725, appointed James Paterson, Clerk, and William Paterson, Fiscall of Regality. James Russell seems to have been appointed Bailie for the first time in 1727 —the superior then being George, Earl of Kinnoull. The Bailie again appointed Serjeants Dempster and other officers of Court. At this time, James Moir, notary in Doune, was clerk, and James Cairns, merchant in Dunblane, fiscal. The Bailie is frequently referred to as the Bailie Depute or Substitute.

On 6th January, 1734, the Bailie Depute James Russell (who was also the Commissary Clerk and the host of the Duke of Cumberland in 1746) appointed Archibald Campbell, writer of Leckropt, Fiscall of Dunblane in place of James Drummond, a former Fiscall, and James Thomson, Merchant in Dunblane, was appointed one of the officers of the Regality and gaoler of the " tolbooth." He had to provide a cautioner for the proper performance by him of the duties of his office, John Cunningham, vintner in Bridgend, acting for Thomson in this capacity.

The tolbooth or prison of Dunblane during the 18th century was a two-storeyed building, situated near the mercat cross, consisting of four rooms and was appointed by the Laird of Cromlix in 1759, then Dr. Robert Drummond of Cromlix, Bishop of St. Asaph and afterwards Archbishop of York, to be used as a prison by his Bailie for rendering effectual the jurisdiction competent to him by law. The tolbooth stood to the east of the present main entrance gate to the Cathedral and was in use until the middle of the 19th century.

The powers of the Bailie were very considerable and the penalties imposed were frequently severe. On the 6th November, 1734, a culprit of the name of Forbes, who had previously been imprisoned and put in the " jugs " for theft and picking, was ordered by the Bailie to remain in prison for five days further and then " to be put in the Jugs and burned in the face with the ordinary marks of this city and afterwards to be scourged and whipped through the city for a terror to her and others for stealing out of a house in the barony of Keir, a plaid, a gown, linens and woollen gown and other articles." The Bailie appointed a deputation of fifteen to go to Stirling and conduct safely the Staffman of that burgh to Dunblane for executing the sentence and thirteen other men to conduct him safely back under a penalty in each case of £10 Scots for failure. In 1734 a woman was driven out of town under a threat of being put in the jugs and burned in the face by the common hangman.

There is recorded in the Commissary Court Books of Dunblane in the year 1686 a submission entered into by James Burden of Feddal on behalf of John Burden, Clerk of the Regality of Dunblane, his brother, and William Young, officer of Dunblane on the one part, and John Burnbank and Graham of Glenny from the Port of Menteithdistrict, " anent what the asythment and satisfaction should be made by either of the parties to the others for the several injuries and bloody riots alleged to have been committed by them upon the others within the town of Dunblane and territories thereof upon 25th May, 1686." The first parties appointed James Robison in Park of Keir as their judge arbiter and the second parties chose Arthur Buchanan of Auchleshie to act on their behalf, and the oversman was John Drummond. The judge arbiters issued their award on 29th July, 1686, decerning John Burden and William Young to deliver to their opponents an "ample letter of slaines and discharge of blood ryots and injuries." Their opponents were ordered to pay John Burden three hundred pounds Scots with £15 of expenses and William Young £36 Scots with £6 of expenses and to Patrick McCarther, surgeon in Stirling, £100 Scots for his pains and expenses in curing them, and Alexander Chisholm, bailie in Dunblane £15 of expenses, and they were also ordained to deliver to the said Chisholm, Burden and Young and their accomplices an ample letter of slaines and discharge of any blood or injury committed against the Grahams and Burnbank.

While the poor to some extent received support from the heritors of the Parish and from the Church, the problem of begging was a serious one during the 18th century. On 20th October, 1756, the Sheriff of Perthshire, John Swinton, issued a proclamation to the heritors, ministers and elders of Dunblane and other parishes with regard to the suppression of vagrants and sturdy beggars with which certain parishes had been grievously infested. The ministers of these parishes were required to call meetings of heritors and elders to put in force an Act passed by the justices and to cause intimation to be made from the reader's desk that before 1st December all vagrants, sturdy beggars and idle persons belonging to other shires should depart to those shires and that all beggars should retire to the parish where they were born or have had most residence for the last three years and that such vagrants keep to the public highways under the pain of being punished as vagrants. Badges for vagrants were made at the foundry at Perth and were sold at 2s. per dozen. In 1756, the number of the poor for whom the parish was responsible was 85, 28 of whom received badges permitting them to beg in the parish. They were known as the travelling poor. The remaining 57 poor persons received money allowances.

The heritors and Kirk Session were also directed by the Sheriff to make provision for the poor of the parish under a penalty of £200 Scots for each month during which provision was not made.

Vagrants were accustomed to congregate when any notable events were celebrated such as a wedding or burial, as also at communion seasons. The Lord's Supper was at this time administered in Dunblane only once in the year, namely, in the month of July. The services lasted from the Wednesday before communion to the Monday after and large numbers gathered to attend, while the church offerings were greatly in excess of those on other Sundays. As a rule, the collections were for support of the poor and money seems to have been distributed among the vagrants, as well as amongst resident poor persons.

The customs of the city of Dunblane belonged to the Laird of Cromlix and were let by him to the highest bidder. They were let in 1742, by public roup for one year from Michaelmas to Michaelmas. On the day of the roup, George Millar, baron officer, advertised by tuck of drum that the customs were to be let before James Russell, Commissary Clerk, who had been appointed Judge of the roup, by James Robertson, factor of the superior. The roup took place at the market cross and was fixed to continue for half an hour and no offer was allowed of less than 400 merks, while each offerer was to overbid the previous offer by at least 5 merks. The highest offerer who could give satisfactory caution was preferred and the rent was payable in three equal portions at Hallowmas, Whitsunday and St. Laurence Fair. In 1742 several offers were made and the highest offer, namely, one of 420 merks, from William Rattray, in Bridgend of Dunblane, was accepted.

A table of the customs of the City of Dunblane to be exacted by the tacksmen and collectors dated 8th October, 1741, and signed by Dr. Robert Hay Drummond, is still extant. Separate lists of charges were fixed for the fairs and for other times, the charges at fairs usually exceeding those of other seasons. A copy of this table is printed elsewhere.

It is not known when the first clock was inserted in the Cathedral tower, but 200 years ago it was described as " the old clock " and was then " in a great measure useless." On 4th April, 1732, James Russell, Commissary Clerk, attended a meeting of Kirk Session and gave in a petition desiring that the Session contribute out of the public funds under their management for purchasing a new clock, alleging for the reasonableness of their compliance with his mission that the Session had the benefit of the bells at burials and that the big bell was hung and stocked at a considerable charge out of the vacant stipends. The Session, after consideration of the proposal, agreed that the elders go from house to house to collect for the said desire of buying a new clock and that they give out their said funds the sum of £4 10s. sterling for the said purpose. The Kirk Sessions had many duties to perform at this period over and above their ecclesiastical work.

During the century the Lodge of Free Masons in Dunblane No. 9 flourished. The oldest minute book in existence contains minutes which date from 6th April, 1695, and it is believed that the Lodge existed for some time prior to that date. The first signature is that of William Drummond, Viscount Strathallan, who was Master of the Lodge in 1696-97. He died in 1702. He was succeeded by Alexander Drummond of Balhaldie, a strong supporter of the Royal Stuarts, and he again was followed by John Pearson, Laird of Kippenross. John Pearson was re-elected on several occasions and his successors Hugh Pearson acted as Master in 1734-35 and John Pearson from 1765 to 1771. Other notable Masters early in the 18th century were John Stirling of Keir and Patrick Stirling of Kippendavie, and Lord John Drummond was Master during the stormy years of 1744-45-46. Lord John Drummond held a prominent command in the Highland army at the Battle of Falkirk. Among later prominent residenters who presided over the Lodge during the 18th century were James Russell, Bailie of Dunblane, Thomas Duthie, writer and Sheriff Substitute, as also other Duthies related to him, Robert and John before him, and William and Thomas Junior, later, several members of the old family of Muschet, John Steven, factor and architect, and several members of the family of Rob.

The schoolmaster of Dunblane at the beginning of this century was James McEchny who was followed by James McGoun, the writer of the short account of Dunblane in Macfarlane's *Geographical Collections* (See chapter xi). Both men were clerks of the Presbytery of Dunblane. Perhaps the most distinguished parish schoolmaster was William Coldstream, appointed in 1743, who was a scholar of some distinction and who took a prominent part in the life of the community. Many of the sons of the local nobility were boarded with him for education. He held various public offices and many of his papers are still extant in the Leighton Library, some of which have appeared in the Transactions of the Society of Friends of Dunblane Cathedral.

Some interesting information may be derived from his old accounts, apart from the records of cock-fighting which are referred to in Chapter xxix. Among some of his purchases are the following :—in 1750, four new shoes, 18/-, in 1754 two large shammy skins at 1/2 each and half a dozen small buttons, 6d. In 1756, he bought a new wig to himself for 14/- sterling and one for John Stirling, his pupil, costing 6/-. In the same year, John Stirling, who was the son of the late Laird of Kippendavie, appears to have passed through an illness in which he was attended by

Henry Christie, surgeon in Dunblane. The treatment began with a bloodlet in the arm costing 2/6 with an emetic 8d. and a fomentation 6d. Doctor Christie supplied· various medicines and gave two injections costing 6d. each, the bill eventually totalling £1 2s. 10d.

Mr. Coldstream had various private pupils, for whom he received reasonable fees. Thus between 1753 and 1756, he taught Latin to Robert and James, sons of William Monteith, smith in Dunblane, for which he received £4 a year. Other pupils included Campbells of Kilbryde and Pearsons of Kippenross. After holding office for a long period he was succeeded by his son, Malcolm Coldstream, who continued in office until his resignation in 1809. His successor was Daniel Stewart whose name is still remembered by the older inhabitants and who carried on his duties in Dunblane for about fifty years. The tenure of the three last named thus covered a period of about 116 years.

On the west wall of Dunblane Cathedral is preserved a mural tablet erected to the memory of William Coldstream, which prior to the Restoration was attached to the north wall of the choir. It bears a Latin inscription in touching terms indicating that it was erected by former scholars in memory of a skilful and faithful schoolmaster, who for 43 years set the youth of Dunblane a living example of a youthful and friendly spirit combined with an earnest desire to assist his pupils. He passed away on 21st December, 1787.

It is interesting to note that at the middle of the eighteenth century, there were representatives of all trades and professions in Dunblane. The professions were represented by a Sheriff-Substitute, writers, Commissary Clerk, schoolmasters and at least one surgeon, while among the shop-keepers, we find wig-makers, book-sellers and vintners, and among the tradesmen are noted masons, joiners, smiths, workers in brass, glovers, belt-makers, skinners, flax-dressers (called hecklers) and harness makers. In 1820, John Ferguson appears to have combined the duties of surgeon with post-master. It may be noted here that at the end of the 17th century, the Kirk Session had difficulty with the darkness of the Cathedral partly due to the large galleries, and in 1693 it was arranged that two windows should be struck out in the south side of the kirk, one on each side of the pulpit, that the people might better see to read. This refers to the south wall of the choir. The pulpit at that time stood in the centre of the choir near the south wall, and if this entry in the Kirk Session book is correct, there must have been two fewer windows, say in Leighton's time, than at the present day.

In 1710, it was agreed to afford the elders, who stood at the doors of the church beside the plates, protection from the weather. The Session then appointed the treasurer to have a porch built over the east door of the church for the elders' accommodation, who collected for the poor. It is not quite clear where this door stood, but there was a door at the east end of the south wall of the choir with a stair leading up to the east gallery.

In 1747 Alexander White, wright in Dunblane, erected a new porch at this door at a cost of £36 17s. 6d. Scots. In 1753 the Session agreed to have a " shade built at the West Great Door of the Church for the collectors, to screen them in winter." This was the entrance door in the chancel arch from the ruined nave to the choir.

The last Episcopalian minister officiating in the Cathedral prior to the Revolution in 1689 was Gaspar Kellie who was deprived for not reading the Proclamation of the Estates and for not praying for William and Mary. A few years seem to have elapsed before a successor was appointed. On 6th September, 1692, a call was given to the Reverend Michael Potter, M.A., who in his earlier life had endured persecution and had been imprisoned in Edinburgh and on the Bass Rock. Mr. Potter died in Dunblane in 1718. His son, Michael, became Professor of Divinity in the University of Glasgow. Reverend Archibald Gibson, M.A., was ordained in Dunblane on 18th August, 1719. He was translated to St. Ninians in 1728. His successor was the Reverend William Simson who was admitted minister of Dunblane on 25th June, 1730. At that time, £135 9s. 10d. was due to the Session Clerk for entertaining ministers, their servants and horses during the vacancy. Mr. Simson was previously minister of Fowlis Wester where he was held in high esteem, so much so, that when it became known that a deputation was to attend service at Fowlis Wester with a view to hearing him, measures were taken locally to exclude the representatives of Dunblane from entering the church. They succeeded by a subterfuge (see p. 189) and thereafter gave a favourable report which led to Mr. Simson's translation. Mr. Simson was a man of considerable wisdom and amiability and a lover of peace as may be inferred from some local incidents during the time of his incumbency. Although he is said to have favoured the claims of the Royal Stuarts, he and Baillie Russell advised the people of Dunblane to go out to the Skellie Braes to meet the Duke of Cumberland when he approached Dunblane with his army prior to the Battle of Culloden. At the time of the Porteous Riots Mr. Simson read the Porteous Act from the pulpit as ordered by the Government which involved him in some local unpopularity. Mr. Simson bequeathed 300 merks to the Leighton Library and 500 merks to the Kirk Session for the poor. It was during his incumbency that dissenters first broke away from the Established Church, and this was partly due to differences between the minister and certain members of his congregation. The body of Seceders was, however, small until after Mr. Simson's death when there was an unfortunate presentation of the Reverend John Robertson to the parish of Dunblane. Mr. Robertson was the son of the minister of Luss and after education at Glasgow University he was licensed in 1747. He was presented to the parish of Dunblane by George II, the Crown having the right of patronage. A call was made out to Mr. Robertson by the principal heritors in the parish and signed also by two heads of families, but some of the heritors were absentees or members of other churches and took no part in the call. Those who favoured Mr. Robertson petitioned the Presbytery to proceed with the call and a strong counter-petition was presented by the whole elders against his appointment. Their objections were based on their inability to hear or understand Mr. Robertson when he preached in Dunblane owing to the forced rise and sudden fall of his voice and they also complained of his slowness of speech and inaudibility. He had preached on two successive Sundays and it was said that on the second Sunday there were only thirty persons present, mainly young people. Three hundred heads of families joined in the petition of the elders. The Presbytery for some time delayed taking action, evidently in the hope that the opposition to Mr. Robertson might die down or that he might withdraw his acceptance of the charge. Mr. William Bryce, Sheriff Substitute, Stirling, acted for the Crown and appealed from the Presbytery to the Synod of Perth and Stirling. The elders, prior to Mr. Robertson's nomination, had had in view a very young, but very popular, minister in the neighbourhood, whom they wished should be appointed. Ultimately the Presbytery carried through Mr. Robertson's ordination and he remained parish minister of Dunblane until his death in 1795. When the Presbytery took him on trial, great satisfaction was expressed with his appearance. It may be noticed that Mr. Robertson was licensed in 1747 and had not previously had a charge, and in October, 1757, within five months of his ordination, he asked the Presbytery to ordain an assistant to him with a salary of £45. A Mr. Ure was ordained assistant in February, 1758. This forced appointment, against the wishes of the elders and the members of the church, led to a large accession to the ranks of the Seceders and left the Cathedral congregation in a weakened condition from which it did not recover for a generation.

On 2nd June, 1791, the Reverend Robert Stirling, son of John Stirling, a local merchant and a Master of Arts of Glasgow University, was ordained assistant and successor to Mr. Robertson. During his ministry a congregation again gathered together within the Cathedral, but his work pertains rather to the 19th century.

The Presbytery of Dunblane, which at first had been united to that of Stirling, was disjoined in 1698 and the first meeting of Presbytery of Dunblane was held on 26th April of that year. With the abolition of Episcopacy the parish ministers after 1689 became Presbyterian, although it may be noted that the Episcopalian minister at Aberfoyle remained in possession for some time, probably with the support either of prominent heritors or of a majority of the parishioners.

At this time the communion utensils belonging to Dunblane were in the hands of the late conformists, and it was agreed to get the help of Lord Aberuchil with a view to their recovery.

From time to time the Presbytery ordained the observation of fasts and in some cases the reasons are given for proclaiming these. In February, 1713, a fast was ordered to be observed on account of the woeful decay of piety and the prevalence of superstitious rites which had aroused God's displeasure as evidenced by violent weather, floods, bad and late harvest and excessive sickness. In other cases while the decay of piety was deplored there was always associated some other ground for holding a fast, such as illness or bad weather, which leads one to conclude that, had the latter not existed, the Presbytery would not have proclaimed a fast merely on account of the decay of piety. In August, 1745, the Presbytery ordained a diet of prayer on account of the threatened destruction of the crops by long rain and in view of the designs of the Popish

Pretender.   A diet of thanksgiving was appointed in February, 1746, on account of the success of the Duke of Cumberland in " quenching the wicked rebellion."   Great sickness prevailed in this neighbourhood in February, 1751, and many very sudden deaths occurred, which the Presbytery accounted to be a judgment for abounding sin and they appointed an observance of a fast.   On 15th December, 1817, the Session appointed the 26th December as a day of solemn fasting and supplication in respect of the deficiency of the last crop occasioned by the wet season and on account of insubordination in the metropolis.

Owing to the disturbed state of the country in January, 1714, the Presbytery resolved to divide into two portions to meet at Port of Menteith and Dunblane for " wrestling and prayer."

There were frequent appeals to the Presbytery of Dunblane for support of public bodies. At the beginning of this century many Scottish people resided in Newcastle-upon-Tyne.   They had difficulty in obtaining suitable rights of burial and the funerals could only be conducted by Episcopal ministers.   Help was sought for acquiring a burial ground for the Scottish community, and it was stated that where members of that community were usually buried the ground was open to dogs and swine who pulled out and ate the bodies.

The Presbytery dealt with many cases of appeal from the Kirk Session, the proceedings in some of which extended over a long period.   In the case of a man residing at Drumdruiles farm which came before the Presbytery, the proceedings lasted for six years.   In the 18th century the translation of a minister from one parish to another was not the formal affair which it now is. Instead of being an occasion for paying compliments the proceedings were usually opposed by the parishioners who were to lose their minister.   The Presbytery, on the other hand, had not a merely formal duty to perform, but had to decide whether it was well to release their brother or to refuse to do so.   Whatever decision they came to, an appeal followed, as a rule, to the General Assembly.   Owing to Perth being the headquarters of the Jacobites in 1715, the Presbytery of Dunblane recommended the Synod to hold its next meeting in Stirling instead of in Perth, while the Presbytery itself resolved to hold its next meeting at Logie as parties of rebels had on several occasions visited Dunblane.   On 8th October, 1715, it was reported that the ministers of Lecropt and Kincardine had been unable to attend a Presbytery meeting owing to the bridge of Teith at Doune having been cut—to prevent the army of the Earl of Mar crossing the River Teith.

Among the objects for which collections were frequently taken was the erection or repair of bridges, a matter of great public importance, as otherwise communications were stopped for periods during winter seasons through the inability to cross rivers.   Help was frequently given to persons for surgical expenses as where they or their children had been " cut for gravel " which must have been a common form of illness at this time.   In 1713 contributions were asked for the support of the Infirmary at Edinburgh, and the General Assembly recommended that this should take precedence over all other objects.   Among other objects to which help was given were the Churches of Lithuania and of Saxony.

On the restoration of patronage opposition was evoked in the Presbytery of Dunblane in 1734, and there was a general desire that this should be abolished.

The Presbytery minutes record the examination of William Coldstream, formerly usher of the Grammar School in Crail, who was appointed schoolmaster of Dunblane in 1743.   His examin-ation included Roman Classics, Greek, the principles of Christianity, and other subjects.   While his appointment lay with the heritors who were responsible for his salary, the concurrence of the Presbytery had to be obtained.   Mr. Coldstream became Presbytery Clerk in July, 1743.

On 31st December, 1745, only two ministers and one elder attended the Presbytery.   It is recorded that the town of Dunblane was crowded and in great confusion owing to the number of rebels who were quartered there.

Reference is made to the old bridge of Kinbuck in 1757.   This had been built with dry stone pillars covered with timber and turf.   A new bridge had just been erected, but had not been paid for.   The Presbytery approved of the Kirk Session of Dunblane giving a subscription out of the Poors Fund towards the cost of the new bridge but not exceeding £5.

Some light on the life of Dunblane in the 18th century is gleaned from the minutes of Kirk Session although the matters dealt with are principally of local interest.   A new volume com-mences with the admission of the Reverend William Simpson to the parish of Dunblane on 25th June, 1730.   At that time the Kirk Session owned very considerable funds for behoof of the poor, that is over 7,000 merks all of which was lent to adjoining proprietors including the Lairds of Craighead, Kilbryde, Balhaldie and Kippendavie. This was almost the only method of investing funds at that time. The other possessions of the Session included four silver communion cups, a pewter basin and ewer for baptism, and two pewter plates and stools for collecting the poor's money, and two minute books, the older dating from 1652.

The earlier portions of this book principally consist of a record of sums collected for public or private objects or for the benefit of the poor. Among the public objects supported were the repair of the bridge over the River Ruchill and the bridge of Feddals. £13 11s. was collected for the latter, but a representation was submitted from Muthill asking for a further sum as the subscriptions of neighbouring parishes had fallen far short of the cost of building the bridge. As the Kirk Session had been generously treated by Muthill on a previous occasion they supplemented the collection by a further sum of £10 9s.

In 1750 a collection was taken for the Protestants of Breslau in Silesia, and in 1752 for the church in Pennsylvania and North America when £39 was contributed.

The Kirk Session had regard for the unfortunate. In December, 1731, they gave a very poor man £6 to help him to buy a horse, and the same sum was given in 1737 to a man who had suffered loss of a leg at Perth, while in the following year £12 was contributed to a student of Divinity who was " in the Straits."

The offence of Sabbath-breaking is less frequently noticed than in the previous century, and where it occurs the fault is usually drunkenness occurring on the Sabbath. Persons were, however, summoned before the Session for offences against morality and they were ordained in most cases to appear three times before the congregation for rebuke, and in one case a delinquent, who was a married man, appeared nine times before he was absolved. Later in the century the custom crept in of culprits paying an increased penalty to save themselves from a public appearance before the congregation. The practice of private rebuke began in 1747. In April, 1718, the Presbytery remitted to Kirk Sessions to consider whether the use of sackcloth by culprits was for edification. It was resolved at a later date to continue its use, but at this time one finds that defaulters began to refuse compliance with the orders of the church in this matter.

About 1738, there was a vacancy in the post of beadle resulting in a joint appointment of two men. Some time after, one of the beadles left the parish with a woman other than his wife. He was deposed from office and the deserted wife was given his salary on condition that she found a substitute to do her husband's share of the work.

Several times during the century there were periods of famine and great and continued severity of weather, and on these occasions extra money was procured and relief given to the community. In June, 1741, during a period of dearth 109 persons received money assistance from the Kirk Session representing a large proportion of the householders in the parish. A favourable harvest followed, but in 1744 the harvest again failed.

The Reverend William Simson died on 17th October, 1755, and, on the occasion of his funeral, a sister and the Laird of Keir gave 100 merks Scots for division among the poor, part of which was divided among vagrant poor persons attending the burial.

The churching of James Campbell, Younger of Aberuchill, and his lady on 10th March, 1754, seemed to have caused considerable local interest, and it is recorded that the bridegroom and bride each contributed half a guinea to the collection which in all amounted that day to about five times the usual sum.

The Kirk Session minutes following on the ordination of the Reverend John Robertson on 12th May, 1757, are barren of interest, being of the briefest description, particularly during the later portion of Mr. Robertson's ministry. At the beginning of Mr. Robertson's ministry there were apparently at least two elders, but latterly the attendance of none is recorded and the Presbytery appointed two other ministers to constitute the Session. For some time during his tenure, communion was only celebrated once in two years and the church collections on these occasions only amounted to about 10s. which contrasts most unfavourably with those noted in earlier times when large sums were given on communion Sundays. Mr. William Coldstream, the Session Clerk, was for some time the only elder whose presence is noted at a Session meeting.

After the appointment of the Reverend Robert Stirling in 1791, a revival of interest is soon noted. At the first communion after his appointment the collection amounted to £1 18s. 9½d., as compared with 6s. 5d. at the previous communion. Three elders were ordained in 1794 and other four in 1797.

The roll of poor persons receiving assistance, was revised from time to time by the heritors and members of Kirk Session and, at the end of the 18th century, the rate usually paid was 10d. a week and the payments were made by the Session Clerk. The necessary money was to a large exte nt supplied from the church collections, but a small sum was assessed on the inhabitants and this in 1792 only amounted to £5 5s. While the sum of 10d. a week seems in these days a very mean allowance it may be kept in view that a man and his wife could, even at a later time, live on about 1s. a week. A tradesman's wage at this time was 1s. 6d. a day.

In 1792, the local sheriff, Sheriff Coldstream, was much concerned over the prevalence of drunkenness in the town and he presented a strong memorial on the subject to the heritors. He mentioned that the number of ale houses had lately increased with most pretentious consequences, and he complained that parents sold and pawned clothing and other necessaries in these houses with a view to procuring drink. He concluded that, unless measures were taken to limit the number of such houses, it would be in vain to attempt to keep order in the town. The heritors agreed to concur with the Sheriff in making a representation to the Court of Session. About this time there were 29 ale houses in Dunblane and 12 in the parish outside the city, for a population of 2750.

While Presbyterianism became formally established in Scotland at the end of the 17th century, trouble arose within the Church early in the 18th century through the foolish restoration of patronage, an Act of Parliament again depriving congregations of the power of election of ministers, a change which met neither with the approval of the clergy nor laity. The chief opponent of patronage in the first part of the 18th century was the Reverend Ebenezer Erskine of the West Church, Stirling, who, with three fellow ministers, was ultimately deposed by the Church of Scotland in 1740. Erskine and his friends formed a Presbytery of their own under the name of the Associate Presbytery, and within a few years numerous Associate congregations were formed in different parts of Scotland. Erskine on several occasions conducted services in Dunblane, usually at the Howmillhead at the top of Braeport, where the congregation sat before him on the grass on the hillside. In 1739 19 persons from Dunblane became members of the Associate congregation of Stirling, but the first congregation in this district was that of Menteith which met at the Bridge of Teith. This congregation was disjoined from Stirling and a minister ordained to it in 1747. The Reverend William Simson was popular as the parish minister, and there was not a large secession from his congregation during his incumbency although, as already stated, his reading in 1737 of the Porteous Act from the pulpit as enjoined by the Government met with some local disfavour, but the appointment of the Reverend Mr. Robertson in 1756 against the wishes of the people led to a large part of his congregation joining the Associate Church. The first church of the dissenters in Dunblane was erected in 1758, and the first meeting of Kirk Session was held on 7th June of that year. The congregation increased in strength, and in 1765 it ceased to be united to that of Doune and it proceeded to elect a minister. Ultimately the Reverend Michael Gilfillan was ordained to the charge in 1768. He spent his whole life ministering to the Associate Congregation in Dunblane.

In 1747, the Associate Church was rent in twain over the wording of the Burgess Oath. The Associate Church in Dunblane adhered to the Burgher section, but a congregation of Antiburghers sprung up in Dunblane and a place of worship was erected in 1765. It is unnecessary here to follow up the history of the dissenting congregation in Dunblane as these particulars are given in a chapter on " Church Unions and Disunions " (Chapter xxx).

Among the leading residenters in the parish in the 18th century were the several lairds of Keir. James Stirling succeeded his brother John who died in 1693 at the age of 15 and was buried in Dunblane Cathedral. He was a strong supporter of the Stuarts and in 1708 he was tried, along with his relatives, the lairds of Kippendavie and Garden, and the Lairds of Touch and Newton on a charge of treason for complexity in a plot to restore the exiled royal family. They were ultimately acquitted. James Stirling fought at Sheriffmuir in consequence of which the Keir estates were forfeited, but these were purchased back by friends of the family for behoof of his eldest son. He suffered imprisonment in Dumbarton Castle, along with his son Hugh, in 1745 or 1746. They were successful in escaping by means of a rope ladder which his daughter, Margaret, conveyed to him concealed about her person. The family consisted of fourteen sons and eight daughters. Several of his sons, as also sons of other local lairds, sought their fortunes in Jamaica and India, and Archibald, his second son, acquired a moderate fortune in Jamaica. Archibald Stirling succeeded his elder brother, John, in 1757, when the latter died unmarried. Archibald was twice married, but had no family, and in 1783, William Stirling, his father's twelfth son, succeeded him. He died suddenly in 1793 of apoplexy while walking within the policies.

Another branch of the Stirlings of Keir was the family of Stirling of Ardoch, the first of which was William, younger brother of the Laird of Keir who married Marian Sinclair, daughter and heiress of Henry Sinclair. The mother of Marian Sinclair was Beatrix Chisholm, who had received a feu of the lands of Nether Ardoch from Bishop William Chisholm in 1543, which was followed by her acquiring a Charter of Chapel-land and Waterside in 1565 from the second Bishop William. William Stirling received from his brother the lands of Glassingall and Dochlewan. Middle Feddal was acquired by the same family in 1577. The third Stirling of Ardoch and his wife had thirty-one children, one of whom lived to the age of 112.

Anne Stirling, the eldest daughter of the fourth Baronet, succeeded to Ardoch in 1799. She married a Moray of Abercairney, since which time the lands of Abercairney and Ardoch have been held by the same laird. A daughter of Anne Stirling eventually succeeded her brother, and as she married Henry Home Drummond of Blairdrummond, the estates of Ardoch, Abercairney and Blair Drummond were united for a time.

One of the nearest branches of the family of Stirling of Keir is that of Stirling of Garden. Archibald Stirling, the third Stirling laird of Garden, was born in 1651, and, as has been mentioned, he was apprehended in 1708, on a charge of high treason. He was taken prisoner to London, but was ultimately acquitted. One of his sons was James Stirling, an eminent mathematician and usually referred to as " The Venetian " as he resided for some considerable time in Venice, where he taught mathematics. His distinguished career at Oxford University was brought to a close through his Jacobite sympathies, while eventually he had to flee from Venice on account of his discovery of the secret of making plate glass, the glassmakers threatening to assassinate him.

In 1735, James Stirling was appointed manager of the lead mines at Leadhills which he conducted most successfully, He died in Edinburgh in 1770. His nephew, Archibald, fifth laird of Garden, was also manager of the lead mines. He added to the estate of Garden. His death took place in 1824. Garden House was erected by John, the fourth laird, in 1751.

For the greater portion of this century the estate of Kippenross belonged to the family of Pearson, having been acquired by the first Pearson laird in 1630 from an old local family of the name of Kinross. John Pearson succeeded to Kippenross on the death of his father in 1694, and he by his son, Hugh Pearson, in 1722. The Beach Walk along the banks of the River Allan was planted by him in 1742. He was succeeded as laird of Kippenross by his son, John Pearson, in 1751, who was followed by his brother, William Pearson, in 1772. William married Jean, daughter of Sir James Campbell of Kilbryde. He was the last Pearson laird of Kippenross as he parted with the estate to John Stirling of Kippendavie in 1778.

The old house of Kippenross was burned down during the lifetime of the last Pearson laird who commenced the present house which was afterwards added to by the Stirlings of Kippendavie. The previous house had been erected by Dean Pearson over the ancient tower of Kippenross about 1646.

Charles Stirling was laird of Kippendavie at the beginning of the 18th century. Born in 1680, he was, as a young man, tried for treason along with neighbouring lairds in 1708, but he escaped punishment. He was succeeded in 1745 by his son, Patrick, born in 1704. Patrick Stirling spent a good part of his life in Jamaica, where many members of the Kippendavie family and other Stirlings from the neighbourhood were resident during this century. Patrick Stirling died in Jamaica in 1775, and was succeeded by his brother, John, born in 1742. It was John Stirling who purchased the estate of Kippenross from William Pearson in 1778. John Stirling was the father of seven sons and six daughters. He died in 1816, having been predeceased by his eldest son. The next laird of Kippendavie was John Stirling, the grandfather of the present laird, who was born in 1811, and was therefore only five years of age at the date of his succession.

One of the most powerful families in the district of Dunblane at the beginning of the 18th century was that of Drummond of Balhaldie, a descendant of the Chief of the MacGregors. After the name of MacGregor was proscribed by Act of Parliament, the family of Balhaldie assumed the name of Drummond.   In 1671, the laird was Duncan Drummond, who was served heir to his brother, John Drummond of Culcrieff, in 1658, and to his father, Patrick of Balhaldie, in 1666. He acquired from Lieut-General Drummond of Cromlix in 1671 the lands of Ramoyle, including Muir of Ramoyle and various crofts in Dunblane under reservation of the dues payable to the Altar of St. Blais.   In 1697 Alexander Drummond inherited these latter lands from his father, but in 1699 gave them in liferent to John Gillespie, who in 1729 conveyed them to Patrick Stirling of Kippendavie.

The Drummonds of Balhaldie were strong partisans of the Royal Stuarts, and on 19th March, 1689, Claverhouse in his march northward stopped at Dunblane to confer with Drummond.   In all probability Claverhouse was entertained in Balhaldie House, where Prince Charles spent a night in September, 1745.   Duncan Drummond's wife was a daughter of Cameron of Lochiel. In Monteath's *Traditions of Dunblane* Alexander Drummond is described as a " Massy built athletic man of extraordinary agility for his weight and a most expert broadsword player, brave but of hasty temper."   He resided in Dunblane during the winter months and during the summer he lived at Lairhill on his estate at Balhaldie, taking an active interest in the farming operations. According to the *Traditions* of Monteath, written about 100 years ago, he exhibited great bravery at the Battles of Killiecrankie and Sheriffmuir.   In the latter fight he had the misfortune of being in the left wing which was driven back by the royal forces and ultimately, when greatly outnumbered, he had to seek shelter in his own kale yard.   Many of the Laird's followers from his estate lost their lives at Sheriffmuir.   For other interesting traditions regarding the Laird of Balhaldie the reader is referred to Monteath's book.   His prowess at Sheriffmuir is recorded in two old songs celebrating the fight.   As has been stated, he was for some time Grand Master of the Masonic Lodge, and his signature of the minutes shows good handwriting.

According to Bruce, the old Laird died in 1749 or sixty years after the Battle of Killiecrankie, and he must have attained a goodly age.

In 1742 the Scottish agent of the Jacobites was William Drummond of Balhaldie.   Prince Charles having gone to France in 1744, information was conveyed by Drummond to Scotland that the Prince might land in Britain at any moment.   It was resolved to send John Murray of Broughton to Paris to set forth the views of his friends in Scotland and to give an account of the conditions of the country.   According to Murray's account Drummond had deceived both the Prince and his adherents.   *The Memorials of John Murray of Broughton*, published by the Scottish History Society, may be consulted regarding this.

The estate of Cromlix which had one time belonged to the family of Chisholm, of which the two last Roman Catholic Bishops of Dunblane were members, was at the beginning of the 18th century the property of Lord Strathallan.   The Strathallan family were also strong Jacobites.   On the death of the third Lord Strathallan, Cromlix, along with the estate of Innerpeffray, passed to his sister, the Countess of Kinnoull, whose second son, Robert, took the estates and assumed the name of Drummond.   In 1745 Lord Strathallan was Brigadier-General of the Jacobite army on the north side of the Forth.

The first Campbell Laird of Kilbryde, Lord Aberuchill, died in Edinburgh in 1704.   His successor was his second son, Sir James Campbell, who lived chiefly in Edinburgh or at Aberuchill and who dispersed a good portion of the wealth which his father had gathered.   Sir James was married on three occasions.   Sir James Campbell, the third baronet, fought with the Scots Greys at Fontenoy.   He had attained the age of 89 in 1812 when his death took place.

The family property of Aberuchill was sold in 1772 as the affairs of the laird had become embarrassed.   The Campbells of Kilbryde took no part in the '15 or '45, and probably their sympathies were not with the Stuarts as there was relationship and friendship between them and the Argyle family.

The proprietor of Argaty at the beginning of the century was George Home, baptised at Kilmadock in March, 1686.   He and his successors are noted on pages 139-142.

Among visitors to Dunblane in this century was Robert Burns who stayed at the Stirling Arms Hotel in 1787, the tenants of which then were Mr. and Mrs. Wetherby.   While living there he wrote a song entitled " My bonny was a gallant gay."

Burns was appointed excise-man at Dunblane, but, owing to his death supervening shortly after his appointment, his transfer never took place.

CHAPTER XXII.

THE OWNERS OF GLASSINGALL.

The lands of Glassingall have been possessed during the past by many different families. In the earliest records, they formed part of the lands of Kinbuck and belonged to a family of that name. The lands of Kinbuck included all the lands in the neighbourhood of the present village of Kinbuck, Glassingall, Ashfield, Cambushinnie and other farms in that vicinity. The " Temple lands of Kinbuck " comprised Easter and Wester Kinbucks, Craigton, Whiteston and part of Sheriffmuir.

Probably the first owner of Kinbuck whose name is now known was Luguen or Lugan, Richard, Knight of Kenbuc, he was a witness to a Charter of Confirmation by Gilbert, Earl of Strathearn, dated about 1208. Richard was the son of Lugan and a brother of Earl Gilbert's second wife, Ysenda. He had a brother named Galfred of Gask. Richard appears as a witness to other charters published in the Inchaffrey Cartulary. In other charters, one comes across the name of Joachim of Kenbuc and Alan of Kenbuc who may have been sons of Richard. Sir Joachim of Kenbuc was a witness to a charter by Bishop Clement in 1247, and in 1258 he was a witness to a charter of Malaise, Earl of Strathearn. In earlier references Kinbuck is spelt Kinboch or Kinbuch. Other lairds of Kinbuck about this time were Gilbert, about 1250, Alan in 1287, and Malcolm at an earlier date when Abraham was Bishop of Dunblane.

In 1261, there was a dispute between Joachim Kuinbuc, Knight, and the Abbey of Lindores as to the right of the Abbey to take wood from Cure Lundyn in Strathearn for repairing buildings on the lands of Feddal. Joachim by a writing undertook to permit wood to be taken and not to disturb the men of the Abbey if they gave him previous notice. A few years earlier there had been a similar dispute about the taking of wood from Glenlichorn which was owned by Robert, Earl of Strathearn.

In 1246, the marches of the lands of Wester Feddal, which were originally lands within the thanage of Auchterarder, were determined by a Jury, of which Sir Joachim of Kenbuc was a member.

In a Lindores Charter of the thirteenth century Sir Joachim is one of the witnesses, as also is Gilbert of Kenbuc who was probably a son.

The place referred to as Curelundyn is now unknown. It is described as being in Strathearn, but this term probably embraces Strathallan. Lundyn means "marshes" and it is possible that Cure Lundyn may have been in the neighbourhood of Braco. " Cure " may be a corruption of " Keir "—that is a fortified post or camp.

The last of the family of Kenbuc, the most powerful in this district in the 13th and 14th centuries with the exception of the Earls of Strathearn and Menteith, was Marjorie, daughter of Malcolm of Kenbuc, who on 1st December, 1458, married Alexander Bruce of Stanehouse, within the Cathedral of Dunblane. The lands of Kinbuck passed to her husband under burden of a yearly payment of 20s. due to the Preceptor of Torphichen of the Order of St. John of Jerusalem.

It has been pointed out that for at least a number of generations about the 13th and 14th century the Archdeaconate of Dunblane was held by the Kinbuck family. Culdeeism survived to a late age in this district and it is thought that the Culdee clergy formed the Chapter of the Cathedral when the Bishopric was first established. John of Kinbuck was Archdeacon towards the end of the 12th century, and his son, Gilbert, succeeded him about 1197. Gilbert of Kinbuck was Archdeacon in 1244, but this may have been a different Gilbert. One comes across the names of other Archdeacons in old charters, but without any indication to show whether they belonged to the Kinbuck family or not. As late, however, as 1360, Sir Nicholas of Kinbuck was Archdeacon. In that year he, and others, gave in an account of the third contribution for the King's ransom from the Stewartry of Strathearn. Thomas de Cascapline (perhaps Corscaplie) gave in a similar account for the Stewartry of Menteith.

In 1382, John of Kinbuck, according to the Exchequer Rolls of Scotland, received a payment of £68.

The name of Glassingall is to be found in varied forms. It is sometimes spelt as at present save that the initial letter is " C." Another form is Glassingawis.

One reads of an Easter and Wester Glassingall. The latter, formerly called Duthieston, was situated about the vicinity and to the south of the modern road to Perth and extended down to the lands of Kippendavie. At one time it was part of the Barony of Drymen.

In course of time, the family of Kinbuck got into straitened circumstances and most of their lands were acquired by the Stirlings of Keir—Glassingall by Sir William Stirling of Keir about 1455—and, save Glassingall, became part of the property of Stirling of Kippendavie. In 1531 " Glassingall " belonged to James Chisholm of Cromlix, brother of Bishop William Chisholm.

In the middle of the seventeenth century, Glassingall was the property of David Muschett, a member of what was probably the family of the most ancient lineage in this district. It claimed that its original name was Montfichet and that the founder of the family had come to Britain with William the Conqueror.

Members of this family owned much property in the Dunblane district in the seventeenth century, including the properties of Burnbank, Spittleton (Spittalton), Mill of Tor and Craighead in Blair Drummond district, and Calziechat, near Drumvaich, as well as Glassingall. Some of the members of the family appear to have engaged in commerce, as about this time, there was an Adam Muschett, a burgess of Edinburgh, and an Adam Muschett, merchant burgess of Stirling. Much wealth appears to have been acquired about this time by persons engaged in merchandise, and its pursuit was not considered unworthy of the oldest families in the country.

In 1651 David Muschett, the owner of Glassingall (the previous owners were Sinclairs), gave an Obligation to Adam Muschett, Burgess of Edinburgh for Robert Muschett of Craighead, and two years earlier he gave another Obligation to David Muschett of Calziechat and David Muschett of Spittleton. David Muschett of Glassingall was succeeded by his son, Robert Muschett, who completed a Title to Glassingall in 1659, the Superior of the lands being Stirling of Keir. Robert Muschett again was succeeded by his brother George who completed his Title in 1714 and conveyed the property to William Muschett, his nephew, who was the eldest son of his brother, James. This was in 1715. William Muschett did not retain his patrimony long as he sold it in 1726 to Alexader Stewart, writer in Stirling, who was the great-great-grandson of Alexander Stewart, the first owner of Annat, who had bought that estate from a Muschett in 1621. William had previously sold Wester Ashfold to Stirling of Kippendavie.

Alexander Stewart was married to Ellen Fleetwood, daughter of John Fleetwood, merchant and maltman, in Stirling, and in 1716 he was himself admitted a maltman burgess and guild brother. He and his wife acquired considerable property in the Middle Bow, Castle Wynd and Meal Market, that is King Street, and in East Craigs, Stirling, as also the lands of Bents and Lochend.

Alexander Stewart was succeeded in Glassingall by his only son, Archibald Stewart, who completed Title in 1748. The only sister of the latter, namely, Janet Stewart, married Bailie John Jeffrey, merchant in Stirling, afterwards Provost of Stirling.

After owning Glassingall for about thirty years, Archibald Stewart conveyed the property to Alexander Jaffray, merchant in Stirling, his nephew. Alexander Jaffray in his turn conveyed Glassingall to two nephews, sons of his sister, Helen Jaffray, namely, Thomas Smith, merchant in Greenock, and Alexander Smith, merchant in Stirling, who completed title in 1802. Thomas gave his half of Glassingall to his brother, Alexander Smith, who obtained a Charter of Confirmation from James Stirling of Keir in 1804.

While thus there were no direct heirs for two generations and the property was on both occasions conveyed to sons of sisters, there was again difficulty in finding an heir on the death of Alexander Smith. The property was ultimately given by the Crown to Thomas Smith residing at Hampstead, London, who was the father of Thomas Stewart Smith who founded the Smith Institute in Stirling in 1869. He latterly resided at Fitzroy Square, London. Mr. Smith was interested in art and antiquities. He had resided for some time about Nottingham and the first trustees of the Institute was a Nottingham friend, Mr. Cox, the Provost of Stirling, and Doctor James Webster Barty.

The next owner of Glassingall was Charles James Henderson, Royal Terrace, Edinburgh, who purchased it in 1863, but who sold the estate in 1874 to George Young, merchant in Glasgow, who, in the following year, disposed of it to Mr. David Wallace, ironmaster, the husband of Mrs. Wallace, who so generously supported the scheme for the restoration of Dunblane Cathedral.

The property was owned by the latter after Mr. Wallace's death and she was succeeded by their only son, John Wallace, whose period of ownership was one of a few years. His son, Captain Euan Wallace, M.P., after the death of his father, disposed of Glassingall to Mr. William Collins Dickson, Glasgow.

THE PEARSONS OF KIPPENROSS.

THE Pearson family, who owned Kippenross for over a century, is one of considerable interest and of somewhat ancient lineage. The name is spelt in numerous ways including Person, Peirson, and Perrison. The Pierissones owned land in Berwickshire in 1296.

The family seems to have flourished in the fifteenth century when John de Perisson was Burgess of Linlithgow and Servitor to King James I, while his brother Henry was bailie of Linlithgow in 1434. In 1450 the eldest son of John held lands at Blackness and at Eister Liff in Angus, while Thomas, son of Henry, was one of the Clerks of the Chapel Royal in 1467, and a nephew acquired land at Arbroath in 1508 which afterwards formed the property of Lochlands, the principal seat of the Pearson family. The Pearsons of Kippenross are a branch of the Lochlands family, the first owner being James, the third son of Alexander Pearson, a merchant of considerable means in Edinburgh, which city he represented at the Convention of Estates held at Holyrood in 1602, and in the Scottish Parliament of 1608. He was on six occasions Moderator of the Convention of Royal Burghs. His father was Walter Pearson of Whitefield, Dundee.

Burke's *Country Gentry* states that James Pearson of Kippenross was born in 1594, studied at Edinburgh University and graduated Master of Arts on 2nd April, 1615. Having qualified for the Church, he was appointed minister of Dunblane by Adam, Bishop of Dunblane, and Dean by James VI on 3rd March, 1624. As Dean of Dunblane, he on 17th February, 1626, raised an action against James Kinross, fiar of Kippenross, for arrears of vicarage dues, in which he proved successful.

In 1633, he and his wife obtained a Charter under the Great Seal of the Barony of Kippenross, which lands had previously belonged to Sir James Chisholm of Cromlix. These lands were held of the Crown in free barony for services due and wont. They had been owned for some centuries by the family named Ros, Kinross or Kippenross. The Barony was created in favour of John Ros in 1507, but there is a record of a charter by Janet of Kinross or Kippenross, in 1448. In 1507 the barony included Kippenross, Kippenrait, Auchlochy, Culinnis, grain mills, fuller's works, cruives and lands of Lettyr. These lands were incorporated in one free barony of Kippenross by James IV for good services rendered. Dean Pearson in 1646 built a house over the ancient tower of Kippenross styled the " Newe house of Kippenross," the site of which was not far from the River Allan, not where the present house of Kippenross stands. His wife was Jean, second daughter of David Drummond of Innermay, a near relative of the first Lord Drummond. He had to resign his Deanship when Episcopacy was overthrown, and although he was anxious to be recalled as minister of the Cathedral, he was not successful in obtaining election. James Pearson obtained a charter of the lands of Auchinlochie, Newtoun and Drumnagoune in or near Dunblane from Oliver Cromwell in 1655. These lands were previously owned by John Ker, burgess of Edinburgh. This also included Spittal Croft and Marions Acre in Lower Bridgend. His death occurred in 1658. His widow, referred to as Lady Kippenross, afterwards married Major John Home of Argaty. She retained Kippenross in liferent till her death in 1691.

The arms of Dean Pearson still adorn the house at the Cross which appears to have been his town residence and which adjoined the residence of the Lairds of Kilbryde, which again adjoined the mansion of Lord Strathallan.

The arms of the Pearson and Drummond families are inlaid together within a border on an oak slab fixed to one of the old stalls of Dunblane Cathedral.

Dean Pearson had three sons and one daughter. James, his eldest son, born in 1637, succeeded him. He married in 1661, Helen, daughter of Sir John Rollo of Bannockburn. He received a charter of the barony in 1676, when it was dissolved from the Barony of Feddills. His eldest son, also called James, was born in 1664, but was one of the victims of Cameron of

Lochiel's " very sad and unwarrantable mistake " during the Argyll Rebellion of 1685, when he and other four men were killed in the belief that they were supporters of Argyll, and it was accordingly the second son, John Pearson, who succeeded to Kippenross. He was served heir on 24th October, 1694.

John Pearson, born in 1667, married Jean, daughter of Sir Patrick Threipland, the widow of Alexander Linton of Pittendreich, who had fallen along with James Pearson. John was distinguished for immense stature and abounding hospitality. His eldest son having died while young, he was succeeded in 1722 by his second son, Hugh Pearson. It was this laird who, in 1742, planted the Beech Walk along the Banks of the Allan water. His wife, Agnes Gibb, whom he married in 1743, was a daughter and co-heiress of William Gibb, surgeon in Edinburgh. He had two sons, John Pearson who succeeded to Kippenross in 1751, but died unmarried, and William Pearson, who succeeded his brother in 1772.

William Pearson was born in 1750 and married Jean, only daughter of Sir James Campbell of Kilbryde. During his time, the mansion house of Kippenross was burned down. He commenced building what was the first portion of the present house, which was afterwards added to in the latter half of the nineteenth century. He was unable to complete the work and in 1778 he sold the estate to John Stirling of Kippendavie, reserving to himself a liferent superiority of parts of the Barony. The boundaries of the Estate were the River Allan on the South, Sheriffmuir on the North, Dunblane on the west and the Wharry Burn on the east.

William Pearson's eldest son, Hugh Pearson, was born in 1776, and entered the Navy in 1793. He took part in the attack by Nelson on the Spanish gun-boats off Cadiz, where he was severely wounded. He had a distinguished career in the Navy and retired in 1815 after the war. Hugh Pearson had a family of seven sons and seven daughters, some of whom died in infancy. The oldest son, William Pearson was born at Kilmany in Fifeshire in 1818. He migrated to Victoria, Australia, in 1841, and had a very successful career.

The following is a copy of the Deed of Presentation by King James VI of the Deanery of Dunblane Cathedral to James Pearson—" Our Soveran Lord being informit of the literatour qualificatioun and guid conversatioune of his hines lovit Maister James Peirsone minister sone lawfull to Alexander Peirsone, Merchant burges of Edinburghe and of his earnest zeall and affectioun borne be him to the functione of the Ministrie and preaching of the evangill of Jesus Cryist and to taik paynes and travell thairin. Ordaines thairfor ane lettre to be maid under his hines privie seall in dew forme. Nominatand and presented lyk as his hines be thir presentis nominatis and presentis the said Maister James Peirsone during all the dayis of his lyftyme to the Deanrie of Dumblaine withe all and Sundrie Mansionies landis tenementis teyndis fructis rentis proventis emolumentis and dewties perteining and belonging lyand within the diocie of Dumblain and scherefdome of Perthe now vacand in his hienes handis and at his Majesties gift and presentatioun be dimissione of Maister William Fogo last Dean of Dumblaine and lawfull possessour of the said Deanrie maid be him of the said Deanrie and of all and sundrie landis teyndis fructis rentis emolumentis and dewties perteining and belonging thairto in his heines handis REQUYRING heir for ane Reverend father in God Adame bischop of Dumblaine to trye and examine the qualificatioun literatour and conversatioun of the said Maister James Peirsone and gif he beis fund apt abill and qualifeit to use and exerce the functioun of the Ministrie to authorise him withe his ordinar collatioun and testimoniall of admissione to the said Deanrie withe all and sundrie Mansiones landis tenementis teyndis fructis rentis emolumentis and proventis perteining and belanging theirto duiring all the dayis of his lyftyme. With command in the said lettre to the lordis of his hines counsall and sessione upone the sicht of the saidis lettres of presentatioun and of the said Reverend father in God his testimoniall of admissione and collatione following thairupone to grant and direct lettres of hroning upon ane simpill charge of ten dayis allenarlie and all other executoriallis necessar at the instance of the said Maister James Persone for causeing of him his factouris and servitouries in his name be thankfullie answerit and abeyit af all and sundrie the said is mansiones landis tenementis teyndis fructis rentis proventis and emolumentis perteining and belonging to the said Deanrie of Dumblaine duiring all the dayis of his said lyfetyme in forme as affaires. And that the said lettre be farder extendit in the best farme withe extensione of all calussis necessar Giwine at Theobollis the third day of Marche the yeir of God j.ᵐ vj.ᶜ tuentie four yeires Six Supra Scribitur James Rex et subscribitur Ad : B. Dumblaine Melros."

Chapter XXIII.

TRADE GUILDS IN DUNBLANE.

THERE were a number of Trade Guilds in the city of Dunblane about the 17th and 18th centuries, but there are few references extant to them. There is, however, preserved among old papers in the Kirk Session safe in Dunblane Cathedral an Extract Decree in a case at the instance of Mr. Archibald Gibson, minister of the parish of Dunblane, and the members of Kirk Session against William Muschett, Deacon, and Christopher Finlayson, merchant, Boxmaster to the Masons of Dunblane, John Henderson, Hammerman Deacon, and James Hart, Boxmaster of the Hammermen, Andrew Bennett, Tailor Deacon, and Walter Lennox, Boxmaster to the Tailors ; James Cairns, Younger Deacon, and William Kerr, Younger Boxmaster to the Skinners, Robert Corsar, Deacon, and Robert Miller, Boxmaster to the Cordiners (that is shoemakers), John Bain, Deacon, and John Riddoch, Boxmaster to the Weavers.   The date of the Decree is 15th December, 1728, and this establishes the existence of at least six trade guilds in Dunblane at that date. The action was one of Declarator that the Kirk Session had the exclusive privilege of keeping mortcloths, of letting out the same and of receiving fees for the use of such to be disposed of for charitable uses and for the maintenance of the poor.   The pursuers complained that these trade guilds had purchased three mortcloths, not only for the use of their members, but for the purpose of letting them to all and sundry at a much cheaper rate than the Session could afford and disposing of the fees received for their own purposes without warrant or authority whereby the Session of Dunblane and the poor were " damnified " in the sum of £400 Scots and upwards. The Kirk Session were successful in obtaining decree and the Extract covers 17 pages of writing.

The Kirk Session following upon obtaining this decree against the Trade Guilds of Dunblane entered into an agreement dated 10th April, 1732, between the Rev. William Simson for himself and the Kirk Session, and the officials of the Guilds of Hammermen, Weavers, Skinners, Shoemakers, Tailors and Masons, whereby it was agreed in order to prevent further debates which they regarded as " most indecent in a Christian Society," that the Trades should deliver to the Kirk Session their three mortcloths with covers and chest belonging thereto for 400 merks Scots money less a voluntary rebate by the Trades of 30 merks to be devoted to pious uses, the Kirk Session discharging the Trades of the sum of £6 4s. decerned against them and all damages and expenses, judging it more safe to give up part of what might be found their due than to use quarrelling and compulsion.   Probably this agreement originated in the wise brain of the parish minister, perhaps backed up by Thomas Duthie, writer, Dunblane, the Clerk of the Masons' Lodge, afterwards to become Sheriff Substitute at Dunblane.   One can understand that the parish minister would dislike being at enmity with the six Trade Guilds of the city embracing many of the most important of his parishioners, while the Trade Guilds would very reluctantly lay aside the mortcloths for which they had expended much money in the hope of receiving a considerable income annually.   A copy of this agreement is annexed as illustrative of the care devoted in the preparation of a legal document over what may seem at this date not to be a matter of the first importance and as also throwing light on the life of an urban community of this period.

It is interesting to preserve a copy of the Charter of Confirmation in favour of the Hammermen of Dunblane, dated 1697, which is in the following terms :—

" Be it kend to all men be thir pnts, US William Viscount of Strathallan, Lord Drummond of Cromlix, heritable baylie of the Lordship and Regallitie of Dunblane, For certain good and onerous causess moveing us, and particularlie for incouragement of the trade of Hammermen within the city of Dunblane.   To have ratified and approven, Lykeas we be thir pnts, ratifie, approve, and for us and oure successours, perpetuallie confirme to and in favours of the said trade of hammermen within the said city, and their successours ALL former chartours Grants, Rights and priviledges whatsomever made and granted, conceived, or that may be interpret in their favours be any of oure predecessours or authors hereth. baylies of the said Lordp and regallity of Dunblane, of qtsmr. dats or contents the same be of, after the forme and tenor yrof in all poynts.　AND specially but prejudice to the generality aforesaid.　We doe hereby ratifie and approve in their favours Ane Lettre of Grant and priviledge made and granted to them be the deceist John Chiesholme of Cromlix, baylie hereth. of the sd. lop. and regallity for the tyme bearing dat the twenty day of Jany javic and fourty nyne yieres (1649), together with the heall liberties priviledges and immunities yrin contained, conceived in favours of the said trade, And particularly with power to them to choice deacons yierlie for regulating the said trade with all vyr members of Court necessyr.　And to hold and continue Courts as oft as need bees. And to judge, determine, and decerne with themselves upon any of that trade within the said regallity according to law, and to impose onlayes, fynes, and expenses upon the absents or delinquents as they shall find just and reasonable and the sds fynes and unlayes to lift and exact and to use and dispone yrvpon, for the use and intrest of the sd trade at their pleasure with power also to them to visite all the jron worke brought in by strangers to the publict mercats of the said citie from tyme to tyme, and to punish and fyne all haveres and inbringers of insufficient jron worke to the sds mercats or aney vyr worke relating to the said trade—And to exact and vplift for the use of ye sd trade the usuall deues of two shilling scots money vpon ilke smith, his stand, or vther Hammermen worke, and sixtien pennies money foresd of ilke stand of a dale lenth from such chapemen as shall bring aney jron worke to the saids mercats for sale or retaile, and lykewise with pouer to them and their sd Deacon within their sds courts to make and inact such statut and ordinances as to them shall seem just for the due regulateing and government of the said trade according to law.　And to cause their sds statut and ordinances to be putt to due execution—And generallie to doe all and sundrie vyr things requisite concerning the premisess, siklyke and as friely in all respects as aney vyr.

The Agreement between the Kirk Session and Trade Guilds of Dunblane is in the following terms :—

"AT DUNBLANE, the Tenth day of Aprile One Thousand seven hundred and thirty-two years it is contracted, agreed and finally ended betwixt the Reverend Mr. William Simson, Minister of the Gospell at Dunblane, for himself, in name of, and as having Commission from the Church Session of Dunblane, Managers for the Poor of the said Parish on the one part, And William McAllaster, Deacon, & David Malloch, Treasurer of the Hammermen there, John Reddoch, Deacon, & John Wright, Treasurer of the Weavers there, James Cairnes, Deacon, & William Kerr yor, Treasurer of the Skinners there, Robert Corsar, Deacon, & Robert Miller, Treasurer of the Shoemakers there, Archibald Buchanan & James & Walter Lennoxes, Taylors there, and John Duthie, late Master Mason, and Thomas Duthie, Clerk and Treasurer of the Mason's Lodge in Dunblane, for themselves, in name of and as representing the whole body of their several trades, and as having their special Commission to the effect underwritten on the other part, In manner following, viz., Forasmuch as the said Incorporations of Trades having, in the year one thousand seven hundred and Twenty two, Purchased three Mortcloaths for the use of their dead, Mr. Archibald Gibson, late Minister of the Gospell, at Dunblane, for himself, in name & by authority of, and as having commission from the sd Church Session, Did Intent Process, before the Baillie of the Regality of Dunblane and his Deputes, against the Deacons and Boxmasters of the sd Community of their several Trades, which was thereafter advocated, by him, to the Lords of Councill and Session,　Before whom he obtained Decreet Declarator, against the said Community and Trades, upon the Fifteenth day of December one Thousand seven hundred and twenty six years, whereby the said Lords of Council and Session Found & declared That the Minister and Kirk Session of Dunblane had the sole Priviledge of keeping and giving out Mortcloaths for hire, for the burying of the Dead, and found & declared That the Incorporations of Trades had no right to keep use or let out Mortcloaths and decerned & ordained the said Incorporations of Trades to desist from using or letting out of Mortcloaths for the burying of the Dead in all time coming, and Decerned & ordained the said Incorporations of Trades to make payment to the said Master Archbald Gibson of the sum of six pounds four shillings Scots as the expenses of the Complaint given in by him against them for not duely returning the process in manner narrated in the sd Decreet as the samen of the date aforesaid, in itself more fully Bears And now seing that the said Kirk Session and Trades, who for a considerable time bygone have been desirous that all differences and pleas betwixt them, with respect to the foregoing affair should be amicably settled and composed, Have at length (for preventing further pleas and debates, which are most undecent in a Christian Society, and for Conciliating and maintaining peace, unity & good agreement together) Condescended and agreed That the said Incorporations of Trades should sell and deliver to the said Church Session their three Mortcloaths wt their covers or wallets and Chest belonging thereto for the sum of four hundred merks Scots money as the value and price thereof, which sum having been numerated and told down They the said Trades, in token of their confidence of the said Kirk Session their faithfull administration and management of the money belonging to the Poor of the said Parish, frankly Returned thirty merks thereof to them to be applyed and distributed for pious uses at their discretion, and on the other hand That the said Kirk Session should Quite and Discharge the said Incorporations of Trades of the six pounds four shillings contained in the Decreet above deduced and of all damages and expenses that could be demanded of them for their keeping, using or letting out of Mortcloaths preceeding this date, which the said Kirk Session (for peace and quietness sake) cheerfully went into, Judging it more safe and convenient to Quite a part of that which, by law and equity, might be found to be their due, than to use quarrelling, pleas and compulsion for the same ; And it having been also agreed that the Right and security underwritten should be granted ; Therefore the said William McAllister, David Malloch, John Reddoch, John Wright, James Cairnes, William Ker, Robert Corsar, Robert Miller, Archibald Buchanan, James and Walter Lennoxes and John and Thomas Duthies for themselves, in name of and as Representating the whole body of their Incorporations of trades abovementioned and as having their special Commission as said is, acknowledging the Receipt of Three hundred and seventy merks scots money from James Ker present Treasurer to the sd Kirk Session (which they accept in full satisfaction of the value and price of the sd mortcloaths &c. Renouncing every exception proponable in the contrary). Have sold & Disponed, and, by the tenor hereof, Sell & Dispone to and in favours of the said Kirk Session of Dunblane All and Whole their said Three Mortcloaths (the two largest whereof are of fine velvet and the other of plush) with the Covers or Wallets for holding the same and chest belonging thereto, together with all right, title and interest they can pretend to the samen, surrogating and substituting the said Kirk Session in their full right and place thereof for ever, With full power to the said Kirk Session to keep, use, let out for hire and otherwise Dispose of the same as they shall think expedient and oblige themselves and whole body of the said Trades to warrand the above Disposition thereof to the said Kirk Session at all hands and against all Deadly as law will ; For the which causes The sd Mr. William Simson for himself and in name and authority foresaid, confessing and acknowledging the Receipt of the foresaid three Mortcloaths and the covers or Wallets for holding the samen and chest thereto belonging (for Implementing the said Kirk Session their part of the sd. agreement) Has Exonered and Discharged, and, by these presents, Exoners, Quite Claims and Simply Discharges the said Incorporations of Trades of Dunblane of the foresaid six pounds four shillings mentioned in the Decreet above narrated, and of all damages and expences that can be demanded by the said Kirk Session from them on account of their keeping, using or letting out of Mortcloaths preceding the date hereof, and of all action, diligence and execution competent to the said Kirk Session thereanent, And of the foresaid Decreet itself, heall force and effect thereof so far as concerns what above discharged allennerly ; which Discharge he the sd Mr. William Simson, for himself and in name foresd, obliges him and the said Kirk Session and their successors to warrand to be good valid and sufficient to the sd Incorporations of Trades and their successors at all hands and against all deadly as law will : Consenting to the Registration hereof in the Books of Councill and Session or others competent Therein to Remain for Conservation, and, if need be, That all execution necessary on six days charge may pass thereon, They Constitute Their Prors. &c. In Witness both parties have subscribed these presents consisting of this and the three preceding pages (written on stamp paper by Thomas Duthie Writer in Dunblane) Place, day, month, &c. year of God and written before these witnesses Charlie Muschet, Wigmaker, in Dunblane and George Muschet, his

(Signed)

John Wright	Wil. Simson, Minr	John Duthie
* A B W L	William McAlester	Robert Millar
Tho. Duthie	Jas. Cairnes	Robert Corsar
Charles Muschet, Witness	David Malloch	John Reddoch
George Muschet, Witness	Will. Ker "	

* *These are the initials of Archibald Buchanan and Walter Lennox.*

The following extracts are taken from the Records of the Burgh of Stirling.

" *4th October,* 1602.—In presens of the baillies and counsall, comperit personallie Johnne Sinclaire, commissare of Dunblane, quha declaret that the provest, baillies and Counsall of this burgh for the tyme, frelie ressavit and admittit him to the libertie and fredome of ane burges and gild brother of this burgh, and that he findis the said libertie and fredome to be now unproffitable to him, thairfoir of his awin fre will renunceit and gaif over the same to the saidis baillies and counsall to be used and disponit upon be thame at thair plesour."

" *3rd May,* 1630.—The Provost and Magistrates considered a complaint by the deacone of the hammermen against the deacone of the cordineris for boisting (threatening) James Henerey belt-maker in Dunblane lately received a burges to enter with the hammermen as saddlers and other belt-makers were in use to enter with, the cordineris affirming on the contrary that the said belt-maker pertained to them. The counsall found that John Henerey ought properly to enter with the hammermen."

" *13th March,* 1665.—The Councill recommended the Magistrates and Dean of Guild to write a letter to the Provost of Perth anent unfree persons in Dunblane who useth merchantdising that he may put the laws to execution against them so they may forbeare."

THE STIRLING GUILDRY BOOK.

The only references to Dunblane in this book are as follows :—

On 13th March 1669 the Guildry nominated Duncan Watson to write to Edinburgh and supplicate the Convention of Burghs for redress of the wrong done by the Burgh of Perth in tolerating unfree persons to exercise merchandise in Doune and Dunblane to the great prejudice of the Merchant Guildry of Stirling. On 3rd April 1669 Watson reported that the Convention had ordained the Agent to agree with the Burgh of Stirling in putting the Acts of Parliament in execution against unfree traders and he was appointed to write to Perth to require the Magistrates to put the said Acts in execution against unfree traders in Doune Cross and Dunblane.

CHAPTER XXIV.

THE BATTLE OF SHERIFFMUIR.

ONE of the most interesting periods of Scottish history is that of the first years of the eighteenth century culminating in the rebellion of 1715. Generally speaking the lairds and clansmen of the north were Tories and supporters of the exiled Stuarts, while the majority of the people south of the Forth, particularly the commercial classes, were Whigs, strong Protestants and opponents of the Stuart family. Dunblane and district were strongly Jacobite. The family of Stirling of Keir had taken part in numerous plots, the object of which was the recall of the Stuarts and their restoration on the throne of their ancestors, while the Lairds of Cromlix, Kippendavie and Balhaldie were alike strong upholders of the Jacobite cause. In the 'Fifteen, Stirling was the headquarters of the Royalist army, and Dunblane was the nearest Jacobite city to Stirling. The River Forth being the natural boundary between the territories of the opposing forces. This district as a result became the centre of the most stirring scenes of the rebellion, while in the neighbourhood was fought the Battle of Sheriffmuir, the last fight to take place on Perthshire soil, the result of this battle proved decisive to the Jacobite cause for the time being.

Before narrating the story of the battle it may be of interest to recall briefly one or two of the causes which led up to this attempt to place the Stuart family again upon the throne of Great Britain. Early in the year 1707, the Union of the English and Scottish Parliaments was agreed to despite great opposition throughout Scotland, many Scotsmen believing that they would lose thereby more than they would gain. Grumbling was increased by the measures taken following upon the Union, particularly through the new taxes imposed on Scotland collected by Englishmen who were sent to Scotland for the purpose, as Scotsmen were not familiar with the English method of taxation. It had been arranged that £400,000 should be paid by the English, partly to develop Scottish trade, but this also was unpopular, as it was regarded as being of the nature of a bribe, while delay in making payment of this sum caused further discontent. The party, therefore, who favoured the restoration of King James, took advantage of the unsettled state of the country, and in 1708 an attempt was made, aided by Louis XIV of France, to restore him to the throne, which proved abortive. The Lairds of Keir, Garden, Kippendavie, Touch and Newton, who were believed to have been involved, were imprisoned in Newgate, but were, after a time, released. During the remaining years of the reign of Queen Anne, 1708 to 1714, the Scots became more and more dissatisfied. They considered that they did not get justice from the United Parliament and were annoyed by Acts passed restoring patronage in the Church of Scotland and imposing a tax on malt. Such then was the state of feeling in Scotland when Queen Anne died in 1714, to be succeeded by George I, a sovereign who was unknown to his people and who had not even learned to speak their language. As, however, George was a descendant of the house of Stuart and a Protestant, his accession to the throne was at first well received, and on 5th August, 1714, he was proclaimed King in Edinburgh amid much rejoicing. On the following day the Duchess of Argyll gave a ball at the Palace of Holyroodhouse to celebrate the occasion.

The Jacobite supporters in Scotland of James and his son were, however, disappointed that neither had been placed on the throne and they commenced working to achieve this object, and they were not long before they found a leader in the Earl of Mar. Mar had taken a prominent part in carrying through the Union, had been a strong supporter of Queen Anne's government, and at the time of her death was Secretary of State for Scotland. Soon after the Queen's death, and before George I landed in England, Mar wrote him a long letter assuring him of his loyalty and praying that he might have a long and prosperous reign. He failed to find favour with King George, who treated his advances with contempt and dismissed him from the offices which he held, dealing with his fellow Tories in similar fashion. The consequence of this was that Mar threw himself into the Jacobite cause. He is said to have been a man of admirable address and of great courtesy but of supple politics, so much so that he went by the name of "Bobbing John." While of some capacity as a diplomat he had no gifts as an organiser or as a soldier. Early in August, 1715, in workman's disguise Mar left London in a coal boat accompanied by General

Hamilton and Colonel John Hay, his brother-in-law, a brother of the Earl of Kinnoull, although on the day previous he had been interviewed by King George. Landing in Fife he proceeded northwards to his estates in Aberdeenshire where a great hunting expedition had been arranged to which he had invited the chief supporters of the Stuart family. This gathering was, of course, but a cloak for assembling the Highland chiefs together to make arrangements for the rebellion, and it was then arranged that on 7th September, 1715, the standard would be raised for James, son of James II, which was accordingly done by Mar on that date at Castleton in Braemar. Among the chief supporters of Mar were the Marquis of Huntly and of Tullibardine, Earls Marischal, Southesk and Seaforth, Lords Drummond and Strathallan, and Generals Hamilton and Gordon. Their plans having to some extent been made, the chiefs returned to their own districts with the view of calling out the clansmen.

The time for raising the standard of rebellion proved inopportune. It had not the approval of the Chevalier, and, as it happened, Louis XIV of France, from whom powerful aid was expected, died on 1st September, 1715. As Louis was succeeded by his great-grandson, a child of five years of age, and as the Duke of Orleans, who was appointed Regent, was opposed to the Jacobite cause, the blow was a serious one, for, although there were many Jacobites in England, they were not prepared to take the field before foreign troops had landed in the country.

It should have been explained that the raising of the rebellion was to some extent precipitated by the action of the Government, who had on 13th August, 1715, summoned a large number of noblemen and gentlemen throughout Scotland, including the principal proprietors in Perthshire such as Lord Strathallan and Lord Kinnoull, Stirling of Keir as also Rob Roy, who were believed to be supporters of the Jacobite cause, to surrender at Edinburgh. This summons was obeyed by one man only, Murray of Ochtertyre. The others, being denounced as rebels, at once associated themselves with the Jacobites.

Following on the raising of the standard at Braemar on 7th September, Mar commenced to march southwards from Aberdeenshire, and the town of Perth was seized by Colonel John Hay, on 16th September, Perth becoming the headquarters of the Jacobite army. While some of the clans delayed and showed reluctance to take the field, Mar had in a short time a very considerable army under his command and one much superior in numbers to that of the Royalists who had only some three thousand men scattered over Scotland. The Duke of Argyll, who had seen service under Marlborough, and who is said to have been the third best general living at the time, was appointed to command the army in Scotland, and on proceeding thither he gathered his forces together in Stirling to prevent the Jacobites crossing the Forth and moving southwards.

About this time a bold project designed by Lord Drummond to seize Edinburgh Castle came to nought through the conspirators tarrying in a tavern to a late hour and through one of their number revealing the secret to his wife who gave information to Cockburn, the Lord Justice Clerk. Had Edinburgh Castle been captured, a serious blow would have been sustained by the Government while the Jacobites would have obtained possession of the £400,000 grant paid by England to Scotland which was then lying there, as well as military stores.

Undoubtedly had Mar moved forward without loss of time as soon as he had a considerable army at his command he would have found the Government ill-prepared to stop his advance instead of which some weeks elapsed without any action being taken. Sinclair writes that after Mar arrived in Perth he did nothing but write. No steps were taken to fortify the town, to procure powder or repair guns. " Whoever spoke of those things which I did often was giving himself airs. We followed strictly the rule of the Gospel for we never thought of to-morrow." Eventually Mar sent a portion of his army under a capable officer, McIntosh of Borlun, to cross the Forth which McIntosh managed cleverly, transporting his men in little boats under cover of night and landing them in Haddingtonshire, avoiding on the way the Government ships in the Firth. McIntosh proceeded to march his men towards Edinburgh expecting to receive aid from the Jacobites there, but Argyll, by mounting two men on each horse, quickly conveyed troops from Stirling to Edinburgh, and McIntosh was thus prevented entering the town. He had ultimately to retire as his force was too weak to withstand an attack from Argyll's troops. He afterwards joined the Jacobites of the south of Scotland and north of England, and his force formed part of the army which marched into England and ultimately surrendered at Preston on the same day as the Battle of Sheriffmuir was fought.

Mar, having learned of the withdrawal of a portion of Argyll's forces from Stirling, resolved on 16th October, 1715, to march on that town. Various reasons have been given for this advance, namely, the taking advantage of Argyll's absence at Edinburgh to seize Stirling or to march southwards avoiding Stirling, or merely the inducing of Argyll to withdraw from the pursuit of McIntosh's force. Mar seems to have been reluctant to move from Perth, he having not yet been joined by all the forces which he had expected, but, the advance being pressed by General Hamilton, Mar's troops moved forward to Auchterarder on 16th October. On the following day (17th October) the infantry reached Ardoch, while the cavalry were pushed forward, at a fast trot and in heavy rain, to Dunblane, which they reached between eight and nine p.m. Nothing came of this preliminary advance. The Jacobite army remained at Dunblane till noon on 18th October in the bitterest cold, according to the Master of Sinclair, that he ever felt, Lord Drummond having meantime at Dunblane proclaimed the Chevalier as King. On that day the horsemen and infantry returned to Auchterarder. The reasons given by Mar for withdrawing his army were that he had learned that Argyll had received reinforcements and that General Gordon with the clansmen had failed to join him. Argyll had returned to Stirling on 17th October. Mar undoubtedly lost a good opportunity at this time of coming to grips with Argyll.

For three further weeks the Jacobite army remained in Perth in a state of inactivity, but early in November, 1715, Mar, having received re-inforcements, had no further excuse for delaying his attempt to cross the Forth and march southwards into England. On 8th November part of Mar's force seems to have set forth from Perth. His army was a considerable one, consisting probably of about seven thousand infantry with horsemen and eleven pieces of artillery for which there was little, if any, ammunition, and supplies were carried for a few days' march. Three battalions were left at Perth and other troops were stationed at Dundee and in Fifeshire. About 9th or 10th November the Jacobite army reached Auchterarder—the various historians differ as regards to the date of arrival there—where they were joined by the Highlanders under Gordon. It would, however, appear that Mar reviewed his army there on 10th November and rested his troops on the following day, but some time at least was lost there reviewing the troops and arranging the order of advance. According to Sinclair's account there were disputes about the position of the squadron, and on the morning of 12th November, before leaving Auchterarder, Mar seems to have challenged Sinclair for having delayed the advance of the army on the day before. The latter was credited with having been the leader of the " Grumbling Club " of the army. Huntly and the clansmen had apparently refused to march without Sinclair and his Fifeshire squadron. Ultimately, Sinclair agreed to accompany them, and, when the army advanced from Auchterarder in the early morning of 12th November, Sinclair led the way in command of three squadrons of horse, followed by the clansmen under General Gordon. He writes in his memoirs that, when the march started south, it was a case of the blind leading the blind, no one knowing where the army was going to or what it was to do. But according to the historian Rae, the plan of the Jacobite army was that three thousand men should be detached from the main force to make sham attacks at the Abbey Ford, a mile below Stirling at the end of the causeway leading to Stirling Bridge (Causewayhead) and at the Drip Cobble, a mile and a half above Stirling Bridge. While these forces were to take up the attention of the Royalists, the main army of Mar was to attempt to cross the River at some fords higher up or at the head of the Forth. Rae estimates the Jacobite army at 12,000 men, but this number is evidently much exaggerated, and Sinclair's number, 8,000, or that of Keith, 6,800, are probably more accurate. Sinclair appears to be correct in criticising the want of preparations. It would seem that the Bridge of Teith had been cut by Argyll to prevent the Jacobite army crossing the Teith and that the principal fords of the Forth had been spoilt by placing therein heavy bars with iron pikes. Mar would therefore have found considerable difficulty in crossing the River Teith in winter flood or in using any of the fords of the Forth had he reached them.

On 12th November, Argyll, who had previously heard of Mar's departure from Perth, marched his army consisting of about 2,500 men and 1,000 cavalry from Stirling, and encamped that evening in the neighbourhood of Dunblane. Mar's delay at Auchterarder had permitted him to do this and also to call up re-inforcements from further south. His army lay that night in the open under arms, despite the exceedingly cold weather. The left of his army was said to have rested in Dunblane and his right on the Stoney Hill of Kippendavie. At that time the road from Dunblane to Sheriffmuir was by Newton and Dykedale Farm; the present Sheriffmuir

Road by Kippenrait and Stonehill had not been constructed. The probability is that Argyll's army was encamped in the neighbourhood of the Dykedale Road about Newton Farm and the Hydropathic grounds extending to Dykedale which is below the Stoney Hill of Kippendavie, or as it is now called Stonehill. As his object was either to attack the Jacobite army or to prevent its reaching Stirling, Argyll would no doubt take up a position not far from the main road by which Mar was travelling southwards, but on higher ground. The Stoney Hill of Kippendavie probably refers to some of the higher fields of Dykedale Farm which are below the present farm of Stonehill, part of the old estate of Kippendavie. Argyll is said to have slept in a sheep-cote on the right of his army—probably in a building about the site of Dykedale Farm. Some writers have thought that Argyll's army was stationed on the night before Sheriffmuir near Kippendavie House which then stood a little higher up the hill than the present Kippendavie Farm house, but from the description of the movements of Argyll's army next day the Dykedale position seems more likely. As Kippendavie was a strong adherent of the Jacobite cause, Argyll would not be desirous of encamping in too close proximity to the household of an enemy.

Meantime, the clansmen under Gordon, with three squadrons of horse under Sinclair, were advancing towards Dunblane to seize the town, it being intended that the remainder of the Jacobite army should encamp for the night at Ardoch. During the day, however, a number of messengers reached General Gordon with information that Argyll's army was on the march through Dunblane. One of these was a woman sent by a sister of Cameron of Lochiel, who resided in Dunblane, and another was a lame boy sent by Lady Kippendavie who met Gordon's army about half-way between Greenloaning and Kinbuck about 3 p.m. It should be kept in mind that the old road from Dunblane to Crieff ran in a line somewhat parallel to the present main north road, past Glassingall Lodges, and keeping, as it went north-east, the River Allan on its left. Gordon sent a messenger to inform General Hamilton, who was in command of the army at Ardoch, while horsemen were pushed forward towards Dunblane to reconnoitre. At first the lame boy's story was not believed, but the lad alleged that he had seen Argyll's army himself, and that he would be willing to be hanged if it was not the case. His story was confirmed by country people shortly after. Gordon and Sinclair then marched their men forward, but as they came to the neighbourhood of Kinbuck, darkness began to fall, and it was resolved to encamp for the night. The forces were halted at two little farm houses near the River Allan in a hollow, with the river to the north and rising ground about two hundred yards off in the other directions. The place of encampment is said to have been north-east of Kinbuck Bridge and was evidently near the present farm steading of Naggy Fauld. The horses were put for the night into the kailyards of two farm houses, while the men rested in the bottom of the hollow near the river. Sinclair criticises the place fixed for encampment, and states that the army had " neither front or rear more than it can be said of a barrel of herring," and that he believed that eight thousand men were " never packed so close together since the invention of powder," and that the most ingenious engineer could not have contrived so fit a place for the destruction of men. The remainder of the army, under Mar, did not reach Kinbuck until about 9 p.m. Mar declined to believe the truth of the news of Argyll's advance to Dunblane, and, when Gordon corroborated Sinclair, Mar replied that he knew to the contrary, to which, Sinclair states, there was no answer to be made.

Next morning, Sunday, 13th November, 1715, about 6 a.m., before break of day, Mar's army was drawn up on the moor of Kinbuck—on the present farm of Lower Whitieston—extended in two lines facing Dunblane and to the left of the road leading to Dunblane—that is, to the left or south-east of the old road between Crieff and Dunblane. When day broke the Highlanders could see on the high ground away to the south at a good mile's distance, a strong squadron of the enemy's horse, this being an advance guard sent out by Argyll to reconnoitre. These horsemen appear to have been on the north-west crest of Sheriffmuir above Dunblane, probably near the Gathering Stone which stands at the highest point of the Muir. They, on the other hand, could clearly see the Jacobite army. Word was sent to Argyll and he went to view the enemy from this vantage point. It has to be kept in view that at this time there were no trees or plantations between Dunblane and Muthill, and, the countryside being bare, Mar's army was fully under observation from Sheriffmuir. Argyll observed that the Highland army was drawn up to point towards his right flank. Meantime Mar had sent out scouts, who had returned reporting the position of Argyll's troops. Evidently he was taken aback by Argyll's advance and by the fact that he could no longer avoid a contest, which left him undecided as to his course of action. Some considerable time accordingly was lost, but ultimately a Council of War was held about 11 a.m. at which the commanders and leading men in the Highland Army were present. They were at first addressed by Mar in what Sinclair described as a very fine speech " being the only good action of his life." The conclusion of his argument was that the enemy should be attacked, and he enlarged on the subject " in very strong and moving terms." There was one dissentient voice, namely that of Huntly, who, while owning the truth of what Mar had said, asked what was to be gained by fighting. Mar, ignoring Huntly, took a vote, and all being in favour of attacking Argyll, those in command went straightway to their posts, while the men received the decision with cheers. Sinclair, who had previously thought little of the Highlanders' fighting qualities, remarks that every Scotsman would have been elevated to see the spirit of his countrymen. Unfortunately for the Jacobite army, General Hamilton appears to have made a mistake in his method of advancing the troops. These, as has been stated, were drawn up in two lines, and four squadrons of horse were on the right flank and three on the left. In marching the army forward to the attack, Hamilton broke the two lines, each into two columns. The four squadrons of the right wing were ordered to advance first, followed by the right column of the first line, the left column of this line following at some little distance. These horsemen were under the command of Lord Drummond and the Earl Marischal, and the first column consisted of the clansmen under General Gordon. The first two columns were in turn followed successively by the right and left columns of the second line, with three squadrons of horse in the rear. Sinclair, in charge of the Fife Horse, was last in the advance. The first squadrons and the first column were already close to the enemy by the time the last of the Jacobites had left the place of parade. Unfortunately the left of the front and rear lines had a further distance to march to get into position and, as has just been stated, they were last to leave for the battle field.

Argyll had been watching the Jacobite army and he was surprised, when they commenced their advance, that they did not come by the main road to Dunblane, as they had faced in that direction when drawn up in line of battle, but had wheeled to the left in the direction of Sheriffmuir ridge where he and his horsemen were standing. (It may be explained that Argyll had also thought that Mar's artillery would cause him to advance by the main road). When he saw this, he hurried back to order his men to march to the higher ground before the enemy would arrive there. He formed his army into two lines, making a change of front to the right. His army then climbed half a mile up the slope of the Stoney Hill towards the east and marched a further half mile towards the north. Argyll's right wing marched first and reached the battlefield before the left of Mar's army was in position, and consequently, when the fight commenced, the right wing of each army was in position and prepared, while the left wing of each army had not had time to draw up in proper battle order and was more or less unprepared to resist an attack. The Highland army in the advance uphill had to some considerable extent got out of position, the front line and the rear having got mixed, but a greater difficulty arose through the leading squadrons of horse reaching the battle field towards the centre of the line instead of being on the right flank. Probably this arose from the infantry following them marching too much to the right. In any event, the three squadrons of horse which were bringing up the rear were ordered to advance to the right wing in place of to the left, and this no doubt assisted to bring victory on that side of the battlefield. It was, however, one of the main causes of the disaster to the left wing of the Jacobites, which was left denuded of cavalry.

The site of the battle has been a subject of much controversy.

The sites marked on the Ordnance Survey and other maps have differed considerably. Thus on Stobie's map of Perthshire published in 1783, the site of the battle is represented as being nearly half a mile north-west of the Sheriffmuir Inn. In the one inch Ordnance Survey maps of 1871 and 1906 the site is shown at about half a mile west of the inn, while in the six inch Ordnance Survey map of 1901 the battleground appears as over half a mile to the north-east of the inn. None of these positions appears to be correct. Although in the accounts of the battle the actual fighting ground is not carefully described, one must consider the position of the armies prior to the commencement of hostilities. As has been stated, Mar's army lay all night near the Allan above Kinbuck Bridge and on the morning were drawn up on Kinbuck Moor to the east of the old road between Crieff and Dunblane, facing Dunblane. Argyll's advance post was on the heights of Sheriffmuir, the highest point of Sheriffmuir where the Gathering Stone lies. When the Highlanders resolved to attack Argyll, the Earl Marischal was ordered to advance and dislodge Argyll's horsemen from the heights, and the Highland army, in place of marching on Dunblane, wheeled to the left. The Earl Marischal was with the right wing, but owing to the infantry not keeping to his left, the Highland army worked round more to the right than was intended and ultimately the cavalry which were to have supported the left wing were extended on the right of the Highland army. Thus the Earl Marischal made for the Gathering Stone with some of the infantry falling into his right and the remainder of the horsemen on their right flank. The remainder of the Jacobite army were extended eastwards, and as the force numbered about seven thousand men, when they got into position they must have extended considerably to the east of the ridge of Sheriffmuir, as their battle front would cover more than a mile. If the right wing of the Jacobite army was west of the top of the hill and their left wing was extended eastwards, the men of the two wings would not see how the fight was progressing on the other side of the field.

Argyll, on the other hand, on the night before the battle, marched his force through Dunblane to the east of the town, encamping on rising ground between Dunblane and " the mountain called Sheriffmuir," on the lower slopes of Stoney Hill of Kippendavie. His force would not be too far removed from the road between Kinbuck and Dunblane. When Argyll from the heights of Sheriffmuir saw the Highland army advance against him on the forenoon of 13th November, he marched his troops half a mile up the hill to the east and then another half mile to the north, which would bring him to the neighbourhood of the Gathering Stone. When his right wing came in sight of Mar's left, the opposing forces were only two musket shot distance apart. It is said that Argyll would have been unable to use his cavalry on the right flank owing to boggy ground had there not been severe frost on the previous night. It is not quite clear what piece of ground this refers to, but it was probably the wet land between the Lynns Farm and the MacRae Monument, where there is a tradition that Argyll's cavalry fought. The site of the battle was carefully inquired into by the Duchess of Atholl in writing her *Military History of Perthshire*, and her conclusion is probably correct, namely, that the Jacobite line was roughly a line from N.W. to S.E. through the Gathering Stone. The Restoration Standard was raised at the Stone according to a local tradition. In Macfarlane's *Geographical Collections* published in 1723, it is narrated that the Kippendavie Burn rising in Glen Tye is crossed by the road by a fine bridge and that this burn formed the eastern boundary of the Battle of Sheriffmuir. The author, McGoun, Schoolmaster at Dunblane, seems to be here referring to the Wharry. While it may be said that there was no fighting across the burn, it is very improbable that part of the contest took place near its banks, although combats may have taken place between fleeing soldiers and their pursuers. It has been pointed out by one writer that the name of Wharry Burn is not mentioned by one of the historians of the period in connection with the fight. Mar talks about advancing on the skirt of Sheriffmuir, and in his first account of the battle he states that he attacked the enemy on the end of Sheriffmuir. Mar was, of course, with the right wing, his left wing being extended eastwards. Mar's account of the battle printed by Freebairn, Perth, is headed " Account of the Engagement on the Sheriffmuir near Dunblane."

The fight commenced with the attack by the Highlanders on Argyll's left wing. Sinclair states that the Angus and Perth squadrons of horse which were in front of his (the Fife) had been excellently posted. The right of the Jacobite line outflanked Argyll's left and the clansmen had possession of the brow of the hill. In addition, Argyll's left were not drawn up to receive the enemy. The clansmen, having fired their guns, threw themselves flat on the ground while the fire was returned, then, throwing off their plaids, they rushed forward to the attack. General Wightman wrote after the battle that he had never seen regular troops more exactly drawn up on line of battle in a moment, and that the Jacobite officers behaved with all the gallantry imaginable. Allan MacDonald, the much-loved Chief of Clan Ranald, who was the only leader on horseback, was killed at the commencement of the fight. The wild attack of the Highlanders with their broadswords soon put the Royalists' left wing to confusion, and, according to Jacobite accounts, their right wing achieved a victory over the left of Argyll's army in a matter of seven or eight minutes. Argyll's left wing was pursued for some considerable distance, Mar stating in one account to the hill south of Dunblane (the writer Mahon says as far as Cornton south of Bridge of Allan, in sight of Stirling Castle). Sinclair did not join in the pursuit, his explanation being that he had heard that Mar's left wing had been routed. Whetham, who was in command of Argyll's left, is stated to have retired slowly with the view of holding Stirling Bridge against the Jacobite advance, but he reached Stirling by 3 p.m., and the Commander of the Castle describes the return of Argyll's men as a rout, while it took about the same time to drive the left wing of Mar's army back to Kinbuck, about a third of the distance.

The fight on the opposite wing ended in a victory for Argyll. As has been explained, Argyll's right wing was in readiness before Mar's left, and the former had the support of the regiment of horse now known as the Scots Greys and other mounted men. The Jacobites made a strong attack, but Argyll, seeing their flank unprotected, sent some squadrons to the right, and the Highlanders, being thus opposed from two directions, gave way and were driven back, being pursued by Argyll with his horsemen and General Wightman with the infantry of the right wing and centre. The commanders of Mar's left wing again and again rallied their men on favourable ground, but they were gradually driven back to the River Allan, the pursuit lasting for three hours until after 3 p.m. Apparently Argyll was still unaware of what had happened to his left wing, and he may have been of opinion at the time that the whole of the Jacobite army was in retreat, but he seems to have acted imprudently in personally following up Mar's left wing for such a time and to such a distance. Moreover, a great opportunity was lost by Mar and his commanders, as his right wing, with Sinclair's squadron at least, were practically intact on Sheriffmuir, while they had been meantime rejoined by some of the horsemen and foot who had pursued Argyll's left past Dunblane in the direction of Stirling. There must have been a Jacobite force on the battlefields of about 3,000 men including some squadrons of horse, but they remained on Sheriffmuir inactive without attempting to pursue Argyll or attack him in the rear or cut off his withdrawal to Dunblane although occupying a position of strength and greatly outnumbering their opponents.

Argyll, after continuing the pursuit of the left wing of the Jacobite army to Kinbuck, returned towards Sheriffmuir. He took up a position at the foot of the hill behind some turf dykes with some pieces of artillery placed on his flanks, in as good a position as possible to meet an attack. Mar's army, however, remained on the western ridge of Sheriffmuir, and when the light began to fail, Argyll proceeded to draw off his troops to the right in the direction of Dunblane. He was joined about 5 p.m. by some remains of his left wing, and, passing over the bridge at Dunblane, he encamped to the south of the city, probably about Hillside, his men remaining under arms all night. While Mar was thus left in possession of the battlefield, he was without supplies. His baggage horses had stampeded, and his bread waggons, which had been left without protection, had been captured. His men were wearied with their exertions of the last few days and from want of food, and Mar withdrew them during the evening to Ardoch. On the following morning, Monday, 14th November, part of Argyll's army returned to the battlefield to collect the wounded and to renew the fight if the enemy were there, but none of the Highland army were visible, and indeed they were then proceeding to Auchterarder, from which town they retired to Perth. General Wightman states that if Mar's troops had had the courage they would have undoubtedly destroyed the Royalist army when stationed at the foot of the hill within half a mile of the strong force of Jacobites on the high ground above them.

So far as one can judge from the figures which have been preserved, the casualties of Argyll's army were more severe than those sustained by Mar's, Argyll admitting a loss of 477 officers and men killed and wounded and 133 prisoners taken. Mar states on the other hand that his losses were not more than 60 men killed, but 82 officers and men were captured and lodged prisoners in Stirling Castle. Amongst the killed was Lord Strathmore, and among the prisoners, Lord Strathallan. Strathmore was only 18 years of age. Of him Sinclair writes that he had the most good qualities and the fewest vices of any young man he had ever seen. The small losses of the Jacobites were partly due to Argyll's cannon having never been in action, while apparently Argyll's instructions were to spare the enemy wherever possible. On the other hand, Argyll seems to have had bigger captures of booty including a large number of flags, among them the Royal Standard of the Chevalier.

Following upon the fight there were very considerable desertions from the Highland army, while, as was the custom after a battle, many of the Highlanders returned to their homes to re-fit themselves as they had lost their clothing in the fight. While it may be said that in the actual fighting neither side achieved a victory, the result of the Battle was undoubtedly a gain for the

Royalists, who had stopped the Jacobites in their objective of crossing the Forth, while it made any further attempt of a similar nature hopeless of achievement, particularly as through the suppression of the rebellion in England by the defeat of the Jacobites at Preston, the Government were able to concentrate their forces at Stirling and place at Argyll's disposal a much more powerful army than he had previously commanded.   In the meantime, the clansmen were weakened by desertions and discouraged by failure.   The fight at Sheriffmuir decided the fate of the rebellion, which would probably have had a different result had the Highlanders been under the command of a competent general possessing military capacity and courage.

In the records of the time it is narrated that the men in the Highland army who specially distinguished themselves were the Macdonalds and the Perth and Angus Horse, while the Seaforths, Camerons and Gordons failed badly and the MacIntoshes are said to have never drawn sword.   One writer blames the Stewarts of Appin, but Paton in his history, published 1717, states that the Stewarts of Appin fought with bravery, although not the other Stewarts.

Mar's army rested at Auchterarder on Tuesday, 15th November, and reached the head-quarters at Perth on the Thursday following.   A party was formed amongst Mar's leaders, including Huntly, to obtain terms of submission from Argyll, but, on the Duke being approached, he replied that, while everyone who appealed to the King's clemency might expect pardon, he could not deal with cases in general.

The Chevalier at last landed at Peterhead on 22nd December, but, in place of being at the head of an armed force, he had only three gentlemen in his retinue.   He found a diminished and discouraged army with divided counsels amongst the leaders, while he himself failed to inspire enthusiasm, and the discovery that his sympathies were with the Roman Catholics proved a disappointment to his supporters.

In the meantime, Argyll's army was being strengthened and early in January his force had increased to threefold its previous strength.   A strong body of horse and footmen were sent to take up a position at Dunblane, while a smaller party bivouacked at Doune.   Argyll, having received urgent instructions to advance against the Jacobites, rode out to Dunblane on 24th January, 1716, with 200 horsemen to view the state of the roads, and proceeded as far as Auchter-arder, which threw Mar's army into a state of consternation and some of his advance posts retired behind the River Earn.   On the orders of the Chevalier, the towns and villages of Auchter-arder, Crieff, Blackford, Dunning and Muthill were all burned to the ground along with all the corn and forage which the Jacobites were unable to carry away, amidst scenes of great suffering and deprivation, the orders being carried out without consideration of age or infirmity and during weather of great severity.   Thus the town of Auchterarder was destroyed on Wednesday, 25th January, 1716, about 4 a.m., without previous intimation to the inhabitants or an opportunity afforded to dress themselves or remove their goods.

Following on Argyll's inspection of the roads on 24th January, there was a sudden thaw, followed by a fall of snow to a depth of two or three feet.   This was succeeded by frost which froze the snow and made the roads extremely difficult.   Argyll, however, made preparations to clear the roads and advance on Perth.   Long debates were held in Mar's headquarters as to whether his advance should be opposed, but on 31st January it was resolved to withdraw from that city, and the River Tay being frozen over, men and horse crossed on the ice and retreated north-wards.   Argyll's dragoons entered Perth on the following day.   The Chevalier embarked on a small boat for France from Montrose on 4th February accompanied by Mar and Lord Drum-mond, and this may be said to mark the termination of the rebellion of 1715.

While one cannot but have sympathy for the gallant Highlanders and for the many lairds who risked all for the cause of the Stuarts, it was well for Scotland that the Stuarts were not again placed on the British throne.

One interesting point in connection with the account of the battle is the alleged abstention from the fight of Rob Roy and his followers.   It has been popularly believed that Rob Roy was present during the battle, but declined to assist the Highland army, and Sir Walter Scott wrote that during the fight he retained his station on a hill in the centre of the Highland position although, had he attacked, the day might have been won by Mar.   Sir Walter proceeds to state that his followers were enriched by plundering the baggage and the dead.   Probably this story may have been based on the version contained in Paton's history of 1717, while on the other hand, an exaggerated and misleading account appears in Haliburton's *History of*

Scotland. The truth appears to be that Rob Roy was, on the day of the battle, never on the east side of the River Allan or near the position indicated by Sir Walter Scott, but on that afternoon was observed approaching the scene of the fight from the west. Cameron of Locheil in a paper, dated June 24th, 1716, narrates that his clansmen, who were on the left wing of Mar's army, made off from the field of battle and were not rallied by him until they had crossed the River Allan. Lochiel then states that at that time he perceived Rob Roy *on his march from Doune*, he having not been present at the engagement. He had with him about 250 men and was only then approaching Kinbuck. There was, of course, an old road from Callander by the Braes of Doune to Cromlix by which Rob Roy no doubt came. It is true that Lochiel then asked Rob Roy to attack Argyll and his victorious right wing and that Rob Roy declined to do so, but this is not surprising considering the cowardly part taken by the Camerons that day and the small number of men at Rob Roy's disposal. It is possible, of course, that he had no great desire to side with either party in the fight and he may have delayed the approach of his men purposely. Probably his men sympathised with the Highland army and the Jacobite cause, but, on the other hand, Rob Roy had adopted the name of Campbell and had placed himself under the protection of Argyll and he would probably have been very reluctant to have opposed his protector. It would, however, appear that he had previously been in touch with Argyll and had given him sundry information as to the Highland army. It is thought that Argyll gladly took him under his wing in order that Rob might plague the Earl of Montrose.

It is strange to think that the Battle of Sheriffmuir was the only fight in the rebellion of 1715, and that this inconclusive action brought to an end for the time being the hopes of restoring the exiled Stuarts. With the army which Mar had under him and with the state of discontent throughout Scotland a leader of capacity and energy might have swept over Scotland before any substantial opposition could have been brought against him, but it was fortunate for Scotland that the Jacobites lacked such a leader and that there was so much jealousy and rivalry between the clansmen.

It may be interesting to recall a few anecdotes connected with the Battle of Sheriffmuir. It is narrated in Monteath's *Dunblane Traditions*, first published in 1835, that some shepherds who were witnessing the battle from Little Hunt Hill, one of the Ochil Hills to the east, observed a number of red coats surrounded by Highlanders in the form of a red diamond, which gradually diminished in size until it was finally extinguished. An old woman who was then living at Lynns Farm House used to narrate that she saw eleven of Argyll's men killed in her own midden. The Highlanders after dispatching the red coats entered her house and robbed it of whatever they fancied. A single dragoon is stated to have been chased to a stone dyke at Wharry Burn by a dozen Highlanders, where he defended himself so well that ten fell under his arm before he himself was slain. Monteath also narrates the tale of the shepherd at Braco, a man famed for his skill in the use of the broadsword, and of a fierce and robust nature. Along with two companions he joined Mar's army on the night before the battle, and took part in the fight with the victorious right wing. He and his companions chased a party of dragoons, seven in number, to a deep ravine in Pendreich Glen from which there was no exit. The three with their two-handed swords attacked the dragoons and three fell in a moment. The remaining four put up a desperate fight, the end of which was that the shepherd alone remained alive. The nine men are said to have been buried in a little haugh of the Wharry, about a mile above the Loup of Pendreich.

The day of the Battle of Sheriffmuir was bright and frosty, and the hills wore a coat of white. The good people of Dunblane had no thought of the kirk—indeed no services were held in the district, but they wandered up Hillside, and from that safe distance watched the battle rage on the western slope of the hill and the Highlanders driving the red coats before them down by Dunblane and Kippenross.

CHAPTER XXV.

DUNBLANE IN THE '45.

AT the time of the " 45 " some of the inhabitants of Dunblane were followers of the Royal Stuarts while other sympathies were with the Whigs.   As an ancient ecclesiastical centre, Roman Catholic until the time of the Reformation, and thereafter from time to time Episcopalian, Dunblane housed many families who were descended from or had been connected with dignitaries of the Church, but among the general inhabitants there was a considerable body of dissenters as well as other men whose political sympathies were with the house of Hanover.   It is interesting to note that following upon the rebellion of 1745, no names of Dunblane men appear in the list of rebels, although 13 names of such are recorded as belonging to Doune.   Of the rebels in Doune, four were slaters, three, of the name of Caddell, gunsmiths, two were carriers and three tradesmen.   The witnesses against these men were principally merchants, innkeepers and millers in Doune.

This difference of opinion may be illustrated by the opposing views of one of Dunblane's leading citizens and his wife, namely, Bailie Russell, the Commissary Clerk and Bailie of Dunblane, a supporter of King George and the Government, and Mrs. Russell, who was a strong adherent of the Stuarts.

Political conditions were in a disturbed state about Dunblane during the latter end of 1745. The city occupied a position at the entrance to the Highlands which, to a large extent, supported the cause of Prince Charlie, while it also lay on the borders of Lowland Scotland, which was predominantly Whig.   At this time there resided in Dunblane Alexander Drummond of Balhaldie and Lord Strathallan and, in the neighbourhood, Stirlings of Keir and Kippendavie, strong supporters of the Prince, as also junior members of distinguished Highland families, whose sympathies were with him.   At this time Highlanders, members of the Stuart army or followers of it, scoured the country for food or pillage, notwithstanding that Prince Charles discountenanced such practices and did what he could to restrain his followers and to penalise culprits.   The inhabitants were afraid to go abroad or strangers to visit the district, and farm houses in special were the scenes of violent pillage.   The inhabitants gladly gave up their possessions to avoid violence and to preserve their homes from destruction by fire.   Such conduct on the part of the Highlanders severed sympathy from the cause they had at heart, although adherence to the Prince may not have arisen in every case from a Highlander's devotion to his cause so much as from the hope of spoil.

Such were the general conditions when Charles Edward Stuart arrived at Dunblane on the march south on 11th September, 1745.   He spent that night in the house of one of his chief supporters, the laird of Balhaldie, Alexander MacGregor, who had adopted the name of Drummond.   Drummond had distinguished himself at the Battle of Sheriffmuir in which fight he prominently figured, but he was now a man of over 70 years.   Prince Charles's stay in Dunblane was a short one, and on the following day he left for Newton House, Doune.   While in Dunblane he received supporters of his cause, and it is narrated in Monteath's *Traditions* that among these was Mrs. Russell, wife of the Bailie, who in bidding him Godspeed pressed a purse of gold into his hand.

The hopes of the Jacobites were soon dashed to the ground and within a few months Prince Charles was returning with the remnants of his army dispirited and beaten.   On his way northwards he made no stay in Dunblane.   He was followed at a short distance by the Duke of Cumberland at the head of the Royal army.   The advance guard passed through Dunblane on the forenoon of 4th February, 1746, leaving intimation that Cumberland with his main army would spend that night there.   Bailie Russell, who in virtue of his office was the leading inhabitant and who occupied the property of Allanbank, at the north end of the Millrow, which faced down the street towards the bridge of Dunblane, resolved to offer the Duke hospitality within his home.   According to Monteath he had to invoke the aid of his friend, the Reverend Mr. Simson, the parish minister, a man of broad sympathies and of wise counsel, but one who was at heart a supporter of the Stuarts. Bailie Russell and the minister then proceeded to the Cross, and from the Tolbooth stair the Bailie addressed the inhabitants, advising them to contro their private opinions and for their own safety and the welfare of their families to receive Cumberland and his forces in a friendly manner. Similarly, Mr. Simson advised the throng to remain strictly neutral and to proceed to the outskirts of the town with a view to giving Cumberland and his army a welcome to Dunblane. The inhabitants took the advice offered, and, led by the Bailie and minister, they marched in a body across the bridge of Dunblane, and a short distance along the Stirling Road until they came to the hill known as the Skelly Braes, where the crowd was drawn up on both sides of the road. On the arrival of Cumberland, with his principal officers, the crowds raised a loud cheer on a signal from the Bailie, who, along with Mr. Simson, stepped forward to greet the Duke and welcome him to Dunblane. The inhabitants and the military then moved forward, and Cumberland with some of his staff accompanied the Bailie to Allanbank, where he was shown to the best room. It is narrated in the *Traditions of Dunblane* that five sentinels stood on guard in the passage leading to Cumberland's room, while two were stationed within the door with loaded muskets and fixed bayonets, to the chagrin of the Bailie, which increased when the Duke's attendants brought forward his bedstead and bedding, as also his provisions and cooking utensils.

Cumberland rose early on the following morning and, having issued orders for his army to proceed, remained to deal with cases of theft from his army equipment. A tailor belonging to Kilbryde who had taken possession of a cheese was captured and it is said that the Duke ordered him to be hanged over the bridge of Dunblane. His life was, however, spared by the intervention of Bailie Russell. Two Dunblane men, by name MacNiven and Brown, were captured in the act of stealing from a baggage or ammunition waggon at what was then known as the Crofts, which lay about Claredon Place and to the north-west behind Springfield Terrace. The Duke is said to have ordered the "Mac" to be hanged, but Brown to be set at liberty as he had many Browns in his army. According to some local traditions MacNiven was the last man to suffer death on the old gallows tree of Dunblane which stood on a little hill in front of what is now known as Keir Street, the portion of the old Doune Road as far as Keir Street being formerly known as the Gallows Loan. According to other traditions the life of MacNiven was also spared. It is also narrated that a bullock and horse belonging to the Royal Army were stolen from the churchyard and that this was undetected. The removers of the spoil, which they termed lawful prey, were afterwards well-known. That MacNiven was hanged under the protection of a guard of Cumberland's troops is narrated by Mr. Bruce in his *Guide to Dunblane* on what he was satisfied was reliable authority.

On the site and to the south of the present prison of Dunblane, opposite the present Union Bank House and the Leighton Library, stood the residence of Lord Strathallan known as " My Lord's House," or " Strathallan's Lodging." The gable of the house, which was a two-storeyed one, was towards the High Street and an outside stair led to the second storey, while, as often occurred in ancient buildings, the front door was below the level of the street. So Mr. W. B. Bruce narrates. Behind this mansion and perhaps below it ran the Minnie Burn, the course of which ran from the Kippenross Park across to the Perth road, thereafter by Woodend House, under Balhaldie House, below the East Church and behind and below the property of Dunblane Co-operative Society. After passing Lord Strathallan's house it crossed the main street, passed down the Millrow and eventually joined the River Allan behind Allanside House. This burn where underground was conveyed in a culvert about 4 feet square and at that time was free from sewage or almost entirely so, but as a rule a greater volume of water now passes down this channel than in former times. There were various openings in the culvert, no doubt for the convenience of the inhabitants, as for the purpose of drawing water. There were such behind Lord Strathallan's house, the Co-operative Society's property and on the site of the East Church where, before that building was erected, there was a garden. At one time the burn came to the surface at the top of the Millrow, where there was a bridge and there was also a bridge near the entrance gate to Woodend House. These matters are mentioned to enable one to understand the event which is now to be narrated of the attempt on the life of the Duke of Cumberland by the maid of Balhaldie.

The Duke, having disposed of matters requiring his attention, proceeded on horseback to follow up the army which had left Dunblane some little time previously. His course was by the Cross and then by Braeport and Ramoyle, along the road which proceeded in the direction of Kinbuck to Crieff. When passing "My Lord's House" a domestic servant, employed by Drummond of Balhaldie at Balhaldie House, endeavoured to pour a pail of boiling oil or water on Cumberland, from a window in the second storey. Her aim was defective, but the liquid fell on the haunches of his horse, which, starting forward, left the Duke stretched on the ground. The maid, who is said to have fallen under the attractions of Prince Charles when a few months earlier he had spent a night in the house in which she was employed, and who may have been instigated to the act either by members of the Strathallan or Drummond households, made her escape in the channel of the Minnie Burn to which she had easy access from the rear of the house. A most diligent search failed to discover her, and the occupants of the mansion house assured Cumberland that they knew nothing of the matter. Bailie Russell greatly feared that harm would fall upon the town, but the Duke and his staff were sufficiently pacified to offer no violence. The owner of a great portion of the town and adjoining land at this time was Robert Drummond, Laird of Cromlix and Archbishop of York, and it is said that the escape of Dunblane from penalty for this attempt on Cumberland's life was due to a promise given by him to the Archbishop that he would not harm the City.

The maid of Balhaldie suffered no penalty for her attempt on the life of Cumberland. Some time later she married a farmer of the name of McLaren, so writes Mr. W. B. Bruce, and a son tenanted the Mains of Balhaldie farm about the period 1770-90. The latter was an elder in the Secession Church at Dunblane. Mr. Bruce failed to ascertain her maiden name.

There are many traditions of violent acts committed in the "45" both by Royalists and Jacobites in search of food or plunder. The latter were ill-supplied with money or provisions and may therefore have had a greater excuse than their opponents, who were in no want. The wants of the Highlanders were simple—a meal of oatmeal and cream was sufficient for their needs. On the other hand Cumberland's men were difficult to satisfy with beef, eggs and bacon. Monteath relates the tale of two soldiers who, at a sitting, ate a large portion of a ham and two dozen eggs. Various stories regarding events in Dunblane in the "45" are recorded by him in his *Traditions of Dunblane* which he, no doubt, gathered from some of the older inhabitants, who, if not alive in 1745, may have heard the tales repeated by parents or friends who were in Dunblane at that memorable time.

A sidelight on how money was obtained for the use of Prince Charles and his forces is obtained from the terms of a proclamation made by William, Viscount of Strathallan, Brigadier-General of His Majesty's Forces on the north side of the Forth, dated at Perth the 18th day of December, 1745, ordering the sundry heritors within the parish of Dunblane to pay up the cess due the 25th March, 1746, and all preceding terms at Alexander Brown's Vintner Inn, Dunblane, on Friday, 27th December, by 9 in the forenoon under the pain of military execution. This peremptory order was addressed to the reader in the parish of Dunblane and he was ordained to obey under the pain of imprisonment and punishment.

In December, 1745, the Jacobite Army were withdrawing from England and they reached Glasgow on 26th December. After a short rest an unsuccessful attempt was made to take Stirling Castle. After a victory had been gained at Falkirk, it was resolved that the army was not fit to meet the Government forces under the Duke of Cumberland, and the Highlanders crossed the Forth at the Fords of Frew and passed northwards to Perth and Crieff. At this time Doune Castle was held for Prince Charles by McGregors of Glengyle commanded by a nephew of Rob Roy, and for fear of an attack from the troops at Stirling Castle the garrison was enforced by Mac-Donalds of Glencoe and Stuarts of Appin. As a further precaution, Dunblane was occupied by the Camerons under Locheil and Bridge of Allan by the MacKenzies under Lord MacLeod.

It was but seldom that any events of a public nature were referred to in the minutes of the Kirk Session of Dunblane, but it is recorded in September, 1745, that "The smallness of the collection now and afterwards, which may be observed, is owing to the uncertainty of public worship in regard that the Young Pretender came to this place on Thursday last (11th September, 1745) with an army of Highlanders and others, his adherents marching southwards and parties passing continually to join them, which created great disturbance in the country." On 27th October, 1745, an intimation was made from the pulpit of Dunblane Cathedral of the appointment by the Presbytery of a fast on the following Wednesday because of the present rebellion in favour of a papist pretender. The collection made on that day only amounted to

19s. 3d. During these disturbed times the Kirk Session had a collection plate stolen by the rebels, causing them to purchase a new plate at a cost of 28s. The Kirk Session gave an allowance to their tenant, Robert Kelly, smith in Dunblane, of 35s. from the rent due by him to the Session. Kelly paid £21 yearly to the Session as rent. In addition, the Session owned a house, let to Thomas Duthie for £16, a bake house and oven rented at £5, and a byre let at £10 10s.

It is noted at this time that a party charged with an offence had failed to appear before the Session, "having joined in the present rebellion." He may have been actuated by motives of loyalty to the Stuarts or he may have joined the Jacobites as a means of escape from the discipline of the Kirk Session.

On 22nd June, 1746, " the Minister read this day from the pulpit with suitable exhortations the Act of the General Assembly for offering a day of public thanksgiving on Thursday next, the 26th inst., for the remarkably great and gracious deliverance from that wicked and unnatural rebellion by the success it has pleased Almighty God to grant to His Majesty's armies at the Battle of Culloden in the North under the conduct of his Royal Highness the Duke of Cumberkand." The weight and influence of the Church of Scotland was thrown into the conflict in favour of the Government principally on account of the Stuarts' attachment to the Roman Catholic Church.

By the west bank of the River Allan close to where Glenorchard now stands was the farm of Easter Corscaplie, tenanted for generations by a family of Finlayson. The last Finlayson who occupied this farm was Christopher, who died there in the middle of the 19th century at the age of 94. After his death the farm was taken over by the Laird of Cromlix along with adjoining lands. A grandson of old Christopher was Thomas Finlayson, who as a lad was trained in the Law Office of Tho. & J. W. Barty, Solicitors. He joined the Volunteer Forces when 16 years of age and took part in the Volunteer Review of 1860. He died on 30th November, 1930.

The following are stories of events occurring in Dunblane and neighbourhood in 1745, and, as they have not been printed previously, it may be of interest to record such, even although the incidents are in themselves of minor importance. They are given as related :

"During the '45 Rebellion the farmers in this neighbourhood were much harried and annoyed with the Heilandmen at that time stealing and robbing everything that they could lay their hands on.

"My Father's Grandmother one day had a washing of stockings, etc., hanging on the paling near the road-side at the Farm, when she observed a Heilandmen passing along when he deliberately went to where the washing was drying and appropriated one of the best pairs and stappet them in his sporran. My Grandmother, having observed the theft, cried out to him, 'he would have to gie an account for that at the Lang Day,' when he replied that it would be a long time before that day arrived, and at the same time took another pair of stockings from off the paling, placing them beside the first pair and marched away speaking to himself in Gaelic—no doubt well pleased with his laudable action.

"Late one night a party of Highlandmen came to the farm when the occupants were all in bed and roused them from sleep demanding that they have the use of their horses to drag their vehicles containing baggage, etc., a certain distance on their march under threatenings that if they did not comply at once, the whole farm premises would be set on fire and burned to the ground. There was, of course, no alternative but to consent with as good grace as possible.

"After getting the horses harnessed and yoked to their waggons and conveyed to the other side of the Forth by the Bridge of Frew, a halt was made on the march there and the horses unyoked and a guard of Highlandmen put on the bridge to intercept all who wanted to cross—orders were given to the men with the horses that they (the Highlandmen) were not done with them as they would require their services to carry them for another stage of the journey. However, when the camp was all asleep and everything quiet, the owners determined to make a bold dash for home, and knowing that the bridge was guarded, they rode their horses straight for the Forth and swam the river all right to the other side, but the bank being steep and high they had great difficulty in getting a landing and the men and horses were nearly drowned, but by swimming down the side of the bank they came to a place where the bank was lower and there they succeeded in making a landing.

M

"It was a very dark night and they were very thankful that they got home with their lives.

"A solitary Highlandman was observed being pursued thro' Dunblane by two horsemen who were on the look-out for stragglers from the Highland Army. The Highlandman ran from the Cross up the bank of the River Allan to a part opposite Easter Corscaplie Farm and the horsemen were overtaking him at this point. A heavy spate was on the river at the time. When the Highlandman saw that he was being overtaken he boldly entered the river and crossed safely to the other side, altho' no ordinary man could have attempted it without being swept away.

"The horsemen, when they saw this, turned their horses and were in the act of going back to Dunblane as they did not think it advisable to cross the river. The Highlandman, seeing this as he was going up the brae-face on the other side, lifted up his kilt, clapped his hand on his bare person and shouted to them at the top of his voice a derisive remark. This was too much for the horsemen to stand, for they immediately turned their horses and crossed over the river and made up to the Highlandman whom they found in battle array in a field in close proximity to the farm house and situated at the back thereof. The fight began without any delay between the Highlandman and one of the horsemen who was a young lad. When he made a lunge at the Highlandman the latter, with his broadsword, managed to cut his bridle rein. When the other horseman, who was an oldish man, saw what happened he cried out, ' Stand off, Jack, and I'll try him,' when he at the same time made a lunge at him with his sword and with the first sweep cut him a great gash in the throat which soon proved fatal. My Grandfather saw all this done and gave the horsemen a snuff from his horn-mull before they left.

"Not long afterwards a party of Highlandmen arrived at the farm and threatened to burn the farm premises because the occupants had not turned out to assist the Highlandman in his difficulty, but they did not put their threat into execution. They buried him under a cairn of stanes where he fell, and I have often played, when a boy, around this cairn when visiting at my Grandfather's farm. It was known as 'Duncan Aubraugh's grave.'

"This apparently was the name of the man who was slain.

"It was on the occasion of the Battle at Falkirk that two of my forbears left the farm and proceeded to that neighbourhood the night before the battle, for the purpose of obtaining ' Spulzie ' (plunder). They obtained lodgings for the night in close proximity to where the battle took place. During the evening and while sitting at the fireside, two Highlandmen came into the house and began at once to search the house for plunder. After searching the kitchen they went into a back apartment or pantry where a large meal girnel or barrel was kept and at this time the meal was pretty far down in the girnel. One of the men raised up the lid and began searching among the meal with his head far down in the barrel, when the other man also put in his head and was assisting in the search when some of the farm hands who saw them in the trap seized the opportunity and turned down the lid of the girnel on the top of the two men and sprang on to the lid top and squeezed in on the men until they were both dead. They knew this to be the case for shortly after the two were trapped, there was a tremendous sleuch came into the kitchen, which was caused by the breaking of the intestines of the two men being crushed by the lid on to the sharp edge of the barrel. It was the custom in these days to hide money and other valuables deep down among the meal when it was known the Highlandmen were on the war-path, and the Highlandmen knew this for the meal girnel was invariably searched by them, and if they did not get money they were always sure of getting their bags filled with plenty of good meal.

"Next morning while the battle was in progress my forbears lay concealed at the back of a dyke on the side of a by-road leading from the field of battle. On this road and not far where they were concealed was a Highlandman with his broad sword intercepting all stragglers from the battle and any one who chanced to come that way. They saw him attack and kill several men until at length a horseman came along. He was bareheaded and had one boot off and the other on, and looked as if his horse had been killed under him. He had no sword. The Highlandman made a lunge with his sword at the horseman who, being on his mettle for fear of his life, luckily managed to pass him without being struck, but he was being followed up hard by the Highlandman until the horseman came to where one of the slain men was lying on the road with his sword beside him. Seeing the sword, he immediately seized it and, turning round, tried its calibre, and at the same time cried out 'Thank God I am saved.' The Highlandman came on with his sword and attacked, the horseman, made a few parries and thrusts, and in a very short time the former received a blow which laid him dead on the road. My forbears were very thankful to get home with their lives, and the ' Spulzie ' they intended to take home with them was all left behind."

CHAPTER XXVI.

THE MILITARY IN DUNBLANE.

DUNBLANE at no time ranked as a military centre although during the centuries from the time of the Roman occupation military forces passed to and fro through the city. A Roman road lay close to the town on its eastern boundary and the Roman army marching from the south used this in going to their camp at Ardoch and to their strongholds in Strathearn and in the north. It is recorded that, about the 10th century, Dunblane was twice pillaged and burned down by invaders when there were no local forces to give protection and to repel assaults. At the beginning of the 14th century Edward I of England passed through Dunblane with his English armies, and, although fighting took place in Stirling and at the memorable field of Bannockburn, and although there may be have been a victory gained by William Wallace at Sheriffmuir, as recorded by the poet, Blind Harry, there is no evidence of there having been a military station in this neighbourhood. Dunblane was noted as an ecclesiastical centre, and from the 13th century to the Reformation was one of some importance and as such was, at that period, the centre of much legal business in the Ecclesiastical and Commissary Courts. Criminal jurisdiction was exercised by land-owners, probably at the castle of Doune, which was the chief stronghold of the district. About the 13th century the Earls of Strathearn were the principal magnates in central Scotland, to be followed as such by the Earls of Menteith. In the parish of Dunblane there were no powerful noblemen and no fortified castle.

Dunblane continued to be an ecclesiastical centre so long as a Stuart king occupied the throne. With the accession of William and Mary, church government became Presbyterian and Dunblane ceased to be of importance as a centre of organised religion. During the 17th and 18th centuries military forces were from time to time temporarily stationed in Dunblane. During the rule of Cromwell a regiment dispersed a meeting of Presbytery, which was being held within Dunblane Cathedral. In 1652 a garrison occupied Dunblane for the Royalists. General Monck passed through Dunblane in June, 1654, when proceeding to the Highlands to oppose the Royalists under General Middleton.

Dunblane was a busy military centre for a short time about 1689, as it was a rendezvous of the levies summoned for the suppression of the Jacobite party under Dundee. Many regiments gathered at Dunblane where they were sworn in and from where they were afterwards marched north by way of Perth. Although the rebellion came to an end at the Battle of Killiecrankie and through the death of Dundee, a garrison of soldiers remained in Dunblane for some time thereafter. Drill took place in the north portion of the churchyard and the soldiers worshipped in the Cathedral, sitting in the east gallery across the large east window, known as Balhaldie's Loft or the Soldiers' Loft. Entry to this gallery was obtained by an outside stone stair which was ultimately removed in 1818. In 1685, troops under Pitkellenzie were quartered in Dunblane. It is recorded that they wooed the fair maidens of the city and then rode away and left them lamenting.

On 19th March, 1689, Viscount Dundee stopped on his march northward to confer with Alexander MacGregor or Drummond of Balhaldie, son-in-law of Lochiel. He received from him an encouraging account of the state of feeling in the Highlands. Drummond played a gallant part in the Battle of Killiecrankie and it was he who afterwards entertained Prince Charles Edward in his house on the night of 11th September, 1745.

During the latter half of 1715 there was no organised camp in Dunblane or immediate neighbourhood, although the sympathies of the land-owners were with the Stuart family, but matters were very unsettled in the district owing to frequent incursions of bodies of Highlanders —so much so that the Presbytery of Dunblane, in October, 1715, met at Logie instead of in Dunblane. Again in 1745, the people of the city abstained from public worship not only prior to the passing of the Jacobite army, but afterwards when parties were passing continually to join the Jacobite forces, and this caused great disturbance in the country. The Presbytery at this time fixed a fast as a time for intercession for the country faced with a " Rebellion in favour of the Papist Pretender."

Although the bridge over the Teith at Doune was cut about October, 1715, to prevent Mar's army crossing the river there, the bridge of Dunblane was not interfered with either then or in other troublesome times. On 13th December, 1745, the town of Dunblane was in great confusion through the number of rebels quartering there, so much so that only two ministers and one elder appeared at a meeting of Presbytery. Cumberland, on his march north early in February, 1746, remained with his army one night in Dunblane, but no military force was stationed there.

The Battle of Culloden ended the hopes of the supporters of the Stuarts, of a Stuart restoration, and probably the excesses of the Highlanders tended to make the public less inclined to take part in schemes of rebellion, and the streets of the city ceased to be troubled by armed forces or Highland marauders.

From the time of Charles II onwards, military forces were raised throughout Scotland, including Perthshire, for home defence. Such forces were at first known as Fencibles or, in England, "Trained Bands." It may be recalled that John Gilpin was a "Trained Band" Captain, a word which is said to have been rarely used in Scotland, save in Edinburgh. A few years after the restoration of Charles II an Act of Parliament was passed authorising the raising of a National Army or militia on a territorial basis, the quota for Perthshire being 1600 soldiers and 176 horsemen. The Crown nominated the Captains of the Horse and Colonels and Lieutenant-Colonels of the Foot, the Colonels having the power of appointment of the Majors. The appointment of junior officers was in the hands of commissioners of the militia consisting of Justices of the Peace and Commissioners of Excise who exercised considerable powers in the matter. The senior officers received no pay, but the others were paid, when in camp, at the rates of the regular army. Lieutenant-General Drummond of Cromlix was in command of the Earl of Perth's Troop of horse in 1669 and was succeeded in 1676 by Sir John Stirling of Keir. In 1681 Harry Home of Argaty was Lieutenant of the Troop and in 1675 Robert Drummond of Kilbryde was Corporal. Prior to this—in 1666—two troops of horse had been raised by the Earl of Atholl and General Drummond for the defence of the country from possible invasion. The first Major and Captain of No. 3 Company of Perth's Foot Regiment was John Home of Argaty, and of No. 5 Company, Sir John Chisholm of Cromlix. The Ensign was John Sinclair of Glassingall. The Perthshire militia formed part of the Highland Host and was sent in 1678 to the counties of western Scotland to enforce the orders of the Privy Council. When James VII withdrew the regular army from Scotland to oppose the landing of the Prince of Orange, the militia of West Perthshire was formed into four divisions and it was arranged that each of these serve for a fortnight in turn. The first division was ordered to muster at Dunblane under the Laird of Pendreigh from 13th to 26th October and the second division under the Laird of Argaty from 27th October to 9th November.

Volunteer forces in Perthshire date from 1794. These were formed following upon a circular letter sent out by Pitt recommending the formation of Volunteer Companies in certain towns for local defence. By 1797 the volunteer movement had spread far and wide. Out of 1200 inhabitants in Dunblane, 100 enrolled at the beginning of 1797. A company was also raised in Doune, and it was proposed that the Doune and Dunblane Companies should form a Corps under the command of Captain Stirling of Keir. In 1799 Volunteers of Dunblane and Culross offered to give their services in any part of Great Britain in case of invasion.

Among the officers in the 9th Local Perthshire Militia at this time was Captain Campbell Younger of Kilbryde who was Captain of the Grenadier Company. Among the Volunteer forces in Perthshire was the 3rd or Menteith Battalion consisting of two companies raised at Doune, Dunblane and Callander, one of the Captains being John Rob, probably the writer of that name in Dunblane.

In December, 1827, the services of yeomanry were dispensed with in Scotland save at four centres, and on 4th January, 1828, the men of the Perthshire Yeomanry delivered up their arms. For a period of 32 years there was no volunteer force in Perthshire, including the district of Dunblane, but, in view of strained relations with France, in May, 1856, Lords-Lieutenant were recommended to form Volunteer Companies which were not to be called out save to repel invaders. Volunteer corps again came into existence and a company of Royal Highlanders or Black Watch was formed at Dunblane, known as the 6th, under the command of John Grahame of Glenny, who was Sheriff-Substitute of the Western District of Perthshire and who resided in Dunblane. For many years thereafter the Volunteer Company was the most active body in Dunblane.

Sheriff Grahame was succeeded in the command of the Company by Captain Harper, Major J. W. Barty, Mr. William Wilson, wool spinner, and, at a later date, Lieutenant-Colonel D. T. Reid, Town Clerk, who latterly commanded the Battalion.

It may be of interest to know that the uniform of the Dunblane Company in 1860 consisted of a grey tunic with scarlet facings, grey trousers with a black stripe and a low cap with a peak in front. The outfit cost £2 7s. 6d. towards which each man of the Company contributed a sum of not less than 2s. 6d. and some as much as £1. The balance of the cost of the outfit was defrayed by public subscription. The cap was in 1868 succeeded by a shako and in 1878 by a busby. Photographs of Dunblane men in uniform are still extant.

Dunblane contributed a number of men to the Forces who fought in the South African War, while future historians will record the great response made by its loyal inhabitants at the time of the Great War and the great sacrifices contributed by its sons to the national cause.

Note.—Much of the information in this chapter has been obtained from the Military History of Perthshire *edited by the Marchioness of Tullibardine.*

Chapter XXVII.

THE GLEBES OF DUNBLANE AND KILBRYDE.

Dunblane.

THE parish of Dunblane was without a glebe for a lengthy period, but ultimately in 1697, a glebe was laid off extending to 4 Scots acres to the west of the public road from Dunblane to the south commencing near the west end of the bridge of Dunblane and extending south and west-wards. This remained the glebe of the parish until the construction of the railway line to the north from Dunblane. It was taken over by the Scottish Central Railway Co., at Martinmas, 1845. In 1848 arbitration was resorted to to determine the compensation money to be paid by the Railway Company, and this money was invested for behoof of the Presbytery and the interest is payable to the minister.

The following is extracted from the minutes of meeting of the Presbytery of Dunblane held there on the 16th June, 1697, which states that up to this time the minister had no glebe in his possession and " yt. yr. is a piece of ground lying beyond the bridge of Dumblain on the west syde on the highway commonly called the Gleib of Dunblane for which yr. is onely fourtie merks payed yearly unto him." The Presbytery accordingly remitted to James Dick, measurer in Stirling, " to goe and measure faithfully four acres of arable ground on that forsaid piece of ground," three ministers along with an Ensign and a civilian, who were elders, to accompany the measurer. Mr. Dick reported that the ground usually called the glebe measured exactly four acres of arable ground, and accordingly the Presbytery designed the same as the glebe. As he had no grass glebe the Presbytery recommended the Judge Ordinary to grant him " twentie pound Scots and yt. he be provided in feall and diffett (divot) feuell and faggitt accord-ing to lawe and as use and wont is with the people of the Bridge end of Dumblain."

The Glebe of Kilbryde.

An interesting litigation took place about 1761 and later as to whether the minister of Dun-blane was entitled to have a glebe at Kilbryde. The minister, Mr. Robertson, raised an action against Mr. William Bryce of Bowtoun and his tenant to have them removed from the possession of the glebe of Kilbryde. The Sheriff allowed the minister to lead proof that he had been in the natural possession of the glebe of Kilbryde, which he did. He produced an extract from the records of Presbytery dated 14th March, 1664, relating to the designation of "glebe of Kil-bryde," as also receipts for the rent of the glebe of Kilbryde granted to the three last proprietors of Bowtoun and a decree he had obtained against Bryce for the rents of the glebe from 1756 to 1760. The Sheriff's decision was against Mr. Robertson and he appealed and Lord Stonefield led a proof of the marches of the glebe libelled. The proof having been led, the Sheriff assoilzied the defender and there was a second appeal which came before Lord Auchinleck, who found that there was not sufficient evidence that Kilbryde had ever been a separate parish or that the minister of Dunblane had right to any lands at Kilbryde. Lord Auchinleck found that the minutes produced did not bear out Mr. Robertson's contentions, that the minutes showed that in 1678 the minister claimed he had right to two glebes, but had possession of neither, only that he received payment from John Drummond of 40 merks.

The owner of Bowtoun had since 1702 paid £20 Scots to the minister of Dunblane. This was sometimes referred to as glebe money or stipend or for minister's grass. Mr. Robertson carried his appeal further and was able to prove that Kilbryde was originally a separate parish and he averred that he had documents to show that he was entitled to a glebe at Bowtoun and he sought to disprove the objections taken by the defender.

About 1575 Elderships or Presbyteries began to be founded in Scotland, and on 8th August, 1581, the Eldership of Stirling was erected by Commissioners appointed by the General Assembly. Andrew Graham, minister of Dunblane, and Michael Learmonth, minister at Kilbryde, were present at this erection, but refused to accept office.   They being censured appealed to the General Assembly which, on 31st October, 1581, found that the ministers of Dunblane ought to enter themselves in the Presbytery of Stirling and that, after increase of their numbers, the General Assembly might be moved to erect a new Presbytery in Dunblane.   Michael Learmonth afterwards regularly attended the Presbytery of Stirling to 9th May, 1584.   The lands of Bowtoun were described at one time as lying within the parish of Kilbryde now annexed to Dunblane.

At a meeting of Presbytery of Dunblane in February, 1654, Mr. Thomas Lindsay produced an old designation of a glebe at the old church of Kilbryde and desired infeftment, and men were appointed to give the minister infeftment, and in the following month they reported they had done so.

In June, 1678, the Dean and Minister of Dunblane declared at a visitation of the Presbytery that he had 2 glebes but that neither of them was in his possession, and that the Lord Lieutenant (Lord Strathallan) paid him 40 merks yearly for one of them.   He also declared he had no pasturage.   In the Court of Session proceedings in 1764 the minister relied on the terms of various receipts by Mr. Potter, minister of Dunblane, for £20 Scots for the glebe of Kilbryde annexed to Dunblane or on other receipts in which similar language was used.

In 1697 a piece of ground beyond the bridge of Dunblane to the west of the highway was marked off for a glebe for which ground it was said 40 merks yearly had been paid to the minister. The area was four acres of arable land and it was also provided that the minister should have £20 Scots for grazing two cows and a horse, a byre, a barn, fuel and faggot as use and wont with the people of the Bridgend of Dunblane.   In reply to the averments of the minister, William Bryce of Bowtoun explained that the lands of Bowtoun appeared originally to have been Church lands, and in 1555 these were feued out by Alexander, Commendator of Inchaffray, in favour of Robert Row and Mary Edmonstone, his spouse.

In 1746 they were purchased by Bryce from Mitchell of Blairgorts who, and his predecessors, had occupied them for nearly 200 years.

A proof as to the marches of the alleged glebe of Kilbryde was taken in 1764-65, but the witnesses examined gave evidence that they had never heard of a glebe of Kilbryde.   In 1766 the building at Kilbryde was known as the Chapel and not as the Kirk, and it was suggested that the building had been erected by the Earls of Menteith for their private use.   There could have been no glebe at Kilbryde unless there had been Church lands, and according to Mr. Bryce's argument there could have been no designation of a glebe before 1593.   If Kilbryde Parish was united to Dunblane in 1594—it was united in 1618—there was every probability that no glebe would be designed in that short period especially as there appears to have been no minister at Kilbryde from 1584 to 1594.   Mr. Bryce's case was that the £20 payable from the lands of Bowtoun was for minister's grass, and the reason that the payment was made by the Laird of Bowtoun was that the proprietors of these lands, which was a feu granted by a Bishop, had not apparently paid stipend.

The piece of ground fixed by the minister as the glebe of Kilbryde was part of the lands of Bowtoun known as the Meikle Kirk Croft.   Another part of the lands of Bowtoun was known as Molland Salt.   John Lennox deponed that the lands adjoining the new chapel and churchyard of Kilbryde were called Meikle and Little Kirk Crofts, Tinklers Yard, Bridge Bank and Molland Salt.   In the minister's proof several witnesses deponed that when boys it was their practice to play football in the churchyard of Dunblane and, when the minister quarrelled with them for so doing, they usually answered that he had £20 paid to him out of Bowtoun for his grass and that he had nothing to do to hinder them to play in the kirkyard, that is that the minister had no right to the grass there.

Chapter XXVIII.

SEATS AND SEAT RENTS IN DUNBLANE CATHEDRAL.

In the Kirk Session records references to the letting of seats and of stances for seats in the Cathedral in the 18th century are very frequent. Many of the seats belonged to the Kirk Session and were generally let for the benefit of the poor of the parish, but sometimes seats were the property of individual members, erected for their own comfort, and in such cases the owners paid a rent for the site to the Kirk Session. Thus in 1730, James Monteath, portioner in Ochlochy, was granted a new seat in the middle of the west loft for a yearly payment of 1s. sterling. The other new seat south and next to it was let to William Wright, also portioner in Ochlochy, for a yearly payment of 8d. with entry in both cases at 1st November. The Kirk Session at that time appointed their Treasurer to employ workmen to repair the southmost seat in the west loft with a view to letting this for the benefit of the poor. The sums charged seem very moderate. In 1730 William Stirling, merchant, paid 2 years' rent of half a merk Scots per annum, while James Hart paid 10d. a year for his seat in the east loft.

Patrick Whitehead, wright, executed the repairs to the seat in the west loft for £8 9s. 6d., and it would thus appear that some years would elapse before this expenditure was cleared off.

In April, 1731, the Kirk Session must have brought pressure to bear to secure payment of rents in arrears, as on 8th April we find that Willian Caiden and Patrick Monteath each paid 5 years' seat rent, and John Hart, 4 years' rent, Hart's rent being 10d. sterling.

The seats in the south side of the west loft having been repaired were re-let, the rents to be received by the Treasurer for the use of the poor. In May, 1732, John Ritchy in Kippenrait paid 2 years' rent, but his next payment was not until 1738, when payment was made of 6 years' rent at one time. About 1744 seat rents seem to have been considerably in arrears, and about that time it is related that Henry Kinross paid 7 years' rent in one sum and James Anderson 8 years' rent.

In 1747, the Kirk Session were disturbed over the action of the tenants of the Barony of Cromlix in asking a new seat which encroached too far into the area and threatened to straighten the room proper for the communion tables and the passages which required to be kept free for use on these occasions. They therefore appointed the Treasurer in their name to call on those tenants to leave sufficient room and not to encroach on the floor of the church beyond the adjoining seats, and should the tenants still insist on their encroachment, he was instructed to take an instrument in the hands of a Notary Public and to make a legal sist to that work. The Treasurer evidently found it necessary to take legal proceedings as it is recorded that he paid a sum of 12s. for a legal protest against the people of Cromlix.

The Kirk Session showed an indulgence towards Patrick Montieth, as in 1748 he paid 9 years' seat meal (or rent) in one sum for the 9 years preceding, while in the following year, William Stirling paid for 7 years in one sum.

In May, 1751, Robert Kelly, smith in Dunblane, applied for leave to erect a seat on the floor of the kirk immediately behind the elders' seat, which, if granted, he promised to remove at communion seasons. The Session considering that the said place was then possessed by other people who had their chairs there and that there was a design to enlarge the elders' seat on that side which might take place when occasion required, with one voice refused the petition and resolved to leave the area of the kirk for chairs and other moveable seats as formerly. In the following year Robert Kelly petitioned to erect a seat for three persons in the east loft of the kirk of Dunblane to the south of the seat of William Wright, portioner of Ochlochy, and on this occasion his application was successful, the following conditions being, however, attached to the grant, namely, that he pay on New Year's day, 6s. yearly for the poor, that he bear a proportion of the cost of repairs of the said loft conform to his number of seats and deliver up the said seats to the Kirk Session when required and that he in no way incommode the entry to other seats. In 1754 we find Patrick Montieth again paying 7 years' rent of his seat in one sum.

In March, 1755, Colin Brown, lately in Balhaldies and then in the parish of Lecropt, as also John Harrower in Dunblane, having at their own hands, without the consent of the heritors or Session, erected seats which they let out for rent, the Session appointed their Officer to warn these persons to remove by Whitsunday and leave their seats "void and redd" so that the Session might let them to other people for behoof of the poor.   Brown and Harrower were, however, allowed compensation for the said seats at prices to be fixed by tradesmen.   In April, 1747, the Clerk was instructed to draw out a list of arrears of seat rents belonging to the poor and the Kirk Officer was instructed to call and collect payment.

In some of the earlier books of the Kirk Session there are further references to seats and seat-letting in the Cathedral.   In August, 1668, liberty was granted to Harie Blackwood to possess that room in the Church of Dunblane under the east loft in the middle of the church as they enter in at the east little door, formerly possessed by him. At this time Alexander Chisholm, Bailie of Dunblane, was permitted to put in a seat consisting of two pews with a footgage for him and his family.   In the same year John Stirling of Kippendavie rendered his desire anent room in the church immediately next and behind the pulpit on the south side to set his seat in.   In May, 1662, the Session built a seat for scholars placed in front of the pulpit.   In 1658 the Session appointed Archibald Duthie to " keep the pews " and ordained that every person who took a pew pay 1s. sterling if they let anyone be within the pews, and 1s. sterling for the pew itself.   A general rule seems to have been made at this time for charging each occupant of a pew a yearly sum of 1s.   In 1660 a foreseeing parishioner who wished to prepare for emergencies was authorised to provide accommodation for a future increase in his home circle by building " ane laigh seat or cheir when it shall please God to enlarge his family."   In January, 1661, John Stirling of Kippendavie, Harie Blackwood, Bailie in Dunblane, and John Graham in Cromlix supplicated the Session for the use of the four pews in the west end of the choir of Dunblane opposite to the entry of Kippenross seat upon the right end as they enter in at "the mickle choir door."   In 1664 John Stirling of Kilbryde made application to the Session for the liberty of a commodious room in the choir of Dunblane for the building of a seat or loft for himself and his family.   The minister and Session granted liberty if Kilbryde thought fit to build a loft joining the great window betwixt the pulpit and the west loft and to enter in at one of the said windows in the churchyard on the south side.   John Stirling was only a short time proprietor of Kil-bryde and the project does not seem to have been carried through, but it is sad to contem-plate the passing of such a proposal and that during the time of Bishop Leighton's ministry in the Diocese of Dunblane.   In 1668 it was minuted that " whoever within the Parish freely gave 30s. Scots for the use of the poor should have liberty to build a seat in the east loft in the most convenient part."   In 1670 an application was made for room before the reader's seat on the south side of the church.   In February, 1671, John Stirling of Quigs was given liberty to set up "a seat or dask at the back of the little door of the Church at Dunblane." In May, 1694, two seats were removed with a view of improving the entrance to the pulpit and to provide room for people at the baptism of their children to the north-east towards Balhaldie's Loft.   In 1670 John Graham, Commissary Clerk at Dunblane, was appointed Church Treasurer, his duties being "the taking up and keeping of collections, pounded dollares penalties morceau silver and sums due for pews in the Kirk."

CHAPTER XXIX.

THE SCHOOLMASTERS OF DUNBLANE AND COCKFIGHTING.

ALTHOUGH there is no continuous record of parish schoolmasters in Dunblane, such are known to have laboured here in as early as Culdee times and the names of all those who held office from the middle of the 17th century have been preserved. The parish schoolmaster in 1652 was Robert Caddell who was succeeded by Mr. Wilson, who was schoolmaster from before the restoration of Episcopacy until after its abolition. He was in Dunblane by 1658 and held the office of Clerk to the Presbytery. Robert Caddell, schoolmaster at Dunblane between 1652-57, was also Session Clerk, Reader and Precentor. He was afterwards transferred to Doune. Richard Franck writing in 1568 tells the story of this dominie whom he calls a formal pedagogue. He states that his good wife " was a notable comer, one of the first magnitude, who, with two more of her consorts at a four hours' drinking, guzzled down as much ale and brandy, wine and strong waters, as mounted to the sum of £40 Scots." Wanting more to pay the reckoning, Mrs. Caddell pawned her husband's trousers, and he, to redeem his wife's reputation, would never redeem his breeches in case they smelt of the tears of the tankard. Robert Caddell was succeeded as parish schoolmaster by Wilson in 1658 and he again by Duncan Niven. In 1670 a school at Duckburn was closed by order of Kirk Session. It was, of course, not a public school, but some private adventure. In 1672, the house-mail, that is rent allowed to the schoolmaster, was fixed at £40 Scots per annum. The schoolmaster in 1694 was a Mr. McEchnie who was also Precentor in the Cathedral and Clerk to the Kirk Session and who was succeeded, about 1700, by Mr. McGown, whose short account of the parish is preserved. His successor was William Coldstream, 1743-1786, a man of considerable scholarship. Malcolm Coldstream, his son, followed him and held office till 1809 when Donald Stewart was appointed. The latter held office for 50 years and his name is still remembered with respect. His successor was Robert Hugh Christie and on his retiral in 1899 Alexander Hamilton was appointed headmaster. Further particulars concerning these pedagogues will be found in other chapters.

The parish school was, of course, not the only school in the town and neighbourhood. There were also schools in Kinbuck, Balhaldie and Kilbryde, as well as adventure schools in Dunblane supported by the fees of pupils and not by the heritors or other public body.

The schoolmaster was, as a rule, a man of very considerable learning, a good Latin scholar with some knowledge of Greek. He held an important place in the parish, not only in respect of his scholastic position, but as holding, as a rule, the posts of Session Clerk and Precentor while he also sometimes held the appointment of Clerk to the Presbytery and reader in the Cathedral.

Among the records left behind by William Coldstream are those of the cockfighting in Dunblane school, known as the Parochial, Public or Grammar School, which was in his day conducted within the Chapter House of the Cathedral or in the organ loft above. These records are almost continuous between the years 1750 and 1774, after which there is a blank for 10 years, and they conclude with the figures for 1784 to 1788.

The cockfighting took place in the " Vasterie," a somewhat wet and uncomfortable place owing to a roof that was not water-tight. This was probably the east portion of the Chapter House. There were no windows towards the choir of the Cathedral and only small ones to the north. While the idea of cockfighting within the hallowed walls may somewhat shock the modern reader, one must recall that the churchyard was used as a playground up to the last half of the 19th century when the school boys played football with human skulls unearthed by the grave digger. It was also used as a drill ground for the military, and was the scene of markets, and the choir itself was embellished with galleries and furnished without any sense of dignity or beauty.

The day of the annual cockfighting fell between 1st February and 3rd March and it was held on the day preceding Festerns, Fastrin's or Fastin's E'en, which was Shrove Tuesday or Pancake Day. Three days before, a ballot took place for order of precedence, and this is preserved for many of the years. Thus the "Ordo Gallorum Gallinaceorum" of 1753 begins "(1) Gull.

Rob., (2) Jac. Stirling, (3) Jac. Paterson, and ends with (68) Geo. Chrystie, (69) Jac. Wright, (70) David Russell." On that occasion Jo. Pearson was the victor, his cock having 8 victories. It is possible that he was a son of the Kippenross family. In the following year the order is termed " Ordo Gallorum Pugnacium " when the scholars numbered 68 headed by (1) Anna Miller and (2) Jac. Hart, finishing with (67) Thos. Duthie and (68) Jo. McAree. The winner was Jac. Hart, Major. Other headings for the list of competitors include " Ordo Pugilium Gallorum," " Ordo Bellatorum Hilarious " and " Gallomachia."

Although many of the pupils competed in the cockfighting, all did not ballot for a place, some declining to take part, while in certain cases a pupil put forward two cocks. Thus in 1767 only 16 took part out of a roll of 49. Each competitor paid 1s. entry money.

In 1761 seventy-one scholars were in attendance at school divided into 7 classes as follows, 2 in the 1st class, 6 in the 2nd class, 10 in the 3rd, 9 in the 4th, 18 in the 5th, 17 in the 6th, and 9 in the 7th. Among the victors was David Russell in 1759, possibly a son of Bailie Russell who entertained the Duke of Cumberland. In 1765 Colin Campbell, perhaps a son of the Laird of Kilbryde, was King of the Cockfighters—his cock scored 6 victories, the victor in the following year being Alexander Campbell with 4 wins. In 1761 there were 71 scholars on the roll, 20 of which declined to take part in the contest, while 2 entered 2 cocks, making a total entry of 53 cocks. In 1773 there were 90 scholars on the roll, but only 27 drew lots. In 1786 the lots were drawn on 25th February and the fighting took place on the 28th. It is recorded that many were absent or declined to draw lots and paid the penalty.

At the cockfighting the schoolmaster took charge of the proceedings and was the umpire. The rules of the contest have been preserved and are as follows :—"(1) No one may lift his cock until beaten or put to flight. (2) No fuges to be counted. (3) The boy or girl whose cock is the champion of the contest shall be the victor or king. (4) The victor may pay an English shilling to the guardian. (5) Those who refuse to take part pay a fine. (6) If four minutes elapse without a cock striking it is to be lifted up and counted defeated."

The slain cocks became the property of the schoolmaster.

The biggest number of cocks recorded as having been slain by the champion was 8.

It is recorded that about the beginning of the 19th century, cockfighting was still held yearly in the parish school in Urr Parish in the south of Scotland. Parents and friends of the pupils were present at the contest and refreshments were provided in the form of negus for the ladies, strong drink for the gentlemen, and a sip of claret for the older children.

CHAPTER XXX.

CHURCH UNIONS AND DISUNIONS IN DUNBLANE—1730 to 1929.

AFTER a long period of strife, Presbyterianism was firmly established in Scotland at the end of the 17th century, but early in the 18th century in the reign of Queen Anne trouble arose through the foolish restoration of patronage by the passing of an Act of Parliament placing the election of ministers in the hands of patrons, thus depriving the congregations of the power of election. This neither met with the approval of the clergy or laity and for some time the Act was ignored. Matters were, however, brought to a head about the year 1730 when a number of ministers were forced on Parishes against the wishes of the people. As already related, the chief opponent of patronage was the Rev. Ebenezer Erskine of the West Church, Stirling (1680-1754), who proclaimed that a church could not be a true Church if it submitted to the placing of ministers over congregations who were unwilling to accept them. This led to Erskine and three fellow ministers being suspended by the General Assembly in 1733, and in 1740 they were deposed, marking the first Secession from the Established Church of Scotland. Erskine and his friends then formed a Presbytery of their own under the name of the Associate Presbytery.

Dunblane was considerably affected by the wave of controversy, and (as noted on page 154) a number of its inhabitants followed Erskine who on several occasions conducted services in Dunblane, usually at the Howmilnhead at the top of Braeport, now enclosed in the grounds of Holmehill where the congregation sat before him on the grass on the hillside while he preached. A wave of secession soon passed over Scotland and in a few years many Associate congregations were founded throughout the country. In 1739 19 persons from Dunblane became members of the Associate congregation of Stirling, but the first congregation in this district was that of Menteith which met at the Bridge of Teith. This congregation seems to have been part of the Stirling Church for some years, but was ultimately disjoined, and the Rev. David Telfar was ordained first minister on 19th March, 1747. It drew its members from Callander, Menteith and Dunblane as well as from Doune and Kincardine. Strange to say, the Associate Church in Scotland did not long remain united. In 1747, it was rent in twain over a controversy with regard to the Burgess Oath, which is referred to later in this chapter.

During this period the parish minister was the Rev. William Simson, who was called from Fowlis Wester to Dunblane in 1730. Mr. Simson was highly popular within his first parish, and tradition relates how a deputation of three who went to Fowlis Wester to hear him preach was received. The three worthy men of Dunblane approached the Church individually, and the first two, admitting that they came from Dunblane, were warned away. When the third was questioned as to where he came from he replied interrogatively " D'ye ken Peebles ? " No danger was suspected and he was admitted to the Church, and having reported favourably on his return to Dunblane, Mr. Simson was duly called and elected.

Rev. William Blair, D.D., has recorded that the first meeting of the Associate congregation in Dunblane was held in a house in the Millrow and that for some time thereafter meetings were held in the Teind Barn at the top of the Braeport. It was some years before the congregation had a permanent home, and Burghers and Anti-Burghers held their services for some time in tents.

From the minutes of the Secession Church of Stirling it appears that Dunblane was still in conjunction with Stirling until after April, 1750, when William Anderson and Henry Clow were elected elders for the district of Dunblane.

In 1755, Mr. Simson, a man of amiable and peace-loving disposition, passed away. He was succeeded, after some trouble (see page 151) by the Rev. John Robertson. He seems to have had a pleasant nature, but to have been entirely unsuited to the ministry, and his forced appointment to Dunblane against the wishes of the people led to a large part of his congregation joining the Associate Church.

Although in July, 1739, nineteen persons resident in the parish of Dunblane joined the Associate congregation of Stirling, and although some in 1740 joined with the seceders at the

Bridge of Teith, it was not until some time later that an Associate Church was established in Dunblane. This was no doubt hastened by the forced appointment of Mr. Robertson. On 4th March, 1758, James Dun and Colin Drummond from the Associate congregation of Dunblane presented a petition to the Bridge of Teith Session for union of their congregation to that of the Bridge of Teith, and requesting that their minister, Mr. David Telfar, receive them as part of his congregation and take them into his oversight. The Bridge of Teith Session approved and negotiations proceeded with regard to the share which the congregation of Dunblane was to have of Mr. Telfar's services. It was ultimately arranged that Mr. Telfar should minister to the affairs of the two congregations to be managed separately, both to have a like claim on the minister's services and to bear an equal part of his stipend. It was agreed that Mr. Telfar should preach alternately in the two churches except during the winter quarter when he should preach twice at Bridge of Teith for once in Dunblane.

The first church of the Seceders in Dunblane was in this year 1758 in course of erection, and the first meeting of its Kirk Session was held on 7th June, 1758. This building was covered with red tiles and was known as the Meeting House or " the Red Hoose," and the road that passes it was known as the Meeting House Loan. The present church—the Leighton Church—was erected at the same place in 1835.

The congregation grew in strength and in 1765 the Presbytery of Glasgow disjoined Dunblane from Doune. The Dunblane members gave a call to Mr. Telfar to minister to them alone which was signed by 350 members and 93 adherents. Mr. Telfar was appointed at this time to proceed to Philadelphia to organise a church there, and consequently his call to Dunblane came to nought and for some time the congregation were left without a pastor. Ultimately, Mr. Michael Gilfillan, a young man described as " a fine lad " who had just completed his college course, was elected and he was ordained in 1768, his stipend being £55. The elder who took the leading part appears to have been Colin Drummond, tenant of the Bows Farm, Kilbryde.

The first church was a long narrow building running parallel to the Loan, the stone of which was taken from the quarry at Whitecross.

On 28th July, 1788, being the day after the July Sacrament, a meeting of the congregation was held to consider the repair of the meeting house, the roof of which was said to be in a ruinous state. The congregation agreed to have a new roof supplied of foreign wood and slated, and appointed a committee to employ tradesmen and to have the work proceeded with in the following spring. The cost of the repair amounted to £108 which included a new stair to the east loft and £3 16s. 8d. for drink for the work people. The old roof realised £13 and the balance of the money was collected from the congregation.

Mr. Gilfillan, who was born in Stirling in 1747, spent his whole life ministering to the Dunblane Associate congregation. He lived on most friendly terms with Mr. Robertson, the parish minister, they frequently walking together and talking over the books which they had read. His virtues were recorded on a tombstone now placed on the east side of the Leighton Church. His death took place in 1816 in the 49th year of his ministry.

In the year 1747, the Associate Church in Scotland was rent in twain over the wording of the Burgess Oath which was administered to burgesses of the principal towns in Scotland. The burgess was required to " allow the true religion presently professed within this realm." The Burgher section were prepared to accept the terms of the oath, but the Anti-Burgher body held that the acceptance implied an acquiescence in the errors of the Established Church and was thus equivalent to renouncing the principles of the Secession Church. The Reverend Ebenezer Erskine, the leader of the first secession, adhered to the Burgher body, the leader of the Anti-Burghers being the Reverend Andrew Gibb, a native of Muckhart. The Associate Church in Dunblane was a Burgher congregation, but a group of Anti-Burghers also formed a congregation at Dunblane, their first minister being a Mr. Ferguson who also had congregations under his charge at Greenloaning and Comrie. A place of worship was erected in 1765, its position being within a gate on the Holmehill road nearly opposite Dunblane smithy, the site being now included in Holmehill grounds. From 1768 to 1803 a Mr. Russell ministered to the Anti-Burghers and he was followed by the Rev. John Wallace (1804-1828) and the Rev. Alexander Henderson who, after 20 years' sojourn in Dunblane, went, on behalf of his church, to Canada. Mr. Henderson carried on a Boys' School in St. Blanes House. He wrote a poem known as " The Pilgrim," and he intended to develop his theme in several cantos, but he gave up his project after completing the first canto.

Lithograph by J. Macpherson, Edinburgh; from "The Kirk and the Manse," by the Rev. Robert W. Fraser, M.A., St. John's, Edinburgh. Published by Fullerton, Edinburgh, 1857.

From a Drawing by L⸍ Co⸍ Murray

DUNBLANE CATHEDRAL
The Nave looking to the West

Lithograph, about 1820, by S. Leith, Banff   By courtesy of the Society of Friends of Dunblane Cathedral

There are some interesting features connected with the early days of the Associate congregation of Dunblane. The names of members indicate that this church included families long resident in the district whose descendants are still in the neighbourhood, many being members of the Leighton congregation. The business of the congregation was carried on very similarly to the methods in use in the Established Church, as also was their procedure in electing ministers and elders. The first congregations contained a large proportion of the farmers in the neighbouring districts who at first took a leading part in the proceedings. A representative to the Presbytery and the Synod was elected yearly and it was the custom to nominate two members and vote thereon, the unsuccessful candidate, however, as a rule, proving successful at the next election. Frequently difficulty was experienced in getting leading members of the congregation to accept the eldership.   When it was thought desirable to elect elders, meetings of members were held in various parts of the parish and one of the number was appointed to report the result of the meeting to the Session.   The words commonly used in reporting the selection of a member was that the meeting had " pitched upon " one of their number as fit for the office.

The seceding congregations were in the habit of looking after their own poor, which duty had previously fallen for the whole community upon the heritors and Kirk Session of the Established Church.   The sums allowed to poor persons by the Associate congregation in its early days were small, usually about 6d. or 1s. at one time.   In 1775 there were 56 poor persons on the roll of the Established Church.   These were divided into two sections, those incapable of doing anything for their own maintenance who were given an allowance of about 2s. a week, and those who were able to do something, but required assistance. Each of the latter was given a badge to wear which conferred permission to beg throughout the parish for their own support on two days a week, but such received no money allowance. Any persons not belonging to the parish who came there to beg were to receive no help.   Any poor persons receiving a money allowance had to hand over all their property in return for the grant.

In January, 1797, the Session of the Associate congregation was much perturbed on account of the trouble which had arisen in the congregation with regard to the proposed alteration by the Associate Church of the terms of the Church's formula so much so that they were doubtful as to whether the spring communion should be celebrated. The hope was expressed that the Synod would come to some harmony consistent with truth respecting the Magistrates' power in matters of religion. The sacrament was duly celebrated in February, but the Session sent several remonstrances to the Synod craving that the preamble should be laid aside.   It would appear that the author of the preamble was Mr. Gilfillan, the much-loved pastor of the congregation.   The trouble resulted in 73 persons leaving the congregation about 1799 and forming themselves into an Auld Licht Body.   The meeting place of the Auld Lichts was Allanside House, Millrow, which became the first home of the Scottish Episcopal Church about 1842. In 1839 the Auld Lichts in Dunblane united with the Church of Scotland.

Matters had been proceeding quietly in the Cathedral congregation during this time, but, under the Reverend Robert Stirling, ordained assistant and successor to Mr. Robertson in 1791, it gradually gained strength.   Mr. Stirling, born in 1765, was a native of Dunblane and continued minister of the parish until his death in 1817.   His brother, William Stirling, was Procurator Fiscal in Dunblane until 1829 and his son, Patrick James Stirling, also followed the profession of the law in Dunblane throughout his long life.

Mr. Stirling's successor in the Cathedral was the Rev. John Grierson, previously minister of the parish of Dunning, who was inducted at Dunblane in July, 1818. About 1836, the degree of Doctor of Divinity was conferred upon him. His death occurred in 1840. In 1806 the heritors had had under consideration the waste, uncomfortable and ruinous state of the church and the damp and unhealthy situation of the parish school. Mr. William Stirling, architect, Dunblane, submitted to them a plan for repairing the church, that is the choir of the Cathedral, and converting part of it into a new school. This was approved by a meeting of heritors, but at the following meeting it was resolved to keep the fabric of the church in its present form. It was, however, agreed that the doors on the front of the church, that is probably two doors on the south wall of the choir, should be shut up, as also the vestry (or Chapel) door, that the partition wall of the school, which seeems to have been a wall across the Lady Chapel, should be taken down, and that the door of the gallery opposite the pulpit, which stood about the centre of the choir near the south wall, should be shut up, the breach in the east end repaired, frames with glass put into the windows and the walls of the choir plastered and white-washed and the floor laid with brick or stone. These alterations were not immediately proceeded with, and in the following year, 1807, it was agreed not to repair the Chapel as a school, but to erect a new building 32 feet by 20 to act as the parish school. The cost of the new school which was built on churchyard ground opposite the Leighton Church was £190. The building up of the doors, and of the window of the west gable of the choir, was proceeded with, and a new pulpit, precentor's desk, elder's seat and communion tables and forms 36 feet in length were supplied, as also an inside door at the west door entering from the ruined nave.

At this time the schoolmaster's house and garden, which were detached, were situated in the Millrow. In 1809, Mr. Malcolm Coldstream, who had with his father, Mr. William Coldstream, acted as schoolmaster for the greater part of a century, retired and was succeeded by Daniel Stewart, a notable figure in Dunblane for many years. The heritors purchased ground from the Earl of Kinnoull in 1811 for a house and garden for the schoolmaster, and a new house was built at a cost of £350. This house was occupied by Mr. Stewart and his successor, Mr. R. H. Christie, until it was removed to allow the erection of a new infant department early in this century.

The condition of the Manse of Dunblane also gave concern to the heritors. Dr. Grierson occupied what had been the residence of the Dean which stood adjacent to the north gable of the Leighton Library in front of the present Manse. The heritors were advised not to spend money on the old building and they desired to erect a new Manse on the Bishop's Yard (that is the Grass Yard), but the Barons of Exchequer refused to give a site there for this purpose. Ultimately the heritors bought two old houses and some ground to the west of the Dean's Manse and erected a new home for the minister with offices at a cost of £1208.

As early as 1807, there had been a proposal in the Associate Congregation to call an assistant to Mr. Gilfillan, but the latter opposed this and continued to labour in Dunblane until his death on 16th September, 1816, in the 49th year of his ministry. The members of his congregation erected a memorial to record their appreciation of his many personal gifts, which for many years stood against the south wall of the choir of Dunblane Cathedral, but was afterwards removed and re-erected outside the Leighton Church. It bears the following inscription:

IN MEMORY

of

The Revd. Michael Gilfillan, Minister of the Associate Congregation in this place, in whom extensive acquaintance with sacred literature, practical wisdom, and moral rectitude were happily united with habitual devotion, cheerfulness of temper, and suavity of manners. Alive to every impulse of benevolence, it was his delight to minister happiness to his friends. Faithful and affectionate in all his official duties, he was loved as the Father of his people, and by his unwearied efforts for the good of Zion, and for the welfare of Society, he was distinguished as a true Patriot, and as an eminent blessing to the Church of Christ. In testimony of their grateful recollection of his labours, and of their veneration of his memory, his Congregation have erected this Monument.

Among Mr. Gilfillan's good works was the founding of Bible and Missionary Societies, a Savings Bank and a Sunday School conducted at one time in the Court Room at the Tolbooth. Mr. McKerrow, long Secession minister at Bridge of Teith, described him as a man of great sagacity and practical wisdom, with great influence in the Church and very patriotic.

Mr. Gilfillan's successor was the Reverend James Anderson from Leslie, who was ordained at an open-air service in April, 1818. The Reverend Mr. McKerrow, minister at the Bridge of Teith, delivered the sermon. About a year later members of the congregation submitted a petition which they asked should be forwarded to the superior courts expressing the desirability of union of the Burgher congregations with their Anti-Burgher brethren on the other side of the Secession Church. The Kirk Session unanimously agreed to forward the petition, the same to be presented by the Moderator to next meeting of the Synod. The union between these branches of the Secession Church took place in 1820 when 154 Burgher congregations joined 129 Anti-Burgher Congregations, forming the United Secession Church. By 1847, it had 400 congregations at which date the Relief Church united with it. While these bodies were then united, separate congregations continued to exist in the same villages although units of the one united church. Persons who remained outside the United Secession Church formed a new church which they called the Original Secession Church. It may be noted that in 1819 the Burgher congregation gave a subscription to a " Broth Kitchen " in Dunblane. There also existed in connection with the Church a Singing Club which had power to appoint a Precentor. This was probably the forerunner of the modern church choir although the members may not have sat together at service to lead the praise.

Church history in Dunblane between 1820 and 1840 appears to have been devoid of much interest. In the latter year Dr. Grierson died, and he was succeeded as minister of the Cathedral by the Reverend William MacKenzie, minister of Comrie Parish. Mr. MacKenzie was a man of some force of character, earnest and strongly evangelical. He had the parish divided up into 14 districts, a custom which had existed in previous generations but had fallen into disuse. He had good business instincts—he was the first Established Church minister who signed the minutes—and he instituted monthly meetings of Kirk Session, held on the first Monday before the full moon at 6 p.m. The duties of elders were all laid down, and it was arranged that they stand at the plate by rotation. It was resolved, in 1842, to have the youth assembled for religious instruction after the dismissal of the congregation. A fortnightly Prayer Meeting was also instituted. These changes all indicate that Mr. MacKenzie was full of enthusiasm for the duties of his office, but, as sometimes happens, the most active and sincere are not the most discreet. Soon after Mr. MacKenzie's ministry commenced, Patrick James Stirling, writer, son of a former minister of the parish, and a man of great intellectual ability, resigned the eldership, and, shortly after, Thomas Barty, also a writer, and son of the manse, resigned his membership. These men, the two leading inhabitants of Dunblane at the time, were chiefly instrumental in founding a congregation in connection with the Scottish Episcopal Church. The first services were held in Allanside House, which had been previously used by the " Auld Lichts." After worshipping for two or three years without a church, St. Mary's was built during 1844-5, and dedicated on 28th May of the latter year.

In the meantime the Disruption in the Church of Scotland had taken place. No reference to this very important event is recorded in the minutes of the Kirk Session of Dunblane parish. A Session meeting was held on 14th May, 1843, and the minute was signed by the Rev. William MacKenzie. This was followed by the General Assembly, when the Rev. Dr. Chalmers led forth a large number of ministers and elders, splitting the ancient Church in twain. On 7th June, 1843, Mr. MacKenzie and his elders met together, when an Act of Demission by the elders was read over, and signed by all present. The absentees were Adam Baird, who was unable to attend, but who afterwards signed the Act, and James Bain, the only elder who did not sever himself from the old Church. The terms of the Act of Demission are worthy of preservation, and are given verbatim :—

" Dunblane, 7th June, 1843.

" We, the undersigned Elders, considering that a large body of the Commissioners chosen to the General Assembly of the Church of Scotland, appointed to have been holden at Edinburgh on the 18th day of May by past, did solemnly protest against the freedom and lawfulness of any Assembly that might then be constituted as an Assembly of the Establishment and against the subversion recently effected in the constitution of the Establishment; and did thereafter, along with diverse other Ministers and Elders, assumed by them, constitute themselves into a Free General Assembly, adhering to the Confession of Faith and the Standards of the Church of Scotland as heretofore understood ; and did agree to adopt an Act of Separation whereby they separated from the Establishment and renounced the rights and privileges thereof, all in prosecution of the claim of Right adopted by the General Assembly of the Church of Scotland which met in May, 1842, and the Protest made on the occasion above-mentioned. And considering further, that we cordially approve of the foresaid Act of Separation, and are resolved to adhere to the said Free Assembly and the Judicatories subordinate thereto, Do therefore now separate from the Establishment, and renounce and abdicate whatsoever status, right or privilege we may have hitherto held as Elders by reason of the Establishment of the Church, and its connection with the State ; Declaring, however, that we do not hereby in any degree affect or impair our status as office-bearers of Christ's Church in our respective congregations, or such portion thereof as may concur with us, or relinquish any of the privileges thereto belonging, which we shall possess and enjoy in the Free Church of Scotland, as fully as if we had not subscribed these presents. And we appoint a duplicate hereof to be transmitted to the legal Administrators of the Poor of this Parish for their information, and another to be transmitted to the Clerks of the Free Church of Scotland for preservation.

(Sgd.)   Donald McDonald, Elder.
Adam Baird, Elder.
Walter Lennox, Elder.
John Gentle, Elder.
John Donaldson, Elder.
Andrew Hart, Elder.
John Stewart, Elder.
James King, Elder."

In this way a new and vigorous Church sprang up in Dunblane, and once more the Cathedral congregation was reduced to a very feeble body. Mr. Bain did not long survive, and it was some time before new elders were secured for the Parish Church.

This Act of Demission was communicated to the heritors with whom Parish Kirk Sessions were at the time so closely associated. Mr. MacKenzie and his elders accounted for the funds for the poor, which had been administered by them, to the satisfaction of the heritors. The new body proceeded to erect a school and church. The first communion was held on Sabbath, 30th July, preceded by public worship at the How Miln on the Thursday previous, and in the Leighton Church on the Saturday. On the Communion Sunday there was service at 11 a.m., again at the How Miln, and the Lord's Supper was dispensed in Mr. Anderson's Church, where there was also a service of thanksgiving at 11 a.m. on the following day. These days and hours were similar to those observed by the Established Church. The Howmilnhead, at the top of the Braeport, in late years a kitchen garden for Holmehill House, had been the scene of many religious gatherings in the time of Ebenezer Erskine, and when a congregation was unable to meet in its church or the building was too small on special occasions, the members frequently worshipped at this place. The first building of the Free Church was opened for worship in November, 1843, and stood to the rear of the hall which is now used by the Territorial Forces. For many years before the Victoria Hall was erected, this hall served as the Public Hall of Dunblane and until 1872 the Free Church day school was conducted there. The accommodation of the first Free Church soon proved inadequate for the congregation, and in consequence the East Church was erected in 1854.

Mr. MacKenzie remained minister of the new congregation for only two years, and he was succeeded in 1845 by the Reverend James D. Burns, a hymn writer, some of whose compositions are included in the *Church Hymnary*. During the fifty years from 1843 to 1892 seven ministers served the congregation. The Reverend Hugh Stevenson alone ministered for 42 years.

To return to the Cathedral congregation—the first minister after the Disruption was the Reverend James Boe, who was ordained minister of the parish on 25th January, 1844. His first communion was held on 21st July, 1844. Mr. Boe records in the minute book that notwithstanding the zeal and activity of the new seceders in advancing their own cause and accusing the Church they once revered of denying that Christ was the sole King and Head of the Church, though the Church of Scotland recognised and rejoiced in that doctrine as fully and reverently as those who assailed her, the church was well filled with a most attentive congregation, and that, inclusive of seven ministers and assisting elders, the communicants numbered 141, all of whom were firmly attached to the church of their fathers.

For some time the duties of the Kirk Session were conducted by Mr. Boe, assisted by Mr. Gordon Mitchell, minister of Kilmadock, and the Reverend Peter W. Young, minister of Lecropt. The first elders to be appointed after the Disruption were Mr. Donald Stewart, schoolmaster,

Mr. Walter McLean, weaver, Bridgend, and Mr. Walter Graham, Ochlochy, who were ordained on 29th January, 1845, Mr. Stewart being appointed Session Clerk.

The Disruption in the Established Church was followed by the union of the Relief Church with the United Secession Church. The Relief Church was formed in 1761 following on the deposition of three ministers who would not take part in the intrusion on a parish of a minister who was unacceptable. They claimed relief from the yoke of patronage and the tyranny of church courts. This body consisting of 136 congregations joined the United Secession Church in 1847, the united church being thereafter known as the United Presbyterian Church. The Anti-Burgher Church was still standing in 1856 when the Reverend William Blair came to Dunblane, but it had ceased to be used for worship, and shortly after this date it was taken down.

In 1854 the Reverend Mr. Anderson retired, his successor being the Reverend William Blair. His examination by the Presbytery took place on 1st April, 1856.

The Reverend James Anderson did not live long in retirement, his death taking place at Leslie on 9th March, 1858, immediately before the celebration of the centenary of the congregation.

Progress in building up a congregation in the Cathedral after the Disruption was slow. Mr. Boe died unexpectedly in 1860, leaving a young family. He had proved a faithful minister and kindly man, one highly respected by his congregation. During the early days of his successor, the Reverend Mr. Ingram, little life was shown. At his first Session meeting in November, 1861, there was only one elder present, but two new elders were appointed a few months later. At the February communion, 1862, the number of communicants was 116 or a smaller number than were left after the Disruption. Although Mr. Ingram's appointment had not pleased everyone the congregation began to increase, but his ministry was short, being terminated by his death in 1869. His successor was the Reverend John Barclay, a preacher of exceptional ability, who remained in Dunblane only about 18 months. In February, 1870, the Session deplored the death of Daniel Stewart, the old parish schoolmaster, who had acted for 60 years as Session Clerk. His successor was Mr. R. H. Christie, who held office for 33 years.

The poverty of the Cathedral congregation or their lack of interest in 1868 was shown by a perusal of the accounts. The collections for that year amounted in all to £27 and the total income of the Session to £41, against which there was an expenditure of £15 on salaries, £5 on the poor and education and £16 on other objects. The Cathedral itself seems at this time to have been in considerable need of repair. Some minor repairs were executed in 1861. Three years previously a gravitation water supply was introduced to the Manse off a pipe laid down by Kippendavie estate to supply the railway station. Before this was introduced, water for the Manse had to be carried either from Bruce's Well or the River Allan, and various proposals had been under consideration such as the pumping of water from the Bishop's Well in the Grass Yard.

About 1872 further repairs were undertaken to the Cathedral. The gallery at the west end of the choir was altered, pews were supplied and a door made between the Chapter House and choir. The work in 1861 included the supplying of a new roof to the choir and Chapel and a parapet on the south wall of the choir. The old roof was made of oak formed out of whole trees rudely squared up with ties and struts tenoned to the rafters and to one another, and the rafters tenoned together at the ridge, all being fixed with oak pins. Many of the rafters were found much decayed although the sarking was good. The slates had also been fixed with wooden pins.

Until the restoration of 1872 the entrance to the gallery had been by a stair which occupied part of the Lady Chapel, but it was then arranged to use the ancient circular staircase which had been previously rediscovered. There was introduced at this time a new apparatus for heating the building with hot air, but there had previously been in use a similar system of heating introduced about 1835 at the expense of the parishioners.

Various changes were introduced during the short stay of the Reverend Mr. Barclay. Thus, the Monday service of thanksgiving following communion, the use of metal tokens and the celebration of the Sacrament at successive tables were all given up. In November, 1870, Mr. Henderson of Glassingall presented cups, salvers and a flagon, also Bibles for the use of minister and elders at the communion table.

Soon after his successor, the Reverend David Morrison, had been inducted, the congregation agreed to a harmonium being used in the Cathedral at the ordinary services of the church, and at this time it was arranged that the congregation should stand during praise and kneel during prayer.   The harmonium was also the gift of Mr. Henderson.

The relationships between the Cathedral and United Presbyterian Congregations seem to have been very friendly, and the use of the Church of the latter was given to the Cathedral congregation in 1818, 1861 and 1872 when repairs were in progress, and indeed in 1872 the Cathedral members, on their own suggestion, worshipped with the U.P. Congregation on Sunday forenoons.

The history of the three Presbyterian congregations of the Parish Church, the United Presbyterian Church and the Free Church in Dunblane up to modern days has been briefly traced, and now all carry on an active existence.   In October, 1900, the latter two became one, and now, since 1929, all are happily reunited in one great mother Church of Scotland.

CHAPTER XXXI.

CHURCH LIFE IN AN EARLY SECESSION COMMUNITY.

THE first entry in the records of the early Secession Church of Dunblane is dated 25th May, 1758, and explains that the congregation of Menteith and those in and about Dunblane had agreed to unite into one congregation. In consequence of a petition from Dunblane and by appointment of the Presbytery, a meeting of Session was held on this date at which the Rev. David Telfar, Moderator, and some elders were present. Two of the elders, Robert Coper and James Hutchon, represented that the people of Dunblane insisted on having a number of men ordained elders and had at a general meeting nominated persons whom they wished the Session to ordain. These included Colin Drummond, Bow of Kilbryde, and others, chiefly farmers. The meeting was adjourned until 18th June when the persons nominated were approved and an extra man added. The Session was known as the Associate Session of Doune and Dunblane. The Session proceeded with the election, but one, Andrew White, objected to one of the candidates, James Wright, in Bridgend, because he had taken away a bill before it was fully cleared. The elders were duly elected after some considerable time, and John McIsack was appointed clerk after he and Colin Drummond had been put on a leet. It is to be noted that whenever an appointment fell to be made a leet of two was drawn up and a vote taken. At the same time Robert Coper was appointed treasurer. These appointments seem only to refer to that part of the business which pertained to the Dunblane members.

In 1759, the Session had much trouble over John Hutchon, who, it was said, had given in a list of four hides to the Gadger (or Excise Officer) when he had drawn five. Hutchon admitted this, but explained that he had done so by mistake. He would not admit that he was guilty of perjury as he was only put on oath once every quarter of a year. He also stated that he had not intended to use this hide until he had drawn more and that he intended to give it in with the other hides he designed to draw. The Session ultimately resolved that he had acted contrary to law and had given an occasion for enemies to reproach religion and he was ordered to be rebuked.

The Session frequently dealt with offences, sometimes grave but often trivial. There are not many cases of Sabbath breaking mentioned in contrast to what is found in the early minutes of the Cathedral Kirk Session. It is recorded on 24th April, 1769, that John Reid alleged that Edam Dawson had broken the Sabbath by drying clothes in his house which he could prove by the evidence of his maid and Dawson's maid. Dawson objected to his own maid being a witness as she had averred malice against his wife, and to John Reid's maid as she was much given to lying and was not a credible witness. A committee who had been appointed to deal with the case then rebuked Reid for not reproving Edam when he saw the clothes drying or telling him his fault in private according to Scripture, and further for charging him when he could not prove the offence. They then admonished Edam to beware of any such practices as those laid to his charge and they then admonished both parties to live in future in love, amity and friendship. The conduct of the committee who had dealt so thoroughly and judiciously with the case was approved of by the Session.

One of the original elders of the congregation was Colin Drummond of the Bow of Kilbryde. On 30th July, 1770, he referred to the scruples some members of the Session had to his practice of making his cheese on the Sabbath day during the summer season. He repeated that he did not see the sinfulness of his practice, but argued that it was a work of necessity and not a profanation of the Sabbath. The Session thought it advisable to refer the matter to the Presbytery. The Presbytery gave the opinion that this was not a work of necessity and that Colin should leave it over. At a later meeting Colin adhered to his previous opinion alleging that it was both a work of necessity and mercy and no breach of the Sabbath. The Session did not agree and recommended Colin to leave off the practice and to fall upon some other way of managing his work. Probably this was not acceptable to him, and it may be noted that his presence at later meetings is seldom, if ever, recorded.

A new member for the Presbytery and Synod meetings was generally elected yearly. The retiring member would mention that it was fitting that a new appointment should be made, and on nearly every occasion two were put on a leet and voted upon. Very often the unsuccessful candidate was renominated in the following year and successfully elected. Elections of elders took place from time to time, and the procedure followed was as follows:—In 1769, for example, the Session took into consideration the many and great disadvantages under which they laboured by reason of the paucity of their number and they appointed their members in certain quarters or districts such as the Barony of Kippenross and the Barony of Kippendavie, the people about the Loaning (that is Greenloaning), Kilbryde and various parts of the town to meet and elect one or more elders. Frequently an elder was appointed to meet the people of the various districts, but in 1769 this was not done and the districts at their meetings each appointed a member to report. Thus, James Scobie was appointed by Kippendavie Barony to report that they had made choice of Archibald Whithead. The words usually employed instead of " made choice of " were " pitched upon." The candidates for the eldership were next invited to a meeting of Session where they were examined as to their fitness for office, and, if they were found fit, the election proceeded much as at the present time. There was practically no difference in the proceedings from those of the elections to the Kirk Session of the Parish Church. It would appear as if a high standard of conduct was expected and was obtained from the members of this Church.

We find the Session dealing with matters such as the forgery of a brother-in-law's signature. A man named John Morrison was rebuked for taking a sneck off a gate at Balhaldie. Another complaint was anent a wife drying clothes on the Sunday. It is noticeable that at first there are few cases mentioned of acts of immorality, but references to such become more frequent later on, that is in the 19th century. This indicates either that the standard of conduct had fallen or that the Session regarded such matters with greater seriousness in later years than at first.

About the year 1777 monthly meetings of Kirk Session were held, the first part of which was always devoted to prayer and Christian conference. This was usually opened by one elder and closed by another, both named. The minutes at this period record that all members were present except A, B, C, D, etc., which is not such a convenient way as stating the actual persons present. The Kirk Session from time to time gave money in support of their poor. The sums voted were quite small, usually about 6d or 1/-, rising to 2/6 on rare occasions. In July, 1775, the minister informed the Session that the heritors of the parish desired to know how much they could spare yearly for support of the poor as the heritors wished to put in execution a plan for the poor which would stop begging.

It was the custom in the congregation to have two communions yearly, and these were very frequently on the fourth Sundays of February and of July, but the days varied a week or two in many years. A Fast Day was usually observed, but there were not so many preparation services as, at one time, were held in the Parish Church.

John McIsack, the first Session Clerk, acted for many years. His successor was Henry Paterson, appointed in 1782, and at that time William Bennett, a tailor, was appointed precentor. Another matter which gave the Session a little trouble was a complaint against four members who had been convicted of using light weights.

On 10th January, 1785, a long petition was presented from Kilbryde against an elder who was accused (1) of some indecent conduct and (2) of stealing limestones belonging to other people. It was common at that time to search for lime stones in the burns and collect and burn them and afterwards apply the product to the land. There was no evidence of the first charge against the farmer, but with regard to the second there seems to have been evidence that he had taken from neighbouring piles, limestones belonging to others. The Session agreed to absolve him from the charges, which did not at all please the congregation, who appeared to be strongly of opinion that the farmer was guilty.

In December, 1785, under the direction of the Synod, a day of fasting and humiliation was appointed for observation as soon after the harvest as convenient on account of the abounding wickedness of the generation, notwithstanding the many mercies enjoyed, and although tokens of the Lord's anger had gone forth. The Session's first resolution was to recommend the Moderator to draft out the reasons for the fast, and the fast was no doubt afterwards held. Collections were frequently given for other churches. Thus, 20/- was contributed in 1762 for a church at

Newcastle. In August, 1786, a collection was appointed for the people of Kirkintilloch, and in the following month it was agreed to take a public collection every two years for the benefit of weak congregations.

The contracting of irregular marriages was regarded as a scandalous matter. In May, 1787, a Mrs. White, from Alloa, confessed having contracted a secret marriage with her husband about 17 years previously. She was appointed to appear before the congregation to be publicly rebuked.

In April, 1787, it was found that none of the candidates for eldership appeared for ordination and consequently none were ordained. It was usual to observe the Wednesday before the communion as a fast day although sometimes the date varied. In March, 1788, a Thursday was fixed as Wednesday was the day of the March Fair in Dunblane. Another man who got into trouble was a carrier who was said to have kept money, and he was charged with dishonesty and breach of trust, as also with the telling of lies and drunkenness.

One finds some difference in place-names. The farm of Dykedale is referred to as "Digdale." Sinclair Street is known as St. Clair's Wynd, and Shanraw appears as Sharow, as also as Shandror. The name Milad's Cottage seems to have been an abbreviated form of Miln Land Cottage.

In January, 1797, the Session were disturbed about a matter—so much so that they were doubtful about holding a spring communion. Some of the members were not clear about the expediency of appointing the Sacrament to be dispensed on account of the ferment which had been in the congregation respecting the proposed alteration of the Formula. They, hoped that the Synod would allow the question regarding the government of the Church to remain as in the old Formula and would come to some harmony consistent with truth respecting the magistrates' power in matters of religion. The members of Session, however, came to an agreement on what steps they should take in this important business, and it was arranged to have the sacrament on the second Sabbath of February. The Session at a later meeting resolved to send a remonstrance to the Synod relating to the alteration in the Formula, and appointed a committee of elders with the minister to draw up a draft petition and remonstrance, which was approved on 6th April, 1797. At this meeting a petition was presented from the congregation for permission to petition the Synod. The congregation met on two occasions and approved of a petition of remonstrance which the Session forwarded to the Presbytery along with their own petition. On 6th August, 1798, the Session were asked to call another meeting of the congregation for petitioning the Synod on behalf " of our received principles." A meeting was held and it was agreed that the congregation petition the Synod craving that they lay aside the preamble of the Formula, which petition was also forwarded by the Session.

In February, 1799, the Church was not available for the sacrament and it was agreed to obtain Mr. Russell's Meeting House for that purpose if such could be obtained. William Mathie, the Church Treasurer, died at this time and was succeeded by Alexander Malloch. Further petitions were forwarded to the Synod in September, 1799, for removing the preamble to the Formula. The subject continued to cause difficulty, and in July, 1800, Thomas Kinross and John Roy required that it be minuted that their continuing to officiate as elders was not to be construed as approving of the Deed of Synod in continuing the preamble. It was noted at this time that Robert Morrison and James Hart had not officiated for some time, being offended with the conduct of the Synod respecting the Formula. In May, 1801, the Session had to appoint an Officer in place of Peter Bell, deceased, John Bruce being appointed. His remuneration consisted of 3d. for opening and shutting the Meeting House each Sabbath, 4/- for the summer sacrament and 3/- for the winter one, 6/- a half year when the stipend was paid, 1/- for each marriage, provided as much was collected, and 3d. for each baptism or 6d. when the parent could afford it. In 1801 10/- was paid for the expense of coals and candles for catechising in the Court Room on Sabbath evenings for the by-past winter and spring.

Some congregations elsewhere got into litigation over the ownership of church property at this time. A congregation in Dundee asked a collection from Dunblane owing to their having joined the "Auld Lichts." The precentor about this time received £1 1/- a year as salary, increased later on to one and a half guineas. The Synod continued from time to time to order days of humiliation or thanksgiving as the profanities and events in the district demanded. In November, 1813, it was agreed to have a solemn thanksgiving on account of the recent plentiful harvest gathered in safely, as also for the uncommon success with which the British armies had been crowned leading to the expectation of an early honourable peace. On 3rd March, 1814, the Session considering that the first lease of 57 years of the Meeting House expired at Martinmas, 1814—that is, it must have been granted in 1757—agreed to take the benefit of the second period of 57 years and to give intimation to John Robb, his heirs or assignees, six months before Martinmas. Mr. Robb was apparently succeeded in the ownership of the ground by a Mr. Nidderly.

The usual procedure in dealing with offences was for the party to appear before the Session when a committee was appointed to confer with the offender and, when the committee at a later date reported that they were satisfied of his or her repentance, the offender was cited to appear before the congregation for public rebuke, following on which he (or she) appeared before the Kirk Session and a vote was taken as to whether he (or she) should be absolved. One case is noted where a person confessed a moral fault after the matter was 15 years old.

In January, 1840, there was an election of elders. One of the candidates, James Eadie, merchant in Dunblane, appeared at a meeting before his ordination and objected to two of the questions of the Formula as a bar to his accepting office. One objection was that he could not go the length of saying that the Presbyterian form of government was the only form founded on and agreeable to the Word of God. His other objection was that he did not believe religious covenanting to be a moral duty. The Moderator mentioned that similar protests to the Synod had been presented from ministers on both of these points, and the Session agreed to receive the protest of James Eadie and to allow it to lie on the table and he was duly ordained.

At a meeting held in December, 1840, the Session considered the proposed union with the Relief Church agreeable to the recommendation of the Synod, and after long reasoning agreed to report favourably of that measure.

In 1842 the minister acted as Session Clerk and continued to do so for some time although previously an elder had always so acted. During Dr. Blair's early days, although there was a Session Clerk, Dr. Blair wrote the minutes. In May, 1842, the death of Thomas Kinross, sen., is recorded, and for the first time one finds a minute of appreciation of his character and good qualities. Later on John Monteith, merchant in Dunblane, became Session Clerk. There seems always to have been considerable reluctance on the part of members of the congregation to accept the eldership, and a number of well-known citizens declined this office on several occasions. Sometimes eight or ten men would be approached and perhaps two or only one would accept office, and these were not, as a rule, the men who received the most votes.

There is no reference to the Disruption in the Church of Scotland in 1843. While in the earlier days of the Church there were only winter and summer sacraments of the Lord's Supper, in the early half of the 19th century the number was increased to three, and about 1844 the Session considered increasing the number of communion celebrations to four. In 1844 it was agreed that the minister should give an address on the subject of intemperance. In 1845 John Monteith, elder, intimated a desire to resign his office as elder owing to natural diffidence disqualifying him for the office. A committee of two other elders were appointed to persuade him to continue, but they proved unsuccessful and ultimately his resignation was accepted. About this time one observes for the first time references to Missions, and, at first, applications for support of such were not cordially received. In 1847 the Moderator proposed that the Session decline any active exactions. At this time reference is made to the United Associate Presbytery of which there were two congregations.

In 1848, the members of this Church who lived in the neighbourhood of Bridge of Allan were disjoined and they formed a congregation of their own. The petition for this purpose was presented by James Ferguson, a member of the Session, who had for some time been worshipping at the railway station, newly erected at Bridge of Allan. The Kirk Session granted the prayer of the petition and disjoined the petitioners numbering 17. It would appear that the influx of men to the district in connection with railway construction had supplied a nucleus for a congregation.

In 1849, the Session was concerned over one of their number, James Eadie, who had been worshipping with the party called the Morisonians. Eadie admitted this and long discussions followed. Ultimately in June, 1849, he was declared to be no longer a member of Session. On 11th April, 1854, Dr. McKerrow acted as the Moderator as it was said that the Rev. Mr. Anderson was in feeble health. At this meeting a petition addressed by James Eadie to the Presbytery craving that he be allowed the privileges of a member of the United Presbyterian Church was submitted. The Session agreed to re-admit only if Eadie withdrew from his erroneous principles. Many meetings followed, but apparently Eadie was unable to satisfy the Session that his principles were in accordance with those of the Church. The views of James Eadie seem to have been quite reasonable, and one wonders at the difficulties made about re-admitting him as a member.

The congregation met on Thursday, 11th October, 1855, at 2 p.m., to take steps for the election of a minister, and on 5th February, 1856, representatives of the congregation appeared before the Presbytery with a call to Mr. William Blair signed by 255 members and by 92 adherents. On 1st April, 1856, the newly-elected minister was examined by the Presbytery. He had to deliver a lecture and sermon and to read a dissertation and polemical discourse after which he was examined in Greek, Hebrew, church history and practical religion. His ordination took place on the 16th April, 1856.

The congregation appears to have had a library for the use of its members, and volumes were added in 1857. In October, 1857, a fast day was appointed, the forenoon to be observed as one of humiliation on account of the disastrous war in India and the afternoon service to be one of thanksgiving for the abundant harvest. In February, 1858, two former members applied for re-admission. They had joined the other Secession congregation which had by this time become defunct.

Peter Gentle, grocer in Dunblane, known in his day to all, and for long an active elder, was admitted a member of the congregation in April, 1858. He had previously belonged to the Anti-Burgher congregation and afterwards to the Morisonians.

During some repairs to the Cathedral in 1861 the Established Church congregations were allowed to worship in the U.P. (now Leighton) Church. A union with the Free Church of Scotland was discussed as far back as 1864. The new United Presbyterian Church was opened in 1835, and it is stated that in 1872 the income from seat rents was the same as in 1835. The Cathedral congregation again in 1872 asked for accommodation in this Church, which they had also had in 1818, and it was agreed that they should worship with the United Presbyterian congregation on Sunday forenoons.

Dr. Blair was pressed to accept a Church in Glasgow in 1874 and one at Bothwell in 1875, but declined in both cases.

In 1878 elders' districts were again formed as such had existed in the early days of the congregation. One of the districts was known as the Suburbs and this included " The Terrace," apparently what is now known as " The Crescent " or " Kippendavie Crescent."

The Session was troubled at this time with members adopting different postures during service—some standing and others sitting to sing and some standing and others sitting to pray. It was its desire that there should be uniformity.

A notable minister in the Secession Church in Scotland in the 18th century was the Reverend Patrick Hutchison, a native of Dunblane and a son of an elder in the Burgher Church in the time of the Reverend Mr. Gilfillan. Mr. Hutchison is understood to have been the son of James Hutcheon or Hutchison, a farmer in the Kilbryde district, and an elder in the Associate Session of Doune and Dunblane, while there was still a united congregation ministered to by a single minister. Patrick Hutchison was licensed as a minister of the Secession and his first congregation was that of the Relief Church of St. Ninians. In 1779 he published a book entitled *Compendious View of Relief Principles* which dealt with points of difference between the Relief Church and the Established Church of Scotland. He soon afterwards brought out a second volume entitled *Messiah's Kingdom* and later a history of the Relief Church.

Though much attached to his congregation at St. Ninians, he was in 1783 transferred to Paisley, where he remained until his death in January, 1802.

CHAPTER XXXII.

CHANGES IN THE CHOIR AND CHAPTER HOUSE OF DUNBLANE CATHEDRAL DURING THE PAST CENTURIES.

AFTER the nave of the Cathedral became roofless, Divine worship was restricted to the choir, and the choir arch between choir and nave was built up to the roof. This was originally done with such thickness that the piers and mouldings of the arch were entirely hidden. The two windows above the arch were also built up. Changes were also made from time to time on the interior of the Lady Chapel or chapter house of which an explanation follows.

Prior to the 19th century the pulpit stood not far from the centre of the choir near its south wall. Entrance was obtained by a doorway on this wall, the position of which is noticeable to the present day. At the eastmost south window there was also an entrance with an outside stair giving access to the gallery erected across the east window and known as Balhaldie's Loft or the Soldiers' Gallery. In the 18th century for a time there were three galleries in the choir, namely, on its east, north and west walls, and the sittings seem to have exceeded 400 in number at all times. With the development of the country following on the close of the rebellion of 1745, the choir would soon have proved too small for the congregation had it not been for the unfortunate appointment of the Rev. John Robertson as parish minister against the strenuous opposition of the members and adherents. This greatly weakened the congregation for many years thereafter, and, while it began to revive at the beginning of the 19th century, and while it became evident that about 1842 further church accommodation must be supplied, the Disruption followed and a great proportion of the members left the Established Church along with their minister and Session to form a congregation of the Free Church of Scotland. The membership being in this way reduced, the need of a larger church was again postponed for a considerable period.

Prior to 1800 there was no heating system in the choir and no lighting unless by lamps or candles.

In 1746, the roof of the steeple seems to have been in bad order and damage was done to the church bells and to the clock. This was duly attended to, and in the following year a new porch was erected at the east church door at the cost of £36 17s. 6d. This was probably at the door entered by the stairway leading to the east loft. In 1749 the windows on the south wall of the choir on either side of the pulpit were in need of renewal. When these had been inserted with lead, wire frames had been put outside which made the choir dark, particularly in winter. It was resolved at that time to have the windows sashed, but this may never have been done. It should be kept in view that these windows were originally much shorter, terminating at a greater distance from the ground than at later times, and it was with the view of improving the light that the windows were lengthened at a later date.

It has already been noted (page 191) that in 1806 and 1807 it was proposed to carry out certain alterations in the choir and in the part of the church used as the parish school. Eventually it was decided to erect a new building for the school. It has to be kept in view that at this time, in addition to the Parochial School, there were country schools at Kinbuck and Kilbryde, and also that " private adventure " schools existed in Dunblane where the teachers depended on receiving fees for their pupils and were not given assistance by the Government or any local body. The proposed alterations were not all proceeded with although it was agreed to close up the doors above mentioned, and to supply a new pulpit, precentor's desk and elders' seats, communion tables and forms 36 feet in length as already mentioned. It was also agreed to repair the roof and to supply an inside door at the west door entrance.

It does not seem clear whether the agreed-on alterations were carried out, as the heritors were concerned in 1815 with the internal arrangements of the choir, and in the following year a memorial was presented to them protesting against certain proposed alterations and, in particular, against the destruction of the old carved stalls, the closing of the entrance door in the centre of the chancel arch and the making of two new doors to take its place, while objection was also taken to retaining the gallery across the east window.   The protestors, who included some of the chief heritors, urged that the features of ancient buildings should be retained. Alternative plans were submitted by Mr. Gillespie, architect, who undertook that no greater expense would be entailed in carrying out his designs than under Mr. Stirling's plan (see page 191), while his suggestions would provide thirty additional sittings.   It was then resolved to proceed with Mr. Gillespie's proposals which involved making passages along the north and south walls of the choir, restricting the west gallery to extend only to the first pillar from the west end and providing for the vestry and session house being in the chapter house.   Mr Smith, of Glassingall, although himself an artist, seems to have favoured the changes proposed by Mr. Stirling, architect, which would have involved considerable structural interference with the choir. While one may not endorse all that Mr. Gillespie proposed, his views seem to have been much sounder than those of Mr. Stirling, and to his credit it should be recorded that, while he agreed to render assistance while the work was in hand, he declined to accept any remuneration.   During the progress of the alterations at this time the Cathedral congregation were accommodated in the Auld Licht Meeting House, that is Allanside House in the Millrow.

After the alterations in the choir had been completed in 1819, the seating was allocated and one learns that the pulpit then stood in the centre of the choir near the east end.   In the first place, the minister was given a pew for himself and his family, which consisted of a square seat to the north of the pulpit and next the vestry door.   The elders were next provided for in a square seat in front of the precentor's desk and the seat immediately below his desk.   The next to be given a pew was the schoolmaster who obtained the eastmost pew on the south side of the pulpit.   Family pews were then allotted to the heritors, Kippendavie receiving the front seat of the gallery on the south, and the Earl of Kinnoull, the proprietor of Cromlix, received the front seat of the gallery on the north side.   It would appear that it is one and the same gallery that is here referred to. The Laird of Keir had allotted to him a square seat on the south side of the pulpit, and the Kilbryde family pew was the westmost seat under the gallery on the south side of the church.

At this time the monument traditionally believed to be the tomb of Bishop Finlay Dermoch, but believed by some to be that of Bishop Clement, was removed across the choir to the south side, the object being to permit of a door being made through from the chapter house about six feet east of the present door from the chapter house to the choir which choir was built up and lost sight of for many years.   According to McGregor Stirling the tomb in the south transept formerly lay on the south wall of the choir opposite that of Dermoch, and this he suggests to have been the tomb of Bishop Clement.   It was removed to its present position to permit of a door being opened through the south wall into the choir.

At the west end of the choir within the entrance door from the ruined nave was a vestibule, and at one time the old stalls stood there and a stair led from the vestibule to the gallery or galleries. From the vestibule the church (that is the choir) was entered either to the left or right, there being no centre passage from 1819 for the next fifty years.

The floors of the choir and chapter house were at this time raised probably with the object of avoiding damp and making the building more comfortable.   The chapter house in the early part of the 19th century was greatly damaged.   The window at the east end was removed and a wall with a door in it substituted.   One bay was used for accommodating a stair to the gallery and, when heating was introduced, the apparatus occupied another bay.   The introduction of " heated air " for making the church more comfortable was carried out by the parishioners at their own expense about 1835.   In 1832, four hundred parishioners complained of the difficulty of hearing the minister on account of the length and narrowness of the church and the position of the pulpit, and they complained that the roof of the church was in bad repair.   Arrangements were made to obtain a report on the roof, as also on the gutters and window blinds.   In 1839 some of the old stalls had to be repaired as they were badly affected by dry rot.

In August, 1842, it appears that there was only the one gallery, namely, at the west end of the choir, and at that time the Rev. Mr. MacKenzie suggested further gallery accommodation. The Disruption, however, came and Mr. MacKenzie left the church, taking with him a large part of the congregation.   No immediate steps for repairs seem to have been taken and, in 1860, a fresh representation was made to the heritors that the roof of the choir was in a dangerous condition.   Mr. Thomas Brown, architect in Edinburgh, was instructed to report on the roof.

He found that it was composed of rafters with ties and struts tenoned to the rafters and the rafters tenoned together at the ridge. The old couples consisted of whole oak trees rudely squared up from four to seven inches square. The different portions were fixed together by oak pins. The wood was found completely rotten except in the case of the larger timbers, but many of the rafters had failed where the ties joined and also at the ridge. The wood seems to have been held together by the sarking which was found in good condition. The slates had also been fixed with pins. Mr. Brown recommended the heritors to renew the roof, as also the roof over the Lady Chapel, and to repair the parapet on the south wall of the choir.

Prior to the Restoration in 1872-73, the choir was much as has just been described, that is the pulpit stood at the east end about the spot where the communion table now stands, the minister facing westwards. The pulpit had two stairways, one on its north side and one on its south, while the precentor had a desk and seat immediately below the minister. The precentor was raised four steps above the choir floor and the minister some three or four steps higher. The floor of the pulpit was about level with the sill of the choir windows. Opposite the door from the Chapel, which was further east than the present door, that is where the Bishop's effigy lies, was a 3-foot passage, and on each side of the pulpit east of the passage were six or seven short pews, each to hold four persons, the occupants facing westwards. Behind the pulpit was a square pew with a table in the centre with sittings for about 12 persons, and it was customary to hold the choir practices in this pew as it was more comfortable there than in the Session House.

In front of the pulpit between the two stairs was a small table on which the communion elements were placed on sacrament Sundays and around which the elders sat. On the opposite side of the cross passage was a long table about 18-in. broad which ran across the church and had a long seat on each side. It was round this table that the communicants sat, but on ordinary Sundays these seats were occupied by members of the congregation. From 30 to 34 people could be seated round the table at one time. About 1870 the attendance at the Lord's Supper numbered about 90 which involved dispensing the elements three or four times. As soon as the sacrament was dispensed, those who had received it left the table, to be followed by other members of the congregation who took their places while verses of the 103rd Psalm were sung. Seats on either side of the pulpit were on different levels, that is each seat eastwards was higher than the one in front. Two passages ran down the main part of the choir along the north and south walls respectively. These walls were lined with Gothic panels and had oak seats which folded to the wall.

The congregation entered by the door in the chancel arch, left their contributions in the plate which stood within the door and then turned to the right or left along one of the passages or took the stair to the gallery which rose from the left side of the entrance vestibule. At the time there was no entrance from the nave into the chapter house, and the circular stair to the apartment above the chapter house was unknown.

The chapter house was, at that time, entered by a door at its east end where the Cathedral War Memorial has been erected. A wall was built across the first archway from the east end and through it one entered by a door into the Session House. There was a door on the north wall of the chapter house, but west of the present north door. The Session House occupied the space between the first and second arches and beyond there was a solid wall built across. Such was the state of the choir and chapter house when Duncan McOwan, joiner, afterwards an elder, until he attained a great age, came from Blackford to Dunblane to act as precentor.

The alterations made in 1872 were of a much more satisfactory character than those earlier in the century. These commenced in September, 1872, the congregation meantime worshipping on alternate Sundays with the congregations of the Free and United Presbyterian Churches. The heritors and repairs committee were guided by a well-known architect, Sir Gilbert Scott. The wall in the choir arch was taken down as being unnecessarily thick and rebuilt to show the piers and mouldings, while two stained glass windows were inserted in this wall on either side of the entrance door by Sir William Stirling-Maxwell of Keir. Sir Gilbert Scott had desired to do away with any wall and to fill up the chancel arch with a screen of oak and glass, but this was deemed too expensive and unsubstantial.

The two apertures above the choir arch, which had been built up, were opened and filled with glass. The floors of the choir and chapter house were restored to their original level and the tomb of the Bishop was put back on the north wall from which it had been removed in

1817. A string course, which had run round the whole interior and had been completely broken off, was replaced, and the original doorway from the chapter house to the choir was re-opened. It was proposed at this time that the walls, which were of rubble, should be left without plaster and whitewash, but this was objected to by a majority of the acting committee. The old stalls were placed below the east window. The gallery at the west end was reduced in size. It had previously extended across an additional window in the south wall.

The chapter house was entirely renovated. The door on the east wall was built up and the window restored. Groined arches which had been damaged were replaced and the aumbries and recess in the east end which had been built up were re-opened.

The three slabs of blue marble said to mark the resting places of three daughters of John, first Lord Drummond, lay, up to 1873, immediately within the vestibule inside the chancel arch. These slabs were lifted and, at the request of the Earl of Perth, the representative of the Drummond family, they were placed in the position they now occupy. No objects of interest were found under the floor of the choir save a stone coffin containing two incomplete skeletons very much disarranged, which was found in the middle of the choir, about 20 feet to the east of the arch. One of the skeletons was believed to be that of a woman, and it is suggested that they may have been those of some notable person connected with the Cathedral or district and of his wife. The treasured Celtic Cross was found in the west end of the chapter house about two feet below the original floor and partly under the foundation. It was at this time that the staircase between the lower and upper storeys of the chapter house was rediscovered. An entrance was made from the roofless nave to the chapter house by removing a low stone wall which had been built up three feet from the ground between the foot of the old stairway, and a small chamber entered from the present doorway.

Certain proposals made at this time were not carried out, one being to have an organ gallery over the Lady Chapel and another to have a porch outside the chancel arch doorway.

It was at this time that the choir was seated with pews which, after the restoration, were in use in the nave, but have since been replaced by carved oak seats. Following upon this restoration, a pipe organ was presented to the congregation by Mr. Henderson of Glassingall. It was stated at the time that Dunblane Cathedral was the first of the Scottish cathedrals to be supplied with such an instrument.

Following on this restoration of 1872, a new pulpit was erected immediately to the east of the door from the chapter house. The side passages were replaced by a centre passage from the main door to the cross passage from the chapter house door. The organ was placed in the gallery where the choir as well as some of the congregation sat. In the winter season the main or west door was closed and the congregation entered through the chapter house.

Such was the church in which the Cathedral congregation worshipped until the great restoration in 1890-93.

CHAPTER XXXIII.

LIFE IN DUNBLANE IN THE 18th CENTURY, AS REVEALED IN THE CATHEDRAL

KIRK SESSION MINUTE BOOKS.

THERE are two volumes of Kirk Session Minutes of the 18th century extant, but apparently a volume pertaining to the beginning of the century is missing. The earlier book refers to the period between 1730-1757 and the second volume covers the later part of that century. Neither volume contains much matter of great interest. Some of the information given in this chapter has already been noted, but it is here repeated for the sake of completeness. The doings of the Kirk Session during this period were very similar to those of the 17th century, but it is noticeable that there are recorded few cases of Sabbath breaking, and those cases which are mentioned are trivial and were not treated with the same severity as those in the earlier volumes. In 1744 Janet Meiklejohn was cited before the Session and, after being seriously exhorted, she confessed that she had been guilty of unnecessary travel and idle conversation on the Sabbath, for which she was sharply rebuked and, having expressed her sorrow, the Session agreed that she be dismissed with certification that if any other aggravations of her guilt appeared at a later date, she would be liable to higher censure.

On quite a number of occasions parties appear to have given offence to the Kirk Session by proceeding to Greenloaning and being there married by a Mr. Robert Drummond, an Episcopal minister. This led to the bridegroom, bride and witnesses of the marriage being summoned before the Session and sharply rebuked for this irregular conduct.

The Kirk Session chiefly concerned itself with sexual offences and with the affairs of the poor. The poor at this time were principally supported by the Sessions, and the church collections were used for supplying their wants. At other times the burden of the poor lay more upon the heritors of the parish than upon the church. In 1756 a joint meeting of the heritors and elders of the parish church was held at Dunblane when statements of the poor's funds were laid before the meeting. Lists of all the poor were given in and these persons were divided into two classes, the members of one of which were continued as pensioners who received weekly or monthly subsistence as formerly according to their necessity, the other class being given badges to permit them to beg, but only throughout the parish. Mr. Coldstream, the Session Clerk, was appointed to give out badges on parchment or cards. This is the only occasion on which the heritors are recorded as taking part in providing for the poor, the roll of persons and the payments to be given being in other years in this century fixed by the elders alone. This meeting was the outcome of an order of the Justices of the Peace and the Sheriff Depute (or Principal) of the county.

There was still considerable severity in the methods of dealing with certain culprits brought before the Session. Such had to make frequent appearances for rebuke both before the Session and the congregation, had to sit on a seat of repentance and on occasion had to wear sackcloth.

The Kirk Session had at their disposal considerable funds, but there were at this time little means of having this profitably invested. Apparently the only form of investment open was a loan to one of the neighbouring proprietors who was called on to sign a Bond usually with two further proprietors as cautioners. Payment of interest seems to have been made very irregularly as in some cases it is noted that a debtor paid several years' interest in one sum.

During this period offerings were taken for repair of bridges, but there were fewer such collections than are recorded in the minutes of the 17th century, and the same may be noted with regard to collections for expenses to defray the cost of surgical operations.

In May, 1740, it is recorded that the season was "very straitning" and that there was "great dearth" and that the necessities of the poor were "clamant." Special provision had to be made for their assistance. The great dearth continued throughout the summer, and in August, 1740, the poor were said to be in extreme necessity and want and their numbers increased. This continued throughout that season and in the following year.

It is noticeable that, when it became necessary to add elders to the Session, this was carried through without difficulty by the existing members of Session and without any consultation with the members of the congregation. It is also noted in contrast to the experience in the Secession Church, that the men who were appointed readily accepted office. The elders were selected principally from the farming class. In 1735 the Kirk Session made choice of James MacFarlane and James Lennox both in Dunblane to the office of beadle, the emoluments of the office to go equally betwix them. In the following century a double appointment was also made, but with unfortunate results.

On 14th July, 1743, William Coldstream, schoolmaster, was appointed Session Clerk and this office he held for many years. He was the successor of James McGoun who was parish schoolmaster and who had died shortly before. Mr. Coldstream having intimated his willingness to accept the office, the oath *de fideli administratione* was administered to him and he was seriously exhorted to a faithful discharge of the important trust reposed on him, which he promised " judicially."

On 7th September, 1742, James Cairns and William Kerr, skinners in Dunblane, met the Kirk Session and intimated that the Skinner Trade was resolved to sell the new house belonging to them and had appointed them to wait upon the Session and make the first offer thereof to them, the house to be afterwards let for behoof of the poor. The Session agreed to meet the Masters of the Skinner Trade to inspect their titles and their property and finish the buying of the same. A month later the Masters of the Trade and Thomas Duthie presented the progress of writs, after which the Kirk Session bought this property, namely, a house and yard in the Millrow of Dunblane, for the price of 650 merks Scots. The Session obtained a substantial rent from the property for many years.

There are several references to the second Jacobite rebellion of 1745-46. Thus, it is recorded on 15th September, 1745, that " the smallness of the collections now and afterwards which may be observed, is owing to the uncertainty of public worship in regard that the young Pretender came to this place on Thursday last with an army of Highlanders and others his adherents, marching southwards and parties passing continually to join them, which created great disturbance in the country."

On 27th October, 1745, by the appointment of the Presbytery, intimation was made for observing a fast on the Wednesday following because of the present rebellion in favour of a Popish Pretender.

On 20th February, 1746, the Session took into consideration the present clamant necessity of the numerous poor occasioned by the heavy oppression of the rebellion raging in the country especially in Dunblane where the road was a public one and where parties of the rebels were either quartered or were passing and repassing continually. The Treasurer was accordingly appointed to be active in using endeavours for obtaining speedy payment of all bygone interest towards settling the wants of the poor.

The last reference to this matter is under date, 22nd June, 1746, when the minister read an intimation from the pulpit from the General Assembly for observing a day of public thanksgiving on Thursday, 26th June, " for our remarkably great and gracious deliverance from that wicked and unnatural rebellion by the success it has pleased Almighty God to grant to his Majesty's armies at the Battle of Culloden in the North under the conduct of his Royal Highness, the Duke of Cumberland."

On 11th March, 1747, John Stirling of Keir, who had for many years faithfully executed the office of Treasurer, communicated his desire " to be eased of the trouble." He received the thanks of his brethren for his faithfulness in the discharge of that trust, and a leet of four elders was made from whom a successor might be selected. It would thus appear that the office was regarded as an honourable and desirable one, and it was arranged, on this occasion, that a new appointment be made at least every third year.

About the middle of the 18th century the fabric of the Cathedral required considerable repair. In August, 1757, Alexander White, wright, Dunblane, presented his account, for erecting a new porch at the east church door, amounting to £36 17s. 6d. Scots. He also gave in a further account for mending the Communion tables and forms.   At this meeting the Session considered the insufficiency of the east and west lofts which had recently greatly alarmed the congregation. White was appointed to provide five good trees for pillars to the east loft and three for the west loft for the further support of these lofts.

In the following month the Session had under consideration the bad condition of the steeple roof whereby the timber of the roof, as also the clock and bells, had been damaged by storms of wind and rain.   White was appointed to provide scaffolding and other materials and to employ William Duthie, mason and slater.   Mr. Duthie was summoned to the meeting and reported that he could not possibly give an estimate of the cost of the work till once he began it and made a trial, but he agreed to do the repairs in the most reasonable manner.

In October, 1749, it was reported that the windows on each side of the pulpit were failing and having wire frames on the outside they gave little light, particularly in the winter.   The Session accordingly instructed Alexander White, wright, one of their number, to execute repairs.

In September, 1752, the alteration made in the calendar by Act of Parliament took effect, and the change is referred to in the Session records.   It is noted that the following Sabbath would be dated 17th September under the new style, in place of 6th September.

The Rev. William Simson, who had been parish minister throughout this period, died on Friday, 17th October, 1755.   His burial took place on Tuesday, 21st October, when it is noted that Mrs. Imbry, his sister, and the Laird of Keir gave 100 merks Scots, to be distributed among the poor, of which £12 Scots were distributed among the vagrant poor at the burial and the remainder at a later date among the poor of the parish.

His poor parishioners were not forgotten by Mr. Simson in his will.   He bequeathed 400 merks Scots to the poor of the parish, which was assigned by Mrs. Imbry.   The Assignation was handed over by Mr. Russell, Commissary Clerk, recorded in the Sheriff Court Books and an extract lodged with the other securities belonging to the poor.

In the Session Book covering the period from 1757 to 1800 there is not much information of general interest.   On 10th February, 1763, the Session resolved to accept the proposal of Thomas Duthie, writer in Dunblane, for purchasing two pieces of land in the territory of Dunblane, extending to rather more than 6 roods, for the price of £420 Scots money.   The rental of the land was at that time £21.   One of the portions of land was St. Michael's Croft, no boundaries of which are given, the second being known as John Moir's Croft.   At this time the heritors purchased from the Kirk Session a house in the Millrow for 650 merks Scots with the view of providing a house for Mr. William Coldstream, the parish schoolmaster.   It had been intended in 1745 to make the purchase, but owing to the disturbed state of the country the matter was delayed.   The heritors also bought, at this time, a ruinous house and yard in the Millrow as garden ground for Mr. Coldstream.   The transaction was completed on 18th May, 1765.

Although no reference is made in the minute book with regard to the disastrous appointment of the Rev. John Robertson to be parish minister of Dunblane, the result of his forcible intrusion is seen in the minutes.   From 1757 to 1781 no sederunt of persons present at any Session meeting is recorded.   On 4th January, 1781, the sederunt consisted of Mr. Robertson, Rev. Mr. Stirling, Minister of Port, and Mr. Coldstream, elder.   The sederunt is always recorded after the appointment in 1791 of the Rev. Robert Stirling to be assistant and successor, but for some little time there were no elders in the congregation save Mr. Coldstream, and Session meetings could not be held as a rule, without two neighbouring ministers being associated with Mr Robertson to make a quorum.   No meeting of Session was held for 9 months after Mr. Stirling's appointment.   The minutes, even at that time, were, as a rule, of the briefest, and it is observed that such were, for the first time, concluded with the words " Closed with Prayer," but were not signed.

Mr. Stirling was ultimately able in 1794 to obtain the appointment of three elders.

It may be noted that for some time prior to Mr. Stirling's appointment, the Lord's Supper was only celebrated in Dunblane Cathedral once in two years.

In 1794, Mr. Malcolm Coldstream, who had succeeded his father as schoolmaster of Dunblane, was elected Session Clerk.   No elder seems to have been suitable for appointment as Treasurer and administrator of the funds of the poor, and the minister accepted the office.

In this year the Session drew up a scale of regulations for proclamation of banns.   They fixed 4/6 sterling as the sum payable where parties were proclaimed on three separate Sabbaths divisible as follows—1/8 to the poor, 2/4 to the Clerk and 6d. to the Officer. Where the proclamation was finished on two Sundays the parties paid 10/6, of which 4/6 was allocated to the poor, 5/6 to the Clerk and 6d. to the Officer. When the banns were only read on one Sabbath a fee of one guinea was payable, 9/6 of which went to the poor, 11/- to the Clerk and 6d to the Officer —this scale also applying to irregular marriages. It will thus be noticed that the Clerk was more highly paid when the work was lightest and, while his remuneration rose very considerably, there was no similar advantage to the Officer.

While there are recorded many cases of discipline, the sentences imposed during this period were less severe than in earlier days. A custom commenced of paying pecuniary penalties to avoid censure in presence of the congregation. The first case in which this is noted is in 1773 where a culprit, after rebuke by the Session, offered to pay one guinea above the usual penalty if public appearance was dispensed with and this was accepted. It is somewhat difficult to justify the action of the Kirk Session in considering it proper to substitute for rebuking a man in public, the acceptance of a money penalty from the wealthier parishioners which a poor person was unable to pay. The penalties were, however, expended for the benefit of the poor, and, in accepting such, the Session seems to have considered that they were acting for the benefit of the latter. In 1775 a local proprietor gave a bill of 5 gns. which was accepted in full of penalties, and, shortly after, one reads of the same proprietor paying a penalty for a woman in trouble.

The winter of 1794-5 seems to have been an unusually severe one. Frost continued from the middle of December to the middle of March. Sums amounting to about £20 were collected from the heritors with which 130 carts of coal were purchased for distribution among the poorer people.

Fasts were appointed from time to time by the Church Courts and sometimes by the King. In March, 1797, a fast was fixed by Royal proclamation and it was ordained that the collection be given to the widows and families of soldiers and sailors belonging to the parish who had suffered in defence of their King and country in the war.

In 1797, the Kirk Session, who had retained the three elders appointed in 1794, elected four other elders. This points to the new minister having been successful in obtaining the assistance of parishioners suitable for eldership and, although no figures are given, one may safely infer that the congregation was increasing in numbers and in zeal.

In December, 1797, a public thanksgiving was held by Royal order in respect of the many signal and important victories obtained by the Navy in the course of the war.

On 17th July, 1799, the names of young communicants are recorded for the first time in the Kirk Session minutes, the Session appointing that such be served with tokens. In 1802, Duncan MacKenzie was elected Beadle, Sexton and Kirk Officer in succession to William Lennox, who had held this office for the previous 7 years.

MacKenzie did not survive many years and, following upon his death, Duncan McLeish was appointed Beadle, Kirk Officer and Sexton and admitted to the emoluments and perquisites pertaining to these offices on 26th October, 1807.

On Thursday, 5th December, 1805, a public thanksgiving was held by Royal Proclamation in respect of the recent " signal and important victories attained by the British Fleet." A collection was taken for the widows and orphans of those who fell or were wounded, which realised £10 sterling, which was sent to the Secretary of the Patriotic Fund at Lloyds, London.

Early in 1807 the Session agreed that the sacrament of the Lord's Supper be dispensed on the first Sabbath of March. Hitherto this had been celebrated only once a year and that usually on a Sunday in July. No intimation is made of this service in the few years following, but, in 1811, a dispensation of the sacrament was fixed for the 4th Sabbath of March.

In March, 1807, James Russell of Woodside, grandson of Bailie Russell, who entertained the Duke of Cumberland in 1746, sent to the minister 5 guineas to be divided among the poor. It is narrated that this money was given on account of his father's death which occurred at this time. About 1809 the Session received gifts from the Lairds of Kippendavie, Keir, Cromlix, and others, including John Rob, Sheriff Clerk, of sums of money to be expended among the poor of the parish.

While persons guilty of offences against morality were still frequently rebuked by the Kirk

o

Session, and, as a rule, paid money penalties, rebuke in face of the congregation had, by this time, ceased to be resorted to.

On Friday, 12th May, 1809 " the Great Bell which had been rent by the carelessness of John Dougall in May, 1795, was replaced in the tower of this Cathedral." It had been sent to London and recast there by Thomas Mears & Son, bellfounders, Whitechapel, out of the funds of the Kirk Session at a cost of £35 18s. 2d.

On 22nd October, 1809, it was publicly intimated from the pulpit that His Majesty would on 25th October, 1809, enter on the 50th year of his reign. It was agreed to celebrate this jubilee by national demonstrations of joy and thanksgiving all over the kingdom and to hold public worship at 2 p.m. on that day when thanksgiving would be offered up for the " many and inestimable blessings vouchsafed to this kingdom during the long and arduous reign of His Majesty King George III."

On 22nd January, 1810, Malcolm Coldstream, who had acted for a lengthy period as Session Clerk and precentor, resigned. The Session appointed Donald Stewart, schoolmaster of the parish, as his successor. A list of the books handed over to Mr. Stewart is embodied in the minute.

Little of note occurs during the next few years.

In October, 1817, the Rev. Robert Stirling died and his interment took place on the 24th day of that month. The Session met on the same afternoon and in their minute he is referred to as " their much respected and sincerely regretted Minister." Mr. Stirling had acted as Treasurer for the Kirk Session, and, in his place, Mr. William Stirling, writer in Dunblane, was appointed. There is no reference in the minutes to his successor's election.

In February, 1818, a meeting of elders was held when an agreement was made for the use of the kirk of the Auld Licht congregation once a fortnight for the sum of 7s. 6d. per day. The Auld Lichts owned the property of Allanside in Millrow and the Cathedral congregation worshipped there for a time while repairs to the Cathedral were being proceeded with. Dr. Grierson's presence at a Kirk Session meeting is first noted on 30th August, 1818.

The Barons of the Exchequer on 3rd December, 1818, allowed the Minister to occupy " a small piece of ground called the Bishop's Yard adjoining to the Manse," conditional on his enclosing the ground in a sufficient manner and keeping the fence in good order during his occupancy, he not to be permitted to plough the land. The following is a copy of the Rev. Robert Stirling's application :—

" Unto the Right Honourable The Lord Chief Baron and other Barons of His Majesty's Court of Exchequer in Scotland.

" The Memorial and Petition of the Revd. Robert Stirling, Minister of the Gospel at Dunblane Humbly Sheweth,

" That your Petitioner in June last presented a Petition to your Lordships representing that in Consequence of a Presentation from His Majesty your Petitioner was ordained on 2nd June, 1791, Assistant and Successor to the Revd. Mr. John Robertson, Minister of the Parish of Dunblane, who departed this life on the 23rd of June last, and praying to be allowed to possess and enjoy a small spot of ground called the Bishops Yard during his Incumbency as Minister of said Parish.

" That it appears from various Petitions and Orders recorded in your Lordships Books, and particularly from the Representation and Petition of the Revd. Mr. William Simson, Minister of said Parish, on 17th July, 1730, That the Ministers of the said Church since the Revolution were before the Union allowed by the Lords of the Treasury, and since that time by the Barons of His Majesty's Exchequer in Scotland to possess and enjoy the small spot of ground called the Bishops Yard lying in the immediate vicinity of the Ministers Manse between his garden and the water of Allan, and by the Report of the Deputy Collector of the Rents of the Bishopric of Dunblane in a Representation by Commissary Finlayson to this Court, 15th July, 1720, it appears ' that the value of the said Grass yard is very small,' and praying to be admitted to the possession of the said Bishops Yard in the same manner as his Predecessors by the favour of this Court were allowed to have, the Barons were pleased to order, that the said Mr. William Simson ' do and shall during his Incumbency in the said Church peaceably and quietly possess and enjoy the said spot of ground called the Bishops Yard.' And by the Representation and Petition of the Revd. Mr. John Robertson, Minister of said Parish, 2nd

July, 1757, setting forth as above the Barons were pleased to order that Mr. Robertson ' enjoy and keep possession of the said Ground ' which he did till the time of his death.

" That this small spot of ground called the Bishops Yard has been kept sometimes under Tillage but more frequently in grass for the conveniency of the Minister, that part of it has been occupied as a kitchen garden for many years, the Minister having a very small allowance of garden ground. That from the circumstances of its being in grass some of the inhabitants in the neighbourhood of the Manse have been indulged by the Minister in having the use of it for bleaching their linen in the Summer months. That it is so situated that the Minister alone can at all times have access to it, the other entries to it, except by the Manse, being thro' the property of Individuals, who at any time they please, may shut up their entries to every inhabitant. That those who have been indulged in the use of the yard, have likewise been indulged in the liberty of using the entry by the Manse. That if it were made a Common to the Town's People the Minister's garden, etc., would be laid open to the Depredation of the malicious and ill-disposed, of whom the number in such Places as Dunblane is not small. That this would be a great Grievance too hard to be imposed upon any Clergyman. That the Petition presented to your Lordships in name of the whole Inhabitants is in Fact and Truth from one, two, or at most three individuals, without the knowledge or Concurrence of any other Person, so that its being in Name of the whole Inhabitants is a gross imposition upon the Court entirely calculated to mislead your Lordships.

" That the Right Honourable The Earl of Kinnoull as Superior of the Town of Dunblane receives annually from the inhabitants Feu Duties which amount to a considerable sum, besides Customs, which are this year let for above £90 Sterl., in return for which the Town receives no benefit whatever. That his Lordship's Property is most conveniently situated along both sides of the River, and it is humbly submitted that an Application from the Inhabitants would with a better Grace be preserved to his Lordship for accommodating his Vassals with washing greens which he can easily and effectually do rather than applying to your Lordships for a small piece of Ground enjoyed and possessed thro' the favour of your Lordships by the Ministers of Dunblane since the Establishment of Presbytery.

" May it therefore please your Lordships to consider the Premises and to grant and allow your Petitioner the use of the said Bishops Yard in the same manner as his Predecessors by the favour of this Court were allowed to have, during his incumbency in the said Parish, and Your Petitioner as in Duty bound shall ever pray, etc."

A volume of Kirk Session records closes in the year 1820, by which time the life of the community as revealed therein bore an aspect of modern days.

CHAPTER XXXIV.

JESSIE, THE FLOWER OF DUNBLANE.

IT is strange, but true, that the name of Dunblane is better known throughout the world by this song rather than by its cathedral, its bishops or any of its sons who have attained to fame. To thousands of people, Dunblane is only known as the home of Jessie, and, yet, who Jessie was is unknown.

The song was written by the Paisley poet Tannahill and wedded to music by his great friend, R. A. Smith, in 1808, since which date, few, if any, Scottish songs have enjoyed greater popularity, due to the beauty of the words and the appropriateness and the melody of the music.

It has never been determined who was the true heroine of the song. A popular belief, at least in modern times, is that she was a Jessie Duncan who resided in Braeport, Dunblane, and who was buried in the Cathedral churchyard near the north-west corner of the Cathedral. Mr. W. B. Bruce, in his *Guide to Dunblane*, refers to a local tradition that a house painter, hailing from Paisley, employed at Kippenross House while it was being built, met Jessie Duncan at social gatherings and fell in love with her. He sought the assistance of the poet Tannahill, with whom he was on intimate terms, to write a song in honour of Jessie, and it was in response to this that the song of Jessie, the Flower of Dunblane, was composed.

The following extract from the well-known book by Mr. P. R. Drummond, F.S.A., entitled *Perthshire in Bygone Days*, quoted by Mr. Bruce, is repeated here.

" William Paterson, long guard on the coach between Glasgow and Perth, repeatedly pointed out to the writer in 1821-22 a lady, apparently about forty years of age, who lived in a house then standing at right angles to Kinross's Hotel, as the heroine of the song. She was a tall, handsome, pale-faced lady-like woman, and wore a black velvet cap or hood, peaked down in the front after the fashion of Queen Mary's day, and was so frequently seen sewing at her window that passers-by concluded that she was a dressmaker, but Paterson was provokingly reticent on that point." Bruce concludes, and the author with disappointment agrees with him, that the most diligent inquiry in quest of a reliable source as to the identity of the fair Jessie is fruitless, and who the famous Dunblane beauty was, must remain a mystery.

Kinross's Hotel is now known as the Stirling Arms Hotel and was then a two-storey building of smaller dimensions than the existing hotel. Little credence can be placed on the coach guard's story. If it had been founded on fact, the tradition would surely have been carried forward to the present day. The tale seems to have been one told for the consumption of his passengers. It is, however, to be noted that this story dates from only about a dozen years after the song was composed.

The following is an extract from *The Liverpool Albion*, dated 16th March, 1829, being part of an article, entitled " Rambles and Sketches," by W. & B. & S., No. VII., " The Romance of Jessie, The Flower of Dunblane," which sketch was re-printed in *The Airdrie Literary Album* for 1829 :—

" The fair subject of this song was a bonnie lassie in Dunblane. Her family were of poor extraction, and Jessie herself was contented with a peasant's lot. When Tannahill became acquainted with her, she was in ' her teens,' a slight, dimple-cheeked, happy lassie ; her hair yellow-coloured and luxuriant ; her eyes large and full, overflowing with the voluptuous languour which is so becoming in young blue eyes with golden lashes. The tinge which lit up her oval cheeks was delicate and evanescent ; and her pulpy lips bubbled with bliss as she gave utterance to her heart.

" Tannahill was struck with her beauty, and, as in all things he was enthusiastical, became forthwith her ardent worshipper. But her heart was not to be won. Young, thoughtless, and panting to know and see the world, she left her poor amourante to con songs to his mistress' eyebrows, while she recklessly rambled among the flowery meads of Dumblane, or of an evening sang his inspired verses to him with the most mortifying nonchalance. This was a twofold misery to the sensitive poet. A creature so sweetly elegant, so dear to him, so very lovely and innocent, and yet, withal, so encased in insensibility as apparently neither to be conscious of the beauty of the verses trembling on her dulcet tongue, nor caring for the caresses of her lover. 'Twas too much—to mark all this, and feel it with the feelings of a poet, was the acme of misery.

" But the ' Flower of Dumblane ' was not that unfeeling, unimaginative being which Tannahill pictured her.   She was a creature all feeling, all imagination although the bard had not that in his person or manners to engage her attention or to arrest her fancy.   The young affections are not to be controlled.   Love, all-mighty love, must be free, else it ceases to be love. Tannahill was plain in his person and uncouth in his manners, and felt and expressed discontentment at the cruel disappointments which it had been his unhappy fate almost invariably to encounter.   Jessie, on the contrary, looked upon the world as a brilliant spectacle yet to be seen and enjoyed—as a vast paradise full of the beauty of heaven and of earth, where men walked forth in the image of their Creator, invested with His attributes, and where woman trode proudly amidst the lovely creation, an angel venerated and adored.   To express dissatisfaction under all these circumstances was to her mind the extravagance of a misanthrope, the madness of a real lover of misery, and a sufficient cause for her not to respect him.   Both viewed the world through a false medium, and their deductions, although at variance, gave colour to their minds and accelerated their fate.

" Jessie could not comprehend what appeared to her the folly of her suitor.   She relished not his sickly sentiment ; and, as all womankind ever did and do, she scorned a cooing lover. The bard was driven to despair, and summoning up an unwonted energy of mind, departed, and left his adored to her youthful aberrations.

" Soon after this period, the song of ' Jessie, the Flower of Dumblane,' together with the music, was published ; it became a public favourite ; it was sung everywhere, in theatres and parties ; a world of praise was showered upon it from woman's flattering lips, and men became mad to know the adored subject of the lay.   In a short period it was discovered. Jessie Monteith, the pretty peasant of Dumblane, was the favoured one.   From all quarters young men and bachelors flocked to see her, and her own sex were curious and critical.   Many promising youths paid their addresses to her, and experienced the same reception as her first lover.   Nevertheless, at last poor Jessie became really enamoured.   A rakish spark, from Mid-Lothians, adorned with education, being of polished manners, and confident from wealth and superiority of rank, gained her young affections.   She too credulously trusted in his unhallowed professions.   The ardour of first love overcame her better judgment, and, abandoning herself to her love passion, she made an imprudent escape from the protection of her parents, and soon found herself in elegant apartments, near the city of Edinburgh.

" The song of neglected Tannahill was to his Jessie both a glory and a curse ; while it brought her into notice and enhanced her beauty, it laid the foundation for her final destruction. Popularity is a dangerous elevation, whether the object of it be a peasant or a prince ; temptations crowd around it, and snares are laid on every hand.   Who would be eminent, says a distinguished child of popularity, if they knew the peril, the madness and distraction of mind to which the creature of the popular breath is exposed.

" When the poet heard of the fate of his beloved Jessie, his heart almost burst with mental agony, and working himself into the enthusiastic frenzy of inspiration, poured forth a torrent of song more glowing and energetic than ever before dropped in burning accents from his tongue.   It is to be lamented that, in a fit of disgust, he afterwards destroyed those poetic records of his passion and resentment.

" Ere three years had revolved their triple circuit after Jessie left her father's home, she was a changed woman.   Her paramour had forsaken her.   She was destitute in her splendid habitation.   Her blue eyes looked pitiful on all things around her ; the oval cheeks were indented by the hand of misery, and the face and person presented the picture of an unhappy but amiable being.   How changed was the figure clothed in silk, which moved on the banks of the Forth, from the happy, lively girl in Dumblane, dressed in the rustic garb of a peasant. But this is a subject too painful to dwell on ; let us hasten to the catastrophe.

" It was on an afternoon in July, a beautiful sunny afternoon, the air was calm and pure. The twin islands of the Forth, like vast emeralds set in a lake of silver, rose splendidly o'er the shining water, which now and then gurgled and mantled round their bases.   Fifeshire was spread forth like a map, her hundreds of inland villages and cots tranquilly sleeping in the sunshine. The din of the artisans' hammers in Kirkcaldy and Queensferry smote the still air ; and Dunfermline's aproned inhabitants scattered forth their whitened webs beneath the noontide sun. On the opposite shore, Leith disgorged her black smoke, which rolled slowly in volume to the sea.   Edinburgh Castle, like a mighty spirit from the ' vasty deep,' reared her gray bulwarks high in the air ; and Arthur's Seat rose hugely and darkly in the background.   The choruses of the fishermen, like hymns to the great spirit of the waters, ascended over Newhaven ; and down from Grangemouth, lightly booming o'er the tide, floated the tall bark.   The world seemed steeped in happiness.   But there was one, a wandering one, an outcast, wretched and despairing, amidst all this loveliness ; her bosom was cold and dark, no ray could penetrate its depths ; the sun shone not from her, nor did nature smile around, but to inflict a more exquisite pang on the unfortunate.   Her steps were broken and hurried.   She now approached the water's edge, and then receded.   No human creature was near to disturb her purpose— all was quietness and privacy ; but there was an Eye from above who watched all.   Jessie Monteith—how mournfully sounds that name at this crisis !   But Jessie sat herself down, and removing a shawl and bonnet from her person, and taking a string of pearl from her marble-seeming neck, and a gold ring, which she kissed eagerly, from her taper finger, she cast up her streaming eyes, meekly imploring the forgiveness of Heaven on him, the cause of her shame and death.   Scarce offering a prayer for herself, she breathed forth the names of her disconsolate parents, and ere the eye could follow her, she disappeared in the pure stream."

" The sun shone on ; the green of the earth stirred not a leaf ; a bell did not toll ; nor did a sigh escape from the lips of one human being, and yet the spirit of the loveliest of women passed (may we not hope ?) to heaven "...S.

It is not known who was the author of this sketch.   One must, however, keep in view that the Editor of the *Liverpool Albion* appended a note to Number IV. of this Series to the effect that the sketches were original work and " have hitherto been founded on fact."   It seems, however, that in this case, the author has written a romantic tale round the song and an imaginary heroine, for which there is no real foundation.   It may be admitted, however, that the name Monteith has been associated with Dunblane for a long period.

The endeavour to trace the original heroine has interested many local antiquarians, but they all eventually came to the conclusion that, assuming she ever existed, it is impossible now to establish her identity.

If anyone should have known who the heroine of the song was, one would imagine that it would be R. A. Smith, Tannahill's friend, and the composer of the music.   Smith wrote " I do sincerely believe the poet had no particular fair one in his eye at the time, and that Jessie was quite an imaginary person."   This was also the belief of relatives and friends of the poet founded on his own assurances.   It is said that Tannahill was never in Dunblane and knew no person belonging to it, and that the words were written to take the place of a well-known doggerell song entitled "Bob of Dunblane."

While the sun certainly seems to descend over the lofty Ben Lomond at certain seasons as seen from Dunblane, such is also visible from viewpoints in the neighbourhood of Paisley.

Smith wrote that the third stanza was not written until several months after the first two were completed, and in his opinion the poet would have been well advised not to have added this stanza, as falling in merit much below the previous verses.   Smith states that this third stanza was published much against his wishes and he believed that every singer of taste would discard it.

CHAPTER XXXV.

DUNBLANE, 1800-1842.

" DUNBLANE lay in the sunshine young in age,
Its mouldering ruins speak of former years.
They teach us man's affairs, like foliage,
Have Springtime and decay.   The spot appears
Where druids taught.   They taught, the people's fears
Subside.   Druidism passed away.
Culdees succeeded them.   The pile still rears
Its massive front where they retired to pray.
Rome sent, the Culdees bowed and owned the papal sway
.... Episcopacy came in state
And lived to worship in the ancient halls.
She too gave way to Presbytery and fate.
Dunblane ! unknown in the decay that falls
On thy Cathedral and its Palace walls
A City once, a city village now
I love thee, home adopted ; nature calls
From thine own River and from mountain brow.
She claims my love, she has it and my fervent vow.

I love thee all unchanging as thou art
In mountain, river, springs and ruins grey.
All beautiful ! thy voice within my heart
Finds a response as it has done alway,
In every heart that loves with thee to stay."

These are the words of the Reverend Alexander Henderson, Anti-Burgher minister in Dunblane for about 20 years in the first half of last century.   A stranger to the ancient city, he had learned to love it, and probably his poetic fancy had to some extent coloured the picture of it in his heart.

Contrast that description with the account of a traveller, who passing through Dunblane in 1843 described it as "the little town of Dunblane, miserable, irregular and dirty—the houses thrown together as if by accident or earthquake and dunghills profusely scattered on either side."

Another author writing in 1839 quoted by Mr. W. B. Bruce in his *Guide to Dunblane* is filled with the same love as the poet above quoted, but his vision is less tinged with poetical fancy. His description of Dunblane is as follows :—

" The Allan rendered classical by that sweet Scottish song ' on the Banks of Allan Water ' is still the same, but Dunblane, the place that gave it all its celebrity and round part of which it sweeps, has felt the pressure of the iron hand of time.   From being a city it has sunk into almost irretrievable decay.   It is now a straggling village with its mouldering Cathedral and escutcheoned houses—once the residences of the dignified and inferior Clergy—the favourite abodes of the Scottish nobility—the fashionable resort of the frequenters of the gay society, and the chosen retreat of the lovers of the learning and politeness of the age.   To many, Dunblane may be a place where one may wish to be born and educated ; but to recluses of taste it attracts, refreshes and delights when the modern Athens and Babylon, with their crowded marts and interminable streets, would be subjects of perpetual annoyance.   Dunblane is one of those delightful loopholes of retreat which the poet Cowper describes as being well adapted to the tastes and habits of those who wish to view from a safe distance the busy crowds congregated in larger cities.   The halo of antiquity rests on it."

It is interesting to note that this writer refers to Dunblane as having sunk into " almost irretrievable decay," and perhaps at this time it was suffering from a wave of poverty and wretchedness which it had not experienced for centuries, but within a very few years it had shaken off its lethargy and was beginning once more a prosperous country town.

Interesting and reliable information regarding Dunblane is given in the *Statistical Account of Scotland* compiled by Sir John Sinclair, Bart., and published in 1793. The article on the Parish of Dunblane was written by the Rev. John Robertson, the parish minister, and the Rev. Robert Stirling, his assistant and successor. They write that the Parish is about nine miles long and six miles broad, but it then included a considerable portion of what is now the parish of Ardoch. A portion consisted of arable land, but the greater part was covered with heath or was swamp. A considerable number of sheep and some black cattle grazed the hills, but the number was small in proportion to the area. Grouse were very abundant, as also hares and partridges on the low ground. While the climate is described as healthy, rheumatism was a frequent disorder and many died of consumption, but in 1839, this is contradicted by Dr. Peter Gordon Stewart in his essay on the " Dunblane Mineral Springs," where he states that consumption was rarely known. The mortality by smallpox was frequently very great and the poorer classes were averse to inoculation. There was no compulsory registration of births and deaths, although a register was kept by the Session Clerk. Births were believed to exceed 70 per annum and the average number of marriages at the end of the 18th century amounted to 23 apart from a few irregular marriages. Burials in Dunblane averaged 30 per annum, but interments also took place at Kilbryde and Ardoch Chapels of which there was no record. The farms were, in general, of small size and about two-thirds of the land was kept in pasture. Rents varied from 5s to 15s. per acre save for land in the immediate neighbourhood of Dunblane, the rent of which ran from 25s. to 42s. per acre. At this time there was a resident Sheriff-Substitute (the salary, even at 1840, was only £250), a Commissary, a Procurator-Fiscal and four writers or attorneys and one surgeon. The demand for legal assistance was therefore apparently more clamant than that for medical aid. There were at this time in Dunblane three clergymen, namely, the pastors of the Established Church and of the Burghers and Anti-Burghers. The parish minister's stipend was originally the living of the Dean and consisted partly of meal and Scottish barley and partly of money, with a manse and a glebe of about four acres, while feu duties were payable from Deans-Keir, near Braco, Deans-Lundie, now known as West-Lundie and Deanstoun, near Doune, and other lands.

While there was much poverty in the parish, the number of poor persons receiving assistance varied from about 34 to over 40, and these were maintained by assessments which were first imposed in 1775 when the number of poor on the roll was only 19. Money was also received for the poor, over and above the assessment, from bequests and occasional gifts from the Kirk Session out of church door collections, dues of mortcloths, etc. In 1798 the heritors were of opinion that a weekly allowance of 9d a head was sufficient for maintaining a poor person. While this may seem an impossible sum upon which to subsist in the twentieth century it may be mentioned that Daniel Cameron, a slater in Dunblane, commonly spoken of as " The Squirrel," (probably from his activity on the roofs) towards the end of last century informed the writer that a shilling a week was sufficient to maintain his wife and himself.

It was still the custom at this time to license beggars who were permitted to perambulate the parish to which they belonged. The heritors in 1802 allowed all poor persons who possessed badges to beg through the parish as formerly, but the infirm, who were unable to beg, numbering about 20, were given pensions. The heritors at this time were not wanting in foresight or kindliness, for in November, 1800, when apparently they anticipated either a shortage of food or high prices in the winter then commencing they resolved to purchase 100 bolls of bear (or Scottish barley) and 50 bolls of oatmeal for the benefit of the poor of the parish, borrowing the price from the Bank of Scotland, Stirling.

The principal crops in the district at the beginning of last century were oats and barley, but flax and potatoes were also cultivated to a considerable extent and some clover and rye grass were also sown, and the crops raised more than supplied the wants of the district with the exception of wheat of which only a small quantity was grown. Turnips were not then a staple crop. Flax was an important crop in Scotland at the beginning of the 19th century, but it ceased to be cultivated and this was only resumed to a minor extent about the time of the Great War.

"DUMBLAIN ABBEY"
Print of Plate in J. W. M. Turner's "Liber Studiorum" (1816).

By courtesy of the Society of Friends of Dunblane Cathedral.

KILBRYDE CASTLE TO-DAY

OLD KILBRYDE CASTLE

While peats were still used by many of the farmers, most of the inhabitants of the parish were accustomed to burn coal, which was brought from pits in the neighbourhoods of Alloa and Bannockburn. In 1843 coal was purchased at the pit for 1s. 3d. a load. As railway construction had not commenced, there was a large traffic by road, and even after the railways reached Dunblane, much coal was brought by cart, as also lime shells (for dressing the fields) which were conveyed to Stirling by river. The farmers applied lime freely to their fields, as also shell marl of which there were good pits within the parish. There was also much passenger traffic by horse-drawn machine or by horseback, and on the day of a court or a fair, Dunblane was crowded with people from the neighbouring districts, many of whom had come considerable distances for business at court or market or to hear and see the proceedings. The public, however, were not afraid to use shoe-leather and the weaver was accustomed to shoulder his web in the morning before daylight and carry it either to the Hillfoots or to Glasgow, returning home on foot in the late evening or next morning with the proceeds of his labour or as much as remained.

The first census of the population of Scotland was made by the Rev. Alexander Webster, D.D., minister of the Tolbooth Church, Edinburgh, and Moderator of the General Assembly, in 1753, the date of which census is 1755. It is said that no census of any country in the world had been taken since the days of the Roman Empire until the 18th century. Such was first made by Sweden in 1749, followed by Austria in 1754. According to Dr. Webster, the population of the parish of Dunblane was 2728 persons, all of whom were Protestants, and he estimated that there were 545 fighting men in the parish. The population in 1793 was 2750, and this, of course, included that portion which is now in Ardoch parish. In 1801 a regular census was taken throughout the country and the returns for this parish were as follows:—inhabited houses, 493; families in the parish, 587; uninhabited houses, 21; males, 1231; females, 1388; persons employed in agriculture, 462; persons employed in trades and handicrafts, 175; other persons, 1982; total population, 2619.

In 1811 the population was returned at 2733, in 1821 at 3135, and in 1831 at 3228, which shows that, while the population at the latter half of the 18th century was stationary, there was a considerable increase at the beginning of the following century.

In 1811 there were only 163 persons engaged in agriculture, showing a large decrease during the 10 previous years, while persons engaged in handicrafts and trades had risen during this period to 293.

In October, 1831, an account of the parish was written by Mr. John Monteath, a schoolmaster in Dunblane, which was published by James Lockhart, bookseller, Dunblane. According to the census of June, 1831, there were 504 inhabited houses in the parish and 3 uninhabited, and there were 699 families. Ninety-seven persons were employed in agriculture and 205 in trades or manufactures. The population numbered 3228 which represented an increase of 93 on the figure of the 1821 census. Thirty-one persons were then receiving poor relief, the allowance given being 1s. per week. Of the three congregations in the town, that of the first United Associate congregation (known as the Burghers) seems to have been the most flourishing. The office-bearers consisted of 11 elders and 11 deacons as contrasted with 6 elders and 7 deacons in the Second United Associate congregation or the Anti-Burgher. In the former there were 570 communicants, and in the latter, 105. The number of communicants in the Parish Church is not given, but the officials were limited to 5 elders. At this time there were two Sunday schools, one conducted in the parish school room with 50 scholars and the other in the Burgher Meeting-house attended by 95. Some signs of growing life in the town were manifest at this time. Apart from the Leightonian Library, a library was founded in 1827 by the Rev. Mr. Anderson, Burgher minister, and there was a reading room open from 8 a.m. to 10 p.m., with London and provincial papers supplied, and the Dunblane Reading Society provided books, principally for the Sabbath School children.

Among the societies which then flourished in the parish were the Free Masons, the Curling Club, a Farmers Club, a Gardeners Friendly Society, a Funeral Society, a Militia Society, which existed for the purpose of procuring substitutes for those members who were balloted to serve in the Militia, a Temperance Society, with 203 members, and a Philosophical Society. Mr. Monteath mentions that, prior to 1831, there were in Dunblane incorporations of hammermen, weavers, shoemakers, tailors, fleshers, and glovers, all of whom enjoyed chartered privileges within the regality of Dunblane under their feudal superiors, the Barons of Cromlix. Several of the charters were still in existence in 1831, that granted to the Hammermen being dated 1649. These Guilds continued to exercise their privileges long after their charters became a dead letter, and even at the beginning of the 19th century contributions were asked to " Crisben's Box " on fair days at the shoe stalls erected on the streets of Dunblane.

In 1831, the Sheriff-Principal was Duncan MacNeil, the resident Sheriff-Substitute Hugh Barclay, the Sheriff Clerk Depute Mr. MacAra, and the Procurator-Fiscal, Mr. Thomas Barty, whose remuneration was by piece work, that is he received a fee for each case conducted by him. There were five other solicitors in Dunblane and four sheriff officers in addition to one resident at Doune and another at Kincardine. Mr. Monteath gives a list of special constables, one or more of whom were elected to the several streets of the town. There was one postman or letter carrier, and letters arrived from Edinburgh and the North at 5 a.m. and from Glasgow and the West at 6 p.m. The postmaster at this time was William Dawson who followed Malcolm Coldstream, retired schoolmaster. Another postmaster about this time was Mr. Bain, solicitor.

The mail coach to Glasgow passed through Dunblane at 5 a.m., and the coach from Glasgow at 6 p.m. took letters to Perth and the North. Dr. Stewart in his essay on " Dunblane Mineral Springs" mentions that "during the watering season Noddies started each lawful day from Sharp's and Clark's Taverns to suit the arrival of the steam-boat at Stirling. Chaises, cars, gigs, etc. are kept for hire at the Inn and at Sharp's." The hotel, known in modern times as the Stirling Arms, was then referred to as the Head Inn, while Clark's Inn was known as the Steam-Boat Inn. Sharp's Tavern was called the Masons Hall.

Visitors to Dunblane were at this time very numerous, the special attraction being the taking of the mineral waters. Dr. Stewart mentions that there was abundance of accommodation in and around Dunblane for strangers of all ranks from the prince to the peasant, but from one's knowledge of the housing in Dunblane at that time such accommodation must have been of a simple or even primitive kind. Visitors chiefly lodged about Ramoyle, owing to its proximity to the Well House on the Laighhills. Travellers to Dunblane from the east came by boat to Stirling and from elsewhere by coach. A noddie was the name originally given to a one-horse vehicle on two wheels which opened from the rear, but latterly the name was applied to a one-horse vehicle of any kind on four wheels.

It may be of interest to compare the particulars of Dunblane given in the *New Statistical Account* of 1843 which was written by the Rev. William MacKenzie, the minister of the Disruption, with those in Sinclair's account of 1793. The population of the parish had grown during these 50 years to 3367 of whom 631 were resident in the portion assigned to Ardoch. The town of Dunblane had about 1800 inhabitants, many of whom, the writer says, were extremely poor and some in the lowest degradation and wretchedness. He refers to the violent settlement of a parish minister in the previous century which scattered the Established congregation which had never been gathered together again. Strange to say, his own appointment to the parish of Dunblane led to a number of the wealthier and more influential members leaving the Established Church and founding a Scottish Episcopal congregation, while, shortly after, Mr. MacKenzie, accompanied by his Kirk Session, seceded from the Established Church to form a congregation of the Free Church of Scotland.

In 1843 there were three manufactories within the parish, namely, at Dunblane, Mill of Keir, and Kinbuck, while there was still a considerable number of weavers working with private looms. Great depression of trade and want of employment, however, prevailed in the district. Many improvements had been executed on the estates of Keir and Kippendavie, but there was at that time no mansion house on Cromlix and little had been done up to that date to improve that property. Three mail coaches and three stage coaches passed through the town daily. In July, 1842, that is the year before the Disruption, the number of communicants in the Established Church was 444, and, the accommodation, which consisted of the choir of the Cathedral, was regarded as very inadequate. There were then three dissenting churches, two in Dunblane and one in Greenloaning, while the Episcopalians worshipped in a room hired by them before the erection of their church. The number of poor on the roll averaged 45, and the provision for their maintenance was chiefly derived from a voluntary assessment as the church collections only averaged £30 a year. The stipends of the dissenting ministers varied from £130 a year to £30. The valuation of the parish was estimated at about £16,000 at this time. Notwithstanding the existence of seven schools within the parish there was said to be a considerable deficiency of education. A Savings Bank had been opened in 1841, but had not made much progress owing to depression of trade. The picture of Dunblane, as presented by the Rev. Mr. MacKenzie, concludes by referring to the evils connected with ale houses, and the only sign of advance recorded by him is the new prison erected in 1842! Dunblane had, however, now reached its lowest ebb and, as this narrative proceeds, it will be seen that its advance in modern times was continuous.

Although modern Dunblane was built after 1840 some building of importance is of earlier date and the town was fortunate in having early in this century two capable architects, namely, Mr. William Stirling and Mr. J. Gillespie. One of the restorations of the Cathedral took place in 1817, the details of which are given elsewhere. Mr. Stirling built Holmehill House about 1820. This property occupies a magnificent site overlooking the town and it was probably on Holmehill that St. Blane had his abode and the Culdees afterwards resided. The policies consisted chiefly of a number of crofts which were bought up by Mr. Stirling and united in one. It was about this time that Mr. Stirling of Kippendavie built the bridge over the Wharry on the Glen Road and made this roadway, leading to Bridge of Allan and also the present roadway to Sheriffmuir. In earlier days the road to Sheriffmuir was by Dykedale.

The discovery of the mineral wells on Cromlix estate brought some prosperity to Dunblane in the earlier half of the 19th century. The credit for making the discovery in 1813 is due to Alexander Coldstream, a son of the well-known parish schoolmaster of Dunblane, William Coldstream, and brother of Malcolm Coldstream who succeeded his father as schoolmaster and of John Coldstream for some time Sheriff-Substitute at Dunblane who died in 1820. One of the springs is situated on Hutcheson Farm and the other on Crofts of Cromlix about 200 yards to the north-west of Well Cottage, the little house across the River Allan from Ashfield. Both are on the estate of Cromlix and about 2 miles north of Dunblane. Well Cottage is believed to have been the " House for South Springs." In accordance with tradition the attention of Alexander Coldstream was attracted to the spot through observing it to be a resort of pigeons which flocked thither from great distances at all times of the day. On tasting the water Mr. Coldstream found it to be distinctly saline. The water was analysed by Dr. Murray, F.R.S., Edinburgh, and it was learned that an English pint gave off 47 grains of solid matter of which the principal ingredients were muriate of soda 24·07 parts and muriate of lime 17·06. A pamphlet from the pen of Sheriff Coldstream was published, and in the *Scots Magazine* of 1815 an account is given of the water. A paper was read by Dr. Murray in Edinburgh and published in the transactions of the Philosophical Society in 1822, while a Professor Jamieson also wrote on the subject a few years later, in the *Glasgow Medical Journal*. Prior to the discovery of these wells the only similar well known in Scotland was at Pitcaithly, near Perth.

Of the two springs the lower is less saline than the higher.

The value of these springs having become known throughout the greater part of Scotland, a well house was erected on the Laighhills in 1828. This well house, which stood near the old football pitch crossed by the path from Braeport to Ashfield, consisted of three apartments, one portion being reserved for ladies and another for gentlemen, while in the central division Katie Malloch in a lavender print dress with white apron and mutch took charge of the water, heating some for those who preferred to drink it warm. The water was brought in a barrel every morning from the springs at Cromlix in a pony cart driven for a time by a man named Gow, popularly known as " Lord Raglan." The River Allan at that time was not confined in the water-cut, but made a big sweep eastwards to the foot of the hill on which the well house stood. The cart was taken by ford through the river opposite the present railway level crossing save when the river was in spate when the water had to be carried across the stream by means of a foot-bridge, a short distance south of the ford. One of the attractions of taking the waters was the caustic conversation of Katie Malloch in her old-fashioned garb.

There was every prospect that the discovery of the mineral wells would bring prosperity to Dunblane, but, while it attracted attention to the ancient city for some 30 years, resort to Dunblane for the purpose of taking the mineral waters in course of time came to an end, and yet the waters were not unpalatable and were undoubtedly beneficial for many in ill-health. The neglect of Dunblane as a watering place seems partly to have been due to the limited accommodation for visitors and the want of local effort to make the town attractive and to advertise its attractions, but what overshadowed the fame of the springs of Dunblane was the reputation gained by the mineral waters of Airthrey discovered shortly after the discovery of the Dunblane wells. Within a short time Bridge of Allan became one of the chief health resorts of Scotland, spreading itself over Airthrey lands upon the high ground and towards Stirling. Previous to this, it was limited to a hamlet on the banks of the Allan.

In 1839, Dr. Peter Gordon Stewart, son of Dr. Cornelius Stewart, who had practised as a surgeon in Dunblane from the beginning of the century, published an essay on the Dunblane mineral springs which he had previously read to the Faculty of Physicians and Surgeons. In the preface to this book Dr. Stewart mentions that the " Dunblane mineral springs have of late years been comparatively neglected." He blames the silence of medical authority and the absence of any work to guide either the invalid or his medical advisor. His essay was published to give particulars of cases of cures and of cases where great benefit had been effected by the use of these waters. Dr. Stewart, after mentioning that the discovery of the springs was due to Mr. Alexander Coldstream, writes that soon after the publication of the analysis by Dr. Murray in 1814 " the little ancient city known formerly at a distance only from its poetic sound or its having been the birth and dwelling-place of the heroine of Tannahill, had to witness almost the congregated fashion of a world, all anxious, some by necessity impelled, searching for a remedy which art had failed in procuring, others accompanying and assisting their weaker friends and relatives ; and a third party from that insatiable curiosity common alike to every age and country, to taste of the springs, which, like the Philosopher's stone, had been represented to them as capable of curing all diseases, of banishing the numerous and annoying race of malaria ; restoring the sickened appetite, substituting the blooming countenance of health and vigour for the sallow aspect or the hectic blush, and even of wooing the mind to sanity when the wild delirium comes and weeping friends are strangers."

It may be said to Dr. Stewart's credit, that he, on his part, did not claim that the waters would cure every disease, and he admitted that their virtues had been by many overrated, while, on the other hand, the merits of the waters had been most unwarrantably detracted from. Indeed, their virtues had been attacked by physicians in Stirling who were more interested in the prosperity of the Airthrey wells. Dr. Stewart claimed that, while the waters would not cure every disease, they cured many and helped many more, and in his booklet he gives particulars of interesting cases in his own medical experience and that of his father. One instance given by Dr. Stewart of a cure effected at Dunblane was that of a clergyman who had fallen into ill-health and was suffering from hypochondria. He had—to use Dr. Stewart's words—" become unfit for the ghostly functions of his office." He was guided to Dunblane and, after partaking of the waters for some weeks, he was restored to a sound body and a sane mind. A Dr. Ainslie, whose sister was seriously affected with arthritis, was sent to Dunblane in an almost hopeless condition. She was soon restored to health and vigour after a course of the waters. Her recovery was celebrated by Dr. Ainslie in a poem of some merit of which the following is a stanza:

" Nor seasons change, nor healing art
Could move the wasting inward ill
Till drink I did from that blest well
And rambled by the Allan side,
When health came o'er me like a spell
And joy resumed her wonted tide."

A writer, also in the *Scots Magazine* of 1817, refers to a visit paid by him to the mineral springs near Dunblane, situated " upon the skirts of extensive and bleak moors, one of which (springs) was enclosed in a wooden shed. In the inside of this temple is hung up a scroll of writing purporting to be the terms on which the proprietor (the Earl of Kinnoull) allows the public the use of the wells. (1) Visitors are to pay his tenants for the water at the rate of one penny per pint. (2) The poor are to have it for nothing on bringing a certificate of their poverty from the Parish Minister. (3) No person is to spit or commit any nuisance in the place. (4) If strangers are found using any other than the public roads about the wells they are to pay damages.

" At the other spring is the chief erection, a kind of lodging house consisting of three small rooms and a cellar for kitchen or pump room into a corner of which the water from the spring is conveyed by means of a lead pipe.

" The house stands in a bog where you cannot stir abroad (as there is no road to it) without wetting your feet, so that a person in a delicate state of health runs a risk of receiving as much wrong from the dampness and wetness of the place as benefit from the use of the water.

" I was informed that some public-spirited gentleman offered to build a number of cottages round the walls for the accommodation of strangers, but the noble proprietor declined listening to the proposal."

The efforts of Dr. Stewart availed nought, and Dunblane, as a watering place, was eclipsed by Bridge of Allan, for he failed to convince the invalid that the milder waters of Dunblane were as efficacious as the stronger wells found elsewhere, as any deficiency in the Dunblane water could be corrected by drinking a larger quantity of it.

When the Dunblane Hydropathic was erected in 1878, the Company rented the mineral wells for some years, and a room at the Hydropathic Lodge was used as a pump room where the public could obtain the waters, but the practice of bringing it there was soon abandoned. The " Well Hoose " on the Laighills had by this time fallen into disrepair and many of the stones had been carried off for building purposes at Shaw's Buildings in Ramoyle and no longer was Dunblane visited by the " Well Folk." Thus, an interesting episode in the story of Dunblane closed, although the waters which could most beneficially be taken by many still flow on as of old, but unheeded.

At the beginning of last century handloom weaving was the chief industry of Dunblane, which was a manufacturing town of some importance before the invention of power looms. In 1818, 700 handloom weavers were employed in Dunblane, chiefly weaving cotton, and there were resident in Dunblane seven agents of manufacturers who employed the weavers to work for their principals. Some weavers also worked for private customers, weaving their wool for blankets and their lint for linen. The looms were commonly 72 inches broad and cost from £5 to £5 10s. Some weaving shops had accommodation for 8 looms. The hours of work were long, namely, from 6 a.m. to 10 p.m. with three breaks during the day, and the wages were fixed by piece work. On the invention of power looms the trade vanished and many of the younger weavers joined the army for want of civil employment. In 1831 there were 274 looms working in Dunblane for the Glasgow cotton trade, 229 being worked by men and 45 by women. Their earnings at that time were very meagre, averaging about 6s. per week, whereas twenty years earlier in Dunblane a weekly wage of 18s. was made. By this time 70 workers were employed in a woollen mill.

In November, 1838, silk weaving was introduced into Dunblane.

In the earlier part of the century there were many weaving shops in Ramoyle and Bridgend and some in Millrow and High Street, but after the middle of the century only a few handlooms were worked and the last disappeared somewhere about 1880.

One or two extracts from the *Glasgow Herald* in 1833 may here be quoted. At a meeting of the master tailors of the City of Dunblane, Mr. Kinnaird—a well-known name in connection with tailoring in Dunblane at that time and later—said that the charge made by him for making a " proper mathematically cut coat " was now 7s. 6d., but, owing to the low wages of other tradesmen, demurring of his customers and the present price of provision, he would move it be reduced to 5s. Mr. McNee moved as an amendment that the price for " a full-bodied coat " be 4s. 6d. For any man to charge more was an act of extortion. Mr. McNee was called to order and the motion carried by ten votes to six. A proposal that trousers be reduced from 3s. 6d. to 2s. 6d. and vests from 2s. 6d to 2s. was met by an amendment that trousers be 1s. 6d. and vests 1s., but the meeting dispersed without coming to anything but blows.

In these days of multiple shops and ready-made clothing it is of interest to note that sixteen master tailors assembled at one time in Dunblane, that the usual practice was for customers to supply their own cloth and that a suit could be made for 9s. 6d. or less.

The *Glasgow Herald* records that about 1st March, 1832, the Highland shepherds before their departure from this neighbourhood in early spring gave a grand ball at the farm of Waterside, when a more brilliant display of rustic mirth and beauty had seldom been witnessed in the district. About one hundred and twenty persons assembled in their gayest attire with " mirth on every brow and love in every e'e." The young shepherds did their guests well and provided them with abundance of mountain dew and substantial viands.

Human nature was then as credulous as now for the *Stirling Advertiser* records about March, 1832, that a female fortune-teller in one hour fleeced thirty blooming damsels in Dunblane at one sitting of their odd pence.   She seemed to have so many peers to bestow as future partners that it was pointed out that her predictions could only be accomplished by the long-talked-of new creation of peers.

The city of Dunblane and the lands of the Bishopric were erected into a free Barony in favour of the Bishop by Act of Parliament in 1442.   At a later date the Laird of Cromlix became the superior and he had power to appoint a Bailie who received a salary and who held courts and administered justice.   A weekly market was authorised by Act of Parliament and was held on Thursdays, and there were (as already noted) three annual fairs, which, in the 17th century, were said to have existed from time immemorial.   These fairs were held at Whitsunday on the last Tuesday of May, known as the May Fair, the Lammas Fair held on St. Blane's or St. Lawrence's day, which was the 10th August, commonly called the Grosset Fair, and the Martinmas Fair which seems originally to have been held on All Hallow's Day, but latterly on 12th November.

There was no proper ground for the holding of these fairs, but stalls for the sale of merchandise were erected at the Cross and in Kirk Street, and live stock, including cattle and horses, were sold at the Howmilnhead, that is in ground enclosed in Holmehill at the top of Braeport, and even in the Cathedral churchyard.   Merchandise coming into Dunblane was brought from the north through the gate of Braeport and from the south through the gate at the Bridge of Dunblane, and, as merchants brought much goods to the town and farmers much stock, these fairs were busy times with the buying, selling and bartering of merchandise.

It was reported to the Convention of Burghs in 1692 that the yearly trade of the Regality and City of Dunblane was estimated at £8000.   The right to receive customs from those who brought goods and animals for sale was let annually by the Laird of Cromlix, and elsewhere will be found a list of the charges which were permitted to be made in the 18th century.   Lieutenant-General William Drummond and his heirs were granted authority by Act of Parliament in 1669 to hold a new fair to be known as St. Monance Fair on the day of St. Monance, that is 1st March.

In 1686 Sir Colin Campbell of Aberuchill was authorised to hold a free fair at Cambusmore on 8th August to be called St. Mary's Fair.   Little is known about this fair which for a very long period has been in desuetude.   By the middle of the 19th century the fairs of Dunblane had lost their original importance, although, in contrast, those in Doune were large and prosperous until the latter half of the century.   At the May Fair at Dunblane in 1837 only 17 cattle were presented for sale, nearly all of which were of very inferior quality and few were sold.   At the Martinmas Fair at Doune in 1838 3000 black cattle, 2000 sheep and other domestic animals were on sale.   Latterly the St. Monance Fair was usually held on the first Wednesday of March, the Whitsunday Fair on the Tuesday following the 26th of May, and the Hallowday Fair on the first Tuesday of November.   There was also for a time a fair for the sale of cattle and horses held in Dunblane on the third Tuesday of October.

Fairs were originally church festivals held on the day when a saint was celebrated.   At such festivals a large portion of the population of the district gathered together to take part in the services of the church.   This involved the provision of refreshments, and the merchants took the opportunity of providing other commodities to attract the people who had gathered.   In course of time, however, these fairs ceased to have any religious connection and became holidays for the general population and opportunities for the sale of merchandise.

After railways became established throughout Scotland markets were instituted at suitable centres where stock could be brought and despatched by rail.   On 4th June, 1871, markets for cattle, sheep and grain were established near Dunblane railway station, the intention being to hold these on the first Wednesday of each month.   These proved unsuccessful at Dunblane, and the old country fairs have to a large extent ceased to exist while markets have been greatly developed at railway centres such as at Stirling and Perth.

Until 1879, the public roads were kept up by means of payments charged at various toll houses and gates over the country and, although the gates have long been abolished, one can readily recognise the old toll houses from their proximity to the public roads and from the custom of having a window extended towards the road to enable one to see approaching traffic from either direction without leaving the house.   The first toll north of Dunblane was at Balhaldie and the next on the Perth road beyond Greenloaning, where the road to Sheriffmuir branches off. The money collected at the toll houses did not go directly to the road authorities. The latter let out the right to the tolls by public roup each year for the period from Whitsunday to Whitsunday. In 1837 the price paid by the man who rented the tolls on the Crieff and Stirling road was £2,308, but the payments for less important roads were, of course, much smaller. There were fixed scales of dues payable by the public using the roads.

In 1793 there were in the town of Dunblane, in addition to the parochial school, three other schools to which most children were sent other than those of the poorer parents. There were also three other schools in country districts of the parish. The number of scholars at the parish school about that time averaged 60 and the salary paid to the schoolmaster was £12 sterling, in addition to which he was provided with a house and garden and 7 stones of cheese. The schoolmaster supplemented his salary by holding other offices, and in 1793 the dominie was likewise Session Clerk, the perquisites of which office amounted to about £10 a year. In 1843 there were four unendowed schools, two schools supported by individual subscription and the parochial school. At the former date there were schools at Kilbryde and Kinbuck, and the heritors contributed 10s. a year to the master at Kilbryde and £1 a year to the Kinbuck teacher. It may be explained, however, that country schoolmasters at Kilbryde and elsewhere were usually young lads who had just left school and who were boarded by the farmers in the district for a period of from one week to one month at a time, and certain fees were also paid by the scholars. In 1796, Mr. Malcolm Coldstream presented a petition to the heritors of Dunblane stating that he had only received 10s. annually for teaching poor scholars, and he prayed the honourable court to grant him such redress as to their wisdom and goodness might seem right. The result of this humble address was that the heritors increased the master's annual allowance to one guinea when the number of poor scholars should amount to four or upwards.

In 1806, the heritors drew up a scale of fees for Dunblane school from which it appears that the master was permitted to collect the following fees—for reading, 2s. 6d. a quarter, for writing, 3s., for arithmetic, 4s., and for Latin and Greek, 5s. It is strange to read of provision being made for the teaching of Latin and Greek in a humble, country school of 60 scholars at the beginning of last century and that there should be a sufficient demand for this instruction to justify a scale of charges. In recent years with thousands of pounds spent annually on education within the Parish there was no such provision and no young persons receiving instruction in these subjects in our local schools. In March, 1843, an advertisement appeared in the *Stirling Journal* for a teacher qualified to teach Latin and Greek for Braco School. The sole emoluments were a free schoolroom and liberty to charge fees.

After the parish scholars had ceased to be taught in the apartment above the Lady Chapel of the Cathedral or in the Chapel itself they were accommodated in a building within the church-yard opposite the Leighton Church entered from the Meeting House Close. In later years the school was transferred to a site in Braeport where the present school, in much extended form, stands. Other schools in Dunblane in the early part of last century included an infant school in the Braeport kept by Jenny Miller, the pupils of which were known as Jenny Miller's Mice, Meiklejohn's school in Ramoyle kept by the father of the late Professor Meiklejohn of St. Andrews University, a well-known authority on education, and Monteath's School in the Millrow con-ducted by three men of the name of Monteath, one of whom was John Monteath, the author of *Traditions of Dunblane*. Later in the century a Miss Campbell taught an infant school at Rose Cottage at the foot of Old Doune Road, and, after St. Mary's Church was founded and after the Disruption, schools were instituted by these new congregations. The Free Church school was held in what was till recently the Territorial Drill Hall, but which for many years was the public hall of Dunblane. One of the teachers in the Free Church school was Buchan, afterwards famous as a scientist and meteorologist.

Children left school at as early an age as 8 to 10, but opportunities were given for further education at evening classes and these flourished generations ago in Dunblane. At one time a school was held at Messrs. Alexander Wilson & Co's mill at Springbank. It is said that, when the young people got out of hand, the master put their heads under his arm and punched them with his knuckles, and if he could not ascertain the principal culprit, he corrected the whole class equally to make sure that he did not miss the ringleader.

In 1831, the number of schools in Dunblane were four, these consisting of the parish school with 108 pupils, Mr. Monteath's school with 70 to 100 scholars, Mr. Bennett's school with 60 to 90 pupils, and a female infant school taught by Miss Archibald and attended by 30 to 40 children. There were also subscription schools at Balhaldie attended by 30 to 40 pupils, Kinbuck by 20 pupils, Greenloaning by 22, and Kilbryde by 24 to 40. The number of children now at Balhaldie is very much smaller, and at Kilbryde those of school age do not exceed a dozen and sometimes are considerably fewer. Only in Kinbuck has the number increased, due to the expansion of the village of Ashfield.

The old prison of Dunblane stood to the east of the entrance gate to the Cathedral churchyard and is said to have been built from stones which formed part of the walls of the Bishop's Palace. There were four apartments in the ground floor, one of which was occupied in the earlier part of last century by Duncan McLeish, the gaoler and town bellman. Another room contained the old lamps of the town, and the remaining two, lumber. The upper floor was reached by an outside stair and consisted of a central apartment called the outer court; the court room was at the west end, and at the east end were two apartments known respectively as the Lock-up and the Black Hole. If prisoners were boisterous, they were placed in the Black Hole and chained there to a large stone, and there was little light in the apartment. In the court room the bench consisted of a platform two feet in height, and on the wall at the west end of this apartment were placed the Royal Arms. There was a table in front of the bench around which the solicitors sat and the boxes for jurymen were placed next the north wall. Witnesses and other persons interested remained in the outer court until they were required. The business of the court occupied the whole time of a resident Sheriff-Substitute and, on days when courts were held, there was great stir in the town. Prisoners serving sentences up to six months were kept in the old prison and they were given a four pound loaf of bread and some water daily. If sentenced to long periods of imprisonment they were taken by coach to Perth prison where they served their sentence. Prisoners were able to vary their fare by obtaining a supply of tobacco and whisky, the *modus operandi* being to lower a stocking from the window sill with a bottle and cash in it, and on the keeper of a neighbouring public house learning of the stocking, the bottle was filled by him.

In May, 1837, a report was published on the condition of Dunblane prison indicating that one of the cells was without any heating and that there was no glass in the windows. It mentioned that it was easy for the prisoners to escape and that several had escaped in recent years, and that the keeper was infirm, unwieldy and enveloped in dirt. In these days it was the custom for prisoners to be allowed home for a change of clothing, if they so desired. When it was proposed to erect a new prison, the suggestion was made that it should be built at Doune. While civil business had been conducted in Dunblane since before the days of the Reformation when church officials held jurisdiction, the principal centre of criminal administration in earlier centuries was at the Castle at Doune, this being a principal residence of the Earls of Menteith. The Laird of Cromlix, however, came forward with the offer of a free site for a new prison where an old property, then in ruins, stood, namely, Strathallan's Lodging, once the residence of the first Drummond Laird of Cromlix. The modern prison was built there and Dunblane has since continued to be the court town for western Perthshire. The foundation stone was laid by Stirling of Kippendavie with Masonic honours on 3rd May, 1842, following upon a procession round the city led by two brass bands. A dinner was thereafter held in Kinross's Inn attended by over 100 persons.

The sentences pronounced for trivial offences were throughout the greater part of the century exceedingly severe. Thus in 1839, four lads were convicted of fruit-stealing and were sent to prison for periods from 20 to 30 days. A local newspaper commented on the gravity of the offence stating that such actions should be punished as severely as possible. Even at as late a date as 1871, similar severity is to be observed. In September of that year two girls aged 14, strangers to this district, were sent to prison each for 40 days for the theft of an old gown taken from a green and were ordered afterwards to be detained in a reformatory, while, in September of the following year, a man was imprisoned for 40 days for the theft of a penny stamp.

At the beginning of last century there was ample scope for temperance reform, and licensed houses were very numerous in the district. The drunkenness of the town was the cause of a memorial addressed by Sheriff-Substitute John Coldstream to the heritors in 1792. The Sheriff submitted that the number of houses in which liquor was retailed had increased to a most improper degree and that heads of families, both men and women, were daily to be found in the lowest of these houses while their children were neglected at home, and parents were in the habit of selling and pawning their goods to procure whisky. The Sheriff stated that, unless the number of public houses was limited, and unless licences were refused to such as encouraged dissipation and harboured vagrants which infested the country, it would be in vain to attempt to keep discipline and order in the society here. The Sheriff accordingly appealed to the heritors to support him in having the number of licensed houses abridged, and he concluded with a request to the heritors for their support which they appear to have gladly given. According to the *Statistical Account* of 1793 there were 41 houses where ale and spirits were retailed in the parish, of which 29 were in the town of Dunblane and 12 in the rural portion, and the writers attributed misery and poverty amongst the community as the result. By 1831 these licensed houses had been reduced in number to 22, of which the following is a list taken from Mr. John Monteath's account of the parish :—

No.	Cognisance.	Persons Licensed.	Designation.
1.	Head Inn	T. Kinross, Vintner,	Bridge, Dunblane.
2.	Black Bull	G. Christie, Glasgow Carrier.	
3.	Star Inn	A. Nicholson,	Bridgend.
4.	Mason's Hall	John Sharp, Innkeeper.	
5.	Temp. Coffee House	W. Faichney, Turner.	
6.	Monteath Arms	G. Monteath, Saddler,	High Street.
7.		Thomas Gow, Grocer,	High Street.
8.		James Wilson,	Ramoyle.
9.		Robt. Moir, Tavernkeeper,	Cross.
10.	Rob Roy's Cave	Jas. McLaren, Weaver,	Cross.
11.	Victuallying Office	J. & G. Burns, Grocers.	
12.	Steamboat Inn	David Clerk, Labourer.	
13.	Carrier's Inn	James Clason, Mason,	Feus.
14.		Andrew Stirling,	Kirk Street.
15.	Balhaldie Inn	Jas. Roy, Innkeeper,	Balhaldie.
16.		John Whyte, Tollkeeper.	
17.		Young, Tollkeeper,	Rottearns.
18.	Sheriffmuirhouse	Robert Menzies,	Sheriffmuir.
19.	Killiecrankie Inn	Peter McKenzie.	
20.	Sun Tavern	Jo. Whitehead, Farmer,	Whitecrosses.
21.	Greenloaning Inn	A. Monteath,	Greenloaning.
22.		Robert Towers, Vintner.	

It will be observed that at this time there were 14 Inns or other licensed places in Dunblane and 8 outside the town principally in the neighbourhood of Greenloaning.

By 1843 the number of ale houses had been reduced to 16, but the evils arising from such were termed " incalculable."

Among the taverns were two situated side-by-side at the west side of the Cross between the Manse and the Cathedral churchyard. In 1831 one was occupied by Robert Moir, a well-known name in the parish 100 years ago. The other was known by the somewhat suggestive name of Rob Roy's Cave. This was for many years tenanted by Rab Bruce, who went by the by-name of " Cash Doon." An old story is told of him and of a local worthy who went into his tavern to purchase whisky, but without the necessary cash. Knowing that he would not be supplied without making payment he armed himself with a bottle which he filled with water. He obtained from Rab Bruce a bottle of the same size filled with whisky, placed it in a pocket and then offered to pay Rab on an early date. The request was at once declined and the whisky demanded back. When the drouthy customer failed to obtain time he handed to the publican the bottle containing water which Rab at once poured back into his jar not observing that he had been taken advantage of. The customer then departed having obtained his order without payment.

When ultimately Rab Bruce retired from his life's occupation, the following verses were written which are printed not for their poetical value, but as illustrative of the life of the day :—

P

BROSE RAB—A DUNBLANE WORTHY.

Anither auld worthie has left our auld toon
Brose Rab, or Rab Bruce, or Alias Cash Doon,
For Rab never trusted a grot a' his days,
An' he sought nane himsel' for meat, fuel, nor claes.

Rab kept a dram-shop for near forty years,
Beside the heigh-kirk, whaur the steeple uprears
Its quaint fashioned pow, 'neath whas dark shadow lies
The remains o' the gay, grave, foolish and wise.

Whaever stepp'd in for a dram or a drink,
Rab aye held the stoup till they doun wi' the clink ;
There's nane could cheat Rab—e'e a Yankee, I guess,
Altho' he had come frae the seat o' Congress.

Rab's house was na braw, as ye weel may suppose
For nae female kept he to mak' his kail-brose ;
He cook'd an' he scrubbed, an' did a' thing himsel',
Frae feedin' the pig to attending the bell.

His wonderfu' inn was a thousan' years auld,
Weel theekit wi' strae to keep out rain and cauld ;
The order nae doot had belanged to the Picks,
Wha's houses were biggit wi' clods, clay and sticks.

But fashions will change, as they often do soon,
Rab's Inn was condemned, to Rag's grief, to come doon ;
The laird had resolved to rear a new biggin',
Wi' good hewn stanes an' sklates for the riggin'.

Rab's bundled up a', to Dunblane bid adieu !
I ken'd by his e'e that his auld heart was fu'
Sae waesome he gazed at the door o' the inn,
Where forty lang years he cried " Doon wi' the tin."

Brose Rab, Fare-ye-weel ! it were good for us a'
To do as ye've doon, that is score nane ava' ;
An' mind aye your mottoes thro' thick and thro' thin
" No tick given here," and " Come doon wi' the tin ! "

The history of the Grass Yard or Bishop's Yard, that is the ground between the Cathedral Manse and the River Allan, is not generally known. Prior to the Reformation it was garden ground attached to the Palace of the Bishop of Dunblane. Along with the Cathedral it became Crown property, but the use of it was given to the parish ministers over a considerable period from 1689 onwards. The Rev. William Simson in the 18th century made application for the possession of this "small spot of ground" as a garden, to the Barons of His Majesty's Exchequer in Scotland and he was given permission to peaceably and quietly possess and enjoy it.

His successor, the Rev. John Robertson, made a similar application and received a similar grant. The ground was sometimes cultivated and a portion was kept as a kitchen garden, and during the summer months the minister was accustomed to allow inhabitants to use a portion for bleaching their linen. The only entry to the ground at the end of the 18th century was through the Manse or otherwise through the property of private persons.

On the death of the Rev. Mr. Robertson a petition was presented to the Lord Chief Baron and other Barons of Exchequer bearing to be on behalf of the whole inhabitants, craving that the ground be given for the benefit of the community. Revd. Robert Stirling, who succeeded Mr. Robertson as parish minister, also submitted a petition asking that a fresh grant of the ground to him as parish minister be given on the same terms as those under which his predecessors held it, and he suggested that the Earl of Kinnoull, who was superior of the town, should provide the inhabitants with washing greens and allow the minister of the parish to continue to possess this ground. The text of this petition is given in Chapter XXXIV. The petition was granted, but ultimately the Exchequer, after the death of Dr. Grierson in 1840, granted the ground to the community, and the use of it was thereafter continued to the public of Dunblane for the purposes of a bleaching green. In 1933 the Bishop's Yard was purchased by the Town Council for the community.

There were some troublesome days in Dunblane about 1828-32. The community was much perturbed by the doings of the Resurrectionists, that is with persons who removed dead bodies from graves for the purpose of supplying these as subjects to schools of anatomy. Devices were resorted to to prevent the uplifting of coffins and at one time a watch was provided in Dunblane churchyard. Men at night perambulated the ruined nave with lantern in one hand and staff or other weapon of defence in the other. When the weather was stormy they found shelter in a little apartment in the west gable of the Cathedral known as Katie Ogi's Hole. Reference is made in the Kirk Session minutes of 8th June, 1828, to what may have been the last case of this kind, when, it having come to the knowledge of the Session that a depredation had been recently committed within the churchyard by the carrying away of a dead body from a grave, the Session resolved that a statement of the above most reprehensible and sacrilegious outrage be made to the Procurator-Fiscal and Sheriff-Substitute with a request that they take immediate steps for the punishment of the depredators, with the view to the setting at rest of the public mind and the safeguarding of the undisturbed repose of the bodies of deceased friends. In reply to the communication from the Session Mr. William Stirling, Procurator-Fiscal, a brother of the Rev. Robert Stirling, replied that the Session had omitted to give a list of the persons who gave the information. The Session Clerk replied that the matter was one of public notoriety and that it fell to the Procurator-Fiscal himself to trace the depredators. He apparently failed to do so and the matter is not further referred to in the minutes of Kirk Session. Mr. William Stirling in the following year was succeeded by Thomas Barty as Procurator-Fiscal.

In the early part of last century the Cathedral churchyard was in a very neglected state. The ground was uneven, the grass was not cut, sheep were grazed there and nettles grew in parts. There was a very old row of houses in Kirk Street standing partly within the present east boundary of the churchyard, and a source of nuisance arose from broken china and other refuse being thrown out by the tenants of these houses from doors and windows opening on the churchyard, some of the houses being of the poorest description and the tenants of the poorest class. The heritors took the matter in hand in 1819 and ordered that all doors and windows opening into the churchyard were to be securely fixed by stanchions, and in course of time animals were excluded and the churchyard ceased to be the playground of the children.

An old story of this period may be recalled. One night the Cathedral bell mysteriously began to toll. It was not the work of the beadle and no one could account for the ringing. The inhabitants could only attribute it to the Devil, and this seemed to be confirmed when a black face and hoofed feet were discerned. The elders, much concerned, proceeded to the Manse to seek the aid of the minister with a view to laying the Evil One by the heels or hoofs. The minister, perhaps bolder than the members of his flock, and armed only with a Bible, marched to the Cathedral to face the enemy of mankind, but, on coming close to close quarters, it was discovered that a practical joker had tied the rope of the bell to the horns of a black-faced ram who had tolled the bell in tugging at the rope in its effort to obtain release. On Sunday, 2nd July, 1842, as members of the Cathedral congregation were dispersing, a sharp earthquake took place. This was thought to have been caused by the rattling of the bones of the clergy of Roman Catholic times.

The year 1832, the time of the passing of the Reform Bill, was marked by much local excitement. On 29th August of that year, Sir George Murray visited Dunblane and addressed a meeting. His supporters evidently feared a disturbance, and, according to local accounts, hired bands of Peace Officers were brought to the meeting with the result that the local constables resigned office. Great excitement prevailed during the election time. The supporters of the Tory Party referred to the Reformers as seditious Radicals. A rumour was spread that the mob intended to assassinate Sheriff-Substitute Barclay and it was suggested that the rumour arose from the Tory Party with a view to prejudicing its opponents. As a matter of fact Sheriff Barclay was a popular figure in the community. One night a cannonade was heard and " a hallowed pane of glass of unalloyed Tory stuff from the crystal works of Bendochy" was demolished at the house of Thomas Barty, the Procurator-Fiscal. While the Tory Party threw the blame of this on the Radicals, the latter replied that the pane had been broken with the object of throwing a stigma on them. At this time a song was written of which at least two versions, only slightly differing from one another, are known to have existed. A copy of this song follows. Although a somewhat scurrilous production it has interesting references to the chief persons resident in the district and illustrates the spirit of the times. Measures were adopted to suppress these verses, which steps were said to have led to greater evils than the measures were intended to prevent, and a protest was made at the character of the notices and proclamations posted up in Dunblane and neighbourhood, as degrading to the character of the inhabitants. There was thus great unrest and mutual distrust between the residenters and the local authorities.

A general meeting of the inhabitants was held at Dunblane on 28th November, 1832, at 8 p.m., within the Meeting House of the Rev. Mr. Anderson (that is the Leighton Church), called by the Reform Committee of Dunblane of which Mr. John Monteath, schoolmaster, was secretary. The chairman of the meeting was Mr. Charles Meiklejohn, and, after he had spoken briefly, Mr. Monteath addressed it at considerable length. Mr. Monteath referred to the song which had created so great a sensation. Neither Tory nor Reformer had ascertained the authorship of it and the authorities had failed to suppress it. Much annoyance had been caused by the youth of the town singing verses about local inhabitants as they passed by. A proclamation bearing the signatures of numerous Justices of the Peace had been circulated and this the Reformers regarded as "foul and insulting." To the proclamation was appended a declaration which bore the names of 36 inhabitants who had declared their abhorrence of the disgraceful proceedings, and had bound themselves to bring the offenders to punishment. The Procurator-Fiscal (Mr. Thomas Barty) had apparently taken special offence at references in the song personal to him, and it was said had rendered himself obnoxious to the public by his having become a hired agent of the Tory Party. The Procurator-Fiscal at that time had liberty to carry on a private practice and had probably acted on behalf of the Tory candidate. Mr. Monteath concluded by stating that there had been no riots or even breach of peace and that the whole trouble had arisen through the publication of the song and the foolish measures taken to suppress it. It was apparently suggested at this time that the Sheriff Court might be removed to Doune in view of the outrageous conduct of some of the local inhabitants. The meeting resolved that, with a view to restoring confidence among the inhabitants, certain individuals should be removed from the offices they held and that a memorial be forwarded to the Lord Advocate giving a narrative of the circumstances from the date of the visit of Sir George Murray. Two inhabitants, Gilbert Reid and David Henderson, afterwards addressed the meeting, commending peace and good order and urging people to prevent their children annoying the poor Tories by lilting the obnoxious song and to refrain from saying or singing it. In a short time feeling died down and Thomas Barty lived to be a highly respected and popular member of the community.

The following are the words of this song :—

I.

The Tories ilk ane, in and near auld D--b--ne
Are the queerest set ever ye saw, man—
This while they've been mad—they are now getting sad
When they think on the depth o' their fa', man :
(*Keir*). Glyed Archie o' K--r, he for mony a year
    The Black men did lash and did ca' man ;
But he had got land, and of course great command,
    And the Whites he wou'd fain keep in thraw, man.
And we sing, and they cling, and they cling, and we sing,
    And rejoice that the Bill is our law, man.

II.

(Blairdrummond).

Blind Harry i' Moss, since his ee he did loss,
 He looks unco dowie and wae, man ;
He may keep up his heart—he is sure o' a part,
 Beside his auld friend Castlereagh, man :

(Wm. Stirling, Esq.,
* of Content).*
(Sir George Murray).

And slave-owner Willie—he looks aye sae silly,
 His friends they're making great moan, man—
He looket sae queer that day Geordie was here,
 When the crowd gied him sic a lang groan, man.
   And we sing, &c.

III.

(A. Smith, of
* Glassingall).*

And road-siller Sandy—he cut quite the dandy,
 Although that his troop was but sma', man ;
On their head he was crouse—in their rear Will Bruce
 Determined to conquer or fa' man ;
And our paper Jock, for the sauls of his flock,
 He doesnae care ae single straw, man,
Nor their moral lives, but some easy chiels' wives
 Ne'er miss their guid men when awa', man.
   And we sing, &c.

IV.

(Wm. Stirling,
* Holmehill).*

There's dunder-head Will, on the tap o' the hill,
 In his gig now does whup and does ca', man ;
Though saul he has little—a famous lickspittle
 He maks to the big and the braw, man.

(Mr. McAra).

Our thick-headed Clark, he keeps much in the dark,
 For he daurna say aye nor say na, man ;
Thae Radical een are sae gleg and sae keen,
 They are apt to find out the least flaw, man.
   And we sing, &c.

V.

(Mr. Barty).

Our thief-catcher Tam, he likes Lancashire ham,
 Fresh beef, and split mutton, an' a', man ;
He took an auld lass for the sake o' her brass—
 He ne'er made his bread by the law, man—

(Mr. Fenton, Factor,
* Kippendavie).*

Mean Jamie frae Angus, he cam here amang us
 A beggar, but now plays the braw man—
His nose he will cock, and insult honest folk
 Wi' his dirty, low Norland jaw, man.
   And we sing, &c.

VI.

(Mr. Finlayson,
* Merchant).*

Then big-bellied James our notice next claims,
 Though he gies a grunt and a roar, man ;
If he is weel fed, he's as easily led,
 And tame as the Dollerie boar, man.

(Mr. Kinross, Baker).

And three neuket Leg, wi' his fair sister Meg,
 Ne'er ought but gentility saw, man—
The vulgar nor rude never tainted their blude
 Nane under a Stallion Bashaw, man.
   And we sing, &c.

VII.

(Mr. Kinross, Farmer).   Lang Lewie himsell, thought nae shame for to tell,
          A brush he wou'd get, and tar pig, man,
(Major Murray, of   And he'd lay a wager it wou'd please the Major
   Abercairney,   To tar ilka Radical Whig, man.
   probably).   Now ye've got a swatch o' that precious batch,
          That has been sic a pest to our land, man ;
        They Freedom detest, but of subjects the best
          For Don Miguel, or mild Ferdinand, man.
        And we sing, and they cling, and they cling and we sing,
          And rejoice that the Bill is our law, man.

In 1837 Dunblane was visited by an epidemic of cholera. With a view to staying its ravages fires of Archangel tar were ignited in the streets as a disinfectant. There was a high death rate and interments usually took place at night. There was difficulty in getting assistance to bury the dead as few had the courage to assist, and it is recorded that the only men in the community who would perform this duty were William McOwan, David Eadie and James King.

Among the principal inhabitants in Dunblane in the first half of the last century, reference may be made in the first instance to the local clergymen. The Rev. Robert Stirling, a native of Dunblane, was presented to the parish of Dunblane by George III and ordained on 2nd June, 1791. He was the son of John Stirling, merchant in Dunblane, and Isabella White, his wife, and was a Master of Arts of the University of Glasgow. During the first four years of his incumbency he was assistant and successor to the Rev. John Robertson who died in 1795. He married Mary, eldest daughter of Dr. James Graham, a lecturer in Edinburgh, and had 6 children, the youngest being Patrick James Stirling, LL.D., writer, Dunblane. The correct date of his birth is 13th November, 1764, and not 1765, as stated in Scott's *Fasti*. He died, as the result of a carriage accident, on 17th October, 1817, when on his way to Alloa to meet his children who were travelling from Edinburgh by boat.

His immediately elder brother was William Stirling, born 1761, who practised as a writer in Dunblane and held the appointment of Procurator-Fiscal. His death seems to have taken place in 1829, although it has also been said to have occurred in 1832.

The Rev. R. Stirling was succeeded by the Rev. John Grierson, an M.A. of Edinburgh University, who was licensed by the Presbytery of Dalkeith in 1813. After three years in the parish of Dunning he was presented by the Prince Regent to Dunblane and admitted on 16th July, 1818. He died in 1840.

During Dr. Grierson's incumbency the first of the modern restorations of the Cathedral took place, of which particulars are given elsewhere.

Although the early portion of the 19th century, particularly between 1830 and 1840, was one of much interest in the history of Dunblane, there are few facts recorded and little light thrown upon it in the records of the Kirk Session of Dunblane, these being practically barren of any reference to historical events or to local incidents. Between 1817 and 1840 Dr. Grierson was the parish minister, and the minutes of the time chiefly refer to the formal fixing of the date of the next communion and to the half-yearly election of an elder to the Presbytery and Synod.

Dr. Grierson, who was made a Doctor of Divinity by Glasgow University, is first referred to by that title in February, 1836, but there is no record as to the conferring of this distinction on him, and no minute was recorded of appreciation or sympathy on the occasion of his death in 1840. During the greater part of his incumbency, Dr. Grierson acted as Session Treasurer, having undertaken this work from 1819 in succession to William Stirling, writer, Dunblane. Offenders at this period still frequently appeared before the Session and on more than one occasion were rebuked in private and not before the assembled congregation, while fines were also frequently imposed.

On 5th December, 1824, the Session were informed of a scandal existing in the parish against a tenant at Cambushinnie who was said to have been guilty of cutting down and carrying away wood, the property of Lord Kinnoull, the owner of Cromlix. He was summoned before the

Session and, at his appearance, he averred that he was unaware how the wood came to be in his stackyard, and that rather than quarrel with Mr. Lorimer, the Factor, he had paid him the sum of two guineas. Consideration of the complaint was deferred till a later date and seems to have been allowed to drop for the time being, but in May, 1842, the case was again mentioned when the Session came to the conclusion that there was no ground for with-holding from the farmer any of the privileges of the church.

Although the number of elders remained small, there seems to have been a considerable increase of young communicants about 1832 and some Seceders rejoined the Church of Scotland about that time.

In December, 1837, Duncan McLeish resigned the beadleship owing to advanced age. He had served for upwards of 30 years. His successor was William McKinlay from whose daughter, Mrs. Bruce, the old bell and sand-glass now preserved in the Cathedral were received. On the death of Dr. Grierson, Dr. Gray, minister of Kincardine Parish, was elected Moderator, and the roll of persons entitled to vote in the election of a new minister shows the names of 151 males, heads of families, and 19 other additional persons who claimed to be put on the roll, but who had not been in attendance at church or communion.

Dr. Grierson's successor, the Reverend William MacKenzie, who has been mentioned elsewhere, was inducted on 30th March, 1841, and was the minister of the Cathedral at the time of the Disruption. He was of an earnest, evangelical type, but was probably deficient in tact. It may be noted that he was the first minister to authenticate the minutes with his signature. In October, 1841, the Kirk Session divided up the parish into 14 districts which were not dissimilar to those of the present time, and an endeavour was made to increase the number of elders from 5 to 14, but the full number was not procured. The families in the parish numbered 543 and these were divided among 8 elders, James King in Ramoyle having 138 families to superintend, and Andrew Hart in his district 132 families. The duties of the elders are laid down in detail in the minute of March, 1842.

Other evidence of Mr. MacKenzie's energy was seen in fixing regular meetings of Kirk Session to be held on the first Monday before the full moon in each month at 6 p.m., in fixing a rotation of elders to stand at the church plate, in laying down a series of questions to be put twice a year to each elder as to performance of his duties as to whether he observed family worship, etc., in assembling the youth of the congregation for religious instruction at the completion of the ordinary service, and in holding occasional Sunday evening services in addition to the forenoon and afternoon services, as also a fortnightly prayer meeting.

About this time the first Associate Congregation, which worshipped in the Leighton Church, was the largest in the city. Rev. Michael Gilfillan, who was ordained in 1768, was still the minister and he continued until his death in 1816. His successor was the Rev. James Anderson from the East Congregation, Leslie, who was ordained on 15th April, 1818. The Rev. William Blair, D.D., wrote of him in 1858 in the following terms. " His talents were of no mean order— his accomplishments very high—his classic taste and sweetness of manner admitted and admired by all. His discourses were models of accurate composition, presenting the picture of a smooth stream stealing through fine landscapes and beautifying as well as fertilising wherever it flowed. He was always well prepared in the pulpit." In 1835 the first Meeting House of this congregation (the " Red Hoose," already noted), was replaced by the present building erected at a cost of about £1500. Mr. Anderson continued minister until 1854 when he retired to Leslie where he died in 1858. In 1804 the Rev. John Wallace was ordained minister of the Anti-Burgher congregation, worshipping in the church in Holmehill Road. He died in Dunblane on 13th August, 1828. At the beginning of his ministry his ministrations extended to Greenloaning, but during his term of office these congregations were disjoined. The Rev. Alexander Henderson succeeded him in July, 1829, his yearly stipend being £40. After about 20 years' service he went to Canada as a missionary of the United Presbyterian Church. Mr. Henderson is remembered as the builder of the house of St. Blane's Rood, now known as St. Blane's, and as the writer of a poem on the city of his adoption entitled " The Pilgrim."

One of the most prominent citizens in the early part of the 19th century was William Stirling, Architect in Dunblane, born 15th October, 1772, the son of James Stirling, wright in Dunblane, and a cousin of the Rev. Robert Stirling. He acquired the property of Holmehill and erected the present mansion house there. His wife was Jean Erskine, daughter of David Erskine, W.S.

He was the oldest son of his father.   His younger brother, Rev. John Stirling, was minister of Craigie Parish, Ayrshire, and Moderator of the General Assembly in 1833.   The property of Holmehill was greatly added to by the purchase of small adjacent properties.   Mr. Stirling had charge of the restoration of the Cathedral about 1817.   His death took place in 1838 and he was succeeded by his son, James Stirling, born in 1816.   Mr. James Stirling's death took place in 1866, his successor being his nephew, John Stirling of Fairburn, who was the last surviving child of Dr. John Stirling of Craigie parish.   The latter was a manufacturer in his early life, but acquired an interest in iron mines near Cockermouth in Cumberland, became wealthy and purchased the estate of Fairburn.   He died in 1907 at the age of 87.

The present property of Holmehill is comprised of a considerable number of tenements and crofts, the most of which were acquired about the year 1820 by William Stirling above-mentioned.

The following properties have been traced as making up a considerable portion of Holmehill.

(1) A tenement to the east of the road leading to Mintoch Myre situated within high walls along with the upper yard of Balhaldie which stood on the opposite side of this road from Balhaldie House.   This road is the continuation of Sinclair's Wynd, Mintoch Myre being the lower part of the Hydropathic gardens and grounds or between these and Ramoyle. Mr. Stirling acquired this tenement in 1820, but sold it to Mr. Alexander Coldstream whose trustees re-sold it to James Stirling of Holmehill in 1852.   Mr. Coldstream's property was the last house in Sinclair's Wynd standing in a court-way and facing to the south.

Mr. Stirling also acquired in 1820 the croft adjoining the above subjects, the croft, house and yard in Ramoyle which had belonged to J. Moir, the Meikle Croft, Long Croft, and How-milnhead Croft, also Ninian Drummond's Croft.

The croft of J. Moir was purchased by Thomas Duthie, writer, in Dunblane, in 1763, and the Meikle Croft, Longcroft, and Howmilnhead Croft were purchased by him in 1762 from Mr. Keltie, blacksmith.   Mr. Duthie also acquired Ninian Drummond's Croft in 1765 from its owner, John Rob.   In 1775 William Duthie, mason, Dunblane, a brother of Thomas Duthie, was served as his heir of line, and in 1777 he disponed the properties to John Rob, who was probably his son-in-law.   William Rob, his eldest son, whose address was Duthieston, Jamaica, obtained a Charter of Confirmation from the Earl of Kinnoull in 1819 and in the following year Mr. Stirling became proprietor.

Longcroft was also known as Lichale Croft and was situated near the Laighills, while How-milnhead Croft was the land to the east or north-east of Glengyle House at the top of Braeport. Ninian Drummond's Croft was north of the croft which adjoined the Coldstreams' House in Sinclair's Wynd and it stood apparently east of Kirk Street.

(2) Another property now embraced in Holmehill was a malt barn which belonged to Alexander Bryce, a maltman and burgess of Stirling.   This was known as the Muckle Barn. It was disponed by Bryce in 1736 to James Gillespie, wright and maltman.   James Gillespie, architect in Edinburgh, his grandson and nearest heir, obtained a Charter of Confirmation about 1824.   He was latterly known as James Gillespie Graham of Orchill.

(3) A third property was acquired by Mr. William Stirling in 1837 from James Bain, writer in Dunblane, consisting of two barns with a back-yard bounded by the property of James McKisick on the east.   McKisick acquired this property from Peter Henderson and George Henderson, masons in Dunblane, tutors of Robert Keltie, who was the only child of Donald Keltie, writer, Dunblane, and grandson of Robert Keltie, blacksmith, Dunblane.   For a time the property belonged to John Monteith, Cauldhame, Sheriffmuir.

(4) The fourth subject is a small one, namely the one-half of the south gable of the meeting house of the second United Associated Congregation which William Stirling acquired in 1833 from Dr. Cornelius Stewart and others, managers of the Anti-Burgher Church.   The Church stood within the present walls of Holmehill inside the cart entrance gate nearly opposite Dunblane Smithy.

(5) The next property refers to a house and yard in Ramoyle with one-third acre of land which had belonged to Marion Moir, daughter of John Moir, and wife of John Paterson.   The latter conveyed the property to Thomas Duthie in 1774 very shortly before his death.   William Duthie, his heir, conveyed it to Joseph Finlayson in 1778, and William Stirling acquired it from him in 1817.

(6) The sixth property consisted of three roods of land in Ramoyle which was conveyed by James Stirling, wheelwright, to William Stirling in 1820.

(7) Mr. Stirling in 1818 acquired the property of Backcroft and part of Howmiln and Howmilnhead from the Earl of Kinnoull by excambion.

(8) By a process of straightening of marches William Stirling acquired some land in 1820.

(9) Property was also bought by Mr. Stirling in 1820 and consisted of a large barn, yard and upper garden conveyed by Alexander McGregor of Balhaldie to John Rob, Jun., in 1781. This building and ground was in all probability situated to the east of the road to Mintoch Mire opposite Balhaldie House.

(10) Property consisted of the meeting house of the Anti-Burghers, afterwards known as the East United Secession Congregation when the union took place between Burghers and Anti-Burghers. The property had at one time belonged to Robert Keltie, hammerman in Dunblane. It was acquired by James Stirling of Holmehill from the Church Managers in 1849.

(11) A property was acquired by William Stirling in 1819 from Janet Miller, widow of William Burn, mason. It was situated where the south wing of the old school of Dunblane stands on the east side of Braeport with the property of Daniel Stewart to its south and Howmiln on the east.

From the Titles of Holmehill one learns that James Burns acquired from Robert Taylor in 1739 the northmost half of Mercer's Croft consisting of one and a half acres of arable land on the north side of Ramoyle—that is the side next the Laighills, described as being between two great green baulks. The southmost half of Mercer's Croft belonged at one time to the first Lord Strathallan. It lay to the west of the teind barn which is understood to have stood where Shaw's Buildings now stand, with other land of Lord Strathallan on the west.

Another portion of ground acquired by Holmehill consisted of part of the yard previously attached to the Manse of Abernethy and bounded by Holmehill on the east. Abernethy Manse stood near Holmehill Lodge in Braeport. Thomas Duthie, jun., Notary Public, whose name appears in some of the titles, was the son of William Duthie, mason, and nephew of Thomas Duthie, writer and Sheriff-Substitute.

One of the prominent men in Dunblane at this time was Cornelius Stewart, who carried on a medical practice in Dunblane and district during the early portion of the 19th century. He resided in the three-storeyed house on the south side of Bridgend, and his garden lay across the street running down to the River Allan. He was known locally as "Corney." In his later years he is said to have been of round, stoutish build, with long grey hair and side whiskers. It was while he practised in Dunblane, that the bad epidemic of cholera occurred which principally affected one side of the High Street of Dunblane, and it was he who ordered fires of tar to be lit in the street to prevent the spreading of the disease to the other side. The epidemic proved very fatal, and the custom of tolling the church bells for funerals was departed from. It is said that when Dr. Stewart was called to a case of cholera his first act was to take measurements of the patient for his coffin.

He was held in high esteem throughout a wide district. In January, 1837, at a dinner given in his honour he was presented by residenters in the Lecropt district with a silver snuff box which was the usual token of public appreciation handed to public men at this time. The people of Dunblane in July, 1837, followed the precedent of Lecropt and presented Dr. Stewart with a horse and gig and his wife with a purse of sovereigns. According to his tombstone in the Cathedral churchyard Dr. Cornelius had a number of sons and daughters, one of whom was Dr. John Stewart, sometime doctor in Doune and afterwards in Bannockburn. During the controversy over the efficacy of the Cromlix mineral waters, an essay on the mineral springs was published by another son, Dr. Peter Gordon Stewart. The essay was attacked in the press in a bitter article by an anonymous writer, said to have been a John Rae, surgeon in Stirling. Dr. John Stewart of Doune replied in forcible language in which he did not hesitate to express his opinions of Mr. Rae. Dr. Peter Gordon Stewart practised in Auchterarder for 10 years prior to emigrating to Cape Town in 1850. He was entertained in Auchterarder to a public dinner before he sailed. He had a successful career at Cape Town, being a member of the council of the Medical Board of that town, but he died in 1883 at the age of 62. He purchased the property of Fernbank in Dunblane, where his maiden sisters, his brother Daniel, who had been for some time in western Canada, and his orphan niece, Dora, lived latterly. Dr. Cornelius had four daughters, two of whom married and left Dunblane, the other two remaining unmarried. In March, 1850, Cornelius Stewart, Junior, surgeon, a son or a grandson of the old doctor, delivered in Dunblane three lectures on electricity, the study of which had made little progress in Scotland up to this time and little was known of it by the public.

Miss Dora or Dorothea Gordon Stewart acquired the property of Fernbank from her maiden aunts. She taught music for some time in Dunblane and, prior to 1881, acted as organist at Dunblane Cathedral. When she resigned this post she was presented with a clock which is now in the Cathedral Hall. A story is related with regard to Daniel Stewart. A large root of a tree had stuck on the dam dyke in the River Allan below Dunblane Cathedral which he coveted for a rockery in the garden in Bridgend. One night about 10 p.m. he took a garden fork and proceeded to push the root over the dam and down the river, taking advantage of the current. While engaged in this operation he was observed and a report spread that someone was murdering a man in the river. People gathered on the banks and the police appeared, but, when the facts were ascertained, assistance was given to Stewart to take the root down to a point opposite his garden and to land it safely there.

The resident Sheriff-Substitute in Dunblane at the beginning of the 19th century was John Coldstream, son of the talented schoolmaster of Dunblane, who was appointed in 1789. He was succeeded by George Baillie, the son of a cotton manufacturer, born in Paisley in 1784 and brought up in Glasgow. Sheriff Baillie wished to follow a mercantile life, but his father, who is described as having been intelligent, but eccentric, made him a lawyer. After practising in Glasgow for some time as a writer, he accepted the office of Sheriff-Substitute in 1823, his salary then being £200. Sheriff Baillie found that local court procedure was very dilatory and this led him into conflict with the local Bar, leading to his resignation in 1829. He thereafter travelled extensively for 12 years and kept a journal of his experiences in 34 volumes. It was due to him that the Law Library of Glasgow Faculty was founded in 1817. In 1863 he transferred his savings to the Glasgow Faculty as an endowment to form free libraries and free schools. His portrait, painted in 1865, is hung in the Faculty Library. He died in 1873.

Sheriff Hugh Barclay was his successor. He was the youngest son of John Barclay, a Glasgow merchant, and was born in 1799. He was apprenticed to Mr. George Baillie, and from 1821 to 1829 he practised as a writer in Glasgow. He succeeded Sheriff Baillie at Dunblane on his retiral. After four years residence in Dunblane he was transferred to Perth. He was greatly interested in Sunday School work and acted as a teacher for over 60 years, and for a long period he represented the Presbytery of Perth at the General Assembly. He was one of the founders of the Infirmary at Perth. In 1868 he was presented with his portrait, silver plate and £500. He retired in 1883 after serving 54 years on the bench and he died in the year following. His successor at Dunblane was William H. Colquhoun whose stay in Dunblane was likewise a short one. He left in 1837. A public dinner was given in his honour in Kinross' Inn, the chairman being Thomas Barty, the Procurator-Fiscal, and the croupiers, Mr. Bain, a well-known local lawyer, who resided in Balhaldie House, and Mr. McAra, the Sheriff Clerk, who resided in the Union Bank House. Sixty persons attended the dinner, the proceedings commencing at 5.30 p.m. and continuing till after 11 p.m.

Sheriff Colquhoun's successor was Sheriff John P. Trotter, who was only two years in Dunblane. He was followed by Andrew Cross, who, like Sheriffs Baillie and Barclay, had previously practised as a writer in Glasgow. Sheriff Cross was described as a man " talented and of urbane manners." He lived in St. Blane's House, was of a religious disposition and at the Disruption became a strong supporter of the Free Church. His son, Andrew Cross, was one of the earliest and one of the most successful tea planters in Ceylon, while a daughter, Miss Margaret Cross, became a missionary in India.

There were about this time four lawyers in Dunblane, namely, Thomas Barty, Procurator-Fiscal, James Bain, already mentioned, and Andrew Malloch and John MacGruther, all of whom seem to have had considerable business. William Stirling, writer and Procurator-Fiscal in Dunblane, died in 1829. At the time of his death clients owed him £1,044 for business charges, which indicates that he must have had a prosperous business. When Andrew Malloch died in 1838 his business creditors were divided as follows :—good for payment 101, dubious 119, very dubious 135, desperate 113.

An examination of the Commissary record books of 100 years ago indicates that there were few estates recorded of any value and those recorded seldom exceeded £1,000. It is interesting to notice how money was invested at that time compared with the present day. Now money is put into Government or Corporation loans or invested in the shares of Limited Companies, but at the time under consideration there were few such opportunities and, if money was not kept in the bank, it was usually lent on bill, frequently to the local landowners. Kincardine-in-Forth was in the district of this court, and the persons whose estates are to be found in the Commissary books are principally shipowners or ropemakers, and their means principally consisted of shares in a sloop or perhaps in several boats.

An old cash book of the Anti-Burgher congregation in Dunblane commencing 27th May, 1809, has been preserved. It may be mentioned that the Ramoyle was sometimes referred to as the Fore Road and the district from the Holmehill Road by Bogside and Backcroft was commonly called the Back o' the Toon. It appears that at this time a property had been purchased for the meeting house, the price being £70. Considerable repairs were required to the property, and the thatch of the meeting house was sold to two purchasers for £1 9s. The Rev. Mr. Wallace was then minister of this congregation. He went in June, 1809, on a mission to Paisley which contributed £21 9s. 4d. at an expenditure on Mr. Wallace's behalf of £1 1s. At later dates Mr. Wallace visited Stirling and elsewhere, receiving further collections to assist his congregation. Only a few seat-rents appear in the treasurer's books, but various donations from time to time are recorded, such as £100 from John Wilson, wheelwright, Dunblane. Dr. Stewart was on several occasions the instrument for handing over donations from sundry residenters. The congregation experienced difficulties, as it is observed that Mr. William Stirling, writer, Dunblane, was paid £3 7s. 6d. for conducting a law process. On one occasion wrights were given cash for drink money. David Young was sent to Methven and Kinkell to seek for help. He collected there £9 9s. 10d at an expense of 15s. There are no payments of stipend recorded, but Mr. Wallace had on one occasion to borrow £25. The congregation owned some property in Dunblane and there is a note of rents collected. In 1818 it had considerable sums to pay by way of interest on loans, but this seems to have been put right in the following year. Mr. Wallace had no manse given him and he had to pay rent for a house which belonged to his congregation. The latter borrowed £440 from the treasurer, Mr. Robert McRobie, which sum, however, was repaid him from a loan given by the Messrs. Hart. The book closes in 1826.

At the beginning of the 19th century a native of Dunblane, Malcolm Gillespie by name, had an adventurous career which terminated in a tragic death. His life story has been sketched by Mr. David Cuthbertson, University Library, Edinburgh. Gillespie, as a young man, appears to have had a strong desire to obtain a commission in the army, but, having no one to assist him, he joined a regiment at Stirling Castle as a private. He was afterwards engaged very successfully in recruiting young men for the army. While he was still hoping to get a commission he found himself in debt and being a married man he sought for some other opening for a career. He joined and remained in the Excise Force for 28 years, until his death. In 1799 he superintended the salt manufacturers at Prestonpans from which he was transferred to Aberdeen near which there was a strong force of smugglers, where his zeal in the performance of his duties told greatly on his health, he frequently remaining out all night to detect contraveners of the law. On one occasion, he tackled about 16 fishermen on their way from the Loch of Lossie, each carrying an anker of spirits and he was successful in capturing their whole cargo. Gillespie was a man of great courage and determination, but, in spite of his abilities and zeal, he was never given a superior position in the Excise. He was transferred in 1807 to Stonehaven and in 1812 to Skene, and some of his adventures with smugglers have been recorded. It is said that at Colliston he destroyed 17 illicit stills, at Skene 330 and at Stonehaven 20.

Gillespie took a lease of Crombie Cottage, Skene, with 18 acres of ground and spent £1,000 on repairs and equipment. His affairs became embarrassed which led him to forge a number of documents involving sums amounting to £230, and in 1827 he was convicted of these charges for which he suffered death at Aberdeen on 16th November, 1827.

Sir James Campbell, Laird of Kilbryde, died in 1812 and was succeeded by his son, Alexander, who had been resident in Jamaica for 39 years. Sir Alexander in 1816, at the age of 59, married Margaret Coldstream and had a family of one daughter and six sons. He died in 1824, his eldest son, James, succeeding him when he was only six years of age. As in the case of Kilbryde, the Laird of Kippendavie at this period was also under age. John Stirling, grandfather of the present laird, succeeded his father in 1816 at the age of 5 years.

At the beginning of the century the Laird of Cromlix was Francis John Hay Drummond, son of the 10th Earl of Kinnoull. He was drowned in the River Earn on Sunday, 28th October, 1810, while attempting to ford the river on horseback. Robert Hay Drummond, son of the 11th Earl of Kinnoull, owned Cromlix until his death in 1833, when he was succeeded by Arthur Hay Drummond, his brother. The latter survived until 1900.

The Lairds of Keir, in the early part of the 19th century, were James Stirling, who died in 1831, and his brother Archibald. James Stirling spent most of his life at Keir and took much interest in improving his property. Archibald Stirling, like some of the Stirlings of Kippendavie and younger sons of county families in the district, was a planter in Jamaica for nearly 25 years. He married Elizabeth Maxwell, second daughter of Sir John Maxwell of Pollok, in 1815. He took a great interest in breeding stock, particularly shorthorn cattle, as also in improving his estate. He was of a benevolent disposition and on occasions returned home minus his overcoat which he had bestowed on someone needier than himself. He was often known to return home on horse-back without his boots, which he had given to some poor person whom he had met on the road. He kept a meal girnel near his front door and, if any poor person called seeking food, he would supply him with meal at his own hand. The infant school at the foot of the Old Doune Road long kept by Miss Campbell, was built by him. In advance of her day, she introduced the teaching of singing in schools, as also physical training, both of which were derided by other teachers of her time. Archibald Stirling died suddenly in 1847 and was succeeded by Sir William Stirling Maxwell. Further information with regard to these proprietors is given elsewhere.

In 1830-31 there was a litigation between certain inhabitants of Dunblane and the heritors, which throws an interesting light on the west side of the Cross, Dunblane, but which litigation does not seem to have been proceeded with to a conclusion. A memorial to counsel submitted by the heritors deals with the ground in dispute. This memorial describes the buildings forming the west side as follows :—firstly, there was the two-storeyed house which contained Bishop Leighton's Library and, next to it, was attached the Old Manse of Dunblane, formerly the Dean's House. The approach to the entrance door of the Old Manse was through an archway commencing at the foot of the stair to the Library which lay partly along the wall of the Library building, and partly along the wall of the Old Manse—Until a few years previous to this date the stair had stood at right angles to the Library building. Beyond the Dean's Manse were two old houses of two storeys in height attached to the Manse. These were the two properties which were bought by Dr. Grierson, minister of the Cathedral, and were sold by him to the heritors, to be added into the property of the Manse. These properties and the Dean's Manse were all in line. Continuing beyond Dr. Grierson's houses and in line therewith, was the house of Robert Moir, which at the beginning of the 20th century was owned and occupied by William Cowper, joiner, and is now the property of the Kirk Session of Dunblane. At one time this house belonged to John Maule, joiner, a leading member of the United Presbyterian Church (Leighton Church), who, it is understood, married a daughter of Moir. The furthest north property on the west side of the Cross—that is beyond Robert Moir's house—was that of John Millar which, however, was not in line with the other buildings. It was also a two-storeyed house and its back wall was nearly in line with the front wall of Moir's house. A run-channel ran from Millar's house in a nearly straight direction past all the other premises till it reached the outside stair of the Library.

There was thus left an area of ground bounded by this run-channel on the east, the south gable of Millar's house on the north and the front walls of Moir's house, Dr. Grierson's houses and the Old Manse on the west, forming a triangular area, over which the dispute arose. This area was covered at the Library corner by the new stair, and at other parts by portions of causeway laid down by Dr. Grierson and by a loupin-on stane—for mounting one's horse.

The two old houses of Dr. Grierson had outside stairs to the upper storeys at right angles with the front wall, the northmost stretching to the run-channel and the other to within a foot of it. The houses had previously belonged to a man McLaren who used the space between the two stairways as a dung-hill, and the space between the northmost stair and Robert Moir's house served the same purpose. At an earlier date, there was a shop in front of the northmost part of Dr. Grierson's property, used at one time by a shoemaker and later by a saddler, which extended almost to the run-channel, with gable-end towards the street, but with a stone seat belonging to the owner between the gable and the run-channel.   This property also belonged at one time to John Millar above-mentioned, a saddler in Dunblane, who disponed it to Duncan McLaren, who sold it to Dr. Grierson.   The two projecting stairs of Dr. Grierson's properties were pulled down in the summer of 1830.

The heritors were anxious to build a wall extending from the Library stair to a point at right angles to the north boundary of what were Dr. Grierson's properties in a line with the front of Millar's house.   After laying the foundation of the intended wall, they were stopped by an interdict from the Sheriff-Substitute obtained at the instance of some of the inhabitants, whose plea was that the proposed wall would be an encroachment on the market place.   It was alleged that 20 or 30 years previous an old wife was in the habit of selling crockery on fair days, which happened four times a year, in front of the Old Manse between the loupin-on stane, and the first stair to the north, and that to the south of the loupin-on stane, a person or persons were in the habit of selling riddles.   Such usages had been given up a considerable number of years earlier.   It was also stated that in 1831 the fairs at Dunblane had dwindled away to nothing, although it was admitted that crockery and wooden dishes were exposed for sale on these dates in front of the Jail, which then stood to the east of the Cathedral gate. It seems that the loupin-on stane was an accessory to the Manse.

The heritors sought the advice of Andrew Rutherford, advocate, as their counsel, and he advised that, although the ground in question was probably private property, the circumstances were not conclusive and he advised the heritors to consider whether their interest in the ground was of sufficient importance to induce them to enter on an expensive litigation in which success was far from being certain.

As has been stated, the action does not seem to have been proceeded with.   If it had been, interesting features of local life and history would probably have been preserved in the evidence.

Chapter XXXVI.

KILBRYDE IN BY-PAST DAYS.

THE charms of Kilbryde are known to the inhabitants of Dunblane. They have walked by its burn and marked the awakening of spring to the song of the lark and the mavis. They have watched the worker in the harvest field, and gazed lingeringly on the foliage lit with the golden tints of autumn. But it may be they passed by flowers, stones, trees, which, had they known, had stories to tell, back from the Ice Age to modern times—stories of crime, love, hate, of tragedy and comedy, of persons high and noble as well as low and noble, of church and fair now long forgotten, of busy life where all is now so quiet and peaceful.

In a field there stand high two lumps of rock—once one—borne thither on a barge of ice perhaps from a mountain side 100 miles away, or, some say, from across the ocean. There, under the friendly arm of a thorn hedge, appears each summer a little flower, to recall to us the tailor's garden where, round the thatched cottage with its honeysuckle, bairns spent happy summer days. There is the spot on the knowe above the burn where green-coated fairies were seen and heard by the miller's daughter ; while not far off is Mattie's Pool, where poor Mattie, the weaver, whose brain became clouded with religious doubts, was drowned.

When we reach the Castle the very air is filled with romance. In the glen below are seen myriads of daffodils, which, tradition says, speak of their first planting by the youthful Mary Queen of Scots and her companions. Not far away is the Wife's Lynn, which tells, in a silent voice, of the women law-breakers who came there to their doom. We pass a wood, a home of the smugglers, from which, at the dead of night, stole forth 30 horsemen with loaded saddle. The circle of trees on the hill reminds us of thieves left to dangle from the gallows. Here and there are grassy patches and stones strewn around, all that remain of happy homes, whither the bridegroom brought his bride, where they spent a simple, happy time until, at the last, they were laid in peace in the old kirkyard, within hearing of the soothing voice of the burn and the song of the birds overhead. It is about such half-forgotten things and days that this is written.

The conditions of life at Kilbryde about 100 years ago are of considerable interest. One striking circumstance is that the district was able to supply its whole wants from within its own bounds. The pendiclers as well as the farmers kept a considerable head of cattle, and on some of the farms, even those now almost solely devoted to the rearing of sheep, 70 cattle, including 20 or 30 milk cows, were formerly kept, and a very considerable amount of butter and cheese was made, not only to supply the wants of the inhabitants, but to bring in revenue from sale in Stirling and elsewhere. Thus, 40 cheese might be seen in the smithy dairy alone, made from the milk of a few cows kept by the smith. The principal articles of diet were porridge, broth, salt meat, potatoes, oatcakes, and cheese. Wheaten flour was in rare use, barley scones and oat cakes taking the place of these, the barley and oats being, of course, grown at home. Latterly the old people had their cup of tea, and a wheaten loaf would be produced in honour of a visitor, but except on rare occasions, all the foodstuffs were produced on the holding. Similarly articles of clothing and linen were made at home ; the farmers' wife and daughter spun the wool, and also the lint or flax grown on the holding, and a local weaver converted the spinnings into cloth, while a local shoemaker made and mended the footgear of the community. Even the blankets were made locally. The evenings were spent by the light of the fire with the help of tallow candles made by the good wife. The children attended the local school for learning. The schoolmaster, who was usually a lad who had not long previously completed his education, received board and lodging at the various farms, where he resided in rotation for a week or two at a time. Part of his salary appears to have come out of the teinds, and probably a part from the laird's pocket, while parents of children in attendance paid certain fees. The pupils brought the peats for the schoolhouse fire. Peats were in universal use, although supplemented by coal. There were no matches in these days, but the kitchen fire was never out. If through carelessness this occasionally happened, the maid had to proceed to an adjoining farm to borrow part of their fire with which to re-kindle her own.   Although the inhabitants travelled little from home, life was not dull.   Many were proficient in the playing of the fiddle, and there were frequent gatherings at one house or another in the winter evenings for dancing.   In the smithy or one of the farmhouses 30 or 40 young people met and spent a winter evening in this way.   On the opposite side of the road from the smithy was a curling pond, where the Kilbryde folk indulged in the national game during frosty weather.   The usual means of locomotion was by foot or on horseback.   Some of the farmers subscribed for newspapers, and these were passed from one household to another, while letters were brought from Dunblane on horseback.   It is said that in the olden times as many as 30 horsemen would be waiting the arrival of the mail at Dunblane to carry the letters home to country houses.   When a wedding took place at a distance the bridegroom's friends went on horseback, and accompanied the married couple to their new home, there being sometimes a race thither, with an award of prizes to the first arrivals.   The scene in the harvest field was an animated one in the days when mechanical reapers and binders were undreamt of, and many hands were required, for each man who used a scythe or heuk had several assistants in attendance, some making ropes of straw for tying the sheaves, others lifting the corn and binding the sheaves together.

In the earlier days at Kilbryde and elsewhere, the crops were reaped by the sickle or heuk, an implement still used by roadmen in cutting the grass on the sides of the roads.   The form of heuk was teethed—that is it had a saw edge.   The blades were like a file with a fine edge like the cutting edge of a triangular file.   As the implement soon lost its edge and as it was almost impossible to renew it, it was replaced by the scythe-edged heuk which was a much more useful implement.

In autumn, bands of harvest workers called shearers or thraivers came from the Highlands or from Ireland to the midlands of Scotland to work at the harvest.   Thirty men might be seen cutting a crop of grain, each thraiver having a rig of corn allotted to him, and working from side to side.   He cut the grain, gathered it together against his leg, and when he had a sheaf he tied it together with his ropes.   He was attended by a man called a banster who was employed to put the sheaves together into stacks, the stacks consisting of twelve sheaves in each case and two stacks made a thraive.   The shearer or thraiver was paid by the number of his thraives. The duty devolved on the banster to see that the sheaves were at full size.   This method of cutting corn continued in the neighbourhood of Dunblane until the middle of the nineteenth century.

Cutting by the heuk was replaced by scythe-cutting when the scythe-man was attended by a lifter—generally a woman—who gathered the grain into sheaves, by a youngster who made the ropes and a banster who tied the bands of the sheaves and put them into stacks.

In these days labour was cheap, and the services of a man could be procured for the harvest season for a sum of £3.

The Kirk of Kilbryde being in a state unfit for worship, and no services being provided there, the inhabitants walked to Dunblane or Lecropt, and it was the custom to carry infants to Dunblane for baptism.   Whether from motives of economy or from a dislike of having their feet cramped, the Kilbryde folk walked barefooted to near the site now occupied by Springbank Mills, carrying their best Sunday shoes and stockings, which they donned before reaching Dunblane, their menfolk meantime passing on.   In some cases old shoes were worn and hid in a hedge, while the owners, in the glory of their best footwear, proceeded to church.   Besides their homespun garments, the farmers' wives and daughters had each a silk gown, and it is noted that the cost of making one in Stirling in the year 1838 was 4s. 6d.   The ladies, when attired in their best, also wore a lace veil, perhaps costing £1 1s. or more.   At the beginning of last century the men never wore caps, but commonly a tall hat of a greyish or snuff colour.   Family worship was conducted by the farmer every evening, and on the Sunday evenings the farm servants were also present when he catechized the company, beginning with his wife.   The Sabbath was then a day of rest, and everything was prepared the night before, even the water required was fetched from the spring.   In these days servants remained in one situation for a lifetime, and maids frequently dropped their surname and were known by that of their employer.   The relationship of laird and tenant was intimate and friendly. Thus Sir James Campbell, in the eighteenth century, visited all his tenants regularly, as did also the members of his family, who were numerous and probably not overfed, and they partook heartily of the farmers' cheese and scones.   This laird was even known to help himself to a potato from the pot on the fire.   When any emergency arose it was to the laird that the farmer went for advice.

Kilbryde smithy was the scene of much activity.   Several smiths were employed regularly, and 40 ploughs, sent from many miles around, might be seen at one time, awaiting repair.   The Laird of Argaty alone kept 21 horses, which were all sent to the smithy for shoeing.   He rode much on horseback, and went about the countryside attended by men servants in powdered wigs and white stockings.   A hundred years ago most of the corn was threshed with flails—that is, a heavy stick, attached to a wooden staff by a thong—and the corn was afterwards riddled.   Threshing of corn was done frequently in the mornings in winter.   Apart from milk, the principal drink was whisky, probably secretly distilled.   One illicit still was in the Tod Holes Wood, on the opposite side of the road which leads to the moor past the Gallows Hill.   The inhabitants were, no doubt, privy to the existence of such stills and, indeed, gave assistance thereat ; and on a fixed night, about 2 a.m., a number of horsemen would gather for the purpose of conveying away whisky to some neighbouring town.   It is said that on one occasion the excise officers captured 50 men engaged in removing spirit, and if this be true it would probably mark the destruction of the still for good.   Another still was situated beside a burn which joins the Kilbryde Burn at the north-west corner of the rabbit warren at Stromavane.   The old road which crossed the Kilbryde Burn at the head of Kilbryde Glen, and proceeded past Heather Jock's House and down to Doune by Lerrocks and Argaty, was known as The Smugglers' Road (it was probably in general use for conveying sheep and cattle to the fairs at Doune), while high up on the moor, on the slopes of Slimaback, there was a fair-sized cottage, near the march with Cromlix, which was known as the Smugglers' Bothy.

In these days beggars were confined to their own districts, and were licensed to beg throughout the parish.   They were frequently aged persons unfit for work, or weak-minded, and were not of the broken-down or lazy type with which the name is now more associated.   When they called at a farm they received a kindly reception, and were given food and a bed of straw in the barn.   Blankets were kept for their use, and washed with those of the household at the blanket-washing season.

Only vague recollections exist as to the hanging of persons at the Gallows Hill, but one inhabitant can remember of hearing of one such case, but cannot recollect the name of the culprit or the crime for which he suffered, and another narrates a tradition that three young lads were at one time hanged for stealing bonnets.   It is said that the laird had a pit or dungeon for confining persons in the Castle, below the scullery, and this is no doubt true, as all barons were ordained to provide a prison, and were under obligation to provide a window for such, enabling anyone to see the interior of the apartment from outside.   It is understood that there was an underground passage from the dungeon in Kilbryde Castle to the side of the Kilbryde Burn, near where there is a gate across the Glen Path, to the south-east of the Castle, which passage terminated at the waterside at the pool known as the Wife's Lynn.   It is probable that in ancient days, if capital punishment was to be inflicted on a woman, she would be taken to this pool and drowned there, and this would account for the name of the Lynn.

At the door of Kilbryde Castle formerly stood a stone, which was known as The Loupin'-on Stone, the use of which was to assist a lady to mount on horseback.   A wall then surrounded the Castle, while a short distance down the avenue there was a tree, known as the Bell Tree, on which a bell was hung, and probably rung morning and evening to denote to the inhabitants the hour of day and night.   A cottage near the church was occupied at one time by a man known as the bellman, but whether he rang the bell at the Castle or perambulated the district giving the inhabitants public notice of important events, or whether he rang a bell for use in connection with church affairs is unknown.   The bellman, however, existed long after the parish of Kilbryde was amalgamated with Dunblane, and when a beadle was no longer required.

The laird at the beginning of the 19th century, Sir James Campbell, sought to improve his estate.   He encouraged his tenants to enclose their lands by building dykes, undertaking to pay for them at the end of the lease or charging 7½ per cent. on the cost where he erected them; 6 per cent. was charged on the cost of erecting palings, making ditches or planting hedges.

Kilbryde had, as most villages had, what was called a Mortcloth Society; and the minute book, with records of meetings from 1758, is still preserved.   The committee usually met at The Green, or at the Kirkton.   They made arrangements for lairs, for the burial of the inhabitants, charging small fees for them, the funds being expended on the upkeep of the churchyard. The chapel dyke was repaired in 1806, and in 1839 a new dyke was erected, at the cost of £2 5s. 2d. Presumably the stone was at hand, as the cost at the present time of erecting a new wall there might amount to £200. Another illustration of the inexpensiveness of manual labour is seen from an item in the blacksmith's account in 1782 for making a new key for a lock and fitting it, which was 2d.

The local farmers founded an Agricultural Society in 1842. For some years they held an annual ploughing match, followed by a dinner, and each year they appointed a committee to examine the green crops on the various farms and the stackyards, and the committee thereafter submitted a report, awarding prizes to the best crops. The first show of farm stock was held in 1842, but the existing records terminate in 1847. In that year the income of the Society was £4, and the expenditure as follows :—Prizes, £1 10s ; dinners, £2 10s ; and liquor, £1 10s. The rents in these days were in many cases higher than at the present time, but in some cases it is difficult to compare them, as the money payment was comparatively small, and the tenant had services to perform and goods to deliver in return for his farm. Thus, in a lease to John Anderson of Dalbrack Farm in 1775, his rent was fixed at £15, and he had also to contribute to the laird 8 bolls of oatmeal, 18 hens or pay 6d. for each hen not delivered, 12 " throavhs " of straw, and 35 loads of peat or pay 1d for each load not delivered, as also to winter two cows for the laird or pay 3s. 4d. for each. He had also to pay his share of minister's stipend and schoolmaster's salary, and he was bound to take all his grain to Kilbryde Mill. Further, he had to plough, manure, harrow, cut, and lead in the laird's crop. In 1839 John Cameron of Easter Bows was bound to deliver a stone of butter and 12 good fowls, and to drive 340 stones of coal or pay 1d for each stone not driven. It may be of interest to note that about 100 years ago the price of a sheep was 18s. and of a lamb or a pig 7s, that meat was purchased at 4d or 5d a pound, eggs cost 5d a dozen, and cheese 4½d. a pound; a pair of shoes cost 5s in 1828, and in the valuation of a deceased farmer's estate blankets were assessed at 1s per pair. While this would not be the full value, probably that would not exceed 3s 6d. At Bows Farm in 1832 ewes and lambs were valued at 7s 6d, rams at 8s, cows at £4 and mares at £9.

There is probably no old Castle in Scotland that has not traditions connected with it of murders committed within its walls, and of ghosts that frequented its neighbourhood, and Kilbryde is no exception to this. Ghosts have been seen at Kilbryde from time to time, according to the statements of persons whose word can, as a rule, be relied on. Thus, a gamekeeper, MacGregor, on one occasion, heard someone knocking at a window of the Castle, and, looking up, saw a strange face at the window. He obtained the assistance of the gardeners, and made a thorough search of the Castle, armed with his gun with which to lay low the spirit, or at least protect himself, but all trace of the ghost had vanished. One of the ghosts that inhabited Kilbryde district was known as the White Lady of Kilbryde; and an old blacksmith used to say that he often saw her, but when he spoke to her, she melted away out of sight. She was usually seen in the neighbourhood of the chapel. In the old Castle of Kilbryde, in a back passage where three steps led up to a room now demolished, it used to be alleged that blood was to be seen on the stone, and that at that place a lady had been murdered. It is strange that there are two stories as to a murder involving one member of the Kilbryde family and one of the Cromlix. One is to the effect that a daughter of the Castle used to go to Kilbryde Glen and cross the burn at the stepping stones and meet one of the sons of the Cromlix family, who came across the moor to meet her, and that the lady was eventually murdered. The other story is in almost identical terms, with the exception that the murdered lady is of the Cromlix family, and her lover is of Kilbryde. It is improbable that two such murders were committed, and probably the latter version is the correct one, as it has been preserved in greater detail and the names of the lady and murderer are recorded. The story is narrated in *Historic Scenes of Perthshire*, also in Monteath's *Traditions of Dunblane* and, according to his version, a young lady of the Cromlix family named Lady Anne Chisholm fell in love with Sir Malise Graham, called the " Black Knight of Kilbryde," but, after some time, he, tiring of her, foully murdered her in the Glen of Kilbryde, and hastily buried her at the scene of the crime. A slight variation of the story is to the effect that she had not been decoyed hither by the Black Knight, but that, when riding on the Cromlix Moor, or perhaps when hawking, her pony had run away with her and had carried her towards Kilbryde. Following upon the disappearance of the lady, every effort was made to trace

Q

her fate. The rumour soon spread that the neighbourhood of the Castle was haunted by a ghost arrayed in the white robes of death sullied with blood. The spirit of the murdered lady was said to have been frequently seen beckoning to inmates of the Castle to approach, but no one to whom she appeared had courage to have converse with her. After the death of Sir Malise in battle, one of his successors welcomed the opportunity of coming in contact with the ghost, who saluted him one dark evening at his garden gate and beckoned to him to follow. This he did, and the spirit led him to the Glen below the Castle, to the spot where the Black Knight had slain and buried his sweetheart. Having marked the place, the knight returned next day, and had the remains of the lady of Cromlix removed for Christian burial, and the troubled spirit was at the same time laid to rest. There seems good ground for holding that no Sir Malise Graham ever owned Kilbryde. Prior to 1643 the property was owned by the Earls of Menteith, except when held by Sir John Graham.

Fairies were not unknown at Kilbryde and neighbourhood in the olden days. One resident can recollect coming home one night, and, as she approached the house, seeing a room lit up, and on peering through the window she saw fairies inside, but when she clapped her hands the light went out and the fairies hastened away. A Kilbryde farmer, many years ago, while on the Stirling road near Keir, met a big company of fairies playing bagpipes. His horse would not go past them, but when he clapped his hands they disappeared. The fairies at Kilbryde chiefly frequented the knowe, above the Kilbryde Burn, not far from the old mill wheel of the meal mill. The daughter of the last meal miller used to tell how she had heard them dancing and singing at the Fairies' Knowe. Monteath in his *Dunblane Traditions* relates that the fairies were more dreaded at Kilbryde than the devil and his witches, and it was supposed that they were permitted to kidnap one-tenth of all unchristened children from their mother's side. It is related that at Brighills, Kilbryde, there resided at one time a solitary pedlar named Scobie, who earned his livelihood by trucking with the fairies. One night he had been with his pack at a farmhouse when he appeared fay-like. The farmer accompanied him part of the way home, and when taking leave of him invited him to return with him as some strange noises were heard. Next morning he was missing, and it was universally believed that the fairies had carried him off, pack and all. Dr. Ure, the warlock, was consulted. Dressed in leather breeches, green-sleeved coat, and red nightcap, with his witch book and black art stick, the doctor proceeded to ascertain the pedlar's fate. He shook with terror, but on recovering said in a piteous voice, " He's awa' wi' the fairies. Ye'll find his corpse in a little glen within sight of the Chapel of Kilbryde." Many little glens were sought in vain, but Scobie's body was at last found some months later in what is still known as Scobie's Wood. It is not recorded what was the fate of the poor pedlar's pack, but it was not the fairies who got it.

In these days there were many weak-witted persons, for whom little consideration was shown. Many such a one came to an untimely end through the superstition and ignorance then current, when sickness or misfortune was attributed to the evil eye, or to the maliciousness of some benighted person whose mental capacity was so affected that he (or she) was incapable of defending himself, or of proving his innocence. It is related that two old women used to be left at the Drum Wood, overlooking Kilbryde, chained, the object perhaps being to prevent them wandering away and being either lost or doing themselves injury, but it seems somewhat extraordinary that no kinder method could be devised for taking care of persons so afflicted.

Kilbryde has also its story of hidden treasure. Many have searched in the Glen of Kilbryde in the hope of tracing it. The key of the chest was found many years ago by a dog at the mouth of a conduit down at the Rowans Stalk, not far from the tree from which one of the young Campbells fell and was killed when bird-nesting. The key is carefully preserved, and will be available if the chest containing the treasure is ever found. It used to be related that in the time of the Grahams, when a warlike chieftain was soon to fall in battle fighting for his country, or in strife with some other clan, his apparition might be seen at the darkening about Kilbryde Glen, while the galleries of the Castle were filled with the wailings of spirits foretelling the mournful event which was drawing near.

A few notes may be of interest regarding a notorious character who long held the neighbourhood of Kilbryde in dread, namely, Heather Jock, or John Fergusson, thief and poacher, who lived for a time at the pendicle of Shank by the Paffray Burn and later in a small thatched cottage near a burnside between Dalbrack Farmhouse and the old farm buildings of Towrie. The site

7

rof the house is still pointed out.   An old road from Cromlix to Doune passed near his cottage, and as it is said that he was born beside the Old Doune Road, it is possible he may have been born in the house in which he so long resided with his mother.   It is not known how he acquired his name, and the suggestion that it was because his hair resembled a heather besom seems far-fetched.   It is more probable that it was derived from his residing amongst the heather, and from his obtaining his livelihood there.   He was accustomed to come to Dunblane to purchase ammunition for his gun, and it is said that he was so notorious that half the population turned out to see him go by.   He seems to have been a skilled shot, and at the matches held on Hansel Monday he carried off the chief prizes.   His mother probably had a miserable existence, and eventually she hanged herself.   A gruesome story is told that, with the rope used by his mother for this purpose, Jock sometime after led home a stolen cow. The owners of the cow, who had followed it to Jock's house, found it shut up in a press bed. They proceeded to remove it home, and he apparently allowed them to do so without inter- ference, except to demand the rope, which he refused to part with, as it was the one used by his mother.   After a long period of crime, he was tried in April, 1812, by the High Court in Stirling for cattle stealing.   He pled guilty, and was sentenced to transportation for life.   It is related that he escaped from Botany Bay, but was recaptured and sent back.   Henderson, the game- keeper at Kilbryde, was a near relative of Heather Jock, and it is said that the shackles put on his wrists were forged at the smithy of Kilbryde by ancestors of the late smith.   He seems to have so far observed the Sabbath by abstaining from his crimes on that day, and devoting himself to music, he being an expert fiddler.

His clock, the works of which are entirely of wood, is still preserved at Kilbryde.   Heather Jock's exploits are all recorded in a well-known song, the authorship of which is disputed.   It is claimed by some to have been written by a Dr. James Stirling, born at Biggings, Keir, who emigrated in the first half of last century to Ontario, where he died in 1857.   Dr. Stirling started life in a draper's shop in Perth, and on one occasion surprised the inhabitants of Dunblane by riding through the town on a " wudden horse "—no doubt a forerunner of the modern bicycle. He afterwards studied medicine in Edinburgh and Paris.   The authorship is also claimed for William Morrison, the first beadle of the Free Church of Doune.

It may be fitting to conclude with the quotation of the following touching verses on the Churchyard of Kilbryde, written by one long resident in the parish, and highly esteemed by all its inhabitants, the Rev. William Blair, D.D., minister of the Leighton United Free Church :

KILBRYDE KIRKYARD.

O bonnie grows the gowan in Kilbryde Kirkyard,
And red-cheekit is the rowan in Kilbryde Kirkyard ;
    But the gowans fade awa',
    An' the rowan berries fa',
When winter haps the graves in Kilbryde Kirkyard.

O the brae is stey and weary tae Kilbryde Kirkyard,
An' the brig is auld and eerie near Kilbryde Kirkyard ;
    'Twas the howff where witches met,
    Ere they forced the iron yett,
Tae keep their midnicht cantrips in Kilbryde Kirkyard.

The auld Castle folks lie sleepin' in Kilbryde Kirkyard,
An' Death his watch is keepin' in Kilbryde Kirkyard ;
    In the vaults are Knights an' Dames
    O' the Campbells an' the Graemes
O' Kilbryde and Aberuchil in Kilbryde Kirkyard.

Fu' sweet's the laverock's sang in Kilbryde Kirkyard,
When the summer day is lang in Kilbryde Kirkyard,
    Frae the sky she sends us hope
    That the sleepers eye shall ope
When the final trumpet clangs ower Kilbryde Kirkyard.

Chapter XXXVII.

AGRICULTURE AT THE BEGINNING OF THE 19th CENTURY.

By the early years of last century agriculture had made comparatively little progress in this district. The fields were to a large extent unfenced and much of the land was undrained consisting of bog and morass. A new interest in agriculture was, however, born at this time, perhaps to some extent due to the Napoleonic Wars. The grain crops then consisted chiefly of oats and barley, the latter being used principally for distilling whisky, but some wheat, beans and pease were also grown. In earlier days proprietors were wont to stipulate that all tenants planted a certain portion of their arable ground in pease on account of the beneficial effects this crop has on the soil. Among green crops, potatoes had chief place and these formed one of the principal sources of food supply of the community. The growing of turnips as a principal crop is referred to in books of the period as an innovation of recent date, and with the successful growing of this crop there spread the practice of feeding cattle within the farm buildings. Prior to this time sheep and cattle had a somewhat precarious existence during the winter months and, when spring came round, they were in a lean and half-starved condition. A plentiful supply of turnips solved the problem of winter feeding and enabled farmers to fatten the young animals and to keep their cattle in good condition, so that they improved rather than fell away during the winter months. Prior to this, the butcher had small supplies during the winter months and it was a common practice in the autumn for the householder to purchase a young cow for salting purposes to provide butcher meat for the winter.

One has to keep in view that at this time there were no railways or steamboats, few vehicles and few roads on which these could travel, no bicycles and no motor cars. Travelling from one place to another in the country could, as a rule, only be done on horseback or on foot. Country people went seldom from home unless it were on Sunday to the nearest church, or to attend an occasional fair at some neighbouring town. Horse and cattle markets were only held at intervals and the housewife seldom visited a town and shopping by post was unknown. The principal articles of food were porridge and cakes made from oatmeal, potatoes, eggs, cheese, butter, milk and salt meat, all of which were produced at home. Broth was made from the vegetables grown in the garden and whisky was produced from the barley grown in the fields. Tea and wheaten bread were luxuries partaken of only on special occasions. Linen was made from lint grown in the district and blankets from the wool of the sheep, while leather was tanned locally and, in the hamlet in this parish, shoemakers made their boots and shoes to be hawked later throughout the neighbourhood. At this time the farms carried many head of cattle, some having as many as 70, of which from 20 to 30 were milk cows. Much cheese was made in the district and as many as 40 cheeses, many of which were afterwards sold in Stirling, might be seen in the dairy of a small farm maturing on the shelves.

The lairds did much to encourage improvements on the farms. Tenants were urged to fence fields and were given allowances for fencing if they gave up their farms, while on some estates tenants were bound to plant a number of young trees yearly, which provided shelter and later supplied wood for repair of buildings and stobs for fencing. Attention was also devoted to the improvement of stock by breeding from good animals and considerable encouragement was given in this way by enlightened proprietors. The improvement of stock and of farming methods received assistance from local Agricultural Societies of which the earliest in this district was that of Dunblane, founded on 1st January, 1804, and originally known as the Strathallan Farmers Club. As the name indicates, the Society was more intimately connected at first with the north-easterly part of the parish, *i.e.*, in the neighbourhood of Greenloaning. The first President was an Ardoch man named William Anderson, the first Treasurer was Henry Monteath of Greenloaning, and the principal members were tenants about Feddal, Cambushinnie and Balhaldie. The Society was founded for the improvement of agriculture and its first active step was to institute a ploughing match. The first match took place in the spring of 1804, on the farm of Whitieston.   Each member of the Society paid 2s. 6d. towards the prize money and 5 prizes were offered ranging from 15s to 5s.   At this match 23 ploughs competed and the awards were made by persons selected from outside the parish.   The first prize-winner was Alexander Glass, servant to David Robertson, Hillside.   After the match the members of the Society dined at the house of James Bruce, Balhaldie—no doubt at the inn there—and the Society then appointed a committee of their own number to go round the farms of the members about June or July following and to report on the state of these farms.   The committee carried out their work very thoroughly and reported to the next meeting which was held on 10th July, 1804, at the house (or inn) of Henry Monteath, Greenloaning.   The committee had the assistance of Sheriff Coldstream as their Secretary and he continued to act during the remainder of his life, and there can be little doubt but that the lengthy reports submitted to the Society and engrossed in the minute book, which is still preserved, were of his composition.   Unfortunately, the reports are written, as a rule, in very general terms, although they sometimes deal with the different farms of the members individually.   While they usually commend the diligence and skill of the farmer, one finds frequent reference to the prevalence of sorrel, nettles and other weeds.   The Society, not content with having a report of the working of the land and the prospects of the crops, directed their committee to inspect the stackyards in the autumn of 1804 and to give a further report to the next general meeting to be held at James Bruce's house on 9th January, 1805.   At this meeting a new President was elected—Mr. Alexander Monteath, Cauldhame—and arrangements were made for the next ploughing match which was held on 4th March, 1805, when 30 ploughmen competed and increased prize money was offered.

At this time rules were drawn up for the government of the Society, one rule providing that the prize money for the ploughing match should be raised by a levy of 1s. from each member, along with fines imposed on members whose crops were deficient or whose land was over-run with weeds due to sloth or bad management.   The minute book and accounts fail to show any signs of the imposition of any such penalties, and, while fault is occasionally found with weedy land, the criticism is expressed in gentle terms.   Members, who were absent from meetings, were fined, the amount of the fine depending on whether the excuse given was a weighty one, but, whether absent or present, each member had to pay the price of his dinner.   Few members would care to miss their dinner when they had to pay for it whether they ate it or not.

At the general meeting on 24th June, 1805, the farms of the members were reported upon individually.   At this time considerable quantities of lime and marl were applied to the land, and the report indicates that the inspectors were of opinion that some farmers were over-liming their fields.   The next ploughing match was held on Christmas Day, 1805, and at the meeting following petitions were presented by Cornelius Stewart, surgeon in Dunblane, and others craving to be admitted members of the Society.   As it was thought that they would make " good and peaceable brothers," the Society duly admitted them.   Unfortunately, although the Society had existed for less than two years, differences of opinion arose at this meeting.   Certain members complained that, owing to the state of the weather and the want of proper intimation of the day of the match, no ploughs from the Loig district competed and the members from that neighbourhood suggested that a second ploughing match should be held for the benefit of the ploughmen in that part of the parish.   The Society did not admit that there was fault on their part and declined to arrange for a second match as contrary to their rules.   The dissenting members being still dissatisfied held a meeting amongst themselves, formed a separate committee and proceeded to arrange another ploughing match.   The Society instructed Sheriff Coldstream to write a letter of protest.   An attempt was made on 27th May following to effect a reconciliation, the members of the western district suggesting that bygones be bygones.   The dissenting brethren from the eastern district, however, declined to do so unless the expenses of the second ploughing match were paid by the whole Society.   No reconciliation, however, seems to have been effected.   The result of this dispute seems to have diverted the headquarters of the Society and its sphere of activities to the Dunblane district, and thereafter the farmers in the Keir, Lecropt and Bridge of Allan districts took a more prominent part in the Society's affairs.   It may be mentioned that, although professional men like Sheriff Coldstream and Dr. Stewart were members of the Society, these gentlemen had qualifications in respect that both cultivated acres of land within the territory of Dunblane.

Attention was drawn in 1807 to a new form of threshing mill invented by Mr. Monteath of

Harperstone which was driven by water power, and it is said that at that time Mr. Robb, farmer, Duthieston, had a mill in course of erection to be worked on the same principles.

There are many references to the fineness or badness of the seasons. Thus in 1807 the spring was late and the summer was cold and wet which led the committee to give way to moralisings. The following year was, however, propitious and the harvest abundant so that moral reflections were not required. The year 1810 is said to have been wonderfully good, both as regards weather and crops, but on the other hand 1811 was disastrous. The weather was continuously wet and from April till July and again between the middle of September and the end of October, when the harvest was due to be ingathered, there was not one dry day.

In most of the old records of Dunblane, such as those of the Kirk Session, references to national events, or even important local events, are very rare. The deaths of men of world-wide fame, as well as of those who had been pre-eminent in local history, pass unheeded, as also do the great events of history. This is not the case in the minutes of the Agricultural Society where there are constant references to the Napoleonic Wars, particularly between the years 1811 and 1815. Napoleon is referred to as a " crewel tyrant " and a " barbarous usurper." The praises of Britain as " the mighty island of the ocean where reigns the most complete system of liberty" are often sung, her prowess in war is praised and her pre-eminent virtues are regarded as inspiring admiration and envy among the other nations of Europe. The hope is expressed that the " downfall of that oppressor of the world will be accomplished by the indefatiguable exertions of Great Britain under heaven the grand instrument of ridding the world from the grip of this tyrenous usurper and restoring to it that peace, order and happiness which had as hitherto been in vain languaging after."

The society continued its course with little change for a considerable number of years. The ploughing match was the chief event of the year, followed, as it was, by the dinner attended by all the members and an evening spent in conviviality. After the first few years of its existence the Society held its functions in Dunblane either in the inn of John Sharp or in Kinross' Hotel, now known as the Stirling Arms. The lairds became interested members, particularly the Stirlings of Keir and Kippendavie and Dr. Henderson of Westerton, Bridge of Allan. The Society prided itself on the improvements effected in agriculture since its commencement, particularly in the amount of peat and moorland reclaimed. While about 1812 there was more land planted with wheat and lint than formerly, this does not seem to have been maintained, and this was attributed, in the case of lint, to the difficulty in getting seed.

About 1814 the discovery of mineral springs at Cromlix brought considerable prosperity to Dunblane for the generation to follow. Many persons were attracted to the district to partake of the waters. In the summer report of that year the Society's committee refer to the discovery and mention that numbers throng to drink the waters, while two eminent gentlemen, Dr. Murray and Dr. Ellis, were then engaged making an analysis which it was hoped would confirm its medicinal value. The Earl of Kinnoull was proprietor of Cromlix at the time and he had works executed for the preservation of " that precious fluid." The committee again refer in the following year to the crowds of strangers who have been coming from distant parts for a cure.

The victory of Waterloo is the subject of comments and appreciations extending over several closely-written pages of the minute book. Britain is referred to as mistress of the world and the French as " that restless, volatile unprincipalled people."

In November, 1815, the centenary of the Battle of Sheriffmuir was celebrated in the district, and the committee record that they had, with others, assembled on the Battlefield. France, as a supporter of the Jacobite rebellion, is described as " dead to all gratitude and alive to perfidy, envy and malignity towards Great Britain." The life of the King (George III) is referred to as one of virtues and excellencies beyond all praise, and it is said that Great Britain and all Europe owed gratitude to him for his beneficent reign. The final overthrow of Napoleon and the establishment of peace did not bring the blessings which were expected. 1816 saw a bad harvest with unprecedented falling away of manufactures and commerce. The price of food-stuffs rose quickly, while the poor had less means wherewith to buy them.

Sheriff Coldstream seems to have died about 1821 when he was succeeded as Secretary of the Society by James Bain, writer in Dunblane. The minutes of the Society become shorter with few comments on public affairs. A new departure was made at this time when a committee was formed in November, 1821, to prepare rules for a proposed show of stock. The first show took place on the farm of Barbush on the second Monday of June, 1822, more than 18 years after the Society had been founded. Prizes were given for the best and second best bull between two and seven years old, for the best and second best milk cow, for the best two-year old stot and quey and for the best brood mare. Prizes of £2 2s. and upwards were given. As the principal object of the show was to improve the breeding of stock, one of the rules was that owners of the prize bulls had to keep them available for breeding purposes at fees of 2s. and 2s. 6d. for a period of three months after the show. Of the seven prizes offered at the first show, James Stirling of Keir won four, Henderson of Craigarnhall two, and McVicars of Keirfield the other. In the following year Mr. Stirling of Keir gave a £5 5s. prize for the best bull and the number of prizes was increased to ten.

The show was gradually developed in various lines as years went on. The principal classes were, however, for cattle. Classes for sheep were introduced some time later, as also one for pigs in which there were, as a rule, no entries. The Lairds of Keir assisted the show and exhibited stock, but ceased to compete. For some time the dates of the show varied considerably, and in 1831 it was not held until 5th October. By 1834 the prize lists were more than doubled, although it was not until 1840 that prizes were offered for sheep, namely, for Leicester rams and ewes.

CHAPTER XXXVIII.

OLD MILLS, THE MARKET CROSS, AN OLD HOUSE AND THE WELLS OF
DUNBLANE.

THERE have been many mills on the banks of the Allan some of which existed centuries
ago. One of the earliest was the mill of Kinbuck. It was no doubt a meal mill in its earlier
days although for some considerable time it was used as a yarn or wool-spinning mill. The mill
at Ashfield was known as Mill of Ash, and it was not originally associated with the river. It was
used for various purposes at different times including the grinding of corn, as a lint mill when it
was occupied by a William Dow, and at another time for distilling vinegar from the bark of wood.
The wood was subjected to heat and the steam arising therefrom was condensed while the char-
coal which remained was used for making powder. It is said that the distilling of the wood gave
off very unpleasant vapours. This mill stood near where the Works Manager's house now
stands.

A short distance below Ashfield on the right bank of the River Allan between the railway
line and the river and opposite Barbush farm stood Reid's Mill or Auchinlay Mill. It took its
name from a tenant of Auchinlay farm. It was occupied at another time by James Kinross.
It does not seem to have been an ancient mill and it was never used after 1819. Its principal
use was for treating lint, although meal was also ground there. Lint was commonly grown in the
Dunblane district about the beginning of the 19th century and earlier and was a usual crop on
Crofts farm where there was a pool beside the Auchinlay road beyond Woodend cottage known
as the Lintstank.

Currie's Mill is said to have stood at the north end of Curries' Haugh near Lower Auchinlay,
and one gathers that its site was about the Water Cut as it has been said that, when the course of
the Allan was altered for railway construction, the ruins of the mill were blotted out. This mill
was at one time a meal or lint mill and the Haugh or Croft was occupied by the miller. The
path leading from the Braeport to the Laighills was known as the path leading to the Waulk
Mill, and probably Currie's Mill was also used for waulking cloth.

Before the Water Cut was made the River Allan flowed round to the east at the foot of the
high ground of the Laighills and there was a bridge over the river at the corner where the path
turns to the right and leads towards Ashfield. There were a few steps down from the path to
the bridge and on the west side of the bridge there were a few further steps.

The next mill on the banks of the Allan was formerly known as Mill of Angry which in
1817 consisted of a single storey building with attics thatched. It was developed at a later date
into Springbank Mills. The first erection was similar to the mill store next the railway. It may
be of interest to note that the windows in this store were the windows of the first Free Church in
Dunblane erected in 1843. Much of the work in Springbank Mills in modern days has been
spinning yarn for carpet and woollen manufacturers.

The old meal mill of Dunblane is probably the oldest mill in the district. It belonged at
one time to the Bishop and Chapter of Dunblane and latterly became the possession of the lairds
of Cromlix. The dam on the River Allan is shown in a picture by Slezer, dated 1693, but a mill
had undoubtedly stood there at a much earlier date. A piece of ground between the mill and the
river now used as a washing green was known as the Sheiling Hill where the grain was separated
from the husks after thrashing, but there was also a Sheiling Hill on the opposite side of the river
near the end house of Mr. Guthrie, joiner, or Ferguson's house opposite the latter. Sheilings
were used at malt kilns for the purpose of maintaining a regular heat for the purpose of drying
malt.

Following down the riverside we come to a waulk mill about 100 yards south of the bridge
over the Allan at Dunblane on the left bank of the river. The remains of the mill lade are still
seen and parts of the stone work are visible, as also a roadway down from the Beech Walk. At
one time this mill was used as a silk thread mill.

Duckburn Park Mill stood on the right bank of the River Allan near the north end of the railway bridge over the Allan at the north of Kippenross tunnel. There is an arch at the north end of the bridge where water for the mill formerly passed through. This mill was also known as the Feus Paper Mill. This mill seems to have had a chequered career. The owner, Ferguson by name, was fined for smuggling paper and the mill was twice burned down. After the second fire it was not rebuilt. There was formerly a road from the end of Claredon to the mill and coming back to the present Stirling road below the entrance gate to Hillside farm, at Skelly Braes.

Only a short distance below the paper mill are unmistakable signs of a mill on the left bank, of the history of which nothing is known. Probably this mill was of an early date.

A short distance further down the left bank is a very large stone known as the washing stone, and a piece of flat grass ground there was known as the washing green and the pool in the river as the washing green pool. At one time there were vestiges of a path leading from there to the Darn Road.

On the right bank of the Allan below the south end of the Kippenross tunnel are the remains of two mills. The one immediately below the tunnel is comparatively modern. It was used at different times as a paper mill, woollen factory and wire factory. The lower mill was originally a corn or flour mill and later a woollen or cloth mill. At one time the occupier of the mill was Baird, tenant of Drumdruils farm, and during his time the mill was kept busily employed and a cart went back and forwards all day to Dunblane.

The last mill in the parish was the Kippenross corn or flour mill on the left bank of the Allan a little above the junction of the Wharry Burn with the river. The mill has sometimes been referred to as the Mill of Ads and the cottage there is still known as Millads Cottage. Various suggestions have been made as to the origin of the name, but it seems probable that it merely stands for Mill Lade or Mill Lands Cottage. The last miller bore the name of Whitehead. It has been thought that there had been a mill at one time to the west of Holmehill where land bore the name of Howmill, and the hollow at the top of Braeport is known as Howmilnhead, but, if there was a mill in that part of Dunblane, nothing is known about it. It is improbable that there was ever a mill there.

A mill bore the name of Mill of Pendrich. This may have been the mill of which the remains were traceable until late years on the left bank of the Wharry Burn below Lynns farm, the site of which is now covered by the Dunblane Reservoir.

Kilbryde, which supported at one time a very considerable population, had a mill on the right bank of the Ardoch below Kilbryde Bridge beside the right-of-way from Argaty to Kilbryde smithy. This mill was, however, driven by water from the Argaty Burn and not from the River Ardoch.

THE MARKET CROSS.

The market cross was a symbol of honest and fair dealing in commercial bargains. When merchants first learned to write and to reduce their contracts to writing, they sealed their accounts with a representation of some form of a cross and frequently began their documents by invoking the name of the Deity. Market crosses were general in English boroughs, and also in Scotland, and even in districts not widely populated, and at a distance from centres of population. In some cases these crosses have survived although there is no longer a village.

The Cross of Dunblane stood near the Cathedral entrance gate, and the street, known as The Cross, sometimes referred to as Cathedral Square, derived its name not from there being cross roads, but from the market cross which stood there. It is greatly to be regretted that, after it had survived some centuries, it should have been removed on false grounds of religion as an object of superstition.

Before the Reformation many business transactions were completed within the Cathedral of Dunblane, and often where sums of money were lent, it was stipulated that such should be repaid at one of its altars.

It has been suggested that there were crosses at Whitecross, Corscaplie, Anchorscross and Kippenross, and that any refugee from justice was safe if he came within the limits of the district enclosed by the crosses. While it is possible, but not probable, that there was a cross at one or more of these places other than Kippenross, it is thought that there are no grounds for this suggestion. Anchorscross was referred to in former times as Ankerscroft and Whitescross as Whitecroft, and it may be noted that there was a croft near the latter known as Blackcroft the site of which is now called Backcroft. The name of Kippenross has existed for many centuries and means the Field of the Promontory. It is possible that at Corscaplie there may have been a cross, the word meaning the cross of the Chapel, but no evidence exists of this, and the oldest spelling of the name—Cascaply—rather negatives the idea.

An Old House in Dunblane about 1741.

The following is a description of an old house in Dunblane. The side walls were six feet high, four feet wide at the base, and two at the top. They consisted of alternate layers of feal and flat stones as bands ; the gavels were six feet thick at least and rose in the common way. The rude, undressed trees of the roof, termed couples, were fixed in the earth at the bottom of the walls and secured side-wa' height, with cross beams or bauks which were fastened to the couple-legs with large wooden pins driven through one and a half inch wimble-bores. Next across the couple-legs were laid two rungs on each side of the roof, and a rigging-tree on the top. Then there were laid on the kebars parallel to the couple-legs next a slating of divots, and last of all a coating of bog-thack and a ridging of flax-mill dust. An aperture of no small dimensions was left in the middle of the ridge to admit the light and " vent the reek." No "winnock-bunker " was otherwise considered necessary. A circular tube of wicker-work, plastered with clay. surmounted the " hole i' the riggin," which was with no impropriety called the lum-head. The door was a frame of basket-work also, and finished with clay.

It may be mentioned that, while walls of a house could not be removed by a tenant, the same did not apply in Scotland, at one time, to the roof. The latter was frequently the property of the tenant and, when he removed, the roof was frequently taken by him.

The Old Wells of Dunblane.

Prior to there being a gravitation water supply for the town, the inhabitants were dependent for their water supplies upon various wells situated within and without the city. The earliest scheme for taking water by gravitation was from the Reivers Burn by Sheriffmuir to Stonehill and other dwellings on Kippenross. When the railway was constructed, Kippendavie made a reservoir above Ochlochy from which the railway station was supplied and off which a supply was taken to the Manse of Dunblane. This reservoir seems to have been fed from the Kippenross supply from Sheriffmuir. Later on, when the Hydropathic was built, a reservoir was made for its supply behind Leewood.

It may be of interest, however, to recall the various wells on which the townsfolk were so long dependent.

Tammie Blair's Well. This well stood beside the path which leads from the Bridgend up the right bank of the Allan to the Haugh. A drawer of water at one time had to go down about 15 steps to the well. It may have been constructed after the making of the railway as previously a little burn flowed from the Bridgend west of the railway down to the Allan, the lower part of which is still open next Willowbank House. This well may therefore have been made by the Railway Company to supply dwellings in Bridgend. It took its name from a man Blair who had charge of the railway gates there prior to the erection of the iron footbridge over the railway line. There was another well nearby to which access was obtained by one or two steps also on the left side of the path leading to the Haugh and which was filled up about the beginning of this century. This well was known as *Walker's Well.* At the west Bridgend there were formerly one or two breweries and it is believed that one of these was owned by a man Walker.

At the top of Bridgend there was another well, known as *Cowan's Well*, which supplied a brewery which at one time belonged to a Thomas Jeffrey, the water being used for brewing or malting and the overflow passing into the little stream above mentioned. This well stood near the property of the late William Ferguson, joiner, at the corner of Upper Bridgend and Doune Road.

Another well stood to the left of the Doune Road beside Wellplace, a row of houses which derived its name from this well. On the Old Doune Road were two wells, one at the back of the one-storey dwelling at the foot of the road which was at one time occupied by the well-known infant school of Miss Campbell, while the other stood in a field nearly opposite Keir Street, opposite Mornish House. The Gallows-tree stood nearby. This well is traditionally believed to have been a Roman well. The overflow ran eastwards for about 100 yards then south-eastwards and eventually past Vicar's Cottage in Claredon.

At the south end of the Feus was *Moulin's Well*, which was probably an overflow from the old Roman well. It was also known as Rab Vicar's Well, bearing the name of a well-known builder in Dunblane of 100 years ago and grandfather of John Robertson, librarian in Dunblane. Many ancient wells were dedicated to saints and were regarded as sacred, and in some parts of the country little gifts were left beside them hung on trees nearby. Moulin is the name of a saint and this well may have been sacred to him.

There was a pump well under the site of the steeple of the former Roman Catholic church in Claredon, and a similar well at the north end of the Feus opposite the close at the shop of James Cameron, joiner, now removed for road improvement purposes.

Christie's Well was in the rock behind the Dunblane Hotel, and it acquired its name from a former inn-keeper. Being only a slight distance above the level of the Allan, it was not available when the river was high, but at other times a good supply of water was obtainable from it.

A well stood behind the saddler's shop in High Street. The house there was at one time an inn with stabling behind.

A well-known well was called *Eppie Easson's Well* beside the Gas Works to the east of the path running along the left bank of the Allan. This well was reached by several steps. It was open to the public so long as it was in use, but now it is enclosed within the boundary wall of the Gas Company's property. Behind the corner house of The Cross in the yard there stood a pump well.

Perhaps the best-known well in Dunblane was the *Bishop's Well*, in the Bishop's Yard or Grassyard. This well is now dry and the explanation is that it was fed by a strong stream from about Kirk Street which was incorporated into the town sewer when it was laid in Kirk Street. There was a right-of-way or at least a privilege held by some of the inhabitants to pass through the north end of the Manse ground out by a gate which still exists and down a path to the well. The line of the path is still visible.

Passing along Kirk Street one comes to the Wellclose in which there was a " dry " or draw well known as *St. Philip's Well*. In the close known as Regent's Square in Braeport opposite the Public School was a well called *Bruce's Well* and also *St. Blane's Well*, and probably water from this supplied a well in Cathedral Market Garden to the west.

A well, known as *Bowsie's Well*, stood at the east end of the East Church, the close there from Sinclairs Wynd being known as Bowsie's Close. It took its name from an old inhabitant who lived thereabouts.

Balhaldie House was supplied with water from a well within St. Blane's where high beech trees stand and which also supplied St. Blane's House.

Water for Holmehill House was at one time pumped from a well near the gardener's lodge by a pump worked by turning a wheel.

The people of Bogside opposite the Hydropathic gardens were supplied from a well within a field on Ledcameroch.

There were a number of wells outside the town. One on Landrick farm, known as *Nancy's Well*, which used to bear a carved inscription. Nancy is said to have been a faithful servant of John Stirling of Kippendavie.

There was a well beside the Darn Road, and *Jean Drummond's Well* was at the side of the fence which at one time divided the Cowpark of Kippenross and the Quarry Park where a Jean Drummond had a cottage and garden. This ground now forms part of the first and last holes of the golf course.

Other wells in the neighbourhood of Dunblane included the *Laighill Well* which flows now as strongly as in past years and which was used by many inhabitants long after they had a water supply within their own houses. Another excellent well is the *Barbush Well* at the riverside on the road to Ashfield.   *St. Duthie's Well* seems to have stood on the south-east side of the Perth Road near Duthieston where formerly stood a temporary hospital.

A well at Glassingall was known as the *Roman Well*.

At the north-west end of Wanderwrang Wood, Keir, there was formerly a built well. Probably there were dwellings there at one time as otherwise such a well would seem to have been unnecessary.

The writer is indebted for much of the foregoing information to notes given to him by the late John Robertson, librarian and local antiquarian.

Some of the wells noted must have had long histories through the past centuries.   In earlier days, however, the inhabitants would be chiefly dependent for their water supplies on the River Allan and on burns in the neighbourhood, particularly the Laighill Burn and the Minnie Burn from Ochlochy down by the Perth Road, the back of the Dunblane Prison and the Millrow, and on streamlets such as that in the Feus and Upper Bridgend.

BEFORE giving an account of some of the principal events in the history of Dunblane during this period, it may be of interest to readers to recall the appearance of the city about the year 1842. On entering Dunblane from the north the traveller came by coach past Whitecross. The main Perth Road was constructed after the middle of the 18th century and at one time there was no road between Whitecross and Duthieston although there had been for centuries a road to Landrick and the two villages of Woodlands and Soutar's Town in the neighbourhood of Kippendavie Farm. The road between Whitecross and Barbush was known as the road to Kinbuck and this joined the Dunblane-Kinbuck Road near the cemetery gate. The oldest road to the north passed up from Backcroft by the nursery garden and along the side of the cemetery. The nearest building to Dunblane at Whitecross was the inn situated where Kippendavie Lodge now stands, and the Whitecross cottages were used as stables for the coach horses. Continuing towards Dunblane one passed Anchorfield, one of the oldest houses in Dunblane, and south of Anchorfield garden wall there was a row of small houses and byres as also a smithy extending alongside the Perth Road to the road which leads to Backcroft and the Ramoyle. These cottages were known as Bogside. In what is now the Hydropathic vegetable garden, there stood at an earlier date a square of houses built on ground known as the Bog, or Balhaldie's Bog, being the property at one time of the Laird of Balhaldie. This low-lying ground running southwards to Kincairn was at one time bog land, there being a considerable stream of water flowing through it which is now piped into the burgh drains.

The land lying between the Dykedale and Glen Roads and north-westwards to the Holmhill Road was at one time known as Bog Green Park.

In 1842 there were no houses about the Crescents or Perth Road, neither was there an Episcopal School, but opposite the present smithy stood the church of the Anti-Burgher congregation which building was situated within Holmehill grounds. The minister of this congregation at that time was the Rev. Alexander Henderson, author of the poem "The Pilgrim," who during his residence in Dunblane erected St. Blane's House then known as St. Blane's Rood Cottage where he conducted a boarding school for boys and where he undertook to impart "a sound classical and commercial education." The ground within the neighbourhood of St. Blane's House was known as St. Blane's Rood, but it is not known whether this name was of ancient origin.

There were no buildings in the Glen Road with the exception of a little cottage known as Drumlochy, situated behind the fine copper beech tree at Overdale gate, whose last occupants were Macfarlanes. About the middle of last century it was occupied by James Drummond, gamekeeper at Kippenross, and afforded a lodging for law clerks and other young men employed in Dunblane. The original road from Dunblane to Drumlochy and beyond was by the Darn Road through the Kippenross Parks past Ochlochy cottages which were situated among trees to the south of the curling pond and out at Drumlochy.

The old city of Dunblane may be said to have been enclosed between the Overport or gate at the Braeport and the Netherport at the east side of the bridge of Dunblane which carries the main street over the River Allan, but there were also communities with considerable populations in Ramoyle and in Bridgend. One, however, finds in old documents, such as in lists of the poor of the parish, that persons are designed as residing "at Dunblane" or "in Ramoyle" or "in Bridgend," this indicating that Ramoyle and Bridgend were considered outside, and not part of, the city. The older inhabitants will recollect that the portion of the High Street from the Prison north-eastwards was called in their younger days "the New Road," and it must have been constructed about the days of their fathers. Going up the hill north-eastwards from the property of James Lennox, grocer, were gardens, and further up on the left, that is about the barber's shop, the houses seem originally to have been entered from the rear, that is from Cross Street by Arnot's Close. This road was made before 1840, but probably not much earlier. Balhaldie House must previously have been entered from Sinclair's Wynd, and it was so called from its being the town residence of the MacGregors or Drummonds of Balhaldie. The portion next Perth Road was added at a later date. It has been stated that it was built for a law office for a local solicitor. At a later time it was used as the local Post Office, Mr. Bain, solicitor, being postmaster. Before the advent of railways, letters, of course, came by mail coach.

Continuing to pass through Dunblane from the north, one comes to Ramoyle—thought to be the oldest part of the town. There was probably a considerable community there before the days of St. Blane. Ramoyle has not greatly changed during the last hundred years save that the houses were formerly of one storey and thatched and that a number of the inhabitants had byres. There were crofts or small holdings in the neighbourhood to north and south. Many weavers resided and had weavers' shops in Ramoyle in the earlier part of last century. At the south end stood a school, the last master of which was Mr. Meiklejohn, father of Professor Meiklejohn of St. Andrews University, the well-known educationist, and grandfather of Major Meiklejohn, a V.C. of the Boer War, who met with a heroic death in Hyde Park, London, in an endeavour to prevent an accident.

The ground at the top of Braeport, used as a vegetable garden or for poultry-rearing, part of the property of Holmehill, was then open land where public gatherings were held and where the Gospel was frequently preached by, amongst others, the Rev. Ebenezer Erskine. The ground lends itself for the seating of large gatherings on its east side where it rises rapidly. Here cattle were sold at the old fairs.

Entering by the Overport one passed into the town by the old road used by the coaches earlier in the century. The houses on the east side of Braeport were the Manses of officials of the Church in pre-Reformation days. At the foot of Braeport the Meeting-house Loan branched off to the right and there stood the meeting-house or church of the Burgher congregation of which the Rev. James Anderson was then minister. Opposite this meeting-house, formerly known as the Red Hoose, stood the Public School and Session House within the ground of the church-yard. Later on the schoolhouse became the Volunteer Drill Hall. There were houses, in these days, on the west side of Kirk Street as well as on the east. Some notable people had had residences there, including the Earl of Perth whose town residence was opposite the Leighton Church where the house of the schoolmaster of Dunblane now stands. There were houses and byres up closes in Kirk Street, and the local custom was to wheel out the manure and leave it in heaps on the street which was then considerably narrower than it is now, there being no place to keep it on the owner's property. The Leighton Church had by this time replaced the red tile house which ran at right angles to the site of the present church. At the east and west ends of the old building were stairs forming entrances to low galleries. Entrances to upper storeys were usually at this time by outside stair.

Sinclair Street, or more properly Sinclair's Wynd, stood much as it stands at present. Sinclair is an old name in Dunblane and some centuries earlier there was a Bailie Richard Sinclair. He or some other prominent man who had lived or owned property there, no doubt gave his name to the street. A Sinclair of Drumdoulis—Drumdruils—owned a house in this Wynd or near-by in 1630.

Passing along Kirk or Cross Street westwards one passed the Tolbooth or Court House and Jail on the east side of the Cathedral gate and entered The Cross. On the left side going south the Rev. Michael Gilfillan had once occupied the corner house, and next it stood the house of Dean Pearson, the first Pearson Laird of Kippenross. The lane known as Towerhead Lane or Bishop's Close ran westwards from The Cross towards the River Allan with buildings on either side. The first house next the west pillar of the Cathedral gate had a room which projected over the churchyard, but it did not rest on the ground. The owner had obtained permission from the heritors, who owned the churchyard, to extend the room in this way as his family was increasing.

There were two public houses on the west side of the Cross. Where the prison now stands was the ruined dwelling of Lord Strathallan. Of the two public houses between the Cathedral and Manse (which had been erected some years earlier) the first one extended into the street considerably beyond the line of the present dwelling and was then kept by Brose Rab. The other was carried on in the building now known as Cathedral Cottage, which then belonged to a Mr. Moir. Mr. Moir's daughter married John Maule, joiner, a prominent man in Dunblane about the middle of last century.

The Leighton Library has stood much as it stands at the present time since its erection at the end of the 17th century, save that the stairway originally stood east and west and not north and south as it is now.

The Union Bank House was formerly known as Greenyards and was the residence at various times of some notable local people including John Rob, writer, and Charles McAra, Sheriff Clerk, and afterwards bank agent. Mr. McAra suffered from baldness, and, whether to hide this or because he felt his head cold, he was accustomed, when sitting in church, to spread his gloves over his bald pate. When the minister prayed for the King and the Government, Mr. McAra was used to make a profuse bow of acknowledgment as a representative of Royal authority. At one time there stood in the garden of Fernbank, Dunblane, 2 pillars taken out of Lord Strathallan's house. These were thought to be gate pillars, but seem to have been the pillars of a large fireplace. They are now erected within the grounds of Cromlix House, which estate formerly belonged to the Strathallan family.

The High Street—at one time known as the " High Causeway "—from the top of the Mill-row to beyond the Bank of Scotland was exceedingly narrow and part of it even narrower than the neck at the Bank of Scotland. The buildings were, however, lower. Where MacEwen's buildings now stand, small houses and shops came out on to the public road beyond the line of the present pavement and all the buildings between the baker's shop and the Bank of Scotland —at least on the east side—have been erected within the last 50 years, replacing the thatched dwellings and weavers' shops which formerly stood there. At the south end of the High Street on the east side was the village smithy, and a little thatched building beyond it served as a Post Office. The postmistress lived in a room above the back office. Beyond that again there stood at one time a cartshed in which the elephants belonging to Wombell's Menagerie found a resting place about 80 years ago. There was, of course, no New Road at that time, and Kippenross Lodge, which at first was situated on the High Street, where also one entered the Beech Walk, was not as yet erected, the drive not being made until 1854-55. The Stirling Arms Hotel, then known as the Head Inn, consisted of two storeys and was tenanted by Mr. Kinross who also occupied the farm of Stockbridge. This inn in 1839 was described as being exceedingly comfortable, and Mr. Kinross was said to supply excellent gigs, chaises and cars, superior horses and superior drivers. It was here that Robert Burns stayed when he visited Dunblane.

It is not known when the High Street was constructed. There must have been houses there 300 years ago, but there were probably none before the first bridge of Dunblane was built early in the 15th century. Prior to the erection of the bridge the river was crossed by a ford from about the Auld Licht Manse to the foot of the lane which comes down from Bridgend to the right bank. The Millrow is a much older street than the High Street and takes its name from the corn mill which existed there for many centuries. The Money or Minnow Burn seems to have flowed down the Millrow above ground and there was a bridge over it at the head of this street. Prior to the making of the High Street of Dunblane there were roads, or at least tracks, from the Millrow through Kippenross Park by Ochlochy and also round the back of the High Street gardens and past the east wall of St. Blane's House. A road through this Park between the Minnow Burn and Ochlochy was known as the Road to Pendreich.

Allanside House, or, as it was called, " the Auld Licht Manse," has had an interesting history. In 1797 there was a breakaway from the Anti-Burgher congregation which worshipped in Holmehill road. Mr. W. B. Bruce narrates that 73 persons left that Church and formed themselves into a congregation of " Auld Lichts," and Allanside House became their meeting place. When there was a breakaway from the Established Church in 1842 and a Scottish Episcopal congregation was formed, their first services were held in this house and, on one occasion, Dean Ramsay, the author of *Reminiscences of Scottish Life and Character*, preached there. At another time the Cathedral congregation found temporary quarters in Allanside.

One of the best houses in Dunblane in the '40s of last century was Allanbank known as Cumberland's Lodging as it was here the Duke of Cumberland stayed in 1746 when passing north with his army prior to Culloden. It was at that time the property of a well-known man, James Russell, Bailie of Dunblane, a solicitor and Commissary Clerk. In later times it was occupied by Mr. John Rob, Sheriff Clerk, and his daughter Jane, and his son-in-law, Mr. James Boyd, and his wife, Elizabeth Rob, lived there at the middle of the 19th century. Attached to Allanbank House was an excellent garden running down to the river bank with the mill lade flowing through it. Opposite the garden were stepping stones for crossing the River Allan. It may be mentioned that at the old ford boats were kept on the west side for taking passengers over the stream when the water was sufficiently high.

To obtain a picture of Dunblane in Bridgend and beyond one must keep in view that in 1840 there was no railway, but that the main road branched at the end of the bridge as at present, one road leading towards Stirling and the other up Bridgend where again after passing the site of the present railway the road forked in one direction to Kilbryde and Auchinlay and in the other to Doune. The Auchinlay Road at Glenallan Cottages is marked on an old plan in *Perthshire Illustrated* as " Gallow Lane," and the land between this and the River Allan as *Fisher's Lands*. There was no road at this time at Springfield Terrace, nor houses, and the land was used as village acres. The railway station and yard extending to fully 4 acres constituted at this time the glebe of the parish minister. It was entirely fenced and in 1843 was let for £15 a year. A little distance behind Springfield Terrace there was a road leading from Claredon to the Old Doune Road. One may still observe that the Stirling Road leading from the Bridge of Dunblane towards the railway continues in a straight line along Claredon. The construction of the line of the Scottish Central Railway northwards through Dunblane on its way to Perth, about 1846, made many changes in the district, but there were at first neither the road bridge on the Stirling Road south of the station nor the foot bridge in Bridgend north of the station. There were level-crossings at each of these points with men in charge of the railway gates, and foot and horse traffic crossed the railway lines on the level.

Save for the house at the foot of the Old Doune Road there were no dwellings between that point and Doune, except farm houses and cottages, and this was the only road to Doune prior to the '50s when the present road to Doune was made.

Calderwood Place or " Chuckie Row " marked the limit of Bridgend of Dunblane on the west and there were no houses beyond. The first house to be built in the present Doune Road was Glenallan, originally occupied by Colonel Campbell, a relative of the Kilbryde family. Birchbank followed many years later and for a considerable time it stood alone at quite a little distance from the town.

Early in the nineteenth century, the Glen Road from Bridge of Allan to Dunblane did not extend beyond Drumdruills Farm. The present Glen Road was constructed by John Stirling of Kippendavie who obtained land from Lord Abercromby at the Wharry Glen to allow a road to be made and the Glen Bridge to be erected. It is said that the men employed at the work were paid at the rate of 1s. per day which was a not uncommon pay about one hundred years ago. Prior to this the road from Dunblane to Sheriffmuir passed by Dykedale towards the Lynns and proceeded down the March Dyke between the Lynns and Stonehill Farms in the direction of Dumyat until it reached high ground on the hill behind the ruined house. The road then turned towards Pendreich, passed behind it and came down by Sunnylaw to Bridge of Allan. There was an old mill on the left bank of the Wharry Burn, the site of which is now covered by the Dunblane Reservoir.

About 1850, there were four public houses at Sheriffmuir, one known as Meg o' the Bogs which stood beside the tall ash trees between Cauldhame and Dumyat. Another public house there was known as Miller's. There were also the Sheriffmuir Inn and Donald MacNab's Inn which stood on Balhaldie's ground. Another old road led from Comrie and the Highlands by Feddal across the River Allan to the east of Naggiefauld Farm coming up by Woodside Farm formerly on Balhaldie Estate then by Balhaldie Hill to Sheriffmuir. When the railway line was made, two railway gates were put up on the line of this old road, which now mark its position.

The builder of the Wharry Glen bridge was Robert MacVicar, a well-known mason who came to Dunblane from Menstrie in 1808, and who also built a bridge over the River Allan near Kippenross House to carry the avenue to the Stirling Road. At one time, the land between the Stirling Road and the river was part of Keir estate. When the avenue was made, the public insisted on the gates being kept open as there had long been a drove road here with a ford in the river near to the site of the bridge.

On the lands of Park of Keir, above the railway line, are two high points, the higher of which is known as the Moot Hill. On it the courts of the Barony of Keir were held. The hill nearer Bridge of Allan, now covered with wood, was known as the Gallows Hill. Traces of an old road are to be seen between the old Castle of Keir known as Arnhall and the Moot Hill.

From the Moot Hill a magnificent view is to be obtained in all directions, and it has been suggested that this was the site of a signalling station of the Romans and that the Roman road from the south passed to the east of it.

The highest point on the Laighills, formerly known as the King's Seat, but now reduced in height, is on the north-west side of the bridge which crosses the railway line. A little further to the north-west, where the green of hole 8 of the old golf course was placed, there was formerly a small lake with an island in the centre which went by the name of the Egg. This had the reputation of being haunted and children used to run round it singing " Whaur's the man wi' the cloven foot ? "

No case of the devil being seen is recorded, but at one time two old women reputed to be witches lived on the island. A Cromlix farmer passing one night at the darkening saw a hare and had a shot at it. The shot was followed by an unearthly but human-like cry. The farmer, McFarlane by name, got the dog to trace the hare and it swam over the water to the island to which the farmer followed. On reaching the Egg, he found that one of the two sisters had been wounded in the thigh. As witches were reputed to have the power of turning themselves into hares, the story was regarded as conclusive, as proving that the injured woman was a witch and that she had run past McFarlane in the form of a hare.

Among old buildings in Dunblane about the middle of the 19th century was the house in Sinclair's Wynd occupied by Sheriff Coldstream, the site of which is now enclosed in Holmehill gardens. The gable of the house was to the street and there were two outside stairs, one to the kitchen-end of the house and the other to the family apartments. There was a court in front of the house and across the court were stables and other offices. At that time, there were few two-storeyed houses in Dunblane save in Kirk Street. Where the Post Office now stands were one-storeyed houses with tiled roofs. The " back of the toun " Church in Holmehill Road had round windows and doors at either end with grass between the building and the roadway. Where the East Church Hall stands were stables where old Donnelly kept the donkeys which drew his small carts when delivering coals in the town.

There were numerous hamlets or small collections of houses standing by themselves in Dunblane and neighbourhood, including the one known as the Bog about the south end of the Hydropathic kitchen garden, which was entered between two tall lime trees. The houses stood in a square, four on each side with one at the end. Another stood at Ochlochy in the Cow Park or Kippenross Park to the south-west of the Curling Pond where again there were two rows of houses with a bigger house at each end. " Woodlands " and " Soutars Toun " situated at Kippendavie had by this time disappeared. At one time 26 families occupying small pieces of land resided at Woodlands, but by 1810 only one remained. At Soutars Toun there were at one time 8 houses, but the last had disappeared by 1805. There was a hamlet at Dalchanzie, between Auchinlay and Grainston, of seven or eight houses, and another at White-hills—that is at the end of the Tinkers Loan which comes down from the Old Doune Road to the present Doune Road and which is marked by tall lime trees. Part of the hamlet stood on the opposite side of the Doune Road. There was a considerable number of houses at Brighills between the tall plane trees and the cross roads near Kilbryde Chapel and extending down the road to Auchinteck. Besides a shoemaker and tailor there lived there, at one time, a clock-maker and a man who kept an electric battery for treatment of rheumatism.

The properties on the west side of Kirk Street, purchased by the Lairds of Keir, Kippendavie and others with a view to demolition to open up the view of the Cathedral and to effect a town improvement, stood one-half on the site of the present street and one half in the churchyard. The property at the corner of Kirk Street and Cross Street belonged to Mary Vicars, daughter of the builder of the Manse at Dunblane and the bridge on the Glen Road over the Wharry Burn. She married a Mr. Phillips who had a contract for erecting a portion of the railway line near Dunblane and who afterwards emigrated to New York, where he was very successful as a public works contractor. This property is described in the titles as bounded on the east and south by the High Street "leading from the Holme Hill and North Port to the Mercate Cross." Next to it going northwards was the property of Whiteheads, and north of this that of Malcolm, the local baker, standing to the south of the gateway from Kirk Street to the churchyard known as Riccarton's Style, a name which is to be found in old deeds from 1763 or earlier. The two houses north of the Style belonged to a man Rattray, and north of his property was that of Maxwell. The stance between Maxwell's property and the corner of the west side of Kirk Street was vacant in the latter portion of the 19th century.

Down the Meeting-house Loan stood the property of the United Presbyterian Church used by the congregation as a Session House. Part of this property was, as already mentioned, at one time the headquarters of the Volunteer or Territorial Force and previously was used as the public school. This property was let on long lease by David Balcanqual to the Rev. Michael Gilfillan and others in 1803. It was described as being opposite the Meeting-house of the Anti-Burghers—a mistake for Burghers—and as being bounded on the east by the High Street of Dunblane and on the north by the commonway leading from the Laird of Cromlix's Yett. The latter was the road from Kirk Street along the river side towards Cromlix. There was no bridge over the River Allan before the latter half of the 19th century and persons going towards Cromlix would probably ford the river at some convenient spot and probably there were stepping stones in the neighbourhood of Glenorchard, or below Auchinlay House.

The long lease was assigned in 1886 by John Monteith, Glenhead, last surviving trustee of the First United Associate Congregation, previously called the Burgher Associate Congregation.

Such was the city of Dunblane when Queen Victoria, at the age of 23, and Albert, the Prince Consort, passed through on Tuesday, 13th September, 1842. Landing at Granton near Edinburgh on Thursday, 1st September, they had visited Dalkeith Palace, Dupplin Castle, Taymouth Castle and Drummond Castle, where they arrived on Saturday, 10th September. On Monday, 12th September, a grand ball took place in Drummond Castle, and in the morning following Her Majesty continued her journey south. When passing through Dunblane she wore a white transparent cottage bonnet trimmed with a blonde veil and small white feather and an exquisite cashmere shawl with gold coloured palms on a scarlet ground. Near Muthill the Royal carriages passed under a large arch which bore the inscription " Adieu, fair daughter of Strathallan." Horses were changed at Greenloaning. It is stated in the Queen's Journal of her visit to Scotland that the inhabitants of the ancient city of Dunblane were not behind their neighbours in giving proofs of their loyalty and affection in token of which " many of the houses were whitewashed for the occasion." A flag was hoisted on the Cathedral spire and the Cathedral bells rang at intervals from an early hour until the Queen had passed into Stirlingshire. A handsome arch was erected by Mr. Stirling of Kippendavie at the entrance to Dunblane and a similar arch stood at Holmehill gate. Flags decorated many houses as at Anchorfield, where Union Jacks were displayed and a large banner having in gold letters " God Save the Queen." The Royal carriage did not pass down the old coach road by Ramoyle, but by Holmehill gate. Along the road to Bridge of Allan were numerous triumphal arches, and in Dunblane it is said that evergreens ornamented every door and window, and that felled trees were planted opposite the doors of the houses although it is not quite clear in what way this beautified the town. The population of Deanston village, numbering about 1500 persons, were gathered near Keir Lodge. Almost every second person carried a flag, and the neatness, nay elegance, of their dress is said to have attracted the attention of all. Three arches were erected at Bridge of Allan, and from the one at the Reading Room was suspended a gilded beehive with a busy bee with gold body and silver wings and the motto, " How doth the good Queen bee improve each shining hour ? "

Dunblane celebrated this occasion in the evening by an exhibition of fireworks obtained from Edinburgh, to the great gratification of the citizens, and a Mr. Currie, lecturer in chemistry, exhibited " the new telegraph light " equal to 864 candle power.

It is said that when the Queen's carriage was passing Woodend gate on its entrance to Dunblane, a postilion stopped the horses and jumped down to examine their hoofs on the supposition that there was a stone in one of them. He appears to have been bribed previously to do this with a view to giving those gathered at the spot a good opportunity of seeing the Royal party.

At the corner house in Bridgend near the Bridge of Dunblane is to be seen a representation in stone of a crown with a blacksmith's tools below. This was the property of Mr. Mackenzie, the local blacksmith, and he in this way commemorated the fact that he shoed the horses which drew the Queen's coach, this entitling him to be considered a recipient of Royal patronage.

It is in the early '40s of last century that Dunblane awakened from its long sleep, and this was closely connected with unrest in ecclesiastical matters. The Rev. Dr. Grierson, inducted as parish minister in 1818, died in 1840 from apoplexy after less than 24 hours illness. He was succeeded by the Rev. William Mackenzie previously minister of Comrie parish. Mr. Mackenzie was a man of considerable ability and an earnest preacher of the Evangelical school, and it is said traces of the impression he made on Comrie are observed to the present day. Soon after his induction to Dunblane he appears to have introduced a number of reforms which have already been noted on page 231.

That Dunblane was keenly interested in Church affairs is shown by the signing in July, 1841, of a strong protest against the action of the General Assembly in attempting to depose some ministers of the Presbytery of Strathbogie. The protest was published in full in the newspapers, the first signatures being those of Thomas Barty and Patrick James Stirling.

The election of the Rev. Mr. Mackenzie to Dunblane in November, 1840, was not a unanimous one, but he received 97 votes against 36 and 25 given for the two other candidates who were voted upon. There was considerable opposition to his appointment among the wealthier classes although this is described in a local newspaper as " a Coatery of a dozen." Following upon his election Patrick James Stirling left the Cathedral, as also Thomas Barty who took offence at the minister not praying for the Royal House. These leading inhabitants with the backing of the Lairds of Keir and Kippendavie were the founders of St. Mary's Episcopal Church. Mr. Mackenzie was of an impulsive disposition and, although active and earnest, he was probably unwise, and, in any event, he failed to keep his congregation together.

In the Minutes of the Kirk Session of the Established Church prior to the Disruption in 1843, there is no record of any difficulties or impending trouble. Mr. Mackenzie presided at a meeting of Session on 14th May, 1843, when ordinary business was transacted and there is no indication that within a few days later the Church of Scotland was to be rent in twain. Later in the month the minister joined the Free secession taking with him his whole elders except James Bain whose death took place shortly after, and leaving behind him only Donald Stewart, Session Clerk, and William McKinlay, the church officer, as representatives of the Parish Church officials. There is no further record in the minutes of Kirk Session until 25th January, 1844, when the Presbytery inducted the Rev. Mr. Boe as parish minister. A copy of the Act of Demission by the Elders of the parish of Dunblane is printed on page 193.

The Free Church Kirk Session met for the first time on 7th June and the following is a copy of the Minute of that meeting :—" At Dunblane, 7th June, 1843, the which day the Kirk Session met and was constituted. Sederunt Rev. William Mackenzie, Moderator, Messrs Donald McDonald, Walter Lennox, John Gentle, Andrew Hart, John Donaldson, James King and John Stewart, Elders.

" The Act of Demission of Elders of the Establishment having been read over and considered was signed and subscribed by all the elders present, and Mr. Adam Baird sent word by one of the members that he is ready to sign it, but is unable to attend this meeting. The only other member of Kirk Session, Mr. James Bain, continues in connection with the Establishment.

" Session closed with Prayer,

" W. Mackenzie, Moderator."

Further meetings were held on 9th and 21st June and 23rd July, 1843, but no matters are recorded therein of interest. Further information about the early Free Church in Dunblane will be found on pages 193 and 194.

The Rev. William Mackenzie only remained in Dunblane till the end of the year following the Disruption when he was transferred to the North Free Church, Leith. He retired from the ministry in 1857 and went to Queensland. He died at the age of 77 on board ship in the Red Sea while on his way home. On the Sunday of the Disruption the minister, elders and people marched to Howmilnhead, that is the hollow behind Glengyle at the top of the Braeport where they worshipped for some time and where in earlier days dissenting congregations had been addressed by Erskine and other famous divines of the earlier Secessions.

Mr. Mackenzie's successor was the Rev. James D. Burns, who was minister from 1845 to 1850, and who is remembered by his hymns some of which are in the Church of Scotland Hymnary, the best known being " Hushed was the Evening Hymn." He was succeeded by the Rev. H. M. Williamson, in 1850, who was followed 5 years later by the Rev. Alexander Paterson, whose successor was the Rev. David Tasker.

The first church of this congregation was opened within five months of the Disruption, namely on 15th October, 1843. It is said to have been seated for 550 persons and on the opening Sunday it was crowded and those who could not gain admittance met in the school adjoining. The collection taken on that day was £42. The building was lit by gas. This congregation (as already noted) erected a new church, which was opened for worship on 5th November, 1854. On the opening Sunday the collections amounted to £230. The building was described in the local papers as an ornament of the ancient city. It was erected more in the style of a parish church than that of a secession meeting-house. The church bell, described at the time as an "excellent" one, but the peals of which to the modern ear are unmusical, was presented by one of the members, Mr. James McCaull, cattle dealer, Balhaldie House.

The Rev. Alexander Henderson continued minister of the Anti-Burgher Church until about 1849 when he emigrated to Canada under the United Presbyterian Church. He was the recipient in December, 1843, of two silver salvers, the Rev. William Mackenzie, Sheriff Cross and other citizens taking part in the presentation. The Anti-Burgher congregation afterwards became part of the United Presbyterian Church and the building was removed in 1857. From 1818 to 1854 the Rev. James Anderson was minister of the Burgher, afterwards the United Presbyterian Church. He retired in the latter year and was succeeded on 16th April, 1856, by the Rev. William Blair, who continued in the active work of the ministry until the close of the century. This congregation had thus only three ministers during the period from 1758 until 1900, that is during 142 years. As has been already mentioned, the first congregation of the Scottish Episcopal Church was formed in 1842, and its first meetings were held in Allanside House. The Rev. J. S. E. Robertson, afterwards of Duncrub, was minister for a short time prior to the induction of Canon Malcolm on 4th August, 1844. St. Mary's Church was consecrated by the Episcopal Bishop of St. Andrews, Dunkeld and Dunblane on 28th May, 1845. Mr. Bruce records that the cost of the new church was £1800, and that the subscribers included W. E. Gladstone and Dean Ramsay.

The Parsonage was erected by Stirling of Keir and St. Mary's School by Stirling of Kippendavie. Canon Henry Malcolm for about 11 years had charge of a mission of his church at Doune and, largely through his efforts, a large sum was collected for the endowment of a church there.

Henry Malcolm was born in Sevenoaks, Kent, in 1810 and was educated at Winchester and St. John's College, Cambridge. He married the eldest daughter of Bishop Terrot of Edinburgh, Primus of the Episcopal Church of Scotland. His first residence in Dunblane before the Rectory was built was at Allanside House, part of which was used for church services until St. Mary's Church was built. He was for nearly fifty-one years incumbent of St. Mary's and was a Canon of Perth Cathedral from about 1889. He loved gardening and his roses were unequalled in the county, and he filled his garden with decorative trees and climbers. Canon Malcolm was without bigotry. He greatly esteemed the parish minister, Mr. Ingram, and, later, the Reverend Dr. Blair of the United Presbyterian Church was a dear friend, while he had the highest regard for Father Paul, the Roman Catholic priest at Doune. He was just and honourable in all his dealings and spoke what he thought to high and humble. His special antipathies were discourtesy and unpunctuality. Sons of numerous well-known families were boarded with him from time to time to whom he acted as tutor. Latterly he suffered a most painful illness with great courage, continuing his pastoral duties to the end.

One of his congregation, and a valued friend, was Miss Helen MacNab, an old lady, who for many years walked from Doune to Dunblane on Sundays to attend St. Mary's Church, remaining till afternoon service and making her mid-day meal of bread and brown sugar. In her last days, she resided at Elmbank, Doune Road. She was of Highland ancestry, being descended from the MacNab of MacNab, her mother being a Stewart of Appin. She had two very old spinster aunts named Stewart who were buried in the family burial ground at Glenfinlas. A story is told that one of these ladies had supplied food to Prince Charlie at the '45 and that Prince Charlie afterwards offered her his hand to kiss and that she remarked that she would rather " pree his mou." He gave her a lock of his hair which is preserved in a ring.

On one occasion, Canon Malcolm returned home after visiting Miss MacNab who spoke with a beautiful and pithy Scots tongue. It was New Year's Day and the Canon announced that Miss MacNab was ruining the morals of her neighbourhood, she having given six of the children in Chuckie Row " a gill apiece." So the old lady had herself told him. Enquiry soon cleared up the matter, her gift having been merely a " jelly piece."

Meantime the Cathedral congregation was passing through difficult times. The first minister after the Disruption was Rev. James Boe, the son of a farmer in the South of Scotland, who was ordained on 25th January, 1844. At the first Communion dispensed after his induction, namely on 1st July following, the number of Communicants present was 141 as contrasted with 444 who partook of this sacrament in the July preceding the Disruption. Mr. Boe was esteemed by his congregation which he greatly built up. It was due to him that the first church choir was formed in Dunblane, taught by a skilled musician brought by him from Glasgow. The singing was at this time led by a precentor whose yearly salary was 30s. and there was then no musical instrument in use to accompany the praise. Mr. Boe died in 1860.

Unfortunately, further trouble arose through the appointment of his successor, the Rev. James Ingram, who at the age of 49 was presented to the parish by Queen Victoria.

Mr. Ingram's first appointment had been to the Scots Church, Amsterdam, where he married the daughter of a Huguenot wood-merchant, and, after 10 years' service there, he was inducted to the parish of Fala. His election to Dunblane did not meet with favour by the congregation. An appeal was presented to the Presbytery signed by 6 heritors and 8 parishioners whose objections were submitted by Mr. Reid, solicitor, Perth, the grounds of these being that his discourses were cold, rambling and unedifying, that his utterance was defective and that his age and infirmity unfitted him for such a parish as Dunblane. The proceedings before the Presbytery were continued from time to time over a period of four months, during which there were frequent meetings and almost weekly discussions. Thereafter the Presbytery took evidence, the proof extending over a dozen sederunts and on some occasions evidence was led during 3 days in succession. The Presbytery, as a rule, met about 11.30 a.m. and their sittings lasted to as late hours as mid-night and 1 a.m. The first witness for the objectors was Robert Dick, age 28, coal agent, who was followed by William Graham, estate worker, Kippenross and James McEwan, jailer, at Dunblane Prison. Other witnesses among the objectors were James McNaughton, game-keeper, Cromlix, Thomas Watson, baker, and Mrs. Watson, Miss Mary Menzies, Sheriffmuir, and Miss Janet Boyd, Allanbank. On 9th May, 1861, the case came to an end at 11 p.m., when the Presbytery by 10 votes to 7 resolved to remit the whole case to the forthcoming General Assembly. The latter on 27th May found that the objectors had failed to prove their case, and on 8th August of that year Mr. Ingram was admitted minister of Dunblane.

Mr. Ingram is described as a man of 6 ft. in height and of fresh appearance and, despite the evidence of the objectors, it is said he was " quite well heard " in the Cathedral, that he preached an average sermon and gave utterance to earnest prayers. He devoted himself assiduously to his work in the parish and proved a devoted pastor, but was handicapped by the loss, at the time of his appointment, of a large proportion of the congregation gathered together in the time of his predecessor. He had the assistance of only 2 elders during part of his ministry. His death, caused through fever contracted while visiting a sick parishioner, occurred in 1869. He was described by Canon Henry Malcolm as a man gentle, loving, earnest and holy, and a friend of the poor.

The development of modern Dunblane dates from the secessions from the Established Church of 1842 and 1843 involving the erection of new churches and residences for their clergy. This was followed by a period of activity arising through the construction of the line of the Scottish Central Railway through the parish on its way to Perth, which involved the housing of a large number of workers and the expenditure of much of their wages in the shops and inns of the town. Whitecross House, now known as Ledcameroch, was probably the first of the larger houses to be erected, namely in 1858. It took its name from the hamlet of that name known as New Whitecross, Old Whitecross being situated on the old road to Kinbuck, halfway between Ramoyle and the road to Barbush Farm. It was also about 1858 that the Leighton Manse was built. Crawford Park dates from 1859, Alford from 1861, Claremont from 1863 and Glenacres from 1866, while numerous other villas were also erected in the '60s.

On 20th May, 1841, a meeting was called for the purpose of forming a gas lighting company at which Mr. Stirling of Kippendavie presided. At that time the only lighting was by lamp and the streets after dark were entirely unlit. The company was successfully inaugurated, and on the 10th December following, gas light was used for the first time in Dunblane. The light was said to be of great brilliancy and cheaper than candles.

Stage coaches in this district had a glorious, but short career. They flourished principally between the years 1820 and 1848. It is true that some mail coaches had been organised and had given a regular service from the latter part of the 18th century, and these coaches carried passengers, as well as mails, but after 1820, coaches for passenger traffic became much more numerous. This was probably due partly to the development of business throughout Scotland with the necessity of travelling to and from important centres, improvement in the roadways, increase of wealth and greater freedom from unrest throughout the country.

During the early part of the 19th century the roadways were much improved by more modern methods and through the system of tolls whereby charges were made for vehicles using public roads, and the income derived from the letting of the tolls was available for improving the highways. During most of the period when coaching was at its height both mail and stage coaches passed through Dunblane while in course of their journeys between Glasgow and Edinburgh and Perth and Aberdeen, but it may be explained that all the coaches between these large cities during the whole period did not pass through Dunblane, but during part of the period some ran by Queensferry to Edinburgh or by Milnathort and Stirling to Glasgow.

Horses were usually changed at Dunblane—in the case of some coaches at Kinross's Inn (Stirling Arms Hotel), some at an inn which stood at Inchallan, south of Dunblane Post Office opposite Dunblane Railway Station, and others at Whitecross where there was for a time an inn and stables. At the beginning of the 19th century the boats on the canal between Port Dundas, Glasgow, and Falkirk formed a most popular means of conveyance and coaches were run from Stirling and elsewhere to meet the arrival of such boats. Sometime after the opening of the Union Canal from Falkirk to Edinburgh in 1822, a coach service was instituted to meet these boats. Some of the most important coaches in different parts of the country were known as the "Defiance." A coach of this name left Aberdeen daily, save on Sunday, at 6 a.m. for Glasgow, arriving there at 9 p.m., and similar coaches ran to Edinburgh. The coach from Glasgow to Perth stopped 15 minutes at Dunblane to allow the passengers to have lunch. It is related that on one occasion a minister, who was one of the passengers, commenced the luncheon with a Grace which continued until the guard appeared to summon the passengers to resume their seats.

On a day in March, 1841, many of the citizens of Dunblane were collected as was their custom to watch the arrival and departure of the coach at Kinross's Inn when a horse yoked to a cart became startled, ran off and knocked over 4 people. In the following week there was a further accident on the Bridge in Dunblane when a gig was upset. It was about this time that the Bridge of Dunblane then about 12 feet in width was first widened. It was originally a narrow saddle-backed bridge as were other ancient bridges in Scotland. About 1825 the levels of the roadway were raised which considerably improved the approaches to the bridge.

In 1838, a regular 'bus service was instituted between Dunblane and Stirling. A 'bus left Kinross's Inn at 8 a.m., returning from Stirling at 11 a.m., leaving again at 2 p.m. and finally returning at 5 p.m. A stoppage was made at Philps Inn at Bridge of Allan and the journey took about an hour to accomplish. The fares from Dunblane to Bridge of Allan were 9d inside and 6d outside and from Dunblane to Stirling 1s. 3d. and 1s. respectively, these fares being for the single journey. A coach also ran from Dunblane to Callander daily, leaving at 9.15 a.m. and returning from Callander at 4.45 p.m.

The day of coaches was a short one. The Glasgow to Edinburgh Railway was opened in 1842, six trains running from the one city to the other daily and leaving on their journeys at the same hours. Railways soon formed a network all over Scotland. For a time 'buses ran from Dunblane to Stirling to connect with coaches to meet the Glasgow and Edinburgh trains, but by 1848 the railway had reached Stirling. Coaches for a time endeavoured to compete with the railways by reduction of fares, but the public preferred the more expeditious and comfortable mode of conveyance, and soon after coaches ceased to run in this district and were only to be found in parts where railways had never penetrated.

The contract for the erection of the railway between Dunblane and Kinbuck was let to a Mr. Philips, a local contractor, married to a native of Dunblane, who afterwards had a successful career as a constructor of railways in the United States and Canada. The contract presented considerable difficulties as it involved the crossing of the River Allan at three places and the construction of a tunnel at Ashfield, while there were cuttings to be made through hills and the erection of considerable embankments. The Ashfield tunnel was made by boring from each end, this being remarkably accurately done. The River Allan at the back of the Laighills was diverted down what is known as the Watercut. Above the Watercut in the River are small picturesque islands called after a little English gaffer whose by-name was " Punch." When unable to get ground for depositing surplus soil out of a cutting at Barbush, he is said to have laid a little rail and tipped his waggons into the River Allan thus creating these islands. About 1400 workmen were engaged on the construction of the railway between Bridge of Allan and Kinbuck. The railway station at Dunblane was opened for traffic on 22nd May, 1848.

As early as April, 1845, there was a project for constructing a railway from Dunblane to Doune and Callander, and the proposal was advertised in a local newspaper. Thomas Barty and Patrick James Stirling were appointed interim secretaries. A rival proposal was put forward for a railway from Stirling to Deanston, Doune and Callander, of which the secretaries were James Chrystal, Junior, and J. & J. Mathie, solicitors, both of whom took leading parts in a number of schemes for new railways branching from Stirling. It was pointed out that a railway was under construction as far as Dunblane and that the distance from Dunblane to Callander was shorter than from Stirling while the work of construction would be easier. The Stirling solicitors mentioned were secretaries for companies which proposed to erect railways to Dunfermline and Queensferry, to Tillicoultry and to Balloch and Glasgow. The proposal for a railway to Callander fell asleep for about 10 years, but on 1st September, 1855, a prospectus was issued with Thomas Barty as secretary. The capital of the company consisted of 6000 shares of £10 each. Work of construction commenced on 17th February, 1857, the contractors being John and Alan Granger. The railway was officially opened on 28th June, 1858, when a special train left for Callander at 10 a.m. conveying the contractors of the railway and a party of well-known people. An excursion was provided to the Trossachs and a dinner partaken of on return to Callander. The construction of these railways involved the extinction of coaches and considerable alteration in the habits of the community.

The level crossings north and south of Dunblane Railway Station were done away with at the end of September, 1866, being replaced by the Stirling Road Bridge and the footbridge at Bridgend.

1851 was the year of the great Exhibition in London. The *Stirling Observer* records that one could travel by boat from Stirling and Edinburgh, pay one's board and lodging for a week in London, visit the Exhibition on one or two occasions and pay the entrance fees to some other shows, all for the sum of £2 10s. London seemed a far cry from Dunblane in those days, but, notwithstanding, Mr. Stirling of Kippendavie paid the expenses of his tenants and servants travelling there and spending a week in the Metropolis.

The habits of the people at this time were simple. Workmen had long hours, perhaps 12 hours per day from 6 a.m. to 6 p.m. and no half-holiday on Saturday, while weavers worked longer hours, but were, of course, their own masters. The only holidays were Auld Hansel Monday, or later New Year's Day, and the two Fast Days. The rates of pay were smaller. At the beginning of the century many worked for a shilling a day and even in the latter half of the century females in factories laboured for 7s. or 8s. a week, and bakers were only paid at the rate of 9s. to 10s. a week. A baker's boy received from 6d. to 1s. weekly, along with half a loaf. A quart of sweet milk, however, only cost ½d. and four glasses of whisky 6d. There was no milk in winter, when treacle was taken with porridge. The workman had brose for his breakfast and broth for his dinner. Wants were, of course, simpler and money went further. From an advertisement in the *Stirling Observer* of 2nd November, 1837, one learns that James Eadie, clothier, Dunblane, supplied shoes for men at from 4s. 6d. to 6s. 6d. a pair, while men's stockings cost only 9d. a pair, women's 6d. and children's 4d. The price of cotton shirting was 2d per yard. In 1846 an advertisement appeared in a newspaper for a female servant of all work with unexceptionable character, the wage to be £6 a year.

The business hours of professional men were usually from 10 a.m. to 4 p.m. without a mid-day break. The dinner hour of such and of persons of leisure was either 3 p.m. or 4 p.m., and lawyers returned to their offices from 6 p.m. to 8 p.m. Ladies paid calls not during the afternoon, but between 12 and 1 p.m. and their entertainment consisted of cake and shortbread with port or sherry wine. It is related that a lady of Dunblane wearied of these refreshments, and on one occasion, when asked of which wine she would partake, remarked " I am tired of port. I am tired of sherry. I shall take them mixed." Manners were dignified and formal in these days. If a dance was indulged in, it was in stately fashion. Whist was played in the evenings at home, but whist drives were unknown. When one sent a messenger to the house of a friend with a request even of the simplest character, the messenger was carefully instructed to make or present compliments to the lady of the house before, for example, borrowing her saucepan. Notwithstanding, there was a greater degree of friendliness amongst all classes of the community and every person knew every other. The community was not divided into sets, but the wealthiest and poorest were on familiar terms and conversed with each other on meeting, greeting each other by their Christian names. The wealthier entertained their friends to dinner, they drank tea together, played cards and afterwards had supper and toddy, but so long ago as the '40's there existed a Mutual Improvement Society in Dunblane, and Penny Readings were instituted in the old Free Church School in Perth Road, which was the place in which local concerts and entertainments were held until the first Victoria Hall was opened in 1887. The culture of music was not neglected in those days, for Dunblane boasted of a brass and two flute bands. In addition to the Leightonian Library which was for a time opened for general reading, there were at the middle of last century two libraries in Dunblane. Before the arrival of the railway at Dunblane, newspapers were less numerous than they afterwards became, but daily papers were received from Edinburgh and Glasgow by coach, and weekly papers came from Stirling and elsewhere. When railway trains first passed Dunblane, one had to meet a train to secure a newspaper by purchase from the railway guard as such were not then for sale in the local shops.

At that time in small towns and villages there was usually one mangle for common use, frequently worked by some widow as a means of making a livelihood. In Dunblane at the middle of the 19th century a mangle was owned and worked by a Mrs. McIlvride in a house in the Millrow near the gas works. The roller moved along a table by the aid of a handle, while her operations proved of great interest to the female inhabitants who discussed the napery entrusted to the good lady's care.

The post office arrangements were likewise of a simple and public character and the letters for the inhabitants were delivered by a woman who was not provided with a bag, but carried the town's correspondence in her apron. Such a one was Nancy McKinlay, who went her rounds adorned with a white mutch. As she passed along the street she and her friends carefully examined the letters which she was distributing, and one can imagine what confabulations would take place as they inspected the correspondence and noted from where it came. There was no cause for hurry in these days, and the post-woman would wait while the letters were opened to hear the news which she would gladly carry with her and pass on to her friends.

If the hours of toil were long and the remuneration earned was small, there were compensations in the greater leisureliness and friendliness of these days. Various societies in Dunblane were active bodies in the middle of the last century, prominent amongst which were the Society of Freemasons and the Curling Club. It was, however, in the last quarter of the century before football occupied a leading place among the interests of the community, while the first golf-course in Dunblane was not opened till 1892. One gathers from the files of the local newspapers that there was a strong temperance movement in Dunblane in the second half of the 19th century. In 1855 a temperance gathering was held in the Leighton Church at which 700 people are said to have been present. For some years the principal item of local news is the record of temperance gatherings. The earliest accounts of the playing of cricket in Dunblane date from 1865, but there were fewer opportunities for sports and athletics a hundred years ago, when, apart from fast days, which were duller than Sundays, about the only holiday in the year was Hansel Monday which, about 1865, was still observed locally in preference to New Year's Day.

For many years there was an enthusiastic Volunteer Corps in Dunblane—the predecessor of the Territorial Force. A company was raised in Dunblane in 1859, of which the first Captain was Sheriff Grahame, the local Sheriff-Substitute, his Lieutenant being William Mitchell, solicitor, Dunblane. A company of about 60 was raised, which included a considerable number of men from Bridge of Allan. Sheriff Grahame was succeeded by J. W. Barty, who in 1872 became Major.   The first Ensign was Mr. Lawrence Pullar of Keirfield, who was succeeded by John Dunn, merchant, a well-known figure in Dunblane at this time.   Among other citizens who obtained commissions as Captain was Alexander Harper, afterwards of Ceylon, who resided at St. Blane's, William Wilson, wool-spinner, brother of Alexander Wilson of Alford, and James Liddell, who resided at Leewood.   Prominent in later years were James Watt, Sheriff Clerk Depute, and Lieut.-Col. D. T. Reid, Town Clerk.   Many volunteers in the earlier days were bearded men—no longer youths—while their uniform was not specially selected for campaigning.   It included at that time a heavy rough beaver hat ornamented with a brush. Company and battalion drills were frequently held in the park between the Crescent and Perth Road, through which St. Mary's Drive now passes.   For many years the Dunblane company contained first-class rifle shots who brought home many trophies from battalion competitions.

The history of the Masonic Lodge covers a period of over 200 years.   It was in an active state during the period from 1840 when Patrick James Stirling, writer, succeeded Thomas Barty as Master Mason.   Dr. Stirling was followed by the Laird of Kippendavie, who was Master Mason many years between 1842 and his re-election in 1866.   He continued Master of the Lodge from the latter year until shortly before his death.   Other Masters during this period included Major Henderson of Westerton, Bridge of Allan, and James Stirling of Holmehill who had two terms of office.

The Curling Club at Dunblane dates from a very early period.   The Royal Caledonian Curling Club was founded in 1838, and Mr. James Boyd of Allanbank represented the Club at its meeting on 18th November, 1840, at which meeting he presented a copy of the Court Rules of Dunblane with a drawing of a curling stone bearing the date 1551, which was found in an old curling pond near the City of Dunblane now drained, the property of Thomas Henderson, New Orleans Cottage.   Mr. Boyd represented that Dunblane should be enrolled as the oldest Club, but his proposal was delayed for consideration at next meeting of the Caledonian Club to be held in July, 1841.   Unfortunately the Caledonian Club does not seem to have dealt with this motion at its next meeting.

The present Club was instituted in 1816, and at the first competition match at Carsebreck the Club played 8 rinks and were 66 shots up—the highest on the winning side.   This was in the year 1853.   In the match at Linlithgow in 1848, Dunblane Club had the highest majority on the losing side when 4 rinks were 27 shots up.   Again in 1912 at Carsebreck 6 rinks had a majority of 40 points.   In early days the entrance fee to the Club was 2s. 6d.   A member was fined 2s. if he did not appear on the ice at least once in the season, and he was bound to bring his besom neatly tied.   Curling is a game which encourages a variety of expressions peculiar to the sport, but strong language is discouraged.   According to the old rules of Dunblane Club a player was fined a penny for an oath and the penalty was doubled on each repetition.   Although there was much jollity on the ice, the punishment for appearing in an intoxicated condition was expulsion.   The Club at one time possessed two ancient curling stones named the "Provost" and "Bailie," each weighing about 60 pounds.   The minute books have been well kept and further interesting information will be found on perusal of them.

Two of the most noteworthy citizens of Dunblane about the middle of last century were Patrick James Stirling and Thomas Barty.   The former was born in the Manse of Dunblane on 13th July, 1809, the son of the Rev. Robert Stirling, minister of the Parish from 1779 to 1817.   His uncle, William Stirling, had a legal practice here until his death, and before him a relative of the previous generation had also practised.   When he was only 8, Patrick J. Stirling lost his father, but he had the opportunity of a university education at St. Andrews whither he went at an early stage.   He had a distinguished university career and in one session gained 4 first prizes.   His work in the Moral Philosophy and Political Economy classes, which were taught by Dr. Thomas Chalmers, earned warm praise.   He afterwards studied Law in the University of Edinburgh where he gained first prize for Civil Law.   Having completed his legal studies, he returned to Dunblane to join his uncle.   Patrick James Stirling was in practice in Dunblane for over a half century and he also acted as factor of the Kippendavie and Ardoch estates, was clerk to the Road Trustees and held other appointments.

Much of his leisure time was devoted to the study of Political Economy and to the writing of articles and books on this subject.   His first published work was entitled *The Philosophy of Trade*, which was highly praised in reviews by Dr. Chalmers and by George Eliot.   He wrote a book on the Australian and Californian gold discoveries which was also favourably received, and both books were translated into French. He also published a treatise on the *Gold Question*. One of his best known works is a translation of the well-known work by Bastiat, *Harmony of Political Economy*, to which he added an account of the author's life and writings. He received the degree of LL.D. from the University of St. Andrews and was a Fellow of the Royal Society of Edinburgh. He died at Kippendavie House on 22nd March, 1891. Dr. Patrick James Stirling was a man of great intellectual ability and one of the ablest sons of the Cathedral City.

Thomas Barty was the son of the Rev. James Barty, minister of the parish of Bendochy near Coupar Angus, in which parish a younger brother, Rev. James Strachan Barty, succeeded his father. He commenced the practice of law in Perth in 1827, where his ability attracted the attention of the Sheriff Principal of the county, Mr. McNeill, afterwards Lord Colonsay, who appointed him to the office of Procurator-Fiscal of Western Perthshire at Dunblane. He was sworn in on the same day in October, 1829, as Sheriff Barclay entered upon his duties as Sheriff-Substitute. In addition to performing the work of this office, he acquired a considerable general legal business which included the factorships of Kilbryde, Argaty and Garden estates. He was a keen sportsman, but met with a gun accident while shooting at Garden and his right arm had to be amputated. He was (as already noted) early faced with difficulties in his duties as Procurator-Fiscal arising out of the elections which followed upon the passing of the Reform Act of 1832, but although some feeling was created against him at that time, he afterwards was said to have performed his duties with discretion, firmness and leniency. Thomas Barty in the prime of life was a man of excellent appearance, with a vigorous and bounding step and a vivacious disposition. He was the life of any social gathering and took pleasure in the associations and amusements of the community, but he had a high standard of what was right and decorous. If somewhat quick-tempered he was ever generous and kindly, a man of quick but warm impulses. He was described by one of the old farm tenants as being " either the lion or the lamb."

A notable figure in Dunblane for a few years prior to 1860 was Alexander Buchan, the headmaster of the Free Church School. He was the son of a weaver in the village of Kinnesswood, Kinross-shire, where he was born in 1829. As a lad he showed great ability and, through the sacrifice of his parents, he was sent to Edinburgh University. He was a prizeman in the classes of mathematics, natural philosophy, metaphysics and moral philosophy. His culture was many-sided—it was not restricted to the sciences with which his life work was concerned. He was well-versed in the writings of the poets and dramatists. He was a student of philosophy and had a considerable knowledge of the classics. Keenly interested in botany, and indeed in all sciences, he had a strong love of all natural objects and a keen appreciation of beauty in nature.

Buchan's stay in Dunblane commenced about 1857 and extended over about 4 years. He was warmly interested in the welfare of his pupils and inspired them with a love of learning and of literature. Some of his older scholars accompanied him on botanical excursions, on which occasions he sought to introduce them to the wonders of nature and to the poets who wrote of them. Owing to voice trouble he was forced to give up the scholastic profession. In 1860 he received the appointment of secretary to the Meteorological Society which appointment he held until his death on 13th May, 1907. In 1887 Glasgow University conferred the degree of LL.D. on him. Dr. Buchan had an attractive personality. He was described as " One of the most lovable of men, simple and erect in all his dealings with his fellows, a man to be trusted in every respect." He had a great power of handling masses of statistics with a view to bringing out underlying facts. He published many valuable books on meteorology and wrote many articles of great value in scientific journals and in the *Encyclopaedia Britannica*. His treatise on *The Main Pressure of the Atmosphere and the Prevailing Winds of the Globe* has been described by Professor Hann, Vienna, as an epoch-making work and as one which has exercised the greatest influence on the further development of meteorology. He is now popularly known as the discoverer of " Buchan's Spells."

Had he remained in Dunblane he would have exercised a powerful influence on the young mind and character, but the sciences might have lost a distinguished personality.

One of the most distinguished sons of this parish was Sir William Stirling-Maxwell of Keir and Pollok, who succeeded to Keir on the death of his father, Archibald Stirling of Keir. His mother was Elizabeth Maxwell, daughter of Sir John Maxwell of Pollok. When Sir William

Stirling succeeded his uncle, Sir John Maxwell of Pollok, he assumed the name of Maxwell. Sir William was Member of Parliament for Perthshire from 1852 to 1868 and from 1874 until his death in 1878. Although an influential member of the Conservative party he did not take a prominent place in the House of Commons. He was much interested in art, literature and history, and during his life-time published a large number of books, the best known probably being *The Annals of the Artists in Spain* and *The Cloister Life of Charles V*. He was a man of wide and scholarly attainments, but he also took a keen interest in local affairs, particularly in the development of agriculture and the rearing of stock.

Few inhabitants of Dunblane were more widely known than Jimmie White, the railway porter, whose face from the opening of the railway until his death was familiar to train travellers. His eyes were china-blue in colour and his face vermilion. In later days his hair and whiskers were snow-white and he had one tooth, a yellow and prolonged one always. He carried a snuff box and a red handkerchief. In winter he bound his boots round with straw to help his walk which was frequently precarious at any season. He was employed to work the bellows of the organ in St. Mary's Church which he attended in a black funeral suit with a large beaver hat ornamented with a crepe band and tied behind in a huge bow. The organ was placed, at that time, at the west end of the church with a screen around it which concealed him and the organist, but this did not prevent him gazing, from time to time, on the congregation as it gathered. Standing on his square seat he would peep over the barrier and remark on the gentry as they came in. One of the best stories connected with Jimmie has reference to a Sunday when he is said to have fallen into a snooze. Canon Malcolm's sermon had for its theme the necessity of a change of heart. The good minister had laid emphasis on the word " change " which caught the ear of the old porter while he snoozed and, not realising that he was not at the scene of his daily labours, he brought out his accustomed cry " Change for Doune and Callander." The story, however, is said to be apocryphal. . While he commented to the organist on the assembling of the congregation he had cause frequently to remark that it was " a weak hive the day."

The first stationmaster at Dunblane was Mr. Dewar, a native of the district, who afterwards became stationmaster at Doune and in his later years at Kinbuck. When he rebuked Jimmie for a weakness which was not unknown among the residents of Dunblane in those days, the latter was accustomed to remark that he was at Dunblane Station before the stationmaster and would be there after he was gone. It is said that he was on duty on the opening day for 4 hours before Mr. Dewar arrived.

The following are some of the anecdotes preserved about old Jimmie. On one occasion he did not observe that a train which had arrived consisted of trucks filled with cattle and was not a passenger train which was about due. He proceeded along the station platform crying as usual " Change for Doune and Callander," and, when his error was pointed out to him, he proceeded on his way shouting "Keep your seats, ladies and gentlemen." On another occasion a young man at the window of a railway carriage called on him to close his eyes and open his mouth and see what he would get, at the same time trying unsuccessfully to throw a shilling into his mouth. The coin fell on the platform and was quickly covered by the old man's foot and he at once invited his friend to have another shot. In his early railway days he acted as a coal agent and kept a number of ponies which in summer he hired out to the "well folk," either for conveying them to the Laighills for the mineral water or for giving them an airing. Jimmie White had an old crony in the fiddler who played on his violin at Dunblane and neighbouring stations. When confined to bed in his last days a local lady who had known him all her life used to sing to him the metrical psalms of his boyhood, while the fiddler rendered old Scots songs. A picture was painted by a well-known artist of the dying man and his fiddler friend playing the " Flowers of the Forest."

There are numerous local surnames which one finds existing in Dunblane over the last few centuries. Among such may be classed Christie and Christison, Eadie, Cramb, Finlayson, and Monteath. The following story is told of Mr. Monteath, saddler in Dunblane, a brother of the school teacher and author of *Traditions*. A travelling showman who had put up at the Cross at Dunblane, as showmen did until recent years, had occasion to have some harness mended at Monteath's shop. When the work was finished the showman came for his harness and asked for the bill. Monteath at first informed him that he would make no charge, but that he would take a dram. His customer stated that that would not do as he required to show a bill in writing to his master. Evidently the saddler was not accustomed to writing accounts, so he went to a brother who was a lawyer in Dunblane to have the bill written out. The latter put it in the following rhyme :—

> " To cutting and contriving,
> To nine nails driving,
> Resin, hemp and leather,
> Five shillings altogether."

One morning a weaver at Dunblane having finished his web set out accompanied by his wife to Alva or some town in that district for which the hand-loom weavers of Dunblane frequently worked. The occasion was one for a holiday and relaxation after the long hours of weaving, but his wife accompanied him in the hope of safeguarding the greater portion of his earnings. She accordingly walked with her husband carrying in her arms their young infant. The day was an enjoyable one and, before returning home, husband and wife became somewhat happy. In passing through Bridge of Allan on their return journey they espied a tasty leg of mutton hanging in a shop and they forthwith went in and purchased it. On the way home wife and husband shared the burden of the child and the meat, taking the infant, the heavier, by turns. On reaching home at a late hour, they put the gigot in their cupboard and the infant in its cradle and were soon fast asleep after the exertions of the day. During the night the neighbours became alarmed by hearing strange noises like the cry of an infant in serious pain. They felt compelled at last to awaken the couple to enquire what was wrong with the bairn. The good wife remarked that there was nothing wrong and that the baby was sleeping quietly in its cradle, but, notwithstanding, noises were to be heard emanating from the cupboard. Further investigation proved that the infant had been laid on an ashet in the cupboard and that it was the mutton that was reposing in the cradle.

On 24th January, 1868, a severe storm occurred in Dunblane and district, accompanied by a heavy fall of snow. Among the damage done was the destruction of the famous sycamore known for generations as " The Big Tree of Kippenross," which is said to have been, in its day, the largest tree in Scotland. It was measured on 26th May, 1821, when it was found to contain 875 cubic feet. The measurements taken in 1841 were as follows, girth close to the ground 42 ft. 7 ins., girth where the trunk branches 30 ft. up 27 ft. 4 ins., extreme width of branches 114 ft., height 100 ft. One of the branches had a girth of 21 ft. which was greater than part of the trunk of the tree. The tree had been previously damaged by lightning during the summer of 1823, but, notwithstanding, it continued to maintain a healthy existence. The age of the tree was estimated in 1842 to be 440 years. According to *The Forester's Guide*, published in 1836 and quoted by Mr. W. B. Bruce, Mr. John Stirling of Keir, who died in 1757, had made many enquiries of old people from 80 to 90 years of age whose memories went back to the reign of Charles II. They unanimously declared that they had heard their fathers say that, so far as their knowledge went, the tree always went by the name of " The Big Tree of Kippenross."

About 1858 a case proceeded in the Court of Session between John Stirling of Kippendavie and MacCulloch and others regarding the Darn Road. It took the form of a Declarator and Interdict. Kippendavie claimed that he was entitled to alter the line and levels of a footpath, called the " Darring Road," between Dunblane and Bridge of Allan. He admitted that the public had a right as foot-passengers to use this footpath. The case was defended, the defenders alleging that the road was formerly used for horses and carts and objecting to the narrowing of part of the road, as also to the proposed alterations. Eventually the action was settled by agreement. Kippendavie admitted that the foot-path ran through his lands from the town of Dunblane to Milland's Brae on the Wharry Burn. Certain alterations on the existing road were agreed to, commencing in front of the inn at Dunblane, all as marked on a plan, but it is impossible to follow the alterations without seeing the plan. Kippendavie was taken bound not to use more than six unlocked gates to be self-acting or easily opened. He and his executors were taken bound to keep the foot-path in good repair. As to the bridge over the Wharry, Kippendavie had the option of maintaining it or allowing other persons to do so, if he did not. The defenders were allowed their expenses as between agent and client. The decision is reported in the *Scotsman* of 23rd July, 1858.

The "Darn Road" case created great local excitement at the time, echoes of which resounded in the district 50 years later. It is related that, at one time, the Laird of Kippendavie employed local masons to build a wall across the road, and that one of the men who built it during the day, assisted some of his friends to knock it down at night.

EARLY SCHOOL BOARD DAYS.

FOR a long period prior to 1873, the parish schools were provided by the local heritors, and education was to a large extent under the supervision of the parish minister. Alongside the parish schools, during the period from 1843 to 1873, were schools kept up by the Free Church of Scotland, and there were usually in each district " private adventure" schools conducted by schoolmasters who were dependent for their salary on the fees paid by their pupils. In 1873, public education was placed in the hands of a popularly elected Board, who were authorised to impose a school rate to meet the expenses of public education, and the heritors and the Free Church of Scotland ceased to provide schools or incur financial responsibility for them.

The first election of a School Board in Dunblane took place on 21st March, 1873, when the returning officer was William Thomson, solicitor in Dunblane, sometime Sheriff-Clerk Depute and afterwards solicitor and bank agent in Callander. He was appointed returning officer by the heritors. The number of the electors on the occasion of the first election was 317, of whom 233, including 42 females, voted, and there were 2 polling stations. The result of the voting was that James Webster Barty headed the poll, followed by Rev. William Blair, James McCaull, cattle-dealer, John Stirling of Kippendavie, Rev. David Tasker, Free Church minister, Alexander Wilson, manufacturer, and the Rev. David Morrison, parish minister. John Cramb, builder, retired before the day of election, and the unsuccessful candidates were, Dr. Thomas Brown, the local doctor, and two farmers, Mr. Kinross, of Upper Whiteston, and Mr. Menteith, Glenhead. The first meeting was held on 29th March, 1873, when Mr. John Stirling was elected chairman, and Mr. William Thomson, clerk and treasurer. The first School Board officer was Thomas Mackinlay, Sheriff Officer, and his salary was £8 per annum. The first school rate imposed was 4d. per pound.

At this time there were in the parish, in addition to parish schools, a Free Church School, a school at Springbank Mills, an infant school and a school at Kinbuck, the latter belonging to Stirling of Kippendavie.

The principal business during the first few years consisted in the taking over of these schools and the erection of new and larger schools at Dunblane and Kinbuck, the pupils being concentrated at these centres. It was a few years later before the rounding up of defaulters figured prominently in the minutes.

In 1875 the male assistant at Dunblane School had a salary of £70. It was agreed, in that year, that the Board should hold its meetings in private.

On the occasion of the second election on 14th March, 1876, there were 336 electors on the roll of whom 250 voted. The successful candidates on this occasion were James McCaull, James Webster Barty, Dr. Thomas Brown, Alexander Wilson, Rev. William Blair, John Stirling of Kippendavie, and William Finlayson, the latter a native of Dunblane employed in Glasgow. The Rev. David Tasker and Rev. David Morrison thus dropped out and their places were taken by Dr. Brown and Mr. Finlayson. William Wilson and James Johnson Thomson were the unsuccessful candidates.

It has to be kept in view that at School Board elections each elector had as many votes as there were vacancies to fill and he was permitted to give all his votes to one candidate or to spread them over the candidates as he thought fit. Considerable feeling appears to have been risen over the election, and a copy of an election address by Messrs. Barty, Blair, Brown, McCaull and Alexander Wilson is preserved—it may be of interest as illustrating how elections were conducted, even only 60 years ago, to give one or two extracts from this address.

" Two Gentlemen, hitherto unknown to fame, of the names of Finlayson and Thomson, have discovered that their mission is to Reform the Educational arrangements of Dunblane. The result is that you will have to pay a heavy expense which is most unnecessarily incurred.

" Persons with less title to be your representatives cannot well be imagined. The one pays no rates and his time is at his master's disposal. The other pays a most trifling rate ; he is resident in Glasgow, and his time is also, we presume, at *his* master's disposal. Your present School Board pay, as individuals, or as representatives of others, school rates exceeding £100 in annual amount. Your would-be public representatives do not pay between them 100d. To be particular they have paid between them 2s. 10½d. ! !

" Are the present Board noted for extravagance ? Three years ago they were charged with parsimony.

" You are asked to discard us in order to admit two parties whose qualifications for the office are of the most meagre character. What great reforms do they contemplate ? They will make the meetings on the Saturday afternoons ! ! ! They will reduce the Clerk's salary."

Words were not minced at election times in those days, but it is strange to find this document emanating from the five staid men whose names are printed thereon.

On the occasion of another of the early elections hand-bills were posted throughout the parish calling the ratepayers at Dunblane to select their own School Board and not to be dictated to by kirk sessions. It may be interesting to preserve the terms of this Bill.

" RATEPAYERS OF DUNBLANE.

Choose your own School Board !
Suffer not to be dictated to in this matter !
Consult your own intelligence !

The law of the land places the matter in your own hand. Why then should seven (7) men be foisted upon you by " Deacons' Courts " and " Kirk Sessions," without your deliberation and without your consent ? It is an overweening conceit on their part, and a despising of the intelligence of the Ratepayers of Dunblane. It is more ! It is an endeavour to frustrate and to stifle a FREE ELECTION.

Why object to a free nomination by the Ratepayers ?

Why object to such men as Dr. Brown, James McCaull, John Bayne, James Gavin, John Cramb ? They are good men, honourable men, and well qualified to secure the efficient administration of the Act, and economy in expenditure.

GOD SAVE THE QUEEN."

Dr. Brown was, for many years, the medical man of the parish, Mr. McCaull, a well-known local cattle-dealer who resided in Balhaldie House, Mr. Bayne and Mr. Cramb, both master-builders, and Mr. Gavin a solicitor who commenced business on his own account, but ultimately left the district.

It is a mistake to think that evening schools are a modern development. Evening schools had been conducted for a long time before the institution of School Boards, and the local Board in its early days arranged for Mr. R. H. Christie, the local headmaster, carrying on evening classes.

This election seems to have satiated the appetite of the electors for the time being, as on the next occasion (1879) there was no poll and the former members were re-elected save that Mr. Finlayson retired and his place was taken by the Rev. J. S. Bowie of the Free Church. In 1882 there was again no poll and no change in the membership.

John Stirling of Kippendavie continued chairman until his death in 1882 when he was succeeded by James Webster Barty and the vacancy on the Board was filled by Patrick Stirling of Kippendavie.

James McCaull, who resided at Balhaldie House, was a member until his death in 1886. He was succeeded by Mrs. Wallace of Glassingall.

At the election in 1885, there were 9 candidates for 7 seats, and on that occasion Dr. Barty retired and another candidate withdrew his name, so that no poll was required. James Gavin, solicitor, Dunblane, took the place of Dr. Barty.

Rev. William Blair was then appointed chairman and continued to hold office until 1909, when he gave up educational work, after having sat on the School Board continuously for 36 years, and acted as chairman for 24 years.

Towards the close of the century several changes took place. In 1898 Dunblane and Lecropt parishes were united and consequently also the School Boards. That year saw a new school erected at Kinbuck and the retiral of R. H. Christie from the headmastership at Dunblane School. He was succeeded by Alexander Hamilton. In 1899 Mr. Wilson, headmaster of Lecropt, retired, his successor being his assistant, Miss Duff. In 1900 Mr. Thomson, who had held the Clerk and Treasurership for 27 years, resigned and was followed by Alexander Boyd Barty, who continued as Clerk until 1919, when School Boards were abolished, to be succeeded for a time by School Management Committees under the County Education Authorities.

In 1903, Mr. Ferguson, headmaster of Kinbuck, retired, and J. M. Chalmers was elected in his place, and in that year Alexander Wilson, Alford, resigned after 30 years' service on the Board.

Dr. Blair's successor as chairman was the Rev. Alexander Ritchie, Dunblane Cathedral, who held office from 1909 to 1915, and he was succeeded by James Rodger, factor, Keir, who occupied the chair until the curtain was finally rung down on School Boards in 1919.

CHAPTER XLI.

DUNBLANE, 1870-1900.

THE year 1870 marks the commencement of a new era in the history of Dunblane. The Rev. James Ingram, parish minister, passed away in 1869 amid general regret, and, following on his death, there was a development in ecclesiastical matters in various directions. In February, 1870, there died at an advanced age, Daniel Stewart, born in 1784, parish schoolmaster for over 50 years, a man of grave but genial manners, esteemed by all sections of the community. On 5th May, 1870, the first Burgh (or Police) Commissioners were elected. Alexander Wilson of Alford was appointed Chief Commissioner and Mr. Boyd, Claremont, and Mr. Grahame—probably the merchant of that name—junior Commissioners. The other members were John Dunn, grocer, Dr. Thomas Brown, and Thomas Watson, baker. Most public offices at that time, as in earlier days, were held by the parish schoolmaster, and Mr. R. H. Christie was appointed Clerk to the Commissioners with a modest salary of £5 per annum. About this time Dunblane was in the course of extension in the neighbourhood of The Crescent, while, shortly before, £4000 had been expended on offices at the County Buildings and £2000 on the prison where eleven additional cells were added and a heating system introduced. The average number of persons in confinement at this time was 8. An attempt was made to develop cattle, sheep and grain markets at Dunblane Railway Station on the first Wednesday of each month. The first was held on 4th June, 1871, but the markets did not prove successful, and in course of time were absorbed into those of larger centres.

Even about 1870, wages paid in this district were small. A local baker received from nine to ten shillings a week and his hours of labour commenced at 4 a.m. Bakers had no blowers for their ovens, and it, therefore, took some considerable time before they were heated with the use of coal, after which the wood of beech trees was burned. Charles McInnes, long a worker at Keirfield, was employed about this time as a baker's boy for a pay of sixpence a week and half a loaf. His employer was a man named Malcolm whose shop stood below the present Burgh Chambers. After a time of service with him McInnes went to Watson, another local baker, when his wage was doubled. In these days many of the inhabitants bore nicknames, by which they were always referred to. Thus, there was Willie Tait, Whitecross, known as "The Old Resurrectionist" as he was blamed for lifting bodies from the churchyard for schools of anatomy, Jimmy Downie, who went by the name of "The Whale" as he was famed for singing a song entitled "The Whale, the Pride of the Ocean," and McEwan known as "The Canary." The Whale was employed as a mason and at the time when Kippendavie endeavoured to close the Darn Road by building a wall across it, Downie was employed professionally building it during the day, and, as one of the public, pulling it down at night. Another old character was Baldie Dougall, barber and hairdresser, and assistant to the Sheriff Officer. His charge for cutting a boy's hair was 1d. At that time two quarts of milk cost one penny and the same sum bought three or four quarts of skim milk. Farm servants had nothing to eat but oatmeal over which hot water was poured and which was supped along with milk. This they had three times daily.

At one time the chief industry in Dunblane was the weaving of shawls. The bulk of the houses in Dunblane were still thatched about 1870. It may be noted that at this time the Laighill Burn passed under the name of the Dalwhommie Burn.

In March, 1870, Peter McCaull, a member of a well-known family of farmers and cattle dealers, took over the tenancy of Dykedale Farm, and 80 ploughs turned out to give him a day's darg. In 1870 Sir William Stirling-Maxwell of Keir was entertained at a public dinner, and in February, 1872, a presentation of a silver sword and an address was made to James Webster Barty at a gathering in the public school at which Sheriff Grahame presided.

The most noteworthy event in Dunblane in the early 70's was the restoration work at the choir and chapter house of the Cathedral. The possible restoration of the nave was talked about as early as September, 1870, but, while this was not proceeded with till many years later, work of considerable importance and interest was carried out on other portions of the ancient building about 1872. At this time there were a number of notable discoveries which included the pillars and mouldings of the transept arch which had been covered up, the doorway on the north side of the choir from the chapter house which had been built up, the old stair from the west end of the chapter house to the apartment above it also built up for a long period, and the Celtic cross found partly under a wall of the chapter house indicating that it had lain there for at least 6½ centuries. This was found on 1st August, 1873, lying 2 ft. below the floor. Among the changes made at this time were the lowering of the floor of the choir and chapter house to the original level, the removal of the Soldiers Gallery across the east window and the removal of the stairway within the choir leading to the gallery above.

Alterations were made in the internal arrangements which included the substitution of a new pulpit erected east from the door of the chapter house in place of the old pulpit which stood near the east end in the centre of the choir. New pews were provided at this time with a centre passage in place of two passages along the north and south walls. Further particulars of this restoration are given elsewhere. The choir was re-opened for public worship in September, 1873.

In May, 1874, the Smith Institute was opened in Stirling. The founder was Thomas Smith of Glassingall who was born near Stirling and educated in France, and who had lived principally in Nottingham. Glassingall was bequeathed to him by an uncle and he came to reside there in 1862. He was a painter and student of the fine arts. After owning Glassingall for a few years he sold it and went to reside abroad. He died at Avignon in March, 1869. He left his pictures along with the sum of £22,000 for the erection of a picture gallery and museum for the benefit of Stirling, Dunblane and district. The first Trustees were the Provost of Stirling, *ex officio*, James Webster Barty and Mr. Cox of Nottingham.

A notable event in 1873 was the formation of School Boards and the taking over of the schools previously maintained by the Heritors and by the Free Church of Scotland, which came under the control of elected representatives of the ratepayers, the cost of public education being henceforth defrayed from the proceeds of the school rate imposed on local owners and occupiers of property, with the help of Government grants. A short account of early School Board days is given in Chapter xli.

An Act of Parliament which helped to modernise public life was the Road and Bridges Act of 1878. Up to that date toll gates were placed on public roads, at distances a few miles apart, and barred the passing of traffic until the prescribed payments were made. By the abolition of tolls there ceased to be any impediment to the free passage of vehicles from place to place, while the expense of upkeep of roads was made by the imposition of rates. On the evening of 22nd March, 1878, the mansion house of Cromlix and its chapel were destroyed by fire. The shooting lodge at Cromlix had been burnt down some 8 or 9 years previously.

The chief event in the history of Dunblane at this time was the erection of the Dunblane Hydropathic establishment which was opened on 13th September, 1878. The local proprietors and leading citizens were all interested in the company which promoted this and they had the assistance of many well-known business men in Glasgow and elsewhere including a Mr. Arthur, a wealthy wholesale draper, Mr. Brechin, a well-known butcher, and Sir Robert Cranston of Edinburgh. The first chairman was John Stirling of Kippendavie, and the first secretary, James Webster Barty. Messrs. Kinnear and Peddie were architects of the building which was said to have been erected in the Italian style. Dr. Clark, who afterwards became a well-known radical Member of Parliament, was the first doctor. The building was inaugurated with the holding of a large ball, and the grounds were illuminated. Prospects of success were at first believed to be good. For some little time there was an average of forty guests resident there, but within a few years the company got into financial difficulties. In June, 1884, Patrick Stirling of Kippendavie presented a petition to the Court of Session for an order to wind up the company. The Hydropathic was sold by the liquidator to Mr. Philp of the Cockburn Hotel, Edinburgh, for £16,000. For some time previous to the sale the Hydropathic had been let to a tenant. Its original cost was £60,000. Numerous changes were made by Mr. Philp which included the removal of the dining-room from the south to the north end and the construction of an addition at the north end where the dining-room now is, with new kitchen premises behind. Originally the kitchen was on the top floor at the south end above what is now the large drawing-room.

KIRK STREET, DUNBLANE, 1883
As painted by Miss Pattie Jack.

Reproduced by courtesy of the Rev. Robert L. T. Blair, B.D., and the Society of Friends of Dunblane Cathedral

SCOTTISH CHURCHES HOUSE
Photograph by Herbert W. Gallagher

In July, 1882, John Stirling of Kippendavie, grandfather of Lieutenant-Colonel John Alexander Stirling, the present laird, died at the age of 70. He succeeded to the family estates in 1816 at the age of five and had possessed them accordingly for over 65 years. Mr. John Stirling was a man of great business capacity and was intimately concerned with railway development throughout Scotland. He was a director of the Scottish Central Railway Company and chairman of the Scottish Midland Railway Company and Scottish North Eastern Railway Company. In 1866 the North British Railway Company got into serious difficulties and he accepted the chairmanship and, largely through his ability, the affairs of this company were put on a satisfactory basis. He was also a director of the Royal Bank of Scotland. He took much interest in the affairs of his estate and tenantry, as well as in matters of local government. He was succeeded by his son, Lieutenant-Colonel Patrick Stirling who, until his death, took a foremost part in all matters of local concern. The erection of the headquarters of the Masonic Lodge was chiefly due to the interest which he showed in and the help which he gave to this project. He was keenly interested in the breeding of Clydesdale horses and other live stock. Colonel Stirling was a prominent Volunteer and, although he did not devote himself as his father had done to company work, he was at the head of all schemes for local improvements, and gave valuable assistance to all local boards.

The year 1884 marks another stage of development in local history. Prior to this time the inhabitants of Dunblane were chiefly dependent for water supplies on public wells or on springs within private grounds. The requirements of the railway company led to the necessity of a reliable water supply which was provided by the construction of a pond at Ochlochy, and from this the first water supply to the Manse of Dunblane was taken. For the benefit of the Hydropathic a pond was made at Leewood, but Dunblane did not have its gravitation supply until after 1884 in which year an agreement was entered into between the Laird of Kippendavie and the Burgh Commissioners to provide for the construction of a reservoir at Waltersmuir with the necessary filters.

A great local improvement was effected in the same year when the houses on the west side of Kirk Street and on the north side of Cross Street were removed, having been purchased, as opportunities presented themselves, by the heritors of Dunblane for the purpose of removal. Their removal enabled these streets to be widened and ground added to the Cathedral churchyard, while, at the same time, an uninterrupted view of the Cathedral was provided.

In the same year the shops and houses forming MacEwen's buildings in the High Street were erected by Messrs. D. & J. MacEwen & Co., merchants, Stirling. These buildings took the place of small old houses and weaver shops which originally extended into the present roadway so as to make it narrower even than the existing corner between the Bank of Scotland and the shop opposite. The thatch of the roofs of these old houses was in easy reach of the average man's hand as he walked by. During the following few years the east side of the High Street was rebuilt in line with MacEwen's buildings. The shop of Mr. Brown, baker, was erected by Lachlan Ritchie, who succeeded an old Dunblane worthy, Thomas Watson, baker. Watson's shop was a low building with a small side window towards the north and a small window to the front, and it also extended into the roadway a considerable distance.

The year 1886 is also notable for the erection of the Masonic Hall with shops below which took the place of the old smithy of Dunblane. Work on the first public hall commenced in that year. It may also be noted that in 1886 the Rev. Alexander Ritchie was inducted minister of the parish, his incumbency being afterwards marked by the great event of the restoration of Dunblane Cathedral.

The erection of a public hall for the use of the inhabitants had been long contemplated. In February, 1860, a public meeting was called to promote a scheme for providing one, and a committee was then appointed to raise funds, but the scheme did not mature until 1886. The hall was completed as a memorial of the Jubilee of Queen Victoria in the following year.

The first Jubilee of the Queen was celebrated in Dunblane in June, 1887. The day's proceedings began with Divine Service in the various Churches. Later in the day a memorial stone was placed in the Victoria Hall and an entertainment followed in the Kippenross Park. Medals were presented to the young folk and a luncheon held in the Victoria Hall at 3 p.m. In the evening a concert was given in the Hall, followed by a performance of " Trial by Jury." The proceedings of the day closed with a bonfire lit at Anchorscross at 10 p.m., and displays of fireworks at some of the principal residences. The decorations in the town were described in the local papers as " simply superb."

Steps of a preliminary nature were taken at this time in connection with the proposal to restore the Cathedral. In March, 1887, a deputation of heritors, accompanied by Lord Balfour of Burleigh and various Members of Parliament, met the First Commissioner of Works in London. Before the approval of the Government was obtained numerous letters appeared in the local newspapers taking exception to the restoration as an interference with the Cathedral for the object of acquiring an uncomfortable church. One correspondent urged that the Cathedral should be left for the reception of the dead. On several occasions reference was made to the proposed restoration as being a " tinkering of a crumbling ruin," and it was said of the Church of Scotland that " its death knell is being loudly sounded." On the other hand Dr. Walter C. Smith, a prominent Free Church minister, wrote to *The Scotsman* strongly advocating the restoration.

While the restoration of the Cathedral was being proceeded with, adverse criticism and comment, which arose almost entirely outside the Established Church, continued for some time. It may be noted, however, that once the work had commenced any feeling of ill-will passed away and the newspapers, which formerly printed views opposed to the restoration, now commented favourably and with interest on the progress of the work.

It was about this time—February, 1888—that the observance of fast days, prior to the celebration of the communion, was given up. Such occasions had ceased to be used for religious worship and had become general holidays.

From time to time the inhabitants of Dunblane took a prominent part in the world of sport. The Volunteer Company (now part of the Territorial Army) was most active in this parish at the end of last century. In their ranks were included many first-class rifle shots who gained distinctions at rifle meetings. Cricket is first heard of about 1865, but, owing to the young men of the neighbourhood leaving the district from time to time for wider fields of advancement in life and also owing to the difficulty of getting a park suitable to the game arising from the hilly nature of Dunblane's surroundings, this fine sport has never taken a hold of the young men of this parish as have other branches of athletics. Cricket was revived with some success from 1899 to 1906, but when the new road was constructed the ground was no longer available and none other being obtained the club was dissolved.

For a number of years the Dunblane Football Club was the strongest in the county. The game was a development of the old game played once a year, or perhaps more frequently, in which the whole parish took part and play was not confined to a park. In earlier times games took place between Dunblane and Kinbuck or between Dunblane and Bridge of Allan, but about 1840 or 1850 football began to be played on a restricted area at the Laighills on Auld Hansel Monday or some other holiday. The players were not hampered at first by rules. Sides were not selected but any person could join either side. The players were not restricted to the use of their feet and head, but could pick up the ball and run with it. When a player got tired he ceased play and the game came to an end when all the players were satisfied to stop. In earlier years games were played between the two ends of our city, and during the play the ball was frequently in the River Allan whither the players followed it. All this added to the excitement of the game.

Modern football in Dunblane is said to date from 1876-77 when clubs were formed by some schoolboys at Dunblane Public School and also by some residenters in the Millrow. A match between these was arranged and took place at the farm of Kippenrait, the goalposts consisting of the players' clothing heaped together. The match came to an untimely end owing to a dispute over a goal.

The first match played by Dunblane Club was with Thornhill in 1877 or 1878 and this resulted in a defeat. For the next match against Bridge of Allan, R. M. Christie, then a schoolboy of 12 years of age, was selected, and through three goals scored by him, Dunblane achieved a victory. In that match only two of the players had jerseys and none football boots or knickers.

Enthusiasm for the game spread and rising players practised on every opportunity and after dark, if moonlight permitted. In these days the players would carry the goalposts 1½ miles from the town to the football pitch and bear them home when play ceased for the night. The Club increased in strength and for several years progressed to the fourth round of the Scottish Cup, to be dismissed on the old Kippenross Park field, now encroached on by the New Road, by the Glasgow Rangers and Third Lanark Clubs. The Dunblane Club's most successful effort, however, was in 1897, when they were defeated in the semi-final of the Qualifying Cup by Kilmarnock, the ultimate winners.

The Perthshire Football Association was instituted at a meeting held in Dunblane during the season of 1884-5. In the first years the prominent clubs were not associated with Perth, but with small country towns. In the first final Dunblane was victorious, their opponents being the Vale of Teith, Doune. They were again successful in the following year, their opponents being Coupar-Angus. After falling in the third year of the competition to the latter, Dunblane had two further wins followed by defeat by the St. Johnstone Club in season 1892-93.

A few years later professionalism was introduced into football and four of the leading local players went to England and this handicapped the local club for some little time.

Dunblane's first colours were blue and white, but about 1884 they adopted the red shirts which they have since worn.

The original success of the club was chiefly due to Robert Main Christie, son of the parish schoolmaster, who was a player from his schoolboy days. He entered Edinburgh University in 1882 and was one of the university team which created a surprise by winning the Edinburgh shield held for some years previously by the Hibernians. In the following year Christie went to Glasgow where he joined the Queen's Park Club, and in his first season he gained Scottish and English cup badges and at the age of 18 represented Scotland in its international match with England, at which match the writer, then a small schoolboy, was present. The newspapers of the day recorded that he was the best forward of the Scottish side. He was famed for his fast runs and superior dribbling, and it was chiefly through his instrumentality that the only goal was obtained which brought victory to Scotland. The following season proved an unfortunate one for the best left winger of his day. He had the misfortune to meet with accidents on the field which prevented him taking a serious part in the game thereafter although for some years he aided the club of his native city.

Major R. M. Christie practised as an architect and civil engineer in Dunblane for many years. He was a keen Volunteer and was one of a small number of Dunblane men who went on active service in the Boer War, being in command of the Service Company of the Black Watch. He again gave his services to his country in the Great War where he met with a soldier's death. On several occasions he skipped a rink in international curling matches.

The only other football player from Dunblane who attained international distinction was his brother, Alexander J. Christie. At first he occupied a position on the left wing, but ultimately became an outstanding centre half-back in the Queen's Park team, and in this position he played against England and in a number of other representative matches. Mr. Christie is in practice as a solicitor in Glasgow.

The game of golf was unknown in Dunblane until 1892 when a course was laid out by Mr. Philp of Dunblane Hydropathic on the Laighills under the direction of Mr. Robert Henderson, the manager of the Hydropathic who was an excellent player, and this was opened for play in April of that year. About this time the popularity of golf as a sport spread with extraordinary quickness from Scotland throughout England and the United States. For centuries the game had been chiefly confined to a few courses on the sea coast, but so popular did this game become that there was soon found a course in every residential centre. Preparations were made for the developing of the game in Dunblane, and the press intimated that Mr. McLauchlan, saddler, had stocked " a supply of the tools " requisite. In the opening match on the Laighills course, old Tom Morris of St. Andrews, who was still able to play a good game despite his years, and Bernard Sayers, of North Berwick, were opposed by two well-known amateur players, Leslie W. Balfour Melville and Alexander Stuart. The former were badly beaten. In the first local competition on this course the winners were (1) Major R. M. Christie and (2) David C. Blair, son of the Reverend Dr. Blair, who, after his retiral from business, became Provost of Dunblane and was one of the promoters of the existing golf course in Kippenross Park.

Three of the leading citizens in Dunblane during the second half of the 19th century were Alexander Wilson, woolspinner, Rev. William Blair, D.D., minister of the United Presbyterian Church, and James Webster Barty, LL.D., solicitor and Procurator Fiscal.

Alexander Wilson was the eldest son of John Wilson of Hillpark, Bannockburn, and was born there in 1834. His early education was at Blair Lodge School, Polmont, and at the age of

14 he matriculated at Glasgow University. After he had contracted typhoid fever there, his parents thought it inadvisable for him to return. He was subsequently sent to Germany for further education, and, whilst still under 15 years of age, he travelled alone to Neuwied on the Rhine. During his stay in Germany he joined a master and other boys in an extensive walking tour, and this may have inspired his life-long love of travel. In later years Mr. Wilson travelled not only in many parts of Europe, but also in the United States of America, Canada, Egypt, and North Africa, but he frequently returned to the country of the Rhine. After completing his education he spent some time in his father's works at Bannockburn and at the age of 19 he commenced business for himself in Dunblane where his father extended and fitted up Springbank Mills for him. This took the place of an old, small mill, known as Walker's Mill. In 1861 he married Miss Isabella Bruce, at which time he built Alford House and took up his abode in Dunblane. As a young man he was always very smartly dressed and he was fond of riding. Before taking up residence in Dunblane he rode on horseback daily from and to Bannockburn.

As business prospered, Mr. Wilson found that there were not sufficient workers locally available for the purpose of his mill, and he arranged for a number of families to migrate from the Isle of Skye to Dunblane to provide additional hands. Accommodation being required for their wants, two blocks of houses, now included under the name of Springfield Terrace, were erected. These were long known as the Skye Buildings. He took a great interest in local affairs. He was the first Chief Magistrate of Dunblane and was long a member of the School Board and Parish and County Councils, while he acted as Session Clerk of the Free Church of Dunblane, now the East Church of the Church of Scotland. In 1875 he purchased the lands of Springbank, including the site of his mills, and land between them and Dunblane, from the Honourable Arthur Drummond of Cromlix. While he devoted much time to public work, his chief happiness was found in his family circle by the domestic hearth. Mr. Wilson died in 1914 at the age of 80.

William Blair, who became minister of The United Presbyterian Church of Dunblane on April 16, 1856, was born at Cluny in the parish of Kinglassie, Fife, on January 13, 1830—the youngest son of George Blair.

The record of his life bears that, after his boyhood's schooling, he and a brother walked from Cluny to St. Andrews to enrol themselves as students in the university. He left the university with the degree of M.A. and in 1879 his Alma Mater conferred upon him the degree of D.D., and still later he was elected to a seat on the University Court.

He had gained experience of the ministry as assistant to Mr. Sorley in Erskine Church, Arbroath, and it was there that he met Elizabeth Corsar, who became his wife in 1858. Then slight of build, six feet tall, dark-haired, with fine cut features, he remained to the end upright in carriage, notable in appearance and courteous in manner. A shepherd-tartan plaid—a gift to him from one of the last handloom weavers in his congregation—in winter time was wont to mark him out, as he wore it on his shoulders.

In Dunblane the United Presbyterian Church stood under the shadow of the Cathedral. William Blair, though a loyal seceder, had sympathies that went out beyond his denomination, and it was inevitable that he should fall under the spell of Robert Leighton, Archbishop and saint of his time. Toilsome happy days spent in the Archbishop's library, among his manuscripts and books, ended in 1883, when he published a memoir of Robert Leighton.

The literary and historical gift thus revealed was recognised and used by his Church. With immense labour, he edited MacKelvie's *Annals of the United Presbyterian Church* in 1873, wrote *The History and Principles of the United Presbyterian Church* in 1888, drew up *The Practice and Procedure of the United Presbyterian Church*, and finally edited *The Jubilee Volume of the United Presbyterian Church* in 1887. These were labours of love and duty, but he was on his own ground when he collaborated with Professor Mitchell of St. Andrews in editing the Wedderburn *Ballads*, when he commenced as a young man, before ordination, dabbling in historical studies which he published under the title of *Rambling Recollections*, or when he essayed a different theme in *Kildermock*. In verse, typical of his style and inspired by a local theme, is " Kilbryde Kirkyard," which has already been quoted.

Musical judgment and gifts were also put at the service of his Church. He was enthusiastic in improving the worship of the sanctuary. Instrumental music was early introduced into his own congregation. His name occurred on all the Praise Committees of his period up to and including that which produced *The Hymnary*. He was himself convener of his own Church'

Praise Committee. From 1870 to 1895, he acted as clerk to the Stirling Presbytery. In 1884, he became, by vote of the Synod, Joint Clerk to the Synod, an office he carried into the United Free Church in 1900. In 1898, he was called to the highest position his Church could offer and moved from the table of the Clerks to the chair of the Moderator.

For forty-four years, William Blair was in sole charge of the United Presbyterian Church, Dunblane, latterly known as the Leighton Church. Though he travelled widely both in Europe and America, sometimes as the representative of his denomination, and though he took more than his share of the work of the Church at large, he contrived to live in closest contact with his own congregation and with the community of Dunblane—a feat only accomplished by being in his study no later, and often earlier, than 6.30 a.m. After 1900 he left the oversight of the congregation in the hands of his colleagues with whom he had the happiest association. But it may be recalled that in education he was one of the most trusted members of the School Board and for twenty-four years its chairman, while he was a member of the Parish Council from its inception and had an intimate knowledge of every person in the parish.

All his life he was unselfish enough to have a genius for friendship. Wherever he went, he made friends with rich and poor. Time and again he impounded the wealth of some to retrieve the needs of others. He lived the life of a Christian man at home in his own family and abroad among his fellows. And when, having celebrated his diamond jubilee, he was in the same year (1916) laid to rest beside the wife who had been his comfort and strength for forty-seven years, it was as though a land-mark had been removed.

James Webster Barty was the son of the Rev. James Strachan Barty, D.D., who was during his ministerial career minister of the parish of Bendochy near Coupar-Angus, and his wife Margaret Webster, daughter of James Webster of Balruddery. The Rev. James S. Barty was a prominent churchman, and was Moderator of the General Assembly of the Church of Scotland in 1868. He was an excellent business man and enjoyed participating in the work of the courts of the Church. He wielded a facile pen and some of his writings appeared in such publications as *Blackwood's Magazine*. He gained considerable fame from a series of letters named *Peter Plough's Letters*, of which he was the author. He was the prototype of the country minister, Dr. Davidson, who figures in the writings of Ian McLaren. After his death in 1874 friends raised a sum of money for a memorial which was devoted to the foundation of a prize for divinity students, known as the Barty Memorial Prize.

James Webster Barty was born at the Manse of Bendochy on 1st November, 1841. He received part of his education at St. Andrews and he afterwards studied Law at Edinburgh University where he unsuccessfully competed for the first prize in Scots Law with a fellow student who afterwards became Lord Wellwood. In 1863 he gained a prize of ten guineas, given by the Society of Solicitors before the Supreme Courts for the best essay written by a student in the Scots Law Class. He commenced business in Dunblane with his uncle, Thomas Barty, in that year and became Captain of the local Company of Volunteers. In 1864 he was appointed an elder of the Cathedral congregation. Prior to his ordination there were only two elders. In March, 1866, he married Ann Moubray Boyd, the orphaned daughter of Alexander Boyd, solicitor in Stirling, who had been brought up with maiden aunts, who, along with their ancestors, had long occupied Allanbank House, Dunblane. Dr. Barty lost his partner and uncle within a few years of commencing business. Thomas Barty died in November, 1867. About this time the former erected Glenacres where he resided for the remainder of his life. In addition to commanding the Volunteer Company, he took considerable interest in shooting and fishing and various forms of athletics, but he devoted much time to public work. He was an excellent rifle shot and competed successfully at open rifle meetings. Under the Procurators (Scotland) Act he acted as a Law examiner while still in his twenties, and along with Professor James Roberton of Glasgow University he was instrumental in the promotion of the Incorporated Society of Law Agents in Scotland. He was the first Secretary of this Society and, save for a short period when he occupied the Chair as President, he continued to act as such until his death. He had a very extensive knowledge of Scots Law, and few, if any, practitioners of his day were better versed in Criminal and Ecclesiastical Law. He was Procurator Fiscal of the Western Division of Perthshire in succession to Thomas Barty for about 50 years, and was President of the Procurators Fiscal Society of Scotland.

For over 50 years he was an elder in Dunblane Cathedral and for a long period he sat

annually as a member of the General Assembly.   In the days when it was sought to dis-
establish the Church of Scotland, he was a keen supporter of its establishment.   Dr. Barty
took a leading part in the committee work of the Church of Scotland, was convener of the
Committee on Libels and wrote a small handbook dealing with such matters for the
guidance of the Church.   Much of the credit of conceiving the idea of the restoration of Dunblane Cathedral and of carrying it out is due to Dr. Barty.   The scheme of the restoration was
mooted at as early a date as 1870 and the proposal was not lost sight of, but it was not proceeded
with until about 1889 when, through the efforts of the Rev. Alexander Ritchie and Dr. Barty,
with the backing and munificent assistance of Mrs. Wallace of Glassingall, the work of restoration was commenced despite some little opposition.   After the restoration was completed he
continued to take steps towards the adorning of the building and was able to influence the
presentation of valuable gifts for the beautifying of the interior.   Dunblane Cathedral was one
of the chief interests in his life.

Dr. Barty led a very busy professional life.   The duties of Procurator Fiscal performed by
him for over 50 years received his personal attention.   He was agent for the Bank of Scotland
and factor on a number of landed estates.   For a time he was partnered by William Thomson,
sometime Sheriff Clerk Depute at Dunblane, but Mr. Thomson left to take over a bank appointment at Callander where he afterwards practised.   For the greater part of his legal career Dr.
Barty conducted a large business unaided, and, as his duties took him frequently from home,
he was accustomed to spend several hours each evening at his office.

Dr. Barty was for twelve years a member of the School Board and for a time its chairman.
He was chairman of the local Parish Council and Parish Councils elsewhere, and perhaps the
most prominent member of the Western District Committee of the County Council of his day.
He continued keenly interested in his business and in all local concerns until his death which
occurred on 23rd May, 1915.

Two contrasting characteristics were combined in Dr. Barty, namely, a certain sternness
and a high degree of kindness of heart.   No one who was under him ever contemplated disobeying
an order, although from no fear of a penalty.   On the other hand, acting as public prosecutor,
he ever sought to lay before the Sheriff any ground for mitigation of penalty, any circumstances
which tended to show the accused party in the least unfavourable light.   Imagine a case of a
man in court charged with wife assault.   Dr. Barty, as Procurator Fiscal having explained to
the Sheriff how the prisoner had hammered the poor woman and severely injured her, to which
the latter had made no reply, would address the accused in words such as these, " Jeemes, my
man, why did you strike your wife—had you taken a gude dram ? "

" Aye, that was it."

" And you did not intend to hit her, Jeemes ? "

" Naw."

" And you love your wife, Jeemes, and will never do the like again ? "

" Aye, aye."

Dr. Barty would then close the case by saying everything a Counsel could have said for the
accused, but probably in a more telling way.

But if one spoke to the Procurator Fiscal later on about the trial and ventured the opinion
that the prisoner was not to be greatly sympathised with, Dr. Barty's reply would have been
that he agreed and that the man was a thorough blackguard.   But notwithstanding, there was
no inconsistency in this.   His experience of human nature could not conceal from him the true
character of the man, but his soft-heartedness caused him to seek out a ground for restricting
the just penalties of the law.   He did justly, but loved mercy.

Dr. Barty abhorred any action bordering on unjustness, unfairness or meanness, so much so,
that, on occasion, there was a danger of his not doing entire justice to a client through fear of
being unfair to his opponent.   He was ever anxious lest he should inadvertently take an advantage which he did not deem that he was entitled to receive.   One might instance this in illustration.   When railway companies first introduced cheap fares for persons travelling on local
holidays, Dr. Barty, for some years, declined to purchase such a ticket on the ground that his
going from home did not arise from the existence of a Dunblane holiday, and that he was travelling on business and not on holiday and that he would have travelled that day and paid the full
fare had there been no tickets at reduced prices.

Dr. Barty had a peculiarly charming manner which put strangers or any persons who felt an awkwardness at their ease, giving them the impression that they were, of all men, particularly welcome. This originated from his kindness of heart and his real desire for the welfare of his friends.

One of the most distinguished sons of Dunblane during the latter part of the 19th century was Thomas Henderson Whitehead, latterly manager of the Chartered Bank of India, Australia and China, who was born on 14th August, 1851. His parents were both of farming stock and he had the good fortune to be brought up in a home in which a high standard was set of straightforwardness, honesty and hard labour. His early education was partly under Dr. Alexander Buchan, afterwards the famous meteorologist. After obtaining a business training in the office of Tho. & J. W. Barty, solicitors in Dunblane, he had a commercial training for two years in Liverpool, after which, in 1873, he entered the service of the Chartered Bank of India, Australia and China, with which he worked for the remainder of his business career. After experience in all parts of the East, as well as in the United States, he was appointed manager at Hong Kong at the early age of thirty-two. In addition to the duties there he added in 1893 those of superintendent of the Far Eastern branches.

In 1901 he went on a special mission to the United States where he was brought into close touch with the financier, Mr. Pierpont Morgan, Mr. William McKinlay, the President, the President of Mexico, and Judge Taft, Governor of the Philippine Islands.

Mr. Whitehead was twice offered the post of financial advisor to the Chinese Government, but declined the appointment, influenced no doubt by difficulties he felt in carrying out monetary reforms.

Mr. Whitehead was greatly interested in the problem of bimetalism, being strongly in favour of the restoration of silver as a recognised standard of value concurrently with gold. He was also strongly in favour of fair trade on the ground that free trade was non-existent.

Mr. Whitehead was held in the highest esteem in Hong Kong on account of his ability and high standard of integrity. He was a member of the Legislative Council and a supporter of reform in the management of Hong Kong.

On leaving Hong Kong for the Head Office of his Bank in 1902, he was entertained to a farewell banquet and presented with an address in Chinese, embroidered on a silk scroll, along with a silver statuette of Confucius. He retired from the General Managership of the Bank in May, 1920. To show the growth of the bank during his period of service, the following figures quoted by Mr. Whitehead may be mentioned. In 1872, the rate of dividend was 1¼ per cent., and in 1919 20¼ per cent. free of Income Tax. In 1872 there was no Reserve Fund and in 1919 it amounted to over three millions. In 1873 the assets of the bank were eight millions and in 1919 sixty-eight millions.

Mr. Whitehead's life after his retirement was a busy one, he taking a prominent part in many schemes for the public good, particularly in connection with the education and advancement in life of young men, in which he was deeply interested. He presented Dunblane with three thousand pounds funding stock, the income to be used for prizes for young people who had distinguished themselves at school or college, as also one thousand pounds of this stock for the benefit of the poor. He helped schemes the aim of which was to help lads to emigrate to the colonies, and in the end a large part of his estate was bequeathed to General Baden-Powell and the Boy Scout movement. In his later years, he endowed two beds in the Royal Infirmary, Stirling, one at Edinburgh in memory of the poet Robert Burns, and one at Perth in which he commemorated Dr. Buchan as his first teacher, Dr. Blair as his first pastor, and Dr. Barty as his first employer.

While he devoted himself whole-heartedly to his business and to advancing the interests of his bank, he was in his youth a notable athlete and sportsman. His kindly nature and his pawky humour made him a most amusing companion.

His death took place in a nursing home in London on 15th May, 1933, and, after cremation, his remains were laid in Dunblane Cathedral burying ground in the grave of his parents whose memory he so greatly revered.

Dunblane owed much in the last years of the 19th century to the Reverend Alexander Ritchie, D.D., minister of Dunblane Cathedral. He was born in Edinburgh in January, 1853, the son of a master printer. His education was at the Edinburgh Institution and University where he graduated Bachelor of Divinity at the age of 21. He was licensed in 1875 and was for a time assistant at St. Giles Cathedral when Dr. Cameron Lees commenced his ministry there. Minister of the Parish of Whithorn from 1879 to July, 1886, he was then translated to Dunblane Cathedral where he laboured for thirty-one years until his retiral in 1917. His name will be kept in everlasting remembrance through the leading part which he took in preparing the way for the restoration of the Cathedral, for helping in carrying out the work thereafter, for his successful efforts in equipping and decorating the building in a dignified and worthy manner, and for building up a large congregation equipped with all modern church organisations.

Dr. Ritchie was well read and drew successfully from his knowledge of literature to adorn his pulpit discourses. His church services were simple and dignified and he adopted a moderate course of neither adhering too rigidly to the older fashions of worship nor adopting too many innovations.

Dr. Ritchie gave considerable time to public work in Dunblane, particularly to matters connected with education and the care of the poor. While a regular attender at church courts, he had little interest in matters of ecclesiastical government.

The anxieties and strain of the Great War told severely on his strength and, in the autumn of 1917, he resolved to retire. In 1919, the degree of Doctor of Divinity was deservedly, but somewhat tardily, conferred on him by his old university. Dr. Ritchie passed away in July, 1931, at the age of 78.

Chapter XLII.

SOME POETRY AND POETS OF DUNBLANE.

Of the poets connected with Dunblane one of the finest, as well as the most voluminous, is Walter C. Smith, the poet-preacher of the Free High Church in Edinburgh, previously minister of the Free Church at Orwell, Kinross-shire. Dr. Smith, a man of much culture and devoid of narrow sectarianism, owned Orwell Cottage, which now belongs to the Ancient Order of Foresters and is used as a convalescent home. It stands above Kinbuck Station and from it in 1902 he issued his collected poetical works extending to over 600 pages. The book was published by J. M. Dent & Co., Aldine House, London. Among the longer poems the best known are " Olrig Grange " and " Hilda among the Broken Gods," but many of his smaller poems are worthy of high praise, as for example, Hymn No. 12 in the revised *Scottish Hymnary*, which, differing from so many of our hymns, is full of suggestive thought and poetical expression,

The poem of Dr. Smith, which specially appeals to lovers of Dunblane, is the first in this volume, entitled " The Bishop's Walk," which seems to exhale the spirit of the little old city in the middle of the 19th century before it wakened up to modern days. This poem is full of beautiful expression and of the spirit of Leighton, the portrait of which is tenderly drawn. A few stanzas are quoted here in the hope that readers may acquire and love the whole poem.

I.

A gray old Minster on the height
Towers o'er the trees and in the light ;
A gray old town along the ridge
Slopes, winding downward to the bridge—
   A quaint, old, gabled place,
   With Church writ on its face.

2.

The quiet Close, secluded, dim,
The lettered scroll, the pillar slim,
The armorial bearings on the wall,
The very air you breathe, are all
   Full of Church memories,
   And the old sanctities.

3

And beautiful the gray old place
With characters of antique grace,
That tell the tale of pious work
Beneath the spire and round the kirk,
   And growth of Law and Right
   Where Christ had come with light.

32

Two hundred years have come and gone,
Since that fine spirit mused alone
On the dim walk, with faint green shade
By the light-quivering ash-leaves made,
   And saw the sun go down
   Beyond the mountains brown.

33

Slow-pacing, with a lowly look,
Or gazing on the lettered book
Of Tauler, or a-Kempis, or
Meek Herbert with his dulcimer,
   In quaintly pious vein
   Rehearsing a deep strain.

37

A frail, slight form—no temple he,
Grand, for abode of Deity ;
Rather a bush, inflamed with grace,
And trembling in a desert place,
   And unconsumed with fire,
   Though burning high and higher.

38

A frail, slight form, and pale with care,
Made paler by the raven hair
That folded from a forehead free,
Godlike of breadth and majesty—
   A brow of thought supreme
   And mystic glorious dream.

Dr. Walter C. Smith was preceded by an earlier ministerial poet, the Rev. Alexander Henderson of St. Blane's Rood, Dunblane, minister of the Anti-Burgher congregation and principal of a boarding school for boys. In August, 1839, he published Canto the First of a poem called " The Pilgrim " with a frontispiece showing the Cathedral, taken from a picture by Sir Noel Paton painted in the same year. The poem is written in the stanza of Spenser and the author intended that this Canto should merely be the beginning of a long ambitious poem. As apparently it proved to be the last, the poem could not have met with popular success, but it is not without merit as may be appreciated from the following stanzas :—

III.

It was a lovely Sabbath afternoon—
A Scottish Sabbath—all above, around,
Bathed in the last beams of a July sun,
Rested in silence, holy and profound.
Nothing was heard, save the soft hum and bound
Of insects wheeling in the tepid air—
The voice of woods—the air's Aeolian sound—
The Allan's roll—the neighbouring tree-perched
  choir
Pouring in one loud song their little souls of fire.

IV.

DUNBLANE lay in the sunshine, young in age ;
Its mould'ring ruins speak of former years,
They teach us man's affairs, like foliage,
Have spring-time and decay. The spot appears
Where Druids taught. They taught—the people's
  fears
Subsided. Druidism passed away.
Culdees succeeded them. The pile still rears
Its massive front, where they retired to pray.
Rome sent, the Culdees bowed, and owned the Papal
  sway.

V.

Mitred Episcopacy came in state,
And loved to worship in thy ancient halls ;
She, too, gave way to Presbytery and Fate.
Dunblane ! unknown in the decay that falls
On thy Cathedral and its Palace walls ;
A City once : a city-village now ;
I love thee—home adopted—Nature calls,
From thine own river, and from mountain brow ;
She claims my love ; she has it, and my fervent vow.

VI.

I love thee !—all-unchanging as thou art,
In mountain, river, springs, and ruins grey—
All beautiful ! Thy voice within my heart
Finds a response, as it has done alway,
In every heart that loves with thee to stay.
Lords of the soil may claim thee—gold their aim ;
They plow—they build—years roll—they pass away
Oblivion shrouds them, and blots out their name ;
But Nature, thou alone for ever art the same.

Among other clerical poets connected with Dunblane is the Rev. William Blair, D.D., formerly minister of the Leighton Church. His works were not collected and published, but poems of considerable merit were published from time to time in the press. His poem entitled " Kilbryde Kirkyard " has already been quoted.

David Webster was the son of a labouring man of Dunblane. He received a good education, but at his own request he was sent to Paisley about the end of the 18th century to learn shawl weaving. He was of a social nature and was a clever mimic, but was led into indifferent company where he acquired habits he failed to throw off. He published a volume of poems in Paisley in 1835, but died about 1836 or 1837 at the age of 50. The following is a good example of his skilful writing :—

TAK' IT, MAN, TAK' IT.

When I was a miller in Fife,
Losh ! I thought that the sound o' the happer
Said, " Tak' hame a wee flow to your wife,
To help to be brose to your supper."
Then my conscience was narrow and pure,
But someway he random it rackit ;
For I lifted two neivefu' or mair,
While the happer said " Tak it, man, tak' it."
Then hey for the mill and the kill,
The garland and gear for my cogie.
And hey for the whisky and yill,
That washes the dust frae my craigie.

It was at this period, namely, the beginning of the 19th century, that " Jessie the Flower o' Dunblane " was written, a song which would have made Dunblane immortal had it no other claims to immortality.   Notes on this song are given elsewhere in this volume, as is also the old ballad known as " Cromlet's Lilt," a romantic poem or ballad connected with the love affairs of Sir James Chisholm, the 5th Chisholm of Cromlix, and Helen Stirling, niece of the laird of Ardoch, in which it is narrated how a false friend, trusted by Sir James, betrayed him and wooed his sweetheart, Sir James returning only on the wedding day in time to throw out the supplanter and to claim the bride.

Poems connected with the Battle of Sheriffmuir and with the notorious Heather Jock are noticed elsewhere.

This short account of poets connected with Dunblane may be concluded with two verses quoted by Dr. Stewart, the author of the booklet on the mineral wells of Dunblane.

> By Allan's banks in wild flowers clad,
> Or resting 'neath the cooling shade
>   Of birch, or oak, or plane ;
> While, robed in white, the hawthorn tree,
> Or daisy laughing on the lea,
>   Says, " Welcome to Dunblane ! "
>
> While birds, too, on the branches sing,
> To Him who made these waters spring,
>   And bade them cure your pain ;
> Who gave the sweetness to the breeze,
> And said to Nature, heal and please
>   The stranger in Dunblane.

CHAPTER XLIII.

THE RESTORATION OF DUNBLANE CATHEDRAL, 1889-1893.

IF the greatest event in the history of Dunblane was the erection of its noble Cathedral, probably the next most important incident was its restoration in 1889-1893. It was no little undertaking for a town of less than 3,000 inhabitants, with a congregation of less than 500 members, to undertake this great work, namely, the re-roofing of the nave, which had stood roofless for 300 years, and the completion of the building in a manner fit for the proper conduct of religious worship. The congregation of the parish church, which had worshipped in the choir of the Cathedral since shortly after the Reformation, had suffered severely on three occasions, namely, at the end of the eighteenth and during the nineteenth centuries on two occasions by the presentation of ministers whose appointments met with general disfavour of the members, and by the Disruption in 1843, when the minister and elders and the majority of the members left the parish church to form a congregation of the Free Church of Scotland. Many years elapsed before such incidents were forgotten and fresh generations gathered together to form again a body of some strength and standing.

The Rev. Alexander Ritchie, minister of the parish of Whithorn, was inducted to the parish of Dunblane in July, 1886. Twenty-five years had elapsed since a minister, undesired by the congregation, had been forced upon them—although it is only right to say that he proved himself a faithful pastor and died at the post of duty. The congregation was again one of some vitality, and it was felt that the accommodation which the Cathedral choir provided was insufficient to hold its members and adherents, and in addition the choir was in need of considerable repair.

On 25th November, 1886, Dr. Ritchie called a meeting of his Kirk Session to consider the question of the insufficiency of the seating accommodation for the congregation. It is recorded that the choir was capable of holding 440 persons, giving the usual allowance of 18 inches to a sitting, while the number of communicants was then 437 and of adherents 373, making a total of 810 persons. The Session came to a resolution that the accommodation was inadequate, and that this was prejudicial to the interests of the Church of Scotland and of the community in general, and it was then agreed to make a representation to that effect to the heritors of the parish, with a view to their taking action. It will be noted, however, that there is no suggestion in this minute that steps should be taken for a restoration of the Cathedral, or in what way the additional accommodation should be provided.

No action having been taken prior to 7th June, 1888, the Session on that date instructed their clerk to direct the attention of the heritors to the uncomfortable condition of the church arising through draughts caused by the decay of the fittings of the windows and the openness of the stone work, and from dampness caused by insufficient conductors to convey rain water from the roof.

It is not known who first conceived the idea of restoring the Cathedral, but it may be of interest to recall that at a dinner given by the heritors of the parish on the day of Dr. Ritchie's induction to Dunblane, Colonel Patrick Stirling of Kippendavie, the principal heritor, referred in a speech to the fact that Dr. Ritchie had at Whithorn achieved some fame through restoration work carried out in that parish, and he suggested that he would find in Dunblane an excellent opportunity for similar work. This may have been intended as a humorous remark, and it was received as such, being greeted with the laughter of those present.

On the Sunday following his induction, Dr. Ritchie was introduced to his congregation by the Rev. Dr. Cameron Lees of St. Giles Cathedral. After evening service, conducted by Dr. Ritchie, Dr. Cameron Lees and he passed from the choir through the ruined nave. After a moment of silence and reflection, Dr. Cameron Lees remarked : " Now you will give neither sleep to your eyes nor slumber to your eyelids till you restore this building." Thus within a few days, at the beginning of his ministry at Dunblane, the suggestion of the restoration was twice made to Dr. Ritchie.

Prior to Dr. Ritchie's induction, the question had undoubtedly been the subject of conversation between James Webster Barty, solicitor, Dunblane, one of the leading elders, and Mrs. Wallace of Glassingall, whose great generosity eventually enabled the work to be carried out.

The suggestion of the restoration was also made by Dr. Ritchie's predecessor, the Rev. David Morrison, in his farewell sermon prior to his leaving Dunblane for the Tron Parish, Edinburgh, in December, 1885, in which he suggested that this work should be undertaken as a memorial to Bishop Leighton. It is very probable that the work might not have proceeded, at least at that time, had the necessity for additional church accommodation and for repairing the choir not become urgent, and it was indeed fortunate that the heritors did not satisfy their legal obligation of providing further accommodation by erecting a new building. This was certainly talked about on more than one occasion, and favoured by some in preference to a scheme of restoration. One site suggested for a new church was in Perth Road, where "Kincairn" now stands.

Few restorations of ancient buildings had been effected up to this time in Scotland and such as had been carried through had not always proved successful. It is not surprising, therefore, that in this little city the project was not received with enthusiasm. Hostility to the restoration came from some who were unfriendly towards the congregation who worshipped in the Cathedral choir and to the Church of Scotland, while other inhabitants allowed their judgment to be warped by fear of the work being carried out in a modern style and without due regard to the features of the original building. Other parishioners regarded the scheme with indifference.

The help of John Ruskin, who had a profound admiration for the architecture of the nave, was sought by the opponents of restoration. He wrote condemning the proposal, and stating that he would rather see a railway driven through the ruins than that the hand of the restorer be laid upon them, and referred to the proposed restoration as the "most vulgar brutality committed since the Reformation."

The preliminary opposition, however, was centred principally around the supposed right of burial within the ruins of the nave, and the doubt as to the strength of the walls and pillars to sustain a roof, while the consent of the Board of Manufactures had also to be procured.

In Dr. Ritchie's last talk about the restoration on 18th June, 1931, about a fortnight before his death, he remarked that the opposition of certain sections of the people, the necessity of raising a large sum of money, and the indifference of the community as a whole, never troubled him so much as the thought that the restoration might be carried through to perfection architecturally but still prove a failure through a want of appreciation of a beautiful place of worship by the parishioners who did not take advantage of it, and through a pulpit inadequately filled by himself. He was able to overcome all opposition, and ultimately to prove that his personal fears had been unfounded.

The work of the restoration was directed by an executive committee consisting of the principal heritors or their representatives along with the Rev. Alexander Ritchie. The first meeting was held in the County Buildings, Dunblane, on 14th December, 1888, at which the Honourable Captain Arthur Drummond of Cromlix presided. The other members present were Colonel Patrick Stirling of Kippendavie, Dr. Ritchie and Dr. J. W. Barty. Mr. William Laird, a relative of Mrs. Wallace of Glassingall, was also one of the original members, and at later stages, her son, Mr. John Wallace, Mr. Montgomery Paterson of Holmhill and General Stirling of Keir were added.

The first meeting elected Kippendavie to be convener, but he soon retired in favour of Captain Drummond. It may be noted that neither was a member of the Church of Scotland. A letter was read to this meeting from the Board of Manufactures intimating that the plans and estimates of the restoration work must be submitted to them for approval at this stage. The executive committee resolved that *further* estimates should be taken and formal contracts made with the contractors selected, and that power be reserved to stop the work at any stage by payment to the contractor for the work actually done, he to have no claim for breach of contract. It was agreed that no work should proceed until any litigation which had been threatened was brought to a successful conclusion. The architect's fee was fixed at 5 per cent. plus travelling expenses. Dr. Ritchie was appointed honorary secretary, Mr. William Alexander, solicitor, Dunblane, clerk to the executive committee, and Dr. Barty, honorary treasurer.

The Board of Manufactures requested a meeting with representatives of the committee which was held on 10th January, 1889. Dr. Ritchie, Mr. Laird and Dr. Barty represented the executive committee. The Lord Justice-General presided. It was explained to this joint meeting that the plans were generally approved except that doubt was felt with regard to the tracery of certain windows, and also as to whether the walls of the nave were sufficiently strong to support a roof. Mrs. Wallace at this stage agreed to be responsible for the expense of an examination of the walls by a practical builder or builders, as also for the expense of raising an action of declarator in court or of defending any action raised by the public to stop the restoration work. The walls were thereupon examined by two Glasgow builders, Mr. Thomas Mason and Mr. Robert McCord. They reported that, when the work proposed by the architect was executed, a roof such as had been designed could be erected with perfect safety. A similar report in even stronger terms was submitted by Mr. David Grant, builder, Edinburgh, who was also consulted. This difficulty having been cleared out of the way, the executive committee proceeded to make good their position as against Mr. Robert Hay, manufacturer, Kinbuck, an owner of property in Dunblane, who had threatened an action of interdict should the restoration of the Cathedral proceed. The Board of Manufactures at this stage submitted a memorial for the opinion of Mr. W. Mackintosh, afterwards Lord Kyllachy, and Mr. A. Low, afterwards Lord Low, with reference to the claims by parties of a right of burial in the interior of the nave. It was explained that interments had occasionally occurred within the nave numbering about one in every second year, but only after the relatives had obtained permission from the Office of Works. Counsel gave the opinion that the proposed operations would not involve any disturbance of graves or any desecration, that the legality of interments within the Cathedral was extremely doubtful, and that no claim of right of burial therein could legally be made in future. The interior of the nave was regarded as Crown property, and not as a portion of the churchyard. It was eventually found unnecessary to take any proceedings in court, and no legal steps were taken by Mr. Hay and his supporters. It was not intended to remove, and, as a matter of fact, there was, during the work of restoration, no disturbance of the remains of persons interred within the Cathedral walls. The surface soil was removed only to a depth of about 8 inches. A layer of concrete was laid about 6 inches thick, and the finished floor laid above it. The existing tombstones were embodied in the floor so far as possible over the position of the graves indicated on the stone of the floor. When this was not possible, inscriptions were cut on the floor above the graves.

The Board of Manufactures having stipulated that the heritors provide a sum of £3,000, the interest of which would be expended on the maintenance of the Cathedral after restoration, the heritors arranged with the Caledonian Insurance Company to advance £3,500 repayable by half-yearly instalments extending over a period of ten years, and the required sum was lodged in the bank. All preliminary obstacles having been overcome and the necessary money for the work having been provided, the executive committee, on 6th August, 1889, instructed acceptance of the offer of James Slater, contractor, Edinburgh, for the mason work, wood-work of roof, floors, drains, scaffolding, etc., and that of James Goodwin & Co., Motherwell, for the iron work of the roof.

The plumber and gasfitting contract was eventually given to Mr. James L. Arnott, Glasgow, whose offer was less than that of Mr. John McLaren, Dunblane, while slater and glazier work were both given to Mr. Robert Graham, Edinburgh. Mr. Graham, however, gave up his slater contract, which was taken over by A. & D. McKay. The actual work of restoration commenced on 16th September, 1889, and by February, 1890, the architect reported that satisfactory progress had been made.

On 12th May, 1890, Dr. Ritchie intimated that, on account of the state of his health, he would be absent from home for a considerable period, and the committee were for some time without his valuable assistance. He obtained six months leave of absence from the Presbytery of Dunblane and, on medical advice, he visited Australia. Much anxious work had told upon his strength.

The congregation last met for service in the choir as the parish church on 21st December, 1890. Thereafter the members worshipped within the Victoria Hall for over two years. The pews and other church furniture had meantime to be stored, and the organ, gifted by Mr. Henderson, some time of Glassingall, was dismantled. It was considered unsuitable for use in the restored building, and was purchased by Mr. Ingram, Edinburgh, the builder of the present organ, for £150. The new organ, which on several occasions has been added to and greatly improved, was bought by funds contributed by the congregation.

During the progress of the work Dr. Rowand Anderson recommended the renewal of the inside of certain walls with ashlar. He was of opinion that at some earlier period this had been picked out and the walls refaced with inferior rubble stone.   Some of this work was undertaken, but other walls remained unaltered, such as the inside of the aisle walls of the nave.

One question that gave rise to considerable difficulty was whether the two westmost windows in the north aisle should be restored as they had remained since the middle of the 16th century or changed into windows similar to the other aisle windows.   It was ultimately resolved to retain the windows as they stood, as forming part of the architectural history of the building.   Dr. Rowand Anderson, however, found evidence that these windows originally had been similar to the other windows in the north and south aisles.   The Board of Manufactures disapproved of altering the windows, and also of introducing ashlar masonry where there was rubble.

At this stage the Marquis of Bute, who had become a Trustee of the Board, was consulted as to the heraldic ornamentation of the bosses of the roof of the nave.   Lord Bute on 24th May, 1890, writing from the House of Falkland, dealt very fully with this subject.   He recommended that the arms of seven Earls of Strathearn should occupy the seven bosses on the north side of the nave commencing from the east end, and that the bosses on the south side beginning from the west end should be occupied by those of the six Earls of Strathearn from Maurice to Walter, along with those of King James II, the first Royal Superior.   The thirteen bosses along the middle of the roof were to be occupied by the Royal Superiors after James II down to William IV, while the Arms of Queen Victoria were to be placed on a boss between the two windows over the chancel arch.

Lord Bute was desirous that a rood-loft should be erected or otherwise that a rood screen be placed in the original holes, and that it such should support a highly decorative piece of work like the front of an ornamental gallery.   This proposal was not proceeded with, but the bosses were decorated in accordance with Lord Bute's scheme.

Arrangements were made at this time with John McLaren, butcher, Dunblane, who owned the river banks at the Haining, to allow a pipe for the removal of roof and drainage water to be laid from the west end of the Cathedral down to the river bank and thence to the River Allan.

Before the restoration work was allowed to be commenced, the Board stipulated that £16,000 be subscribed.   Of this sum Mrs. Wallace and some relatives contributed £14,000, to which she afterwards added £2,500.   Other subscriptions received ran from £2 to £500.   The total sums subscribed amounted to £19,573 15s., apart from the £3,000 paid to the Board by the Heritors.   No contributions were made by the ordinary members of the congregation.

Considerable correspondence passed between the architect, the Restoration Committee, and the Board of Manufactures with regard to the tracery of the choir windows, which was generally disapproved of.   Dr. Anderson prepared plans for renewing the tracery more in accordance with the style of the building, but these were not adopted.   Later on in the progress of the work of restoration he prepared a further set of plans, but these again were not approved.

In November, 1890, the architect intimated that he proposed altering the system of heating which he had intended should be installed in the Cathedral and replacing this system by hot water pipes.   He suggested that a house should be erected on an unused portion of the churchyard with the heating boiler in a portion of this house.   This arrangement had certain drawbacks, and the proposal was dropped in favour of heating boilers placed below the Lady Chapel.   In view of the additional work proposed to be put in hand, Mrs. Wallace of Glassingall gave her further contribution of £2,500.

It was at first intended that the nave of the Cathedral should be lit by gas standards set on the floor between the pillars.   It was, however, agreed to abandon the standards for pendants suspended from the roof.

As already mentioned, it was arranged that where there were flat and regularly shaped grave stones within the nave, these should form part of the floor, but in the case of irregularly shaped stones or carved surfaces that these should be laid aside, and that the names and dates thereon should be inscribed on the floor of the nave where the stones had formerly lain.

The north wall of the choir had, prior to the restoration, no windows or openings.   It was resolved to form a triforium by the opening up of arches, ashlar stone work taking the place of rubble in this wall.   The cost of this work was about £700.

On 19th December, 1891, plans for the pulpit, choir screen, communion table, gas pendants and interior porches were all approved by the committee, but, in the case of pulpit, table and screen, difficulty arose with the Board, who disapproved of the design in each case.

T

Dr. Anderson was also desirous of colouring the roof of the nave.　This was opposed by Kippendavie as " an entire mistake."　The committee held the proposal over, according to the minutes, for financial reasons.

On 4th February, 1892, the Board of Manufactures passed a unanimous resolution that the style adopted by Dr. Anderson in his designs for pulpit, choir screen and communion table was not so suitable as one less decidedly departing from the general Gothic character of the building particularly as the Prebends' stalls offered an appropriate model on which to base the designs of these fittings.　While the minute was carefully framed so as to hurt the architect's feelings as little as possible, it apparently did not achieve that end.　He addressed a long letter to the Board complaining that their finding inferred that he had committed an error in violating the traditions and practice in the decorative fittings of Dunblane Cathedral, and alleging that the views of the Board were entirely unsupported by the history of art.　The Restoration Committee sent a deputation consisting of Dr. Ritchie, Mr. Stirling of Keir, and Dr. Barty to discuss with the Board the designs which had been disapproved.　The deputation found that the members of the Board held very strong opinions against the designs, which were expressed by Sir Noel Paton, the Lord Justice Clerk and Sir George Reid, P.R.S.A.　In view of the strong opposition of the Board, the deputation recommended the Restoration Committee to give way to their wishes.　It was accordingly resolved to ask Dr. Anderson to submit new designs for the pulpit and communion table and to leave over the question of the choir screen.　Dr. Anderson seems not to have received the decision of the Board with good grace, and a short time later he informed the Restoration committee that he had not prepared new designs and was too much occupied to do so.　The committee afterwards instructed Dr. Anderson not to proceed with designs for a new pulpit. Mr. Archibald Russell of Auchenraith, coalmaster, for many years tenant of Kilbryde Castle, at a later date, offered to pay the cost of a pulpit.　Dr. Anderson made a new design which was ultimately accepted by the committee.

The tomb traditionally believed to be that of Bishop Dermoch was, in the opinion of Dr. Anderson, the tomb of Bishop Clement.　It is understood that the chief grounds for his opinion were that the tomb presented the characteristics of a thirteenth century one, and that its position indicated the position where the builder of a cathedral, as a rule, was interred.　The tomb was restored at this time.　It is understood, however, that this tomb formerly stood at the south wall of the choir opposite its present position, but it is probable that it was removed there from its present site.

The Kirk Session and congregation were met with disappointment on several occasions by the delay in the completion of the work and by postponement of the re-opening of the building for public worship.　It was at one time intended that the Cathedral be used for worship in September, 1892.　This was afterwards postponed to October, then to December, and afterwards to the following year.　One cause of the delay was an alteration in the heating of the choir from radiators placed against the wall to an air-duct formed under the floor which is filled with heated air from a powerful radiator in the heating chamber below.

A new design for a communion table was submitted in March, 1893, and approved by the Board of Manufactures.　This was an anonymous gift.　A modified design for a choir screen was also approved in June, 1893.

The principal contractor was Mr. James Slater, who executed both mason and joiner work at a figure of about £10,500. Mr. James L. Arnott, plumber and gasfitter, was paid £1,675, which included the lectern, which cost £112.　A. & D. McKay, slaters, received £612 16s. 8d., and R. Graham, Glazier, £337 3s. 2d.　The heating arrangements were supplied by Mosgrave & Co., Ltd., Belfast, costing £696 1s.　The architect's fee amounted to £1,500, and Mr. Alexander, Secretary to the Committee, was paid £250.　Considerable work was carried out under the Clerk of Works at a cost of over £5,000.　The price of the choir screen was £643.　The painters account only amounted to £148 19s. 11d.

A special service to commemorate the completion of the restoration was held on Saturday, 28th October, 1893.　At the beginning of this service Mrs. Wallace of Glassingall handed to the Marquis of Lothian, Chairman of the Board of Manufactures, the golden key which Lord Lothian in turn handed to Patrick Stirling of Kippendavie as representing the heritors, to whom the right of use of the Cathedral as a parish church had been given.　The latter then handed the key to Dr. Ritchie as parish minister.　The ministers who took part in this service were Dr. Ritchie,

Rev. David Morrison, Tron Church, Edinburgh, who preceded Dr. Ritchie as minister of Dunblane Parish, Rev. Wm. Blair, D.D., minister of Leighton Church, and Clerk to the Synod of the United Presbyterian Church, the Right Rev. Walter C. Smith, D.D., Moderator of the General Assembly of the Free Church, and the Right Rev. J. Marshall Lang, D.D., Moderator of the General Assembly of the Church of Scotland. While this marks the completion of the work of restoration, it may be mentioned that the Cathedral had been open to the public from 31st March, 1893.

On the following Saturday (4th November, 1893) Dr. Peace of Glasgow Cathedral gave a recital on the new organ.

The Restoration Committee met for the last time on 27th February, 1894. The total sums subscribed for the restoration as at that date amounted to £26,091 18s., of which Mrs. Wallace, with the help of her brother, Mr. Weir, and her immediate friends, contributed about £19,000. Since that date as large a sum has been expended on the interior decoration of the Cathedral as the cost of the restoration of the fabric.

A Masonic ceremony had taken place at the Cathedral on the 6th October, 1892, when a memorial stone of the restoration was laid by the Grand Master Mason of Scotland, the Earl of Haddington. In a cavity of the stone were placed photographs of the Cathedral, an account of the restoration written by Dr. Ritchie, a newspaper of the day, and coins of the realm within a sealed bottle. The memorial stone stands in the south wall of the choir opposite the communion table at a height of 3 or 4 feet from the floor.

The nave was first used for worship after the restoration on 5th March, 1893. The service was one of Communion in which Dr. Ritchie was assisted by Dr. Cameron Lees of St. Giles. Forty-three young persons communicated for the first time, and thirty-nine new members were admitted by certificate. There was no formal opening till the following October.

The condition of the fabric of the Cathedral before its restoration was in some parts serious, and, had the restoration not proceeded, much of the building might have crumbled by this date into irreparable decay. Piecemeal restoration or repair had been executed from time to time. Thus about 1860, Sir William Stirling-Maxwell of Keir restored the north aisle wall east of the north doorway and inserted tracery in its windows. Considerable repairs were executed about 1871, principally to the choir and chapel, and some years later the top of the walls of the nave, which had been previously covered by sods, were covered with cement, and some of the tracery in the west window was renewed, while repairs were also executed on the clerestory particularly on the north side. The string course on the south side had also been renewed, but the moulding was not correctly reproduced. The string course on the north side is a facsimile of the original. Such partial works indicate how necessary it was that the restoration should have proceeded when it did, if the building was to be saved for posterity, particularly when one considers that rain had, before the cementing of the tops of the walls, run down the inside of the pillars and caused many of the stones in the bases to decay.

It is impossible to indicate all the work executed during the restoration. In the nave the wall-heads, gables and jambs, sealed arches and tracery of windows, as also the clerestory arches, were repaired and renewed when necessary, decayed stones replaced and the walls pointed. The two windows at the east end of the nave in the north and south aisles were carried to rise into a gable projecting above the aisle roof, there being clear evidence afforded in the nave walls, and on the sills and jambs of the windows of this being their former condition. The nave and aisles were entirely roofed and the windows glazed. The pillars of the nave were left precisely as they were found, subject to minor repair. Ashlar work was substituted for rubble in the clerestory walls between the clerestory string course and the pillars, also beneath the west window and on the wall of the south-east aisle. A course of ashlar was also carried round the nave at the floor level to permit a further extension of this work at any time without disturbing the floor. The wall which filled up the chancel arch was removed. Considerable repair was done in the choir. A flattened deal roof had been supplied in 1862 in place of the ancient one. This was replaced by a roof of oak at the original pitch. The tracery of the large south choir windows was renewed in a manner appropriate to the period to which they belonged. The wall heads required considerable repair, and the east gable was raised to its original height. The cross above the east gable which has its upper south arm broken off was replaced as it was, but the crosses on the west and middle gables were placed there for the first time at the restoration. The parapet along the north wall, which had been taken away, was replaced. The turrets in the east gable were rebuilt and their decayed tops run up into finials. The walls of the Lady Chapel were much bulged and had to be taken down and rebuilt stone by stone. In the north wall of the chancel were inserted three arches at the level of the floor of the chamber above the chapel. The west-most arch is not filled with tracery, and is concealed by the organ pipes. The interior walls of the chancel, which were of rubble partly coated with modern plaster, were lined with ashlar. A doorway and porch were inserted in the north wall of the chapel to form an independent entrance. Dr. Anderson being satisfied, from the character of its decayed mouldings, that the tomb said to be that of Bishop Dermoch belonged to the thirteenth century, it was restored in Gothic style. These notes may serve to indicate how extensive was the work of restoration and how thoroughly it was executed.

It is somewhat remarkable that there is no reference in the Kirk Session books to the opening ceremony, nor any comment therein on the work while it was in progress.

It is only fitting to record the valuable services to the work of restoration rendered by Mr. George Kermack, clerk of works. Mr. Kermack was not only skilled in all building operations, but he was a man of sterling character who refused to pass any work that was not executed in a first-class manner, and he was above corruption. He was thoroughly interested in his duties, and was never absent from his post. One interesting fact was determined during the work of restoration, namely, that the choir had been erected prior to the nave—the stone-work of the nave having been built on to the choir walls which had been constructed at an earlier date.

While the restoration of the fabric was completed in October, 1893, comparatively little had been done by that time for its internal adornment. Munificent gifts were afterwards received from Sir Robert Younger, now Lord Blanesborough, Mr. John Graham Stewart, Ault Wharrie, Dunblane, and many others, and there has never been a time during which some fresh gift for the beautification of the Cathedral has not been in course of preparation.

The Executive Committee of the Restoration, the Architect, the Clerk of Works, Mrs. Wallace, Mr. John Wallace, have all passed away—Dr. Ritchie, whose death occurred on 3rd July, 1931, was the last survivor, but happily the spirit which inspired their great work survives in the present incumbent, in members of Kirk Session and in many friends of Dunblane Cathedral all of whom are filled with a great love for this noble building, cherished by them as the fairest House of God in the kingdom of Scotland. Before his death, Dr. Ritchie read the church notes in manuscript and his comments thereon are now given in full.

Notes by the Late ALEXANDER RITCHIE, D.D.

I have read the foregoing account of the restoration of Dunblane Cathedral, and would first say that it is absolutely correct in all its details. It is interesting to find that in many points there was a variety of opinion. I recollect that the architect's original drawings for the woodwork such as the pulpit, choir screen, table, etc., were more of a Gothic design and less ornate. After Dr. Anderson had made his later plans I informed him that I preferred the earlier plans to the second. He replied by asking me if I never re-wrote a sermon, and I answered that I had done so and spoilt the original. Dr. Anderson was of a very determined nature, and it was very difficult to get him to alter his views to conform to the wishes of others.

When the two north-west windows were being restored Dr. Anderson discovered the springs of the old Norman windows. I wished these restored to make them the same as the others of the north aisle. Dr. Anderson, however, thought that these should be restored in the form which they had been in for some centuries, although it was not in accordance with the remainder of the Cathedral. In most cathedrals the windows, etc., are divided into three, five or seven portions, but in Dunblane Cathedral the windows have usually four lights. Sir Robert Lorimer at the time of the restoration was with Dr. Anderson as his chief draughtsman. In the first design for the roof of the nave tie-rods were shown in the inside of the roof. It was said to me, if the roof were made in that way, it would be like St. Pancras Station. I repeated the remark to Dr. Anderson with the result that after a time I found that he had altered the plans of the roof.

The original intention of the donor of the large east window was to insert two of the south choir windows in coloured glass. I went to London to see the artist, Mr. Kemp, and on presenting him with the measurements of the east window, I found that it would cost little more to insert it in stained glass than to insert two of the south windows. The donor agreed to insert the east window accordingly. This was well, as had two of the south windows been put in then and others later, the south windows would not have been of a piece, having been executed by different artists.

INDEX

(This Index is not, and is not intended to be, exhaustive. It contains, however, the names of all important or noteworthy people and places, and a comprehensive list of the subjects treated in the text).

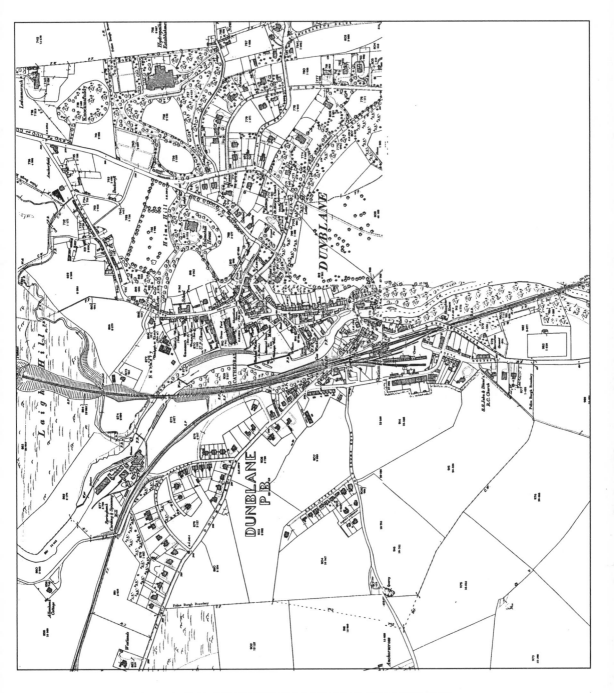

Figure 1: 1900 ORDNANCE SURVEY MAP OF DUNBLANE
Reproduced by kind permission of the Trustees of the National Library of Scotland

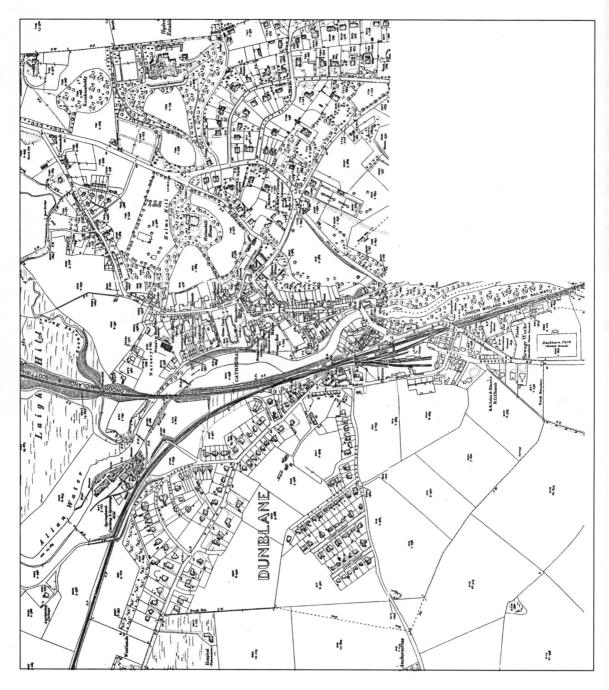

Figure 2: 1932 ORDNANCE SURVEY MAP OF DUNBLANE
Reproduced by kind permission of the Trustees of the National Library of Scotland

CHAPTER XLIV

A BRIEF HISTORY OF DUNBLANE FROM 1900 TO 1994

INTRODUCTION

The History of Dunblane traced the history of Dunblane and the surrounding area up to AD 1900. This additional chapter continues the history of the town from 1900 to 1994.

The Ordnance Survey map of 1900 (second edition), see Figure 1, shows a small town dominated by several large buildings, the Cathedral, the railway station, Springbank Mill, the 'Hydropathic Establishment' and large private houses such as Holmehill House. Then, as now, the town was split by the river, the Allan Water, and by the railway line. There was, however, little housing to the east of the Perth road, the road which later in the century, as the A 9, was to form a third dividing line through the town. In 1900, people travelling south and entering Dunblane along the Perth road continued as far as St Mary's Episcopal Church. There it was necessary to turn sharp right and follow the road all the way down the High Street to the Old Bridge, to go up past the station and hence reach the Stirling Road which crossed the railway line before leading out of the town. The road from St Mary's Church to the Stirling Road did not then exist.

The map of 1900 shows that many public buildings in use today were in existence then, although not all bore their modern names. These include, for example, the Cathedral and three other churches, the station, the Victoria Hall (marked 'Hall') and the Stirling Arms Hotel (marked 'Hotel'). The open areas of the 'Laigh Hill' to the north and what is now Ochlochy Park to the south are clearly visible, the latter with the curling pond marked. Housing was mainly concentrated around the central area, from the Cathedral to the station, although there were also dwellings in the 'Brae Port' and Ramoyle, in Keir Street and in the Springfield Terrace and Doune Road area. A few larger houses had been built further out along the Doune Road and to the east of the Perth Road.

There are then many similarities between the Dunblane of 1900 and the Dunblane of 1994, but there are also significant differences. Some of these differences can be seen in the form of buildings in use then which no longer exist today. Examples of these are the jail, two mills, the gas works and the smithy, all of which are marked on the 1900 map. On the other hand, some of the facilities which we now take for granted did not exist in 1900, facilities like car parks, petrol stations and the health centre. Housing has increased enormously in quantity this century, both private and council houses, out of all proportion to the increase in population. Most people in Dunblane in 1900 lived in more cramped accommodation than today and life for many people was considerably more restricted in terms of mobility and of opportunity.

In what follows, the points touched on above are expanded and others are discussed as the authors trace the history of Dunblane since 1900. It should be noted that only the history of the town itself is covered, although *The History of Dunblane* included information on some of the surrounding villages like Ashfield and Greenloaning and also some of the nearby estates, for example, Argaty, Cromlix, Glassingall, Kilbryde and others. This omission is not because the authors lack interest in the surrounding area. It is rather because the town of Dunblane has expanded and changed so much in this century that tracing its history has become a subject in its own right. For the same reason, the history of Dunblane is not compared in detail with the histories of other towns in Scotland, interesting though such a comparison might be.

One of the great merits of *The History of Dunblane* is the author's meticulous attention to accuracy. The present authors, aware of the tradition they are following, have checked every statement for accuracy. Where, for instance, a particular date has proved difficult to verify, they have preferred to give a general indication of dating rather than an unchecked statement of fact, for example, 'in the 1960s' or 'between the wars' rather than '1963' or '1935'. For any errors or inaccuracies that remain the authors take full responsibility.

1.THE TOWN

a) Population and housing

The most obvious change in Dunblane during the twentieth century has been the increase in population, an increase that has mostly taken place since 1960. The 1901 Census recorded the population of Dunblane burgh as 2516; up to and including 1961 the population was recorded as under 3000, see Table. In 1981, the latest year for which census figures are available, it was 6661. Between 1981 and 1994 there has been further significant increase.

Table: Population figures for the Burgh of Dunblane

Date	Population
1891	2186
1901	2516
1911	2978
1921	2931
1931	2692
1951	2985
1961	2923
1971	4497
1981	6661

Source: General Register Office of Scotland.

The number of houses in Dunblane has increased even more dramatically than has the population. The rise in the number of houses is due partly to the increase in population and partly to the rise in living standards of that population. In 1891, there were 2186 people living in the town, in 518 houses (*Census 1891*, p. 39), an average of 4.2 persons per house; for Scotland as a whole the figure was 4.9 (*Census 1891,* p. 2). By 1981 the population of 6661 lived in 2265 households (*Census 1981, Central Region* 4, p. 36), the average having fallen to 2.9 persons per household, a figure comparable with Scotland as a whole. At the turn of the century living conditions were low by modern standards. In 1891, for example, 51% of the population of Dunblane parish lived in houses where only one or two rooms had windows (see *Census 1891*, p. 316). The figure for Scotland as whole was 61% (see *Census 1891*, p. 308). At the turn of the century many households in Dunblane lacked the exclusive use of a bath and toilet, but by the 1981 census, 99% of Dunblane houses enjoyed these amenities, a figure comparable with the rest of Scotland.

Following the Housing (Scotland) Act of 1919, the first council houses in Dunblane were built in Backcroft and were let in 1922; the next to be built were the houses in the Ramoyle in 1926 and in Claredon Place in 1929. Demand for housing continued to outstrip supply and in 1944 the Town Council made an application for 20 temporary houses to be erected in George Street. These were eventually replaced by permanent houses during the post-war expansion of council housing. The proportion of the Dunblane population living in municipal housing has, however, remained low by comparison with the rest of Scotland. In 1981, 65% of houses were owner-occupied, 26% rented from Stirling District Council (*Census 1981, Central Region* 4, p. 36). The percentage of council-house and Housing Association tenants in Scotland as a whole was 56%, almost double the rate of England at 31% (figures supplied by the General Register Office for Scotland).

By the 1990s, sheltered housing for the elderly was provided in Dunblane both by the Hanover (Scotland) Housing Association, which ran three schemes, and by private organisations administering retirement accommodation such as that in Holmehill Court. Owner-occupiers have been responsible for improving areas of Dunblane that used to contain houses in a poor state of repair, for example part of the Ramoyle. Houses here have been renovated and restored and by 1994 the area had become most attractive.

b) Shops

By contrast with dwelling houses, the number of shops in Dunblane did not increase over the century, and food shops have in fact decreased in number, despite the large rise in the population. This is particularly obvious in the second half of the century and can be explained in terms both of people's increased mobility and of the appearance of super-markets in large places nearby. By the 1990s many people preferred to do their food shopping in these large shops, mainly in Stirling. The super-market prices were lower, the produce fresher and the variety greater than in shops with a smaller turnover of goods. In 1950 Dunblane High Street had the following food shops: five grocers, two butchers, two bakers, two fishmongers and the Co-operative Society store which had all these departments. By the 1990s only a reduced Co-operative store, one grocer and one fishmonger remained in the High Street although there were still three butchers, one having replaced the butchery department of the Co-operative Society, and a delicatessen had also opened. In place of the food shops there have appeared a book shop, craft shops, gift shops and estate agents. There is apparently a possibility that a super-market will be built in Dunblane on the Doune Road before the end of the century.

c) Other buildings

Dunblane has always had a large number of public houses and hotels relative to its population. In 1793 there were 29 such establishments, although this figure includes premises that today might be described as licensed grocers or off-licences; by 1831 the number had fallen but there were still 14 establishments (Barty *History* p. 225). In 1993 there were seven fully-licensed hotels in Dunblane: the Dunblane Hydro Hotel; the Stirling Arms Hotel; the Dunblane Hotel and the Railway Tavern (for many years called the Railway Hotel) in the Stirling Road; the Chimes in Kirk Street; the Red Comyn Inn in the Perth Road; and Westlands Hotel in the Doune Road. Hotels just outside Dunblane included Cromlix House and the Sheriffmuir Inn.

Dunblane Hydro Hotel was built as a hydropathic establishment and opened in 1878; the venture not being a commercial success, it was sold in 1884 (Barty *History* pp. 221, 274). It has been run as a hotel since then, except during the two world wars, see below. The Stirling Arms Hotel, the Dunblane Hotel, the Railway Tavern and the Chimes were all in existence in the early nineteenth century. The Stirling Arms Hotel and the Dunblane Hotel were both at first leased, and then bought, from the Kippendavie estate. The Red Comyn Inn was originally the Leighton Church manse, which was built around 1858 (Barty *History* p. 261); subsequently it became a private house but by 1955 it was the Ardleighton Hotel, a private hotel, before being extended to become the Red Comyn Inn.

As the twentieth century proceeded, Dunblane acquired a number of private hotels and guest-houses; before the advent of sheltered housing, some of these catered for the elderly who could afford to live there. Increasingly, however, these have accommodated visitors to Dunblane. Some have become licensed hotels while others have remained private. The 1993 brochure produced by the Loch Lomond, Stirling and Trossachs Tourist Board listed seven establishments, over and above those already mentioned, including some offering bed-and-breakfast accommodation. Also listed were seven establishments offering self-catering accommodation in and around Dunblane. There were also several not listed by the Board.

Since 1900 various cafes and restaurants have appeared in Dunblane, for example the long-established Allan Cafe in the High Street as well as several fast-food and Chinese restaurants. The India Gate Restaurant at the Fourways roundabout occupies premises which were opened in the 1930s as Laidlaws Tea Bungalow. In the 1950s this establishment became the Fourways Restaurant before being turned into the Indian restaurant in 1991.

Other public buildings included the jail, the Sheriff court, the Victoria Hall, the Burgh school, the tuberculosis sanatorium and the Scout hut. The jail and the police station were in the same building until a new police station was built in the late 1950s. (On this and other local government buildings, see 7. LOCAL GOVERNMENT). The jail building, built in 1842, was demolished around 1963 and a small garden established in its place. Both the old jail and the new police station had two or three cells for overnight accommodation, but those sentenced by Dunblane court to periods of imprisonment went to Perth. After 1975, when the court itself ceased to exist (see 7. LOCAL GOVERNMENT), men sentenced to imprisonment by Stirling Sheriff Court were committed to Barlinnie prison in Glasgow while the women went to Cornton Vale prison in Stirling.

The original Victoria Hall was opened in 1887, the first jubilee of Queen Victoria, as a public hall (Barty *History* p. 275). In November 1925 it was burnt down at an estimated loss of £3000. At a public meeting in February 1926 support was given to the idea of building a replacement hall on a different site as long as this was not paid for by an increase in rates. When an attempt to raise money failed, this scheme was abandoned and the hall was rebuilt on the same site. It was reopened in October 1927.

The Burgh school in the Braeport consisted of several school buildings as well as the head-teacher's house. These were in use until the new school opened in 1962 (see 3. EDUCATION). One part of the school was incorporated into the Scottish Churches House (see 5. PLACES OF WORSHIP); another part, which had been the Infant School, eventually became a furniture store. The head-teacher's house was sold as a private dwelling house. The remainder of the school was used as a youth club until it was taken over, following the 1975 reorganisation of local government, as premises for the Youth and Community Service of Central Regional Council. In addition of, the building now houses various sporting and cultural groups (see 6. RECREATION) as well as religious groups and pre-school play-groups.

The tuberculosis sanatorium was erected in 1909-10 by Captain Stirling of Keir and remained in use until 1930. It was situated at the junction of what are now Scott Drive, Wallace Road and Murdoch Terrace. In 1934 the building was turned into a Youth Hostel and remained in use for some years until it was demolished. In the early years of the century there had been an 'Iron Hospital' at Wellpark near Dunblane and a 'Small Iron Hospital' at Duthieston, just north of Dunblane. Both of these had been run by Perth County Council. They were closed soon after the opening of the 'Combined Hospital' in Stirling which subsequently became Stirling Royal Infirmary.

The Scout and Guide hut was built at the bottom of the Glen Road in 1919. A larger hall was subsequently built on the same site.

d) Parliamentary representation

From the beginning of the century until 1923 Dunblane was in the constituency of West Perthshire which during this period returned four members of Parliament: John Stroyan (1900-1906), David Erskine (1906-1910), John George Stewart-Murray (1910-1917), who succeeded as eighth Duke of Atholl in 1917, and James Gardiner (1918-1923). From 1923 to 1983 Dunblane was in the constituency of Kinross and West Perthshire. Five members of Parliament were returned in this period: Katherine Marjory, Duchess of Atholl, (1923-1938), William McNair Snadden (1938-1955), William Gilmour Leburn (1955-1963), Alexander Frederick Douglas-Home (1963-1974) and Nicholas Hardwick Fairburn (1974-1983). Since the boundary changes of 1983, Dunblane has been in the constituency of Stirling whose member of Parliament is Michael Bruce Forsyth.

e) World wars

Dunblane suffered no material damage during the two world wars although it was not unaffected by them. During the second world war, troops were stationed near Dunblane and evacuees from Glasgow were accommodated in the town. Schiehallion House on the Doune Road was opened as an Auxiliary Hospital. Dunblane Hydro was requisitioned during both wars. During the first war it was known as the Dunblane War Hospital and drawings dated June 1918 show the internal layout at that time. During the second war it had several uses, from housing a girls' boarding school from England to being used as a military convalescent home. A photograph dated April 1941 shows military personnel and nursing staff in front of the building. The 1918 drawings and 1941 photograph are preserved in Dunblane Hydro Hotel. In August 1944, under the Holidays-At-Home scheme, a week of holiday activities was organised. These included four dances and a concert in the Victoria Hall, a band-performance and a children's entertainment on the Laighills and an open-air dance in the street outside the Cathedral. The War Memorial, set up in 1922, commemorates those who died in the two world wars. The memorial was originally sited opposite St Mary's Church on the corner of the Glen Road and the Stirling Road. It was moved to its present position on the Haugh in 1959 when the Stirling Road was widened.

2. Employment and services

The changes in employment patterns are partly the cause, partly the effect, of the changes in the population of Dunblane over the last century.   In 1900 many of the inhabitants of Dunblane worked within the burgh, just as they shopped and took their recreation there.   Some people from surrounding farms and villages came into Dunblane to work and to shop.   Today many of the inhabitants of Dunblane work elsewhere.   The 1981 census gave the percentage of the Dunblane working population who travelled to their employment by car as 66.1%, compared with the national (UK) average of 50.2% (*Key Statistics* p. 54).   From this time onwards, people with access to cars, many of whom drove outside Dunblane to go to work, also did the bulk of their shopping outside Dunblane.   Dunblane shops provided a considerably greater range of the available goods, and much greater job opportunities, in 1900 than they did in 1990.

In 1900 cars were rare and horse-drawn transport provided employment in the form of blacksmiths, grooms, coachmen and others; in 1906 Mr Andrew Morrison was advertising his livery-stable and coach-hiring service in the Millrow.   The 1900 Ordnance Survey map, see Figure 1, marks a smithy in Smithy Loan but this is no longer marked on the 1932 Ordnance Survey map, see Figure 2.   Before the first war, however, a garage had been opened at the upper end of the High Street, near St Mary's Church.   By 1950 there were four garages in Dunblane and in 1994 there were three.

This movement form horse-drawn to petrol-driven transport can be illustrated by the history of the business which became King's of Dunblane Ltd on the Doune Road.   Early in the century an establishment on this site was run by Mr George Morrison and during his time the change was made from horse-drawn carriages to limousines.   When Mr Walter King bought the business in 1929 there were no longer any horses left.   From 1929 to 1973 Mr Walter King ran the business as a taxi and car hiring service, including car hire for weddings and funerals; in 1951 he introduced coaches.   Since 1973 the business, run by his son, Mr Charles King, has been exclusively a coach hiring company.

Throughout the century, firms of builders, joiners, plumbers and similar establishments have operated in Dunblane, providing both services and employment to the town.   The number and type of services have of course altered over the years.   In the early years of the century, for example, many people in Dunblane were employed in private domestic service.   By the 1990s, very few people were employed in domestic service and the majority of those who did this work were employed by Central Regional Council as 'Home Helps' for the elderly and/or the disabled.

In 1900 there were two mills providing employment in Dunblane, the last two of a long succession of mills operating on the banks of the Allan (see Barty *History* pp. 248-9).   The meal mill in the Millrow, marked on the 1900 Ordnance Survey map as 'Corn Mill', which had been in existence for several centuries, was finally demolished in the early 1950s.   The other mill was Springbank Mill or Wilson's Mill, marked on the 1900 and 1932 Ordnance Survey maps as 'Springbank Carding & Spinning Mill'.   This was a textile mill that continued in operation until the last quarter of the century.   Many of the mill buildings were subsequently demolished to make way for private housing but in the 1980s one of them was converted into luxury flats.

Agriculture, although traditionally a large source of employment for the Dunblane area, was never as important for town workers.   With increasing mechanisation, the number of people employed as agricultural workers has been in decline all century.   Small enterprises have however flourished in Dunblane, for example the market garden on the Haining, marked on the 1900 Ordnance Survey map, which continued for over half a century, and the mushroom farm in Atholl Place which operated successfully for some years after the second world war.

A gas-lighting company had been formed in 1941 (Barty *History* p. 261) and gas was manufactured at the gas works in the Millrow, seen marked on the 1900 map.   Gas continued to be manufactured there until around 1950 and the manufacturing building was demolished around 1951.   Gas was then piped from Stirling to the Dunblane gasometer.   This gasometer remained in use until around 1967.   In common with the rest of the area, Dunblane was subsequently converted to natural gas.   Gas manufacturing remained in private hands, supplied by the Dunblane Gas Company Ltd, until the nationalisation of gas in 1949 when it was supplied by the Scottish Gas Board. Following privatisation in 1986 the company was renamed British Gas plc Scotland.

Electricity was introduced to Dunblane in 1923, supplied by a private company, Dunblane and District Electricity Supply Company Ltd. In 1947 electricity was supplied to Dunblane by the Grampian Electricity Supply Company. In 1948, following the nationalisation of electricity, Dunblane was supplied by the North of Scotland Hydro-Electric Board. From the 1990s, after the privatisation of electricity services in Scotland, Dunblane was supplied by Scottish Hydro Electric. By the 1980s virtually all dwelling houses in Dunblane had a supply of electricity.

The professions in Dunblane have always provided not only services but also employment, in terms of clerks, typists and similar jobs. In the early years of the century there were two banks in Dunblane; subsequently this rose to four but by 1994 there were only three. Throughout the century there have been two flourishing firms of solicitors. The firm of Tho. & J. W. Barty was established in 1829. The firm of McLean and Stewart took this name in 1906 but they were the successors of Stirling and McLean, established in 1863, which was the successor of even older firms. Solicitors used to offer services also provided nowadays by estate agents, accountants and insurance agents, all of whom by the 1990s had separate establishments in Dunblane.

Health care has been provided in Dunblane throughout the century, in the early years by doctors like Dr Lindsay and Dr Buist practising from their own homes. In 1924 the first District nurses were provided for Dunblane under the Maternity Service and Child Welfare Scheme. In 1939, the three Dunblane doctors amalgamated to form one practice, Laird, Macfarlane and Fairley, although they still worked from their own houses. A surgery in Well Place was opened in 1968 for the use of the combined practice. The Health Centre, across the road from the Well Road surgery, was opened in 1986. In 1990 there were seven doctors, three practice and six community nurses, three health visitors and eleven receptionists working from the Health Centre. Health care services in the 1990s were also provided in Dunblane by, among others, dentists, chiropodists and opticians.

By the last decade of the century, such employment possibilities as there were in Dunblane were provided by establishments such as those noted above, by shops and hotels (see 1. Town) and by a limited amount of light industry. In the Duckburn Industrial Estate on the Stirling Road are located firms such as glaziers, medical suppliers and suppliers of technological services. In Springfield Terrace there is Dunblane Light Engineering Ltd, established in 1957, which replaced Dunblane Engineering Industries, set up nearby in 1947 on the site of an old smithy.

As noted above, for many years a large number of people have lived in Dunblane and travelled to work elsewhere, usually in Edinburgh or Glasgow. What has changed in the last decades of the century is that people have started to commute to other places as well as to Glasgow and Edinburgh: to Stirling, to the University of Stirling (founded 1967), and to other places throughout central Scotland.

3. EDUCATION

In 1900 Dunblane Burgh School in the Braeport was still administered by a locally elected school board. These boards had been set up by the Education (Scotland) Act of 1872 at which time the parish schools run by the Church of Scotland and the Free Church of Scotland ceased to exist. The school board continued to administer Dunblane Burgh School until 1919 when, following the Education (Scotland) Act of 1918, the administration was taken over by a school management committee under Perth County Council. The 1918 Act also enabled denominational schools to transfer to the management of the county council. The only such school in Dunblane was St Mary's Episcopal School. It had been founded some time after 1843; permission for the erection of the school building in Smithy Loan was given in 1849.

In 1900 elementary education was compulsory and free from the ages of 5 to 14. In that year there were 331 pupils on the roll of the Burgh School, taught by eight teachers under the head-master Mr Alexander Hamilton. Continuation classes were offered in the evenings for children over the age of 14 and for adults. In the session 1902-3, the continuation classes proposed included elementary English, arithmetic, geography and drawing as well as advanced classes in six groups of subjects: commercial mathematics, book-keeping, electricity; needlework;

shorthand; wood-carving; building construction and mechanical art and drawing; and cooking. From 1903 secondary schooling took the form of Supplementary Courses for those who passed the qualifying examination; in 1918 these became known as Advanced Divisions.

In 1921, the first year this century for which figures are available for St Mary's School, there were 83 pupils on the roll under the head-teacher Miss Munro. From 1940 to 1944 St Mary's School building was requisitioned for military use. Two rooms in the Burgh School were provided for use by St Mary's pupils and teachers. Since 1970 Miss Isobel Barker has been the head-teacher of St Mary's School. St Mary's School is a primary school only and in 1990 had 56 children on the roll.

Following the end of the war, the Education (Scotland) Act of 1946 changed many aspects of education; crucially, the Act included the provision of free secondary education for all. Dunblane Burgh school was now divided into two parts, a primary school and a junior secondary school. At the age of 12, pupils sat the qualifying examination and those who passed, about 35%, were eligible to enter a senior secondary school. The nearest such school in Perthshire was the McLaren High School in Callander and the Dunblane children travelled there and back daily by train or by bus. The 65% who failed the examination remained in Dunblane junior secondary school. In 1947 the school leaving age was raised to 15 but pupils at the senior secondary schools usually remained until they sat the Scottish Leaving Certificate at the age of 17. In 1950, under the headship of Mr D. M. Bell, there were 356 pupils on the roll of Dunblane school, including primary and junior secondary pupils, and 56 on the roll of St Mary's under the headship of Miss Paterson.

In December 1962 the new Dunblane school was opened on the Doune Road, the official opening taking place in May 1963. The school still catered for both primary and junior secondary pupils and the headmaster was still Mr Bell. However, the Education (Scotland) Act of 1969 merged junior secondary and senior secondary schools under 'Secondary Schools'. Following this, phase 1 of Dunblane High School was opened in 1974 with a fully comprehensive intake and gradually increased in size until it contained the full six-year complement. No pupil was then obliged to leave Dunblane for secondary education. In 1972 the school leaving age was raised to 16.

In 1990 there were 695 pupils on the roll of Dunblane Primary School, which included 80 nursery pupils. In 1993 Dunblane High School had 709 pupils on the roll. The numbers of staff have risen proportionately much more over the century. In 1990 Dunblane Primary School had 24 teachers under the headship of Mrs I. J. Rae and in 1993 Dunblane High School had 47 full-time and 7 part-time teachers under the Rector, Mr J. L. Gardner.

As well as these schools, there is the Queen Victoria School situated just north of Dunblane. It was officially opened in September 1908 by King Edward VII as a boarding school for the sons of Scottish soldiers, sailors and airmen, and of service men and women who are serving or who have served on a regular engagement in Scotland. The first boys were admitted in June 1909 and by the end of that year there were 145 boys under the headship of Lieutenant W. L. B. White. In 1950, under Major D. G. Washtell, there were around 250 boys. Until 1973 the headmaster was an officer in the Army Education Corps but since then the school has had civilian headmasters. In 1990, under the headship of Mr J. D. Hankinson, there were 265 boys aged from 9 to 18 and around 70 members of staff. The Queen Victoria School pipe band is well known throughout Scotland. It has, for example, played at the Edinburgh Festival Tattoo and, for many years, at international rugby matches at Murrayfield.

4. COMMUNICATIONS

In 1900 Dunblane was situated at the junction of two railway lines going north from Stirling, one to Perth and Inverness and one to Callander, Crianlarich and Oban. Both lines were then run by the Caledonian Railway Company. In 1923 the lines were taken over by the London, Midland and Scottish Railway Company which ran them until the nationalisation of the railways in 1948. The lines were then run by British Railways, Scottish Region, subsequently renamed ScotRail. The line from Dunblane to Crianlarich was closed in 1965. Because of its historic importance as the station at which to change to the Crianlarich line, a role subsequently taken over by Stirling, Dunblane retained the privilege of being a stopping station for the

London to Inverness trains. By the 1960s, however, the express trains stopped at Dunblane only if a passenger requested it. On occasion the request was overlooked and the unfortunate passenger was carried on to Gleneagles. During the century the number of railway employees has been much reduced. A photograph (preserved in the Cathedral Museum) taken around 1920 shows thirteen staff employed at Dunblane station; by 1993 the staff had been reduced to two.

In 1900 Dunblane was also of course situated on the main road from Stirling to Perth. As already noted in the Introduction, the road from St Mary's Church to the Stirling Road did not exist in 1900 and through traffic had to pass through the High Street. The bypass was constructed during 1904-6 and consisted of a road on the line of the present dual carriageway as far as Beech Road and of Beech Road itself. The latter was made on the line of the Beech Walk, an entrance drive to Kippenross House. The entrance lodge to Kippenross was dismantled and rebuilt on the other side of the main road, where it remains. Despite strong arguments put to the Town Council as to the desirability of building a new bridge over the river, this was not undertaken. After the opening of the new road, traffic had still to cross the Old Bridge by the Stirling Arms Hotel. In 1927, however, this bridge was widened and pavements added. In August 1920 the Town Council noted with concern that many vehicles were exceeding the speed limit of 10 mph inside the town.

The first bypass to Dunblane was completed in 1940 with the building of St Blane's Bridge so that through traffic did not need to enter Dunblane town at all. The bypass formed a portion of the A9 and was made into a dual carriageway in 1959. In 1969 the Scottish Development Department put forward a plan to upgrade the A9 into a major trunk road, complete with flyovers and tunnels, which would have effectively sliced Dunblane into two parts. This plan met with considerable local opposition and the Dunblane Society was formed, whose main aim was to oppose it (see 6. RECREATION). Eventually it was agreed that a new bypass should be built instead; this was finally opened in 1990, to the west of Dunblane. The A9 through the town was then reclassified as the B8033.

The roads of Dunblane began to be surfaced in the early years of the century. As mentioned earlier, car–ownership increased dramatically during the century, from a handful of car-owners in the early years of the century to 74% of Dunblane households by the 1981 census. In the 1920s, there were frequent motor bus services. Indeed in 1929 the *Stirling Journal* (14 March 1929) reported that, due to rivalry between bus companies, no fewer than 280 buses per day were passing through Dunblane. By 1939 the number of companies had dropped and most services were run by W. Alexander & Sons Ltd. Regular bus services to north and south were maintained for many years. By 1993, however, following the deregulation of bus services, their frequency was much reduced; most people travelling to and from Dunblane by public transport then found it more convenient to use the train.

Postal services in Dunblane were conducted in 1900 from a building at the lower end of the High Street, near the junction with Beech Road; the present post office was opened in 1905. When postal codes were introduced, Dunblane was designated as FK15.

Telephone services operated by the National Telephone company were introduced into Dunblane in July 1890. There were then four subscribers: the Hydro, MacEwen the grocer, McLaren the ironmonger, who also housed the public call office, and Mrs Dewar the draper who also housed the exchange. In 1898 a separate exchange was opened at Bridgend. On 1 January 1912 the whole system operated by the National Telephone Company was taken over by the Postmaster General. This remained the position until 1981 when the telecommunications system was separated from the post office. The telecommunications system became a public corporation, British Telecom, which was privatised in 1984. Meanwhile, a new manual telephone exchange for Dunblane was opened in the Millrow in 1914 and remained in use until 1939 when it was converted into an automatic exchange building. When this automatic exchange became too small it was replaced by an electronic exchange on the Stirling Road. The new exchange was opened in May 1976 and was updated in 1992. The old exchange in the Millrow was subsequently converted into a dwelling house. Following the introduction of subscriber trunk dialling to the area in 1968-69, the STD code for Dunblane became the same as that for Stirling, 0786.

Radio broadcasting in Scotland began between the wars and television broadcasting after the second world war. Along with television subscribers in the rest of central Scotland, subscribers in Dunblane in 1994 had a choice of four channels, BBC1, BBC2, ITV Scottish and Channel 4.

5. PLACES OF WORSHIP.

In 1900 there were five churches in Dunblane, marked on the 1900 Ordnance Survey map as the 'Cathedral', the 'U. P. Church' (that is, the Leighton Church), the 'Free Church' (the present St Blane's Church), 'St Mary's Church (Episcopal)' and 'S. S. John & Blane's R. C. Church'. In 1994 there were still five churches: part of the Leighton Church had been turned into a private house, part into Leighton House (see below), but a Free Church of Scotland had been built in Beech Road. Church membership has declined sharply in Scotland since the middle of the century and Dunblane is no exception to this. Although numbers of church adherents have risen in absolute terms, these numbers represent a smaller proportion than before of the population of Dunblane. Nevertheless, by the 1990s the churches had enthusiastic, if reduced, congregations; as well as services in the churches, church-related activities were held for the young, the elderly and other groups in the churches, in church halls and in the Braeport Centre.

a) The Cathedral

The restoration of the Cathedral building was completed in 1893 during the ministry of the Rev. Dr Alexander Ritchie who remained minister of the Cathedral until 1917. The cathedral building has belonged to the state since 1888, the date of the Crown Charter, and since 1978 has been in the care of the Secretary of State for Scotland. The Cathedral Hall was built in 1904.

Throughout the present century, the inside of the cathedral building has been restored and improved. Stained glass windows were added, for example the choir windows from 1901 and the west window in 1906. The woodwork in the choir was restored and this new woodwork was inspected in 1914 by King George V and Queen Mary. In 1935 electric lighting was installed throughout the building, at a cost of £1250, paid for by an anonymous donor. Some of the calligraphic work of the artist Helen A. Lamb, a resident of Dunblane, is preserved in the Cathedral, for example the Cradle Roll and the Rolls of Honour commemorating those who fought and died in the two world wars. A peal of bells was donated in 1907 by Mr Robert Younger, later Lord Blanesburgh, and a new organ, the Flentrop Organ, was provided in 1990.

The Very Rev. J. Hutchison Cockburn, minister of the Cathedral from 1918 to 1944, founded the Society of Friends of Dunblane Cathedral in 1929-30. The Society started with around 250 members, a number which had risen to around 900 by 1950; in 1992 there were 639 members. One of the aims of the Society is 'the adornment and equipment of the Cathedral and its further endowment' (quoted in the Society's *Journal* vol. 16, part 4 (1993), p. 114). In pursuit of this aim, the Society has over the years done much for the Cathedral. In 1934, for example, the Chapter House was floored with marble and was subsequently panelled with wood. A vaulted chamber at the west end of the nave was turned into the St Clement Chapel, dedicated in 1964. In 1980 the Prince of Wales visited the Cathedral for the fiftieth anniversary of the founding of the Society. (On the Cathedral Museum and the Leighton Library, see 6. RECREATION).

Membership of the Cathedral congregation has remained fairly constant in absolute terms, although (as noted above) this increasingly represents a smaller proportion of the population of Dunblane. In 1900 the congregation numbered 762; in 1950, during the ministry of the Rev. J. Chalmers Grant (minister from 1945 to 1965), it numbered 1083. In 1992 membership of the Cathedral congregation stood at 1377. Since 1965 the Cathedral has had three ministers, the Very Rev. Dr John R. Gray, 1966 to 1984, the Rev. J. F. Miller, 1984 to 1987, and the Rev. Colin G. McIntosh from 1988.

Services from the Cathedral have been broadcast on radio and television on a number of occasions; in 1967, for instance, three services were televised, a parish service, a schools' service and a service of Songs of Praise. In recent years, particularly since the arrival of the new organ, organ recitals and other concerts have taken place there. In 1992-93, for example, the Dunblane Cathedral Arts Guild (founded 1976) promoted a series of concerts; there were also visits from the Academy of Music Chamber Choir of Vilnius, Lithuania, from the Scottish Ensemble, from the Stirling University Choir and from the Rosenethe Singers.

b) Other Church of Scotland churches

The Leighton Church appears on the 1900 map as the 'U. P. Church', that is, the United

Presbyterian Church, and the present St Blane's Church as the 'Free Church'. (On the early history of these churches, see Barty *History*, especially pp. 194, 231, 254, 259-60, 278-9). In 1900 there was an amalgamation throughout Scotland of these two churches to form the United Free Church of Scotland. The Dunblane churches were then known as the Leighton Free Church and the East United Free Church. In 1929 most of the United Free Church congregations, including both those in Dunblane, joined the Church of Scotland. From 1929 there were therefore three Church of Scotland congregations in Dunblane, each with their own church and minister. This remained the position until 1952 when the two smaller congregations were officially united. Thereafter they worshipped in the East Church, which was renamed St Blane's Church, under the Rev. Alexander Roberts, who was minister from 1952 to 1973. From this time the Leighton Church was no longer in use; it was subsequently turned into a private dwelling house and a hall. In 1967 the hall, Leighton House, became part of the Scottish Churches House, see below.

In 1900 the minister of the East Church was the Rev. Hugh Stevenson (1893-1935) and the minister of the Leighton Church was the Rev. William Blair (1856-1916). Both churches had then around 300 parishioners. In 1940 the East Church, under the Rev. J. Oswald Welsh (1935-51), had 315 parishioners and the Leighton Church, under the Rev. A. S. Dingwall (1938-51), had 308 parishioners. In 1953, after amalgamation, the number of St Blane's parishioners was 504 but this had risen to 646 in 1990. The Rev. George G. Cringles has been minister of St. Blane's Church since 1988.

In 1993 the Free Church of Scotland opened a church in Beech Road, the minister being the Rev. D. Allan MacLeod.

c) The Episcopal Church

St Mary's Episcopal Church was consecrated in 1845 (Barty *History* p. 260). In 1900 the Rector was the Rev. W. D. Crighton and the congregation numbered 180. By 1950, under the Rev. W. Goring, it had risen to 349 and in 1990 to 435. The present Rector, the Rev. Canon Dr G. Tellini, has been in Dunblane since 1985. Around 1845, St Mary's Episcopal school in Smithy Loan was established; see under 3. EDUCATION.

d) The Roman Catholic Church

In 1883 a Catholic chapel dedicated to St John and St Blane was opened in Claredon Place. The chapel house was named St Clare's after the Order of Poor Clare Sisters who stayed there between 1884 and 1885. The chapel was replaced in 1934 by the present Church of the Holy Family, erected as a memorial to General Archibald Stirling of Keir by his widow and family. The Hon. Mrs Stirling sold an El Greco painting to the National Gallery to help pay for the new church. At first priests served Dunblane from Doune but since 1948 there has been a parish priest resident in Dunblane. Between 1934 and 1948, sisters of the Order known as Helpers of the Holy Souls stayed in the chapel house, mainly at weekends, to arrange retreats and to undertake parish visits and other duties. In 1950 the number of parishioners was around 120 but by 1990 it had risen to 700. The present priest, Canon Basil O'Sullivan, has been in Dunblane since 1988. In 1992 there was a Solemn Dedication of the church and of its new stone altar which replaced the wooden one of 1934.

e) Scottish Churches House (see photograph facing page 275)

This ecumenical meeting house and conference centre was opened in 1960. Several eighteenth-century houses in Kirk Street were restored to form the main building and a cellar excavated during the restoration work was made into a small chapel. In 1966 an adjoining building, which had belonged to Dunblane Burgh School, was renovated to form an Annexe to the main house. In 1967 Leighton House (see above) was added to the complex. The Scottish Churches House is owned jointly by nine Scottish churches and is run by a warden; since 1993 the warden has been the Rev. Bryan Owen. The house is used by ecumenical and other church groups as well as by some secular groups and can house up to 54 resident visitors. A new extension is due to be completed in 1994.

a) Sport

Apart from those played at schools, three main sports played in Dunblane this century have been golf, tennis and football although a large number of minority sports have also been enjoyed.

The Laighills belonged originally to the Cromlix estate but the land was bought for £800 in 1909 by Mr R. H. Martin of New York, originally of Dunblane, and presented to the people of Dunblane. In 1892 a nine-hole golf course had been laid out on the Laighills by Mr Philp and Mr Henderson of Dunblane Hydro (Barty *History* p. 277). Subsequently this course was taken over by the Town Council who maintained it until 1925. Meanwhile, in 1923, a private company, Dunblane New Golf Club Ltd, was formed and the present golf course laid out. This was done on land leased, as it still is, from Kippendavie estate. A wooden hut served as a club-house until the present club-house was built. Near the club-house there was a putting green until it was turned into a car park. Both ladies' and men's golf teams have flourished throughout the century.

The Town Council opened the first two municipal tennis courts in the same area, at the foot of the Glen Road, in July 1923. Two more courts were soon opened and subsequently another two. These were managed by the Tennis Club, a flourishing concern with teams that have continued to do well and have attracted enthusiastic members, including junior members. In the early 1980s Dunblane Sports Club, a limited company, was formed and the Club took over the tennis courts. Four of the courts were retained; a building containing two squash courts was built on one and the other was held in reserve for future use.

Football has been a popular sport all century. The Dunblane Football Club was founded around 1877 (see Barty *History* pp.276-7) and its team was known as Dunblane Heather. In 1905-6 Dunblane Heather won the Perthshire cup, beating St Johnstone in the final. Dunblane Heather was disbanded in 1914. After the first world war, a new team, Dunblane Rovers, was started and was a successful Junior Club in the local league, recruiting most of its players from outside Dunblane. There were also two other teams playing in Dunblane at this time. Dunblane Thistle was a juvenile team, recruited mainly from local players, and the Wednesday Club had a team recruited from shop-keepers and employees playing on their half-day. Both of these were permitted to use the Dunblane Rovers' football ground. The football ground was situated at the back of the India Gate restaurant, near the present Drummond Rise, from before the turn of the century until around the time of the first war. It was then moved to Duckburn Park.

Football ceased during the second war but afterwards a new Juvenile club was formed called Dunblane Victoria and, in the 1950s, another Juvenile club which took over the name Dunblane Rovers and continued until around 1960. Dunblane Victoria used the football ground at Duckburn Park until the 1950s when the ground was moved to the Laighills where the new Dunblane Rovers played. In the later years of the century only amateur teams played on the Laighills and Dunblane ceased to have a professional football team.

One sport which has died out locally is cricket; it had been revived in 1899 but ceased in 1906 when the ground became unavailable due to the building of the new road (Barty *History* p. 276). Curling had had a long history in Dunblane even before 1900 (Barty *History* p. 265) and remained popular for some time. In a famous 'Grand Match' at Carsebreck in the 1930s, Dunblane supplied no fewer than twelve rinks, 48 curlers. In the early years of the century curling took place both on a flat part of the Laighills and on the Curling Pond in Ochlochy Park. This Curling Pond is marked on both the 1900 and 1932 maps and is still in existence although by the 1990s little curling was taking place outdoors in Dunblane. Ochlochy Park originally belonged to the Kippendavie estate but in 1943 it was donated to Dunblane as a recreational area by Colonel John A. and Mrs Stirling of Kippendavie to commemorate their twentieth wedding anniversary.

Other minority interest sports have included, for example, horse-riding, bowling, rambling and badminton. A riding stables was run by Mrs D. Macfarlane from the cathedral manse stables in the Cross from the early 1950s to the early 1960s. The riding stables then moved to Greenloaning and was later named the Scottish Equitation Centre. The bowling green in Duckburn Park was opened between the wars and is still well-patronised. The all-male Rambling club is, however, now defunct. A photograph of the club members, taken in 1919, suggests that it was then a popular pastime. (The photograph is printed in McKerracher *Portrait* p. 31, figure 54). A new Dunblane Ramblers' Club was formed in 1975 from the Footpath section of the Dunblane Society (see below). Badminton has been played from time to time in the Victoria Hall and in church halls and in 1993 there were three Badminton clubs meeting regularly in the Braeport Centre.

b) Entertainment and leisure activities

Dunblane has never had a cinema or theatre but professional and amateur productions have been regularly staged in the Victoria Hall and, to a lesser extent, in the church halls. Following the Cinematographic Act of 1909, cinema licences were granted on an annual basis to companies to show films in the Victoria Hall. Music hall, orchestral concerts and silent films were all popular in the early years of the century. Around this time too Dunblane had a town band; in 1905 the Town Council paid it £5 to perform twice weekly during summer in the town. As the century progressed, entertainment became less communal, more private. In the place of the amateur theatricals of the inter-war years, for example, families have acquired televisions, music systems, video players and computers in their own homes. However in 1994 Jim MacLeod and his Scottish dance band were still playing regularly at Dunblane Hydro Hotel as they had done full-time since 1964 and on an occasional basis since the 1950s.

The Dunblane Library and Institute was built in 1905 in the upper part of the High Street. It started as a private concern but was later taken over by the Town Council. It housed billiards and a reading room as well as the lending and reference library run by Perth County Council. Since 1975 it has been run by Stirling District Council Community Services who rent out the library to Stirling District Library.

The Leighton Library in the Cross, illustated on the front cover, was built soon after the death of Bishop Robert Leighton in 1684 to house his books which he had bequeathed to the Cathedral of Dunblane and the clergy of the diocese (see Allan 'The work was much forslowed'). At the turn of the century the library building was in poor condition due to damp and neglect. During the second world war an air-raid shelter was constructed in its vaults. In the 1950s financial help was given by, among others, the Pilgrim Trust and the Society of Friends of Dunblane Cathedral for repair work. This was completed in 1957 but the building still lacked any heating. Between 1976 and 1979 a new catalogue was prepared in the Department of Rare Books and Manuscripts, University of Stirling Library, by Gordon Willis. In the 1980s further restoration and renovation work was undertaken to both the books and the building and heating was installed. The Library was officially re-opened in May 1990 and is now open to both scholars and to the public. In 1967 the library was visited by Queen Elizabeth II. Since 1990 the honorary librarian has been Mr D. W. Moore.

The Cathedral Museum was founded by the Very Rev. Dr J. Hutchison Cockburn and officially opened in May 1943. It was extended, and the contents re-catalogued, under the curatorship of Miss Elizabeth R. Barty, curator from 1954 to 1972. The present curator, Mr John G. Lindsay, has held the position since 1988. Under his care, the exhibits are being preserved in an up-to-date manner with, for example, temperature and humidity being carefully controlled.

In 1959 the Rank Organisation made a film of John Buchan's *The Thirty-nine Steps*, starring Kenneth More as Richard Hannay. Some scenes were filmed in Dunblane, including one where Hannay escapes by jumping from an upstairs window; this is illustrated by McKerracher (McKerracher *Portrait* p. 40, figure 80).

The Cathedral and the other churches in Dunblane have throughout the century run their own clubs and societies for children and for adults. These have included Sunday schools, the Mothers' Union, the Boys' Brigade, the Cathedral bell-ringers, the Dunblane Cathedral Arts Guild and many others. There have also been many town societies. In the early years of the century, for example, the Temperance Union, the Scotch Girls' Friendly Society and the Mutual Improvement Society all held regular meetings but none of these societies has survived. In 1993 there were, however, societies such as the Dunblane and District Gardening Club, the Dunblane Embroidery Club, the Dunblane Local History Society, the Ladies' Wednesday Whist Club and the Doune & Dunblane Bridge Club, among others.

In 1969 the Dunblane Society was founded to protect the environment and the amenities in and around Dunblane. One of its particular aims was to oppose the plan, put forward by the Scottish Development Department, to upgrade the A9 to trunk road standard (see 4. COMMUNICATIONS). Instead the Society advocated the building of a bypass. Dr Neil Fairley was chairperson of the Society from 1977 to 1990; in that year the Society's aim was at last achieved with the opening of the new bypass. Since then the Society has concentrated on the amenities of Dunblane and the surrounding area.

One society has flourished with great success for almost 300 years: the Society of Free Masons, Dunblane Lodge no. 9. Their earliest records go back to 1695 (Barty *History* p. 149). The present lodge was built in 1886; it is situated above shops at the lower end of the High Street, in the place of an old smithy (Barty *History* p. 275). The private house Ault Wharrie, at the top of Leewood Road, was acquired by the Society and opened in 1951 as the Royal Scottish Masonic Home, a residential home for elderly people associated with the Society.

7. LOCAL GOVERNMENT

a) Organisation

In 1900 Dunblane was classified as a burgh, as it had been for many hundreds of years, probably since the fourteenth century (Barty *History* pp. 30, 38). It was administered by Dunblane Town Council under Perth County Council and had a Sheriff Court serving West Perthshire. This remained the position until the Local Government (Scotland) Act of 1975. Dunblane then ceased to be a burgh; although it remained in Perthshire, it has since then been administered by Stirling District Council as part of Central Region. Dunblane Town Council was never elected on a party political basis although Stirling District Council is so elected. A Community Council was set up in Dunblane after 1975 and has remained active. The duties of Dunblane Sheriff Court, in so far as they related to Dunblane, were taken over by Stirling Sheriff Court. The services previously provided by Dunblane Town Council and Perth County Council remained broadly unchanged under Stirling District Council and Central Regional Council.

After 1975 some buildings became redundant. The Registry for Births, Deaths and Marriages, which had been situated in Beech Road from 1928, was converted into shops and the office was moved to the Burgh Chambers. The Burgh Chambers are used as the local offices of Stirling District Council. In 1982 the Court House was converted into private flats for entry in November 1983.

b) Services

(i) Water and Sewage

A reservoir and filters had been provided at Waltersmuir by the Burgh from 1884 (Barty *History* p. 275). In 1934 the new Wharry Burn reservoir was built on Sheriffmuir which, under the control of Dunblane Town Council, supplied the town's needs until 1968. Since then water has been brought in from Loch Turret Filtration Unit outside Crieff under the control of the Water Board. During the century an increasing number of dwelling houses obtained a supply of running water and sanitation. By 1951 only 10% of Dunblane households lacked running water and a toilet (*Census 1951*, p. 51); by 1981 only 0.6% of Dunblane households had no bath or shower (*Key Statistics* p. 45). Although sewage tanks were in existence in Duckburn Park from the early years of the century, they were clearly not very efficient; an Inspecting Officer's report of January 1905, quoted in the Town Council Minutes, noted that untreated sewage was being allowed to enter the river. In 1925 the Town Council agreed to provide a new sewage scheme and these sewage works are marked on the 1932 map. Public toilets have been provided for men since before 1900 but those for women date from later in this century.

(ii) Rubbish collection and disposal

At the beginning of the century a new site had to be found to replace the refuse depots at Stockbridge and Clayhill. In 1901 land was leased from Sir James Campbell of Kilbryde for a new depot at Corscaplie farm. This site was used until 1930 when the Town Council leased a new site at Barbush. The Barbush depot remained in use until around 1965. Rubbish was then taken to various places including Argaty quarry, Sheriffmuir and a depot near Thornhill shared with Perth County Council. The depot at Fallin has been used since 1991.

(iii) Street lighting

Street lighting was introduced into Dunblane after the manufacture of gas began in the town in 1841. The gas lighting was gradually replaced by electric lighting from 1931 and the conversion of the last gas lamps was in 1955. For some years in the middle of the century a special street lamp was placed outside the private house of the provost, necessitating a change in the location of the lamp with each change of provost.

(iv) Social services

Social services include the District Nursing Service, started in 1924 (see 2. EMPLOYMENT AND SERVICES) and now run by the Forth Valley Health Board. The Social Work Department of Central Regional Council runs both the Meals on Wheels service and the Home Help service; the latter provides domestic help and shopping for the elderly and/or disabled living in their own homes. Day care for frail and confused elderly people has been provided in the Braeport Centre since 1990. It is organised by the Social Work Department, with the co-operation of the Health Board, but relies on volunteer workers from Dunblane. In 1993 there were two local authority residential homes in Dunblane.

(v) Fire Brigade

The fire-fighting service was set up by the Town Council in 1901. The eight volunteers were to be paid 2/6d for each drill, with six drills per year; they were also to be provided with a helmet each at a cost of 15/- per helmet. The actual fire-fighting equipment was kept in premises on the Doune Road, latterly, at least, in the stables of a house called Rokeby. In 1952-3 the present Fire Station was built in Anderson Street. The Dunblane Fire Brigade has always consisted of volunteers but since the end of the second world war they have been paid a small retaining fee.

(vi) Police

The police station was in the same building as the jail in the High Street until the late 1950s when a new police station was built on the west side of the Stirling Road, between St Mary's Church and St Blane's Bridge. Until 1975 the police came under the authority of Perth County Council and the new Dunblane police station was a Perthshire divisional headquarters. It therefore had several CID officers as well as police officers; in 1974 there were 16 police officers. Since 1975 the Dunblane police have been part of the police force of Central Region. Because the police officers based there serve only Dunblane, fewer are needed than before. Although there has been a marked increase in the population of Dunblane since 1975, there has been a decline in the number of police officers; in 1993 there were 14 officers. Since the building is a large one, Central Region police force utilise it by housing in it several units concerned with the whole of the Region. In 1993 these included, for example, the Accident Prevention unit and the Animal Welfare unit.

(vii) Slaughter house

Animals have been butchered in the slaughter house under the control of the local authority all century. The slaughter house is shown on the 1900 map, situated just off the Stirling Road, between the road and the river, near to where St Blane's Bridge was built in 1940. The old slaughter house had to be demolished when the bridge was built but a new slaughter house was built nearby and opened in 1940. It has remained in use since then.

(viii) Cemetery

Dunblane cemetery was opened in September 1914 to replace the Cathedral graveyard which was over-crowded and due to be closed. From 1923 no burials were permitted in the Cathedral graveyard except for those of unmarried women resident in the parish, the direct issue of people already buried there. St Mary's Episcopal Church has a graveyard which is still used for Episcopalian burials. All other burials take place in the cemetery.

On library, sports and recreational services, (see 6. RECREATION); on educational services, (see 3. EDUCATION); on roads, (see 4. COMMUNICATIONS).

CONCLUSION

It is perhaps a common human tendency to look back on one's childhood and conclude that, compared to the present day, it was a golden age of peace and charm. The present authors, father and daughter, have personal memories of Dunblane which span a large part of the twentieth century. Tracing, however briefly, the history of the town over the last hundred years may help the reader, as it has helped them, to look afresh and more objectively at Dunblane.

There have certainly been great changes in Dunblane since 1900, changes in population, in employment patterns, in leisure pursuits. For many people, life in Dunblane in 1900, and indeed in 1950, was more austere than in 1990: houses were colder, food was less varied, there was greater risk of disease. There were, however, compensations. The streets were safer, for example, and fewer elderly people lived alone. The greatest difference, perhaps, is more nebulous. In 1900, even to some extent in 1950, Dunblane was a community: the inhabitants worked, shopped, worshipped and enjoyed their leisure within the town. The second half of the century has witnessed a large growth in population, greatly increased car-ownership and hence mobility, a higher standard of living and a falling-off in church adherence. Dunblane is no longer able to provide most of its inhabitants with work, shopping facilities, recreation or entertainment. It has, however, become increasingly popular as a town for commuters to live in and for tourists to visit.

These are important changes but they need not be exaggerated. The character of Dunblane has changed greatly and many times during the last millennium, as was so ably charted in *The History of Dunblane*. Viewed in this historical perspective, the changes of the last century fall into place.

WORKS USED

1. J. MALCOLM ALLAN, '"The work was much forslowed": building and restoring the Leighton Library', *Journal of the Society of Friends of Dunblane Cathedral* 16, part 1 (1990), pp.11-22.
2. A. B. BARTY, *The History of Dunblane* (Stirling, 1944).
3. A. C. MCKERRACHER, *Portrait of Dunblane 1875-1975*, revised edition (Stirling, 1991).
4. General Registry Office, Edinburgh: *Census 1951, Report on the Fifteenth Census of Scotland* 1, part 26 (Edinburgh, 1954).
5. *Key Statistics for Urban Areas, Scotland, Localities*, HMSO (Edinburgh, 1984).
6. Registrar General Scotland: *Census 1981, Report for Central Region* 4, HMSO (Edinburgh, 1983).
7. *Tenth Decennial Census of the Population of Scotland taken 5th April 1891, with Report* 1 (Edinburgh, 1892).
8. Dunblane Town Council Minutes.
9. *Stirling Journal*.

NOTE

Two typographical errors in the *History of Dunblane* should be corrected:
1. p. 187: for 'chapt er' read 'chapter'
2. p. 196: for 'happilly' read 'happily'

J. W. Barty
Elisabeth Okasha